IN THE COUNTY OF HUNTINGDON.

THIS *Beautifull brick Palace and it's Manor belong'd formerly to the Abby of Ely which was then in the Diocess of Lincoln; untill Richard the last Abbot obtain'd Leave of K. Hen: 1.st to turn his Abby of Ely into a Cathedral: and to make himself by this means first Bishop thereof: but this not being to be done without y.e cons.t of his Diocesan he was oblig'd to purchase that, at y.e Price of three Manors, of w.ch this was one: w.ch in process of Time became y.e Palace and Residence of y.e B.ps of Lincoln as it now continues. Russel y.e 47.th B.p created An.1480 built great part of it as appears by his Arms on y.e Wall. D.r Sanderson created B.p An.1660. bestow'd much cost in repair.g & beautifying it. It was confirm'd to y.e B.p of Lincoln by Patent 4.th Edw.d 6.st*

S.t & N.t Buck delin et Sculp.t 1730.

THIS *Beautifull brick Palace and it's Manor belong'd formerly to the Abby of Ely which was then in the Diocess of Lincoln; untill Richard the last Abbot obtain'd Leave of K. Hen: 1.st to turn his Abby of Ely into a Cathedral: and to make himself by this means first Bishop thereof: but this not being to be done without y.e cons.t of his Diocesan he was oblig'd to purchase that, at y.e Price of three Manors, of w.ch this was one: w.ch in process of Time became y.e Palace and Residence of y.e B.ps of Lincoln as it now continues. Russel y.e 47.th B.p created An.1480 built great part of it as appears by his Arms on y.e Wall. D.r Sanderson created B.p An.1660. bestow'd much cost in repair.g & beautifying it. It was confirm'd to y.e B.p of Lincoln by Patent 4.th Edw.d 6.st*

S.t & N.t Buck delin et Sculp.t 1730.

An enlarged copy of the text for easier reading

BUCKDEN

A
Huntingdonshire
Village

Editor: Mike Storey
Consultant Editor: Susan B. Edgington
Production Editor: Robin Gibson

Published by:
Buckden Local History (Publications)Ltd
P O Box 282
St Neots
PE19 9EF
buckden-books@buckden-village.co.uk

First Published 2010

The Book Group

Les Button
Sue Edgington
Robin Gibson
Peter Ibbett
Barry Jobling
Mike Storey
William Tackaberry
David Thomas
Clive Thompson

ISBN 978 0946965 61 8

Printed in Great Britain by the MPG Books Group, Bodmin and King's Lynn

Contents

Preface

The germ of the idea for this book lies with Buckden Parish Council back in the 1970s. In 1976, the year I arrived in the village, the council announced an essay competition with a cash prize for the winner, the theme being the history of the village. Since I was young, naive and unemployed that summer, and I had a fairly recent degree in history, I thought that at the least the research would help me to get to know the village and its history. I never did find out how many entrants there were, but I rather think there were only three, so coming first was not too great an achievement; nevertheless, I duly pocketed the prize, and then I found out that it came with strings attached: the Parish Council wanted a village history in booklet form. Producing this modest publication (about 9,000 words) took another four years and ended thus:

> *Finally: this is not a definitive work, but intended only as an interim guide to Buckden's history. The Buckden Local History Society is working on a much more detailed study, and it is hoped that if you would like to contribute to it you will contact the group.*

The Buckden Local History Society (BLHS) had been set up as part of the same initiative, and continues to flourish. An updated version of the original booklet will be found as the second of the chapters later in this book.

Now, nearly thirty years later (and much aided by the invention of the internet, the world wide web, and the personal computer in the meantime) BLHS is making good its promise of 1980. Some of the founding members, including three former chairmen, have been part of the committee that has produced this book, we have also benefited from the financial advice of our founder treasurer, Eric Nash, who still holds the post, and special mention should be made of Les Button, who has been honorary secretary since the very first meeting of BLHS. As we foresaw, a more comprehensive village study has only been possible thanks to the contributions of very many other people. Except in the case of people who have written entire chapters, we find it impossible to acknowledge by name all the individuals and organizations who have assisted in so many ways, from sharing single memories and photographs to providing access to major archives. We thank you and hope you approve the finished product. Mike Storey conceived the idea of the A-Z section, and compiled most of the entries, as well as producing the whole typescript. Robin Gibson has been the driving force behind the project, chairing meetings of the committee, pursuing finance, finding and negotiating with printers, finding storage space, corresponding with overseas contributors ... and has also edited the illustrations throughout. Robin's indefatigable efforts gained us generous grants from Buckden Parish Council and from the Goodliff Fund administered by the Huntingdonshire Local History Society, for which we are pleased to record our gratitude. Nevertheless, publication would not have been possible without generous loans from five individuals, whom we hope to repay from sales of the book.

I have the pleasure of seeing that germ of an idea from 1976 coming to splendid fruition, and the honour of writing this preface.

Susan B. Edgington
February 2010

ILLUSTRATIONS
Between pages 80 and 81

Buckden – A Huntingdonshire Village

Key to map

Ref	Street	Modern name or use	Historical Interest or previous use
1	Burberry Road	Buckden Millennium Centre	Village Hall (20thC)
2	Church Street	No. 48	Headmaster's House; village schools (19thC to date)
3		The Hoo	19thC farmhouse (rebuilt 1907)
4		No. 57	J.J.Milner & Sons, grocers
5		The Beauty Room	Village Reading Rooms; Pipe's shop
6		No. 42	'Hinsby's Corner' (sweets, tobacco)
7		Burberry Homes	Site of Rifle Range 1921 to 1969
8		Methodist Chapel	Founded 1876 as Wesleyan Chapel
9		South's Almshouses	Founded 1840; altered 1897
10		Bridge House	15thC hall house
11		The Manor House	May have originated as late 15thC guild house
12		The Old Vicarage	Vicarage site for over 300 years (to 1980)
13		Church of St Mary the Virgin	Carvings, architecture, memorials; war memorial
14		Lion Hotel (kitchen wing)	Methodist Gospel Hall
15	George Lane	Part of Anne Furbank shop	The Old Tap Inn
16	Great North Road	Mill House	Buckden windmill (resited)
17		No. 135	Crown public house
18		Park Farm	Bishop's deer park to end 17thC
19	High Street	The Gables	Page family residence
20		No. 21	Windmill public house
21		The Vine	Public house and brewery
22		Nails at the Forge	Smithy and goose barn
23		The George Hotel	17thC/18thC courtyard coaching inn
24		The Lion Hotel	15thC coaching inn and brewery
25		The Green Memorial	Commemorates two brothers, one a VC
26		Buckden Towers	Bishop's palace until 1837
27		Coneygarths	Green family home for over 100 years
28		Laundry Cottage	Home of Towers laundress (19thC)
29		York House	18thC merchant's (butcher's?) house
30		Nos. 61-63 Equilibrium	Girls' school; cycle shop; café; curio shop
31		No. 67 Sherwood House	Housed Second World War evacuees
32		No. 77 Jessamine House	A Bowyer family farm until 1970s
33		No. 79	Spread Eagle coaching inn
34		The Old Chapel	Baptist/Congregational chapel
35	Hunts End	Hunts End Green	Site of village pound and pond
36		No. 15	Black Horse public house
37		Vine Cottages	At one time known as Navigation Cottages
38	Lucks Lane	No.16 The Beehive	Cottage; beer house/brewery
39	Mill Road	The White House	17thC farmhouse
40		Oak Lawn	19thC girls' school; 20thC doctor's surgery
41		Low Farm	Early 19thC estate farmhouse
42		Buckden Day Nursery	Buckden Hosiery Mill (20thC)
43		No. 5	Approximate site of Buckden workhouse
44	Perry Road	No. 36 Nutfield	Bowtell family home; originally known as Ellerslie
45	School Lane	Buckden Primary School	Village farm/industrial area; engineering; building yard
46	Silver Street	No. 4	White Horse beer house (with forge)
47		Bowlings	Site of Buckden's first tennis and bowls clubs
48		No. 33 Field House	Home of botanical artist E.W.Hunnybun
49		Beech Lawn	'A charming, old-fashioned, Bijou Residence'
50	Stirtloe Lane	Stirtloe House	Home of the Linton family for over 100 years

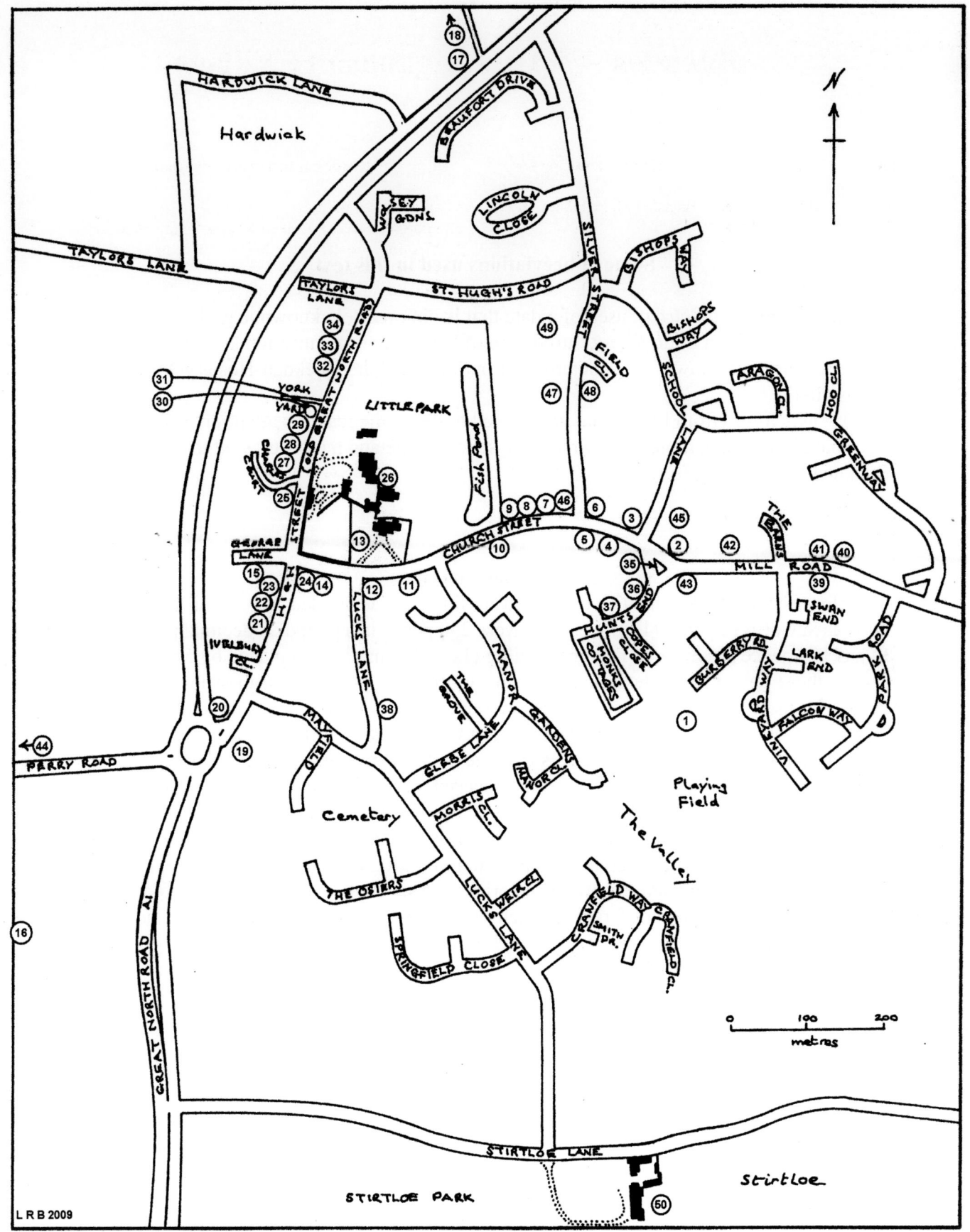

BUCKDEN

Street map showing some of the interesting buildings and places referred to in the A to Z Section

See key on facing page

Some abbreviations used in this text

c. = about (from Latin *circa*): used of a date that is not precisely known, e.g. 'born c. 1671'.
fl. = flourished (from Latin *floruit*): used here of a person or organisation known to be alive or active during a known but undetermined period, e.g. 'the Buckden Hosiery Mill (fl. 1930s/40s)'.
(q.v.) = which see (from Latin *quod vide*): used to direct the reader's attention to further information or explanation, e.g. 'On leaving school, Ellie and her sister went to work at the Buckden Hosiery Mill (q.v.)'.

A note on currency

Before decimalisation in 1971, the pound sterling (£) was divided into 20 shillings (20s or 20/-) each worth 12 pence (12d), i.e. there were 240 pence in a pound. A decimal pound (still £) has 100 pence (100p) in it, i.e., one shilling (1s or 1/-) has been replaced by 5 pence (5p).

But these conversion rates relate only to the moment of decimalisation in 1971. They cannot be used simply to convert earlier amounts (prices, income) into modern values. A meal that cost one shilling in, say, 1840, couldn't be bought for 5p today.

Furthermore, not everything changes in value at the same rate. In 1932, the price (£1,350) of a five-bedroom semi-detached house in a pleasant, rather than fashionable, London suburb was almost exactly equal to twice the annual salary of a middle rank civil servant (£650). In 2009, the price of a similar house was just under £700,000: no longer double but over twenty-two times the modern civil servant's salary of £30,500 a year !

As an added complication, economic historians use several ways of converting 'old money' into new; the results are different in each case. On the whole, therefore, we have not attempted to give modern equivalents to sterling sums !

A

A1. Had the founder of the Michelin Tyre Company had his way, Buckden today would be sitting astride the N1. The rapid spread of motor traffic in the first decade of the 20thC meant that the signing and maintenance of the road system needed to be drastically overhauled. A Roads Board was established in 1910, and in 1913 set about devising a numerical classification that would make it simple to identify the route of every road in the country. The First World War then intervened, and it was not until 1919 that the new Ministry of Transport was able to return to the problem. During 1920, it worked out a scheme which owed something to that already adopted in France. Under this, major thoroughfares such as the Great North Road would be given a number with an A prefix, and lesser roads a B number. André Michelin, who had been advising the British government urged that the French of use of N (for National routes) was a more sensible classification than A, but Sir Henry Maybury, senior MOT engineer, was having none of that.

So as from the summer of 1921 A1 it was.

A1, bodies buried under. According to dowser David Trump, there are 234 bodies buried under the central reservation of the A1 just south of its junction with the road from Brampton. The signpost at this junction features in an 1859 water-colour sketch; an accompanying note states that there were once five stumps at the foot of the post, 'with a fifth which was driven thru the body of a murderer buried according to custom of the time, at this spot'. The signpost may have given its name to White Post Close, a small field shown on the Buckden enclosure map.

See also **Cruel Tree** and **Cut Throat Clos**e.

accidents, shooting. In May 1901, Walter Harry Brightman of Buckden Wood Farm accidentally discharged his shotgun into his left hand while out shooting crows. As a result his fourth finger 'and part of the hand below it' had to be amputated at Huntingdon Hospital. Fortunately this did not prevent his marrying Abbotsley farmer's daughter Amelia Jane Sheard in 1904.

Accidents of this kind were rare but sometimes memorable: a St Neots hairdresser's son accidentally shot his own arm off on Christmas Day 1837, and in September 1819 it was reported that

'Last Sunday a gentleman on the Union coach having stopped at Buckden to take some refreshment, a double-barrelled fowling-piece which he held betwixt his legs, by some accident happened to slip from his hand, when it instantly went off, and the charge lodging in the back parts of his leg and thigh, they were so lacerated, that amputation was rendered indispensable, which the patient next day underwent with the greatest fortitude, and, we understand, is *going on well.*'

Happily, there is nothing in the Buckden burial register to suggest that he stopped going on well.

Acheulian hand axes date from between 400,000 and 200,000 BC; one was unearthed at 28 Vineyard Way in April 1977. This type of crude stone implement was developed during the lower/middle Palaeolithic period (the Old Stone Age), when early man was living within the ice age with its alternate glacial and mild periods. The earliest type of hand axes, known as Abbevillian, were produced 500,000 to 450,000 years ago by striking flints with stone hammers and are characterised by large deep flaking. The Abbevillian people were driven from Britain (which was then still joined to the European continent) by the second glaciation. During the warmer second interglacial period some 400,000 years ago, Britain was re-populated by the Acheulians, who brought with them a better made and less crude type of hand axe. This was almond-shaped with shallow flake scars made with a bone or wooden baton. These were the early men generally referred to as Neanderthal. Buckden's hand axe would therefore appear to be from the early or lower Acheulian period.

See Plate 3.2.2

aggregate extraction: see **mineral extraction.**

agriculture in Buckden. From the 17thC onwards, Huntingdonshire was known as an area of exceptionally fine meadows and pasture, and productive arable land. How well these natural resources were managed varied over the years, but in the course of the 19thC, some of the county's larger farmers became nationally known for their innovativeness and willingness to adopt new techniques. Prominent among them were the Cranfield family, whose farming activities were mainly centred on Buckden and Brampton. Like the Cranfields, the Bowyers – a long-established Buckden farming family – were millers, with a keen eye for making use of new technology such as the railways to increase their productivity and expand the market for their produce.

Alongside these large holdings were the many small and medium sized farms and market garden that used to characterize the English rural scene. The gradual reduction in their numbers, as food production became dominated by economies of scale and competition from imports, means that farming is no longer the major contributor to Buckden's economy; nor does it dictate the village's social structure.

Nonetheless, and despite the loss of land to housing, roads, recreation and mineral extraction, agriculture still unmistakably shapes the parish's landscape – except in one major respect. Well within living memory, you could not have walked far in any direction from, or even within, the village without coming across cattle, sheep, pigs, poultry and working horses. There is now very little livestock visible in Buckden.

For more on farming and land use, see **Chapter 9.**

Alderson, Sir Edward Hall (1787-1857). When still an eighteen year-old, this humane judge and light versifier spent several months in Buckden being coached by the vicar, Dr **Maltby** (q.v.), before going up to Caius College, Cambridge. In March 1831, chance brought him back to Huntingdon as one of the justices presiding over the trials of the sixty or so prisoners accused of taking part in the previous winter's agricultural riots. They included five Buckden labourers, and one of the prosecuting lawyers was his old tutor's son, E. H. Maltby. See under **machine-breaking.**

Allen, William (1770-1843) was a Quaker scientist and philanthropist whose interest in education led him to rescue the Royal Lancasterian* Society from financial disaster. The aim of the society, later renamed the British and Foreign School Society, was to extend education to the largest possible number of children of the poor by setting up monitorial schools (schools in which senior pupils helped teach the younger ones).

* This is was the preferred contemporary spelling.

With his friend Joseph Fox, Allen embarked on a fundraising campaign that in October 1814 brought them to Buckden to meet the vicar, Dr **Maltby** (q.v.). He was more sympathetic to their cause than most of his Anglican colleagues and over breakfast agreed to try to raise £100 for their funds (Maltby was clearly a morning person: he once entertained Sir Walter Scott to breakfast).

The three men may also have talked about teeth: Fox was the country's leading dental lecturer and author, and Surgeon Dentist Extraordinary to two royal dukes.

See also the **National Society.**

allotments. There were at least three distinct types of village allotment:

1 Parish land or property let out to provide income for church, charity or parish officer expenses;

2 Parish or private land let to specific groups (such as the 'deserving poor') to allow them to produce their own food; and

3 Statutory allotments.

For more information, including maps, see **Chapter 10 Gardening in Buckden**.

almshouses [MapRef 9]: see under **charities.**

Amers, Captain Henry Gallon (1875-1944). By the time Harry Amers became a Buckden resident in 1937, he had been a famous man for over forty years. A child prodigy who played several times for the future Edward VII, he grew up to be a conductor, a composer and the musician of choice when entertainment was required for fashionable Edwardian occasions on both sides of the Atlantic. After serving with the Northumberland Hussars during the First World War, he embarked on a new career as a musical showman. Between 1920 and 1936 he was contracted by Eastbourne Town Council to provide their

'municipal music': during the day as Captain H. G. Amers and his Famous Band, and during the evening as Captain Amers and his Famous Orchestra. BBC broadcasts from Eastbourne made him a stalwart of the new medium of the wireless.

His arrival at **Beech Lawn** (q.v.) must therefore have aroused considerable local interest, not only because of Buckden's strong musical tradition, but also because he was 'a handsome fellow...always immaculately dressed with a red carnation in his buttonhole and red hair to match [and] much admired by lady members of the audience.' Alan Cockburn, a schoolboy evacuee in Buckden, remembers him as being still immaculately turned out even in his late sixties.

He stayed in Buckden for five or six years, then moved to Devon, where he died in 1944. He was survived by his wife, Kate, and probably some of the Siamese cats he had bred while at Beech Lawn.

Anchor. The 1861 census lists two beer-houses called the Anchor. One was at the river end of Mill Road, beside the Coal Wharf, in the home of Samuel Gaunt, wharfman. The other was on the north side of Mill Street, not far from

The one-time Anchor beer-house, Mill Road

Hunts End, and was kept by William Clarke, agricultural labour. It was a few doors along in one direction from another beer-house, the Quart Pot, and in the other direction a public house, the Falcon.

anni horribiles: see **Maltby, Edward Harvey** and **Scarborough, Mrs Jane**.

Aoltia (sometimes **Aolti** or **Aolte**) is a female forename of local origin and unknown etymology, first appearing in the 1830s. Almost all the handful of Aoltias in the UK census records were born in a small area of Huntingdonshire: Grafham, Buckden, Hail Weston; those born elsewhere are descendants of Aoltias. For the curious marital history of Aoltia Mira Thomson, see under **Langley family.**

Aragon Close, Greenway, is a residential cul-de-sac named after **Katherine of Aragon** (q.v.).

Aragon House stands on the corner of St Hugh's Road and the High Street. A dated brick suggests it was built in 1851, probably replacing an earlier house. It is believed that at one time the occupier supplied horses for the coaching trade, the land behind being used for grazing and fodder. If true, the grazier is likely to have been the occupier of the earlier house, as the demand for coach horses would have been in decline by the 1850s, although he (or she: grazier Sarah Cope appears as a High Street resident in the 1851 census) may have found it almost as profitable to supply horses for the new network of local hauliers and carriers that the railways brought into being.

Aragon Singers. In 1985, Margaret Moore moved to St Neots from the north of England, where she had been born into a musical family with a particular interest in singing. She had grown up to become a keen member of church choirs. Thus it was natural for her to join the St Neots Choral Society. The following year one of her fellow singers, Sue Webster, asked if she would be interested in forming a choir for people in Buckden who would like to broaden their repertoire to include more secular music. The Aragon Singers came into being at a meeting held in September 1986, with Margaret as its Musical Director. The name was chosen in tribute to that unwilling resident of Buckden Palace, Katherine of Aragon. The choir's first performance was at a preview of a Festival of Flowers (which Margaret had designed) in Buckden Towers. So began a long journey – a journey of many happy times singing to people who love to listen. Along the way, the choir has raised many thousands of pounds for local and national charities. The choir had twenty-five members in 1986; by 2008 it was some forty voices strong, made up of sopranos, altos, tenors and basses. Its musical director is now Grenville Gutteridge, and its activities include performances of popular choral works in local churches, particularly at Christmas and Easter.

Membership of the National Association of Choirs, and in particular of Group 20 Anglia, has given the choir a wider view and the stimulus and encouragement to improve performance and extend its repertoire.

arson: see under **fires and fire-fighting equipment**.

ash, the Bugden. The 17thC saw a bizarre flurry of interest in finding ways of creating life without going through the natural processes of procreation. For some reason this included 'creating' new ash-trees out of dead ones. A Dr Lister was shown one such tree near Buckden. Despite being without bark and clearly dead from the roots upwards, it had a 'fine young shoot, very vigorous and flourishing' growing out of the very top. He rushed home to write a paper for the Royal Society on his miraculous discovery. Fortunately for his reputation, he was still writing it when word came that 'some inquisitive Body or other' had climbed the tree and discovered that the shoot was not the dead ash reborn: it had grown from a seed dropped from one or other end of a bird and had taken root in the decaying top of the dead tree.

See also **elm**, **plane** and **sycamore**.

B

Baby Show. No longer held, alas: it was once a keenly fought event at the Horticultural Society's annual show, revealing, said the *St. Neots Advertiser* in 1923, 'what fine babies Buckden can produce'.

Other favourite competitions of old Huntingdonshire, such as Best Homemade Calico Knickers and Most Queen Wasps Killed By An Allotment Holder, are perhaps best left unrevived.

Bakers Lane [MapRef 45] now lies under School Lane, but was once the industrial heart of Buckden, housing an agricultural machinery manufactory, complete with its own forges. It was also an area of considerable poverty, overcrowded and often unhealthy: in June 1905, a diphtheria outbreak led St Neots Rural District Council to test a well in the yard of Miss Sarah Thomson (of the inventive **Thomson family** (q.v.)). Finding it highly polluted with organic matter, they successfully applied for a court order to have it closed for three months.

balloon dance: see following entry.

Balls. To the nobility and gentry of Huntingdonshire, as of all counties, balls were the highlights of their social year. At the top were those held at the great houses such as Hinchingbrooke House and Kimbolton Castle, to which few people in Buckden could expect to be invited. In February 1868, for example, the Prince of Wales spent a week at the Castle, and was entertained by two dances: one for 'a number of the aristocracy of Cambridgeshire and Huntingdonshire' and the other the annual Regimental Ball of the Duke of Manchester's Light Horse Volunteers and friends.

At balls in the houses of local squires, such as Stirtloe House, Little Paxton Hall, and Gaynes Hall, one might meet a wider range of guests: not only landowners but also the families of lawyers, military men and the clergy (but probably not curates). At the level of both the great house and the local manor, these entertainments were also likely to reflect shared political interests, especially during elections or times of constitutional crisis such as parliamentary reform.

These dances were private occasions; in addition there were public or semi-public balls, held in such locations as the assembly and public rooms in Huntingdon and St Neots, or hotel ballrooms (such as the Manchester Room at the George in Huntingdon). The County Subscription Ball held for New Year 1909 took over most of the rooms in Huntingdon Town Hall, and some of Buckden's great and good were among those who danced to the music of the White Viennese Band until 4.00 a.m. Foreign bands were hugely popular at the time, and the White Viennese was probably the most popular. In truth, the only foreign thing about most of the players was the accent they adopted to disguise their mainly Yorkshire origins! (For seven years one of their trombonists was Gustav Holst, composer of *The Planets*.)

Fancy dress events were popular and there were also what today might be called niche balls: entertainments for a specific group. Local examples, which some from Buckden may well have attended, include the Bachelors' Ball; the Spinsters' Ball (held at the Fountain, Huntingdon), and the Governess and Servants' Ball.

There were, of course, numerous dances outside these events, but they were normally referred to as dances, not balls.

For many years, dancing was certainly one of the favourite pastimes of Buckden's residents: indoors, outdoors, often in the street. One resident still remembers when the Buckden Band used to play regularly outside the Lion: 'The women danced, the men and boys all gathered together across the street outside Alf Papworth's bakery.' Buckden being Buckden, these occasions sometimes became riotous; but not, surely, on those evenings when the Women's Institute 'indulged' (their description) in dancing in the Rifle Range: not even when the indulgence was a balloon dance (in those days a lively comic competition, with couples being eliminated if they dropped the balloon held between their knees or foreheads; it did not, as sometimes happens today, involve nudity punctuated by loud bangs).

See also **Brass Band; entertainment in Buckden,** and **Smith, Francis James.**

Barson, James (b. 1872). On 11 January 1909 the gardeners and smallholders of Buckden crammed into the village schoolroom to hear the first of a series of eagerly-anticipated lectures by Mr James Barson, the much respected head gardener of Hinchingbrooke House and winner of many horticultural awards (thirteen firsts and seven seconds at the 1905 Ramsey Horticultural Show alone). Unfortunately, the series was doomed to remain incomplete. On 8 February, Mr Barson returned home from London on the 5.16 p.m. train to find that his cottage had been raided by the police. To the astonishment of the county he was arrested on charges of forging and uttering receipts with intent to defraud. Further charges followed, and from a succession of court cases emerged a sad story of an able and ambitious man whose promotion to heavy responsibilities while still under thirty had tempted him into living above his means, and thereby sinking into debt, drink and deceit. At the summer assizes, he was sentenced to fifteen calendar months' hard labour; the judge said that in rejecting the harsher penalty of penal servitude, he had taken into account Barson's guilty plea, the time he had already spent in prison and the probability that he would never again climb above the bottom rung of his profession.

Barthram family members played a respected part in the commercial and church life of Buckden in the latter years of the 19thC. Joseph Barthram (1842-1921) was born in Stokesley, Yorkshire, and grew up in the household of one of his uncles. Like his father, Joseph became an assistant highways surveyor, but left while still in his twenties to work for the railways. In 1867, he married Elizabeth Hedge, a bonnet-sewer of Luton. By 1870 (perhaps earlier), he was a stationmaster. At least two of his postings were in Lincolnshire, of which the first was to the newly enlarged Horncastle station on the Horncastle & Kirkstead Junction Railway (seven and a half miles of track, three trains each way each day, extra market specials on Wednesdays and Fridays)

Some time after 1876, Joseph changed careers again: the 1881 census lists him as a provision merchant in Somersham. The household comprised himself, his wife and a son, Joseph Arthur, apparently born in Horncastle in 1870. By 1885, the family had moved to Buckden to open a provisions store in **Falcon Yard** (q.v.), probably on the site of what is now 87 High Street. (gone today, the yard was just to the north of the Spread Eagle public house). In about 1900, Joseph retired and handed over the business to Joseph Arthur, who had worked with him in the shop for at least ten years and had, according to his descendants, qualified as a Master Grocer.

But this Joseph Arthur was not Joseph's son. He was his nephew, who had also been born in 1870, the son of John and Betsy Barthram of Hull. Curiously, the two young men never appear in the same census: furthermore, the 'Horncastle' Joseph Arthur seems to have no existence outside his inclusion in the Somersham household in 1881; further research suggests that he may never have existed.

Within a few years, the Barthrams gave up the Buckden shop. The older generation remained in the village, but Joseph Arthur followed his uncle's footsteps in reverse, and went to work for the railways, as a goods checker in Lincoln. Both his son, Arthur John (born Buckden 1893 and known as 'Jack'), and his eldest daughter, Florence Celia (Buckden 1898), served in the Air Force during the last year of the First World War. Arthur was in the Royal Flying Corps, and Florence was a clerk in the WRAF.

Barthrams Yard: see Falcon Yard.

Barton, John (c. 1839-1868) was nearly 5' 7" tall, middling stout and sallow-skinned, with brown hair, hazel eyes and a long face. We know this because he was one of the few Buckden residents – perhaps the *only* Buckden resident – to be sentenced to transportation. For his story, see under **fires and fire-fighting equipment.**

Bateman, Oliver. In 1607, this keeper of the bishops' park in Buckden was accused of killing a red deer on (probably) the Grafham estate of Sir Thomas 'Swiftsure' Lake, the king's favourite hunting companion. The justice who examined Bateman decided that the killing had been an accident, and 'entreated favour for him, being a poor man, and very useful to the Bishop'. The plea was apparently successful, as Bateman was still alive nine years later.

bath chair, the Buckden (invalids, for the use of). Purchased in 1909 with the proceeds of a concert

organised by Mr Pat Howson, it could be had on application to the Vicarage. This photograph of the High Street is thought to show the chair in use.

Baxter, Joseph (1797/8-1886). 'The oldest inhabitant in the village has just passed away,' said a local paper in its tribute to a respected resident. Born in Offord Cluny and married in his wife's home village of Great Paxton, he began his working life as a carpenter. By 1851 he had become a brewer and the landlord of the Lion and Lamb, but left there some time in the 1860s and thereafter defined himself by his old trade of carpenter (albeit now a retired one). He lived first out on Mill Road beyond Burton's Lane (now Leadens Lane), and then in Silver Street. His wife Ann survived him by only a few months; their marriage had lasted nearly seventy years.

Beaufort Drive is at the time of writing (2009) the most recent large housing development in the village. Bordered by Silver Street to the east and the A1 to the northwest, it stands on land previously leased from the Church Commissioners as Parish Council allotments. The name was chosen through a competition run by the developers in conjunction with Buckden School; the winner was Alex Day. It commemorates the formidable mother of Henry VII, Lady Margaret Beaufort (1443–1509), who spent the summer of 1501 at Buckden Palace. An earlier Beaufort, Cardinal Henry, had been Bishop of Lincoln from 1398 to 1404.

Beaumont. Frances (Fanny) & Laura Beaumont were Houghton-born sisters who ran a girls' boarding school in Buckden through most of the 1830s and 1840s. Having your own school was one of the few acceptable occupations then open to an unmarried or widowed middle-class woman whose family could no longer support her, either because its income had died with the death of the father/husband (the situation in which the Beaumonts found themselves) or because an excess of daughters strained even a respectable income (as was the case with the Beaumonts' near-contemporaries, the Fox sisters, four of whom ran a girls' school in Huntingdon).

A school proprietress had a degree of independence and respect not found in such under-paid alternatives as being a governess (an employee 'uncomfortably stranded between the dining-room and the servants' hall'), or a companion (i.e. dogsbody) to a richer relative. (But see under **Motley** and **Stoneham** for happier examples of companionship.)

Unfortunately, the lure of independence sometimes tempted people into setting up schools they were not competent to run. Fanny and Laura, however, were better-qualified than many. They were following in the footsteps of their mother, Sarah Robson. Born into a Cambridge family of musicians, artists and clergymen, she had opened a girls' school in Huntingdon after her husband's death had left her with a large family and little money. Some of the children were sent to live with relatives; Fanny and Laura stayed with their mother. Early in the 1830s the three women moved the school from Huntingdon to Buckden, leasing **Oak Lawn** (q.v.) from the Reynolds family. Fanny was now in charge, assisted by Laura. Twenty pupils were present on the night of the 1841 census (day-pupils, if any, would have been recorded in their own homes). They ranged in age from fourteen down to four; three of them were boys (all with older sisters to look after/suppress them). They were typically from moderately well-to-do farming or business families. Although most of them had been born outside the county, some came from as near as Kimbolton or Offord. To be boarded this close to one's home was not unprecedented: Jane Bowyer Cope of Buckden boarded at the Misses Foxes' school in Huntingdon, and horse trainer's daughter Clara May Hawkes of Brampton boarded in Buckden at the Ladies' School run by Mrs **Bowling** (q.v.).

Sarah Beaumont died in 1842, and is buried in St Mary's churchyard (though not where her headstone now indicates). The inscription on her grave is from the Book of Job and confirms that life had not always been kind to her: 'There the wicked cease from troubling; and there the weary be at rest.'

At the end of the 1840s, something, probably the sale of Oak Lawn, prompted the sisters to move the school to The Limes in St Neots, where they ran it until their retirement in about 1870. They later moved to Folkestone, where Fanny died in 1891, aged 84, and Laura in 1893, aged 83.

Two of their siblings were also teachers: Caroline was a schoolmistress in Alconbury Weston until, in her forties, she married and became a shopkeeper in Huntingdon. Their brother William, after a false start as a printer's compositor (during which he lodged with a wheelwright in Buckden), taught at a boys' school in Huntingdon New Town.

See also **balls; Bowling, Mrs Sarah; Cartwright, George;** and **Langley family.**

Beckwith, Audrey, author, lived in Buckden from 1974 to 2009. She knew during her teenage years that she wanted to write, but she led a very active life and could not concentrate on her writing till later. In her twenties she worked for the BBC East and Central European News Department in Bush House in London. Later, she was in the Drama Department.

After her marriage, Audrey and her pharmacist husband, Roy, moved to Derbyshire. Here she wrote her first novel, which was set in Italy. Her first accepted novel, however, was mainly set in Jamaica, and published in America. She had chosen the title *Martha's Cottage*, but the publishers thought it would sell better as *Midnight Heiress* - with the cover line

SHE HAD INHERITED A LEGACY OF TERROR.

Audrey wrote from inspiration, sometimes finding one line enough to set her going. This would develop into a plot, and then the characters would take on a life of their own. But she was always in charge, and was ruthless with them if the need arose. She used two pseudonyms. As Dawn Stacey she wrote historical novels, of which the first was *Man of Principle* and concerned the English Civil War. As Kate Frederick, she wrote gothic novels, such as *Midnight Heiress*. Gothic romances were out of fashion by the beginning of the 21stC, but she had several ready, she would say, for when the fashion changed.

Several of her books were on the best seller list; some were issued as audio books, in large print and in translation.

Audrey was an accomplished and intelligent actress, and happily her and Roy's arrival in Buckden coincided with the revival of Buckden Theatre Club, of which they both became active members.

Audrey died in May 2009; Roy had predeceased her in 2008, at the age of 91.   Janet Ingamells

Beech Lawn, Silver Street [MapRef 49], was described in 1898 by St Neots auctioneers Dilley and Son as 'a charming, old-fashioned Bijou Residence, secluded in its own grounds, with Ornamental & Kitchen Gardens (well planted with Shrubs and Fruit Trees), Orchard and Paddock of Rich Old Pasture Land, Stabling, Coach House, Harness Place, Cow House, and other convenient Outbuildings, Gardener's Cottage, Laundry & small Yard.' More prosaically, it is a Grade II listed residence erected in the mid 18thC and altered several times since.

Census returns, directories and title deeds give us a glimpse of some of those who occupied it (some for quite brief periods). They include the Warsops or Worsops): Mary and her seventy-nine year old husband John, a retired farmer from Alconbury. They moved in during 1862. Mr Worsop died towards the end of 1866; and in October 1868 his widow sold up and returned to Alconbury. The new owner was a retired London merchant, Charles Frederick Mann. He and his wife Caroline employed two resident house servants, and a gardener and his wife (both of whom came, like Mrs Mann, from Yorkshire). Mr Mann died in 1875.

By 1877 the occupier was the adjutant of the Hunts Militia, the recently-married Captain Hillyard H. A. Cameron of the Royal Marines (later a Colonel in the Bedfordshire Regiment). He was the son of a controversial Canadian Attorney General, fathered four children in rapid succession, preferred good plain cooking and was posted to Hampshire in 1881. Beech Lawn's gardener, James Dawks, and his daughter Susan then acted as caretakers for a time while the house was untenanted (they normally lived with the rest of their family).

The next named occupier was Felix Cottrill, who was living in Buckden by 1885 and was still there in 1890. We have no other direct information about him; a person of that name graduated from Cambridge in 1886, studied medicine and ended up a director of T. & M. Hesketh & Sons, his brother-in-law's Lancashire cotton manufactory. Whoever he was, he was gone by 1891, when the George Augustus Cumming Elliotts were in residence, a Scots-Irish couple with a groom/gardener, cook, German butler and no visible means of support. It seems likely their occupancy was brief, as in May 1892 this 'charming country residence' was again being advertised to let, with immediate possession.

By the time it was put up for auction in 1898, Beech Lawn was in the ownership (but not necessarily occupation) of E. Henry Cragg, Esq., who also sold (for £200) the nearby 'brick and slated dwelling house' occupied by the widow of Henry **Hyde** (q.v.). Beech Lawn was bought by Dr F. E. **Williams** (q.v.) as a home and surgery. After his death in 1923, it remained the home of his widow Laura (his successor, Dr Robert **Wallace** (q.v.), had to live elsewhere but continued to use the surgery). Mrs Williams was still there in 1936, but from 1937 to 1942 or 1943, the occupier was the celebrated Captain H. G. **Amers** (q.v).

For a short time after the war, the occupiers were the Elliott-Binns family. The Rev. Dr Leonard Elliott Elliott-Binns (1885-1963) – who until 1936 had been plain the Rev. Dr Leonard Elliott Binns – was a respected ecclesiastical lecturer, historian and author. In 1946, he wrote to *The Times* from Beech Lawn to suggest that tobacco should be included in the sweet ration: but for adults only! For the information of young readers, say those under fifty-five, sweets were rationed from July 1942 until February 1953 (except for four blissful months in 1949).

Another occupant of interest in the late 1940s/early 1950s was Edward Cranfield Rose, co-inventor and patentee of an apparatus for heating tarred and bituminous road surfaces.

In the early days of the Huntingdonshire Constabulary, Beech Lawn was a police conference point, a place where the local constable could be contacted by his seniors at a fixed time (and woe betide him if he wasn't there).

Beehive, 20 Lucks Lane [MapRef 38]. The Beehive, a thatched cottage in Old Lucks Lane, was formerly a brewery. In 1841 it was occupied by an elderly couple, Jane and William Cambers - the cottage does not appear in the census by name, but the Cambers are the only brewers shown in Lucks Lane. They were not Buckden people and when they fell into poverty, they left (or were sent) to live on parish relief in William's village of birth in Bedfordshire. The 1851 census again does not list the Beehive by name, nor is anyone in the lane described as a brewer. It may therefore have been one of the two houses recorded as uninhabited. Later, members of the Lymage family were its tenants: Richard Lymage was in occupation

The Beehive

when the Beehive was included in the dispersal sale of the late Robert Whitehead's Buckden estate in April 1864. In 1899, it was one of three Buckden premises among a hundred Huntingdonshire properties listed as being part of the Jenkins and Jones (Falcon Brewery) estate. The other Buckden properties were the **George** (q.v.), and the **White Horse** (q.v.).

Belgian refugees. One of the earliest events of the First World War to impinge on Buckden was the arrival in September 1914 of refugees from Belgium. They were lodged with widow Rebecca Hubbard in Taylors Lane.

They were part of the biggest refugee movement Britain had ever seen, totalling over a quarter of a million people.

bells, the silence of the. Not as bloodcurdling as *The Silence of the Lambs* but bizarre enough in its own way, this story of Buckden's prolonged campanological hiatus is revealed in **Chapter 5**.

bier, parish. This was a four-wheeled hand-cart which a bereaved family could hire for three shillings to carry the

The Bier   L.R.Button

coffin to church. It was used by all classes of society: as, for example, in the imposing funeral of Alexander **Copping** (q.v.).

An inventory of 1709 includes the parish bier as one of the items of furniture kept at (or possibly in) the church itself. In later years, however, its successor was kept in an old barn at Hunts End; a resident can remember as a boy peering in fearful fascination at it through a crack in the door. This bier was made by Dottridge Brothers, of Hoxton and Shoreditch, London N.1. They founded their company in 1835 and were renowned for the quality of their coachbuilding, moving easily from Victorian horse-drawn funeral cars to hearses converted from classic 20thC cars such as the Silver Wraith. In 1985 the firm moved to Hoddesdon in Hertfordshire, and later to Sutton Coldfield, but by 2009 it was no longer trading.

The Buckden bier was thoroughly restored in the late 1970s by a small group of villagers including Brian Smith, then Chairman of the Parish Council, and Leslie Button, secretary of the Local History Society, and it is now in St Neots Museum.

Bishop, John (c. 1789 – c. 11.20 a.m. on Saturday, 4 April 1829). 'The facts [of the case],' reported *The Times* laconically, 'were wholly uninteresting; and the prisoner was found *Guilty*.' The prisoner was John Bishop, a failed shepherd, and the uninteresting facts were that he had stolen sheep belonging to Mr Thomas Lindsell, gent., of Hemingford Grey. Unfortunately for Bishop it was not his first offence; as a result he became the first and last person to be hanged outside the new county gaol in Huntingdon; the last person, indeed, to be judicially hanged anywhere in Huntingdonshire for a crime other than murder. In passing sentence, the judge held out to him 'no hopes of mercy this side of the grave, *in consequence of the magnitude of the theft*' (twenty sheep).

Two men with ties to Buckden were associated with John Bishop's last days. The case against him was laid out by Buckden-born lawyer E. H. **Maltby** (q.v.), while his burial in Hemingford was overseen by the Rev. James Linton, a relative of the Stirtloe Lintons. Perhaps, too, some Buckden inhabitants were among the small, subdued crowd that gathered before the scaffold: Saturday was a market day, drawing in people from the surrounding villages.

Bishop's death left several children fatherless.

Bishops Way derives its name from Buckden's episcopal associations – not from the unfortunate John Bishop of the previous entry. At first sight it appears to form a crescent, connected at both ends to Greenway; in fact it comprises two short roads that are prevented from meeting by a privately-owned grassed area.

Bixissitt, John died on 3 March 1736 and is buried in St Mary's churchyard. He is included here because of his most unusual surname. No search engine has ever heard of it.

Black Horse, Hunts End (MapRef 36) is one of several of Buckden's licensed premises that are now private houses. It stands to the south-west of the Green, recognisable by its exposed timbers and cement rendering. At one time it was one of the village properties on which an annual dole, or customary payment, of five shillings was levied for the relief of the poor of the parish. Among those who kept it were John Adams (about 1840), Charles Storey (1847) and, in 1861, shepherd's son Joseph Kiteley – or more probably his wife, Mary. It was also occupied by a butcher at one time.

black sheep, absence of in Buckden: see Pusey

blankets to help the poor through the winter were distributed from Stirtloe House each October (and presumably taken back in the following spring to be washed and stored ready for the next winter). It is not known for how long this continued; it was certainly done in the early 1920s.

Bonomi, Colonel Joseph Ignatius, CBE (1857-1930) was a career soldier, the son of an architect, and the grandson of the apocalyptic artist John Martin. He lived in Buckden for a time in the early 1900s (he had left by 1914) and was an enthusiastic participant in the Buckden Reading Rooms' entertainments, both as performer and stage manager.

Boswell, James (1740-1795) was a lawyer, diarist and biographer, and never one to miss the chance of chatting up the ladies. He sometimes passed through Buckden when travelling between his native Scotland and London. But we know of only two occasions when he actually stopped in the village. One was when he and three companions travelling north in a private coach arrived in Buckden on the night of Friday, 21 December 1787 and took 'tea and white-wine whey' at one of the inns. White-wine whey appears in cookery books of the time under the heading 'Recipes for the Sick'. Sick they probably were, having bounced up thirty miles of bad road from Stevenage with beefsteaks, chicken, malt liquor and a bottle of port apiece swilling around their stomachs. The other occasion was in November 1778, when Boswell changed conveyances at Buckden. If the change took more than half-an-hour, some of his descendants may still live here.

Bourne, Gilbert was the last Catholic Bishop of Bath and Wells. He was deposed by Elizabeth I in 1560 and in 1561 was removed to Buckden, into the keeping of Nicholas Bullingham, the (Protestant) Bishop of Lincoln. By June 1562 he was back in London (in the Tower), only to be returned to Buckden in 1563 to avoid the plague. By late 1565, Bullingham had tired of acting as gaoler and succeeded in having Bourne transferred to the custody of the Archdeacon of Exeter.

Bowling, Mrs Sarah (1832-1907) was a fixture in Buckden for over 30 years as a music teacher and proprietress of a small day and boarding school. She was born Sarah Rowell Banks in Spalding, Lincolnshire. In 1858 she married William Bartholomew Bowling, the son of Silver Street farmer Bartholomew Bowling. They had four children, the eldest born in Buckden, the remainder in Colmworth.

The family then moved back to Buckden, but after 1871 Sarah and William were no longer living together - nor would ever do so again. William was on his own at 16 Church Street, calling himself a retired farmer (aged 39). Sarah and the children were at 7 Lucks Lane; she gave her occupation as 'instructress'. Thereafter the course of her life is spelt out in trade directories, the census and advertisements; William's is glimpsed only fitfully in the census and a brief, brutal newspaper report of his death.

By 1881, Sarah was the proprietress of a school near the Spread Eagle, her daughter Beatrice acting as her assistant. They had four boarding pupils: two sisters and their brother from Lincolnshire, and a girl from Brampton. Ten years later, Sarah was running a boarding and day school from a cottage beside Ivelbury. She was on her own (and had knocked 10 years off her age), but the absence of boarders may simply reflect that the census took place in the school holidays. The same 1891 census reveals that her husband, now a maltster, was lodging in a beer-house in Yorkshire; he died the following year, run over by a train.

According to the 1901 census, the now-widowed Sarah was still a private school proprietor, living in what is today 61-63 High Street. She had one boarder, a nine year old girl. Sarah also advertised herself in the 1901 *Eastern Counties of England Trades Directory* as a music teacher 'happy to receive a limited number of pupils for the pianoforte. Terms very moderate'. And then, in July 1905, the *St. Neots Advertiser* announced that she was 'giving up Housekeeping'; the contents of her home were put up for auction. As well as the usual household effects, there were quantities of books, a 'capital' cottage pianoforte, six deal forms, school desks and slates, iron bedsteads and an iron doorplate: 'Ladies School'. After the sale, the house was taken over as a bicycle shop (see under **Robinson's Garages**).

bowls [MapRef 47]. No-one knows when bowls was first played in Buckden, but the game has a long history. There is a document in the Norris Museum which states that in Buckden in 1647 there was a manor house with 'a Bowlinge Greene sett about with sycamore trees'. From its description, this 'manor house' is clearly the Bishop's Palace. This was just 59 years after Drake finished his game before chasing the Armada!

The modern era began with the inauguration of Buckden Bowls Club on 21 November 1929, when a meeting of interested members was offered shares in the club. The green was in Silver Street, where the house called 'Bowlings' now stands, and there was a pavilion of sorts from early on. The green must have already been in use: the first drive was on 3 May 1930, and it is impossible to get a green up to playing standard in a few winter months. Unfortunately, the club soon got into some financial difficulty, and in 1933 had to cut the groundsman's annual

"The first drive" by Mr Robinson 3rd May 1930

Photo courtesy of Ken Spencer

remuneration from £12 to £6, apparently without consulting him.

From the beginning, ladies were allowed to bowl and become active members of the club, the first lady president being elected as early as 1934. (At that year's AGM a tennis section was also formed: see under **tennis in Buckden**).) The purchase of a motor-mower in 1939 shows that the club was willing to embrace new technology, although the year war broke out and a decade of petrol rationing began was perhaps not the most auspicious time to demonstrate this!

The club carried on throughout the war; one of the few references to prevailing conditions was the rejection of a proposal to let evacuees use the garden grounds of the club. The war was still casting its shadow long after hostilities ended, however: in 1952 the club had to ask for fats and sugar coupons to hold a social function.

By 1956 the facilities had deteriorated, in part no doubt because of long neglect during the war: in 1940, complaints had led to the groundsman being paid off and relieved of his duties for not fulfilling his obligations, leaving members to maintain the greens and pavilion.

In 1972 the Playing Field Trust offered the bowls and tennis clubs the use of land at the village playing fields, and this offer was accepted. From then until 1976 the new green area was drained, prepared and levelled and a green was laid. The cost ran into several thousand pounds, paid for by social events and weekly lunches as well as the membership fees. An official opening match took place in 1977 against a county team.

Professional help was used and the green, maintained by the members, is of an excellent standard. This was underlined on the club's 75th anniversary, when the President of the Bowling Association visited with a team.

See also **Price, James.**

Bowtells of Buckden, High Street, was the village's own department store, founded by Mr Percy H. Bowtell. The business had previously been managed as a grocery and drapery by Dennis Russell Hardley ('Sole agent for Ceylon tea and Lifebuoy Royal Disinfectant Soap'). Hardley had taken it over from the Langley family in the 1880s but in 1902, after having seven children, he decided to emigrate to New Zealand.

Mr Bowtell later wrote that the premises looked 'not much more than a cottage village shop' but that the books revealed an unexpectedly thriving business. Under his guidance it continued to flourish and in 1911 he was able to buy the building. In 1922 he built the post office – now the ladieswear shop Elouise Lingerie – and in 1923 had the main centre building rebuilt and faced in an Elizabethan style. 'Thus,' he wrote, 'modern, up-to-date business premises were erected, adapted to the surrounding architecture.' The work was designed by Huntingdon architect William A. Lea and carried out by Buckden builders George Page & Son. The premises were further modernised in 1936 when fire destroyed a barn at the rear, making room for new warehouses and garages.

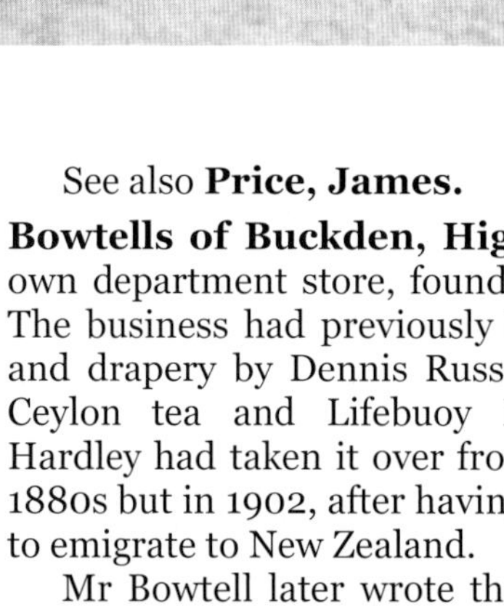

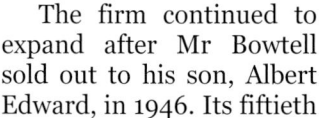

P.H.Bowtell   Barry Jobling

The firm continued to expand after Mr Bowtell sold out to his son, Albert Edward, in 1946. Its fiftieth anniversary brochure listed its many departments with justifiable pride:

Grocery and Provisions; China, Glass and Earthenware; Ironmongery; General Drapery; Ladies' and Children's Outfitting; Gents' Outfitting; Footwear; Linoleum and Carpets; Furniture

Mr Bowtell lived at Nutfield, Perry Road, a large house which, as Ellerslie, had previously been the home of, among others, Dr Hillyer. Mr Bowtell liked his staff also to live 'near the shop' and houses were made available for departmental managers and others.

A Methodist, Mr Bowtell was a 'passive resister', that is to say someone who refused on principle to pay their rates towards the upkeep of church schools; for this he, like many respectable people, was fined.

Brandreth, Thomas Shaw, MA FRS (1788-1873) was a pupil of Dr **Maltby** (q.v.). He grew up to be a mathematician, inventor, classical scholar and barrister. A close friend of the engineer George Stephenson, he played a prominent part in the development of the Manchester & Liverpool Railway. Later in life he took a lively interest in the affairs of Worthing, especially its drainage.

Brass Band, Buckden. It's a fine summer evening in Buckden in June 1904. You and your loved one are discussing how to spend it: a stroll down Cemetery Road and across the fields to Diddington? Or down Mill Road to watch the bathers in the Ouse (a bit risqué that, perhaps)? A sudden burst of music reminds you that there is a more interesting alternative. The local paper has reported that the Buckden Band

'now play for dancing on Wednesday and Friday evenings in Mr Brown's paddock at the back of the George Hotel. As only 2d is charged, which includes instruction in dancing, the attendance has been good.'

The band was reputed to be one of the largest village bands in the country. The most authoritative account to date can be found in Appendix no. 2 of 'Bands in St Neots and District' by David Bushby published in 1997.

The Buckden Band. Date and location unknown   Gale family collection

Entries in the *Hunts Post* for 1922, record that the band was in abeyance in June of that year but in July it was revived by Mr W. Hodson sufficiently to play sacred music in the High Street on a Sunday evening. The band is often referred to during the following year as providing entertainment in the village – as it had done throughout its history, leading processions mounted on a wagon, and playing at special celebrations (such as the Nelson Centenary and the end of the Boer War), shows, fetes and sports days.

There had always been rival bands and other makers of music. Initially these had been other brass bands, such as the Hunts Militia Band, which occasionally played in Buckden. After the First World War the challenge came from new directions: the exotic, like Madame de Siro's Hawaiian Orchestra, and the modern, like the County Syncopated Dance Orchestra.

See under **Edleston** for a note about an unusual event at which the band played.

Brickyard Lane was the name used in the 1891 census for what in previous censuses had been an unnamed alley off the High Street, which subsequently became **York Yard** (q.v.). The only known brick and tile pits in Buckden were to the west of what is now the A1. The 1926 Ordnance Survey map shows what appears to be a large excavated area almost due west of, and possibly accessible from, the lane, but it is not clear whether the two are connected. According to the late Maurice Milner, it was also known as Brickle – a local abbreviation of 'brick kiln'.

Bridge House, Church Street [MapRef 10] is believed to be the oldest surviving building in Buckden. The house was built in 1458 and when first completed was an open medieval hall and a building of high status. It takes its name from the humpback bridge that used to carry Church Street across a stream directly to the west of the main building. The house has been painstakingly restored by Mr Christopher Bates, wherever possible using materials and techniques sympathetic to the building. For his own story of the problems and pleasures involved in returning a historic house to its former glory. See **Chapter 6: Bridge House, Church Street**.

Brightman, Mr [Walter] Harry: see **accidents, shooting.**

Brown, Lancelot (1748–1802) was a barrister and MP whose hopes of augmenting his pension were thwarted by the clergy of Buckden. Known as 'Lance' or 'Capey' to distinguish him from his famous father, the landscape gardener Lancelot 'Capability'Brown, he was the tenant of Stirtloe House for several years at the turn of the 19thC. In 1784 he became one of the two 'borough' MPs for Huntingdon Town. He resigned in 1787 but in 1792 was asked to take over one of the two 'county' seats representing Huntingdonshire. Viscount Hinchingbrooke, the seat's previous occupant, had been obliged to resign when he succeeded his father as the Earl of Sandwich. He asked Lancelot Brown to keep the seat warm for a year or two until the new Viscount Hinchingbrooke was of an age to bring it back into the family; in return, he would secure Brown a Crown post (i.e., an undemanding government job with a good pension). Brown agreed, was elected unopposed, and kept his side of the bargain by resigning in 1794. Six years later he was still 'violently enraged' that no Crown post had yet come his way. Lord Sandwich's friends claimed that he had made every effort but had been constantly thwarted by his political enemies – who included the Bishop of Lincoln and the Vicar of Buckden!

Lancclot Brown died in 1802 ('carried off on Sunday morning last, after lying ill about a month'). He left no children, and the tenancy of Stirtloe House seems to have passed to Lawrence Reynolds (see under **Reynolds**).

Brown, Richard was a Buckden resident whose obituary reported that he had had an idea '*to which, possibly, few other people have given thought, viz., that Buckden is situated in the crater of an extinct volcano.*' Mr Brown's working life was very practical one. The son of a watchmaker, he was apprenticed to a basket–maker and used his skill to develop a considerable business which would now be described as vertically integrated. He bought osier beds and organised the necessary harvesting. The osiers were prepared and used for basket-making in Brown's Yard in the village and also despatched for use elsewhere in the country. His son Alfred, who added market-gardening to the family's occupations, was the grandfather of Frederick (Freddy) Brown, once Buckden's postman and for many years noted for his gooseberries.

Bruce, Robert (1810-1883), the son of Hardwick labourer Thomas and Ann (née Virgin), was an agricultural labourer and shepherd who became a Wesleyan preacher. As a young man, he was something of a serial wedding witness, attending the weddings of:

Thomas Pettit and Sarah Clark on 28 September 1829

Joseph Virgin and Martha Beresford on 6 January 1830

Joseph Russell Sallaway and Mary Audley on 18 October 1830 (the other witness was Rebecca Berrill, his own bride of 3 days before) and

his brother Thomas to Sarah Wright on December 22 1836

He may have been in demand because he could write his name.

By 1861, he and Rebecca had left Buckden for Eaton Socon.

Buckden by-pass. There is no Buckden by-pass, only a four-lane stretch of highway opened in October 1962, which diverts the A1 away from the High Street and splits the village.

Buckden Gas & Coke Company is known to have existed in the late 19thC, one of many such small town enterprises. Its chairman was Samuel Day, a St Neots attorney. At an Extraordinary General Meeting held in the Buckden postmaster's office on Friday, 19 December 1873, it was resolved that the company should forthwith be voluntarily wound up. Unlike some, it does not seem to have produced its own gas, at least not for general use: a local historian has suggested its primary purpose may have been to provide a supply for The Towers.

Buckden Hosiery Co. Ltd, 168 Regent Street, London, was the company behind the Buckden Hosiery Mill. See under **stocking factory.**

Buckden in the 14th century: names, numbers and tags. One of the frustrations of finding out about the more distant past is that there is so little documented evidence of what life was like for the common people. However, Buckden is lucky in having two sets of names of people who paid their taxes. Moreover the two sets are from only five years apart, so that it is not unreasonable to assume that a name on one roll is the same person as one of the same name on the other. **See Chapter 20** for a detailed examination of these lists, showing who paid what; how such factors as bad weather, enclosures and disease affected the size of people's tax bills; and how people's names were derived: for example, from
- occupations (Webster, Clerk)
- nicknames (John le Long)
- places local (Attwell = by the well)) and more distant (Chatteris), and
- Christian names (Saunder from Alexander).

Some may even have arisen by mistake: wrongly copied between documents or just misheard – something that occurred again from 1841 onwards, when the national census enumerators came up against unfamiliar accents or people who had no idea how to spell their own name.

Buckden, Moses (b. 1857), master of the Grimsby fishing smack 'Fairy', owed his name to the fact that as an infant he was discovered abandoned in a ditch at Buckden. He was raised in the St Neots Union Workhouse and when old enough was apprenticed aboard a Grimsby fishing vessel. (Workhouse boys were considered to make reliable fishing apprentices, because Union guardians insisted that they were given the chance to experience life at sea before agreeing to sign on.) The 1871 census records him as a cook aboard an unnamed vessel working the Dogger Bank. By 1881, he was married (to Mary Jane Hudson, in 1879) and living next door to his in-laws in Grimsby. 'By energy and perseverance,' said the *St. Neots Chronicle* of Moses in October 1884, 'he has worked his way up, and is now a skipper'. (He had in fact achieved this in 1880, aged only 23.) By 1886, he had become not only the skipper but also the owner of a larger vessel, the 'Queen Victoria'.

Sadly, *The Times* for 21 March 1894 records an adjudication of bankruptcy against his name; the 1901 census records him as a fisherman not at sea and with no indication of whether he had regained the rank of captain or even mate.

Moses and Mary Jane had at least six children, one of whom died in infancy.

Another boy from St Neots, James Freeman, was the cook on another vessel in the same fleet as Moses. He was not, however, from the workhouse; his unusual choice of career may have been inspired by his having grown up in the yard behind the town's leading fishmonger.

Buckden Palace [MapRef 26]: see **The Towers.**

Buckden Roundabout is a monthly parish journal started in 1979 by Buckden Churches Together. Its history is described in **Chapter 15**.

Buckden Station was open from 1866 to 1959 – but in the parish of Brampton, not Buckden. Almost all physical trace of its existence now lies beneath the (now closed) household waste recycling centre and a derelict fuel depot; they in their turn are likely to be obliterated by a new relief road. See **Chapter 19** for the full story of Buckden and the railway.

Budge, Miss Mabel Beauford. A Brampton rector's eldest daughter (and housekeeper), she moved to Buckden and became a weathergirl, supplying the *Hunts Post* with regular meteorological reports during the 1920s. She lived in 'The Cottage' in old Lucks Lane, and threw open her garden during Feast Week (but not to unaccompanied children).

Bugden is one of at least 15 known spellings of the village name. It is still used in speech by Huntingdonshire people (not necessarily only Bugden residents).

Burberry Homes, Church Street [MapRef 7], are almshouses, originally provided for by the Charity of William Burberry for Almshouses – see under **charities.**

Burberry Road [MapRef 1], a modern residential street that leads to the village's community centre and playing field, is also named for Buckden's 16thC benefactor William Burberry.

Burder, Thomas (fl. late 17thC) Buckden resident who fathered 18 children, all of whom are said not only to have survived into adulthood but also to have married.

buses - and before the buses There is no record of what local public passenger transport served Buckden before 1915 apart from the railways. People wanting to visit nearby villages or market towns would have had to make their own way. Depending on their social station, they would have driven or ridden in carriages, traps or farm-carts, or gone on horseback; the great majority would have walked. A few might have been taken as passengers by the ubiquitous carriers, the commercial conveyors of goods, produce and small livestock by cart or van. Among the most notable of these were:

HENRY CREAMER, one of Buckden's leading Methodists and its first recorded carrier (*Robson's Commercial Directory* 1839). A cooper and trunkmaker by trade, he brought out his cart on market days (to the Dolphin, Huntingdon, on Saturdays, and to St Neots on Thursdays). Some time after 1851, he moved to Great Paxton (where he had been born) and changed career, working with his son as a clock cleaner and repairer. By 1871, however, he had returned to Buckden and was living in Lucks Lane – with one of the most precise job descriptions to be found in any census: 'Maker of 30 hour clock lines' (presumably the chains on which hung the weights).

By 1847 he had acquired a rival in:

JOHN RISELEY of Mill Street, who added St Ives market to those of Huntingdon and St Neots. He ran the following timetable with returns the same day:-
Mondays: Huntingdon & St Ives: Dep. 9 a.m.
Thursdays: St Neots: Dep. 9 a.m.
Saturdays: Huntingdon: Dep. 9 a.m.
However, John died in 1848 and was succeeded by his widow, Mary – already in her sixties – who ran the business through the 1850s, until ill-health forced her to pass it on to their son, also John, who was still at work as a carter in the second decade of the 20thC.

MICHAEL REDDEN (1823-1910) of Church Street was primarily a butcher by trade, but ran similar services on Thursdays (St Neots) and Saturdays (Huntingdon).

Buckden has been served by buses to the local market towns. In 1915 F. J. **Hinsby** (q.v.) and his brother started a service two days a week from St Neots to Godmanchester via Buckden and Huntingdon. By 1921 this had grown to services on Thursdays (four times) and Saturdays (five times). They also served St Ives once on Mondays and twice on Sundays. The vehicle was an open-top double–decker. In 1922 the National Omnibus & Transport Co. (NO&T), centred on Bedford, joined in and shared services were operated with Hinsby until 1931, although in 1930 the NO&T had become Eastern National. This company name survived until 1952 when Eastern National became part of United Counties.

In 1967 on Mondays to Fridays there were fifteen daily services southbound between Huntingdon and St Neots and twelve northbound. It is not reported why there was such a difference! Five of these journeys extended to St Ives and Aylesbury via Roxton and Woburn, with six in the opposite direction. On Sundays there were four each way.

For a few years towards the end of the 20thC, the village found itself on a long-distance route that it had not enjoyed since the end of the stagecoach era: a daily commuter service to and from London. This was run by Whippet Coaches of St Ives. During the same period the aptly-named Stagecoach company enabled Buckden residents to travel direct to Peterborough in the north and Gatwick in the south.

Stagecoach returned to the area in 2008 to operate the local services to St Neots and Huntingdon. This was in succession to Cavalier Travel, a Norfolk company that had in turn taken over from United Counties' successor, Huntingdon & District.

There are now no buses on Sundays.

Byng, John, 5th Viscount Torrington (1743-1813) was a soldier, angler and civil servant who used his annual holidays to tour much of England and Wales, writing a diary as he went. He often passed through Buckden, and was greatly taken by the George, with its 'good cream', its amiable landlord (William South) and especially its resident barber ('a political barber – as barbers should be'). This was in contrast to his experience in most inns, whose disgusting food and slovenly service drove him to heights of inspired vituperation.

Although he disapproved of the bishops of Lincoln living so far from their cathedral, he was keen to see inside their Palace. When he finally succeeded in 1790 he was impressed by what was left - but sad that so much had disappeared. Afterwards he walked down to St Neots by way of Diddington church ('dirty and gloomy') and Southoe ('a mean dwindling village').

C

Canal, the. There are various theories as to the origin of the stretch of water west of the recreation ground, commonly known as the Lake or the Valley. Was it a clay pit? A series of fish-ponds? Or does it represent an abandoned early 19thC attempt to give Buckden a direct waterway to the Ouse, thus doing away with the need to haul goods up or down the hill between the village and the river wharves?

The last of these theories seems implausible. The investment required to construct and maintain such a canal and its locks would appear to have outweighed any conceivable benefits.

The rumour of a Buckden canal may have arisen from a meeting in 1924 between Dr Edleston, the eccentric antiquarian owner of The Towers, and a mapping surveyor noting revisions for a new edition of the 1886 OS plan. That plan had The Towers' lake labelled 'Fish Pond', and indeed it is known that it had originated as a series of

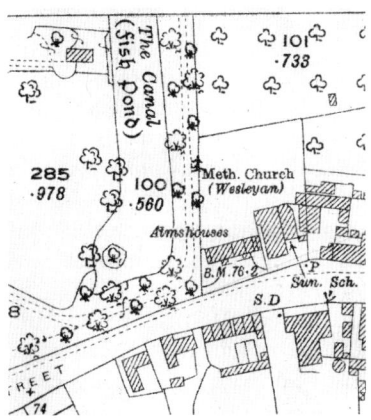

Extract from 1924 revision of OS plan.

ponds in which fish were raised for the bishop's table. From the 17thC onwards, however, it became fashionable to treat such ponds as ornamental rather than merely useful: small ponds were run together and their edges straightened out, turning them into water features—known as garden canals—which it was pleasant to stroll beside, around or, less wisely, on (see **Hodgson**). As the 18thC progressed, the term 'canal' was also applied by designers such as 'Capability' Brown to the long narrow artificial lakes they incorporated into their landscapes. Mr Edleston would have been well aware of this, and quite likely to have pointed out to the surveyor that the Towers' lake had been informally called a canal since at least 1820: with the result that the 1926 OS plan identified it as "The Canal(Fish Pond)".

Thus an antiquarian's desire for precision may have led people to think the Towers' garden canal and the equally rectilinear stretch of water in the Valley were actually the remains of an abandoned commercial waterway.

(A cottage terrace in Hunts End is said to have been built to house canal engineers, and hence has become known as Navigation Cottages. It may be it was actually built for the navvies (navigators or diggers) working on the *railway*, although if so, it was remarkably soundly built for men who were essentially itinerant labourers. The terrace has also appeared in at least one census as Vine Cottages.)

Canning, Percy World Men's Conker Champion 1992 renowned for his prize-winning vegetables and home-made wines.

Captain Green's golden eagle achieved international fame when the following report from *The Naturalist for May 1837* was reprinted throughout the 19thC in several newspapers, magazines and annual reviews – abroad as well as in Britain:

'Fierce and wild as the golden eagle generally is instances have occurred in which it has been thoroughly tamed. Captain Green of [Coneygarths in] Buckden in Huntingdonshire has now in his possession a splendid bird of this description which he has himself trained to take hares and rabbits.'

The Captain also owned a transvestite chicken – see under **cross-dressing**.

Carters Boatyard, Mill Road, situated between the Ouse and Mill Road on the bend before the Offord and Buckden flour mills bridge, was founded by Brian Carter, who bought the land in 1949 and developed it as a boatyard and residential caravan site. In the early 2000s, some time after it had passed out of Mr Carter's ownership, developers submitted a number of proposals for more intensive use of the land for (mainly) second homes.

Cartwright family. George Cartwright (1787-1850), keeper of coaching inns, came to Buckden from Eaton Ford to take over the Spread Eagle. With him came his family, including his wife Elizabeth Henson (1785-1856), the daughter of a Yaxley blacksmith, whom he had married in 1808.

A sociable man, he soon became a familiar figure in Buckden. As well as being an innkeeper, he was also a minor national celebrity, famous as the skilled and unusually polite coachman of the York express. According to the sporting journalist 'Peter Pry', he was 'bony, without fat, healthy-looking, evidently abstemious; moreover not too tall, but just the proper size to sit gracefully.' He was considerate of his horses and his 'personal equipment' was 'modest, respectable, in good taste'.

He could also be sharp-witted. Driving back from Welwyn one night in 1834, he overheard a passenger reading out the description of John Ellis, a young clerk employed by the Cubitt brothers, London's leading builders. He had absconded with the firm's weekly wage payout: £600 in sovereigns and new half-sovereigns (over one thousand gold coins – 'It was certainly not a convenient parcel for a man to carry along the road who was walking,' said a witness). While enjoying breakfast in the Spread Eagle, Cartwright noticed his wife serving a man matching Ellis's description, who paid for a glass of brandy and water with a new half-sovereign. He immediately took him into custody and with the help of one of his neighbours, farmer and churchwarden Thomas Bowyer of **Jessamine House** (q.v.) and conveyed him before the Huntingdon JPs. They ordered Mr Bowyer to take him to London, to Bow Street Magistrates' Court. The following month both Bowyer and Cartwright had to give evidence at Ellis's trial at the Old Bailey. He was convicted, but received only three months' confinement thanks to pleas for mercy both from his employers and from the jury, who all agreed that he had acted while driven temporarily mad by the death of his baby son.

Presumably George Cartwright's prompt action earned him a share of the £50 reward offered by Cubitts.

Sometimes, however, he was less perceptive. In 1833, while surveyor of the highways for the parish, he allowed a Buckden labourer, Samuel Plumb, to con him out of 7s. by pretending to be destitute. 'Whereas' – according to the case presented to the Huntingdonshire Quarter Sessions – 'Plumb had just received 1s. 6d. from Robert Circuit [Sirkett] for work done and he could procure more work to keep his family and himself.'

In October 1836, the Cartwrights moved on to the George, a big step up but not a well-timed one: the railways were coming.

In his eulogy of Cartwright, Peter Pry wrote that towards the end of his life his excellent qualities 'had gained their reward; he was well-to-do, lived regularly, [and] had a happy family'. This was an incomplete summing-up. His last years were not without tragedy. In 1839, the Cartwrights' younger daughter, Mary Anne, had married a London 'man's mercer', Henry May. In 1847, aged only 28, she died suddenly while in Buckden. She is buried in St Mary's churchyard.

Cartwright himself died in February 1850 from 'suppression of urine' (thought by the Victorians to be associated with corpulency, so he may have lost the elegant figure admired by Peter Pry). He had lived long enough to see the unstoppable spread of the railway bringing an end to his kind and a temporary end to Buckden's prosperity. His widow took over the George and the farm. This was not an unusual occurrence: women, particularly widows, were often active in the village's commercial life. Nineteenth century trade directories list not only Elizabeth Cartwright but also several others who succeeded husbands or other male relatives, among them Martha Perrin (blacksmith and wheelwright), Jane Faulkner (pork butcher), Charlotte Smith (beer seller), Elizabeth Clack (builder) and Mary Riseley (carrier).

The Cartwrights' eldest daughter, Elizabeth Henson Cartwright (b. 1816), became a teacher, specialising in music; she is shown in the 1864 Post Office Directory as having a ladies' boarding and day school in the High Street. Like most such schools, it also took in small boys. One of these was six-year old J. R. Langley, the sub-postmaster's son; looking back sixty years later, he remembered her as an 'acid spinster from 40 to 50 years of age' who 'instructed me in the usual approved branches of knowledge'. The 'instruction' consisted chiefly of his having to learn Mrs Sarah Trimmer's *Catechism* by heart.* Despite this unpromising start to his education, he ended up going to university.

*Sarah Trimmer (1741-1810) was a Sunday School reformer and writer of children's books; some of her works, including the scriptural catechism and the perhaps less intimidating story of three birds called Dicksy, Flapsy, and Pecksy, remained in print for over a hundred years

Miss Cartwright gave up teaching to become housekeeper to the **Cranfield family** (q.v.), one of whom had been her pupil.

One of George Cartwright's sons, John, followed his father into the hotel trade, becoming an innkeeper in Huntingdon. Something of George's passion for coaches was passed on to another son, George junior, albeit in less dashing form: the boy grew up to be a London omnibus driver, a job he was still doing into his 70s; he ended his days in St Anne's Home, a branch of the St Pancras Workhouse. *His* son, George W., known as William, was a carman, that is, the driver of a horse-drawn van or tram.

Catherine of Aragon: see **Katherine of Aragon**

Cavell, Nurse Edith Louisa (1865-1915) is well known for her heroism in the First World War when she ran a Red Cross hospital in Brussels. For assisting British and French soldiers to escape to the Dutch frontier she was arrested, tried and killed by firing squad.

She was a cousin of Mrs Kathy Coles, who lived in the double-fronted house adjacent to Lucks Cottage. A woman who considered purchasing the house in the 1980s reported that it still had earth floors.

Cawcutt, Ann. 'I have a scarce little tract by a Cawcutt of Huntingdonshire,' wrote Herbert E. Norris, benefactor of the Norris Museum in St Ives, '[and] as it is little known and rather an interesting account of two persons, mother and son, I give the title':

'A
MOTHER'S PRAYER ANSWERED
Being
PARTICULARS
Of a remarkable
MANIFESTATION
Witnessed by
ANN CAWCUTT
OF STIRTLOE HUNTS
ON SATURDAY 4TH AND SUNDAY 5TH
FEBRUARY 1865
AS NARRATED BY HERSELF'

Ann Cawcutt (née Eaden) was the wife of John, who worked his way up from labourer to farm bailiff. They lived in Bowyer's Farm House, Stirtloe, and had three children: Charles, John and Ann. The manifestation which Mrs Cawcutt witnessed was of Charles, of whose death at sea she had recently learnt. He had been on board HMS *Bombay*, a teak-built line-of-battle screw steamer that caught fire and sank off the coast of Uruguay in December 1864. The cause of the fire was never determined, but it spread so rapidly that the order to abandon ship had to be given only seventeen minutes after the alarm had first been sounded. Just over ninety of those on board perished.

In her vision Mrs Cawcutt saw her son in the company of Christ. He told her that though he had found a watery grave, her prayers had moved God to deliver him out of the hands of the devil and that his spiritual salvation was assured. After urging her to tell the rest of the family and 'my sinful companions' to follow him to Heaven (i.e., lead godly lives), he left her with the comforting thought that she would soon be dead and reunited with him. Her last glimpse of him was of a hand and arm waving to and fro out of a small cloud.

That Charles had indeed perished may be inferred from the fact that he never appears in any of the subsequent Buckden censuses or parish registers. However, nor does his name appear in the official list of those who died. This may simply be a transcription error, though none of the Charleses listed has a surname at all similar to Cawcutt. Or it may be that he joined up under an assumed name: the reference to the 'sinful companions' he had left behind in Buckden, suggests he might have been a bit of a bad lad who had seen the error of his ways (with some help from his mother) and decided to make a new life for himself.

Ann lived almost another ten years, dying a few weeks short of the anniversary of Charles's death; within twenty-four hours, her husband was also dead. Their grave is in St Mary's churchyard, not far from the westernmost path.

cemetery. St Mary's churchyard closed in the summer of 1883, to be replaced from 1 September by a new cemetery in Lucks Lane. The first burial, which took place on 20 October, was of Florence Morley, an infant of 3 months and 4 days.

The cemetery was administered in turn by St Neots Rural District, Huntingdonshire District Council and Buckden Parish Council. Its maintenance is part of the duties of the parish handyman, but for several years there was a dedicated cemetery supervisor or keeper.

"Cemetery Lane"   Barry Jobling

Cemetery Lane appears to have been briefly used as the name of that part of Lucks Lane that runs past the cemetery.

census, dates of. Beginning in 1801, and excepting 1941, a census has been held in Britain every ten years. The first four censuses were little more than simple head counts of the population. In 1841 the first modern census was held. Each householder was required to complete a census schedule giving the address of the household and for each individual residing in his or her accommodation, and their name, sex and occupation. In 1851 householders were asked to give more precise details of the places of birth of each resident, to state their relationships to him or her, marital statuses and the nature of any disabilities from which they may have suffered. Apart from a few minor changes the basic structure of the census schedule did not change until 1891. Householders were then asked how many rooms (if less then five) their family occupied. Additional occupational data were collected and, in Wales, people were asked to say if they spoke the Welsh language.

13

After being collected by enumerators the census schedules were copied into census enumerators' books (CEBs). The CEBs were then sent to London where census clerks used them to compute various local and national statistics. Although the original schedules up to and including 1901 were destroyed, the CEBs were kept and were made public after 100 years.

6	June	1841	3	April	1881
30	March	1851	5	April	1891
7	April	1861	31	March	1901
2	April	1871	2	April	1911

Chadwick, Elizabeth, the Amateur British Golf Champion in 1966 and 1967 and Curtis Cup golfer, was known when living in Buckden under her married surname of Pook (Liz to her friends). Her abilities in sport were cruelly altered by an operation on her back which went wrong. The quotation 'Misfortune is an occasion to demonstrate character' most certainly applies to this courageous woman. For more information, see Chapter 16 of *One Hundred years of Women's Golf* by Lewine Mair (1992).

Chandler, William (c. 1808-1850) was a post office employee who lived in Church Lane (Lucks Lane). In the 1841 census he appears as a 'Postboy', the 'boy' being part of the job description rather than a description of William himself: he was thirty-one, married for nine years and had four children (at least one other had died in infancy). There were several types of postboy: some travelled, riding with the mail coach or driving a post-chaise, others - including William - worked out of a post office, delivering mail to their own and nearby villages (in William's case with the handicap of not being very good at reading or writing). In 1849, alas, he was convicted of a rather pathetic fraud: 'embezzling 2 pence, monies of H. M. Postmaster General, at Southoe' - i.e., having been paid to frank two letters, he pocketed the money and franked them with old stamps. For this he was sentenced to three months' hard labour. Other petty crimes followed and he ended up in the St Neots Union Workhouse, dying there in 1850. Left to bring up their children (six of them now), his widow, Catherine [née Middleton], spent the rest of her life in poverty, living in a stud and thatch cottage in Lucks Lane and working as a laundress. She died in October 1877, on the eve of what would have been her forty-fifth wedding anniversary. Although both she and William were buried in the churchyard, there is no record of their grave[s].

charities. Buckden has been blessed with a number of benefactors over the years, who bequeathed money, land or buildings to be used to improve life for the poor and the old. Among them are:

William Burberry. Under his will of 1558, the rental income from property in Buckden and Stirtloe was to be distributed to poor families each Good Friday. (In time, part of the distribution took place in mid-December.) By 1825, it was no longer enough just to be poor: you had to be deserving and industrious. There was to be nothing for families where either or both parents were of a notorious bad character, i.e. 'idle or drunken, continually quarrelling in the neighbourhood, or regularly absenting themselves from Divine Service.' In 1850, a further condition excluded 'any parents who permit their children on the Lord's Day, and at other times, to wander about the village, and create disturbances, to the annoyance of the other inhabitants'.

The Burberry endowment included fields bordering the western side of the Great North Road, a hundred yards or so south of its junction with Perry Road. They are now known the Windmill Allotments (see under **police trap** for a less charitable use to which they were once put).

Susannah Travill. In her will of 1692, she left £100 to be invested, the income to be given to the poor widows of Buckden.

James South (1768-1834) was a half-pay infantry captain whose will provided funds for the building, furnishing and maintenance of almshouses for 'four of the oldest poor women and four of the oldest poor men born in the parish of Buckden'.

Edward Maltby (1770-1859) left £100 to the poor of Buckden. This may have come as a surprise to them: by the time he died, he hadn't been in the village for nearly thirty years, having in the interim become a bishop (first of Chichester and then of Durham). They probably remembered him - if they remembered him at all - as someone given to preaching very long sermons.

These bequests, together with *The Dole Charity* and the *Allotments for Reeveman, Constable and Hayward,* are now known as the Buckden Parochial Charities. For a detailed description of how they are administered, see **Chapter 12**.

Other benefactors had a particular concern for education. They included:

Robert Rayment, who died in 1661 and in his will instructed his heirs to arrange for an annual payment of £10 to be made to the vicar and churchwardens to enable them to employ someone to teach the children of poor families.

John Green (1706-1779), Bishop of Lincoln, who in his will gave the vicar and churchwardens £200, the dividends or interests of which were to be paid annually to the parish schoolmaster. According to the Charities Report of 1836, he had already donated a house and garden for the schoolmaster's use.

John Linton (1792-1877), of Stirtloe, who in the early 1850s enlarged the schoolhouse at his own expense.

Miss Mason, who left the endowed boys £1. 9s. a year in her will.

George Cornelius Swan, sometimes *Swann* (1716-1788) gave the parish £80, which enabled it to erect a small workhouse in Mill Road. For more details, see **parish workhouse**.

For further details, see **Chapter 12** 'Buckden Parochial Charities' and **Chapter 13**: 'Education in Buckden'.

Charles Court, High Street, is a late 20thC courtyard development in the grounds of **Coneygarths** (q.v.).

Chequers, the. There can be no doubt that Buckden once had an inn of this name - it and its landlord, Thomas Smith, are both mentioned in the *London Gazette* for the 26 October 1686 - but knowing where it stood is another matter.

Cherry, Edward (1842-1927) was the great-grandfather of Ann Brown, wife of Frederick Brown, popular Buckden postman and smallholder. Mr Cherry's retirement, due to rheumatism, at the age of 83 from his job as roadman after 56 years' service was reported in the local press. He experienced the end of road tolls and considered that the road surfaces deteriorated afterwards because people did not have to pay.

He and his wife Mary had at least nine children, one of whom, William Henry, was also a roadman.

cherry orchards were once a feature of Buckden. Eighteenth century records show Thomas Ford, baker, enjoying the fruits of one in Silver Street (1763), and in 1780 a cherry orchard was among several pieces of land of which Mary Russell Burder became tenant. There are still individual cherries trees in the parish, but the orchards do not seem to have survived into the 20thC.

chickens and ducks seem to have thrived in Buckden at the end of the 19thC. The *St. Neots Advertiser* carried more small ads from Buckden than from any other village, offering eggs at so much a sitting from prize-winning White Leghorn and Buff-Orpington hens, and Aylesbury and Minorca ducks. Among the advertisers were miller Joseph Lantaff, one of the two Robert Kings (both brewers by trade), and Sidney Green and Miss Louisa Green of the High Street. The latter were members of the gentry, as was Alfred Hallett Esq, whose effects - auctioned when he left the village in 1898 - included 'Six Capital Poultry Houses with Runs' together with 150 prize fowl, a large number of egg-boxes, a grand piano and a Cakebread's Patent Egg Preserver.

Allen **Cope** (q.v.) continued Buckden's poultry tradition well into the 20thC with the large flock he kept at Hunts End; a later (1940s/1950s) poultry farmer was Mrs H. M.(Peggy) Rogers of Kenways, Lucks Lane.

Children's Home, Silver Street. This small home was built and run by Huntingdonshire County Council on a site just north of the old White Horse forge. One of those brought up there has fond memories of both the home and the kindness of Buckden people.

In 1974, the Local Government Act 1972 led to the County Council becoming part of an enlarged Cambridgeshire. Two years later the home was closed, and is now a private house.

A row of cottages previously stood on the site; as late as the 1940s, their occupants took their Christmas birds to the bakery across the road to be roasted.

circuses used to visit Buckden from time to time, sometimes pitching in a field behind the Spread Eagle. A small one arrived in the village on 10 July 1899 (probably to coincide with Feast Week). Short-staffed, it sought to recruit two handymen to help with ring work and clowning. Sadly, history does not record whether any resident took this opportunity to pack their trunk and say hello to the circus.

Cobbett, William (1763-1835), who is known to have visited Buckden in 1806, was a radical politician, journalist, farmer and hater of tea (he thought it made men effeminate, led women into prostitution, and killed pigs).

College Farm is a lost name; it was presumably the nearest farmstead to **College Green**, a name once given to the area now known as Hunts End.

Collins, James (1869-1920) was one of three Buckden residents included in a list of suspicious characters 'residing within the Buckden beat' that appears at the front of the police journal for 1887/8. From this we learn that he was 5' 3" with blue eyes, light brown hair and a fresh complexion. It comes as small surprise that the 1901 census finds him in Cambridge prison. However, by 1904 he was out again and working as an ostler at the George. We know this because he was involved in a fight with a customer (see under **entertainment in Buckden**).

When he died in 1920, the *Hunts Post* referred to him as a 'somewhat remarkable character', whose amusing antics had offered a good deal of merriment at local fetes (they included doing a striptease in the middle of a Feast Week celebration). Sadly, he fell out of a tree while working at Coneygarths, permanently injuring his back, and for the last six or seven years of his life was confined to bed at St Neots Workhouse Infirmary, the cost of his maintenance being met under the Workmen's Compensation Act.

He was known locally as 'Ikey' and may also be the 'Long Tip' Collins whose nickname arose from his having celebrated the completion of repairs to the church steeple in 1895 by standing on his head on the very top of the scaffolding. It certainly seems in character.

Coneygarths (sometimes **Coneygarth** or **The Coneygarth**) [MapRef 27] is one of Buckden's more interesting listed buildings, unusual among the older High Street houses nearby in that it has a front garden rather than giving straight on to the road and is not in the red brick that characterises the street scene. In part it goes back to the 17thC and has strong associations with the Bishops' Palace across the road, but of all its successive occupants it is the Green family, who lived there from the end of the 18thC into the 19thC, who played the most prominent part in Buckden life. For more on the Greens and on the house itself, see **Chapter 8**

Cook, Edward was a Buckden postman who developed a new strain of wheat shortly before the First World War. His round included Graveley where, one day in 1910, he plucked an unusual ear of corn from a field. It was peculiarly thick, exceptionally long, had an extraordinary number of grains and was on a remarkably thick, strong stalk. He took it and grew it on the following year. By 1913 enough grain had accumulated to sow three acres (1.2ha). The height of straw was about five feet (1.5m).

Unfortunately, it has not (so far) been discovered whether the wheat eventually met with commercial success. The lengthy trials required before a new plant variety can be marketed might have been discontinued when the First World War began, or the upheavals of war may have led to the relevant records being lost.

Cooper, Amy née **Royse (fl. late 16thC).** 'It was a blonde,' Raymond Chandler's detective Philip Marlowe once observed. 'A blonde to make a bishop kick a hole in a stained-glass window.' We don't know the colour of Amy's hair, but she was the wife of a bishop – Thomas Cooper (Lincoln 1571-84 and Winchester 1584-94) – and if ever there was an episcopal wife likely to drive her husband to kick a hole in something, Amy was it. Thomas's friends found her 'too light' for him from the beginning; in the early days of their marriage she was believed to have had affairs with at least two men; her behaviour inspired undergraduates to compose admiring (but rude) rhymes; and perhaps most exasperating of all she threw the manuscript of the bishop's dictionary into the fire.

In one important respect, however, she was beyond reproach. Like her husband, she was very fond of Buckden; so much so that she returned here after his death and leased the parsonage, from which she ran a working farm with the help of her brother, Richard.

Cope, Allen Edward (1905-1977), farmer and livestock transporter, was born in Chichester and moved to Buckden when quite young. Having tried various jobs after leaving Huntingdon Grammar School, he decided to go into business buying and selling fruit. One day he was at Buckden station with a load for the local goods train. A cattle dealer who was there collecting calves remarked that if only Mr Cope had a van he could take the calves to Little Paxton for him. This gave him food for thought, and he

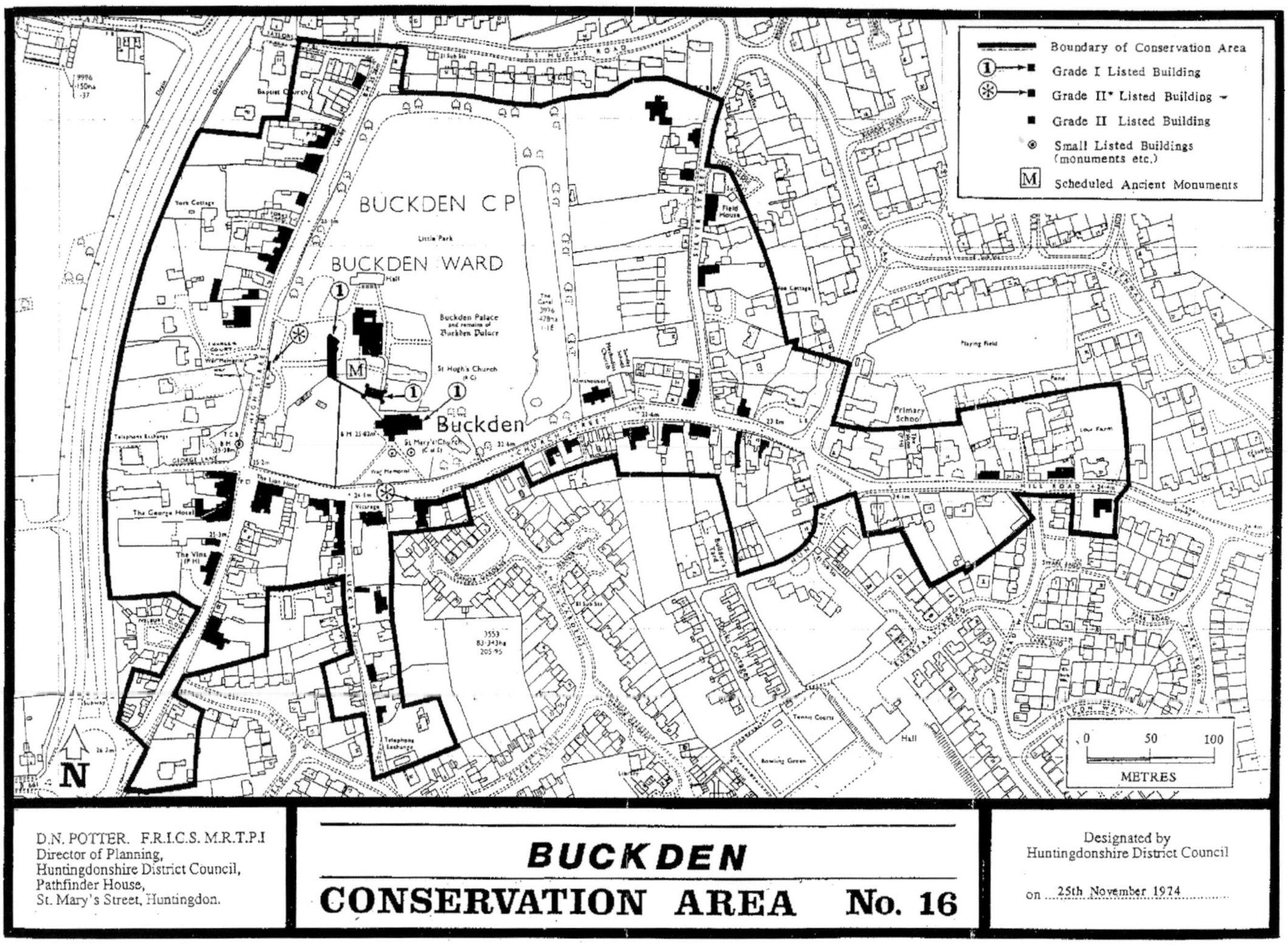

D.N. POTTER. F.R.I.C.S. M.R.T.P.I
Director of Planning,
Huntingdonshire District Council,
Pathfinder House,
St. Mary's Street, Huntingdon.

BUCKDEN
CONSERVATION AREA No. 16

Designated by
Huntingdonshire District Council
on 25th November 1974

Conservation Area. The Buckden conservation area was designated by Huntingdonshire District Council in 1974, and justified by them in a 1995 Conservation Area Character Statement. The area has to be one that the Local Planning Authority considers to be of special architectural or historic interest, the character or appearance of which it is desirable to preserve or enhance. The Buckden area broadly covers the historic built village. Within the boundaries of this area the planning authority has stronger control over development, whether demolition, new builds or extensions or alterations to existing properties. There is also extra protection for features that enhance the street scene, like open spaces, old walls, and mature trees such as those opposite The Towers. Development outside a Conservation Area, but directly affecting it, must also satisfy strict criteria.

A detailed description and justification of the Buckden area may be found in the District Council's *Conservation Area Character Statement* (1995). Some of the most important buildings are also considered in **Chapter 3: Buckden's Buildings**.

---

bought a van, and that was the start of a very successful livestock transport business. It was based at 12 Hunts End (which is now Copes Close): two cottages that were eventually knocked into one and later extended to make a four bedroomed house. With it was a holding formed from four different smallholdings, each purchased when they came on to the market.

As the business progressed Mr Cope bought two lorries, both built by Mr Williamson, a coach builder from St Neots. He was also now employing Mr Sid Gilbert, who asked for part-time employment but managed full-time for 30 or more years.

Soon Mr Cope's nephew joined the business and another lorry was bought from Williamson's. Mr Cope was very particular about his lorries, which in the early years were always built with parana pine, stained, lined and varnished. Mostly the timber was collected from English Brothers wood yard at Wisbech. The cabs were grained and sign-written by Mr Albert Hester from Biggleswade, who was still applying his art at the age of 81.

Mr Cope also had garages built, together with a fully-equipped workshop and a high pressure washer unit to make sure the lorries were kept clean at all times.

The next part of the fleet were built in aluminium so that the lorries were lighter and could carry heavier loads. The sense of pride was retained and with his skills, Albert

A new Cope cattle truck   Angela Bruce

was still able to make the cabs look as if they were made of timber.

By now, Mr Cope had seven lorries and employed six drivers. They travelled far and wide, no longer serving only local farms. Often the firm was asked to undertake quite special jobs, such as fetching show animals from as far away as Scotland to start new herds. One of Mr Cope's proudest moments was when he was asked to transport a horse to the London stables of the Royal Horse Guards. It had been chosen as their next Drum Horse, and he remembered it as a beautiful giant of an animal, yet so gentle.

Some of the land at Hunts End was orchard, and here some two hundred hens were kept, the eggs going to the Egg Marketing Board.

During the late 1940s, pig-rearing was added to the holding. At any one time he had up to three dozen animals in successive stages of fattening.

Cope, Thomas (born c. 1822; died 1895) was a Buckden carpenter whose adventures as parish constable in the mid-1850s demonstrate why those elected to this post were often prepared to pay someone else to do the job. The Huntingdonshire Quarter Sessions records show that during those years he was beaten up by several disgruntled (or drunken) residents while trying to carry out his duties. Most of his assailants came from the same family, one of Buckden's more rambunctious and, when it chose to be, elusive clans. Animosity boiled over in 1855. On 4 October, Thomas Cope attended St Neots magistrates' court to lodge a complaint that one member of the family, Jonas, had been selling beer from his house on a Sunday 'during the hours of Divine Service'. Jonas did not react well to this, or to being fined £1. 0s. 0d., and Thomas begged the magistrates to bind him over to keep the peace: 'for I am,' he said, 'in bodily fear of him.' The magistrates complied.

Two days later, Thomas spotted one of Jonas's younger brothers, William, on whom he had been trying since May to execute a warrant for poaching. William fled through a hedge. As Thomas pushed through after him, William seized a stake, hit him over the head - 'smashing his hat to pieces' - and repeatedly struck him across the body. Another brother, Samuel, then appeared and began kicking Thomas in the ribs, giving William the chance to escape. Thomas was saved by the arrival of his fellow-constable, William Ekins, and the two of them subdued Samuel and dragged him off to the village lock-up (a cage at Hunts End). Before they could finally get him inside, however, the constables had to fight off an attack by Samuel's mother, two of his sisters and yet another brother, James. A large crowd watched with interest, but pointedly refused to offer the police any assistance.

Samuel, James, their mother and their sisters were brought up before the St Neots magistrates on 10 October. The womenfolk were fined 5s. 6d. each, with costs, and the men were committed for trial at the next Huntingdon Quarter Sessions, where each was sentenced to three months hard labour.

Thomas Cope did not appear at the magistrates' court, Mr Woolley, Buckden's surgeon, having certified him as unfit to attend through injury.

Justice did not catch up with William until June of the following year, when he, too, received three months for his assault on Thomas.

Copping, Alexander Charles Edward (1859-1924) was a prominent resident of Buckden for forty years. He was born in Yaxley, but grew up in St Neots. His father

John was a remarkable policeman, one of the first senior officers (superintendents) appointed to the newly formed Huntingdonshire County Constabulary in 1857. He remained in service for fifty years, rising to hold the twin posts of Chief Superintendent and Deputy Chief Constable. He was a very 'hands-on' policeman, often taking a close interest in quite minor cases, particularly those in Buckden. This may in part have been because Alexander moved to the village in 1883, shortly after marrying Annie Sarah Harrison, a farmer's daughter from Great Staughton.

Alexander did not follow his father into the force. He found work as a corn merchant's clerk, then became a flour salesman for Buckden & Offord Flour Mills. So successful was he, the firm made him a partner in 1916. In the same year he represented the company before a military appeal **tribunal** (q.v.) in an unsuccessful attempt to prevent their stockman Stanley Currington from being drafted into the army. A leading freemason (Past Master of his lodge), he also he played a prominent role in the social life of the village: Hon. Sec. of the Reading Rooms, actor in comic plays, leading light of the Buckden Choral Society, cricketer (in his youth), cricket and athletics competition administrator, and member of Buckden Golf Club. In his spare time he particularly enjoyed gardening: the grounds of his home at Oak Lawn were much admired, and he was a committee member of the Buckden and Diddington Horticultural Society. He also shot, and played bicycle polo and tennis. He had in fact been playing tennis on the day he fell terminally ill. His funeral began with a 'sadly imposing' procession accompanying his body on the parish bier from Oak Lawn to the gate of the churchyard. Here it was met by three clergymen, the choir, and an escort of freemasons carrying sprigs of acacia in their white-gloved hands. These 'emblems of brotherly affection' were later dropped on to the coffin as it lay in its grave. The *Hunts Post* description of this funeral is detailed and fulsome, perhaps to make up for the unfortunate heading in the previous week's paper:

DEATH OF MR A COPPING
IS IT ECONOMICALLY NECESSARY?

Coulson: see Zachariah.

County Gaol and House of Correction, Huntingdon. Sixty years after its opening in 1768, conditions in the first county gaol had become so frightful that a replacement had to be commissioned. It opened in 1829, and the inside of this 'spacious pile of buildings', became familiar to some residents of Buckden. The 1851 gaol census, for example, includes six people from the village. Two were not prisoners: Elizabeth Sladen was the wife of Thomas Smith, the gaol's First Turnkey for several years in the 1840s and 1850s, while Elizabeth Eady, the Smiths' fifteen-year old nursemaid, was the daughter of a Stirtloe labourer. The prisoners from Buckden were three labourers and a beer-house keeper. No doubt it was of comfort to them to know that the gaol was 'situated in a convenient and healthy situation', although this may not have been immediately apparent to anyone unfortunate to be in the extension built in 1850: its defective air-shaft left some prisoners half-suffocated in their cells and others seriously ill from breathing 'the impure atmosphere'.

Discipline was imposed through the 'silent and separate' system: individual cells, no talking in the exercise yard or the chapel, the threat of regular visits from the chaplain, and spells on the tread-wheel (which one member of the governing body defended as relieving the monotony of the prisoners' day).

In the old gaol, how you fared had depended on whom you knew: Buckden innkeeper Mrs Jane **Scarborough** (q.v.), for example, had always been regarded as a respectable woman. When she was gaoled for a year for theft, therefore, she was treated well while serving her sentence, being put in a cell with congenial companions already known to her (which prompts the question: *how* did she know them if she was so respectable?).

Cowling, John George (b. 1863) was a Buckden-born plumber and decorator who became Mayor of Northampton in 1925. At his installation, he reminisced about the early 1880s when he was courting his future wife, Annie Coomber, a railway porter's daughter from Offord Cluny. In those days, he said, there was still no bridge over the Ouse. To reach her he had to be rowed across or even carried over on a man's back.

Cowslip, Mrs Dolly, spirited daughter of an inn landlady (or is she?), is one of the heroines of Tobias Smollett's novel *The Adventures of Sir Launcelot Greaves*.

See **fiction, Buckden in.**

Craft, Percy Robert (1856-1934) started his working life as a repertory actor, sometimes playing twelve parts in a week. When influenza damaged his ability to remember his lines, he went to art school – where he was a multiple medal winner – and became known as an organiser of exhibitions and a painter and illustrator in oil, water-colour and pastel. Between 1899 and 1905 he and his wife lived in 'The Cottage', Lucks Lane. During this time he exhibited at the Royal Academy in at least two years, 1901 and 1902. He was a member of the Reading Rooms committee and a popular participant in its entertainments as a singer, recitalist and comic actor: music-hall interests shared by a later artist who lived in Buckden, H. J. Sylvester **Stannard** (q.v.).

Percy Craft at work

Craft was also a keen fisherman and towards the end of his life gave a series of radio talks on deep sea angling – which he knew well, having spent ten years in Newlyn before moving to Buckden (their Cornish maid, Annie Cotton, came with them).

A devout Christian and a man of strong principles, he volunteered for the Royal Army Medical Corps early in 1915 (despite being at fifty-nine well over military age) and served until summer 1918.

Prints and posters of some his works are still sold; unfortunately none seems to be of Buckden or its environs. There are, however, some of his paintings on display in Hinchingbrooke House, portraits of three members of the Linton family of Stirtloe. They were moved to Hinchingbrooke after being found in a barn. There is also a tantalising reference in the *St. Neots Advertiser* to the 'much coveted prizes' offered by Mr Craft to the winners of a sedentary village triathlon (whist, dominoes and draughts); might these been examples of his own work?

And if so, might they still lurk unrecognised in a Buckden home?

They might, of course, have simply been freshly caught fish.

Cranfield family, farmers and philanthropists. There were Cranfields in Buckden in the 17thC and early 18thC; they may or may not be related to William Cranfield (1831-1901), who came from Bedfordshire to Buckden in the late 1850s to take on the tenancy of Park Farm. At its peak (1871), the 1000 acre farm employed 59 workers: 35 men, 17 boys and 7 women.

William Cranfield was a national figure on the agricultural scene: an exhibitor of prize-winning Lincoln sheep and Shorthorn cattle at Smithfield, and a member of the Royal Agricultural Society's judging panel for 'miscellaneous inventions'. It was, however, three of his children who were to make the most lasting impact on the parish: Mary Cranfield OBE, and her brothers William Walker Cranfield and Henry Cranfield. They were the children of their father's first marriage, to Mary Walker (1826-1866), also from a Bedfordshire farming family.

Mary (1855-1940) and her brother William Walker (1856-1931) were born in Bedfordshire, Henry (1862-1916) in Buckden. There were no children from William senior's second marriage, to Jane Bowyer Burrell, the widow of a retired Yorkshire farmer.

The two older children were privately educated: William Walker in Kempston at the uncompromisingly named Bedfordshire Middle Class Public School, and Mary at Boswell House College, a small boarding school for girls somewhat inappropriately sited next door to a pub (the Railway Arms) in Croydon.

As a family, the Cranfields had a strong social conscience, from which Buckden benefited greatly. They were the moving force in the provision of the **Rifle Range** (q.v.) and its associated recreation rooms, and gave strong practical support to local sports, particularly cricket. Henry played a leading role in the organisation of local military training during the First World War and was held in high esteem throughout the county for his work on council and other public committees. He was clearly a man of more than ordinary energy, who caught people up in his enthusiasms. His sudden and early death in a freak riding accident was mourned in local newspapers under headlines that would not have disgraced a major national tragedy. The Cranfield tendency to think big was very apparent in him. In July 1908 the *Hunts Post* reported that he had twenty-seven of his own carts and wagons simultaneously engaged in carting hay on his meadows at Brampton.

cricket in Buckden. Sadly, there is no formal record of Buckden Cricket Club's history but it is known to have been founded in 1891. Its centenary was celebrated with a dinner at the George Hotel in Buckden for about sixty members, including past and present players. The George had also been the preferred venue for the club's 19thC annual dinners (and had catered its smoking concerts, held in the Maltings in George Lane).

The founding date of 1891 suggests that the moving spirits included Buckden's two doctors of the time, Frederick Good and W. H. Hillyer, both young men, both sports-mad. Other useful players in the early days were W. H. Deane, vicar from 1901 to 1911; Peter McLeod, a Scotsman who worked as coachman/groom to Sir Arthur Marshall at The Towers and then took over the Spread Eagle; John Wallage, Buckden's policeman from 1887 to

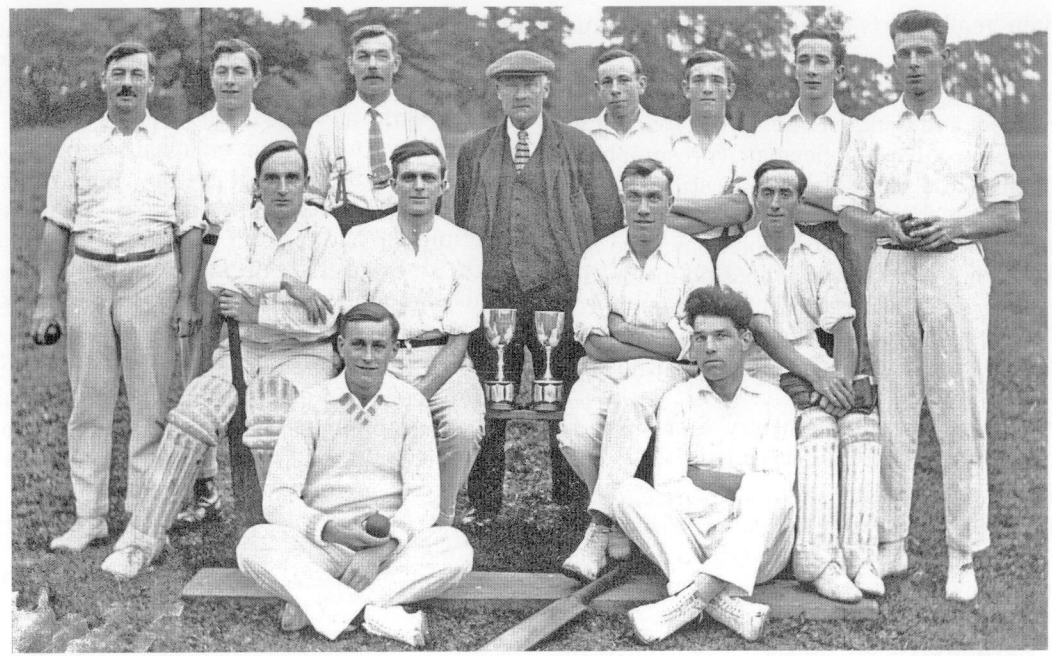

A Buckden XI with W.W.Cranfield c 1930   Alice Whitmee

1900, and his successor John Purser. Alexander Copping, all-round sportsman and an employee (later partner) in Offord and Buckden Mills, continued the police link: he was the son of a Deputy Chief Constable.

The club now plays on a square and outfield provided through the efforts of the War Memorial Playing Fields Trust, with the use of a pavilion put up as part of the village's millennium improvements. For much of its history, however, it led a nomadic existence within the parish. Some matches were, in fact, played on the present field, but that was when it was still known as the Vineyards, and the ground had not been levelled. Other venues included 'somewhere in Stirtloe' (memories disagree exactly where, so perhaps there was more than one site), and fields at Coneygarths and Park Farm. The minutes of the club's 1952 AGM record that Mr Noel Thornhill 'has consented to the club playing a number of matches on his ground at Diddington.' In fact, the Diddington ground had previously been put at the disposal of players from Buckden, this time in the early years of the Second World War, when it was used by the Tollington School evacuees from London. The boys also played on a matting wicket laid down in the Towers and on the Buckden Cricket Club ground 'in Lucks Lane' (one of the Stirtloe pitches, perhaps?).

A book of press cuttings kept by the club secretary gives some idea of the Buckden's prowess and fortunes on the field from 1947 to 1952. They seem to have varied greatly from disaster to success – but as newspaper reports from the club's earliest years confirm, there was nothing new in this!

Fund-raising is always a headache for any sports club. In 1949 the cricket club held a fête at **Beech Lawn** (q.v.), then the home of Mr Edward Cranfield-Rose, the club's president and chairman (a pair of whose cricketing flannels passed via a jumble sale to one of the Tollington boys back in 1941, lasting him until he went into the army in 1945). The fête raised about £100, a remarkable amount for sixty years ago. (How, incidentally, does one play pig skittles? If anyone still has a set, perhaps it is time for a revival...)

The 1949 Annual Dinner took place in the Rifle Range. Seventy attended. The presentation of the Cranfield League (South) Cup to the club's captain W. R. Boddy was made by Mrs Cranfield, the widow of William Walker Cranfield, a lover of cricket who had done much to encourage the game before his death in 1931; his support included funding the purchase of the kit for three teams and donating two cups.

The 1951 AGM listed improvements which the club had been able to make during the year including a concrete wicket and a water supply. The War Memorial Committee had made a grant towards the cost. Among the thanks recorded were those to Mr Mailer (Park Farm) for 'many kindnesses'.

In one year in this post-war period several matches had to be cancelled due to the demands of the harvest – a reminder that agriculture still dominated the economy of the parish.

Cricket had, of course, been part of life in Buckden and its neighbouring villages long before the founding of the club in 1891. Indeed, the Rev. Henry Linton, of Stirtloe House and Diddington vicarage, produced two sons who played for Oxford University: Henry junior who batted and bowled in four matches in 1858-9, and Sydney, a batsman who took part in eight matches between 1861 and 1863. Neither exactly distinguished himself in these matches, but Henry in particular was regarded as an excellent player. He joined the Madras Civil Service and rose rapidly through its ranks until felled by dysentery at the age of only 28. Sydney went on to become the first Bishop of Riverina, New South Wales, where he constructed his official residence out of sawdust, wood and corrugated iron, and had a rose named after him (and another after his wife).

Finally, no mention of cricket in Buckden would be complete without a reference to Bernie Facer – not a member of Buckden Cricket Club (he played for Kimbolton), but one of the leading makers of bats, with over forty years experience with Hunts County Bats, Double-B Bats (his own company), and more recently Hawk Cricket of Worcestershire. His 'Baronet' is highly regarded: a 'hard pressed' bat that takes some time to play itself in, but then 'really starts to ping' (to use a technical phrase).

Cross, the was the name given to the junction of High Street, Church Street and George Lane. In the 1920s it was a duty point for the village policeman (presumably to control traffic, since the High Street was still the Great North Road and the junction was a dangerous one). On hot days, when the windows of the Lion Hotel bar were open, the policeman could hear what was being said inside. This was how Buckden resident Frank Petherick ended up before the St Neots magistrates on a charge of using 'very indecent language' while arguing with a man who owed him money.

Mr Petherick, who lived in Cemetery Lane, pleaded 'guilty under great provocation'. He was fined half-a-crown.

cross-dressing in Buckden has, as elsewhere, tended to be a private activity. (Two men who were prizewinners in the Ladies Competition at a 1929 whist drive each 'played as a lady' but without, presumably, being required to dress as one, too.)

In May 1836, however, an unusual occurrence was reported to the Zoological Society of London by Captain Green of Coneygarths. He owned a 'fine specimen of the barn-door IIen, which has assumed the Cock plumage: the change took place about three years ago.' Captain Green later presented the hen to the Society. History does not record whether they kept it or ate it.

See also **Captain Green's golden eagle** and **Thurlow, Thomas.**

Crown Inn or Crown Commercial Inn, Hardwick [MapRef 17], on the west side of the Great North Road, is now a private residence. Within living memory it was still a public house, owned for many years by Jenkins & Jones

The Crown Inn 1898 with members of the Middleton family
Leslie O. Glessner

of the Falcon Brewery, Huntingdon. 19thC licensees included draper and master tailor Robert Robinson (1860s); Mrs Bass (1870s) and, by 1891, farm labourer George Middleton (assisted by his wife Eliza), who was still there in 1924.

But even this long tenure was eclipsed by that of Mr Middleton's successor, George Stocker, who did not retire until the late 1970s, aged nearly 90. Mr Stocker also farmed a couple of fields at opposite ends of the village and had a few cows. These were housed in the barns behind the Crown, but they were not milked there: his granddaughter Margaret Benjamin (née Laxton) remembers that she and her siblings were often called upon to drive them down the

old Great North Road, round the Lion corner and along Church Street to the sheds beside the Manor House. Mr Stocker sold the milk in Buckden, delivering it on his bicycle with a very large can on either side of the handlebars. Only when milk had to be processed more thoroughly did he give up the round and the cows. Margaret Benjamin's mother had quite a shock the first time she had to pay a milk bill.

On Mr Stocker's retirement, the Crown was de-licensed and became the home of his son-in-law and daughter, Mr and Mrs Bert Lumbers, who lived there for a number of years before moving into a house in the High Street.

Cruel Tree. Its indication on an early map, makes it look like a field name rather than the name of an individual feature. But in a talk on Huntingdonshire artists which

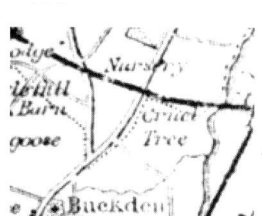

Michael Knight gave to Buckden Local History Society in 1999, he included a lithograph of a watercolour entitled 'The Felo da Se, Cruel Trees [on A1 near Buckden]'. 'The cruel tree' is a phrase found in hymns for Christ's cross but here seems to have more sinister connotations. It has been suggested it was either a tree (or post) under which suicides or executed murderers were buried; or possibly a real tree used for hangings – an idea given weight by the stark description of Site 00664 in the Cambridgeshire County Council's Historic Environment Record: 'Gallows, Buckden'. The site is placed in the fork of the A1/Brampton Hill junction; the supporting references are [1] tradition and [2] a watercolour in a family scrapbook - presumably the same picture that Michael Knight showed.

The matter is made all the more sinister (but no more explicable) by the mass graves allegedly hidden under the A1 central reservation south of the gallows site, and by the chilling name of a small field shown on the village enclosure map: Cut-Throat Close.

All in all, this junction seems somewhere best avoided by lonely travellers, especially after dark

Cuewen or Coren, Hugh or Hugo (d. 1568). The career of this lawyer and cleric took him from Vicar of Buckden (1514-1530) to Archbishop of Dublin and both Lord Chancellor and Lord Justice of Ireland. Along the way he served as chaplain to Henry VIII, strongly defending the king's marriage with Anne Boleyn. He was known as 'Hugh the Complier' for his readiness to change his religion to suit each of the five monarchs under whom he served.

Curtois, Major Chauncey (1841-1905), of Perry Road, was a sociable, cigar-smoking bachelor who played an active part in local events wherever he lived. Son of the Vicar of Hemingford Grey, he served with the Madras Infantry until placed on the reserve list in 1880. In 1891, he returned to the Hemingford vicarage, now occupied by his brother, the Rev. Peregrine Edward Curtois (1837-1899), a short-sighted campanologist who had the melancholy distinction of being almost certainly the last 19thC Anglican priest to be run down by a GNR locomotive on a GER track; in his case while absent-mindedly smoking a pipe in the middle of Houghton Viaduct. Following Peregrine's death, Major Curtois moved to Buckden, taking over Ellerslie, a large house in Perry Road recently vacated by Dr **Hillyer** (q.v.). His brother's widow and at least one of her daughters came to live with him, and he took care to provide for them in his will.

On the morning of 27 June 1905 his gardener brought him his customary glass of milk, only to find him lying on his bedroom floor, dead of a cerebral haemorrhage.

His hobby was woodworking.

Cut Throat Close: see Cruel Tree.

cycling played a major part in restoring the fortunes of Buckden after the lean years following the collapse of the coaching trade in the 1850s. It is hard today to understand the social changes brought about by the coming of the

The Rudge "Three in Hand"

bicycle - or more precisely, by the coming of the safety bicycle in the 1880s. Relatively cheap, relatively easy to master, it offered an exhilarating freedom to both men and women. (Particularly young men and women on sociables (cycles with side-by-side seats): mixed bicycling parties were not as easy to chaperone as the traditional Sunday afternoon walk.) The railway had accustomed people to travel farther from their home town or village, but it was a formal method of transport that took them at speed through the intervening landscape. The bicycle enabled people to use their brief leisure time to explore a wider world than ever before. Urban clerks and shop assistants could exchange the gloom of the city for the fresh air of the countryside; farmworkers could expand the rural gene pool.

Not everyone welcomed the new freedom. Debates raged in newspapers and medical journals about the health benefits or risks of bicycling, especially for women. By 1902, however, *The Parson's Handbook* (a sort of liturgical workshop manual) was advising clergy faced with badly-attended Sunday morning services to ensure they finished Matins early enough to allow young people time to get their bicycle rides in before lunch.

cycling clubs and cyclists. From the early 1880s onwards every self-respecting town and large village acquired a cycling club. A snide item in a local paper suggests that Buckden Cycling Club was not always taken seriously by non-members:

'It is whispered,' said the *St. Neots Advertiser* in May 1901, 'that the Buckden Cycling Club will have to purchase an Ambulance to bring home the pieces when they go for a run.'

In 1904, an anonymous correspondent in the village drew the attention of the *Advertiser's* readers to the strange behaviour of a handful of 'Buckden cyclers', who regularly rode to St Neots and back. The writer clearly expected his readers to recognise the sinister purpose that

lay behind this apparently harmless exercise. The freedom to drink in the town pubs, safe from the disapproving eyes of 'her indoors' back in Buckden? We shall probably never know.

As well as its own cycling club, Buckden hosted some of the national clubs, for whom it was a useful staging-post on competitive or recreational rides to and from the north, such as the popular 'Dick Turpin's Ride' between London and York. Members of the prestigious North Road Cycling Club, founded in 1885 to 'promote fast and long distance cycling on the Great North and other Roads', had a particularly close association with the George, which they used as a training centre.

A world quadricycling record was established at Buckden in 1888. The machine was the large and peculiar 'Three in Hand', built by the Rudge Cycle Company. It was nearly five feet high, weighed 120 pounds, had four 30-inch wheels and three riders. The lead rider was a world-famous American cyclist, Stillman G. Whittaker, known as 'the Little Yankee'. He and his team set up their headquarters at Buckden's George and Dragon in November and spent the next six weeks in training. They decided to go for the record on 14 December. Fog and a head wind delayed their start until after lunch. Despite the surface of the Great North Road being described as 'half frozen, half mud and all rutty', they flew along the measured mile in 2 minutes 29 seconds (four days later they bettered this time by ten and four/fifths seconds). Their amazing speed of over 24 mph was claimed to be the fastest man had ever travelled under his own power. The machine went into production the following year, selling for £36 ('suitable for two ladies and a gentleman, or three gentlemen – can be made suitable for three ladies if desired').

In 1891, Buckden was the starting point for a successful attempt on the 12 hour cycling record for ordinaries: Mr R. C. Nesbitt completed a round trip of one hundred and seventy-five and a half miles in the allotted time, taking in Hitchin and Peterborough (twice) on the way. Sadly for the village he was *not* a member of the Buckden Cycling Club. ('Ordinaries' were the ungeared bicycles popularly known as penny-farthings.)

But cyclists, especially racing cyclists, were not always popular in Victorian Buckden (or Huntingdonshire generally). They might be welcomed as good customers by blacksmiths prepared to repair broken frames and chains, and by the keepers of inns such as the George and the Spread Eagle, but many people regarded them as a menace as they sped along the Great North Road in near silence – no tell-tale clatter of hooves – alarming livestock and knocking down pedestrians. Indeed, when in July 1894 a group of tricyclists competing in a 50 mile race rode into a horse and trap just south of Buckden, the Chief Constable seized on the accident as an excuse to ban road racing in the county, even though the fault lay with the driver of the trap. 'Paced races' (timed trials) were permitted a couple of years later, but were not without incident: one competitor's record-breaking ride through the Fens took him through the jurisdictions of eight separate magistrates' courts. Each of them summonsed and fined both him and his support team for furious and dangerous riding.

See also **Robinson's Garages** and **Shelton, Henry.**

D

Davie, Robert Elliott, MA MD ChB MC was Buckden's doctor in the 1920s. See **Chapter 14 Medical Practice in Buckden**.

Deane, the Rev. William Hodgson MA (Oxon) (1857-1932) was vicar of Buckden from 1901 to 1911. An energetic music-loving Mancunian, he was an admired singer who founded and conducted the Buckden Choral Society. He was also a considerable all-round athlete: a leading amateur golfer (probably one of the founding members of the Buckden golf team); the captain and opening bat of the Cricket Club, and still a tennis player in his seventies. He was also a St Neots Rural District Councillor. He arrived in Buckden with his wife – a Northamptonshire rector's daughter – three children, a governess (the delightfully named Lizzie Lilley), an elderly nanny, a young (22) cook, and a housemaid.

Deaths from Wild Beasts in India. This Government report that appeared annually for over 40 years must have made nostalgic reading for Buckden's several old India hands. Deaths from wild beasts were not unknown in Buckden, either - at least, not if you count bees as wild beasts. An unfortunate donkey was stung to death in Mill Road by bees in 1886; the village rallied round and bought the owner a replacement.

deer park. The bishops of Lincoln had a deer park in Buckden from early in the 13thC. Royal permission was needed to enclose land for keeping deer, and the original grant was made by King John to Bishop Hugh (not yet too saintly to enjoy hunting) 'in recompense for injuries done during the interdict'. Further grants were made, and the park finally took a crescent shape, in the north-west of the parish, curving round to accommodate the hamlet of Hardwick. There was a moated house for the parker (the moat was to keep the deer out of his garden). We know from parkers' accounts and from a survey made in 1647 that as well as providing food for the bishops' table, and recreation in the form of hunting for him, his household and for the king whenever he chose to exercise his rights, the park was an important source of wood, both timbers and coppicewood. In 1647 the park contained 425 acres of land; 200 fallow deer; 28 coppices of different ages; and nearly 7000 oak trees. It was sold to a London alderman, Christopher Packe, who seems to have presided over its destruction. By the end of the 17thC all the deer were gone and the park was enclosed into fields. It survives in the name of Park Farm.

Defoe, Daniel. Between 1724 and 1726, the author of *Robinson Crusoe* published a series of letters under the title *A Tour Through the Whole Island of Great Britain*. 'Bugden' is briefly mentioned in Letter 7: Defoe visited the Bishop's Palace with its 'very pretty, though small' chapel, and was enchanted by a *trompe l'œil* organ in an organ-loft 'so properly placed and well painted, that we at first believed it really to be an organ'. The lifelikeness of the organ is also mentioned by James Sargant Storer in his *The Antiquarian Itinerary* (1818), although he places it in St Mary's Church rather than in the palace chapel.

De Grammont, Corisande ['Corise'] Armandine Sophie Léonice Hélène (1782-1865) was a sensual, intelligent, ambitious French aristocrat whose rise to the heights of English society nearly came to a premature end in a Buckden fireplace. On their way to Edinburgh in the winter of 1802, she and her mother stopped to spend the night at one of the village inns. As a frozen Corise twirled eagerly round in front of the bedroom hearth, her gown billowed out and caught fire. Hearing shrieks, her mother rushed in, saw her daughter engulfed in flames, threw her to the ground, found herself on fire also and fainted – as did Corise. Luckily this enabled a passing manservant to extinguish both ladies by rolling them up in the carpet. Having thus escaped a death that befell all too many fashionably-dressed women in the early 1800s, Corise went on to marry the hereditarily grumpy heir of the Earl of Tankerville and eventually become London's most scandalous and sought-after political hostess.

Douglass, Frederick (c. 1817-1895) was one of Buckden's most distinguished 19thC visitors – possibly the only person to have both visited Buckden and appeared on a US postage stamp (though some people think he must  share this honour with Clark Gable). He was an escaped slave who became America's most charismatic black abolitionist, a noted orator, writer and editor, and a friend of Abraham Lincoln. He and his second wife visited Buckden in the autumn of 1888, while on their honeymoon. They were staying in St Neots with an English friend and supporter from his early days, Julia Griffiths (c. 1810-1895). Now she was Mrs Henry Only Crofts, a Methodist preacher's widow in poor health earning a precarious living from a small girls' school. To cheer her up he drove her in a donkey-cart to Buckden to visit the graves of two of her nephews. They had apparently both died young, while students at Cambridge; unfortunately it has not yet proved possible to identify them.

dovecotes, like fishponds and coneygarths, were a welcome source of fresh meat for the better-off and their households, and for poachers. In return for minimal husbandry, each pair of dovecote pigeons not only produced up to sixteen chicks ('squabs') a year but also provided valuable dung, feathers for pillows, quarry for falconry and, later, targets for shooting-parties (see under **Pigeon Shoot Committee**). In the 17thC, a royal proclamation required dovecotes to have soft earth floors: this was because the birds' droppings were a source of one of the ingredients of gunpowder (potassium nitrate, known as saltpetre). The impregnated earth belonged to the king, who licensed saltpetre-makers to dig it up and cart it away, so giving shot pigeons the unenviable distinction of having been, as it were, dropped by their own droppings.

Buckden had at least two dovecotes, both now gone: one to the west of the George Hotel and one on the north side of Mill Road.

The first of these, a two-storey brick building with a pyramid roof, dated from the late 17thC or early 18thC. It was demolished in 1961. It may originally have been built to supply birds to the Bishop's Palace, but by 1722 it was being included in the lease of the George.

The second was described as 'an 18thC square building with a pyramidal roof, located to the north west of Oak

Lawn'. In fact, it belonged to the farm next door, which was occupied at one time by Benjamin Faulkner. In 1834 he accused four villagers of stealing a number of birds out of the dovecote. William Reason and William Burton were labourers and Robert Holmes and John Smith alehouse keepers; this suggests that a traditional rural back-of-the-pub delivery chain had been established. The outcome of the case has not been traced but the 1841 census shows that John Smith at least was still keeping an alehouse (the George Tap), while Robert Holmes had become a farmer. However, he appears to be living in the Silver Street building later known as the White Horse beer-house; certainly his son George Holmes became an alehouse keeper (and ended up in the county gaol in 1851).

An idea of what these dovecotes may have looked like can be gained from the one still standing at Boughton Grange Farm south of Diddington.

A 1535 survey of the manor of Buckden mentions a dovecote, which may have been an earlier version of one of the two already mentioned. A dovecote also formed part of the amenities of Stirtloe House (as did a slaughterhouse).

drama in Buckden. The plays and other distractions put on in Buckden Palace for bishops and their entourages hardly count as village entertainments, and although the antiquity of Buckden's inns, and their location on one of the country's main highways, may have made them occasional venues for travelling actors, we have no evidence of it. But we do know that as the 19thC progressed, the schoolrooms were used not only for educational and religious entertainments but also for plays (see, for example, under **Wyles**). When the Church Street Reading Rooms opened in 1891, they, too, became the venue for enthusiastic amateur performances of one-act plays, recitations, songs and on at least one occasion a Gilbert and Sullivan opera – an ambitious production of HMS Pinafore by the choral society.

Those taking part were usually members of the more genteel end of Buckden society. So were the audience, apart from an unwanted hard core of loud persons who stood at the back and were regarded as being unable through drink or ignorance to properly appreciate the entertainment on offer.

The South African and First World Wars saw regular evenings devoted to mocking the enemy and raising funds for the soldiers.

The Reading Room gave way to the Rifle Range where Gilbert and Sullivan operettas and plays were performed.

After some years of neglect, the Theatre Club was revived in the 1970s to take advantage of the new village hall, with a formal constitution being drawn up in 1979. The first chairman was David Thomas; Frank Mace, a

"The Yeomen of the Guard" performed in the Rifle Range in 1937.
Alice Whitmee

stalwart of earlier productions, agreed to be Life President. The club aimed to put on at least two productions a year; these included pantomimes and musical evenings as well as straight plays. Bespoke facilities including a large scene store were incorporated in the Millennium Centre, opened in 1999; unfortunately falling membership and shrinking audiences meant that the club gave its last performance (to date) in May 2006. Appropriately enough it was an evening celebrating village life, linked by readings from 'Buckden: a Christmas Ballad.' by Archdeacon **Knowles** (q.v.).

In recent years the Towers has also provided a venue for drama, including professional performances of Shakespeare, Goldsmith and Gogol in the knot garden, and in the courtyard amateur Shakespeare (*A Midsummer Night's Dream*) and a large-scale community play put on by the Theatre Club itself.

Dudley, [Mary] Edna (née Healey) was born on 21 May 1927 in French Park, Co. Roscommon, Eire, the second daughter of farming parents. When she reached 17, lack of work made Edna decide to travel to England. She had friends in Cambridge, and this was where she initially found work. She met her future husband, Albert Dudley, when she moved to Buckden, where she was employed at the Lion Hotel and then at the George. They were married on 6 September 1952 at St Joseph's, the Catholic Church in St Neots to which Edna often walked on a Sunday to hear Mass.

Edna became actively involved in village life, and played her part in the 1954 May Day celebrations. The Rifle Range Whist Drives and the Over Sixties were where Edna discovered her organisational skills. In 1954 she and Albert had a daughter Linda, followed the following July by a second daughter, Hazel.

There was a very small collection of Catholics at this time, Edna, Mr Frank Mace and Mrs Grey. When the Claretians moved to Buckden, Edna began fund raising in earnest; whist drives, dances, jumble sales, barbecues and the popular annual fete, all accompanied by a raffle.

It was not only the Claretians that benefited from her fund-raising skills: so did the Royal British Legion, and the Tennis Club, where Edna was a regular on a Sunday afternoon, not playing but organising the teas.

Durst, John (fl.-1789) was an early Buckden schoolmaster. He seems to have lived both in Stirtloe and in Mill End, Buckden.

E

early closing day for Buckden shops was traditionally Wednesday.

earthquake, Buckden hit by small. Shortly before 1.00 a.m. BST on Monday 23 September 2002, several parts of Britain including Buckden were shaken by an earthquake. Measuring between 4.8 and 5.0 on the Richter scale it had its epicentre at Dudley in the West Midlands. Although no reports of serious damage were received, it was forceful enough to make the yard gates of the Spread Eagle crash together so loudly the landlord thought the pub had been hit by ram-raiders. Other residents reported feeling and hearing a 'rushing wave' pass underneath their house, and seeing a fridge move several inches sideways. Perhaps the most worrying side-effect was the rapid collapse of the emergency services' telephone system under the weight of anxious enquirers.

One Buckden resident who would have enjoyed the experience (had he still been alive) was Thomas Tenison, Bishop of Lincoln from 1691 to 1694. In October 1692 he wrote rather wistfully to his friend the diarist John Evelyn about a recent earthquake that was 'discerned in divers neighbouring towns' though 'none in Buckden were sensible of it'.

Edleston, Robert Holmes, FSA, FRGS, Baron de Montalbo (1868-1952), owned Buckden Towers from 1919 until his death. He was a wealthy and eccentric antiquary, a racehorse owner and breeder, a member of Buckden and Diddington Horticultural Society, and the Consul for the Republic of San Marino. He shared many of his antiquarian enthusiasms with his sister Alice, including the history of their native county, Durham, monumental brasses and inscriptions, Napoleon III, buying old property and acquiring manorial lordships. Following the premature death of his wife in 1915, he also developed a deep interest in the old Roman Catholic Church. Buckden provided him with a focus for many of these activities: as Lord of the Manor of Buckden Brittens, for example, he was able to preside over a customary court (see below), and as owner of the palace he was free to carry out an archaeological dig in its tennis courts. (The aim of the dig was to find the foundations of, and partially rebuild, the former chapel of the Bishops of Lincoln, who as Catholic prelates had been among the most powerful men in the realm.)

The following notes relating to this engaging, eccentric and occasionally infuriating man, supplement the information in **Chapter 4 Buckden Palace to Buckden Towers**.

1. At a curious party held at the Towers in August 1922, one of the guests was a member of the Afghani nobility. Among the entertainments, the village band played for them. (See Photograph) One of the visitors was invited to lay a brick in part of Mr Edleston's reconstruction work.

2. The following quotation from 'It's a Don's Life' by Dr Frederick Brittain, published by Heinemann in 1972, may be of interest:-

> 'I also did a little excavating with pick and shovel at Buckden Palace in Huntingdonshire, where Mr Edleston was busy digging up the tennis courts to discover the foundations of the former chapel of the Bishops of Lincoln. When he had done so, he rebuilt the walls with the old material to shoulder height. Inside them he erected the stone altar-tomb, with a high-sounding Latin epitaph, which Alan Hay had hesitated to allow him to place over Bishop Matthew's grave at South Mimms until he had obtained the approval of his bishop. Mr Edleston had taken umbrage at this delay and had chosen to construe it as a refusal. As he never finished anything, the unfinished chapel was crowned with a hideous galvanised iron roof and left to be a nesting place for birds. It was still like that when he died thirty years later.'

3. The Edlestons' archives contain over a thousand records dealing with Buckden matters: among them plans, drawings, maps, posters, newspaper cuttings, details of property deals going back to the 18thC, the prospectus of

David Thomas

Buckden Towers College, and photographs (including fifteen of the famous Pageant of the Centuries), Sadly for Buckden's local historians, much of this documentation is deposited with the County Record Office in Durham.

4. In July 1923, Edleston, as Lord of the Manor of Buckden Brittens, called a meeting of the General Court Baron and Customary Court, apparently to record a change of copyhold tenancy. It made a very pleasant occasion it seems.

He held other such meetings, the most notable being that of 30 December 1925, which attracted national press interest as the last of its kind: the Law of Property Act 1925 came into effect two days later and swept away these particular manorial courts.

education in Buckden was well established two centuries before the Elementary Education Act of 1870 made its provision statutory. A prominent member of the community died in 1661 and in his will instructed his heirs 'every yeare forever as long as the world indures' to arrange for money to be provided for the appointment of a schoolmaster to teach English and religion to girls and boys whose parents could not afford to pay for their education. His example was followed by the 18thC Bishop John Green, who provided a house and garden for the schoolmaster, and in his will left the interest from a £200 trust fund to augment the teacher's salary.

By the 19thC, however, schooling was being provided only for boys. The lack of opportunity for girls was rectified in 1842 by the opening of a National School **[MapRef 2]**.

Later in the century, the squire of Stirtloe enlarged the schoolhouse at his own expense, and a Miss Mason left the endowed boys £1. 9s. a year in her will (she may have been Sarah Mason who was herself a schoolteacher).

Not everyone was in favour of compulsory education. Children, of course, could always find more exciting ways of passing the time – whatever the consequences:

> 'Punished eight boys with one stroke of the rod for coming late to school. They stayed rat killing at Farmer Cranfield's stacks in Silver Street' (school log book, 1890)

There were parents who needed their children to help out at home or go out to earn. And there were employers, the farmers in particular, who had no compunction about luring children away from school when they needed extra labour.

But it was Henry, farmer Cranfield's son (and heir to the family farming business), who held the most extreme views. In 1901 he told a visiting writer that the compulsory education of working class children 'was doing a great deal of damage to England.' He had, he said, every faith in education, but felt that how much of it a child should have was a decision for its parents, not the state. Parents were the political equals of anyone in the land, now that they had been given the vote. (This would have been news to the mothers of Buckden: women did not have the vote!)

The writer, who was H. Rider Haggard, the author of *King Solomon's Mines*, and an agricultural reformer, found this opinion 'ingenious and plausible'; i.e., wrong.

See **Chapter 13 Education in Buckden**, where this topic is dealt with at length.

Elima is a word with several meanings: it is a name given to sheepdogs; an Irish travellers' word for 'milk'; a variant of the Hebrew Elohim (God), and the Tswa pygmies' name for the divine force (the Congolese Tswa are Christians, and believe themselves to be descended from the children of Israel). By 1905 it was also the name of the Buckden house occupied by the Rev. Herbert Russell Hurditch (born 1875), minister of the Union (Baptist) Chapel. The son of a Devon saddler, he came from a distinguished evangelical family. His uncle Charles Russell Hurditch founded the Evangelistic Mission and was a renowned preacher who could fill London's Oxford Music Hall to overflowing, while his cousin Ruth Hurditch, later Mrs R. B. Fisher, (1875-1959) worked as a missionary in Uganda and wrote *On the Borders of Pygmy Land* – possibly the source for Elima?

Although the Buckden chapel was in the High Street it is not clear exactly where Elima itself was, as the name fell out of use.

Ellerslie [MapRef 44] was a popular 19thC house name, of which there were at least two examples in Buckden. The first was the home and surgery of W. H. Hillyer, Buckden's resident doctor during the 1890s. It was a substantial property in Perry Road: a six-bedroomed house with stabling, coach house, gardener's cottage, ornamental and kitchen gardens, and two tennis courts. It appears in the 1901 census and several Kelly's directories from 1903 onwards. By 1901, it had become the residence of a retired Madras Army officer, Major Chauncey **Curtois** (q.v.). On the major's death in 1905, occupancy passed to Thomas Coxon, draper and deputy mayor of Huntingdon, and then in 1910 briefly to a Cornish farmer called John Gundry. By 1914, the house had been renamed Nutfield, and at some point in the next ten years became the home of the **Bowtell family** (q.v.), probably in 1920 when it was sold by its owner, Mrs Hall (née Page).

The second Ellerslie was a smaller, semi-detached house at 8 High Street, one of whose occupiers was Leonard Sampson Butcher, born in 1893 into a family of Essex tailors and drapers. This background suggests that he may have been one of the departmental managers in Bowtells store. Mr Bowtell liked his staff to live close to the shop. Later it was the home of, first, Mrs Violet Kate **Stannard** (q.v.) and later Frank Mace, first Life President of Buckden Theatre Club (see under **drama in Buckden**).

elm, the Buckden. This was once regarded as one of the finest varieties of the smooth-leaved wych elm *Ulmus montana vegeta* (or possibly *Ulmus glabra var.*). It was first grown commercially in the mid 18thC, from seed collected in the neighbourhood of Hinchingbrooke and hybridised at the Brampton grounds of nurserymen Wood and Ingram. By 1842 it was particularly common in and around Buckden. A quick-growing tree of 'peculiar growth and appearance' it was said to produce excellent timber and to be a desirable ornamental for parks and gardens thanks to its large and 'cheerful green' leaves, which it retained into the autumn. Sadly, it is only moderately resistant to Dutch elm disease, and it is unlikely any specimens still grow in Buckden. It is to be found in arboreta all over the world, however, and possibly at Twizzell, Northumbria.

Also known – but not in Buckden – as the Huntingdon elm or Chichester elm.

See also **ash**, **plane** and **sycamores**.

enclosure [or inclosure] award. That for Buckden was made in 1813, but had still not been ratified seven years later. The award is held in the Huntingdonshire Archives, together with its accompanying map; the map appears on the rear endpapers of this book.

endowed boys: see e**ducation in Buckden**.

engine shed: see **fires and fire-fighting equipment**

entertainment in Buckden. According to the *St. Neots Advertiser* in July 1886: '*What with the feast, a general election and a school treat, this village was pretty lively on Tuesday*'. But then the inhabitants of Buckden have always enjoyed being entertained. As far back as 1713, they celebrated in the street when the end of the Wars of the Spanish Succession was proclaimed. In Victorian and Edwardian days the main indoor venues (apart, obviously, from the many licensed premises) were the schoolrooms and the Reading Room in Church Street. Later on came the Rifle Range (particularly popular for dances during the Second World War); St Stephen's Hall in the grounds of the Towers; the village hall; the Village Club, and, from 1999 the Millennium Community Centre. As well as dances, entertainments included plays, operettas, monologues, recitations, song recitals, musical evenings, parties for the children of the poor, and talks and magic lantern slideshows (some more educational than entertaining).

In April 1886, Colonel Marshall of The Towers presided over two 'popular and pleasing' evenings of ballads and comic songs interspersed with jokes. They would not be so popular today: the performers were an amateur group calling themselves 'The Buckden Minstrels', and were, said the *St. Neots Advertiser*, 'faultlessly attired in the costumes affected by the 'sable brethren', not by any means omitting the war paint'. Such groups had long been a well-established feature of both amateur and professional theatre: in January 1864, for example, the Saint Ives Private Amateur Elocution Society presented a programme of 'drawing room entertainment', which included Ye Ivian Minstrels ('seven Gentlemen of Colour') singing 'refined negro melodies'. They were followed by an extract from Shakespeare's *Othello*.

Outdoor sites for fêtes, bonfires, fireworks, plays, pageants, athletics meetings, flower shows, political gatherings, gymkhanas, bicycle polo and dancing included land attached to the George (often used for dances) and to the Spread Eagle (where within living memory there was a field large enough to host a circus), and fields belonging to, among others, Mr Looker of Church Street and Mr Mann of Perry Road. In addition, large private grounds and gardens were often thrown open for village events, including those attached to Ivelbury, Coneygarths, Stirtloe House, Buckden Towers and Field House. In the early 1900s Field House, sometimes known as Greenfields, was the residence of E. W. Hunnybun, and 'Mr Hunnybun's Lawn' was a popular venue for an evening of dancing to the Buckden Band. It must have been a large lawn: it had space for 200 guests. It now lies under the houses and gardens of Field Close.

The Lion should have been at a disadvantage when it came to offering outdoor entertainment: it had no gardens. But successive landlords got round this by using the High Street instead – as for example on 2 June 1902, when Buckden's celebrations of the end of the Boer War climaxed with the village band playing for dancing in the street outside the Lion (see also under **balls**).

Another popular entertainment was the spontaneous punch-up. A typical example, witnessed by between 80 and 100 excited spectators, was a fight that started late on Boxing Day 1904 in the George. It began when the acting manager told the hotel ostler, James Collins, to eject a drunken Diddington farm-worker. A row ensued. Words and furniture flew back and forth. A Mr House from Brampton chose this moment to come in for some refreshment. Seeing a lamp in danger of being knocked over, he cried out 'Steady, you'll have the place afire!' and was promptly knocked onto all-fours by two blows behind the ear from Collins, whose shout of 'I've owed you that for some time!' indicated that he had recognised House as the witness whose evidence had earned Collins his recently completed prison sentence (for being drunk and disorderly). Pc Hodson, arriving to restore order, was nearly knocked over when Collins, House, Collins's mother (Mrs Mills) and another man tumbled out of the hotel door. House started to complain to Pc Hodson, whereupon Collins punched him in the head again and Collins's mother started to scratch his face. Hodson tried to prevent House retaliating, which only allowed Collins to hit him yet again. They all fell on to the ground fighting, Mrs Mills 'shrieking and using bad language'.

Peace finally prevailed, and the spectators melted away into the night, having had a thoroughly entertaining time.

The subsequent court case ended with Collins being fined 15s. and his mother 10s. (the magistrates rejected the acting manager's claim that it was really Mr House who was the offending party). Mr Murray, landlord of the George, paid Collins's fine for him, saying he was a good worker and trying hard to reform. The man from Diddington, who had taken no part in the main bout, was fined 7s. 6d. Mr House left court bemoaning the half-crown he had dropped when first hit: 'I never saw it again.'

'Girl-on-girl action' – fights and swearing matches between women (usually neighbours) – was even more popular, particularly if some foolish male tried to intervene. See also **Band, Buckden Brass**.

excursions by charabanc and later motor-coach have been a feature of village life for nearly a century. Some took, and still take, the form of visits by groups or societies to appropriate locations – gardens, theatres, markets, places of historic interest. Others, such as Sunday School treats, were outings to the seaside, although there was one annual Combined Sunday Schools outing at the turn of the 19thC which wasn't all that exciting for the children of Buckden – it took place in The Towers. It was exciting for the adults of Buckden, however, many of whom would have been among the 1,200-1,300 people who danced the evening away in the park in the glow of paper lanterns.

Usually all went well with the excursions, although Mrs Billee Lumbers remembers one year when the Sunday schoolchildren were marched off to catch a train at Offord & Buckden station, only to be turned back because Mill Road was flooded.

A truly disastrous outing was reported by the *Hunts Post* in July 1923:

A CHAPTER OF ACCIDENTS

A party of juveniles and adults from Buckden, who went to Hunstanton for a motor excursion last week, had a most eventful outing. The day was enjoyed at the seaside, but troubles commenced on the return homewards...

.....when someone noticed that one boy had been left behind. The drivers stopped and got out to discuss what to do. A little boy also got out, to pick some heather for his mother, and was promptly run over by a passing car which broke his leg. He was rushed to Norwich Hospital in one charabanc while the other returned to Hunstanton, where the forgotten lad was found and bundled aboard. Unfortunately, when the driver started the engine for the homeward journey it burst into flames... .

explosion. On the morning of Monday, 7 March 1887, Mr Priestley, co-proprietor of Messrs Bowyer & Priestley's steam-roller flour mills, had just walked past the engine-house when it blew up, taking the end wall of the main building with it. Debris flew six or seven hundred yards, partially destroying two nearby houses en route. Miraculously, neither Mr Priestley nor any of the thirty men in the mill suffered injury.

F

Falcon public house. Buckden has had at least two pubs of this name. The earliest (also known as the Old Falcon) was in the High Street, just to the north of the Spread Eagle. It was sold in about 1840 and within a year or two had been de-licensed and converted into a shop and cottages. These were demolished in the 1960s to make way for the houses that are now 87-91 High Street, but they can be clearly seen in a late 19thC photograph in the Francis Frith collection

The Falcon name was transferred to premises in Mill Road, just to the east of Hunts End. Some 150 years later, in October 1995, it was closed by its then owners, Bedford brewers Charles Wells, and is now a private house, Crown Cottage.

The Falcon P.H. Mill Road c 1960   Angela Bruce Collection

Falcon Way is one of the short, bird-related streets leading off Vineyard Way. The name may have been suggested by the nearby Falcon public house in Mill Road (see previous entry).

Falcon Yard, High Street, lay between the Old Falcon pub and Taylors Lane. By 1911, it was called Barthrams Yard, after the family of grocers who had settled there some years before (see under **Barthram family**).

family, keeping it in the, was a feature of some of the early horticultural society shows. For example, from 1898:

Special Prizes

Arrangement garden flowers (prizes by Mrs Linton) - 1st Miss L. Linton, 2nd Miss Linton

Spray for a lady's dress (prizes by Mr J. Linton) - 1st Miss Linton, 2nd Miss H. J. Linton, Highly Commended Miss L. Linton

Six stocks (prizes by Mr J. Linton) - 2nd Miss O. H. Linton

Six roses (prizes by Dr W. H. Hillyer) - 1st Dr W. H. Hillyer (!), 2nd Mrs Linton

Six varieties cut flowers (prizes by Mrs Linton) - 1st Dr W. H. Hillyer

Dr Hillyer later married a lady whose sister had married a Linton!

Fawkes, Francis, MA (1720–1777) was a Yorkshire poet and clergyman. His works include an epistle to his wife, called 'A Journey to Doncaster, or, a Curious Journal of Five Days wrote with a Pencil in a Chaise'. It includes the lines:

'And shortly, o'er the rising steep,
We saw the spire of Bugden peep :
At breakfast near an hour we waste,
'Twas coffee, grateful to the taste,
With dulcet cream, and nut-brown toast ;
Then bid a Valeas [farewell] to our host.'

He does not name the inn at which he stopped, but his praise of the cream suggests it was probably the George, – if the experience of John **Byng** (q.v.) is anything to go by.

Feast or **Festival Week** has been celebrated in July for many years, but has been accompanied by some dispute about which is the correct week and by which name it should be known. The origin may well be found in the parish church's annual celebration of the life of its patronal saint, Mary. It may be that the church was first dedicated to St Mary in July (which could explain why the chosen week was a popular one in which to have one's children baptised); but if so, the actual date is lost in the mists of time. It may also be that July was, conveniently, a time of comparative quiet in the old farming year: not an idle month, for it was dominated by the hated daily grind of weeding, but one free of the frenzy of haymaking and harvest when all hands – men, women and children – were needed in the fields. With grain stocks at their lowest, July was also the hungry month, thus providing an opportunity for the better-off to exercise some Christian charity towards their poorer neighbours.

Over the years, the secular side of the Week has become more prominent, with events such as dances, stage shows, competitions, raffles, fairs or fêtes, and exhibitions (including, on one occasion, an impromptu striptease – see under James **Collins**). But a strong church connection is maintained, with St Mary's being decorated with flowers for the Week and a Songs of Praise service held on the last Sunday.

fiction, Buckden in. The village is mentioned, usually as a miserable, miasmic place of exile, in virtually every novel written about Anne Boleyn or Katherine of Aragon. But it appears in a handful of other works, of which Tobias Smollett's story of an English Don Quixote, *The Adventures of Sir Launcelot Greaves* (published 1760-2), is possibly the only work of fiction by a major author to have a scene set in Buckden. It occurs in an inn; sadly, Smollett does not identify which one, though on his own travels on the Great North Road he must have stopped off in Buckden for refreshment or even to spend the night.

Next came *Emmeline; or The Orphan of the Castle* (1788) by Charlotte Smith, a lesser-known 18thC novelist much enjoyed by the young Jane Austen. Emmeline's aristocratic cousin Delamere wishes her to elope ('Go with me to Scotland!'). Emmeline has other ideas ('No! no! never! never!') but is promptly carried off 'with a sort of gentle violence' in a chaise and four. Pursuing them up the Great North Road to Scotland, Delamere's irate father stops in Buckden for refreshment. He asks for news of the runaways at all the inns and public houses. Everyone denies seeing them. This is not because the villagers are trying to live up to Buckden's occasional reputation for being unhelpful: the young couple had never reached the village. They had left the north road at Stevenage and were safely hidden in Hertford; the elopement was over; they were on their way home.

In Lauren Royal's Restoration romance *Emerald*, the hero (a marquess pretending to be a commoner) and the eponymous heroine (a lovely, stubborn, independent Scots heiress whose real name is Caithren and whom the hero mistakenly believes to be a bounty hunter) are pursued down the Great North Road by murderous villains. Believing they have outpaced their pursuers, the pair stop off at the Lion for backgammon, beer, soup and Dutch pudding (a buttock of beef rubbed with brown sugar, salt and saltpetre, left for a fortnight, squeezed in a cheese-press for a day and a night, hung in the chimney to dry, boiled in a cloth and left to cool; it can then be cut out into shivers [i.e., flakes]). But they have underestimated their adversaries, and as Caithren steps out into the stable yard... .

Roseanna, heroine of Victoria Henley's erotic medieval romance *The Raven and the Rose*, is the love-child of Edward IV. During a frantic ride from Yorkshire to London to warn the queen that the king has been imprisoned by the Earl of Warwick, she stops the night in a Buckden inn. She awakens feeling so nauseous that she throws up twice (luckily the chamber-pot is to hand). No food, not even a Dutch pudding, is the cause, as she realises when sickness strikes again the next morning... .

Field Close: see following entry.

Field House, Silver Street [MapRef 48], a Grade II listed mid-18thC red brick house of three storeys (including attics). Its striking front doorcase met with the approval of Nikolaus Pevsner (*Buildings of England: Bedfordshire, Huntingdon and Peterborough*, 1968).

At the beginning of the 20thC it was the home of Edward **Hunnybun** (q.v.), a Huntingdon solicitor and distinguished botanical artist. Its gardens, extending over two acres, were a popular venue for fêtes and dances, but are now for the most part covered by Field Close, a 1970s residential housing development.

A modern single-storey, flat-roofed annex that stands beside the house was built as a doctor's surgery in 1969. It was superseded by a new surgery in Mayfield in 1993, and converted to offices. In 2008, planning permission was given for its return to medical use, this time to house a dental practice which opened in November 2009.

fires and fire-fighting equipment:

The Mischiefs from Fire Act of 1707 required that each parish should provide a means of fighting fires. (It also authorized payments of up to 30 shillings for the operators of the first three parish pumps to reach a fire, but this was probably implemented only in large cities – and sounds like an incitement to arson.) To this end the parish church purchased a fire pump and erected a building for it in the north-east corner of the churchyard. The brick floor and foundations are still present but below ground level.

Unfortunately, the pump could not always be produced when needed. According to *The Annual Register* for 1770:

'This morning [March 6] between ten and eleven o'clock, a most dreadful fire happened at Sturtley [i.e., Stirtloe], half a mile from Bugden in Huntingdonshire. In less than an hour, three capital farm houses, with their out-houses, stacks of corn, &c. were intirely consumed. The fire was raging at the same time in distant parts of the place. There was a great want of water, and no fire engine nearer than St Neots (four miles), and before it could arrive the whole of that beautiful village, with granaries, stacks, barns &c. was reduced to ashes.'

As ever, it was the poor what got the blame:

'This dreadful catastrophe was occasioned by the carelessness of a servant girl heating the oven.'

(An alternative version places the fire in 1790 and ascribes it to 'malcontents' – a reflection of contemporary fears of a radical uprising inspired by the French Revolution.)

It seems that the Huntingdon engine finally managed to reach the village: the archives of the Borough Council record a payment of 5s. to a William Beard for his attendance at Stirtloe on the day of the fire; the payment document confirms that he was connected with the fire engine.

Another Stirtloe fire, this one a mercifully rare case of arson, occurred in the early hours of 28 December 1863. John Barton, son of Buckden miller Richard Barton and described at his trial as 'a young man in a respectable position in life', 'unlawfully, maliciously and feloniously' set fire to farm buildings and corn stacks in the possession of Thomas Topham. The buildings belonged to the unlucky Mr Topham's landlords, Messrs Thornhill and Duberly, two local magistrates against whom John Barton was known to hold a grudge. The fire burned for two days; the resultant damage was estimated at £1,500-£1,600.

Despite a stranger having been seen in the vicinity at about the time of the fire, the jury took only a few minutes to find John Barton guilty; they were possibly swayed by both his father and brother giving evidence for the prosecution; by his own admission to a policeman's wife that he regretted having done it, and by Superintendent Copping's virtuoso demonstration of the footprint evidence. Barton was sentenced to twelve years' penal servitude and was transported on the *Vimiera* to Western Australia, where he died of fever only four years later.

In the early hours of 24 January 1898, the village fire brigade was unable to prevent two of 'the most picturesque specimens of old timber and thatch buildings in the county' burning down. Henry Mann, cowkeeper and dairyman, owned them both and lived in one of them. Fortunately he had fire insurance.

This fire followed closely on one at the George just before Christmas 1897. A servant was woken early one morning by the sound of the ceiling in the room next door crashing to the floor. It had been set alight by flames spreading from an 'oddly-constructed chimney'. Fortunately the parish engine was soon on the spot and little damage was done. But there was a sequel. The George's insurers, the Royal Exchange, refused to pay the one guinea attendance fee. The Parish Council indignantly instructed its clerk to point out that the fee represented only a small part of the cost of maintaining the engine and that other companies had paid it 'without demur'.

He was also instructed to find out whether the Council actually owned the fire-engine and was therefore responsible for insuring it and the engine-house against...fire.

Just over a century earlier, in October 1788, another servant had been awoken by a fire in the George. Staggering through the choking smoke, he was horrified to be met with 'a most shocking spectacle': his master, Thomas Bartlett, was lying in flames in front of the bedroom grate – indeed, almost under it – his shirt and waistcoat already reduced to ashes. The servant's intervention saved the unfortunate man from being 'absolutely roasted', but could not save his life: despite attendance by the best of local medical assistance, Mr Bartlett expired within a few hours. At the 'inquisition' held next day, the jury brought in a verdict of accidental death after hearing that the deceased had been in a state of almost continual intoxication for the previous six weeks. (See also **De Grammont**)

The weather during much of May 1803 was, according to *The Times*, 'ungenial': high winds trapped ships in port, and inland parts saw the fur tippets and fur-lined coats of January hastily retrieved from storage. An unfortunate moment, this, for an ostler at the Spread Eagle to be careless with a candle. On the morning of Monday, 9 May, he had been using it to singe the hairs out of a horse's ears (a practice furiously opposed by veterinary surgeons but widely believed to improve the animal's hearing), but forgot to put it out when he left the stable. Shortly afterwards, passers-by saw smoke issuing from the building. They rushed to open the door; the incoming air turned a smouldering fire in to an inferno. In minutes the winds had spread the flames in every direction. The Spread Eagle, its neighbour, the Falcon, and thirteen small tenements were burned to the ground, as were haystacks two hundred yards away. At one point, there were even fears that the Bishop's Palace would catch fire. Catastrophe was averted only after two days and nights of ceaseless effort by labourers and soldiers and the fire engines from Brampton, Godmanchester, Huntingdon, Offord and St Neots (at a cost to the parish of £25. 9s. 0d. in payments to the fire-fighters). In all, property worth more than £2,000 was destroyed, very little of it insured. The churchwardens' accounts record that donations totalling £560. 0s. 0d. were received from Buckden itself and the surrounding towns and villages.

A pair of cottages, this time owned by the parochial charities, burnt down in the early hours of 27 April 1898. They were thatched, of mud and plaster construction, stood on the south side of Mill Road near Hunts End and may have originally been the **parish workhouse** (q.v.). The respective occupiers were bricklayer's labourer George Bellamy and stockman William Livett and his family. Awakened by a crackling sound, Mr Livett opened his bedroom door. Flames leapt towards him, singeing his beard, and in the words of the local paper 'he hurriedly made an exit'. He discovered that his roof was on fire, woke

Mr Bellamy and roused their near neighbour, plumber William Stoneham, captain of the fire brigade. The engine quickly arrived, but despite there being no shortage of water, both cottages having their own wells, the fire had already taken hold and there was nothing to be done but concentrate on saving an adjacent barn and pigsty. (And the pigs.) Most of the contents of Mr Bellamy's cottage were rescued, but a little downstairs furniture was all that the unfortunate Livetts could save.

An even more disastrous fire broke out at the south end of Silver Street on the evening of 3 March 1909. Just after six o'clock flames were spotted in the thatched roof of a house, hard by the chimney; by the time the fire was contained some seven hours later, three properties had been totally destroyed. One was a large part-thatched property on the corner of Silver Street and Church Street, occupied by Mr T. J. Phillips as a general shop; he also ran an extensive coal and offal business, but fortunately did not store these items on the premises. The other two were rubble-and-thatch buildings: the house and bakery of William Andrews, where the fire started, and a cottage owned by Leonard Mann and occupied by William Gore. (There were two William Gores living in the Silver Street/Church Street area at this time – a retired grocer and a horsekeeper; the fact that the William Gore who lost his home was insured suggests that he was probably the grocer. If so, his death a few weeks later may have been partly due to the shock of the fire).

William Stoneham and the Buckden engine were on the scene within five minutes, soon followed by the engines from both St Neots and Huntingdon (summoned by telephone). There was no shortage of water: the St Neots engine was fed from the lake in The Towers, and the Huntingdon firemen broke into the well that supplied the village pump by the Wesleyan Chapel. But fanned by a north-east wind the fire spread through the three properties so rapidly that the brigades could concentrate only on keeping it away from neighbouring buildings. The cost of attendance for three brigades was estimated to be nearly £60.

In July 1923 – a month of exceptionally hot weather – the *St. Neots Advertiser* reported on a fire in the centre of Buckden that was witnessed by 'hundreds of people, who had come from miles around.' It broke out at 4 p.m. on

Ernest A Gale in WWII NFS uniform

Gale family collection

Tuesday, 17 July, being first spotted by two gardeners working in the grounds of Coneygarths. H. Cook and W. Gore noticed smoke coming from a large thatched barn belonging to Arthur Brown at the end of **George Lane** (q.v), and called Buckden's fire crew, later to be followed by the St Neots and Huntingdon fire engines. The fire quickly spread to Thomas Bowyer's thatched barn, which held many agricultural implements. Mr Brown's barn held **osiers** (q.v), and adjacent buildings included stables and pigsties. Many local helpers arrived and removed the implements and some pigs, but the burning thatched roof collapsed on and killed many pigs, piglets and hens. A haystack and eighty yards' length of buildings were destroyed by fire, fanned by the strong south-westerly wind. The malting barn opposite was now in great danger, its roof smoking in the intense heat, but the risk was got under control by the Buckden firemen. Flames continued to the east end of the buildings, and there were grave fears for the old buildings of the George and the Old Tap Inn. Once again the Buckden firemen soaked the structures, and fortunately the wind eased. When the Huntingdon and St Neots firemen arrived they pumped water 500 yards from the lake in the Towers. All the firemen stayed until the early hours of Wednesday, by which time the affected buildings had been razed to the ground. An inquiry concluded that the cause of the fire was unknown, but that all the property had been insured.

Later History. The Buckden pump was eventually re-housed in a brick building adjacent to the Hunts End shops

The 1879 fire engine from Buckden (Yorkshire). The Buckden (Hunts) machine was similar in operation. The long timber handles worked by perhaps four men each side can be seen. One is not in position.

Photo : Thimbleby & Shorland Auctioneers

(there is now an electricity sub-station on the site). The parish council assumed responsibility for the building's upkeep, repainting its doors in April 1901. Many years later, in the 1970s, the pump was bought by Buckden resident Brian Carter. For his story of what happened next, see Mr. Carter's contribution to **Chapter 21 'Remember when ....? '.**

Second World War. In 1941-2, a National Fire Service station and garage was built in the grounds of the Towers, probably from a kit of parts and largely by the firemen themselves. From photographs it appears to have had a brick front wall with a roof of corrugated iron or asbestos. At the rear was a pre-fabricated mess room with a pool or billiards table. Known as the NFS recreation hut, it was sometimes used for dances.

The equipment allocated to Buckden comprised a medium pump, a light pump and two trailer pumps. The first two were towed by box-type vans but the trailer pumps were capable of being towed by a car commandeered when required.

A photograph shows a staff of twenty-nine including six women but at least one other member is not visible. The officer was Frank Woodhouse of Field House.

There are no records of what fires were attended but Alice Whitmee of Diddington recalled telephoning to report a fire in a barn in her village. Since she was one of the staff, the fireman on duty thought that she was joking. It was suggested that he get outside to look. The glow in the sky provided the proof that the call was genuine.

As a change from fires, see **explosion.**

fish ponds. There are two ponds, one in the grounds of the Towers and the other further south in the **Valley** (q.v.) beside the village playing fields. The two are joined by a stream, now culverted for most of its length. Both have been cleaned out, the latter in 1990 by 'Mac' and his friends known as Waders Anonymous. A painting of the restored Valley by Australian Eileen O'Meara is reproduced at **plate PB2.5.2**. The Waders were rewarded by gaining joint first place in the Conservation Section of the Cambridgeshire Village Ventures Competition in 1991. A cheque for £175 came with the prize and was spent on extending the footpath around the Valley.

The pond in the Towers' grounds was originally three ponds belonging to the Palace: one for carp, one for tench and one for pike. Like the dovecotes and the deer park, the ponds were there to supply the bishops' lavish feasts.

In 1812, these ponds (by 1924 combined into one and labelled The **Canal** q.v.) were the scene of an accident that could easily have ended in tragedy: see **Hodgson, John**.

football in one form or another was probably being played in Buckden even before the first inflated pig's-bladder came bouncing along the great north road at the feet of the children of the camp followers trailing along behind the Roman legions. The first indications of there being a formal team, however, appear in newspaper reports in 1894, the date that the present football club takes as marking its foundation. Initially the side was called the Buckden Reading Room Team; the early reports don't say who was the captain, but we know that the centre-forward was the village doctor, W. H. Hillyer, who was also the Reading Rooms secretary. In 1898 he broke his collar-bone in a match against Catworth.

Fox, Joseph: see **Allen, William**

fox-hunting. Buckden was within the country ridden over by the Cambridgeshire (now the Cambridgeshire with

Date and source unknown.   The Cambridgeshire Hunt leaves the George Hotel. Note the dovecote in the background.

Alice Whitmee

Enfield Chace Hunt). The hunt met regularly at several places in the parish, including The Towers, Stirtloe, Buckden Manor and Park Farm (whose occupier in the early 20thC, Henry Cranfield, was an enthusiastic hunter). It also met at the George where the quaintly eccentric landlord 'old George Cartwright' would host the traditional end-of-season hunt breakfast.

Buckden Station was another popular site for the meet. The spread of the railways hugely increased the popularity of hunting (and racing) by making it easy for riders, horses and followers to come from a distance. It also provided injured huntsmen with a relatively comfortable journey home, especially those wealthy enough to have the stationmaster telegraph their doctor and order him to be waiting to meet them off the train!

Friar John de St Giles (fl. 13thC) was a Dominican theologian and one of the most eminent physicians of his age. For how he came to be in Buckden in the late summer of 1253, see **Chapter 14: Medical Practice in Buckden.**

Frost, Henry (1829-1905) Buckden-born farm worker who passed his whole life in one of the Mill Street (now Mill Road) cottages between the Anchor and the Quart Pot public houses. He collapsed and died suddenly after fetching a pail of water on a hot July evening. At the inquest held next day in the Silver Street pub, the White Horse, Dr Williams ascribed his death to a syncope, brought on by the close, thundery heat. Henry's neighbour, William Riseley, described it rather differently, with an almost Shakespearean vividness: 'He just twittered his lips, and he was gone.'

Henry, who grew excellent currants, probably worked on nearby New Farm (later Low Farm). He was married for over 50 years to Susannah [sometimes called Susan] Bason, also of Buckden. She outlived him by six years.

By 1901 there were three Mrs H. Frosts in the village, one of whom came joint first in the Married Women's 100 yards at that year's Buckden Friendly Societies' Athletic Sports. This is unlikely to be either Susannah (by then aged 72) or Mary Ann Frost, 60 year old wife of Henry's nephew. The most likely candidate is therefore 28 year old Southoe-born Amelia Elizabeth [Ashford], wife of Henry's nephew's son, Harry.

Furbank's corner is the local name for the junction of George Lane and the High Street, so called after the corner shop, Anne Furbank. It was previously known as Papworth's corner, Gale's corner or simply Watkins.

G

Gale family: There were Gales in Buckden over 300 years ago. Among their many descendants are Jocelyn, Judith and Barbara (twins) and Celia, the daughters of Stan and Wyn. Here they tell the story of their father's life and share memories of their own happy childhood.

We lived at numbers 18 and 20 Mill Road. When we were growing up there were no housing estates, just fields and farmsteads to roam and play in and where we lived we could play tennis in the road – it was that quiet!

A photograph of 1953 showed the family outside our house which was gaily decorated to celebrate the Coronation of Queen Elizabeth II. You wouldn't see our Dad as he was behind the No.2 Brownie box camera.

We sisters hope to portray the lively and colourful side of our mum and in particular our dad.

He was born in October 1912. He grew up in Buckden and lived here all his life. He attended the village school until the age of 13 years. On leaving he went to work next door to his home, at the Hosiery Factory (now Buckden Day Nursery). He was a keen tennis player, playing both on the courts behind the factory and at the vicarage. It was at the vicarage where he met Winnie Kiteley, who was in service and lived there. They eventually married at St Andrews church in Kimbolton, and soon afterwards he went to work at Harley's Aircraft Landing Lamps based at Great Paxton.

Together with his wife and several village friends, Dad inaugurated the Lincoln Imps Concert Party, putting on several shows before the outbreak of the Second World War in 1939. He also thoroughly enjoyed playing the piano at the Falcon on Fridays and Saturday evenings. As our dad was a volunteer member of the Fire Service he was exempt from call-up. He was a keen gardener and poultry man, he had an allotment in Silver Street and at one time was helped on it by an Italian prisoner of war. He reared hens and pigs at the bottom of the garden and we as young girls used to help with the feeding and collecting the eggs. He was a keen member of the Parish Council and for some time was its Chairman.

There were the occasions of the village May Days on the village green. All of the villagers became involved in the event. We have a photograph of our dad leading the procession dressed in a white fur coat and top hat and striding out carrying a mace, this just sums him up.

The over-60s nights were another occasion where our mum and dad were part of the committee that entertained the over-60s in the Rifle Range, where the Burberry Almshouses now stand. Our mum, along with the others, was responsible for the catering, all of which was produced in the Rifle Range kitchen. Our dad was responsible for the entertainment and we as daughters also had to be part of the show. I played my piano accordion and my cousin Marilyn Flint and I would sing. Even my sisters' husbands didn't get away with not being involved in the shows. Whether or not our dad wrote the scripts for the shows (which would not have surprised us) he certainly directed them. I remember those evenings being such good fun and there was always an appreciative audience all of whom were our neighbours and friends.

Gale's corner was once the local name for the junction of George Lane and the High Street, so called after the corner shop kept by baker and bootmaker William Gale. The bakery was later taken over by John James Papworth and the junction then became known as Papworth's corner.

gardening, both for pleasure and a source of food, has long been a popular pastime in Buckden, with the later years of the 19thC seeing the annual gardening shows establishing themselves as a major village event complete with athletics and Buckden's other favourite recreation, dancing. For a detailed look at gardening in all its aspects, see **Chapter 10**.

George, Prince of Wales (1762–1830). 'Bishop Tomline had the honour [on 10 January 1814] of entertaining the Prince Regent, afterwards King George the Fourth, to dine and sleep at Buckden.' The Prince charmed his host and hostess and the other guests, as Mrs Tomline made clear in a long letter to her sister. While at the palace he interviewed some French officers, who were being held at the notorious Norman Cross Prison Depot near Yaxley.

This was far from being the only time he was in Buckden, however. In 1818, Mrs Scarborough, landlady of the George, wrote of her respect for the Prince 'whose favours I have often been honoured with at Buckden'.

George Hotel or **Inn, High Street** (at times also known as the **St George & Dragon**, the **George and Dragon Commercial Inn** and (Heaven help us) as **Ye Olde George) [MapRef 23]**. The present hotel takes up only part of what had been a substantial inn, famous in coaching days for its 'vast size and elaborate arrangements'.

The first surviving written reference to the George as an inn was on 14 May 1662, when the churchwardens recorded spending two shillings for drinks, food and the use of a room there when collecting a levy and tax. A fortnight later, Samuel Pepys's diary records 'Mrs Pepys and maid by coach from George Holborn Conduit [in London] to Bugden', possibly to the George, where one can imagine them being collected by Pepys's uncle and aunt, then living at Brampton.

A reward notice in the *London Gazette* of 14 July 1687 suggests that the landlord of the time was a Mr John Spencer; if so, he may be the person of that name whose burial in June 1695 is recorded in the parish register. His successor may have been William Longland, who was certainly the landlord at the time of his death in March 1714. Longland was succeeded by George Lake (or Late), who seems to have left in or by 1722, when the lease of the inn was put out to tender. It was no longer the building that Pepys would have known:

'..there is a new Brick Building erected of Eleven Rooms, sashed [i.e., with sash windows, made fashionable by royal patronage], and a new Wine Vault and Granary, with other new Buildings beside the old Inn, which consists of large Brick Buildings, with very good Stabling, Out-houses, and a large Brick Dove-House, with Orchards and Gardening, and with other necessary Conveniences for an Inn.'

The George appears to have been one of the Thornhill Estates' Buckden holdings at this time: those interested in further details of the lease were directed to see either George Thornhill or William Hook, vicar of Doddington (i.e., Diddington, home of the Thornhills).

An exact chronology of the inn's 18thC landlords is not easy to determine but in December 1760, William South announced that he was succeeding his uncle John Hastings, who had died the previous month. The Hastings family were active in village life for most of the century: at one time or another, Thomas, John, and John junior were all churchwardens, and one of the Johns was a highways surveyor, charged with persuading nearby villages such as Southoe to contribute towards the costs of keeping the turnpike road in repair. William South assured the nobility and gentry that he was well-qualified to take over from his uncle (and aunt, who had died earlier in the year) since he had been living in the George for the last fourteen years. This suggests John Hastings had become landlord no later than 1746 and possibly earlier if he was already managing the George before William came to live with him.

William South himself died in 1795, and it may have been then or a few years later that the inn passed into the long tenure of John Scarborough, a former butler to the aristocracy, and his wife, Jane. They were popular with all classes of society, local and visiting, and successful enough to set up Mrs Scarborough's son in an inn of his own at Stilton. Unfortunately this well-intentioned act sowed the seeds of their abrupt and catastrophic decline into bankruptcy in 1816 and 1817 – see **Scarborough, Mrs Jane** for details.

The best-known of all the George's landlords were the **Cartwright family** (q.v.), who took over in 1836. George Cartwright was the first, and was succeeded on his death in 1850 by his wife, Elizabeth, who died in 1856. Managing the George did not simply mean running a hotel; it came with its own farm, which, as Mrs Scarborough once pointed out, tended to leave the wife in any partnership carrying the main burden of dealing with guests and travellers. Since George Cartwright was a coach-driver as well as an innkeeper, it is not surprising that the Cartwrights appear to have taken on a manageress or possibly a brewer: during a court case in 1844, the victim of a robbery was said to have foolishly spent too much time in the George sampling 'Mrs Herbert's ale'.

On Tuesday, 16 May 1837, a traveller stopping off at the inn for mid-day refreshment would have been startled to find himself sharing the premises with nearly sixty clergymen. This was neither a temperance protest nor a gathering of Anglicans for Real Ale; these were the clergy of Huntingdonshire assembling before going over the road to the palace to present a farewell address to their retiring bishop, the last of the bishops of Lincoln.

The George changed proprietors as well as landlords several times in its history. In August 1849, for example, it was one of several Buckden lots included in a sale of properties belonging to Pumfretts Brewery, Huntingdon. The adjoining George Tap, two shops and some pasture land were also included.

When Mr Edwin Murray left the George and Dragon (as it was by then) in October 1905, all the household furniture and effects were auctioned, ranging from the contents of seven bedrooms to two rustic seats and 'a useful chestnut pony'.

Because of Buckden's position sixty-one miles from London on the Great North Road, the George was well-placed to recover from the loss of the coaching trade by taking advantage of, first, the cycling boom that started in the last quarter of the 19thC and, second, the advent of the motor car. An early 20thC postcard carries the legend 'Quaint, Clean, Comfortable, Garage, Billiards,'. In the 1920 *Michelin Guide* it is described as a 'comfortable hotel, with modern improvements', RAC (but not AA) Appointed; its per person charges are 3/- for breakfast, 3/- for lunch, 4/- for dinner, and 4/- to 5/- a night for a room 'with large bed, light and attendance' (there is, oddly, no indication of how many rooms there are). One's chauffeur is fed and accommodated for 8/6 a day, and can use one of the three on-site garages to house, clean and repair one's car. For more serious repairs and new tyres (Michelin, of course), the A. T. Robinson Garage is just down the road with its inspection pit and spaces for thirty cars.

The serious unemployment in the years following the end of the First World War was forcefully illustrated in September 1923, when the George advertised for a porter. It received nearly 100 applications in two days, some from as far afield as Scotland and Wales.

The hotel was bought by the Anne Furbank Group in August 2003 and re-opened after eight months' refurbishment as the George Hotel and Brasserie, with a distinctive sign depicting twelve celebrated Georges (sadly, George Cartwright is not among them).

George Lane [MapRef 15] is now a cul-de-sac, but was once an ancient way which led to Shooters Hill and beyond to the Midlands. It was, in fact, a continuation of Mill Road and Church Street as they ran up from the old ford over the Great Ouse at Offord. Until the 18thC it was known as Perry Way, before the New Road (now Perry Road) was built. It ran along the northern side of the George Inn, of which two edifices remain, the **Old Tap** (q.v) and an old storage building. At one time, before the fire of 1923 (see under **fires and fire-fighting equipment**), there were large stables and farm buildings here including a huge thatched barn, the bishops' ancient **dovecote** (q.v), a slaughter house and an **osiers business** (q.v).

Barry Jobling

Georges, the. 'Catalogues may be had, at the George, Huntingdon, Kimbolton, Buckden, Potton, and Bedford'; Although they were not formally linked by anything other than name, these George inns made a convenient network for distribution of auctioneers' catalogues and other sales particulars.

Girls' Friendly Society. A decorative cast-iron cross in the Lucks Lane cemetery lych-gate is a poignant memorial to Grace E[mma] Luff, a blacksmith's daughter who died of tuberculosis in 1912, aged 16. The cross was provided by the Buckden branch of the Girls' Friendly Society. Founded in 1875 and affiliated with the Church of England, the Society's original aims were:

> to maintain a high standard of purity among British girls;
> to obtain for every working girl of unblemished character a friend in a class above her own.

The Society later helped women and girls to emigrate to the colonies (particularly Canada), or, if they wished to stay in England, to find work as pupil teachers, shop assistants, dressmakers or domestic servants: at the time of her death, Grace was working as a kitchenmaid for the Moody family, stationers of Huntingdon High Street.

The cross (*see photo*) was placed in the lych-gate early this century after being cleaned and repaired by Councillor Peter Bush, then the parish handyman, who found it discarded under the cemetery hedge. Unfortunately, no records of the Society's Buckden branch appear to have survived, but we know from newspaper reports that it raised funds through an annual sale of work and dance (music, as always, from the Buckden Band). One such event was held at Beech Lawn in 1908. It included a 'Do without stall' and a pastoral play acted by children imported from Huntingdon. One of them was Phyllis Goodliff (1897-1993), later a founder member of the

This memorial in painted cast iron is located in the roof of the lych-gate to the cemetery.

Huntingdonshire Local History Society and, through the fund established in her name, a benefactress of many local history societies – including Buckden's.

Glebe Lane is a short residential street running between Manor Gardens and Lucks Lane, which it joins opposite the cemetery lych-gate.

Gloria Patri, the Bugden. This scurrilous late 18thC or early 19thC rhyme is thought to be aimed at the Bishop of Lincoln of the day:

'To the Father and Son/All praise must be given/Their spirit is even,/ And their lying is one. The father lies well/The son is as clever/They have lied, they do lie/And will lie for ever.'

If anyone knows what lies behind this attack, the Local History Society would be pleased to hear from them!

golf course. Unlike the **Buckden by-pass** (q.v.), Buckden golf course is not a myth – although its exact location has passed out of memory. It is known to have been somewhere on the eastern edge of the village. It flourished at the beginning of the 20thC. That it was open only between August and April suggests it may have been on rented farmland which was returned to livestock grazing during the spring and summer. No mere pitch-and-putt course, it was the home of the Buckden golf team and was extended in 1902. The last known reference to it is during the First World War (in 1916): it may well have fallen victim to the drive to grow more food.

Good, Dr Frederick Thomas MRCSEng LSA (c. 1855-1894) was for six years senior partner in the Buckden practice of Good & Hillyer – although he never actually lived in the village. See **Chapter 14.**

goosing shed [MapRef 22]. Also known as the goose barn, this was part of the blacksmiths' premises just north of the Vine inn. The Great North Road was one of the main routes along which flocks of geese were once walked on their way to London's great Christmas goose fairs. Buckden was one of the staging-posts on this long journey, giving the drovers an opportunity to prepare the geese for the rigours of the miles still to come. They did this by herding them through the goosing shed, whose floor was a mixture of sand and heated tar that left the soles of the birds' feet with a protective coating.

Grafham Water is England's third largest inland water. Although no part of the 1,500 acre site falls within Buckden's parish boundary, some older residents are in no doubt that the reservoir has had an effect on the village. They believe that Buckden's exceptionally dry climate is caused by the temperature difference between the huge expanse of water and the surrounding land. This causes rain clouds approaching from the west to divide, so that they pass to the south (and more often) north of the village.

Great Buckden Hay Robbery. A frisson of disapproval or of amusement, depending on which side of the social divide you stood, ran through the district in 1885. James Matthews, a carter employed by the Rowley family of Priory Park, St Neots, was directed to carry several loads of hay from the Rowley farm to Buckden station for onward transport and sale. It subsequently became apparent that less hay arrived at the customers' end than started out from St Neots. It was first thought the 'shrinkage' took place during the railway journeys. Then the police received a tip-off from a boy who had occasionally accompanied the carter and had been uneasy at what he saw. As a result, they searched two Buckden pubs, the Windmill at the south end of the village, and the Crown at the north. They discovered quite large amounts of hay concealed on both premises. It turned out that on arriving at the station, the carter would 'find' a broken truss of hay and keep it back as fit only to 'feed the horses'. In fact, the horses saw little of it, as on the way back he would stop off at one or other of the pubs and exchange the hay for beer. (No money seems to have changed hands.)

After the carter had been found guilty by the St Neots magistrates, the two licensees were also charged. With a notable lack of chivalry, both put the blame on their wives.

Great North Road. One has only to look at a map of Britain to see why this road was so important in opening up and maintaining trade and communications between London, the north of England and Scotland: a direct route for goods, livestock, passengers, royal messengers, postal services and armies. At times its importance—and the prosperity of Buckden—has diminished, as with the coming of the railways in the 19thC, and the 1959 opening of the M1 motorway and its later extension to Yorkshire.

Several other entries in this book attest to the continuing presence—for better or worse—of the Great North Road (or A1 as the relevant stretch now is) in Buckden's life. A good place at which to start is Chapter 18 which describes why its adoption as a turnpike road was regarded as a priority in the early 18thC and led to the sidelining of the more easterly Old North Road from Shoreditch to Alconbury via Royston.

Green family. The Greens of Coneygarths (and other houses in the village) were one of Buckden's leading gentry families throughout the nineteenth and early twentieth centuries. They were related to John Green, Bishop of Lincoln, and connected by marriage to Edward Maltby, Vicar of Buckden and later Bishop of Durham. The best-known member of the family was Captain John George

Green (1789-1882). Their story and that of their house is told in **Chapter 8**; see also **Captain Green's golden eagle; Hodgson, John,** and the following entry.

Green Memorial, High Street [MapRef 25]. This was erected in September 1923 by John Green in memory of those from the village who had died in the First World War. They included his two sons, who were:

Second-Lieutenant Alan Green of the 1st/5th South Staffordshire Regiment, who was killed on 13 October 1915 during the 46th Division's assault on the Hohenzollern Redoubt near Loos-en-Gohelle, Belgium. The Division lost 180 officers and 3,583 men in the first 10 minutes of battle. Alan Green's body was never recovered. He was 20 years old.

Captain John Green, RAMC, Medical Officer to the 5th Battalion, Sherwood Foresters, who was awarded a posthumous VC for his conspicuous devotion to duty during the morning of 1 July 1916 – the first day of the Somme. Approaching the enemy lines he found a badly wounded fellow-officer, Captain Frank Robinson, caught up in the wire. Although himself injured, he managed to free him and drag him to a nearby shell-hole. Here he dressed his wounds while under almost constant attack from bombs and rifle grenades. He then sought to guide him back across No Man's Land to safety. They had almost succeeded when Captain Robinson was wounded again. John Green stopped to help him, only to be hit and killed instantly. His body was not recovered until the following spring.

At the time of his death he was 27 years old and had been married for six months – to the day. Frank Robinson died of his wounds two days later.

The memorial stands on land that belonged to Coneygarths, the home of the Green family for several generations.

The brothers are also remembered on the war memorials of both Buckden and Houghton-with-Wyton.

green, the village: see **Hunts End.**

Greenway is a long, curving residential thoroughfare joining School Lane to Mill Road, and is a central part of the road network built to serve the new houses erected during the major expansion of Buckden in the latter half of the 20thC. It was engineered to form part of a new bus route, but is not now used for this purpose. The name reflects the fact that it is on land once owned by the Green family.

H

Haigh, the Rev. Daniel (1812-1875) was Buckden's vicar from 1850 until his death, which occurred at the vicarage. He was the son of a Leeds merchant (although he was born in Manchester: perhaps his mother returned to her own family for the birth). He was educated at Leeds Grammar School and Catherine Hall, Cambridge.

Hardonian Farm, Hardwick Lane, now Hardwick House, was a dairy farm with a prize-winning Channel Island herd kept by Reginald Mann, whose father Ernest had become the landlord of the **Spread Eagle** (q.v.)

before the First World War. (Ernest also kept cows, milking them in the paddock behind the inn.)

Miss Gladys Mann, Reginald's daughter, remembers life on the farm in **Chapter 9**

Hardwick Dene, Hardwick Lane, built in the 1920s in

The outbuildings of Hardonian Farm, Hardwick Lane now part of the private dwelling Hardwick House.

the style of an Edwardian gentleman's country residence, stands overlooking open countryside to the west of the A1. Since 1990, it has been a residential retirement home, at present (2009) managed by Sohal Healthcare Ltd.

Hardwick Lane is a narrow, deep-sunk, badly maintained, poorly drained road that was once effectively the main street of the tiny hamlet of Hardwick. It was never intended to bear the weight of traffic that it now does. Irritating as those who live along it today find the way its surface is regularly broken up by running water after heavy rain, they are at least spared the equally regular flows of sewage that their 19thC predecessors had to bear.

Hide (*sometimes* **Hyde**), **Henry (1811-1889)**. His is a classic Victorian rags-to-respectability tale. Born in Buckden, the son of a shepherd, he began his working life as a farm labourer. According to his obituary in the *St. Neots Advertiser*, he left while still a young man to try his luck in the Australian goldfields. There is a problem with this story: the discovery of gold in Australia was not announced until 1851, by which time Henry was already 40 years old – and, as we know from the census, was still in Buckden, living with his brother's family in the High Street. 'Young man', therefore, is a journalist's touch of romance. But there was every reason for a man in his forties to consider leaving the village. With the coaching trade and its ancillary employments being driven out of business by the railways, the local working population had already begun to decline. To Henry – middle-aged, unmarried, without a home of his own – his fate must have seemed all too likely to match that of his elderly parents: pauperism and the almshouse (or, worse, the Union Workhouse.) No surprise, therefore, that some time in the early 1850s he decided to emigrate.

It was the right decision. He made enough money as a 'digger' to buy a farm in Australia. After 16 years he sold up and returned to Buckden as a man of independent means – which meant the name of 'Henry Hide, esq.' appeared among those of the gentry in local directories. He was, said the *Advertiser*, 'a person of a very retiring disposition and much respected'. Towards the end of his life he was in ailing health, and his death was hastened by a fall from a cart in Huntingdon, which dislocated his thigh.

His wife, Ann, stayed on in their Silver Street home, which adjoined Beech Lawn, with a niece as companion. She died in 1909.

Henry's younger brother, William (1815-1861), was an agricultural labourer all his working life, mostly on Park Farm. He became a Wesleyan in 1838, but in 1844 was one of the first to be converted by the Primitive Methodists' Buckden mission in 1844. Despite his having had almost no education, his obituary in *The Primitive Methodist Magazine For The Year Of Our Lord 1860* described him as 'a useful local preacher', 'generally [well] received' for his 'pretty good' preaching abilities. He died at his home in Lucks Lane five days after the 1861 census. His last words to his widow and seven young children were: 'All is well, I am now going home.'

High Street. Buckden's stretch of the great north-south route between London and Scotland has had several other names during its history: the Old North Road and the Great North Road were still appearing in addresses until the last years of the 20thC; and, less romantically, to the Ministry of Transport and Civil Aviation it was 'a length of the London - Edinburgh - Thurso Trunk Road to be superseded'.

High Street shops. Starting on the east side of the High Street, the corner now occupied by the cosy bar of the Lion Hotel was a butcher's shop with a house behind where the butcher's nephew, veteran retired postman Fred Brown, was born.

Moving southwards, there were two premises in what is now the entrance to the Lion car park. One was occupied by a tailor.

On the south side of that entrance is 40 High Street. Since 1995, this has housed Elouise Lingerie, which sells ladies' wear: night, swim and under. From early in the last century to 1952, No. 40 was part of the Bowtell building (see below); from 1922 it was occupied by the post office (see under **Post Offices**.).

Bowtells was the major retailer in Buckden from its start in 1902 until the 1960s, when its range of services began to be run down. The shop built in April 1923 has now been split into three parts. The larger part is One Stop, a convenience store which incorporates the sub-Post Office. Next to it at No. 34 is Susan Peters, a shoe and ladies' accessories shop, and at No. 32 Tangles hair studio.

The butcher's shop at No. 28 , briefly Scotts Rare Breed Meats Ltd (formerly G. Day & Sons) and now under the name Day again, stands on the site of a terrace of cottages. Families known to have lived there include the Chandlers and the Sabeys.

The north end of the **Vine** public house (q.v.) was variously occupied by a tailor and Buckden Farmers Butchers, a co-operative venture. The entrance was in the north wall.

Two hundred years ago, the area of the present access road to King George Court and the George Hotel was occupied by a house and garden that were home to the George's innkeeper. In the 19thC the house was converted into two shops, one of which was the Post Office, which also sold stationery.

The ground floor of the George Hotel extended from its south end to the archway. North of the archway was the establishment of Mrs Ethel M. Lofts (née Bayley), which combined the sale of newspapers, books and antiques. Until 2008, one of her invoices was still displayed in Days' butcher's shop opposite the Vine. She also ran a lending library (1924 motto: 'Why buy Books when you can borrow

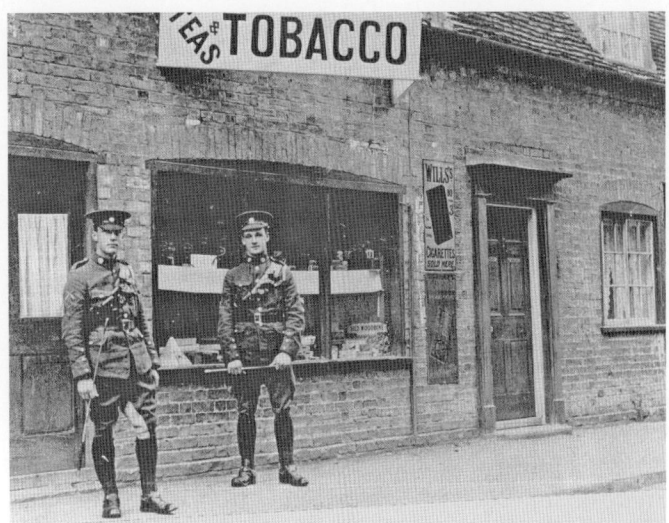

Two WWI troopers of the Lovat Scouts who were based at the Towers at the time. The left side soldier is a marksman and may also be a farrier. The shop-cum-café behind is now 'Equilibrium', the owners having loaned the photograph.

one for 2d? Over 800 up-to-date Novels.'). Her husband, Arthur Henry Lofts, was a Londoner. The son of a fishmonger, he first visited Buckden in 1911 as a collector for the Fishmongers' and Poulterers' Institution. In about 1913, he settled in the village and started an antiques business. He married Ethel in 1915. They had met as neighbours: she had been employed at the Post Office next door.

He died in 1943, aged 85. During the 1920s, he had been a bailiff of the Bishop of Peterborough's Court in Buckden, in which capacity he attended the General Courts Baron and Customary Courts held at Buckden Palace by Robert Holmes **Edleston** (q,v,).

On the corner of George Lane was John James Papworth's bakery which later became Watkins' newsagents. For a time, Watkins' also incorporated the Post Office, where Buckden's incoming mail was received and sorted before delivery.

A hundred yards northwards are Nos. 61-63 High Street, to which the beauty salon Equilibrium came as the latest in a long line of businesses. The premises began life in the early 18thC as two cottages. During the early years of the 20thC they housed a small private school for girls (see **Bowling, Mrs Sarah**) and then a bicycle shop (see **Robinson's Garages**). Later, in the days when the Great North Road traffic ruled the High Street (before the A1 was dualled), the premises were run as a café for perhaps fifty years by, among others, Robert Townsend and the Geerings. It was much patronised by truck drivers, to the irritation of residents who had to cope with the resulting noise and parked lorries. It was then for some years a jewellers and gift shop, Rings and Things.

Equilibrium is now the most northerly retail enterprise on the High Street. Until 2003, however, there was also the **Spread Eagle** (q.v.), a public house that had started life as coaching inn. For many years its northern wing was used as a shop, notably as a picture and art gallery into the 1990s. But like the pub itself, it is now a private house.

A few yards further on, in front of the old Baptist chapel (also now a house), there is a terrace of 1960s houses. These replaced a row of ancient cottages, which had originally been yet another public house; the southernmost of these was a greengrocers shop for a time. It was reported that sales were not good largely because so many villagers grew their own vegetables.

A tiny outbuilding on the south corner of Taylors Lane has also occasionally served as a shop for a time. Just after the war, it was where butcher Jimmy Hunt sold pork pies and other meat products, but forty or so years later, in complete contrast, it was briefly a vegetarian shop.

In Taylors Lane itself is a well-known nursery, Adams Plants.

Hillyer, William Henry MD[Durham] LRCP MRCS (1863-1945) was a canoeist, golfer, actor, cyclist, footballer, tennis player, beekeeper, balneologist, parish councillor and Buckden's doctor through the 1890s. See **Chapter 14**

Hinsby family. Shrewd St Neots traders with business interests in Buckden, they came from a family that exemplified the geographic and social fluidity of the Victorian class system. Robert Hinsby (1821-1856) was a Somerset-born railway worker whose job as a platelayer took him about the country: of the four children he had with his wife Martha (1819-1892), two were born in Somerset, one in Northamptonshire and one in Norfolk. At the time of his early death, the family was living at Tempsford in Bedfordshire and five years later was still living there in some poverty: the painful illness from which Robert suffered for the last five years of his life must have restricted his ability to earn. Yet by 1871, one of his sons, Samuel, had become a successful carrier, operating between St Neots and Bedford. A few years later he had extended this run to St Ives and Cambridge.

By 1879, Samuel and his brother, James, were in partnership not only as carriers but also as farmers, and as corn, coal and grain merchants trading from purpose-built premises in Huntingdon Street. In the 1900s, they introduced a goods and passenger horse-drawn omnibus between Bedford and St Neots. With painfully bad timing they replaced this with a motor bus in 1914; it was almost immediately requisitioned by the army and shipped to France!

Samuel Hinsby and his wife Alice had several children, of whom the following had connections with Buckden:

Transport F. J. Hinsby and one of his brothers are credited with starting the first bus service from Buckden (see under **buses**).

Shop Samuel Ernest Hinsby (1882-1973), brother to the bus operators, appears in a 1920 Buckden directory as a shopkeeper. He owned a tobacconist's shop still remembered by a few as Hinsby's Corner, since it stood on the eastern corner of Silver Street and Church Street. It was officially 1 Silver Street as that was where the entrance was; it is now 42 Church Street **[MapRef 6]**, the front door having been moved round the corner when the

building was converted to a private house in 1974. In one of the rooms it is still possible to see where the counter was.

There is some disagreement among the few residents of Buckden who remember the shop, as to whether there was a sweets machine or a cigarette machine outside. Perhaps there were both. The cigarette machine allowed you to buy three Crail cigarettes for a penny.

The row of buildings of which the shop was part, replaced a group of thatched cottages demolished after the disastrous Silver Street fire of March 1909 (see under **fires and fire-fighting equipment**). An auctioneers' notice of June 1920 referred to the building as 'newly-erected business premises'.

Mr Hinsby's wife Maud (née Lee) ran the tobacconists until her death in 1962. The shop was then rented by Mr and Mrs **Pipe** (q.v.). After Mr Hinsby died in 1973, his trustees unsuccessfully applied for permission to convert the premises into a fish and chip shop. The family then sold all their Buckden properties. Among these was a shop at 49 Church Street (once the village **Reading Rooms** (q.v.)), which was bought by Mr and Mrs Pipe, who had rented it since 1945.

Coal, coke and corn In the family tradition, Mr Hinsby also dealt in these goods, the station at Offord being his source of fuel. The premises were between the shop and bakery – the double gates to the yard are still visible today. A similar business – coal and flour – had existed on this site since before 1891.

Farming At his death in 1973, Mr Hinsby was described in the *London Gazette* as a retired farmer; he had been involved in agriculture since at least 1942, when a local newspaper report of a court case referred to him as a Buckden farmer.

Other family activities In his spare time Mr Hinsby helped found the Bowls Club and bowled the first wood at the opening of the greens in Silver Street. He was a Methodist, a parish councillor, a first-class billiards player, a committee member of the Horticultural Society and a long-serving Special Constable. His son, Mr Spencer Lee Hinsby (1916-2003), took several parts in the Pageant of the Centuries held at The Towers in 1932 (see under **pageants**).

Hodgson, John, Esq. MA (c. 1740-1822) was an ecclesiastical lawyer who acted as secretary to three bishops of Lincoln (Drs Green, Thurlow and Pretyman). He was able and energetic, necessary qualities in a post which required him to work not only in Buckden but as far afield as London and Durham. His period of service lasted fifty-four years (1766-1820), but nearly came to an abrupt end after only forty-five. In January 1812, he, his daughter, his son, his son's wife, two of Bishop Pretyman's sons and Captain Thomas Green of Coneygarths were strolling on the frozen canal in the palace grounds when the ice gave way. The whole party except Miss Hodgson descended into eight feet of water. The young men struggled to the bank, only to see Miss Hodgson now disappearing through the ice as she tried to rescue her aged father. Her brother rushed to help her; ice cracked; he sank.

Fortunately, Captain Green and the young Pretymans kept their heads. The adventure ended, not in tragedy, but in warm beds and cordials for all.

While in Buckden, John Hodgson married widow Sarah Douglas, like himself a native of Northumberland. After his death, she returned there and died in Newcastle upon Tyne in 1836.

A new Hinsby cart   Barry Jobling

Home Counties Trust Houses Ltd. Owners of hotels on the Great North Road, including the Lion.

Hoo Close, a short residential cul-de-sac off Greenway, was built in 1968 on land that had formed part of Hoo Farm.

Hoo Farm. From various papers regarding mortgages, tenancy agreements and so on it appears that Hoo Farm was never large, at least by present day standards.

The Enclosure Award had awarded the land to the Trustees of the Hurst family in 1820. It comprised 165 acres in two parts. The larger part, which included what is now The Hoo on the corner of Church Street and School Lane, extended about 1.4 km. in an ENE direction from it. The smaller part was on the south side of Taylors Lane.

In 1831 the farm was included in the estate of Robert Hurst Whitworth, whose striking memorial in St Mary's Church was designed by Thomas Rickman, a leading architect of the Gothic revival. The estate was divided among his three surviving sisters by lot and Harriet Hurst by that unusual means acquired Hoo Farm and the land in Taylors Lane as part of her share of a will valued at about £57,000.

An acre of land connected to Silver Street by Public Road No. 11, an exhausted gravel pit owned by the Surveyors of Highways, was sold to Harriet Hurst in 1855 for £60 and became part of Hoo Farm with the agreement of a Vestry Meeting (see **parish councils**) in Buckden.

In 1856 Harriet Hurst sold her land to Mr Francis Green for £9,000.

The number of documents relating to the ownership of the land is large and in 1862 a Mr Dubois was asked to advise on behalf of the proposed mortgagors on Mr Green's title to the estate. His work ran to about ten sheets of legible longhand!

John Green gained possession of the lands from Francis Green for £4,600 in August 1895 by taking over existing mortgage responsibilities within the family. This figure also included the four closes totalling 56 acres in Taylors Lane but Francis was to have the use of this at a peppercorn rent.

The last farmer was Mr George T. Page who also traded as a builder. His land was that east of Silver Street (including where the gravel processing plant was until 2006) and was bought from John George Green in March 1912 for £2,200 with F. C. Sydney Green as sitting tenant for the land; the farmhouse had recently been rented by a Bedfordshire farmer's son turned fruit salesman, Frederick Coxall. F. C. S. Green's tenancy ended at Michaelmas 1913. The land comprised fifteen fields or closes totalling 109 acres. There was included also a cottage and blacksmith's shop in **Bakers Lane** (q.v.) tenanted by Mr Morris (sic) Milner from October 1882. The fields were all named including, for example, First Turnip Close. The gravel pit referred to earlier had been added to this close.

The story of the ownership of the Taylors Lane land is less clear. Certainly some fields were exchanged with the Ecclesiastical Commissioners. One was called Twigdens Piece – a possible early connection with the builders who are now part of the very large Kier group.

The fields which comprised Hoo Farm are still mostly under the plough as part of Lodge Farm. Of the rest, some lie under parts of School Lane and Greenway, while a smaller area was occupied by the Lafarge Redland aggregate processing plant until 2008.

Hoobags: see under **The Hoo.**

Hopkins, Matthew (c. 1619/20 - 1647), the son of a Suffolk vicar, became notorious during the first English Civil war for his career as a self-styled 'Witch Finder Generall' . He is said to have married a Peterborough girl, Mary Starling, in Buckden Church, and to have lived here for about a year, using the village as a base from which to conduct his activities. The absence of evidence for this, however, suggests the story is apocryphal.

Hornsby, Robert (b. 1814) was Superintendent of Police for Buckden and the other villages in the Toseland division in the early 1850s. As this was before the formation of the county constabulary, he reported not to a chief constable but to the local district magistrates – who dismissed him after he had 'incurred their displeasure'. It was then found that he had been fiddling his expenses, falsely claiming reimbursement for tolls paid while making official journeys in his horse and cart. In fact he had never paid any tolls, using his position in the police to claim exemption.

Hornsey, Mrs Fanny (c. 1828-1924) was one of Buckden's longest-lived residents. When she died, just a week after her 96th birthday, the *St. Neots Advertiser* said of her that until the last year of her life she had a wonderful memory and *told many interesting stories of the village in her youth*. As this would have covered years of great change for Buckden (for the worse when the railways killed off the coaching era, and for the better with the opening of the National School), it is a pity that no one seems to have written them down!

She was the daughter of John Favill, shepherd and veterinary surgeon, and the wife of George Hornsey, who worked as an agricultural labourer and later as a gardener (they lived in a cottage near the Church Street end of Lucks Lane, so he may have been the vicarage gardener). At her death she left six children, eight grandchildren and six great-grandchildren.

Hostelries Ltd were early 20thC owners of hotels on the Great North Road, including the George.

Hunnybun, Edward Walter (1848-1918), Huntingdon solicitor, amateur golfer and distinguished botanical artist. He lived in Field House, Silver Street, for a time before retiring to the Isle of Wight in 1912. In 1911 he presented some 1,700 botanical drawings to Cambridge University; they were to be used to illustrate a new ten-volume set of British flowering plants. Unfortunately only volumes two and three were ever published. The drawings remain in the collection of the University Herbarium.

His sons William and Kenneth served as officers in the First World War with the Huntingdonshire Cyclist Battalions (and other units). William (1883-1960) was a member of the Buckden Golf Club and took part in Buckden Reading Room entertainments. Kenneth (1887-1972) won the DSO and joined his father's firm; one of the officiating clergymen at his wedding was Archdeacon **Knowles** (q.v.).

hunting: see **fox-hunting**

Huntingdonshire Association, the. Instituted 25 May, 1787 for 'the speedy Apprehension, and effectual Prosecution, of HORSE and SHEEP STEALERS, FELONS, and THIEVES of every Denomination, and other DISORDERLY PERSONS committing Offences in the said County, or elsewhere, within the Distance of 15 Miles from the Town of Huntingdon, on the Person or Property of any of the Subscribers'. One of the founder members was the father of Fanny and Laura **Beaumont** (q.v.). The list for 1812 includes several subscribers from the Buckden area, among them Thomas Usher, Captain Green, William Chapman, William Bowyer of Diddington, James Mann of Leighton (father-in-law of John Gace **Langley** [q.v.]), Mark Moon, Charles Norman, John and William South, the vicar, the bishop, the bishop's son, the bishop's steward,, and brewer Joseph **Baxter** (q.v.).

Hunts End [MapRef 35] is an area south of the Church Street/School Lane junction that includes a triangular **green** bounded by roads and surrounded by shops and houses. A plan in the Norris Museum shows that the green once contained a pond, apparently bounded by a wall on the north side. Adjacent were a **pound** (q.v.), and at one time a set of stocks, as well as a cage where less law-abiding villagers were placed ready for transit to the local jail (this was later used to house the parish fire-engine). One 17thC source places the stocks near the church gate; perhaps the increasing secularisation of the law or the fastidiousness of later generations led to their removal to Hunts End. By the early 20thC the pond had fallen into disrepair and was filled in by a local farmer – see under **pond**. (It appears to have dried up – or at least shrunk – even earlier: Pc Tom Jarvis recorded policing Salvationist meetings on 'Pond Green' in the summer of 1887.)

In his 1971 history of Buckden School, the then headmaster records that in Edwardian times the children would be assembled on the village green on Empire Day (27 May) 'to salute the flag and sing the National Anthem'. One present resident remembers attending a fair on the green in the years before the Second World War. During the war itself the green was the scene of a startling encounter between a lady of quality and a small field gun; this is described in **Chapter 17**

The green is now home to a bus shelter, the village sign (erected at the millennium), two of three trees planted on the occasion of the coronation of King Edward VII, and, to replace a decayed horse chestnut, a young oak tree planted and donated by Mr T. F. Hayward OBE to celebrate his ten years as chairman of the parish council. In 2001, the late Tilly Farmer-Wright, parish council chairman 2000-2003, instituted a tradition of decorating one of the trees with lights over Christmas and New Year.

Hunts Game Protection Association was set up in the summer of 1898 to discourage poaching. In 1901 it successfully prosecuted two Buckden labourers for stealing 29 partridge eggs. In an uncharacteristic fit of leniency, the St Neots bench fined them only 2s. 6d. an egg (the recommended rate was 5s.) plus costs. Two of the magistrates were Buckden landowners, and probably had a shrewd idea of the amount the two men could afford to pay: one had at least eight children (two of whom were to die in the First World War). It would be nice (but probably sentimental) to think that the magistrates may also have felt some slight distaste at the way the arresting officer had gone about his work: he had effectively persuaded one man's wife and son to shop him. The Association lasted until at least the 1920s; as well as working closely with the police it used to employ two detectives of its own.

Hurditch, Rev. Herbert Russell: see **Elima**

ΩΩΩΩΩ

I

Ilsley, Joseph Charles (1861-1884). Enter Buckden Cemetery by the lych-gate in Lucks Lane, walk straight ahead until the path has passed through a row of trees, and look to your right. A few yards away you will see a grave quite distinct from those about it: not grey and upright, but a polished pink coped stone. It bears the names of Joseph Charles Ilsley and his mother, Eliza Thomson.

Joseph was the manager of the brewing department of the Lion and Lamb public house. In this, he was following a family tradition. His father, his mother and both his paternal grandparents had been in the licensed trade (his maternal grandparents, however, had been Northamptonshire fishmongers). His mother had taken over the Lion on her first husband's death in 1873; in 1877, she married Henry Thomson, member of an inventive Buckden family. Henry then became the licensee ('publican and engineer').

On the morning of 7 June 1884, Joseph had gone to work in the Lion's brewery. At one o'clock his mother goes to fetch him through for lunch. At first she finds no sign of him, but on a second visit is horrified to see his hat lying at the bottom of a fume-filled fermenting-vat. She raises the alarm—'Send for the doctor!'—family and neighbours come running—brave young man is lowered into the vat on a rope—brave young man is frantically hauled up again, insensible—iron hooks are found—Joseph finally dragged out—Dr McRitchie arrives—one look: 'Life extinct, carbonic acid gas'—can do no more than resuscitate brave young man.

The funeral took place on 17 June. Shops were closed as a mark of respect, and the route to the cemetery was lined with villagers. Joseph had been a popular young man.

His mother outlived him by nearly forty years. Even before her death in 1922, at the age of eighty-four, many had forgotten the real, harrowing circumstances of her son's accident. 'Drowned in a tub o'beer,' they would say, looking into their tankards with a shudder. Then, cheering up, 'What a way to go!'

In October 1888, a painful, but less serious, accident befell Eliza Thomson's 11-year-old nephew, Frederick Putman. He was drawing beer in the Lion, when the barrel rolled on to his foot, crushing the big toe, part of which had to be removed by Dr Good. This experience seems to have led him to opt for a safer career as an apprentice in the neighbouring shop of Buckden's musical butcher, Francis James **Smith** (q.v.).

inclosure award: see **enclosure award**.

Ivelbury Close, High Street, is a small late 20thC housing development. It was built on the site of a large private residence, Ivelbury, which with its gardens was lost to the 1962 by-pass of the High Street.

ΩΩΩΩΩ

J

James, Charles is shown as the Charity School master in Pigot's 1830 Directory, but died the following year and was succeeded by his brother:

James, Henry (1814-1854), who was born in Hemingford Grey. His mother was a butcher in Fenstanton. According to his epitaph in St Mary's churchyard he was '23 yea~ ~~hoolmaster of this parish'. This means he was only s...   ...appointed. Sadly, his long tenure ...   ...ith the school managers. A few r...   ...smissed he was dead of 'consu...   ...' and the contents of his house...   ...le to commence punctually at Ele...   ...mber of lots' (including his brew...   ...ried Anne Fox in 1838; after his d...   ...cook to a Yorkshire farmer.

Jam...   ...), king and weeder-out of 'toba...   ...ertained at Buckden Palace at le...   ...6 by Bishop Richard Neile, and...   ...ccessor, the 'canary-sucking and...   ...ge Mountain (or Montaigne). The...   ...autumn clearly left James in a n...   ...ts went on to become Prince-Bis...   ...bishops of York.

...   ...present during James's visits we...   ...side on the banks of the moat, re...   ...he first hint of a royal footfall.

J...   ...**cis, MA (1795-1838)** was a C...   ...f Buckden and much-loved v...   ...338). On 14 April 1833 he n...   ...den. Two months later Sophia...   ...r son, Theophilus. Theophilus...   ...n a year later.

...   ...**Street [MapRef 32],** was ...   ...Nikolaus Pevsner in 1968 ...   ...*dfordshire, Huntingdon and* ...ly the house achieved its ...   ...f alterations over the course of ...   ...believed to have begun as two ...   ...e in the early 1700s; further ...   ...ng prosperity of its owners. The ...   ...ltsters and millers, and by the ...   ...y listed among the leading ...   ...The Victorian period saw the ...   ...t at the rear so that its Georgian ...   ...nt part of the street scene), and ...   ...n the style of the time – gravel ...   ...orders, lawns and later a grass ...   ...now that the property is no ...   ...n orchard and vegetable garden ...   ...original livestock buildings.

...   ...family ended their connection ...   ...mid-1970s, they took the name ...   ...in Taylors Lane, west of the A1. ...   ...essamine Houses in Buckden.

PUBLISHER'S NOTE

The publishers regret that the last article on page 39 has been cut short. It should continue as follows: "Mr E. E. Mann's field. The evening ended with the singing of God Save the King. The jubilee was also marked by an outdoor production of *Merrie England*. See also **soup kitchens**." Please also note that the cross-reference to the **Phoenix Memnon Company Limited** on page 42 should be to the **Thomson family.**

1897 Jubilee Celebrations   Philip Gale

Jolly, Eric James MB, ChB, Aberdeen (1899-1968) was another of Buckden's Scots-born doctors, and one of its longest-serving. See **Chapter 14**

Jones, the Rev. Timothy, MA (1812-1875), the ninth son of a Cardiganshire gentleman, was the vicar of St Margaret's, Leicester, when in June 1875 he accepted a transfer to Buckden. He arrived in July; on 3 August he died. He had been in poor health for several months, and for a sick man it was an unfortunate time to move to Huntingdonshire: torrential rains had submerged low-lying areas (and would return in October, forcing the inhabitants of Buckden and Offord to flee upstairs).

Jubilees. Queen Victoria's Diamond Jubilee was celebrated on 20 June 1897. Happily for the vicar this was a Sunday, enabling him to preach 'appropriate sermons' to large congregations at the morning and evening services. Celebrations proper began at 10.30 a.m. on Tuesday, 22 June with cycle races. Unlike those in some other villages, these were for men (and boys) only. At 1.30 p.m., a cycle parade was held on the village green and prizes were awarded for the most tastefully decorated machines. Next came the customary cycle procession through the village. As Buckden's official tribute to the Queen, the parish council installed new staircases in South's **almshouses [MapRef 9]** (q.v.); these allowed upstairs residents to reach their rooms without going through the rooms of their downstairs neighbours.

The Silver Jubilee of Their Gracious Majesties King George Vth and Queen Mary was celebrated on Monday, 6 May 1935. The day began with a peal of the church bells, followed by a United Thanksgiving Service. At 12 noon the Schoolroom was the venue for the presentation of Jubilee cups and saucers to all children up to 15 years of age. At 2.30 p.m., the traditional parade set off from the village green for the Towers. After the best decorated bicycles and prams had been judged, an afternoon of sports began. This included several events that today would probably be banned on grounds of health and safety (riding the plank on a bicycle), hygiene (the boys' mixed boots race), or sexism (ladies could not enter the obstacle race; they had to make do with an egg and spoon event).

After the presentation of prizes, the village dispersed home to have its supper, milk cows, feed livestock, bed down babies, house hens and change into its gladdest rags for two hours of dancing on the Towers lawn to the men of the Buckden band (those of them who had recovered from running in the afternoon's 'bandsmen only' race). At 10 p.m. all still on their feet went up Taylor's Lane and cheered on the Boy Scouts as they lit the grand bonfire in

K

Katherine of Aragon (1485–1536), an unfortunate Spanish princess, was married to Arthur, Prince of Wales, in 1501. Arthur promptly died. She was then betrothed to his brother the future Henry VIII and kept in seclusion and poverty until their marriage in 1509. Their only surviving child was Mary (later queen). The loyal support Katherine gave to her husband included making his shirts and leading an army northwards to fight invading Scots; but it was not reciprocated. Henry had their marriage annulled in 1533, having already married a pregnant Anne Boleyn, by whom he hoped to have a son. Katherine was downsized to 'princess dowager' and exiled first to Ampthill in Bedfordshire and then to Buckden. The latter move particularly incensed her supporters, and continued to do so: 'Ampthill is humid like the county of Bedford,' wrote Jean Marie Dargaud in his *Histoire de Jane Grey* (Paris, 1863), 'but less submerged than Buckden in fogs. At this time, Buckden was above all rendered almost pestilential by the pools of fetid, stagnant water that covered Lincolnshire [sic].'

Although the villagers are said to have faced down an attempt to transfer her to the even more unhealthy Somersham, they could not prevent her removal to Kimbolton the following year. Never a well woman, she fell ill in December 1535 and died the following month. She was buried in Peterborough Abbey (as it then was).

Katherine was not the only distinguished 'involuntary guest' to be lodged in Buckden – see also Gilbert **Bourne.**

Kaye, John (1783-1853), churchman, Cambridge academic and supporter of the anti-slavery movement, lived in Buckden from 1830 to 1837.

In 1820 he had been made Bishop of Bristol, a run-down diocese so poor that he preferred to manage it from Cambridge, where he was a professor and Master of Christ's College. This did not stop him from working actively to restore Bristol's finances and improve the discipline of its clergy, or from preaching against the port's dependence on the slave trade.

In 1827 he was translated – spiritually, but again not physically – to the huge Diocese of Lincoln. However, he remained at Cambridge until 1830, when he moved to Buckden Palace. Here he continued the programme of repairs and improvements undertaken by his predecessor, George **Pelham** (q.v.). When Huntingdonshire was transferred to the See of Ely in 1837, Kaye had to leave Buckden and spent the rest of his life in Riseholme Palace, Lincoln.

For a man who required the highest standards from his clergy, he was surprisingly kind to the candidates for ordination who came to Buckden. He would put them up in a local inn (the George) and on the eve of the ordination service would entertain them at the Palace with a good dinner: 'sumptuous – venison – all kinds of wine etc'.

The description 'sumptuous' was also applied to the hospitality of one of his 17thC predecessors, Bishop Williams; Williams was even said to have turned the palace hall into a theatre, where on one Sunday evening he entertained his newly ordained priests with a performance of *A Midsummer Night's Dream.*

Kidman, George (fl. late 18thC) was a 'person of ill name and fame' from, regrettably, Buckden. In 1782 he was involved in a conversation that must have gone something like this:

> **Mrs May Bray of Stilton:** Oi, George Kidman. You owe my husband four shillings.
>
> **GK:** So I do, missus. But bugger me, I've only got a guinea on me. (Brightens up) Tell you what, give us seventeen shilling and I'll give 'ee the guinea.
>
> **Mrs MB:** Oh, all right. (Pays over the money)
>
> **GK:** Thank'ee, m'duck. Isn't that your old man coming now?
>
> **Mrs MB** (turning round): Where?
>
> **GK:** (legs it)

This trick works better if your victim doesn't know who you are and where you live. At the Midsummer Quarter Sessions of 1782, Kidman was indicted for defrauding Mrs Bray of seventeen shillings, and sent for trial at the next sessions.

King, Charles Richard (c. 1870-1950) was a cobbler whose premises consisted of what was described as a hut on the north road. He did sufficiently well to have a bungalow built in 1932 in Perry Road, where building plots were sold by the length of their frontage; the rate was £45 a foot.

Mr King had been born in Yelling, where he lived until at least 1914, working with and in succession to his father in the family bootmaking business. In 1901 he married Agnes Annie Smith (1872-1959), the daughter of an Offord Cluny railway worker. The exact year they moved to Buckden has not been traced, but it must have been between 1920 and 1924. He was still active in 1940.

King George Court, High Street, a quadrangular development of sheltered and retirement housing, was opened in 1997. It stands to the southwest of the George Hotel, and is built partly on land once down to orchard and partly on the site of demolished outhousing.

Kirton Builders. This company was formed in 1969 by William Render and David Pope in partnership, with Mr Render being the developer and Mr Pope organising construction. The name may come from Kirton in Lincolnshire. Its first offices were on the upper floor of a converted warehouse behind Bowtell's shop in the High Street.

In the early 1970s, Kirton bought the building business of J. W. **Smith** (q.v.), successor to George Page and Son. The business was then being run by Jack Peacock, who had up to a dozen men on the books executing small works locally. Later that decade David Pope took over the whole Kirton business.

Kirton did not wish to retain J. W. Smith's scattered yards. They therefore built two maisonettes (Nos. 9A and 9B) on the Silver Street storeyard, and sold the yard behind the school to the education authority. They moved their own business into the main yard in Hunts End, where the joiners' shop had been. They remained there until the early years of the 21stC, when the yard was sold and the business moved to Caxton. The offices left behind were converted into residential use. The site is now known as Hunts End Court.

Although Kirton's work was mainly residential (new homes, extensions and alterations), it also built the original village hall in Burberry Road, and until recently was responsible for all the maintenance work for the Thornhill properties in Diddington.

For the record, there is now no connection between Kirton Builders of Caxton and Kirton Construction Ltd of Huntingdon.

Knowles, Kenneth Davenport (1874-1944) was the Archdeacon of Huntingdon (1921-1943) and for at least nine years (1923-1932) the occupier of the White House in Mill Road. Between 1914 and 1917 he was chaplain to the 1st Huntingdonshire Cyclist Battalion, to whom he preached 'a very practical sermon on manliness'. At various times he was also Rural Dean, vicar of Woodwalton, rector of Brampton and, from 1938 to 1944, vicar of Diddington. He was also the president of the Buckden, Diddington, Grafham and Offord Branch of the British Legion, and the author of *The Huntingdon children's service and prayer book* and assorted light verse including the amiably nostalgic 'Buckden: a Christmas Ballad'. His sister, Miss Knowles, was the co-proprietor of a Buckden school.

L

Lafarge (and predecessors): see **mineral extraction**

Landowners in Buckden. In 1873 the Government published the results of a survey of all land owners in England and Wales (outside central London). All those who owned one acre or more were listed, together with the address/location, the amount of land and its value. Those listed for Buckden were:

Ann Cope
Arthur W. Marshall (Buckden Towers)
Barley Hubbard
Bowyer & Priestley
Captain Green
Charles Hubbard
Churchwardens of Buckden
Colonel James Linton
Executors of Robert Moon
Frank Green, Coneygarths
Frederick Charles Mann, Beech Lawn
Henry Hyde
John Goodgames
John Milner
Joseph Baxter
Joseph Bowyer
Miss Margaret Green
Mrs Bowyer
Mrs Burton
Mrs Usher
Mrs Wormsley
Rev. D. Haigh (Vicarage)
Rev. R. H. Gatty (The Manor)
Samuel Taylor
Thomas Cope
Thomas L. Priestley
Trustees of Charity
William Bartholomew Bowling (Church Street)
William Baxter
William Bowyer
William Clark
William Nicholls
William Usher

Landsman's (Co-ownership) Ltd started in 1949 and moved to a Buckden field about 1955. It traded in residential caravans and eventually it designed and built specialist mobile units for the construction industry. In 1964 the proprietor and his wife turned the business into a limited company entitled Landsman's (Co-ownership) Limited, and the twenty-five employees became the owners of the company. The annual trading surplus was distributed to all employees as cash and shares with each share representing one vote. Eventually the workers were able to buy out the original proprietors. The Board of Directors had co-opted directors from outside and had worker directors as well as a works committee.

The concept of worker/owners was developing rapidly in the 1960s and many small co-ops and medium to larger companies accepted the principle of worker ownership and participation in the running of companies. Indeed legislation was introduced to allow more enlightened firms to adapt to the method of management organisations.

Although Landsman's was one of the first smaller companies to start there were already some large well-known companies in existence namely Scott-Bader Chemicals of Wellingborough and the famous John Lewis Partnership, which includes Robert Sayle and Waitrose. Landsman's continues to trade in its original premises on the outskirts of Buckden.   Anne Spreckley

Langley family. John Gace Langley (1807-1892) and his family were High Street shopkeepers for some eighty years; for over fifty of these they also ran the village sub-Post Office.

Mr Langley was born in Bedfordshire, the son of a surgeon, but by 1844 had settled in Buckden as a grocer and draper. In 1851 his household contained himself, his wife Elizabeth (née Mann), a grocery apprentice, a domestic servant, a dressmaker and six children under nine years old – all but the first born in Buckden. Over the years, he expanded his business to include ironmongery, insurance, provisions (i.e. a wider range of food than the usual grocery staples) and, some time before 1869, the Post Office. He was still postmaster in 1891, by then aged 84! He died the following year – died young by Langley family standards: his father was said to have lived to 93, his grandfather to 95 and his grandmother to 105.

Education was important to the Langleys. Only **Mary Ann and John Gace Junior** appear to have worked solely in the business, Mary as a draper's assistant and John as a grocer, draper, news agent and stationer. All the other children had some association with teaching, as follows:

Sarah As well as helping in the Post Office, Sarah ran a private ladies' school in the High Street.

Millicent taught music until her marriage to Thomas Moore, tailor, cycle agent and (later) 'preacher of the gospel'.

Edward Mann (BA London, MA Trinity, Cambridge), known to his friends as 'Triangles', married his Australian-born cousin and taught mathematics at his old school, Bedford Modern, for 40 years. He was also Hon. Sec. of the Mathematical Association, and Founder-Editor of its journal.

Elizabeth *junior* married Buckden teacher William Baxter, who became the headmaster of a boys' boarding school in Windsor.

There was one more son. **James Robert** went up to Oxford as a non-collegiate student, obtaining his BA in 1879 and MA in 1883. In between the last two events he got married.

Twice.

In the same year.

To the same woman.

She was Aoltia Mira, daughter of Buckden engineer and inventor James Thomson. Their first wedding was in January 1881, at the Church of St Philip, Battersea. It seems unlikely that either of their families knew about it. The only recorded witnesses were two Battersea residents from the house where Aoltia had stayed long enough to obtain the necessary residence qualification (James Robert came down from Oxford, giving his occupation as 'tutor').

In June 1881 came the census. It recorded Aoltia and James living back in Buckden with their respective families; both referred to themselves as 'single'. Their 'official' wedding took place in Buckden in October. Perhaps family disapproval had driven them into their first, clandestine wedding – it is noticeable that the second was witnessed only by Thomsons: Aoltia's brother Henry and her sister Sarah (another schoolmistress). Against this, however, is that the following year the two families co-operated in a joint business venture, the **Phoenix Memnon Company Limited** (q.v.).

James and Aoltia's son, Arthur Gace Langley, was born in Buckden in 1882. In 1891 he was living with his paternal grandfather in Buckden, while his parents were in a two-room flat in Oxford where James was now studying medicine, his twelfth year as a student! Ten years later all three were living in an apartment in Clerkenwell. James was now a freelance writer and Arthur a draughtsman. Some time before the First World War the family returned to Buckden, where James and Aoltia lodged with Aoltia's eldest sister, Sarah, while Arthur, now an art editor for an international news service, lived at the Post Office in an otherwise all-female household (his aunts Mary Ann and

Sarah, and their two young assistants, aged 19 and 17 respectively).

James thereafter earned his living as a lecturer and unofficial village historian. In 1932, he took part in the '**Pageant of the Centuries**'(q.v.) at The Towers. He died in 1939 and is buried in Buckden Cemetery. Arthur also acted in the pageant. He had joined the East Anglian Royal Engineers at the outbreak of the First World War, rising to the rank of Captain and winning the Military Cross. His post-war career has not been traced – unless he is the Captain Arthur Langley who practised as a bonesetter in Paddington through the 1930s.

Between 1881 and 1885 the Langleys seem to have given up their retail business: Kelly's Directory for the latter year lists them only as running the Post Office. The grocery and drapery side had been managed by John Gace junior and the wife he married in Wiltshire in 1879, Edith Caroline [Kidner]; but by 1885 it had been taken over by a Russell Hardley. By 1888 John and Edith had emigrated to Canada, settling in the Vancouver area. Their family papers are now in the library of the University of British Columbia. They include two letters written by John Gace senior in 1891, the year before his death.

Sarah Langley succeeded her father as sub-postmistress (postcard views of Buckden occasionally surface, issued by 'S Langley of Buckden Post Office'). She was assisted by Mary Ann, who had been running the household since their mother died in 1889. They continued the business until the 1920s; Mary Ann died in 1926 (and was buried in Bedfordshire); Sarah died in 1929. Both sisters are commemorated on the headstone to Sarah's grave near the lych-gate in Buckden Cemetery.

The three employees from 1851 soon moved on to other things. The house servant, Hannah Gore, left to marry Thomas Gore (a cousin, perhaps). In 1886, by an odd twist of fate, their daughter Mary Ann married a member of the Thomson family, Aoltia Mira's brother James. The apprentice, Edward Titchmarsh, left to found a long-lived family grocery and drapery in Royston High Street; one of his grandsons became a senior mathematical professor at Oxford. The dressmaker, Elizabeth Piggott, married Dennis James Robinson in 1856. Born in Hardwick, he was a tailor and the son of a master tailor (and publican). By the time of his marriage, he was working in London. Elizabeth returned there with him as did her brother John, yet another tailor.

See also **Aoltia, Bowtells of Buckden, Post Offices, telephones, Thomson family.**

Lark End is one of the short, bird-named streets leading off Vineyard Way.

Lauder, Sir John (Lord Fountainhall) (1646–1722) was a Scottish criminal advocate, judge and political commentator. In 1667 he found the road between Biggleswade and Buckden a 'sad way' (it obviously got no better: many years later Daniel Defoe called it a 'frightful way' and 'terrible road'). Lauder stayed the night in Buckden when he met a party of fellow Scots coming down from Edinburgh. The countryside between Buckden and

Huntingdon reminded him of Holland, being 'all covered with willows'.

Laundry Cottage, **High Street [MapRef 28],** is an early 19thC house, so named because its excellent water supply made it ideal for washing clothes, linen, etc. In 1891 it was occupied by widow Eliza Jubb, laundress to the Marshall family at the Towers across the road; the family also employed her daughter Louisa as a domestic servant. Mrs Jubb later moved to Yorkshire as a tobacconist.

Between the two world wars, the cottage was the home of the Brown family, whose father brought up six children after the death of his wife. They are best-known for their **osier business** (q.v.) and the large fruit enterprise they ran on land to the west of the A1: apple and plum orchards and thousands of gooseberry plants.

Leadens Lane. This rural thoroughfare linking Stirtloe and Mill Road also gives access to the 'Water Board Road', a favourite area for walkers. It was for a time in the 1860s/1870s also known as Burton's Lane or Stirtloe Road; its present name probably derives from the time of John Leaden (fl. 1890 1910), who had a market garden at the junction of the lane and Mill Road.

The lane has one dwelling, Martins Farm (formerly Leaden House), and Buckden Sewage Works.

Library, **Buckden.** Few of those using Buckden Library will be aware that it owes its existence to the advent of unrestricted submarine warfare during the First World War. Residents had previously had access to private circulating libraries and the Reading Room library in Church Street, but had not had their own public library. The war brought home to the government the vulnerability of Britain's food supply. In a few decades the nation had moved from producing four-fifths of all it ate to producing only about a half. As the war ended, therefore, the government set out to attract people back into the countryside and into commercial and home food production. Agricultural Training Centres were set up to help wounded ex-servicemen become smallholders, and the Land Settlement Facilities Act 1919 and Allotment Acts in 1922 and 1925 opened up allotments to the whole population (not just the labouring class). Ministers also

hoped that better facilities might encourage those moving into the countryside to remain there. Hence the Public Libraries Act 1919, which transferred responsibility for libraries from borough councils to county councils and removed some of the restraints on the opening of new libraries in rural areas.

In 1926, Huntingdonshire introduced a village libraries scheme, with the new post of county librarian attracting a large number of applicants. It is not known when the first public library service reached Buckden; it was certainly served by a library van in the 1930s, one of whose drivers was the Buckden author Frances **Turk** (q.v.). During the Second World War, the village schoolroom was opened on one evening a week as a branch of the public library.

By the 1970s, a library was established in temporary accommodation at what was then the south end of Manor Gardens. The County Council's threat to close it in 1995 led to the largest and most agitated public meeting seen in Buckden for many years. It was reprieved and incorporated into the Millennium Community Centre in 1999.

Library, the Buckden is a collection of works on theology, archaeology and local history founded by William Wake, Bishop of Lincoln from 1705 to 1716. For the next 120 years, every clergyman preferred to a living in the diocese was expected to donate a book to the library. The practice ceased in 1837, when Buckden was transferred to the Diocese of Ely. The books continued to be housed in a room above the inner gatehouse, but responsibility for them passed to the vicar of Buckden. There had in fact been a separate parochial lending library, a Bray library, in the parvis at St Mary's Church since the mid-1690s. (Thomas Bray (d. 1730) was a Wiltshire clergyman who encouraged the setting up of parish libraries throughout England and Wales; he kick-started the one in Buckden with a grant of £1.)

In 1874, the two libraries were combined and their contents removed to Huntingdon, initially to the Grammar School and then, in 1890, to the newly erected Archdeaconry Library. In the 1960s the collection was finally transferred to Cambridge University Library, where it was stored as 'Huntingdon Rare Books' in the Bible Society Library.

Lincoln, bishops of, two buried in one grave, not. The scholarly Bishop Thomas Barlow (1608/9-1691) is said to have asked to be buried in the same grave in the chancel of St Mary's Church as his equally scholarly predecessor and namesake, William Barlow. The reason for such a request is unclear (the two were not related). Perhaps it was modesty, meanness or just a desire to face the resurrection in the company of a fellow-intellectual. Sadly there is no evidence to suggest that his wish – if indeed he ever expressed it – was acted on.

See also **Suffolk, dukes of, two buried in one tomb.**

Linton family. The Lintons of Stirtloe House, who came from Lincolnshire, were major landowners and one of Buckden's leading gentry families throughout the nineteenth and early twentieth centuries. Their story is told in **Chapter 7**

The Manor Gardens Library August 1999 after closure

The Lion Hotel including its modern annexe and also on the right the one-time Gospel Hall with its hipped roof.

Lion Hotel, The The origin of the Lion, or Red Lion or the Lion and the Lamb as it has been variously known is obscure. A study of an aerial view and its elevations show that the building as we see it today has clearly developed piecemeal.

The present bar area on the northwest corner was once separate from the hotel and was occupied by a butcher with his shop and living quarters. These extended along Church Street as far as the slate–roofed section with a window at half height. That was labelled *Gospel Hall* on the 1924 OS plan and was built as a non-conformist chapel in the 19thC.

The hotel once presented a medieval jettied façade to the High Street, but this was sacrificed to 18thC and 19thc improvements. A filled-in archway suggests there was once a rear courtyard with the stabling and stores needed to allow the hotel to compete with the George across the road. However there is no evidence yet for the Lion's having been a staging place for coach traffic needing regular changes of horses. Above the archway the structure resembles a warehouse and luccam. The latter's projecting roof might have accommodated a lifting point and winch to allow luggage to be lifted to an upper floor, but it is more likely that it was used to raise the raw materials for beer making, the Lion like the Vine having its own brewhouse. According to Maurice Milner, the structure was put up by a late 19thC landlord, Henry Thomson, and housed the vats (four foot square and seven and a half feet deep). Mr Thomson was a member of the inventive **Thomson family** (q.v.) and referred to himself as a publican and engineer; unlike his predecessors, Joseph Baxter and Joseph Ilsley, he was not himself a brewer, leaving that side of the business to his stepson, Joseph Charles **Ilsley** (q.v.; he died in the brewhouse from carbonic acid gas poisoning).

The modern side access to the rear of the hotel, its car park and a 20thC annexe was made possible through the demolition of two ancient shops.

Owners of the hotel in the 20thC included Trust Houses and private individuals, but now Churchill Taverns of Wellingborough run it.

local history society. In 1978 a course on the History of Buckden was conducted at the village school by a local professional historian, Sue Edgington, under the auspices of Huntingdon Technical College. The course proved to be very popular with those who attended, and the formation of a society was proposed so that talks and other activities could continue the following year. Sue Edgington agreed to be chairman, Les Button, secretary, and Eric Nash, treasurer.

The society met at the school until 1984; since then the beautifully restored Conference Room in Buckden Towers has provided a suitably historic venue. The society's year runs from September to July.

With the exception of the July meeting, which takes the form of an outing to a place of historical interest, meetings take place at 7.30 p.m. on the first Wednesday of the month. The June meeting opens with the Annual General Meeting, which is traditionally followed by a short talk, usually given by the chairman or a past chairman.

The Society is affiliated to the Cambridge Antiquarian Society.

An album of photographs of the village received from various sources is being assembled with some financial support from the Parish Council. Views from times past are being accompanied by present-day photographs from similar viewpoints. When possible photographs of areas in the parish where change is imminent are being taken.

Lofts, Arthur (antique dealer) and **Ethel** (stationer and newsagent) – see under **High Street shops**.

Low Farm. There are two properties of this name in the parish. The original Low Farm is in Mill Road **[MapRef 41]**, and was part of the Reynolds family estate until its purchase by the Lintons of Stirtloe House in 1849. Its other names included Faulkner's Farm (after the tenant of the time) and New Farm. George Page, a prominent Buckden builder, also ran it for a time, as did one of the Cranfield family.

In 1989, the then occupiers moved to Stirtloe, and took the name with them for their new farmstead. The property in Mill Road, a Grade II listed building dating from the early 19thC, is no longer in agricultural use.

See also **dovecotes**

Luff family. Thomas Luff (born London 1866) was a journeyman blacksmith who lived with his wife and family in **Barthrams Yard** (q.v.). His children included:
William Henry (born 1888), painter's apprentice and athlete, whose achievements included winning three of the four cycle races at the Choral Society's open-air fete in 1905, and being placed in five events in the 1909 annual Friendly Societies' sports held at Coneygarths.
Grace Emma (1896-1912), for whose poignant story see under **Girls' Friendly Society.**

M

Mabel of Bugdene, the 12thC nun who testified that her fellow-religious, Emcina, was saved from choking on a fishbone by being made to swallow water in which the dead body of Master – later Saint – Gilbert had been washed, is now thought more likely to have come from *Bowden* in Leicestershire.

machine-breaking. In March 1831, five respectable farm labourers from Buckden stood in the dock of the courtroom in Huntingdon. They were John Ladds, John Cawcutt, Samuel Smith, Thomas Franklin and William Murden. The charge they faced arose out of the wave of riot, arson, vandalism, extortion and maiming that had swept across southern and eastern England the previous year: a part-spontaneous, part-organised revolt by a rural working class driven to despair by the effects of the agricultural depression that had followed the end of the Napoleonic Wars in 1815. British farming had flourished during the wars, but poor harvests and the return of cheap imported food forced farmers to reduce wages, lay off workers and increasingly mechanize labour-intensive tasks such as threshing. But threshing (the beating of harvested corn to separate the grains from the husks and straw) was traditionally one of the few paid employments by which labourers could lift themselves and their families out of starvation during the miserable winter months, particularly in the predominantly arable areas of the country (on livestock farms the animals still needed to be fed and cared for). The new machines (and their owners) became prime targets of the rioters.

Among those arrested in Huntingdonshire were the men from Buckden. The charge against them was not one that carried a likelihood of capital punishment, as did arson or sending threatening letters; but it was serious enough. They were accused of destroying a threshing-machine belonging to a Silver Street farmer, Henry Cope. They would have been aware that in other parts of the country, machine-breakers had already been sentenced to transportation for up to seven years.

In the event, William Murden was acquitted and his companions sent to prison for a few months. Their light sentences and their subsequent acceptance back into village life suggest that not only their neighbours but the judge himself understood the fear and rage that had provoked their desperate act.

One of the prosecutors at the assizes that week may well have already known some of the five accused: Edward Harvey **Maltby** (q.v.) had been born in Buckden, the son of the vicar. He certainly knew one of the judges: as a young man, Mr Justice **Alderson** (q.v.) had lodged at the vicarage as a pupil of Edward's father.

McLeod, Peter (born Scotland c. 1859) came to Buckden as coachman/groom to Sir Arthur Marshall at The Towers; he was also a useful member of the Buckden cricket team. By 1898 he had moved up the High Street to take over the Spread Eagle Hotel, where he offered 'good stabling accommodation for cyclists'. He lived there with his wife Emma (a schoolteacher's daughter), three children (all born in Buckden) and a mother-in-law. They were still at the Spread in 1903, but by 1910 it was being run by a young Buckden couple, farmer Ernest Mann and his wife Lily.

McRitchie, Donald MB, CM Aberdeen, LRCS & LRM Edinburgh (1854 - 1926) was possibly Buckden's longest-serving doctor. See **Chapter 14**

Mafeking, Relief of. The South African War (1899-1902) between the Boers and the British began in October 1899 with siege of the town of Mafeking. For 217 days up to 8,000 Boer troops tried in vain to overcome a British garrison of some 2,000 men under the command of Colonel Baden-Powell (founder of the Scouting Movement). The siege was followed with intense interest back in Britain, for whose forces the war was otherwise not going well.

Rumours of the lifting of the siege reached Buckden on Saturday, 18 May 1900, resulting in a spontaneous procession, patriotic music from the village band and rejoicings that were 'maintained until very late'. The following Monday a Committee was formed under the chairmanship of the indefatigable Mr S. Green to arrange for a joint celebration of the relief and the Queen's Birthday, which fell on Thursday, 24 May. The evening began with a parade of sixty gaily-decorated bicycles, some of their riders in pretty costumes and some in grotesque. Led by the village band in a wagon, the parade started from the Lion corner and circled the village, its houses 'brave with bunting', via the Hoo Baulk, Lucks Lane and Stirtloe. After more patriotic airs and the National Anthem, a torchlight procession (some 100 torches) paraded round the village cheering, singing and letting off fireworks, and ended up at a huge bonfire in a field on the Grafham Road.

If anyone finds an old-fashioned policeman's helmet gathering dust in their attic, it may be the one 'lost' during the celebrations by the unfortunate village constable, Pc Purser. Such dereliction of duty would have earned him an embarrassing few minutes at the next inspection parade at St Neots police station– doubly embarrassing for him: he had only been in post a couple of months.

Mahomed, Sake Deen of Brighton, 'shampooing surgeon to the Royal Family', was an early Victorian medical entrepreneur whose book *Shampooing; or, Benefits Resulting from the use of the Indian Medicated Vapour Bath as introduced into this country by a native of India….containing a brief but comprehensive view of the effects produced by the use of the warm bath* went into several editions. It includes a long list of distinguished and grateful patients, one of whom was Dr Maltby, Vicar of Buckden (see following entry).

Maltby family:
Edward Maltby, DD FRS FSA (1770-1859), long-serving vicar Vicar of Buckden, later a bishop, was a man who aroused conflicting feelings. Some contemporary views:
'Dear Ned – grave, unaffected, and very impressive' – Samuel Parr, his first headmaster
'The best and most amiable of young men' – Dr Joseph Warton, headmaster Headmaster of Winchester College
'One of the great scholars of the age' – John Johnstone
'It was unworthy of him, as a Christian, to assume the virtues he had not.' – Mrs Jane Scarborough, landlady of the George, Buckden
'An excellent man and a great fool' – Sidney Smith
'…distinguished above all his brethren …[a man of] learning, piety and talents' – *The Times* 1830
'…this loose and lordly priest .. time-serving remonstrant .. slippery prelate .. consecrated culprit .. licentious speculatist .. has disgraced himself for ever .. ought to be drummed out of the Church.' – *The Times* 1838
'one of the first scholars, and most respectable clergymen, in England' – John Britton
'…a bishop unworthy of [his] huge income, unworthy of the church, unworthy of the age in which he lives:' – *The Daily News* 1849

'I like the Bishop very much… [only he] is very deaf with one ear, which is rather disagreeable' – Emily Pepys, aged 10
'*Remarkably* maladroit' – Queen Victoria (after he nearly dropped the orb at her coronation)

Edward Maltby was born in Norwich, the fourth son of a master-weaver. A clever child, he was fortunate enough to have his cleverness noticed and developed by the headmaster Headmaster of Norwich grammar school. At fifteen he moved on to Winchester College, and from there was entered at Pembroke Hall, Cambridge, by his cousin's husband Dr George **Pretyman** (q.v.), the bishop Bishop of Lincoln and lately privately secretary (and still close friend) to the Prime Minister, William Pitt.

Maltby continued to distinguish himself while at Cambridge, winning prizes and medals (for academic achievements: he was decidedly not an athletic man). In 1794, Bishop Pretyman brought him to Buckden as his domestic chaplain; he also gave him three other church appointments including that of vicar Vicar of Buckden. In the same year, Maltby married Mary Harvey, with whom he had several children. (Perhaps anticipating this prolificacy, the bishop had the vicarage extended in 1795.) In 1820 they lost their eldest son, George Rivers Maltby (see below); another son died in infancy.

Maltby became widely-known as a fine classical scholar, an impressive preacher (appointed to speak at both Cambridge University and two Inns of Court) and a political pamphleteer, This last was unfortunate, as his politics (Whig) were not those of the government (Tory). As a result, his career in the church stalled and he remained in Buckden, unpromoted, for over thirty-five years.

Nonetheless, this did not prevent his becoming something of a national figure through his preaching, his publications and his tutoring of private pupils, some of whom went on to distinguished careers. He was a passionate advocate of education, political reform and religious free speech: he befriended both dissenters and Roman Catholics (but later opposed the re-establishment of a Catholic hierarchy in Britain). Despite his fame, he seems, so far as Buckden at least was concerned, to have been a reasonably diligent vicar. This cannot be said of all parish clergy of his time.

His wife died in 1825. Just over a year later, Maltby married Margaret Mary Green, one of the Greens of **Coneygarths** (q.v.). The new Mrs Maltby was related to yet another bishop, the Bishop of Lincoln Dr John Green, a rare bird in that he was happier living in London than in Buckden.

Maltby's second marriage connected him more or less closely to some of Buckden's leading yeoman or gentleman farmers, including the Wallers, the Longlands and the Priestleys. Politics continued to absorb his interest and that of his son Edward Harvey Maltby (see below). Much of the routine church life of the village now fell to his curate, the tragic Francis **Jefferson** (q.v.).

The long years of Tory rule ended in 1830, and in 1831, the new prime minister hurriedly made Maltby bishop of Chichester to help push the Reform Bill through the House of Lords.

But Maltby was no time-server. In 1836, he became Bishop of Durham and played an important part in the establishment of that city's university. As was customary at the time, he did not forget his family or friends: among the canons of his new cathedral were his youngest son; his nephew, and Professor John Edwards, the son of his predecessor as vicar Vicar of Buckden.

In the mid-1850s, failing eyesight finally made it impossible for Maltby to continue his duties and at the age of eighty-five he offered to retire. However, no bishop had been permitted to retire for over three hundred years, and his request for a pension of £4,500 a year aroused widespread outrage, coming as it did at a time when the public had become aware that many of the lesser Anglican clergy were living on the edge of poverty (Maltby had already been fiercely criticised for drawing an income from Durham far above that which he was supposed to have, and for diverting – legally, but not exactly ethically – several thousand pounds in revenue from an ecclesiastical post to his son, Edward Harvey).

In the end, the government reluctantly passed legislation that released Maltby and an elderly colleague into retirement – and granted Maltby his pension.

He died in London in his ninetieth year and is buried in Kensal Green Cemetery. Margaret Mary outlived her husband by nearly ten years. Like his first wife and his eldest son, she is commemorated in Buckden church.

Edward Harvey Maltby (1798-1867) was a Buckden man who made frequent appearances at the Huntingdonshire Assizes but not, as some of his fellow-villagers did, in the dock: he was a barrister. He was educated at Cambridge (where, like his father, he wrote prize-winning Greek and Latin epigrams), and was called to the bar in 1824, taking chambers in Paper Buildings, Inner Temple. He specialized in criminal law, practising on the Norfolk Circuit, where he usually appeared for the Crown. Huntingdon was in this circuit; among the cases in which he acted there, and which attracted national attention, were the 1827 prosecution of Joshua Slade for the murder of the octogenarian vicar Vicar of Little Stukeley, and the March 1831 trials held in the wake of the previous winter's agricultural riots (see under **Alderson** and **machine-breaking**).

By 1840, however, he had become a London magistrate, presiding over Marlborough Street and several other courts. Newspaper reports reveal an unexpectedly likeable man, unimpressed by rank or status, ready to deflate the self-important, often sympathetic to the poorest defendants (whom he sometimes helped out of his own pocket) and given to telling disputants to go away and settle their quarrels out of court. He retired from the bench in 1847, suffering from a severe nervous indisposition caused by a 'too anxious attention to his duties'.

He had something of an *annus horribilis* in 1832. In January he lent £800 to a shopkeeper who later went bankrupt; in June he failed in his bid to be chosen as a parliamentary candidate for Huntingdon; and in July his chambers were broken into and 'every portable and valuable article' stolen except his books. The thieves were soon caught and despite their lawyer's attempt to get them off on a technicality were sentenced to seven years' transportation. The judge seemed depressed that he no longer had the death penalty at his disposal; Maltby was depressed by not having recovered more than one-twentieth of his property. In December, having after all been adopted as a parliamentary candidate, he came bottom of the poll.

Maltby was well-off. A resident of the Albany, Piccadilly, London's most exclusive bachelor address (later dismissed by Charles Dickens's son as 'a collection of queer houses, let as chambers'), he was something of a dandy, given to velvet-collared coats and green silk handkerchiefs. He never married.

George Rivers Maltby (1795-1820), was born in Buckden, the eldest son of Edward and Mary Maltby. Unlike his brother Edward Harvey, he did not go to university but joined the army. In the summer of 1820, following his promotion to Captain in the Sixteenth Regiment of Foot, he was posted to Ceylon. Almost immediately on arrival, he was killed when his horse bolted and he was struck on the head by a tree branch; he is commemorated in St Mary's church.

Manor House, Church Street [MapRef 11]. The significance of the manor house is discussed in **Chapter 3: Buckden's Buildings**.

Among its more interesting occupants over the years have been:

Major-General George Cleland Rowcroft (1831-1922), who was a member of a distinguished military family. Born in Delhi, he spent his career in India; this included service during the Indian Mutiny and on the North West Frontier. In 1889 he came to England, having been placed on the army's Unemployed Supernumerary List.* He moved to Buckden sometime between 1898 and 1901 and left at Michaelmas 1919, when the manor was sold.

* A depressing title if ever there was one.

By the time he settled in Buckden, he listed his recreations rather wistfully as 'formerly, shooting, polo, etc.'

In its obituary, *The Times* pointed out that his death had severed one of the last remaining links with the famous – or infamous – East India Company, for which he had briefly worked as a very young man.

Surgeon-Commander Arthur Sydney Gordon Bell RN MRCS LRCP (born 1869 into a naval family) probably succeeded General Rowcroft; he was certainly living in the Manor House by 1924, the year in which he celebrated his silver wedding anniversary. Remembered by at least one resident as 'a nice man, a gentleman', he had a strong sense of public duty, serving as a parish councillor, president of the horticultural society (1935), Deputy Lieutenant of Huntingdonshire (1936), and Hon. Sec. of the Association of Air Raid Precaution Officers (from 1938).

Major Teddy Chubb MC (1917-2007) was educated at Oundle, and began his working life with Vickers, Barrow. In 1936 he joined the army, and was commissioned in the Royal Artillery 1940, winning the Military Cross in Italy. He was promoted Major in 1952, moved to Buckden in the mid-1960s and retired in 1971. A keen gardener, he became President of the Buckden Gardeners' Association, but was

The Manor House with the Vicarage beyond   Philip Gale Collection

perhaps best known for his service with the Buckden Branch of the Royal British Legion: as Chairman (1982-92), President (1996-98) and Vice Chairman (1998-2007). He was married for some forty-seven years to Jean Bartram (1921-97).

marina, Mill Road. Buckden Marina is a 92 acre leisure development on the banks of the Great Ouse. Its tranquil surroundings include facilities for water- and jet-skiing, holiday lodges, boat moorings, chandlery and a Royal Yacht Association Training Centre. It is one of the village's largest employers.

Marshall, Sir Arthur Wellington (1841-1918) was the co-owner of Huntingdon Brewery. His marriage into an old-established Huntingdon banking family and subsequent occupation of Buckden Towers made him one of the area's leading residents between 1872 and 1911. Both the Towers and the brewery were bought for him by his father James Marshall, co-founder of the famous London store, Marshall & Snelgrove.

He served with the King's Royal Rifle Corps, reaching the rank of Lt-Colonel and Honorary Colonel. When he resigned in 1886, he was permitted to 'retain his rank and wear the prescribed uniform'. The local papers liked to refer to him as Colonel Marshall until his knighthood in 1898 enabled them to use the even more impressive title Sir Arthur.

He was Deputy Lieutenant of Huntingdonshire, Sheriff of Cambridgeshire and Huntingdonshire, and thrice Mayor of Huntingdon,. He was president of the Huntingdon & Godmanchester Conservative Association and would almost certainly have become Huntingdon's MP in 1885 had not the Redistribution of Seats Act earlier that year disenfranchised the town by absorbing its seat into the two county constituencies. These were the preserve of well-connected county families – no admittance for tradesmen, however distinguished.

In April 1893, he was elected first president of the newly formed Diddington and Buckden Horticultural Society. He also offered the grounds of The Towers as the venue for its first show.

See also **Laundry Cottage.**

Marshall's Corner was a late 19thC name given to the junction of Church Street and the High Street; it was derived from the then occupier of The Towers, Sir Arthur Marshall. It was also known as the 'Lion' corner.

Maurice, Rev. Lionel Selwyn [Powys] (1899-1991), sporting clergyman who spent his latter years in Buckden, was a canon, the son of a canon, the father of a canon, and both the grandson and great-grandson of Anglican priests. He grew up in Kimbolton, where both he and his father (the vicar) were enthusiastic members of the local Rifle Club. But his great love was for cricket. A right-hand batsman, he played two first class seasons for Northamptonshire, in 1922 and 1923, making 156 runs in 19 innings at an average of 8.21. His highest score was 65. He then dropped the Powys from his name, and played one season for Blackheath, his first curacy. He was also a keen golfer, and became a leading light of the Ely Diocesan Golf Team. He served as parish priest of, among other places, St Peter's, Offord Darcy, and All Saints', Cottenham. On his retirement from Cottenham in 1964 he and his second wife Molly moved to Buckden, first to Hardwick Dene and then to Perry Road. During the active years of his retirement, he played his part in Buckden life, helping out with church services and encouraging the young to take up sport – particularly cricket.

Mayfield joins the southern end of the High Street to Lucks Lane. Although quite short, it was an essential link in the residential expansion of Buckden in the late 20thC.

Medical Services in Buckden is the title and subject of **Chapter 14** which in particular contains biographies of many of the doctors who have contributed to the health of Buckden's population. A characterful group, they also enriched village life by being sportsmen, parish councillors, gardeners, club secretaries, singers of comic songs and (sometimes) eccentrics.

meeting houses. Under the Toleration Act 1689 and an amending act passed in 1812, protestant dissenters had to petition their local bishop or archdeacon to certify and register any premises in which they wished to assemble for worship. Several such petitions are known from Buckden, which has a long tradition of non-conformity. They include:

1811 Francis Pestill and others, to use the house of William Holmes

1811 Charles Green and others: to use own house

1815 Thos Usher and others: to use house occupied by Samuel Chapman

1816 Thos Usher and others: to use house occupied by Robert Moon

1828 William Whitney and William Cade, to use the house of one of them

1838 John Roberts, to use chapel situate in Buckden

1839 Henry Creamer of Silver Street, trunk maker: to use own house

1844 James Thomson of Bakers Lane, carpenter, later inventor and engineer: to use own house

1845 William Pole: to use Edward Attwell's house

1846 Richard Wimpress of the High Street, shoemaker: to use chapel in Buckden

Registered premises could not be 'locked, bolted, barred, or otherwise fastened' while a meeting was being held.

Memorial Playing Fields, Burberry Road. The land which forms Buckden's main recreation area was at one time owned by the Church of England; in the middle ages it was part of the bishop's **vineyards** (q.v.).

Methodist chapel: see Wesleyan Methodist Church and Gospel Hall

Midnight Butcher, the, was the nickname of Mr Sydney William Peck, who had his shop on the corner of Church Street and Silver Street for over twenty years. He worked long hours and his customers received some surprisingly late deliveries– sometimes via the bedroom window.

Mill Road runs between Hunts End and Station Lane (which starts just before Offord Mill Bridge). In the 19thC, the stretch between Hunts End and White House Farm (which marked the edge of the built-up part of the village) was usually referred to as Mill *Street*. To make matters more confusing, Mill Road was also called the Offord Road or Mill Lane – and sometimes still is.

Millennium Community Centre, Burberry Road [MapRef 1]. In 1997 the Parish Council and the Village Hall Trust agreed that the 1970s village hall was reaching the end of its useful life. With the help of the Lottery Millennium Fund, grants, donations and a loan of £110,000 repaid through the parish precept, they realised an ambitious project for a large building that has provided new and improved facilities for village organisations, an extension for the village club, accommodation for the branch library and room for the village nursery school. Together with the adjacent recreation ground, tennis club, bowls club, valley conservation area, new sports pavilion and new children's play area, the Centre has become a focal point for village activities, as well as being a popular venue for wedding receptions, antique fairs, dog shows, visiting theatre companies, conferences and other events.

Millennium Record. No-one who has seen this photographic record of the village at the turn of the millennium could fail to be impressed by the quality of the pictures and their presentation. Buckden will always be in debt to those responsible: Celia (Ce) Walker, her husband Tim, her sister Judith and Judith's husband Michael Alban. How it all happened follows in their own words:

Ce Walker, née Celia Gale, a native of Buckden, felt strongly that there should be something permanent to mark the millennium. She hit on the idea of a photographic record of all the village's inhabitants.

The project went ahead with the support of the Parish Council and with part-funding of £500 from the Huntingdonshire Local History Society's Goodliff Fund. Ce, Judith, Michael and Tim (who was to be the photographer) set about the daunting task of carrying the project through. This began with finding volunteers in each street – or section of a long street – who could persuade their neighbours to pose as a group. In addition, the staff of each shop and members of many of the village clubs and societies were asked to pose in further groups. The organisation required was very great and took the whole year to complete – but thanks to the weather not one session was hindered by rain.

Having arrived on the day and time arranged, Ce, Judith and Michael would marshal the group while Tim mounted his steps to obtain the necessary elevation. Curtains would move, doors would open and out would come a whole street of residents. Everyone posed, smiling: adults, children, babies (some newly born) - even pets had to be in on the photograph.

Once the photographs had been taken, there was the further task of adding the names of everyone in each picture. This was the particular responsibility of Michael.

The completion of the work was marked by a hugely popular exhibition at the village hall of all the photographs. The data was stored on computer and the Walkers demonstrated its use to all who asked and took orders for prints, which were duly fulfilled.

Also on exhibition were some photographs of Buckden from the early 1900s. Visitors found it fascinating to compare the two sets of pictures and to see the people who had once lived where they now lived. Perhaps someone in 2099 will make a similar record to allow future generations to enjoy the same experience

Copies of the photographs are in albums in Buckden Library. The negatives have been deposited with the County Record Office in Huntingdon. Buckden Parish Council holds the picture files on CD.

Milne, Miss D. M. was the Principal of the Buckden Palace School and Kindergarten for a period between the two world wars.

mineral extraction. Construction whether of buildings, roads, water works or other uses requires concrete, mortar or asphalt. These require aggregates, i.e. sand and stone in a range of sizes. Aggregates must be clean, that is free of organic material and dust, and so water is needed. In turn the washings have to be disposed of into a temporary pond until a worked-out pit can be used. The all but filled pit dug for the purpose behind Bishops Way and Aragon Close is being steadily colonised by scrub willow and other vegetation.

One can obtain aggregates by blasting and crushing rock, but in the Buckden area the source is the river gravels at various levels along the Ouse laid down as the ice retreated 10,000 years ago.

On the 1813 enclosure map there is a gravel pit, half a hectare in area, east of what is now Silver Street, but there is no sign of it on aerial photographs of 1948. There is another on an OS plan of 1926, 300m north of Mill Road. The aerial photograph shows that in 1948 it was overgrown. Who worked it and when is not known

The area bounded by the Scout Hut, the cemetery and Mayfield was a gravel pit, its product being stored along the verges of Lucks Lane until required. The empty pit, which was said to be 5-6 metres deep, was purchased from the Brown family for £143 in 1943, used for the disposal of household refuse and then grassed over. The resulting field was used for some years by the Scout Group. For pioneering exercises the scouts wished to dig holes but when, almost immediately, glass and other items began to appear the holes were filled in and other methods had to be devised! Now the site is largely occupied by the Mayfield Surgery which stands on piles sunk through the rubbish beneath.

Moving on to larger operations, the first company mentioned in Kelly's Directory is Inns and Co (gravel merchants) in the 1940 edition. The earlier quarry workings were opened east of Lodge Farm and connected by a road to the grading and washing plant adjacent to the village. The company is of some interest as its original business was that of supplying fodder etc. to London stables. The drop in demand as the motor vehicle replaced the horse was countered by Inns and Co moving into aggregates.

This company and its successors have been responsible for the majority of the quarrying in the parish. The large-scale winning of sand and gravel started in the early sixties when the dualling of the A1 began; the contractors will probably have been either or both of A. Monk and Co Ltd and Sydney Greene & Co.

Another destination for gravels was the dam and water works at Grafham Water built by W. & C. French and Company, and opened by the Duke of Edinburgh on 6 July 1966. In this case W. & C. French and the St Ives Sand and Gravel Co worked a pit in conjunction with Mr W. Brian Carter. As a result of their work a marina pool came into being thus extending the business of Carter's Boatyard. Mr Carter was awarded the 1970 European Conservation Award by the Duke of Edinburgh and also the Sand and Gravel Award.

Part of the sand grading plant which was removed along with the rest in 2006

Another pit worked to supply the Grafham dam etc was that north of the pumping station on the river.

Inns & Co. were eventually purchased by a larger winner and supplier of aggregates, Redland Aggregates Ltd, who were in turn taken over in 1997 by the French construction group Lafarge, and have since operated as Lafarge Redland Aggregates.

The materials won from yet more areas south of Mill Road were transported by conveyor – a very quiet method – via a tunnel under Mill Road to the grading and washing plant close to the original site.

One of the works Lafarge will be undertaking while reinstating the sites will be the filling of the tunnel with concrete. Some pits have been left as open water with islands. One area east of Leadens Lane has been restored for agriculture. Lafarge will be the last quarry worker in the parish as all the sites permitted by the planning authorities have now been worked out.

In March 2001, Lafarge and Buckden Marina Ltd. were awarded the Cooper-Heyman Cup by the Quarry Products Association for the year's most outstanding restoration project in England.

Over the years aggregate extraction has both provided local employment and contributed to major national construction projects. But it has not been without controversy. There are disadvantages for a community in having an invasive industrial process on its doorstep. Some people believe that these disadvantages are outweighed when the eventual levelling or submerging of the temporary 'moon landscape' turns old gravel workings into sites much favoured by birds both for nesting and for resting places during migration. Others, however, feel that this is insufficient compensation for the loss of so much of the traditional landscape of the Ouse valley. The two points of view are unlikely ever to be reconciled.

See also **marina** and **Carter's Boatyard**.

miracles. Two Buckden residents are associated with miracles. The first is St Hugh (Bishop Hugh D'Avalon, bishop of Lincoln 1186-1200) whose tame swan may have been seen in the village, as commemorated in a modern statue in the grounds of the palace. Another was probably a gardener from Normandy employed at the palace. His story was recorded in the 12thC among the miracles of St Ivo (who gave his name to St Ives, formerly Slepe).

'A certain foreigner was staying with his little family in the village called Buckden; he was from overseas, a gardener by trade, and very poorly off. What is more, he had a son whom he loved very dearly who was eager to copy his father's skill with growing things and worked hard, but he was paralysed. Of course his paralysis was very disagreeable and it disfigured his face, so that he offered a very wretched sight to others, with eyes askew, nose crooked, spreading lips and his mouth almost curving from ear to ear without a break. The father indeed was not a little anxious about treatment for his son, and he spent out what little he had or could get hold of on doctors, but all in vain. ...'So one Saturday he came unawares (yet straying to his advantage) to a certain village which the common people call Slepe. This mean village, about five miles away from Buckden, is yet greatly renowned almost everywhere on earth for the greatness of St Ivo and the frequency of his miracles. When he arrived there and he realised the reputation of the saint he soon hurried to church with his son. Then, just like the tax gatherer in the gospel, he turned his gaze to the ground, fixed his eyes on the earth, watered his cheeks copiously with tears, and on the altar of his heart he made a burnt offering which was most pleasing to God.

'When he had been quite a long time at prayer, and had called on God and St Ivo on behalf of his son, he stood up at last, and deservedly he found his son, whom he had brought there paralysed a little while before, completely well, no doubt through the favours of St Ivo. When the father looked at the boy he clapped his hands in delight, and, capering about in the way the French do, in a loud voice he blessed God as wonderful in His saints. Then, his mood transformed by an expression of thanks to the great and blessed Ivo, he returned home the happiest of men, whose arrival had been of the saddest.' [from *The Life and Miracles of St Ivo*, by S. B. Edgington, 1985]

For a miracle once, but no longer, associated with Buckden, see **Mabel of Bugdene.**

Mitre, the. A messuage [house and grounds] in Buckden 'formerly called the Mitre, and before that the Crown or King's Arms' was once part of the Buckden estates of the Thornhill family of Diddington.

Moore, Major Geoffrey, MBE, lived in Ivelbury Close, and in the late 1970s published several well-regarded booklets on military subjects; one is quoted as a source in Lawrence James's monumental history of the British Raj. Major Moore was also a parish councillor.

morality in Buckden. 'No doubt the morality of some of the inhabitants of Buckden is not all it should be.' Chairman of the Bench, St Neots Petty Sessions, dismissing a case against a Buckden labourer for indecent assault.

Motley, Susan (1810-1893), born in Lincolnshire, was in service with the Green family of Coneygarths for 62 years. She rose through the ranks of house servant, parlour maid and housekeeper to become personal attendant to the unmarried daughter of the house, Frances Elizabeth. When Frances moved a few doors further north in the High Street in the late 1880s, she took Susan with her, more as companion than servant. The 1891 census deals delicately with Susan's changed status. Since she is neither a member of the family or any longer a servant, she is categorised as a visitor 'living with head of house'.

Susan Motley never married; her grave in Buckden Cemetery lies among those of the Green family. Its inscription pays tribute to a family friend and loyal servant.

motorcycles were often a cause of complaint to people living on the High Street (or trying to cross it). This is not surprising when one remembers that until the 1960s the High Street was also the Great North Road. The same qualities that tempted cyclists and motorists to speed through the village inevitably attracted motorcyclists too, with night time races from London to York a particular bane. In 1913, the Chief Constable ordered his men to pay special attention to the fast driving of motorcycles in towns and villages: 'It must be stopped!'

There was a brief respite in February 1924 when major roadworks meant that traffic was routed through Church Street and Silver Street.

Occasionally Buckden's own motorcyclists found themselves before the bench. Two from the 'respectable' classes were Dr Wallace (failing to stop) and the Rev. Cornelius Mensink, the Baptist minister (riding at night with an unlit lamp). The latter case caused much merriment at the Huntingdon Police Court. The Mayor wondered aloud whether Mr Mensink was one of the foolish virgins. Yes indeed, said the police witness, who knew his Bible ('They that were foolish took their lamps, and took no oil with them:' –Matthew 25.3.)

Mountain, Jacob (1749-1825) was Vicar of Buckden 1790-1793/4. During this time he was also examining chaplain to the Bishop of Lincoln, Dr Pretyman, on whose recommendation he was made the first Anglican Bishop of Quebec. His son, George Jehoshaphat Mountain, became its third bishop. An earlier George Mountain had been Bishop of Lincoln and a severely abridged Archbishop of York (he died on the day of his enthronement), but seems not to have been a relative (see also **James VI**).

N

National Society, the. Founded in 1811, it was later incorporated as the National Society for the Education of the Poor in the Principles of the Established Church throughout England and Wales. Its mission was to found a church school in every parish. It did this by offering grants for the erection, enlarging and fitting out of schoolrooms. By the 1850s there were some 17,000 National Schools; that in Buckden was opened in 1842. In September 1843, *The Times* included Mrs Linton of Stirtloe House in a list of those who had subscribed to the Society (£10 in her case).

Navigation Cottages, Hunts End (also known as Vine Cottages) [MapRef 37]: see under **Cana**l.

New Farm, Mill Road, was most recently known as **Low Farm** (q.v.); when occupied by Benjamin Faulkner it was called Faulkner's Farm and similarly as Park's when the last farmer James Park ran it. See under **dovecotes**.

Newton, John (1725-1807) was a slave-ship master turned evangelical clergyman. He is best known today as an anti-slavery campaigner and a writer of hymns, most notably 'Amazing Grace'. Buckden was a place especially dear to him: after several years of failing to be accepted into holy orders, it was here, at 11.00 a.m. on Sunday 29 April 1764, that he was ordained deacon, and on Sunday 17 June was welcomed into the priesthood. Bishop Green of Lincoln presided over both ceremonies. Newton was appointed curate-in-charge of the parish of Olney, Buckinghamshire, a posting that did not appeal to his wife. While still in Buckden he wrote to her at their home in Liverpool, assuring her that he would 'prefer the little vicarage of Olney, with you in it, to the palaces of kings, without you.' It worked. She joined him.

John Newton's earliest known literary efforts were ribald ditties written to amuse his fellow sailors, but 'Amazing Grace' was one of the *Olney Hymns* (1779), on which Newton collaborated with his friend and follower, William Cowper, the fragile and occasionally insane poet and one-time resident of Huntingdon High Street. Its continuing popularity has earned Newton a place alongside Elvis Presley, Pat Boone and Tennessee Ernie Ford in the Gospel Hall of Fame, Nashville, Tennessee (but not, so far, in either the International Gospel Music Hall of Fame, Michigan, Detroit, or the Southern Gospel Museum and Hall of Fame, Dollywood, Tennessee).

night-soil – putrescent manure derived from the contents of outside lavatories, cesspools, etc – was a valuable fertilizer, and its collection was a vital service in the days before mains drainage was installed. Among the places it was spread were the Mill Road allotments on Van Diemen's Lane (one resident recalls that immediately after spreading, the ground would 'glisten attractively in the sun') and on fields up Perry Road, where on one disastrous occasion a broken chain resulted in the cart releasing its contents backwards down the hill.

The cart was washed out at the village pump near the almshouses. This may have been the inspiration for the following lines from 'Buckden: a Christmas Ballad' by Archdeacon Knowles:

'Here old men sit on rustic seat
Watching the doings in the street'

During the Second World War, the cart (well cleaned) was sometimes used to ferry the men and women of RAF Graveley to and from Buckden for the dances at the Rifle Range.

O

Oak Lawn, Mill Road [MapRef 40], was for several hundred years one of the two easternmost houses in the main part of the village (the other was the White House across the road). According to the particulars in a 2008 sale brochure it was originally two cottages, one 17thC, the other 18thC, which were joined together in 1820 to provide a house for the village surgeon. If so, the surgeon may have been Henry Waller, who is known to have been in Buckden by 1822. By the time of the 1841 census, however, it was home to a girls' boarding school run by Fanny and Laura **Beaumont** (q.v.). At the time Oak Lawn was owned by one of the leading local families, the Reynolds of Little Paxton. They put it up for auction in 1849, where it was bought by John Linton of Stirtloe House, with whose family it remained until 1964. During this time its occupants included Francis Cheere, a bachelor barrister (not in practice), Miss Catherine Usher (and her companion Miss Clarkson); Miss Mary A Duberley; William Cawcutt – who farmed neighbouring Low Farm but preferred to live at Oak Lawn, putting his bailiff in the farmhouse itself – and Mr Alexander **Copping** (q.v.). Mr Copping died in 1924 and in 1927 the house again became a surgery as well as a home, first for Dr Robert Davie and then, from 1927 to 1964, for Dr Eric Jolly.

Old Tap, the, in George Lane has also been known as the Old Tap Inn, the George Tap and, in the 1980s, 'Endways'. Probably originally constructed in the 16thC, the Old Tap formed the north side of the George Inn's courtyard and may have accommodated the innkeeper and less wealthy travellers. Much of what remains was probably rebuilt in 1688. There used to be a large wooden beam leading from the rear of the building across some stables, bearing the carving 'RL 1688', regrettably this was cut down with a chainsaw by an owner's wife in the 1980s (she feared that the beam would fall on her head...). 'RL' may have been Robert Longland (1656-1728) or Robert Langley, both of

whom were recorded as innkeepers at that time. Or, indeed, it may have been Richard Lillingstone, who was the Buckden school teacher in 1688. The bricks used in the stables (now garages) facing the lane are certainly pre-1750 (they are identical to those used in the Towers c.1485), but may be reused.

In 1716, the churchwarden accounts record George Lake as being the tapster at the George. During the 1820s, John Blincow was probably resident. After the coaching heyday, when the George was tenemented, the owners or tenants of the Old Tap become more traceable, and the censuses record: 1851-61: Samuel Middleton (publican), 1871-81: David Pratt (beer-seller and shepherd), 1887-1901: Owner, William Reeves, Tenants, David Pratt (licensed 1887-89; he then took over the tenancy of the Spread Eagle) and Henry Usher (licensed 1889-1901).

By the 1930s, the tenant was Frederic John Pond (a former soldier in the Huntingdonshire Cyclists Battalion during the First World War). He was released from the copyhold tenancy to the Bishop, by the Ecclesiastical Commissioners in 1938, for £6. 12s. 0d., at which time the house became freehold. The Ponds had a 'football team' living in the house, i.e. Mr and Mrs Pond and their nine children. Alice Whitmee recalled Mr Pond as driving a horse and cart, collecting rabbit skins, rags and bones etc., while of Mrs Pond, she remembered 'a small lady dressed all in black including her head dress, with an immaculate white apron' in the 1940s. Mr Pond died in the house aged about 90, in 1972; and thereafter the house has changed hands several times. For more on Mr Pond, see **Slippery Road Surfaces Committee.**

Osborn family. We are grateful to descendants of the Osborn family living in Victoria, Australia, and New Jersey, USA, who have provided information about their ancestors. Members of it have crossed tracks with at least one of the evacuees from **Tollington School** (q.v.).

The family originated in Buckinghamshire and Bedfordshire. The first to make Buckden his home was ELIPHAZ OSBORN (1817-1893). According to researchers Wendy Rutter and Leslie Osborn Glessner, Eliphaz was

The Old Tap Inn when a residence   Barry Jobling

born in Thurleigh, Bedfordshire. Census returns and trade directories reveal that he lived and worked in several places before settling in Buckden in his late fifties. He variously referred to himself as a miller (as his father apparently was), machine maker, engineer, machinist (the description that also appears in his burial entry) and miller/millwright. He is said to have been self-taught, and a mechanical genius, having built Buckden's first bicycle and the first pipe organ in the church. It is clear from a photograph of the yard in which his engineering was done, that he must have worked for or with the **Thomsons** (q.v.) in Bakers Lane. Whether it was Eliphaz or a Thomson who was the genius cannot be known but it was the Thomsons who took out several patents in the 19thC.

Eliphaz and his wife Ann are known to have lived in Providence Cottage which was just south of Hardwick Lane on the west side of the Great North Road. After Ann died in 1889, Eliphaz was looked after by his granddaughter Sarah Jane Kennedy, who had been living in his household since at least 1871; it is not clear what had happened to her parents.

NB The name 'Eliphaz' is from the Old Testament. Eliphaz the Temanite was one of the original 'Job's comforters', the three friends who sat with Job in his misery and made him even more miserable. This may go some way to explaining why it has never been among the most popular of christian names.

John Bradshaw Osborn (1848-1909), Eliphaz's son, was a blacksmith (burial record) and had his shop in the High Street next to the Vine public house. He is listed in the 1881 census as an 'Enginere and Ag. Imple. Mkr'. He and Eliphaz were both preachers at the Methodist Chapel.

John George Osborn (1875-1926), the son of John Bradshaw Osborn, was born in Buckden. He was listed as an engine driver in the burial record but the type of engine is not known. In the 1901 census, however, he was listed as a carpenter and joiner.

George Leslie Osborn (b.1908) is presumed to be the son of John George and his wife Maude, and is the father of Greta (see below). He is said to have been the first owner of a motor car in Buckden. Perhaps he was the first MG owner? But not to spoil his grandson's story which follows:

My grandparents claimed to be the first family in Buckden to own a motorcar. He bought the car from some wealthy person in the Lion Hotel one night in the pub. Seems the wealthy person, who did not live in the village, had bought it for his daughter's 21st birthday. She did not like the car so the wealthy man got angry and told anyone in the pub they could have the car for 100 pounds. My grandfather produced the money and drove away with the car.

George was working at Park Farm when he married Alison where she was cook. He later became head carpenter for a Huntingdon builder and also had his own outdoor sawmill in George Lane.

Greta Osborn, the mother of Leslie Osborn Glessner, was a child in 1939 when evacuees from **Tollington School** (q.v.) arrived. Two teenage boys, Alec and Dick, were billeted with the family, much to the chagrin of her parents who had been expecting girls half the boys' ages. There seems to have been some friction as well and the boys were moved to Stirtloe House, but not before Greta had relayed to Alec the announcement of the declaration of war with Germany and Alec had seen his host burying cans of petrol under the garage floor. (This was not uncommon.)

osiers business, the. Willow canes had been cultivated in **The Osiers** (q.v) area of Buckden, probably since at least medieval times, for basket making, construction and other uses. Since before the 1860s, Richard Brown (1827-1912) had employed local labour, usually women, to cut and collect the osiers and bring them to his business in the field and large thatched barn at the bottom of **George Lane** (q.v) (approximately where the A1 dual carriageway is today). The barn was largely destroyed in July 1923 (see under **fires and fire-fighting equipment**).

In 1927, a local newspaper reported: 'A familiar scene is now taking place at Buckden in Mr Brown's paddock; rod or osier peeling. Mrs Mills has turned 77 years and is again rod peeling. She has worked for Mr Arthur Brown and the late Richard Brown for upwards of 60 years.'

ΩΩΩΩΩ

1875 "Grandfather Eliphaz's workshop in Buckden. Uncles William and John in the picture."

The Lorna Baptist Collection, Victoria, Australia

P

Page family members played a significant part in Buckden life for the best part of fifty years as carpenters, builders, farmers, wheelwrights, undertakers and parish councillors.

In about 1856, Thomas Page of Hail Weston moved to Diddington to work for Squire Thornhill. He was a carpenter, as were the two sons who came with him. His wife may have been skilled in brewing: their new home was the Black Horse, a recently vacated beer-house.

In 1869, the elder son, Philip, married a Brampton tailoress, Jane Alger, and settled down in Buckden on the corner of Hunts End and Church Street. The following year, his brother George also wed. After briefly living with his parents, George and his new wife, Caroline (Carrie) Stevens, also moved to Buckden, where Philip and George went into partnership as P. & G. Page (later Page Brothers), carpenters and builders.

The business expanded rapidly, but it was George, not the older Philip, who became the dominant partner. In the 1881 census, Philip is listed simply as a builder, while George is described as a builder employing twenty-four men and four boys. Philip and his family had in fact moved to the other side of Hunts End, allowing George and his family to take over the house attached to the firm's workplace.

This change may reflect declining health on Philip's part: he died towards the end of 1884, aged only 47.

George then continued under his own name until his son, George Thomas, was old enough to join him in a new partnership, George Page and Son, builders, undertakers and wheelwrights.. In 1898, George Thomas married his cousin Jane (Philip's daughter), rescuing her from life as a dressmaker in London, where she and another young woman from Buckden, Louisa Hornsey, were boarding in the house of a War Office computer. (At that time, a 'computer' was still a person who worked with figures.)

Although George senior died in 1912, George Thomas continued to trade as George Page and Son until his death late in 1928. The business was then taken over by builder and undertaker J. W. **Smith** (q.v.).

George Thomas had added farming to the family business interests. At one time or another he occupied the White House, Low Farm and (from 1913) The Hoo.

A particular style of brickwork characterised the buildings of the Pages. Among examples still to be seen in the village are The Gables and Hinsby's Corner (42 Church Street). The mock-Elizabethan facade of the One Stop shop in the High Street is also their work. The firm was also heavily involved in the building of new houses after the First World War; these took priority over its completion of the now demolished **Rifle Range** (q.v.) in Church Street.

See also **Stannard, Violet Kate** and **The Gables.**

pageants had been a popular entertainment in Edwardian times, and were revived in the 1920s and 1930s - this time, perhaps, to reassure people that the First World War and the momentous social and economic changes it brought about had not cut Britain off from its glorious past. Pageants were staged at castles, churches, schools and stately homes; in town squares and municipal parks; on humble village greens. Buckden's most notable contribution, the *Pageant of the Centuries: 1086 to 1814*, attracted national attention in 1932 because of its setting –

the romantic, part-restored Palace – and because of the unusual circumstances of its coming into being. It was written, produced and presented by a young dance band leader from London, Arthur Harold Capel, who wished to raise money for Huntingdon County Hospital, one of whose doctors had saved his father's life.

Capel's 'Tale of Fair Ladies and Gallant Gentlemen' drew its cast from almost every social group in Buckden and several neighbouring communities. The *Hunts Post's* enthusiastic review took up almost the whole of one of its (very large) pages, and included a photograph of the Chief Constable, Captain Rivett-Carnac, looking particularly fetching in Tudor costume as the lover of one of Henry VIII's wives. Unfortunately, an accident removed him from the show after only one night. Among the local performers were three generations of the **Langley family** (q.v.), one of whom, Captain A. G. Langley MC, played the only major speaking role, the Marshall who introduced each scene.

"The Marshall and attendants"   Judith Addington

There was an unscheduled diversion one night, when pale hands were seen moving along the parapet of the Great Tower. 'This had a terrifying effect on all the lady folk,' according to Maurice Milner, because at this time the tower was a potential death-trap, with crumbling brickwork, damaged stairways, no roof and no floorboards. The hands belonged, in fact, to cousins Harold and Cyril Milner, who challenged the very large policeman sent to bring them down to 'come up and fetch us' – a challenge he wisely declined. They made their escape in their own time and were sensible enough not to repeat the escapade.

The pageant was scheduled to run for a week in July/August, but ticket sales were badly hit by unsettled weather at the start of the run. The decision was therefore taken to extend the run to a second week: an extraordinary commitment on the part of all those involved. Newspaper accounts indicate that audiences were enthralled by the setting, the costumes, the skilful deployment of over one hundred players, and the spectacular lighting effects – including the flickering flames that consumed the unfortunate 'Witch of Warboys' (who in reality had been hanged). Electric lighting on this scale must have been a revelation to many villagers, whose homes had only recently ceased to be lit by paraffin lamps and candles and whose windows still looked out on to streets sparingly lit by a thrifty parish council.

Other large-scale productions have been mounted at the Towers, including two productions of 'Merrie England', Edward German's comic opera. The first was in May of the jubilee year 1935, and the second was held to mark the coronation of Elizabeth II in 1953 (one of over 500 such productions in Britain that year).

Papworth's Corner, at the junction of George Lane and the High Street was named for Papworth's Bakery. It had previously been known as **Gale's Corner** (q.v.).

parish boundaries: see Plate PB1.2.

parish constables were originally conscripted annually from among the residents of the parish to apprehend rogues and vagabonds. Service was unpaid, so rarely popular: it could even reduce a small tradesman to bankruptcy. Richer parishioners usually employed someone to stand in for them. The system changed gradually through the 19thC, the general appointment of parish constables being rendered unnecessary by the introduction in 1856 (1857 in Huntingdonshire) of fully professional county constabularies. However, even after the Parish Constables Act 1872, vestries could still appoint paid constables under the chief constable of the county. Buckden availed itself of this right into the 1930s.

A look at **Cope, Thomas** will reveal why a constable's lot was *not* a happy one.

parish councils as we know them today were introduced by the Local Government Act 1894. Buckden's first such council came into being on 4 December of the same year, when about 150 electors met in the Girls School Room to scrutinise the twenty-five candidates for the thirteen places available. Voting was done by a show of hands; it was not until 1949 that councillors were elected by full secret ballots. Meetings were held quarterly, the first of them in the Girls School Room on 31 December 1894; it included the election of a Chairman (who remained in office for the next fifteen years). For more information, see **Chapter 11**- 'The Parish Council: a History of the Governance of Buckden Village'.

parish workhouse [MapRef 43]. This was erected in 1766 by the churchwardens and overseers with the help of a gift of £80 from George Cornelius Swan[n] (c. 1716–1788). According to the Gilbert Report of 1777, it was designed for sixteen inmates. The Buckden Inclosure Map shows it sited on the south side of Mill Road, just to the east of Hunts End, describing it as '0a.1r.7p. Tenements and orchard.'

Next door was a cottage and small garden which the workhouse overseers rented from Burberry's Charity. As the property could only be occupied by 'some honest man to be hoggard [i.e. a gardener or farmworker who usually, but not necessarily, looked after pigs]', it was presumably used to provide the inmates with fresh produce and meat.

It is important not to think of this workhouse as one of the oppressive institutions so vividly described by Charles Dickens. Those were a result of the Poor Law Amendment Act of 1834. The Act was intended to modernise a failing system of poor relief that had developed piecemeal from Tudor times. Unfortunately the legislation was drafted in haste under pressure from the public and rushed through parliament without a proper debate.

The outcome was a system widely criticised as 'legalised cruelty in the treatment of the poor'. Particularly offensive to feminists was the 'Bastardy Clause' which freed fathers from any legal responsibility for their illegitimate children.

This forced mothers unable to support themselves and their offspring to enter the workhouse.

Thus from 1836 the paupers of Buckden were no longer to be looked after in their own village by their own neighbours. They should have been sent away to a new Union Workhouse in St Neots (a Union was a group of parishes – in this case, St Neots and 30 outlying villages – that contributed to the running costs of a central workhouse, and were entitled to send it their poor). However, problems with finding a suitable site meant that the old parish workhouses in St Neots, Eaton Socon and Eynesbury had to stand in for the Union house. The latter was finally built in Eaton Socon in 1841/2 at a cost of £8,145 for 338 inmates. In 1849, John Hale, a Buckden labourer, was one of four inmates convicted of absconding from the Union with workhouse clothes. In 1851, twelve inmates were Buckden-born; in 1861, only one; in 1871, two; in 1881, seven; in 1891, nine, and in 1901, six.

Park Farm, Great North Road [MapRef 18], was previously known as **Rectory Farm**. The present house and farmstead were built by the Ecclesiastical Commissioners in 1857, and were described six years later by a contributor to *The British Farmer's Magazine* as standing 'bare and bleak upon a hill'. The magazine's correspondent did not mean this to be critical: he approved of the fact that the surrounding fields had been cleared of trees and scrub in order to allow better use to be made of modern farm machinery. For more of the history of this important agricultural holding, see **Chapter 9**

Park Farm–the Foreman's House 1995   Joy Freeman

Park, Jim Crowther (1896-1988) farmed Low Farm, Mill Road for many years, starting in the 1930s. He was born (and is now buried) in Grove, Nottinghamshire. A bachelor, his recreations were hunting and cricket: he played for Buckden and was also treasurer of the Cranfield Challenge Cup League.

Parris, Thomas. From the late 1890s to the end of October 1923, Buckden would receive a regular Friday visit from Mr Parris, hair cutter of St Neots. On his retirement he was succeeded by Cecil Sims, who combined hairdressing with running the Spread Eagle Inn.

patients, mental, passing through Buckden. In July 1841 the unhappy poet John Clare left Dr Allen's private asylum in Essex, and set out to walk to his native village of Helpston near Peterborough. He passed through Buckden on the fourth day of his journey, having eaten little but chewing tobacco and grass. He succeeded in reaching home only to find himself unwanted and formally declared insane. He spent the remaining twenty-three years of his life in Northampton's General Lunatic Asylum (later re-named the General Lunatic Asylum for the Middle and Upper Classes in order to exclude the likes of Clare). Coin-cidentally, Buckden's earliest known resident doctor, Henry **Waller** (q.v.), also died there. (In another coinci-dence, John Clare had, in his better days, received a visit from the Rev. Chauncey Hare Townshend, a clergyman, poet and mesmerist, whose cousin, Major Chauncey Curtois, lived in Buckden.) Clare's passing acquaintance with the village is commemorated in 'Buckden, the Bishop's Palace', a lithograph by the artist Rigby Graham**(See plate PB2.6.2)**

On Saturday, 14 March 1931, Police Sergeant Sydney Staughton of Buckden found himself giving lunch and tea to a passing stranger who had very little money and wanted to get to London. Early on Sunday morning Sgt Staughton flagged down a passing motorist and asked him to give the man a lift. The driver, Mr Charles Clapham of 'Clapham and Dwyer, the broadcast comedians', agreed to take him as far as Golders Green, saying later that the policeman 'assured me the gentleman was quite all right'. The gentleman turned out to be a mental patient who had jumped out of the window of the train taking him to an asylum in Salisbury. He was recaptured in London. See also **Pilgrim, Ernest.**

Peach, Maurice was a Buckden writer and owner of the well-regarded small press, Fensedge, whose publications include *Buckden: a concise survey of places of historic interest in the village* (1951, 1957); *The Palace of Buckden: A Concise Survey* (1957); *Vignettes* (1959), and the magazine *Twicer's Tatters.*

Peacock family. Charles Thomas Peacock (1884-1974) was one of eight children born to painter and glazier Thomas Peacock and his wife Fanny [Baker]. The two oldest children, sisters Florence and Margaret, were born in Eaton Socon (as their mother had been); Charles and his five younger brothers and sisters were all born in York Yard.

When his father died in 1896, aged only 39, Charles was thrown into work at the early age of 13. He went as a labourer for Hardwick farmer William Cranfield (as, later, did his younger brother William). In 1908, he married Sarah Ann Bolton and in time became the father of six children (Jack, George, Geoff, Edward, Kathleen and Louie). Home was a two-bedroom cottage on the Great North Road.

Charles served in the First World War, was wounded and after discharge returned to Buckden to work for Mr J. Mailer at Park Farm. In 1926 the family moved to one of the first council houses in the village, at Monks Cottages. Charles was a keen gardener and worked at Diddington Hall, winning prizes with his redcurrants. He would also mend shoes in a shed at the bottom of the garden.

During the Second World War, Charles and Sarah shared their home with two of the boys evacuated from **Tollington School** (q.v.), Alan Loughlin and Ken O'Dell, who still visit Buckden in passing. While the sons of the family were away on active service, Charles and daughters Kath and Louie joined the local Fire Service.

Until he died aged 90, Charles lived in Church Street with his daughter Kath, filling the last of his days with a round of village shows, fetes and outings to the sea.

Kath, who died in 2004, also lived all her life in Buckden. When she left the village school her first job was as chamber maid at the George Hotel. During the Second World War she worked for the Rev. Atkinson and began courting Harold Milner (son of the local grocer). They married in 1942 and initially lived with Kath's parents. Harold worked away during the war in the power stations in Wales. In 1949 they moved into a brand-new council house, No. 1 Lincoln Close. After eight years and two children they moved to Church Street.

peasers, the Biggleswade. Marcus James King (1919 -2000) lived in Biggleswade. His father died when he was only two, leaving his mother to bring up their three children. To supplement her income there was the peasing (pea-picking) season during June and July. The peasers' day began as early as 5 a.m., with the clatter of buckets as they set off for work. Often this meant boarding a lorry for a trip to fields as far away as Buckden.

Pea-picking was one of the field tasks undertaken by the London schoolboys evacuated to Buckden during the early years of the Second World War. One of them, David Rhodes, remembers being amazed at the speed with which local women picked their way up and down the long rows.

Pelham, the Hon. George (1766–1827) was an aristocratic, ambitious – and in the eyes of many, frankly greedy – cleric who agreed to become Bishop of Lincoln in 1820 only after '[going] sulkily down to look at Bugden...to see whether he will condescend to take it' (he had hoped for somewhere more influential, like Winchester, the country's second richest diocese). He was a friend of the Prince Regent and something of a dandy. He attracted criticism for his habit of augmenting his income by collecting minor but lucrative church appointments and hanging on to them, but he was hardly unique in that.
He avoided Buckden in death as well as in life: he was buried on his family estate in Sussex after catching a cold at a royal funeral and dying of pleurisy.

Penny Lane. The Parish Council fought a long battle to obtain the slip-road on the southbound A1 between Bramp-ton Road and Silver Street. When it was completed in 1999, it was suggested to the relevant authority that it be named Penny Lane as a light-hearted (but deserved) tribute to Jim Penny, a councillor for whom road safety was a passionate concern. The response, sadly, was 'We do not name slip-roads; it would be confusing.'

Pepys, Samuel: see **George, the** and **Stan[c]kes, Will.**

Perry Road, which runs westward from the A1 Buckden roundabout, was originally known as New Road, but has been known as Perry Road since at least as early as the 1861 census. Known, that is, to everyone except the Ministry of Transport, to whom it was still officially New Road as late as the 1950s.

Pigeon Shoot Committee. This early 20thC body was responsible for arranging the shooting handicap held at Coneygarths each New Year (weather permitting). This meant ensuring that a stock of 150 or so captured wild birds had been built up for release from traps on the day. In the early 1900s the shoots were still receiving a warm write up in the local papers, although such events were already widely regarded nationally as an 'ignoble sport'. They continued to be popular for several years more, despite attempts by MPs and the RSPCA to have them banned and the scorn of heavyweight papers such as *The Times* ('What sort of 'sportsmen' are they that who need two barrels to bring down a bird released at 30 paces...').

Pilgrim, Ernest was an unfortunate man from Saffron Walden who was found by Pc Wallage wandering about Buckden one wet winter evening in an exhausted state. With the kindness that occasionally characterised Buckden policemen faced with respectable-looking men behaving oddly, Pc Wallage took Mr Pilgrim home for a cup of tea, only to discover that he was labouring under the delusion that he owned Buckden Towers. Pc Wallage therefore thought it wise to escort him down to St Neots police station, whence he was taken to the workhouse (where, it turned out, he had once worked as a porter). Having no visible means of support he was brought before the magistrates – who gave him the money for his fare back to Saffron Walden.

See also **patients, mental, passing through Buckden.**

Mrs Pipe and Colin 1996

pinders were for many centuries among the most important local officials in England; the post dates back to at least the early 13thC. It was their job to protect lives, property and bloodlines by rounding up stray 'beestes', mainly horses and farm livestock, and taking them to the local pinfold or pound to await collection by their owners – for a fee. They were the forerunners of today's vehicle impounders, and about as popular. In Buckden in 1827, pinder Samuel Saunders alleged that he had been horsewhipped and threatened by William Cope, publican, the owner of two pigs Saunders was driving to the pound (they had been found trespassing in the garden of one of Buckden's two Mr Henry Wallers). The case went to court, but unfortunately research has not yet revealed the outcome. Perhaps there were other such incidents, because within a few years Saunders had exchanged the life of a pinder for the comparative comfort of an agricultural labourer in Wyton.

The Buckden pinder was appointed not by the parish authorities but by the Bishop of Lincoln's manorial court. The expenses of the post were met from the income generated by the letting of a piece of land known as Pinder Lane. See also **pond.**

Pipe family. In October 1945 Arnold Sydney Pipe and his wife Sylvia Joan came to Buckden and rented a shop at 49 Church Street from Mr Hinsby Senior, who also had a tobacconist's shop directly across the road at 1 Silver Street. Mr and Mrs Pipe carried on a grocery business at number 49, but right from the start Mr Pipe introduced radios and electrical equipment into the shop and with the help of the *PYE* television agency introduced televisions to Buckden when they reappeared after the war. He also worked as an electrician; for example he wired the house of the late Alice Whitmee in Silver Street.

His friend Mr Gerald Finch worked for the business for some thirty years and later became caretaker for the school. He was also godfather to Mr and Mrs Pipe's son, Colin.

The tobacconist's at 1 Silver Street was managed by Mr Hinsby's wife until her death in 1962, when the Pipes took it over. However, when Mr Hinsby senior died in 1973 his son, Spencer, disposed of all the family's Buckden properties. As a result, the tobacconist's closed in 1974, and has since been a private house. The following year, Mr and Mrs Pipe and Colin were able jointly to buy the freehold of 49 Church Street. Mr Pipe continued with his electrical business until he retired in 1981. After his death in 1984, the grocery side of the business was greatly expanded (Mrs Pipe was deservedly well-known for her home-cooked ham) and an off-licence added. Customers who did not know of Mr Pipe's previous enterprise might be surprised by the range of electrical fittings to be found in the shop.

Pipes Stores continued successfully until 1996, when Mrs Pipe retired and she and Colin left Buckden. Since then the shop has been the Beauty Room.

For many years a small bow-fronted window in a tiled gable on the first floor survived as a reminder that the building had once housed the village Reading Rooms. Unfortunately, while the roof was being refurbished in 1983, it was found that the gable was rotten throughout and beyond any economic repair.

In 1970, the family moved in to a newly built bungalow on the corner of Manor Gardens and Church Street. Mr Pipe had bought the land in 1962, on the death of the previous owner, Miss Sybil Smith of the Manor House. It had been used for pigs and as an orchard in its time.

Piper, John (1903–1992) was a Neo-Romantic artist and designer, one of whose best-known works is 'Buckden in a Storm', a striking picture of The Towers and St Mary's Church. It exists in several versions (some known as 'Buckden Palace, Cambridgeshire)', both as a painting and as a screenprint, and has found its way into locations as diverse as the Tate Gallery and the Chartered Accountants' Great Hall in London, as well as on to greeting-cards. See plate PB2.6.1.

Pitt the Younger, William (1759–1806), politician, lawyer and duellist, was a son of William Pitt the Elder. Each served as Prime Minister, the son from 1783 to 1801 and again from 1804 to 1806; many regard him as the most successful parliamentary leader Britain has ever had. Some of his success he owed to his tutor at Cambridge, the Rev. Dr George **Pretyman** (q.v.)(later Sir George Tomline), who remained his friend and political adviser for life. In return, Pitt appointed him Bishop of Lincoln in 1787, and would come to visit him at Buckden from time to time. After Pitt's early death – he always enjoyed port but never good health – Pretyman was his executor and partial biographer. (Partial in that he was both uncritical of his subject and failed to finish the biography.)

plane, the Buckden. The grounds of Buckden Towers can boast several impressive trees. Among them is a large *Platanus x hispanica* or London plane, believed to have been planted in about 1660 by Bishop Sanderson, who had been charged with restoring the bishop's palace and its surroundings after the depredations of the Commonwealth. If true, this makes it one of the earliest planted in this country. In 2000, it was measured at nearly 114 feet high and 23 feet in circumference.

See also **ash**, **elm** and **sycamore**.

police in Buckden. County forces were introduced by the County Police Act of 1839. However, the legislation was permissive not compulsory and Huntingdonshire took little or no notice of it. The government tolerated this until 1856, when a new act made the formation of county forces compulsory. In 1857 Huntingdonshire became the last county of all to enrol its constabulary, which it put under the shared command of the existing Chief Constable of Cambridgeshire, Captain George Davies RN (Rtd). This resulted in Buckden having its first resident professional policeman. His beat – there was no possibility then of 'her beat' – took in not only Offord Cluny, Diddington and Southoe but also Perry and on occasions Kimbolton – all to be patrolled on foot! (His superintendent had the benefit of a horse – provided out of his own salary – and a cart – provided by the county.)

The daily life of a late 19thC Buckden policeman was governed by routine tasks – looking out for (and if appropriate, moving on) tramps, gypsies, rowdy boys, stolen horses, straying livestock, bicycles without lamps and unlicensed vehicles (horse-drawn, of course), keeping an eye on pubs at closing time and 'attending divine service' on Sundays. This would be enlivened from time to time by intervening in street fights (often between women), trying to identify sheepdog poisoners, serving summonses on poachers, travelling to Newmarket with fellow officers to keep the peace at race meetings, searching the Ouse for persons feared drowned, and, during animal disease outbreaks, helping to slaughter and bury dead stock

In 1903/4, seven Huntingdonshire police stations, one of them Buckden, were linked by a private wire leased by the constabulary from the National Telephone Company (**see** under **telephone service**). Among other things, this enabled the Norman Cross police station to ring the Buckden constables to forewarn them of speeding motorists! In 1908, the Buckden police constable was allowed his house rent-free in return for undertaking the extra duty of 'looking after the telephones'.

police trap, the infamous Buckden. From 1901 until at least the mid-1920s, the local police and the implacable magistrates of the St Neots Petty Sessions turned Buckden into the most-feared speed trap (or 'police trap' as it was then commonly known) on the Great North Road – and possibly in the country. In July 1914, for example, *The Times* reminded its readers that 'On the Great North Road there are 'straight controls' between Hatfield and Peterborough, *and the neighbourhood of Buckden, which is in the county of Huntingdon, is especially to be avoided by motorists.'!*

Distinguished solicitors and barristers appeared before the bench to protest (in vain) the innocence of their no less distinguished clients, and to draw attention to the inherent flaws in a system that depended on the miraculous synchronicity of two constables – one hidden in what are now the Windmill Allotments (see under **charities**) with a stop-watch – timing the passage of a vehicle between two telegraph poles, one of them three fields away. The magistrates took the view - shared by the higher judiciary - that motoring was a rich man's pastime and it behoved the rich to set a good example.

One of the defence solicitors was Earl Russell (1865-1931), aristocrat, electrical engineer, accidental bigamist and motoring enthusiast. He was the first owner of the number-plate A1 and became a Labour Cabinet Minister.

THE flight of centuries effects very little change in human nature— thus the prehistoric policeman was doubtless as remorseless in his enforcement of the traffic laws as the most modern member of the force, and the ancient sundial at least as reliable as the up-to-date but erratic stop-watch.
In order to evade such pressing attention, the motorist's mind must be at rest about his car. The users of

AVON TYRES

have no road worries, and so can easily keep a sharp look-out for traps. AVONS are British made by British Labour, and only the finest materials are utilised in their manufacture, thereby ensuring perfect resiliency and remarkable wearing capacity.

London 25, Long Acre. Birmingham—95, Corporation St.
Manchester—35A Deansgate. Glasgow—101, Stockwell St.
Head Offices and Works: MELKSHAM, Wilts.

The Modern Method.

Reprinted by kind permission of Cooper Tire & Rubber Company Ltd

He was also on the committee of the fledgling Automobile Association. Incensed by what he saw as the unfairness of the Buckden police trap, he persuaded the committee to send the secretary to Buckden to arrange for a large hoarding to be erected outside the village, warning motorists of the dangers ahead. The secretary rented space for the sign from a local cowkeeper, who was probably happy to take a guinea a year off the toffs of the AA while simultaneously thwarting the police and magistrates. The police appeared to have the last laugh, however: they used the hoarding to hide behind before leaping out, stopwatch in hand. They were temporarily routed in 1930 when Earl Russell, by then a junior minister at the Department of Transport, succeeded in getting the speed limit for cars abolished (it was partially reinstated five years later).

In the winter of 1912, a correspondent wrote to *The Field* effectively accusing Alan Chichester, the Chief Constable, of conniving in the running of an unscrupulous speed trap in Buckden, one intended to 'catch the autumn exodus to [the game moors of] Scotland'. Col Chichester responded with a furious defence of himself and his officers and denied any bias against motorists. In later life, John **Wallage** (q.v.), Buckden's resident policeman from 1887 to 1900, admitted that he been posted to Buckden expressly to help reduce the speed of traffic.

The writer Dorothy L Sayers (1893-1957), herself a keen motorcyclist and fond of fast cars, was well aware of the irresistible attraction that the 'long, flat, steel-grey ribbon' of the Great North Road held for lovers of speed. In her 1926 short story 'The Fantastic Horror of the Cat in the Bag' her detective hero Lord Peter Wimsey admits to 'furious driving' up the north road as he pursues two motorcyclists: 'though I do plead in extenuation that I spared the women and children and hit up the miles in the wide open spaces.'

Nor was it only motorists who sped through Buckden. On Sunday 22 May 1898, two cyclists hurtled through the centre of the village at midday 'at 30 miles an hour, quite regardless of folk in the road'. This 'disgraceful racing' must have particularly irritated the vicar. Some of these folk would have been returning from morning service, which he had dedicated to the memory of the recently deceased statesman, W.E.Gladstone. The eruption of the demon cyclists probably swept his 'graceful remarks' and careful choice of solemn music clean out of his congregation's minds.

See also **motorcycles**.

pond. The village pond was part of the manorial pound or pinfold, an enclosure in which stray animals were kept until their owners paid for their release. It was situated on what is now **Hunts End** green (q.v.). Being close to the schools, the pond was regarded as a nuisance by most mothers because of their youngsters 'trying the quality of their shoes' in it. It is not known whether the pond was ever used for evangelical baptisms, as it was in some villages, but it was the scene of a Salvation Army band concert –

after a local farmer, Mr Cranfield, had filled it in early in the last century. His infill included the stones of the surrounding wall, which he apparently demolished on his own initiative. The resulting level area became a popular area for public entertainments. It is noticeable, however, that the pond still re-emerges under heavy rain, flooding the roadway at the northwest corner of the green.

See also **pinders**.

Poor Law: see parish workhouse

Post Offices. The location of Buckden's sub-Post Office has changed several times – once, in the early 1980s, with extraordinary speed.

The first known location was next to the George Hotel in a shop which stood across what is now the entrance to King George Court and the hotel car park (this shop had earlier been the house in which landlords of the George lived.). We know from trade directories that an early (1839) postmaster was George Usher; he was also a shoemaker. The 1841 census is silent on the identity of the postmaster, but there is no reason to suppose it was not still Mr Usher. The census does identify the village post boy, who was William **Chandler** (q.v.). By 1869 the sub-postmaster was Mr John Gace **Langley** (q.v.), who took over from Thomas Darlow. As happens today, he ran the Post Office as part of a larger business: he was also a grocer, draper and ironmonger.

When Mr Langley died in 1892, aged 85, he was succeeded by his daughter Sarah, who ran the business – including selling stationery and insurance – with the help of her older sister Mary. By 1901, the sisters had added a young Telephone Clerk to their establishment. Sarah retired in December 1922 after thirty years as postmistress and over fifty years' association with the Post Office. At a ceremony at Stirtloe House, she was given a cheque for £61.0s.0d. in recognition of her long service. The Post Office was then moved across the road to a shop presently called Elouise. A postbox was mounted in its wall. This property was part of the new building built for **Bowtells** (q.v.) by Pages (see under **Page family**.). The new postmaster was Arthur M. Poulton from Brampton, an ex-army man. Later custodians included a Mr Peach..

On the corner of George Lane and the High Street (formerly known as Papworth's Corner) was Watkins Newsagents. The Post Office had its third location here for a time in the 1970s. The postbox in the wall at this corner is long-established and looks very similar to that which was across the road and may be the same one. In the early 1980s, a dispute led the Post Office to take the business away from the newsagents (the box was not removed and is still there today) and set up a temporary office in the inner gatehouse at the Towers until a new home was found for it. A planning application was submitted to Huntingdonshire District Council in March 1980 seeking a change of use for No. 42 Church Street from dwelling to Post Office; simultaneously there was an application for the installation of Post Office facilities in the SPAR store on Hunts End. The first application was withdrawn, and the Post Office moved to Hunts End.

But still not to a permanent home! Finally or, perhaps, just for the present, the sub-Post Office has come back to the Bowtells building, this time inside the shop itself (now a 'One Stop' store, owned by Tesco), its fifth resting place.

postal service. In 2009, the last collection from the box in the centre of the village was at 4.45 p.m. Monday to Friday and 11.10 a.m. on Saturday. Trade directories show that in 1903, it was 7.50 p.m., in 1885 and 1855 6.30 p.m., and in 1839 9.00 p.m.!

No collection (or delivery) times are shown in the 1940 directory. But then there was a war on....

pound, the village: see pond and pinders

Pretyman, **Dr George** (later Sir George Pretyman Tomline) **(1750-1827)** was one of those bishops of Lincoln who preferred to live in Buckden. He was appointed in 1787, the objections of the king ('Too young, too young!') being overborne by the prime minister, William Pitt; Pretyman had been Pitt's tutor at Cambridge and since 1783 had been living with him in Downing Street as his friend and financial policy adviser. To the annoyance of them both, however, the king was less amenable in 1805 and refused Pitt's request to make Pretyman Archbishop of Canterbury.

Pretyman remained in Buckden until 1820, when he was translated to Winchester. He was highly regarded for his good works: one supporter described him as 'ever searching after new objects of benevolence....a father to the friendless throughout the neighbourhood [i.e. Buckden]'. He was also popular with young clergymen for his book *The Elements of Christian Theology*, a revision crib that allowed them to mug up essential facts before facing their ordination examination.

There were, however, others with whom he was less popular. One was fellow cleric Richard Waldo Sibthorpe, who after visiting the bishop in his Buckden Palace called him uncivil and the most uncouth being he had ever known: 'I like him neither as a Bishop or a gentleman.' This dissenting view may have owed something to the bishop's not inviting him to dinner and being distinctly unsympathetic when Sibthorpe caught a cold in the palace chapel. See also **George, Prince of Wales** (who found Pretyman a more congenial host) and , **Pitt the Younger** and **soup kitchens.**

Price, James. In 2002, the Buckden Bowls Club team of Bob Price, James Price and Peter Holmes won through to the quarter-finals of the Yoplait English men's triples championship – a remarkable achievement made even more remarkable by James Price's age: he was only 10. That the Buckden trio's winning streak was then brought to an end by a team from Kent did not detract from James's fame as the 'four-foot tall wizard of the green': the youngest player to compete in the final stages of the national championships.

Providence Cottage: see Osborn family.

public houses and **beer-houses**. Buckden's 19thC residents would be disappointed or elated, according to taste, to find so few licensed premises in the village today. To take an imaginary walk round a Buckden more adequately provided with places of refreshment, see **Chapter 16**. **Where to Get a Drink.**

pump, the village. This was situated in Church Street, on the boundary between the Methodist chapel and the present Burberry Homes. It had two orifices, one above the other. The higher of the two was used for filling water carts and washing out farm and other carts (see **night-soil collection**). In February 1891, the parish council discussed the 'water cart nuisance on the footpath at the Wesleyan chapel'. The solution proposed was to require the carts to draw their water from a new well to be sunk beside the village pond; the pond itself would then be filled in.

Although the bricks of the wall surrounding the pond could have been used to line the well, this idea was not taken up. However, the pond was indeed filled in, mostly through the efforts of Mr Cranfield of Park Farm. Within two weeks the village band was able to perform where the pond had been.

Pusey, Dr Edward Bouverie (1800-1882) was pale, thin, fair-haired, blue-eyed, a crack shot and a leading Anglican cleric, preacher and academic who devoted his life to reaffirming the Catholic inheritance of the Church of England. Widely thought of as 'austere and gloomy', he was at least able to look back on a happy fifteen months spent in Buckden as a pupil of the vicar, Dr Maltby. 'There were,' he said, rather cryptically, 'no black sheep in Buckden.'

Q

Quarrying: see under **mineral extraction**

R

railway mania-1 The 'railway mania' of the 1840s manifested itself in the hundreds of companies that sprang up to promote new lines (each of which required parliamentary approval). The coming of the railways struck a devastating blow to those who drew all or part of their livelihood from the flow of traffic along the Great North Road. In places like Buckden, these included innkeepers, their staff (maids, boot boys, cooks, cellarmen, laundresses, ostlers, stablehands) and their suppliers (brewers, graziers, coach-drivers, hirers of flies and chaises, horse-dealers, long-distance carriers, and farmers and smallholders). But some local people were quick to see that there was money to be made from railways. Not surprisingly, the gentry such as the Duberlys of Gaynes Hall, Thornhills of Diddington, Reynoldses of Paxton Hall and the Lintons of Stirtloe (who spread the risk by investing in canals as well), all invested in one of the larger schemes, the London and York Railway. In Buckden itself, Captain John George **Green** (q.v.) of Coneygarths was a member of the provisional committees of two small railway companies, the **Ely and Bedford** and the **Wisbech and Huntingdon.** Also on the Wisbech & Huntingdon committee was the Offord and Buckden miller, Thomas Bowyer, who had previously given evidence to a parliamentary inquiry into the commercial imperatives for expanding the rail network.

No more than a five mile stretch of the Ely and Bedford had been built (at the phenomenal cost of £130,000 a mile) before, in 1847, the company was formally amalgamated into the East Anglian Railway Company – which in turn became part of the Great Eastern. The Wisbech & Huntingdon railway (or as it was also known, Huntingdon and Wisbeach) became part of the amalgamated Huntingdon and St Ives and Wisbeach and Sutton company, which was eventually wound up in 1846 – perhaps not surprisingly, given that the leading railway engineer Robert Stephenson was complaining of the chaos and inconvenience being caused by the simultaneous

ELY AND BEDFORD RAILWAY.

existence of fourteen different railway schemes within half a mile of Wisbech.

railway mania-2 A form of melancholia that overcomes researchers who seek to unravel the evolution of individual Victorian railway companies.

Randall, [William] Arthur (1926-2003), who lived in Buckden all his life, is remembered as a raconteur and long-serving member of St Mary's choir. He joined at the age of nine and celebrated his sixtieth anniversary in April 1996. See also **Wyles.**

Reading Room (or, sometimes, **Rooms**) **[MapRef 5].** The building in which the village Reading Room was situated is now the shop called The Beauty Room. It is in Church Street opposite Silver Street.

The decision to try to open a reading room coincided with the arrival in Buckden of the irresistibly energetic young Dr Hillyer at the beginning of the 1890s (see also **cricket in Buckden**). Fund-raising proceeded apace, and the rooms opened in November 1891. They got off to a good start: 'everything has gone on as merrily as the marriage bell' said the *Hunts Post*. There were over eighty patrons, honorary subscribers, and members (who paid 2d. per week). The space – including a library where people could read a daily newspaper, and a recreation room – was well-lighted and commodious, and there was accommodation for the caretakers. From 1891 to at least 1917 these were Frederick and Lydia Allsopp, formerly of Hardwick. In the First World War, their only son, Thomas Charles, enlisted with the Northamptonshire Regiment. He was killed in

1985 Mr W. F. Smith, son of an earlier occupier and provider of the photograph, in front of what had been the reading rooms before his father ran a clothing and general store there. At the time of his visit it was Pipe's shop.

Belgium on 1 October 1917, aged 29.

The institution was run by a committee supported by an Honorary Secretary, the first of whom was, inevitably, Dr Hillyer; his successors were Alexander **Copping** (q.v.), and George Hall of Low Farm.

In 1898, a year of 'great and uneventful prosperity' according to the chairman's report to the AGM, the committee bought the freehold of the property of which the Reading Room formed a part. The price was £241. 12s. 0d., which also included neighbouring stables and enough land to allow for future expansion.

The facilities were in use for nearly thirty years, until the opening of the **Rifle Range** (q.v.) and its Recreation Rooms. The building was then bought by Mr S. E. Hinsby in February 1921 for £300.

The Reading Room was converted to a general store which stocked whatever the tenant felt would sell. Among the services remembered by the late Alice Whitmee was the borrowing of clothing or shoes on approval from Barratts in St Neots. Mr W. F. Smith of South Africa recalls that his father Frank Smith ran it as a draper's shop (his memories are of being there in the mid-1920s). Later the building was first tenanted and then bought by the **Pipe family** (q.v.).

External changes in the building can be traced in photographs. They were limited to the removal of elaborate doors and windows from the front elevation, the brick structure being unchanged. There is a curious finial on the gable end which, we have been reliably(?) informed by a white witch, is to keep away the other sort.

Reynolds family. There have been Reynoldses in Buckden since before the mid-16thC. What their status was in the early years is not always clear, but in the 18thC a Cambridgeshire branch of the family came to play a prominent role in the social and economic life of the parish and, indeed, the county. Although they eventually established their seat at Little Paxton Hall, they remained influential in Buckden, where they continued to own or occupy land and property until the mid 19thC.

Their association with the village began with Richard Reynolds, Bishop of Lincoln 1723-1744, who found Buckden Palace ideally placed as a centre from which to tour his huge diocese. Several of his sons were ordained, six of them enjoying suspiciously successful careers within their father's diocese. The eldest of these, Archdeacon George Reynolds, followed his father's example and lived in or near Buckden for a time. At least three of his children were born here. They were Anthony and Lawrence (yet more clergymen!), and Richard, a lawyer. Richard inherited Paxton Hall from the archdeacon, to whom it had been transferred by *his* father, the bishop.

Next to Bishop Richard, Anthony's son Lawrence (1771-1839) was the family member most closely connected with Buckden. He too became a lawyer after graduating from Cambridge (where he had been kept under surveillance by government agents as a suspected radical). He occupied (but did not own) Stirtloe House from about 1803 until 1814, when he in turn inherited the Paxton Hall estate – he was a favourite of his aunt and uncle, who had no children of their own, and had been helping them to manage the property for some years. He was an irascible and argumentative man whose courtship of Miss Bromhead, a Lincolnshire heiress ('more of a law suit than a love suit', said his aunt drily) came to an abrupt end when Lawrence and her clergyman father quarrelled furiously over the size of her dowry. Fortunately, his eventual marriage in 1802 to Mary Cole was both happy and busy, producing about 15 children despite Lawrence's suffering much from 'Pains in his Loynes'. These were a legacy of his time in Lincolnshire - not inflicted at the hands of his first prospective father-in-law, but the result of a hunting accident.

Others with whom Lawrence fell out included his friend and political ally Edward Maltby, vicar of Buckden; his aunt's protégé and tenant the Rev. Isaac Nicholson; the poor of Buckden; the Charity Commissioners, and the Inclosure Commissioners. His quarrel with the poor and the commissioners arose when he was accused of having abused his position as a trustee of Burberry's Charity during the inclosure of Buckden: giving the charity some land and decayed old buildings at Stirtloe in exchange for a more valuable cottage and garden. This might seem questionable behaviour in one who was at various times High Sheriff of the county, a captain in the militia, and chairman of the Huntingdonshire Quarter Sessions; and indeed, 'You, Sir, should be ashamed of yourself,' was the barbed subtext of the commissioners' conclusion. Although finding that the charity had probably not actually lost by the transaction, they added:
'...but, as Mr. Reynolds was a trustee at the time, an exchange of part of the charity-estate for premises belonging to him could not properly be made at his instance, unless some positive advantage would manifestly result from it to the charity.'

One of his sons, Captain Richard Anthony Reynolds, inherited his father's volatile temper and put paid to a promising army career by sending his commanding officer a letter accusing him of insulting behaviour and, in effect, of cowardice. He then challenged him to lay aside their differences in rank and meet him in a duel. Unfortunately for him, his commander was the equally short-tempered James Brudenell, Earl of Cardigan, who declared the letter 'disrespectful, insubordinate, offensive and insulting', ordered Reynolds's arrest and prosecuted him before a court-martial. Reynolds was found guilty and cashiered for conduct unbecoming an officer and gentleman. This caused public outrage, not least because in the meantime Cardigan himself had also been arrested – on a charge of attempted murder, having shot another of his officers in a duel. Cardigan was tried by the House of Lords, found not guilty and survived to lead the charge of the Light Brigade at Balaclava in 1854. Captain Reynolds was quietly reinstated in rank and lived out the rest of his life as a reasonably popular squire and magistrate. Ironically, history had already linked the Brudenell and Reynolds families: both had held the Manor of Buckden Brittens (which included land at Stirtloe), the Brudenells in the 17thC and the Reynoldses in the 19thC.

Bishop Reynolds died in his London house, but is buried in St Mary's Church, as are his wife and other members of the family, including Lawrence Reynolds's first born son, who died in infancy.

Richard III (1452–1485, king 1483-1485) On 15 March 1484, Richard arrived in Buckden to enjoy one of the few quiet interludes in his troubled reign. He and his queen, Anne, broke their journey between Cambridge and Nottingham to spend a pleasant few days here with the Bishop of Lincoln, John Russell, who was also Richard's Lord Chancellor.

Barely a month later a messenger arrived at Nottingham Castle with the news that Richard's eleven year old son, Edward, was dead. The loss of his only legitimate heir strengthened his enemies and accelerated the disintegration of his rule.

He passed through Buckden at least twice more during his frequent forays to protect the north – by force or diplomacy – from the ever-troublesome Scots.

Rifle Club, Buckden: see the following entry.

Rifle Range, Church Street [MapRef 7]. 'A movement is on foot to establish a Rifle Club in this village' – *St. Neots Advertiser* 27 January 1900. It took a long time before the club had a permanent home, known as the Rifle Range. This was a building later presented to the village by William Walker Cranfield and his sister Mary and conveyed to the village on 21 December 1920 at a formal ceremony. However, the club itself was already active by then. Indeed, in June of the same year, it had met and narrowly vanquished its Kimbolton counterpart to win the Astor County Cup for the second time. (In an echo of old-fashioned village cricket matches, one of the umpires, Frank Lyttleton Powys Maurice, was also a member of the Kimbolton team –as was his son – but he was the local vicar, so presumably his integrity was not to be doubted!)

The Rifle Range was situated in Church Street where the Burberry Homes now stand. Before the Range was built the area was occupied by three low two-storey buildings, two of which had dormer windows lighting the top floor. Two were occupied by tradesmen, one a hairdresser, and the third was a malting. It was the malting which had been converted into a rifle range by Alderman Henry **Cranfield** (q.v.) of Cranfields Farm (now Park Farm). His brother, William Walker Cranfield, who took over the farm after Henry's untimely death, added the reading and billiard rooms. The building was handed over without its brick frontage because the donors had asked the builder, Mr George Thomas Page (see **Page family**) to give priority to new houses and house repairs. It was hoped that completion would be achieved in the following summer (1921).

Later photographs of the Range show the completed building having a substantial frontage of brick, double-fronted with six projecting string courses between pavement and sill level generally, and string courses at the corners at one foot intervals. Over the entrance was a large canopy supported by steel ties. Above that was a central gable end with a tall vertical flagpole bracketed out from it. The roof was tiled and overhung the walls by a foot or so.

The hall was used every Wednesday by the Rifle Club and the smaller rooms by club members for various activities. These included billiards on a full-size table bought second-hand from Hartford House, draughts and – very popular – whist. The Reading Room superseded the previous one across the road. The Range also served as the

The Rifle Club pre 1930   Alice Whitmee
From L. to R.-   T. Milner, M.Milner, S Whitmee
                    W.W.Cranfield (President),
            C.Pond,   J.E. Varley,   E Watman

raised £3,300. It was agreed that half the funds should go to Buckden people serving in the forces and the other towards a memorial.

See Memorial Playing Fields.

A new village hall with more room and more facilities was mooted and in 1969 the momentous but not entirely popular decision was made to build one. The Rifle Range, regarded still with affection by those who remember it, was demolished in 1970 and thus made way for the **Burberry Homes** (q.v.)   Robin Gibson ~June Woods

riots, agricultural: see machine-breaking.

riots and tumult in 1641. Authority has not always thought highly of Buckden, whose residents have sometimes been condemned as obstinate, quarrelsome, sullen, unhelpful, even violent. The following entry in the House of Lords Journal for 1641 records one such instance - although today our sympathies are more likely to lie with the rioters than with the target of their rage...:

'Whereas the Bishops of Lincolne, having quitted their Commons to the Tenants of Buckden, have, by Order and Licence, inclosed some Parts of their Demesne, which lay next unto the Parks and Woods in that Place, which bore neither Corn nor Grass, and having fenced those Grounds, and enjoyed them quietly in their own Possession, and the Possession of the King (upon an Extent), some for Twenty-four Years, and the rest for Fourteen Years; yet now of late, and sitting this present Parliament, *videlicet*, on Friday last, the 18th of this Instant June, some Hundreds of Women and Boys, armed with Daggers and Javelins, in a very tumultuous and riotous Manner, entered upon the Grounds, threw open the Gates, and broke down the Quicksets of the said Inclosure, and turned in great Herds of Cattle upon the Premises, to disquieting of the present Possession, and to the great Damage and Loss of the now Bishop of Lincolne (a Member of this House): Whereupon it is Ordered, by this House, That the said Lord Bishop of Lincolne, and all claiming from and under him, shall quietly and peaceably hold and enjoy the possession of the said inclosed Grounds, lying near to the Park aforesaid, as it hath been possessed and enjoyed for the Space of Seven Years last past, until the Houses of Parliament, or some other of His Majesty's Courts of Justice, shall give Order or determine the contrary; and that Three of His Majesty's Justices of the Peace next adjoining, *videlicet*, Mr Ravenscrofte, Mr Paine, and

The Rifle Range   (Supplier's name mis-laid)

Mr Barnard, or any Two or One of them, shall, by virtue thereof, view the Place, and certify unto this House the Value of the Loss and Damages so done by the said riotous and tumultuous People as aforesaid; and that the said Riot and Tumult shall be considered of, and proceeded against, according to Law, by His Majesty's Justices of the Peace for the County of Huntingdone, at the next Quarter Sessions to be held for the said County; before which Justices of Peace, the Persons offending are to be produced, and proceeded against, in Manner as aforesaid; the Principal of which Actors are to be sent for as Delinquents unto this House, and proceeded against here, as this House shall think fit: And lastly, it is Ordered, That, until the Parliament, or some other of His Majesty's Courts of Justice, shall order the quiet Possession from the said Lord Bishop of Lincolne, that none shall disturb the quiet Possession of the said inclosed Grounds, either by throwing down of the Mounds, pulling up the Quicksets, or throwing open the Gates, or wilful turning in their Cattle upon the Premises; but that the said Lord Bishop, and all claiming from and under him, shall and may peaceably and quietly enjoy the said Grounds, according to the true Intent and Meaning of this Order.'

A day or two later the order was modified:

'Ordered, That the Men which committed the Riot upon the Lord Bishop of Lincolne's Grounds at Buckden shall be sent for as Delinquents; but the Women are to be spared.'

Robinson, Peter Dennis (1923-44) was the son of Arthur and Dorothy Robinson; his father was the proprietor of Robinson's Garages (see following entry). A lieutenant in No. 41 Royal Marines Commando, Peter died during the fighting following the D-Day invasion. He is buried in the Ranville War Cemetery, and is commemorated in Buckden on the St Mary's war memorial.

Robinson's Garages were established by Arthur Thomas Robinson (1881-1938). He grew up in Kimbolton and Brampton, the third son of gardener William Robinson. Although he too started his working life as a gardener, he changed career in 1903, moving to Buckden to start making and repairing cycles in a disused part of the George. In 1905, he took over the High Street premises where Sarah **Bowling** (q.v.) had kept a ladies' school. By 1907, he was doing well enough to marry Dorothy Annie Seymour, whom he may have known (and been courting) since 1901, when he was working in her home town of Watford.

Although the 1914 Kelly's Directory still lists him only as a cycle maker, he had begun repairing motor cars at least three years earlier. He was clearly enthusiastically embracing this new world; so much so that by November 1915 he was proudly advertising 'immediate delivery' of the 1916 model Studebaker car for £250 plus £45 tax. It comes as something of a surprise to realise that fifteen months into the First World War valuable transatlantic shipping space was still being set aside for the import of private motors. The cars were also available for hire 'with experienced drivers'.

In the 1920s, he rapidly expanded and diversified his business: from having been able to garage five cars at a time in 1913, by 1935 he could accommodate 100 cars and ten motorcycles. His premises had moved to just south of where the Great North Road entered the village, almost opposite its junction with Perry Road. The end of the war had left an enormous number of surplus road lorries. In a contemporary photograph of the High Street it is just possible to make out two lorries of the type without cabs; this gives credence to the story that Robinson made much money from the paving and improvement of the Great North Road through hiring out trucks. But he was after a much wider customer base than that: his advertisements in the *Hunts Post* were addressed to farmers, market

Robinson's garage c.1935   Sam Malt

gardeners, coal merchants, builders and brewers among others. He also claimed the first bulk petrol storage in the county (two pumps). His phone number was Buckden 2.

By the 1930s the business was employing a dozen men and boys.

The business name was changed in 1957 from Robinson's Garages (Buckden) Ltd. to simply the Buckden Garage.

Managing to survive the coming of the roundabout in 1962, the garage continued as a repair workshop and petrol station until the 1980s, when the site was bought and flattened to make way for a Shell service station. Since then the house and once attractive garden that went with the site have been sadly neglected.

Mr Robinson was active in village affairs, serving as chairman of the parish council and on the committee of the Horticultural Society. In 1916, he was a member of the jury at the inquest into the death of Buckden philanthropist Henry Cranfield. He was also called as a witness, having driven the dying man home from the scene of his accident.

Roxby family:

Henry Meux Roxby (1832-1900) was the vicar of Buckden for twenty-five years (he died in post) and a founder-member of the village **Reading Rooms** (q.v.). He was the son of a clergyman - and the brother of two more. His children included:

Lt-Col Francis Maude-Roxby OBE DFC Legion of Honour, who had an unusual career that spanned sea, land and air. He was only forty-five when he died of pneumonia in 1922, but in that time he had spent fifteen years as an officer with the P&O shipping line, fought as an infantry officer in the First World War trenches, and ended up in the Balloon Section of the RAF, serving both in the front line and in England, where he was responsible for the balloon defences over London. In 1912 he married Louise, one of the Lintons of Stirtloe House.

Henry M Roxby, an art teacher who became a poultry farmer.

Rev. Wilfred Maude-Roxby, grandfather of the actor Roddy Maude-Roxby.

Royal Observer Corps Monitoring Post. Those who have had business at the gravel pits north-east of the village will have seen two concrete structures beside the track partly obscured by scrub. One consists of a box on stilts with the remains of a ladder leading to its doorway. The other is a manhole over a 5m. deep shaft.

The first is an 'Orlit B', being a pre-cast concrete hut used for aircraft observation by the ROC in their original role until 1965.

The underground shelter was built sometime after 1956. There were 1,563 of these in Great Britain and Northern Ireland in use until 1968 when the number manned was cut by half. Another reduction in numbers was made in the 1980s. Each post was equipped with instruments of various degrees of sophistication to record nuclear bomb explosions, the intention being to provide some information on the location and power of each detonation and the consequent radioactive fall-out.

In the early 2000s the parish council, in association with Dr Mike Osborne of The Defence of Britain Project, sought unsuccessfully to have the post accepted as a Listed Building.

Russell, Lord John (1792–1878) was Britain's shortest and cleanest prime minister - less than 5' 5" high and one of the first Englishmen to have a bath every day. His elder brother, and possibly Russell himself, spent time

An ROC Orlit B observation post

in Buckden being coached for university by the vicar, Edward Maltby. As a result, Maltby became Russell's friend and political ally, helping him with his election as a Huntingdon MP in 1820 and later supporting his party (the Whigs) from the bishops' bench in the House of Lords. In 1847, Russell offered to make him Archbishop of York; Maltby, old and weary, turned him down.

Not Russell's cleanliness, not his use of *Tyzack's Rhodora Shaving Paste* nor the fact that he was the only one of her ministers she could (almost) look straight in the eye, cut any ice with Queen Victoria; she called him 'a dreadful old man'.

Buckden was also familiar to Lord John's grandson, the second earl Russell, though for rather different reasons – see under **police trap**.

S

Scarborough, Mrs Jane (fl. late 18thC/early 19thC) The years 1816 to 1818 were, to say the least, not kind to Mrs Scarborough, much-respected hostess of the George Inn. Her woes – her family's woes, as it turned out – began in November 1816 when she was accused by the Post Office of having a year earlier stolen a letter containing twenty pounds in order to help pay off her son's debts. In the eight months before she came up for trial, creditors put a lien on both the George and the Bell at Stilton, which was managed by her son from her first marriage. The two inns were links in one of the long-distance stagecoach lines. Other innkeepers in the line immediately decided to bypass the Scarboroughs' premises, thus hugely reducing their value. In the spring of 1817, both she and her son had to attend bankruptcy hearings; the inns and other family properties had to be sold at a substantial loss and the Scarboroughs found themselves without home, business or reputation.

Matters were made worse when legal bungling meant that her case was not tried at the Spring Assize, when she had all her witnesses in place, but was postponed to the 28 July, by when it proved impossible for her to present a convincing defence. The case had attracted widespread interest, and on 4 August the national newspapers reported that she had been found guilty and SENTENCED TO DEATH. The next day, however, the papers admitted that their informant had got it wrong: she had in fact been sentenced to only twelve months' imprisonment in the county gaol. The mistake was understandable: if she had been an employee of the Post Office she could indeed have been hanged.

She had constantly maintained her innocence of the charge. Visiting her in gaol, her lawyer, whose inadequate trial preparation was in large part responsible for her being found guilty, sought to console her by remarking that her case was not the hardest in the world, for he knew of two other innocent people in the gaol who were at that moment 'suffering the punishment due only to the guilty'!

She was not consoled.

Although she was given as comfortable a stay as the gaol could offer, her unhappy year stretched on until her release in August 1818. On the day she was freed, a sympathetic Stamford newspaper proprietor, John Drakard, published an eighty-page pamphlet in which she described her ordeal and pleaded for the justice that had been denied her 'at the hands of a suspicious magistrate, an inattentive advocate, and an ignorant jury'. It is a startlingly direct and vigorous narrative, clearly not all her own work, but not the less effective for that. Its publication was noted by some national journals, and reviewed by at least one of them. The reviewer agreed that her case had been badly conducted, but reluctantly admitted that some of the evidence against her could not easily be explained away.

Her troubles clearly aroused public sympathy; but whether her pamphlet had any practical outcome remains unknown; it seems unlikely. Nonetheless, as the years went by, the possibility that she was innocent became a certainty in village memory – to such an extent that in the 1930s, a respected local historian could firmly assert that Mrs Scarborough's conviction was one of the worst miscarriages of justice in English history.

The 'suspicious magistrate', incidentally, was Dr Maltby, the Vicar of Buckden.

sewerage and sewage disposal. Before the laying of sewers and the construction of a sewage works, sewage or 'night soil' was either discharged into cesspits or septic tanks or into buckets. The bucket was in the little house across the yard known to some as the 'bucket and splash'. One resident claimed that his mother used to use her bicycle to get from the house to the end of the yard. Some yard! An early reference to such arrangements comes in a terrier (inventory) of Buckden vicarage taken in 1709, which refers to 'a little necessary house covered with thatch and walled with rodds and clay' standing at the bottom of an orchard that ran alongside Lucks Lane. Another fraught journey for those in need!

Night-soil was so-called because the excrements from the buckets were collected usually at night and taken away to be spread on the fields as fertiliser. The vehicle used for the purpose was garaged in what is now the Scout Hut in Lucks Lane, along with the refuse lorry.

Bad behaviour or mis-applied high spirits are not new. One resident recalls that one morning a night-soil bucket was found upside down on a street light in the High Street; no other details. Senior villagers were not amused.

In January 1898, the Parish Council was asked to deal with a letter of complaint sent to (and rapidly passed on by) the District Council. The writer drew attention to the nuisance caused by drains in the village, particularly near the Wesleyan Chapel. (As the pump outside the chapel was used to wash out the night-soil cart, this probably came as no surprise.) The Parish Council decided that anything less than a complete reconstruction of the drainage system would be a waste of money, but that the problems were not so bad as to justify so radical an overhaul. It therefore instructed its District Councillors to draw the Sanitary Inspector's attention to certain individual drains.

The laying of sewers is recalled as starting in 1939 but the full scheme proper was begun in the 1950s. We should be grateful that this work was done before the huge increase in motor car numbers. Any narrow street such as Silver Street would have been passable only by nimble pedestrians for several weeks at a time. The alternative route would have been via the High Street.

Silver Street–Laying sewers   Robert Baxter

Something as apparently simple as drain-laying has its dangers. A workman was killed by a fall of soil in a trench in Lucks Lane.

The sewage is treated at the works off Leadens Lane. Effluent was discharged into a ditch running due eastwards across the field to Diddington Brook. The destination is still the brook but the ditch has been diverted along the edge of 'Waterworks Road' to allow more gravel to be won and to create one field from the two before. See also **night-soil collection.**

Shelley. Not the poet, but an unfortunate tax-collector wrongfully imprisoned in Buckden in 1636 by the bishop of Lincoln, who objected to his attempt to assess Buckden for ship-money (a deeply resented tax). A local magistrate promptly released Shelley on bail.

Shelton, Henry (sometimes Harry) Robert (b. 1860) was a Bedfordshire-born cycle dealer who used The Hoo, Church Street, as his home and place of business at the beginning of the 20thC. His landlords were the Green family, who rented out the house while farming the land (Hoo Farm) that went with it. There was clearly money to be made in the cycle business: it is a substantial house.

Sherwood House [MapRef 31] is a late 18thC/early 19thC Grade II listed residence standing on the corner of the High Street and **York Yard** (q.v.). Census returns and directories show it was often occupied by the families of professional men such as horse and cattle doctor Edward Cope (1881, 1891), whose widow, Frances, remained there until her death in 1923; Dr R. A. R. Wallace (1920s); Dr Draper, head of Tollington School (1940s) and some of his pupils; and possibly surgeon Henry Waller (1841, 1851). For a time in the late 1930s it was the Sherwood Private Hotel. It may also have operated as a refined lodging-house earlier in its history: doctors Woolley and Meaney both stayed there when undertaking locum duties. In September 1923 this 'old-fashioned country residence' (the local auctioneers' standard description of virtually every sizeable pre-Victorian house in the village) was bought at auction for £610 by Mr P. N. Burrows, in whose family it remained until 1998.

Shooters Hill Farm, Perry Road, was also known as Linton's Farm (and may at one time have been owned by the Thornhill estate). It lay to the south of the road, opposite the entrance to Buckden Wood Farm. Its size during the 19thC varied between 123 and 174 acres; some of the land was in the parish of Grafham.

The occupier in 1871 was a young, temporarily deaf bachelor called James Topham (1836-1912), middle son of Offord farmer Thomas Topham (whose Stirtloe farmstead was destroyed in an arson attack: see under **fires and fire-fighting equipment**). By 1881, James had married and moved to a larger farm in Perry, where he remained for the rest of his life. Shooters Hill seems not always to have had a farmhouse attached, although there was nearby accommodation for at least one labourer and his family, probably on Perry Road itself. The farm was sold for £3,000 in 1887.

Shooters Hollow Farm, Perry Road, lies to the west of Shooters Hill Farm, and was at one time known as Darlow's Farm, after its occupier.

shops. The row of shops at **Hunts End** (q.v.) is a rather neglected example of the architecture of the 1960s. It was built on the site of a farmstead and barns, including a tithe barn. The fire hooks from the latter are now kept in the shop - once a barn - between the George Hotel and the Vine.

Sherwood House High Street

Although architecturally unexciting, the usefulness of the four shops and flats cannot be denied. Starting from the left-hand side, it is understood that the first shop has always been a grocers and general store, though the wholesaler to which the owners have adhered has changed from time to time. Londis, Spar, DayToday, and Premier, are four. From the spring of 2006 until 2009, the Premier mini-market incorporated a pharmacy, Buckden's first apart from dispensaries in doctor's surgeries.

The second shop has been taken by a number of traders including a hairdresser, a haberdasher and a kitchen installer. In 1992 it became a greengrocery, Top Banana, which was declared best independent retailer in the Huntingdonshire Food and Drink Awards 2008. The third is run as a Chinese takeaway, Sunflower House. The fourth, Knit-Knax, was a newspaper, sweets and stationery store until late in 2009 when it was replaced by the pharmacy.

Short Lane connects Taylors Lane and Hardwick Lane; the name is not often used today, and the road is officially regarded as part of Hardwick Lane.

Silver Street, great fire of: see under **fires and fire-fighting equipment**

Slate Club. A group of people who agree to contribute to a common fund to be used for a specific purpose, such as saving for Christmas or providing small sickness or unemployment payments. One such club was started in the Lion Hotel in January 1909. Members subscribing 3d a week were to be eligible for a 6s weekly sick allowance. Mr William **Wills** (q.v.), bootmaker and sexton, was appointed secretary; he died a few weeks later.

Slippery Road Surfaces Committee. In December 1919, the Minister of Transport asked the Society of County Surveyors to investigate complaints received from horse owners and users that their animals could not keep their footing on the new 'scientific' surfaces designed primarily for motor vehicles. The Society set up the Committee, which also had members co-opted from organizations such as the NFU, the RSPCA and road haulage groups. It was probably inevitable that fourteen months and fourteen meetings later, the committee admitted that it saw no way of finding a surface suitable for both classes of road user, and was therefore concentrating on trying to find an improved 'foot-pad' to replace horseshoes.

This 'solution' did not go down well with farmers and other horse users, who found themselves paying for the upkeep of roads that were no longer safe for them to use. Among them was Buckden's Frederick Pond, who was brought up before the St Neots magistrates for refusing to pay his rates: he claimed that he could no longer earn a living as a carter. The magistrates (horsemen all) were deeply sympathetic, but explained that they could not let him off (but they did waive the court fee).

small, but clean see **Russell, Lord John** and **Wesley, Rev. John.**

Smith, Francis James (b. 1858) was a professor of music (i.e., music teacher) who became a butcher in Buckden. Frank J. Smith, as he was more often known, was the eldest son in the large family of master butcher James Smith, whose shop in Huntingdon (now a bookmakers) was on the corner of George Street and the High Street. Frank was taught music by Thomas Embury, Chelsea pensioner turned bandmaster of the Hunts Militia, and by 1881 was himself teaching music in Folkestone. Asthma forced him to retire to Buckden and the family trade: his butcher's shop was on the Church Street/High Street corner of the Lion Hotel. In October 1890, he founded the Buckden Village Band, helping its members with loans to buy their instruments and uniforms. In 1893 he was elected secretary of the new Buckden and Diddington Horticultural Society (bands and flower shows went together in those days). However, by 1894 he had again exchanged butchery for music, becoming a piano tuner, and by 1901 he had left Buckden to become a professional bandmaster in London.

Alfred Brown (and later his widow, Emma) succeeded him in the shop.

See also **Brass Band, Buckden.**

Smith, J. W. (1869-1950). Mr Smith took over the business of Buckden builders George Page and Son in about 1929. He and his family lived in Montague House on the corner of Hunts End Green. He had four small yards around the village. The office and one yard with a carpenters shop were on the site now occupied by 63 Church Street; Mr Peacock, who was Smith's clerk, lived next door at No. 61. A joiners' shop and yard stood where Hunts End Court now stands. The other two yards were in Silver Street and behind the village school.

Like the Pages, Mr Smith was an undertaker as well as a builder. This was often the case with builders in villages and small country towns, since they were usually the main employers of the local carpenters, who would be responsible for making coffins, sometimes in an evening. As a boy in Buckden, Horace Haynes remembers seeing Jack Cawcutt and Albert Wallis at this aspect of their trade. Come the day of the funeral, Jack would also don his bowler-hat to precede the bier through the streets and oversee the bearers at church and graveside.

Mr Smith was even more versatile than his predecessors: Alan Cockburn, an evacuee from **Tollington School** (q.v.) billeted with the family, recalled that Mr Smith was not only a builder and undertaker, but also a corn merchant, a coal and coke merchant and an insurance agent – besides being a church warden!

The firm was well-known for its church restoration work, Jack Cawcutt being entrusted to undertake whatever required the most skill and experience.

Smith's continued after its founder's death in 1950; it was finally taken over by **Kirton Builders** (q.v.) in the early 1970s.

soup kitchens, and their predecessors, **soup shops**, were an occasional feature of Buckden life in hard times. At Christmastide 1799, for example, the then Bishop of Lincoln, George Pretyman, distributed three meals of meat and bread to 225 poor people of the parish; in the following week he distributed 300 quarts of meat and vegetable broth with bread. The Christmas fare cost him twelve guineas, the soup only two.

Fifty-six years later, the *St. Neots Chronicle* reported that on New Year's Day 1856, the Buckden Soup Kitchen had resumed its twice-weekly distribution of soup. By this time, however, Buckden had no resident bishop and the kitchen was overseen by George Woolley the village doctor, Mr Langley the village's leading shopkeeper and some of the local gentry, including the Greens of Coneygarths and the Misses Mann. Nor was the soup now free: the grateful poor had to pay a halfpenny a quart. This not being enough to cover the full cost, the balance was made up by a list of subscribers – among whom was Dr Maltby, formerly vicar of Buckden, now Bishop of Durham. The *Chronicle* pointedly contrasted his generosity with the absence from the list of the vicar of the day, who apparently refused to contribute towards a charity that helped non-conformists as well as Anglicans.

Food charity was sometimes also distributed on days of celebration. On the occasion of Queen Victoria's Diamond Jubilee in 1897, for example, Mr and Mrs Marshall not only entertained 850 people to tea at The Towers, but ensured that anyone unable to attend received a 'substantial meal' in their own homes; if they were aged, sick or infirm they received a double portion and a gift of tea, sugar and groceries. Any left over food was distributed the next day to 50 or 60 of the village's poorest families.

South, James: see under **charities.**

speed traps: see **police trap.**

Spread Eagle, High Street [MapRef 33]. This Grade II listed building is a former coaching inn. That any of its early architecture survives is surprising, given that much of the property and surrounding area was reported as being destroyed by fire in May 1803 (see under **fires and fire-fighting equipment**).

What remains is a 17thC cross-wing linked by an archway to the inn proper, which dates from the early 18thC and is notable for its large bay windows flanking the front door. There was a hatch in the underside of the arch through which baggage could be passed up from the roof of a coach to the bedroom corridor on the first floor. A similar arrangement was in place at the **Lion** (q.v.).

In 1840, the Spread (as it was commonly known) was one of fifty inns and public houses included in a two-day sale held in St Neots. The auctioneers' notice describes the inn as having 'extensive stabling, a garden, paddocks &c., together with a compact farm of 30 acres, lying at a short distance.'

One of the other lots in the sale may have been the old **Falcon** (q.v.), which stood a few yards to the north of the Spread.

Among the coaches that used the Spread were the Boston, the Leeds Union, and the York Highflyer.

A coach driver was in fact one of its landlords in the 1830s. He was the famous George **Cartwright** (q.v.). His successors included Charles Okins; William Chapman (1840s/1850s); William **Worley** [q.v.] (1860s to 1880s); Diddington-born David Pratt (1880s/1890s) and by 1898, Peter **McLeod** (q.v.). By 1901, Mr McLeod was catering for a new type of customer, the touring cyclist, but as might be expected of a former private coachman, he had not entirely abandoned the horse: he hired out flies.

In July 1908, the then landlord, Mr Ernest Mann, lost a horse in the inn's paddock when it was struck on the head by lightning during one of the worst local storms for several years. There was even more excitement in June 1922, when the Spread was the scene of a highway robbery 'of exceptional audacity': six men in a large car drove off with a Gladstone bag which a Mr and Mrs Crisp of Letchworth had left strapped to their motorcycle and sidecar when they went inside for a drink. The bag was later recovered from under a hedge – minus £8 in sovereigns.

Landlords who came in after the First World War included hairdresser Cecil Sims, and George Edward Brighty. One resident remembers that during the Second World War, Mr Brighty used the well in the backyard as a hiding place for bottles of whisky – or more probably, whiskey, since their provenance was almost certainly some US forces store.

The Spread retained its licence until early in the 21stC,

The Spread Eagle in 1992   David Thomas

when like so many other pubs it succumbed to changing drinking habits. A final attempt to make it viable by giving over one bar to a part-time Thai restaurant did not succeed, and in 2003 the Spread Eagle was closed. It was subsequently sold for redevelopment as private housing – an echo of the 1840s fate of its old neighbour, the Falcon.

See also **earthquake, Buckden hit by small.**

Springfield Close is a residential cul-de-sac off Lucks Lane. For the significance of its name, see **Weir Close.**

spy story: a tale of a Second World War mystery passed down to Leslie Osborn Glessner, who now lives in New Jersey, USA:
'During the war due to the bombing and destruction the government ordered anyone who had extra rooms in their house to take in boarders to relieve the burden of displaced

people. Much against my grandmother's wishes they had to take in a lady boarder who was a stranger to Buckden. My grandmother was not very keen on the idea of a stranger in the house and made her discomfort known to my grandfather rather regularly. After realizing her unjustified complaints were falling on deaf ears she decided to observe the stranger's daily activities. In a very short time she noticed that the stranger would have dinner with them until about 7 p.m. then leave for the evening. The stranger then would not return until late at night well after the pubs had closed. She would then stay in her room and not come out until dinnertime the next day then repeat her daily mission.

So after observing this activity for a few weeks my grandmother decided to pass this information on to my grandfather. At this point my grandfather is working 12 and 16-hour days at his saw mill or doing contractor work on the military airfields. He really did not want to deal with this nonsense since he felt it was just my grandmother wishing the unwanted guest gone. Finally to keep peace in the house my grandfather agreed to follow the stranger's activities one night. So my grandfather follows the stranger to a pub where airmen from the pathfinder's squadron enjoyed themselves.

I am not sure what pub he went to, whether it was a local pub or one far away since my grandfather did have an MG motorcar at the time. Anyway, once in the pub my grandfather noticed the stranger flirting with the airmen and coaxed them to drink but did not drink herself. The stranger at first would make small talk with the airmen about their families or girlfriends. After a few rounds the stranger would move into talking about what missions they had flown or if they were going to fly the next day.

Now my grandfather was convinced my grandmother might be correct in her observations and went to the local constable. The constable told him this information was sort of out of his jurisdiction but would pass it along to the authorities. The next day officials showed up at my grandparent's house eager to talk to the stranger. When they went upstairs to her room they found she and all her belongings had disappeared during the night never to be seen again.

I have told this story to a friend of mine who was involved with the military and understands their methods. He said the stranger was most probably working for the RAF and just trying to see if any airmen had loose lips. So when my grandfather reported his findings to the RAF they just moved their informant elsewhere and made it appear like they were investigating a possible spy. My friend felt no spy would be so obvious but it is the story my grandmother and grandfather told me many years ago.'

St George's Place, High Street, is another name no longer on today's village street map. It was part of the George at a time when the inn went under the name of the George and Dragon (hence, presumably, the 'St'), and had been divided into several tenements. The 1891 census lists 'St George's' as a three room household between the inn itself and the shop on the corner of George Lane (which belonged to William Gale, boot maker and baker). The occupants were young Dr William **Hillyer** (q.v.) and two elderly ladies, a housekeeper and her sister.

St Hugh's Road, a residential thoroughfare, was constructed as part of the late 20thC expansion of Buckden; it runs between Silver Street and the northern end of the High Street.

St Mary the Virgin [MapRef 13] in Church Street, is the parish church of Buckden. Its proximity to the striking remains of the old bishops' palace sometimes leads visitors to overlook its merits. The full story of this fine, predominantly medieval, building and the central role it has played in the life of the village is told in detail in **Chapter 5: A History of St Mary's, Buckden Parish Church**.

stagecoaches to and from London are known to have passed regularly through Buckden before the middle of the 17thC. The trade that these early coaches brought to the village varied according to the season of the year: in summer, the northbound coaches might pause to drop or pick up passengers, but would push on to Huntingdon for the dinner break and then to Stamford for the second overnight stop of the journey (the first having been in Biggleswade). In winter, the timetable had to be adjusted to allow for less daylight, bad weather and deteriorating road surfaces. This meant that Stamford could not be reached until the third evening, the first overnight stop being in Stevenage and the second in Buckden. Travellers of the time wrote bitterly of the dreadful road between Biggleswade and Buckden; thus even in summer poor weather could work to Buckden's advantage by delaying travellers and making them less likely to press on to Huntingdon.

The spread of the railway network put an end to the age of the long distance stage lines, and in 1854 a trade directory spoke of there being 'Not one coach...to be seen in the streets of this once bustling village.' Despite this, the last scheduled coach and four to depart from the George ran for a week in the summer of 1932: it was the *Vivid*, once of the Windsor and Reigate line, and it nightly ran from the inn yard to Buckden Towers, carrying passengers at half-a-guinea a head to see the ***Pageant of the Centuries*** (q.v.).

Stan[c]kes, Will, of Brampton, was Samuel Pepys' bailiff, dealing with the tenants of his land and houses, including his properties in Buckden and Stirtloe. Pepys admired his wife's home-brew: 'small and refreshing, with a taste of Wormewoode'.

Stannard, Henry John [Harry] Sylvester, RBA (1870-1951) was a well-known water-colourist of rural scenes. These were mainly set in Bedfordshire, but he was also active in Buckden between 1911 and 1920. He achieved national renown and enjoyed the patronage of several members of the royal family, including Queen Alexandra and the Duke of Windsor. He was the son of a popular painter, also called Henry and well-known for his landscapes and sporting scenes. His brother, his sister-in-law and his niece were also all professional artists, as was his daughter from his second marriage, Theresa Sylvester Stannard (1899-1944), a water-colourist specialising in gardens. She is also known to have visited Buckden to paint (see **Sycamore House**).

Harry married Violet Kate Page of Buckden (see the following entry).

Stannard, Violet Kate (1883-1969), an accomplished pianist and the youngest daughter of George and Carrie Page of Buckden, became the third wife of Henry John Sylvester Stannard. They married in London in April 1917, at the Hampstead Register Office. On the marriage certificate both gave their address as 35 Parkhill Road, Hampstead. This was the home of H. E. Anstee, a solicitor, who attended the wedding as a witness. The other witness was the daughter of a Methodist minister.

The newly-weds returned to Buckden to live at the Page family home, The Gables. Violet's widowed mother was the head of the household, but she died barely five months after the Stannards' wedding, and the house passed to Violet. (Her sister, Clarissa, already had a home of her own, having married George Hall of Low Farm in 1903. She seems also to have been bequeathed several Page properties, including Nutfield (see **Ellerslie**), Hinsby's corner shop (see **Hinsby family**), two cottages in Church Street, and houses and cottages in Mill Road, all of which she put up for sale in 1920.)

The Gables was a large detached house on the High Street facing the junction of the Great North Road and Perry Road. At that time, the junction would have been literally just over the road from the house not, as now, separated from it by a roundabout and four lanes of traffic.

A view from the house seems the probable subject of a large watercolour which Henry exhibited at the Royal Academy in May 1918. It is catalogued as, 'The group of ancient elms at the corner of Perry Rd [Buckden] – in the evening light with rooks, a sheepfold and an old shepherd at the turnip-cutter making the evening meal for his sheep, a hedge lee, in a rough corner field. The trees silhouetted in the sunset'.

On at least two occasions, Violet gave paintings as wedding presents to Buckden friends; perhaps these, too, were by her husband. Could they still be in the village?

Violet remained in Buckden for the rest of her long life, living in The Gables until 1947, when she moved to Ellerslie, a much smaller house just up the road at 8 High Street.

Barry Jobling

Sterne, Laurence (1713-1768), volatile clergyman and writer, was ordained deacon in Buckden in 1736.

Stirtloe, a hamlet south of Buckden, has a name whose spelling has often caused problems. **Stirtley, Stirtlow, Sturtley** and **Sturtlow** are some of the attempts.

Stirtloe House, Stirtloe Lane [MapRef 50]. This impressive late 18thC country house set in its own park and surrounded by country teeming with game was much admired by 18thC and 19thC gentry in search of a rural retreat within reasonable distance of London. See for example Launcelot **Brown, Reynolds** and **Linton. Chapter 7** describes the history of the house.

stocking factory, 16 Mill Road [MapRef 42]. The large double-fronted house occupied since 2002 by Buckden Day Nursery was for many years a factory producing not just stockings but all manner of knitted goods.

Its first incarnation was as Murray & Co. Ltd, hosiery manufacturers, a firm known to be in existence by 1924. The presence of two colonels and a major (Major Murray) on its board of directors suggests they may have founded it with their war service gratuities or pensions. The major may have been Francis James Stuart Murray, late of the Supply and Transport Corps (India), who was living in The Manor House in 1920, and later moved to Hardwick Dene.

In the early 1930s, the premises became the Buckden Hosiery Mill, owned by the Buckden Hosiery Co, Ltd from Leicester and managed initially by a Mr King, and after him by a Mr Brown who lived at Ellington Thorpe in a house called the Crooked Billet. The father of Mrs Cook from Offord came to Buckden to train the operatives in the use of Jacquard looms.

Between 20 and 30 people are reported to have worked there. Mrs Betty Bunnage (née Stannion) was a quality

inspector. In its heyday the mill's products included Fair Isle jumpers and men's pullovers for Austin Reed, Marshall & Snelgrove and Simpsons of Piccadilly. (The company had an office in London's Regent Street.)

Products in the Second World War included webbing.

No extra buildings were added and so the tennis court behind the house remained, allowing some employees to take advantage of it (see, for instance, under **Gale family**).

In 1957, sample products from the Buckden Hosiery Mill were included in one of the eighty 'treasure chests' carried across the Atlantic on the maiden voyage of the Mayflower II (built to replicate the voyage of the Pilgrim Fathers in 1620). The contents of these chests were subsequently exhibited in several American towns and cities 'to represent the highest standards of British

The one-time Stocking Factory in 1994

manufacture and craftsmanship'.

The company was dissolved in May 1972. Subsequent owners or occupiers of the premises included Old Mill Enterprises (Services) Ltd; Bi-Electric Limited; Scanlec Ltd; Stonecare, a specialist building company, and STACS, which until 1998 ran an industrial training and consultancy centre. In early 2000, the building was occupied by Sedgemoor College of Hertfordshire. (Some local residents were unhappy to learn that teenage children from that county with 'severe learning difficulties' were to be tutored here.) The college closed in 2002, and later that year the building was taken over by its present occupant, the Day Nursery.

Stoneham, Miss Elizabeth Reading [or Redden] (1872-1942) was the eldest daughter of Buckden plumber, decorator, and fire chief William Stoneham and his wife Catherine [Redder]. A good dressmaker, she was employed by the Hon. Mrs Rosa Duberly of Gaynes Hall as a lady's maid and stayed on to become her 'faithful friend and companion' for 55 years. Her funeral service at St Mary's drew a large congregation, among whom was her cousin Mrs Harry Worley. Mr Harry Worley was unable to attend, being in the County Hospital; the night before Miss Stoneham's death he had been found in the road near Buckden Station having fallen from – or been knocked off – his bicycle while returning from Home Guard duties.

Also absent was Mrs Duberly herself, too frail to travel at the age of 95. But the wreaths and flowers included 'lovely floral tributes' from her and Arthur and Brenda. Arthur and Brenda were her Pekinese.

Suffolk, dukes of, two buried in same tomb. A table-tomb near the east end of St Mary's Church is said to cover the bodies of Henry Brandon, (1535——-14 July 1551) and his younger brother Charles (1537/8–14 July 1551), respectively the second and third Dukes of Suffolk. They died within an hour of one another, victims of the fifth and (to date) last major outbreak of the 'English sweate', a frighteningly rapid and lethal malady whose causes are still unknown and much debated. The brothers were students at Cambridge when the disease struck the city in the summer of 1551. By the time their mother sent them to Buckden for safety, they had already been infected. The absence of contemporary burial records means we have no idea whether this resulted in other deaths in Buckden (rural communities are thought to have been particularly susceptible).

Sunnyside, 14 High Street: see **Valency House.**

Sutter, Robert Ross MD Aberd MC CM MRCS LRCP was a Warboys doctor who provided locum services to Buckden after Dr Williams died. He was succeeded by a characterful Australian, R. A. R. Wallace.

Swan End is one of three streets off Vineyard Way named after birds, though it serendipitously commemorates both the Swan, a beer-house believed to have once stood nearby, and Buckden benefactor George Cornelius Swan, who paid for the erection of a workhouse not far away on Mill Road.

Sycamore House, 16 High Street, is a Grade II listed townhouse dating from the late 18thC. The name does not appear in any of the county directories that are readily accessible for Buckden, making it difficult to identify past residents. We do, however, know firstly that it was the surgery and family home of Dr Morris from 1964 to 1969; and secondly that the painter Theresa Sylvester Stannard stayed there in about 1916, and perhaps on other occasions as well: she and her father, the artist Henry John Sylvester **Stannard** (q.v.) made several painting trips to Buckden in the second decade of the 20thC.

sycamores, odd, in Buckden. In 1925, two sycamores were found to be flourishing in the roof an old brick kiln. They were in no way connected to the earth as their roots were visible hanging in the air on the underside of the roof.

See also **ash, elm** and **plane.**

T

Taylors Lane once joined the High Street to the fields and woods to the west of the village; the re-routing of the A1 in 1962 cut it in half. Both halves still share the same name, as though the highways authority could not resist the chance to confuse and infuriate strangers to Buckden.

The lane may have been named for the Taylor family, who occupied what is now No. 93 High Street. Taylors appear in the parish registers, in various spellings, from the middle of the seventeenth century. They included blacksmiths, plumbers, castrators and glaziers. At its sale in 1892, No. 93 was described as a substantial brick and tiled four-bedroomed dwelling-house, with an enclosed paved yard, dairy, cellar, pump, WC, bidet, barn and other conveniences.

It is also possible that the lane received its name in the middle ages, long before there was a blacksmith – or a house – at No. 93: this may have been the route that took the bishops of Lincoln's 'tailleurs' or woodcutters to and from their work among the trees and coppices of the Great Park.

telephone kiosk, High Street. Buckden's smallest listed building (Grade II) is a Type K6 cast iron kiosk made to the classic design that architect Giles Gilbert Scott produced for George V's silver jubilee in 1935. Vandalism and mobile phones threaten to reduce it to the status of an ancient monument in spite of BT giving it a new but possibly temporary lease of life as a card-only kiosk.

telephone service. Buckden has had a telephone exchange for many years. The first – a manual exchange – was in Aragon House on the corner of St Hugh's Road and High Street. As was usually the case it was rumoured that the operators knew as much about the subscribers' business as anyone and could save the cost of a phone call by telling a caller that the intended recipient had gone out. There were more than 40 lines available in 1931.

The second exchange was in a purpose-built structure in Lucks Lane almost opposite the Scout Hut. It has been converted into a dwelling. The third and present utilitarian building is in George Lane.

The name of one of the first 'telephone clerks', perhaps the first, appears in the 1901 census. She was Hilda Jessie Shearn, the 18 year old daughter of a Wesleyan minister, and seems to have 'lived in' with her employers, the Langley sisters.

In the Kelly's Directory for 1910, the George Hotel is shown as having a National Telephone Company call office. (A call office was usually a wooden kiosk in which you could operate the telephone yourself or, if you were particularly timid or refined, have an attendant make the connection for you). Photographs of the time show the south-east corner of the building dominated by a large telegraph pole.

The National Telephone Company (NTC) had been founded in 1881; it was far from being national and was not noted for its efficiency. From 1892 onwards it became government policy to take over and extend the NTC's trunk network. The full transfer of the company's plant, property, assets and staff finally took place on 1 January 1912.

See also under **police.**

tennis in Buckden. Tennis as we know it today began in England in the second half of the 19thC (the first tennis club was started in Leamington in 1872). Originally an amusement for army officers, it eventually spread through all classes of society and around the world. Houses in Buckden where lawn tennis is known to have been played by or around the end of the 19thC include Ellerslie in Perry Road – a sale notice of 1898 reveals that it had two courts – and Jessamine House in the High Street. The latter's grass court still has an unusual pavilion thought to be late Victorian or early Edwardian, with two changing rooms. There were also courts at, among others, The Gables, Oak Lawn, Nutfield and the Towers (later dug up in the interests of archaeology by R H Edleston!).

It was not until 1934, however, that a village tennis club was established. It was founded by members of Buckden Bowls Club, whose Silver Street site it shared (along with the mosquitoes from the Towers fishpond). The club's first grass court was followed by a second in 1935.

As with the bowls club, women were welcomed as members from the start. To encourage the young (of both sexes), a junior section was formed in 1948.

The 1950s were a period of expansion and innovation. The club's first two annual singles trophies were donated in 1954 – the Patrick Cup for ladies and the Nutfield Cup for men. Within two years, friendly matches were being played against as many as thirteen neighbouring clubs. The following year, 1957, saw play allowed for the first time on Sundays (but not during the hours of church services!). Club funds were 8s. 6d, but rose to £4. 4s. 5d in 1958, a year that also brought the club its third trophy, the Greta-Osborne Glessner Cup for the under-sixteens.

The 1960s, however, initially saw a decline in membership. The courts were closed in 1964 for lack of playing members, which at least had the merit of allowing them to be partially re-turfed. Club funds varied wildly: £4. 5s. 0d in 1966 (when the club finally became independent of the bowls club), and nil in 1967! Spurred on by this, a few dedicated members came together in 1968 to improve finances and membership. Before the end of the year, a membership of fifteen had become seventy-six, funds stood at £4. 1s. 0d, a programme of monthly fund-raising events had been established and a team had been entered in the new Hunts/Peterborough League. All this led to the club ending the decade with all its debts paid off and £20. 18s. 0d in the bank.

The 1970s brought great changes to the club, including a new home and the end of play on grass. In 1972, the club was offered the use of a piece of the village recreation ground sufficient to accommodate three courts and a pavilion – with the proviso that the club had to raise the money for any works needed to make the land suitable for play. As it was flooded for much of the year, the committee decided that grass would be an impracticable surface and that the club should go over to hard courts. Six-foot high fencing was erected around the whole site, and the first court constructed. The cost of the work was mainly funded by grants and loans, with the balance coming out of club funds. By the end of that year, there were seventy-two members and £76 in the funds; by the end of 1979 these figures had increased to 120 and £630. Membership had fluctuated in the intervening years, but the club's financial position remained sound, enabling it to contribute to the cost of the second and third hard courts (in 1975 and 1980) and to meet the whole cost of erecting a clubhouse and storage shed in 1976. These buildings heralded the club's formal move from Silver Street to the new site, which was now held on a twenty-one-year lease from the Parish Council.

Throughout the decade, the club continued to enter teams in the local leagues, often meeting with success. Two more trophies were donated for internal club competitions: the Romulus Cup for mixed pairs (1971), and the Peter Smith Cup for men's pairs (1979).

This pattern of consolidation and improvement of facilities and success in external competitions continued through the 1980s, with membership reaching over 250 shortly after the club celebrated its first fifty years in 1984. The surround fencing, renewed to between nine and twelve feet high, was augmented on the car park side by a conifer hedge. The three existing courts were resurfaced, and a fourth constructed in 1989. A perimeter drainage system was excavated. Two new trophies were donated: the Caroline and Andrew Pook Shield for under-12s singles, and the Park Cup, which replaced the Romulus Cup for mixed pairs. The club's league successes included divisional wins and promotions for several teams, and the lifting of the Don Brace Cup in 1985. In 1989 the club and the parish council entered into a second twenty-one-year lease.

The 1990s brought both successes and frustrations. Buckden continued to shine in league competitions, with the club becoming the first ever to have three teams playing in the top division in the same season. In 1993 the ladies won the final of the Grays k/o Cup, and the mixed team the Don Brace Cup (again). A new internal trophy, the Albert Dudley Memorial Cup, was donated for mixed veterans pairs.

The planned expansion of the club facilities, however, ran into difficulties, practical and legal. As a result, an ambitious project to extend the clubhouse and floodlight courts three and four required four years and fifteen meetings to reach completion. In the end, all came good and in 1997 a new (rather than extended) clubhouse was officially opened by the then Prime Minister, John Major, in the presence of local and league dignitaries and many members. (Courts one and two had to wait until 2005 to be floodlit.)

A feature of the early years of the new century has been the club's success in attracting young players. The need for this became clear in 2001, when the under-12s singles competition had to be cancelled for lack of entries. The following year saw the first Saturday morning 'Fun Hour', when the courts were set aside for any youngster, member or not, wanting to play or practice. This continues to be popular, with some Saturdays having as many as fifty participants. Coaching sessions and a summer camp have helped build up a strong junior presence. The 2005 season, for example, saw three boys teams entered in the National Club Junior League, and two boys win through to the regional finals of the Road to Wimbledon National 14 and Under Challenge. Further encouragement came with the donation of the Norman Poulter Trophy for the most improved junior member.

It is a mark of the dedication of so many members and hard-working officials that nearly 70% of the £114,000 spent on the projects described has been met from club funds.

Maurice Pepper

Theatre Club: see drama in Buckden.

The Gables, High Street [MapRef 19], was erected some time between 1903 and 1910 by George Page, one of the area's most respected builders, as his family home. It was (and still is) what one would expect from a successful Edwardian businessman: a substantial detached house in gault brick with red brick banding, complete with cellar, stableyard, large gardens and tennis court. The kitchen still has the original servants' bell panel (although we know of only one live-in servant, eighteen-year old Florrie Kent, the step-daughter of a horse keeper on a farm in Mr Page's home village of Hail Weston).

The house stands to the east of Buckden roundabout, where the High Street joins the A1. In the 1900s, the Perry Road junction would have been much closer than it is now, literally just across the road.

Mr Page did not long enjoy his new home: he died in 1912. His widow continued to live there until her own death in September 1917, when the house passed to her recently married youngest daughter, who lived there for much of the rest of her long life.

See **Stannard, Violet Kate.**

The Grove, a residential enclave off Glebe Lane, was previously a paddock attached to 'Foyers' in Lucks Lane, owned by Walter Milner, in which he kept two donkeys,

Mary and Joseph. (Hence a proposal, made to the parish council but rejected by the developers, that it be called Bray Close.)

The Hoo, Church Street [MapRef 3], a large Edwardian house, began life as a Georgian farmhouse, traces of which have survived the rebuilding undertaken in the 1900s by, almost certainly, the builders G. Page & Son. (The 'Son' of the partnership, George Thomas Page, moved into the house in 1913, and remained there until his death twenty-five years later; his widow continued to live there.)

Later in the 20thC, The Hoo became nationally known as the home of Herbs from the Hoo, an enterprise run by Elizabeth and Reginald Peplow. Among their admired products was the Hoobag, a small sack of mixed herbs. When hung in a car, its lemony aroma neutralised the smell of stale cigarette smoke and other unwanted odours.

See also **Hoo Farm.**

The Osiers is a residential cul-de-sac off Lucks Lane. For the significance of its name, see **Weir Close.**

The Towers (also known as **Buckden Towers**) **[MapRef 26]** is built on the site of the former **Buckden Palace,** the remains of which are a monument to the influence of the bishops of Lincoln on the religious and political life of England from the 12thC to the early 19thC. Their presence also brought added prosperity to the inhabitants of what might otherwise have been a convenient but unremarkable way-station on the Great North Road, as well as the occasional excitement of visits by great personages of the day.

No doubt the excitement wore off – ('I see that Pitt the Younger fellow's hanging about the bishop again. Time 'e growed up and stood on his own two feet.') – but at least they must have been better informed about the world beyond the parish boundaries than many villagers.

The Palace became The Towers in 1872, when the house was built for the Marshall family. In 1919, its new owner Robert Holmes **Edleston** (q.v.) reverted to the old name in both its forms, sometimes The Palace and sometimes Buckden Palace.

Since 1947, after a century or so of variable fortunes, Buckden Towers has reclaimed its strength and peace as a retreat and conference centre run by the Claretian Missionaries.

Its architectural importance is explored in **Chs 3** and **4**; its historical importance is a theme running through the whole book.

Thomas, John (1691-1766) was Bishop of Lincoln (1740-61) and Salisbury (1761-66). He was best known for having a sense of humour, four wives and a squint (bizarrely, Salisbury had three bishops in 1761, two of whom were called John Thomas and had a squint). He claimed that his first three wives sank into lethargy and death because he never argued with them. It was said that the following motto was inscribed on the ring he wore for his fourth wedding:

'If I survive,
I'll make them five'

Thomson family. A remarkably inventive Buckden family of carpenters, builders and agricultural machinists. On 9 December 1859, James Thomson and his sons Robert and Henry 'all of Buckden, in the county of Huntingdon' were granted patent No. 2799 for their invention for 'An improved agricultural implement.' At the time, James was forty, Henry seventeen and Robert only nine! On 31 October 1862, Henry branched out into a different line of

"The Towers" built in 1872.
St Hugh's late 20thC statue in the foreground.

business with provisional patent No. 2944 for an invention for 'Improvements in railway signals'.

The family were still at it some fifty years later. In March 1899 the *St. Neots Advertiser* reported that Mr J. Thomson was patenting an improved hoe, and in February 1900 that he had applied for a patent 'for an adjustable double or multiple brush or squeegee.' Only a few weeks later, on 28 April, it was the turn of another member of the family: 'Mr H. Thomson has taken out a patent for an improved tobacco pipe.' These may have been sudden bursts of millennial inspiration, but it seems more likely that further research will reveal there had been other patents applied for and possibly granted in the intervening years. Certainly a company, the Phoenix Memnon Company Limited, with a capital of £1,600 in £8 shares, was registered in 1882 to construct and supply mechanical and electrical appliances; in practice, it was set up to take over the business of James Thomson senior.

In 1861, the family (except for Henry whose whereabouts are obscure) was living in **Bakers Lane** (q.v.); From 1871 onwards, the censuses show most of them as living on the south side of Church Street, towards Hunts End, though Henry for a time lived in and managed the Lion and Lamb, having married the previous host's widow.

See also **Langley family** and **Osborn, Eliphaz**

Thornhill Estate. Although the Thornhill family had their seat at Diddington Hall (described in 1854 as 'a good modern mansion with a small but picturesque park'; demolished in 1962), they held land and property in several parishes in at least three counties. Towards the end of the 19thC, they are recorded as being one of Buckden's chief landowners, along with the church, the Lintons of Stirtloe, William Bowyer and the Green family. In the early 18thC, one of their properties was the **George** Inn (q.v.). See also the **Mitre.**

Throckmorton, Robert (c. 1662-1699) was one of the MPs for Huntingdonshire 1698-1699. Born in America, he lived in Stirtloe from the late 1680s until 1693, when he bought, and moved to, the manor of Little Paxton. He was a member of the 'Country' Party (forerunner of the Whigs) but 'left little, if any, impression on the House [of Commons]'.

Thurlow, Thomas (1737-91) was – at times simultaneously – Master of the Temple, Dean of St Paul's and Bishop of Lincoln (1779-87), after which he became Bishop of Durham. It was said the qualities that carried him to such high office in the church were 'great energy and vast legal talent'; only they weren't his own, they were those of his brother the Lord Chancellor. There seems to be no record of what he thought of Buckden, but in June 1780 he probably wished he was there rather than in London: he got caught up in the Gordon Riots and had to escape from the mob by scrambling across the rooftops disguised as a woman.

Tollington School. The boys from this North London school were evacuated from to Buckden for the first few years of the Second World War. Staff and pupils were billeted with families around the village, but met for lessons in the Towers.

For vivid descriptions of what it was like to be an evacuee, see the articles by Alan Cockburn, Alec Owen and Harold Randall in **Chapter 17.**

Top Farm, west of the A1, was the site of a decoy airfield during the Second World War. This was not a comfortable role to play, but the original alternative sought by the USAAF – to plough it up and lay a real airfield – might have been even more traumatic in the long as well as the short term. Buckden was fortunate that the ministers of food and agriculture successfully argued that land of such productive quality would best serve the nation by feeding it.

town. Buckden has usually been called a village, although sometimes in a way that suggested it was bordering on being a small town ('A large and respectable village' – Cassey's Directory 1862; 'A large and populous village' – Post Office Directory 1854). Some legal documents, such as the agreements listed in the minute books of the early 18thC turnpike trust, speak of the 'town of Bugden'. Residents would occasionally refer to it as a town: the first field at the east end of the village was called 'Town's End Close', and in an 1864 court case a man mentioned meeting his son 'coming from the town'. But in both cases 'town' clearly meant the built-up area of the village as opposed to the surrounding countryside.

It came as something of a surprise, therefore, in March 2001 when the Parish Council was told that under English Heritage's 'Extensive Urban Survey', Buckden had been designated one of Cambridgeshire's thirty historic towns. Not all residents were happy with this – not because it seemed historically wrong but for a more practical reason: a house in a village is a more desirable residence (i.e., worth more) than the same house would be in a town.

Estate agents will be relieved to know that at the time of writing (2009), Buckden is still officially a village.

Town's End Close was a field beyond Oak Lawn, the most easterly house in the village. Paradoxically the next, even more easterly piece of land, was called the Home Field.

Travill, Susannah was a 17thC benefactress (see under **charities**). She is not to be confused with Susannah Travel, a lady of 'no questionable character' who in 1830 was convicted at Huntingdon Assizes of stealing £22 from farmer Thomas Gale, and sentenced to transportation for life (and possibly to a reunion with her husband, who had been transported some years previously).

tribunals, local military. A grim feature of life during the First World War, these tribunals assessed whether men were undertaking civilian work of sufficient importance to the war effort to justify their being given total or partial exemption from military service. In one week in 1916, there were nine cases from Buckden alone.

Most applications to tribunals were from employers seeking to retain essential workers; in the case of family businesses, as many were, this often meant a father or mother pleading to save their son. Sometimes applicants sought exemption for themselves. At one such hearing, a Buckden tradesman successfully argued that, much as he would like to answer the call to arms, he was the only man in the village with his particular, vital skills. This drew a sharp response in the following week's newspaper from another Buckden resident who pointed out that he, too, had the same skills (albeit as an employee rather than self-employed) and being past military age was not liable to be called up, so 'Mr S------ need hesitate no longer to put himself at the disposal of his country.'

The tribunals were no respecters of persons: a lady of the Duberly family appeared before an appeal panel to argue the case for retaining a young horse-keeper and was told in no uncertain terms that she had no idea of what she was talking about.

trouble at' mill: see **explosion.**

Turk, Frances (1915-2004). Not every village can say that it had an author of sixty or more published novels living within its bounds for most of her life. The books were written in long-hand, and nearly all were published by Wright and Brown from the 1930s down to 1969. Copies of fifty-nine of her titles may be seen in the Local History Reserve of Huntingdon Library. Ulverscroft large print editions are also to be found. In general they may be described as romantic novels.

Miss Turk came to Buckden in 1925 with her parents and lived in Lucks Cottage for a year while the new bungalow in Brampton Road was being completed and its well commissioned. She was old enough to attend Huntingdon Grammar School and did so until obtaining her school certificate. Thanks to her father she also learnt shorthand and typing and on the strength of these and possibly some paternal influence started work for the electricity supply company office in St Neots to which she cycled daily. She had a number of jobs after that including one at the mill in Godmanchester where Farmers Glory Wheat flakes were made. Later she helped to provide a library service for Buckden: she delivered books driving an Austin 7 van. The Women's Voluntary Service in Huntingdon employed her on office duties, and from 1940 to 1948 she was Assistant County Secretary for the Huntingdonshire, Cambridgeshire and Ely Women's Land Army.

Miss Turk started writing while she had paid employment. One of her novels 'Angel Hill' was written between June and October 1941 and took up about 570 pages of quarto paper. All the corrections were done in the longhand version. When complete the whole was then typed on a Patria portable typewriter bought through a salesman who called at the WVS office. She had a study in the garden at the family home in Brampton Road where she could write undisturbed. Her father worked at home as an accountant and used the dining room table for his business so 'they always ate in the kitchen'.

The Women's Institute was a long-term interest of Miss Turk. At various times she was President of the Buckden branch or its delegate to the national conferences and also Voluntary County Organiser.

In later years she came into the village to live at the Burberry Homes, and for the last months of her life moved to Rose Cottage at Broughton.

turnpikes. A turnpike road was one run by a trusts whose costs were met by fees charged at toll-gates. See **Chapter 18** for a description of the turnpiked road that ran through Buckden.

U

Union Chapel, High Street [MapRef 34]. This small place of non-conformist worship was built in what had been the backyard of a public house, the Falcon, which was sold and closed down in about 1840. In the 1861 census it is referred to as 'the Primitive Methodists' Chapel'.

Over the years the congregation dwindled and in 1862 the chapel had to be closed. In the summer of 1905 the congregation celebrated the renovation of the chapel and the erection of a new schoolroom; the pastor at the time was the Rev. **Hurditch** (q.v.). The Rev. Cornelius Mensink was in charge of the Buckden pastorate (it included Spaldwick) between 1923 and 1926 (see also under **motorcycles**). He was succeeded by the Rev. W. Smith, who left in 1929. A later pastor was the Rev. C. E. Duffy, who left in 1936. The building remained in religious use as a joint Baptist and Congregational chapel until 1984, when it was converted to a contract furnishings showroom. A plaque dedicated to four men of the congregation who died in the First World War was removed during renovations in 2000 and taken to Trinity Baptist Church, Perry.

In 2006, the chapel was converted to a house, The Old Chapel.

Usher family. This large and long-established family was at the heart of Buckden life for over 200 years, both commercially – as shopkeepers, skilled tradesmen and beer-sellers – and as holders of public offices, such as parish clerk or collector of taxes.

V

vaccination. Parental concerns about 'jabs' are nothing new. Vaccination against smallpox first became compulsory in 1853; from 1867, parents and guardians could be repeatedly fined for refusing to have their children vaccinated. This severe approach caused public unease: many people felt that children should not be exposed to the associated risks, especially as the alarming array of symptoms caused by a vaccination sore gone wrong - snuffles, thrush, nodes on the head, bubo in the armpit, phagedaenic sores, abscesses and eruption on the infant's genitals – included some that suggested that some vaccine might be contaminated with syphilis. A Royal Commission was appointed to review all aspects of vaccination. This took so long that a fifth of its members had died before it issued its final report in 1896/7. However, the government responded swiftly with the Vaccination Act 1898, which included a provision whereby people could obtain an exemption if they satisfied the local magistrates that they 'conscientiously believed' that vaccination would be prejudicial to the health of their child.

This part of the act came into force in August 1898. One of the first people to seek an exemption certificate was Buckden market gardener John Leaden (of Leadens Lane). In October, the St Neots bench accepted his application, which was based on the fact that vaccination had caused one of his children to break out in sores.

The child in respect of whom he sought the exemption was a son, Joseph Herbert. Sadly, the boy died early the next year – but of bronchitis, not smallpox. He was six months old.

Curiously, 33% *more* children were vaccinated in the year after the new Act than in the year before: exemption applied: confirmation, perhaps, of the Victorians' resistance to being bullied by government into doing something that most of them were reasonably happy to do of their own free will.

Valency House, 14 High Street, is a Grade II listed 18thC house. The name is relatively new: it was previously known as Sunnyside. Unusually for Buckden, the house stands at right angles to the street: most people of the time rich enough to build a substantial house preferred to present its façade to the passing world. It emphasised their new status.

Valley, The. The preferred name for the conservation area south of Manor Gardens and west of the playing-fields. The stretch of water that forms its main feature is known as the Lake; to call it a pond in the hearing of a Buckden resident is to invite a sharp correction. On the other hand, to call it the **Canal** (q.v.) shows one is aware that there is more than one theory about its origins.

Vellacott, George Harold (1920-2008). 'Buckden man's name will live on in London' said the local paper in November 1989. The man was George Vellacott OBE MA, holder of the Housing Corporation and National Federation of Housing Associations Certificate in Housing Association Finance and Administration. Mr Vellacott settled in Manor Gardens in 1983 and became active in village affairs, joining the Village Hall Trust, the British Legion and the Parish Council; he was particularly interested in the parochial charities. A varied life before coming to Buckden had included Second World War service in Burma with the Royal Engineers, 20 years with the Church Missionary Society in Nigeria and 20 years with the Postgraduate Medical School at Hammersmith Hospital, first as its secretary and then, from 1972, as the project manager for the Ducane Housing Association. The Association was set up to purchase and develop nearby land to provide accommodation for the hospital's postgraduate students and their families, an aim that had been unsuccessfully pursued for many years but was finally achieved with the opening of five residential blocks in 1976-77. A further block was opened in 1989 and named Vellacott House.

vermin. Acts of Parliament passed in Tudor times allowed churchwardens to pay from the parish rate a bounty for certain animals which were considered to be pests. Buckden churchwardens listed details of the vermin bounty in their account book (1627-1774). Mole-catching required some expertise, and attracted payment at the rate of 9d a dozen; in the twenty-year period 1632-1653, 2,227 moles were accounted for, but for some reason very few were recorded after that. Hedgehogs were believed to steal milk from cows and dozens were turned in for every decade in the book. The rate paid varied from 1d each in the 1630s to 4d each in the 1720s. Polecats are no longer found in Huntingdonshire, but the account book suggests they were common throughout the period. The reward for killing a polecat was 1d at the beginning of the accounts and 4d at the end. Bounty payments for foxes were usually paid to a huntsman, and they and badgers rated a shilling each. Otters appear only twice, in spite of their being worth 3s 4d each in 1731. Only five weasels, at 2d each, were recorded. In the 18thC sparrows became the target of systematic extermination: in 16 years from 1717 well over 8,000 sparrows and eggs were destroyed – the birds fetched 2d a dozen and their eggs 1d a dozen. Animals that were specifically mentioned in the Vermin Acts but absent from the Buckden records included stoats, rats and mice.

Rabbits and rooks were not mentioned then, but their killing was encouraged during the Second World War; the war also put sparrows back in the firing-line (eggs 2d a dozen, heads 3d a dozen), together with rats, pigeons and cabbage-white butterflies.

It is tempting to draw conclusions about the early modern ecology of Buckden from the bounty figures: in particular the ubiquity of polecats reflects a wooded landscape (see **deer park**) while the determined effort to eliminate sparrows may indicate the increasing importance of arable farming.

veterinary surgeons were not always people with an educational qualification in animal husbandry – or indeed, with any education at all. Before there was a veterinary profession, it could be used to describe anyone thought by his or her neighbours to have a gift for healing animals. In 19thC Buckden these included:

J. Searle (Post Office Directory 1869)
Edward Cope, 'Horse and cattle doctor' of Sherwood House, High Street (Kelly's Directory 1890)
John Favill aka Shepherd Favill.

vicarages. The Old Vicarage **[MapRef 12]**, as it is now known, stands on the corner of Church Street and Lucks Lane and is now in private hands. The Commonwealth survey in 1648 recorded a building 'of timber & covered with tile, hall, parlor, kitchen, five chambers, beerhouse, three barns, stables, garden, orchard, barnyard, close abutting street to North', which was occupied by Edward Powell. Much of this was pulled down, but parts of these earlier buildings may still remain on the vicarage site.

The vicarage was re-fronted in 1783 by Jacob Leroux, a well-known (but not universally respected) architect and speculative builder. However, a more thorough rebuilding was undertaken only a dozen years later, probably prompted by the very severe winter of 1794/5 and the arrival of a new vicar, the Rev. Edward **Maltby** (q.v) in 1794. A fine Georgian double-bayed vicarage was constructed in the summer of 1795. A mortgage for £260 was taken out, signed by Maltby, Bishop George **Pretyman** (q.v), Archdeacon John Pretyman and John **Hodgson** (q.v.), the bishop's clerk, to cover the expenses as follows:

Thomas and John Hipwell, Buckden Brickworks in West Field, 1 June-18 August 1795; 36,000 bricks at £1/10s/0d per 1,000, £54
Charles Clark, bricklaying & labourers, tiling, plastering £92
Thomas Mahew, scaffolding & hair £2
John Lindsell, timber £10
William Ayers work £12
Thomas & William Usher, nails, screws, laths £10

"The old vicarage"　　　　　　　　　　Barry Jobling

William Usher, sand timber poles hair and carriage from Huntdn; clay hard lath, fir lath and carriage of fir timber from St Ives £16
Henry Maule, lime poles, deals, one piece of Riga timber 40feet long £3/6s/8d
ditto, polished flag stones, delivered 3 April-6 July 1795 £98

This vicarage was sold in 1980; its replacement, at 16 Church Street, was completed and handed over to the Rev. Stanley Griffiths on 13 August 1981. It was built on former Palace land at a cost of £80,000. See also **sewerage** and **water supply.**　　　　　　　　　　　　　Barry Jobling

Village Hall, Burberry Road. The hall succeeded the **Rifle Range** (q.v.) and preceded the **Millennium Community Centre** (q.v.) as the recreational centre of Buckden. See **Chapter xx.**

Vine, The, 33-35 High Street [MapRef 21]. The building housing Buckden's only remaining traditional pub dates from the 18thC, but there was an inn on this site in the early years of the 17thC. We know this from the record of legal proceedings held between 1650 and 1653, in which Elizabeth Kirby, a London merchant's wife, sought to regain possession of 'a freehold messuage and 25 acres called Le Hyne in Buckden' which had been left to her as a child, after the deaths of her father and mother in 1615. Before she could enjoy her inheritance, however, it had been taken away from her by William Clement. Since then, it had been sold at least four times and by 1650 was in the hands of Thomas Jackson, Gent.

The grounds of the dispute were whether the property had been subject to a mortgage, and if so, whether the mortgage had been discharged before the death of Elizabeth's parents. If it had, Mr Clement and all the subsequent purchasers were entitled to possession; if not, the property should have remained with Elizabeth.

There followed a long-drawn out examination of the conflicting claims. This involved sundry aged Buckden residents – yeomen, labourers, 'gents' and craftsmen – trying to recall what had happened in the preceding 35 thirty-five years.

From them we learn that 'Le Hyne' was indeed an inn called the Vine, and that even before 1613 it had been 'very old and ruinous', the owners at the time having cut down all the trees in its orchard, demolished a barn and a hovel [a framework for a corn-stack], and left the rest of the property to decay. Repair and restoration had cost William Clement and his successors dear.

Nobody could remember the existence of a mortgage, nor was there a record of it in the court rolls. One witness claimed Elizabeth Kirby's father had 'confessed' to having sold all his estate in Buckden, i.e. outright, without mortgage or other encumbrance. 'Confessed' suggests he had not told his family of this.

Fascinating as it is to hear across the centuries the actual words of long-dead ancestors, the papers are frustratingly silent on the outcome of the proceedings. All that one can say is that the incomplete evidence we have is more favourable to Thomas Jackson's cause than Elizabeth Kirby's.

(One of the yeomen witnesses was a Robert Raymont; he is probably the Robert Rayment who at his death in 1661 left money for the employment of a schoolmaster to teach poor children – see under **charities**).

The southern end of the rebuilt Vine of the 18thC incorporated a stable with a hayloft over. The dividing line between stable and inn remains clear even now: the inn walls are rendered, but the stable is only painted, with the outlines of its brickwork showing through. The Vine was also a brewery.

vineyards. According to a correspondent in *Notes & Queries*, Vol. 2 (57) 30/11/ 1850 p. 446

'In the fields between Buckden and Diddington, in the county of Huntingdon, there is what is called 'the Vineyard' at the present day; and connected therewith is what is called, and evidently from the shape has been, a fish pond....there is no doubt but what the above was, in olden times, belonging to a religious house in that part.'

In the Middle Ages viticulture was practised over a large part of England, including the north, and was almost always associated with monasteries and other religious foundations. The Domesday Book does not mention vineyards in its description of Buckden, but they are likely to have been introduced once the Palace became the principal residence of the Bishop of Lincoln in the mid 13thC. The leasing of 'closes and vineyards' by the queen (Elizabeth I) to the bishop of the day is referred to in 1558/9. There were several acres of vines, known as the great and the little vineyards, and as the name of the modern road **Vineyard Way** suggests, they were situated in the area of what is now the recreation ground.

Thanks to the enterprise of members of the Wine and Beermakers Society, vine-growing has returned to Buckden in recent years, though not as yet on a commercial scale.
The Claret Centre at Buckden Towers is not, to the disappointment of some visitors to Buckden, the Society's headquarters.

W

Wallace, Robert Allez [sometimes Allen or Aller] Rotherham was one of Buckden's more colourful doctors – see **Chapter 14 Medical Practice in Buckden**.

Wallage, John (c. 1854-1939). The Cambridgeshire-born son of a woodsman, he was Buckden's resident policeman from 1887 until his retirement in 1900 on a pension of £47.13s a year. He married Sarah Smith (1853-1911) in 1883. They lived in the Buckden police house, which was then at the southern end of the village. After nearly twenty-eight years on the force he retired to Little Paxton. The *St. Neots Advertiser* praised the way he had 'discharged his important and oft-times unpleasant duties with zeal, conscientiousness and tact, and gained the esteem of all classes.' In line with his image as a 'proper' village bobby, he played in the village cricket team and won prizes for gooseberries, blackcurrants and roses at the Buckden Horticultural Society's first annual flower show in 1893.

He was succeeded by Pc John Purser.

Waller, Henry MRCS LSA (1787-1873) was one of Buckden's earliest recorded resident physicians – see **Chapter 14 Medical Services in Buckden**.

Walpole, Horatio (aka **Horace**), **4th earl of Orford (1717–1797)** was the son of Britain's first prime minister (although the post at the time was usually referred to simply as 'the minister'). His interests included gardening, history, politics, and the arts. He wrote that the first sight of Buckden Palace in 1756 'surprised one prettily in a little village'. In 1772 he was shown round the palace by a housemaid (the Bishop, John Green, was probably absent: he preferred living in one of his London houses). A portrait of a Mrs Newcome, who had been the mistress of his father's main political opponent, so tickled Walpole's fancy that he prevailed upon a clergyman friend to get him a print of it. He was less impressed by some of the other pictures, including one of 'some lads'.

war memorials. Buckden has remembered its dead of two world wars in a surprising number of ways. There is the memorial at the front of St Mary's churchyard, erected in 1920 and realigned in 1947 when the names of the Second World War dead were added; the Green memorial stone in the High Street; also in the High Street, a memorial in the old Baptist Chapel (but now at Perry Baptist Church) dedicated to four of the congregation who died in the First World War; a memorial in the Methodist Chapel; the Memorial Playing Field off Burberry Road; and a framed First World War roll of honour that once hung on a wall in the High Street, was lost for over twenty years but is now in St Mary's Church.

water supply. Settlements appear where there is a supply of water. Before the installation of a piped supply Buckden's inhabitants obtained most of their water from wells, most of them private ones. The Board of Agriculture's Great Britain Agricultural Survey of 1811 recorded that most places in Huntingdonshire were watered by ponds, but that Buckden was supplied by 'good springs'. More than 150 of them were known when the piped supply was begun. Bishop Williams's fishpond in the grounds of the Towers is still fed by one, for example, and old OS maps show a distinct line of springs or spring-fed wells running through the gardens of houses lining the west side of the High Street. Hand pumps over wells can be seen in one or two places from the road even now but they are not in use. However, Oak Lawn in Mill Street still has a working well.

Not surprisingly, the Board's report noted that gravel formed a third of the parish's 2,500 acres, the remainder being good quality clay. Its author also thought that the lie of the land suggested there was probably coal to be mined in several areas round Huntingdon. Buckden was presumably not among them, or the Church would have enthusiastically exploited such a source of revenue, as it did in other areas of the country such as Durham. It is hard to avoid a shudder at the thought of Buckden as a landscape of slagheaps, abandoned pitheads and subsided tunnels.

One hears the traditional comments that the mains water does not taste as good as the well water. Perhaps it doesn't, but it is generally more reliable: towards the end of the 19thC, many wells were drying up and householders, unwilling to approach their landlords, were urging the recently-formed Parish Council to do something about the failing supply. Nor was having to fetch water in a bucket good for the health: see the entry for Henry **Frost**.

A Francis Frith photograph taken in Church Street shows a tank on a horse-drawn cart being filled from the public pump outside the Methodist church. The tank was used to distribute water to those without a well.

In the 1920s, Buckden resident Mr J. M. Brown was respected throughout the county as a successful water-diviner. His work in Buckden included testing prospective housing sites for builders such as Hardwick & Burrows, and G. Page & Son.

Another source of water was from roofs. One major one was the church roof. The rainwater is said to have been led to the vicarage across the road where there was the daily chore for someone to pump water to a tank in the roof. Since the water was well fouled with pigeon droppings one hopes that it was filtered and boiled before use! (Perhaps it wasn't: a resident who grew up in Lucks Lane remembers the then vicar regularly sending over for buckets of water from her family's well 'as it tastes so much better than our supply!'.)

Another resident remembers Buckden's water being put to good, if unconventional, use during the Second World War by one of the village innkeepers – see under **Spread Eagle.**

The wartime hospital and camp for displaced persons in Diddington drew its water from wells there; when the hospital storage tank was full, this supply was pumped to the reservoir above Buckden on the Perry Road. This source was augmented in 1952/3 and 1954.

The scheme for the provision of piped water to Buckden and ten other villages began in 1946 and continued until the early fifties. The reservoir for the scheme was at Great Paxton.

That water undertaking was instituted by the St Neots Rural District Council. On 1 April 1963, it was taken over by the Nene and Ouse Water Board, which reinforced the Buckden supply in 1965 by a 12-inch main from Brampton. The village supply is now (2009) the responsibility of Anglian Water Services Limited, an appointed water undertaker owned by AWG plc, which in 2006 was bought for £2.25 billion by Osprey Acquisitions Limited, a Huntingdon-based company set up for that purpose by a consortium whose members include the Commonwealth Bank of Australia, several Australian superannuation funds, the Canada Pension Plan Investment Board and an international venture capital and private equity business. Welcome to the global village pump!

Weighbridge Cottage was, according to the 1881 census, located at the northern end of Buckden. It was occupied by a shepherd and his young family. Since operating a weighbridge seems an occupation not easily compatible with being a shepherd, it may be that it was no longer in use or was supervised by his wife – the machinery

had been looked after by two women forty years before, a lath-render's widow and her young daughter, both called Mary Newman (Mrs Newman died in 1842; Miss Newman married William Picking, a thatcher, in 1848 and died in 1915).

Weir Close is a small development of local authority housing off Lucks Lane. As nearby streets include *Spring*field Close and The *Osiers*, it is not surprising to find that older residents remember the area as a water-meadow.

Wesley, Rev. John (1703–1791) visited Buckden on at least three occasions, and was probably the shortest and cleanest of the founders of Methodism: barely 5' 3" high and a meticulous recorder of how many items of clothing he sent out to the laundry each day. His energy bordered on the superhuman. A typical week in his diary for 1781 shows him preaching in Kent on Wednesday and Thursday, and Sussex on Friday; back in London on Saturday; preaching there on Sunday evening before taking the overnight coach north; preaching in St Neots on Monday evening, Buckden on Tuesday morning and Huntingdon Tuesday evening; and on Wednesday arriving in Bedford. This itinerary is the more astounding for being undertaken in December by a man of seventy-eight. But he was rarely worried by winter weather: in February 1747 he stopped off in Buckden for 'a short bait' (refreshment break) on his way north to Grantham. The journey had not been easy – the roads were invisible under snow, and the wind rose to gale force – but he insisted on continuing, undeterred by a storm of hail and rain that 'froze as it fell, even on our eyebrows'. Despite arriving exhausted in Stilton, he battled on to his destination through snow-drifts almost deep enough to swallow his horse.

Wesleyan Methodist Church, Church Street [MapRef 8]. A Methodist Class was formed as part of the Bedfordshire Circuit in 1781, but without established premises. Its fortunes at first ebbed and flowed. According to Samuel Lewis's *Topographical Dictionary of England*, there was a place of worship for Wesleyan Methodists by 1831. By 1838, however, a leader had emerged: a Silver Street trunk-maker (and later carrier), called Henry Creamer (c. 1802-72). There were soon sufficient members and funds to justify starting work on a 100-seater chapel. The £100 debt that the work incurred was paid off by 1842 (pew-rents helpfully raised over £7 a year). The building, sometimes known as the [Old] Gospel Hall **[MapRef 14]**, was in Church Street, and now forms the east end of the Lion Inn.

The present chapel in Church Street was opened in July 1876 by Charles Roberts BSc of Peterborough. In June 1878 it was registered for the solemnisation of marriages, and in 1915 was the scene of an event that caused considerable local interest. This was the wedding of schoolmistress Evelyn Marjorie Phillips and Teiji Orihashi, a native of Japan. Mr Orihashi had come to Buckden as batman to a Lovat's Scouts officer (Buckden Towers was requisitioned as a convalescent home by the Scouts during the First World War).

Westfield Farm, Great North Road, was for many years one of Buckden's dairy holdings, farmed by members of the Mann family. Since the death of Mary Mann in 2004, the land has attracted interest as a possible site for residential, employment and leisure use.

The name derives from the fact that the farm is on the site of the West Field, one of four large open areas that prior to the implementation of the 1813 enclosure award were cultivated communally (as described in **Chapter 2: The History of Buckden**).

whist drives were an always popular evening out and often used for fund-raising. One in March 1908 attracted forty people; although it was a ' very pleasant evening', the general feeling was that 'these gatherings would be much more enjoyable if a larger percentage of ladies were present'. This was clearly a persistent problem: at a Christmas whist drive held in 1929, two of the prizewinners in the Ladies Competition were men 'playing as ladies'.

White Horse [MapRef 46]. This was a beer-house at the southern end of Silver Street. It was next door to a forge, and census returns suggest that initially selling beer was a sideline for the blacksmith – or, more likely, for his wife. Thus John Jeakins appeared in the 1851 census only as a journeyman smith; by 1861, the previously unnamed property had become the White Horse, and John had added beer-seller to his job description. By 1871 his son, also John, had taken over as blacksmith and publican, and

Westfield Farm 2004. The farmhouse and buildings out of use.

was still there in 1881. In 1890, he died and the beer-house was run by his widow, Jane. There is no reference to the forge; however, later that same year, Jane married a blacksmith sixteen years her junior, Amos Arthur Fowler. Amos was himself the son of a smith who sold beer (at the Plough in Offord Darcy). It comes as no surprise, therefore, to find him once again combining the two roles in the 1901 Buckden census. By 1914, he was still selling beer but was no longer a smith, the forge having been taken over a few years earlier by a blacksmith from St Neots, Albert Edward Seer (known as 'Doughy' Seer). Albert later took over the beer licence as well, and his wife, Sarah Ann, ran the house after his death. Albert was born in St Neots in 1863, the son of a tailor from Somerset.

White House, Mill Road [MapRef 39]. This Grade II listed 17thC timbered-framed farmhouse was for many years one of the two houses marking the eastern edge of the village (the other was Oak Lawn across the road). Its occupants have included the Hon. Mrs Rosa Duberly, George **Page** (q.v.) and Archdeacon **Knowles** (q.v.).

White Lion: see the **Lion.**

Williams, Frederick Edgar BACantab MRCSEng LRCPLon (1863-1923) was Buckden's doctor (the first to own a motor-car) for nearly 25 years – see **Chapter 14**.

Wills, William (1850-1909), boot and shoemaker, came to Buckden from Oundle in about 1875. At first he lived and worked in Church Street, between Page's workshop and Gore's (later J.J.Milner & Sons') grocery

shop **[MapRef 4]**. Later he moved to Lucks Lane. For thirty-three of his thirty-four years in Buckden he was the village sexton.

windmill, the Buckden [MapRef 16] stood on a slight eminence west of the Great North Road and south of Perry Road. It was a tower mill, now severely truncated and converted into a private house. One of the longest-serving millers was Richard Barton, who appears in the 1841, 1851 and 1861 censuses. For the unhappy, if self-inflicted, fate of his son John, see under **fires and fire-fighting equipment**.

Windmill, 21 High Street [MapRef 20]. This small public house sited at the southern entrance to the village was demolished in January 2010.

Wisbe[a]ch & Huntingdon Railway: see **railway mania.**

Wine and Beermakers Society: see under **vineyards.**

witchcraft. There appear to be no records of witches operating in Buckden. This doesn't necessarily mean none was suspected of doing so: it would be an unusual village in which fear, malice, ignorance and jealousy never gave rise to such rumours. That they never led to official action might reflect the relative sophistication of a village exposed from its earliest days to the influences of the wider world.

Nevertheless, Buckden had at least one brush with witchcraft. This was during the infamous ordeal of the 'Witches of Warboys', as the victims became known. On 26 December 1592, the elderly Alice Samuel of Warboys was brought to the Palace to be examined before the Bishop of Lincoln (William Wickham) on a charge of bewitching members of the wealthy Throckmorton family (also of Warboys) and causing the death of Lady Cromwell, wife of the Lord of the Manor. Three days later Alice and her daughter, Agnes, were further examined before the bishop and two local justices, Francis Cromwell and Richard Tryce. Alice, who had already been hounded by accusations for several years, finally 'confessed' – or, in the words of author Moira Tatem, 'confirmed all the current witch fantasies that clearly filled the minds of her interrogators' (*The Witches of Warboys*, 1993).

Alice and Agnes were immediately committed to Huntingdon gaol; they were tried and hanged in April 1593, as was Alice's husband John. The 'evidence' against Agnes amounted to the fact that the girl had hidden in the coal-hole when the mob stormed the house in search of her mother.

See also **Hopkins, Matthew.**

Wolsey Gardens is a small group of affordable housing bordering Lincoln Close and Beaufort Drive. The name refers to the one-time Bishop of Lincoln, Cardinal Wolsey, whose idea of an affordable house was Hampton Court Palace.

Women's Institute. The WI movement arrived in Britain in 1915, having begun in Canada in 1897, when country women in a man's world came together to learn skills to benefit their families and to help their communities. The Buckden branch was formed, as were many others, in 1919, a year that saw national membership surge to over 55,000. At that time it was not unusual to elect the local 'lady of the manor' as President of the Branch Committee; and Buckden chose Miss Philippa Linton (1878-1962) of Stirtloe House. The committee first met in Field House, Silver Street, where it set the subscription at 6d. The members met for the first time at the Rifle Range, where they learnt how to re-bristle a brush. Under the supervision of committee member Mrs A. Stoneham as Librarian, books bought secondhand from Boots were lent for a fortnight. No figure exists for the size of the membership in the early days but a tea party held in 1920 for the children of members catered for fifty children.

From the beginning, besides the undoubted educational lectures and demonstrations which covered many useful subjects such as cookery, upholstery, poultry keeping and disease prevention, there were also magic lantern shows bringing the exotic sights of Mesopotamia and Egypt to Buckden, and evenings devoted to historical subjects, the Great Duke of Marlborough and General Wolfe among them. It is interesting to note that a glove-making class simply assumed that its participants would supply their own rabbit skins (in 1973 a similar class offered the name of a firm who would supply them). In addition, the social life of Buckden was enhanced no end by a startling number of whist drives, dances and garden parties in members' gardens – or fields. One such event in 1923 resulted in a donation to the hospital of £5. A dance competition held in the garden of the White House in Mill Road in 1929 offered prizes of cigarettes and stockings!

The ladies of Buckden also busied themselves in the knitting of mufflers for the patients at Wyton Sanatorium during 1925, and in 1926 undertook to provide the cricket teas.

Throughout its history the WI has always sought to support and help good causes. In recent years, Buckden has helped to provide clean water for Lesotho, kit out the Cheshire Home at Brampton and, for several years, to organise the house-to-house collection for Cancer Relief. However in 1933 the Institute found itself organising a house-to-house collection for its own distressed areas when hard times came upon Buckden itself.

A gap appears in the recorded history for the years 1933–1951. No minute books for either committee meetings or monthly meetings are available, although the branch is known to have continued in being. Apparently this is not an isolated case: other local villages have a similar gap in their histories. It is sad that the war years are not covered as these saw the W.I. come into its own in 'keeping the home fires burning'. However, when minutes start again in 1952 it is with another garden party, and in the following years there were fêtes and fun aplenty.

It became usual in the early 1950s for dances to be held with either a hired or borrowed radiogram – several in the garden of Ivelbury, where Ivelbury Close now stands. Although interesting and informative talks and demonstrations were still given, social changes seem to have made the lifeline to further education which the early Institutes had offered, less important to the health and well-being of rural families.

In the light of present attitudes, it is interesting that in 1957 the provision of cigarettes and chocolates on the table at the Christmas Party was preferred to the more traditional crackers! Indeed, smoking and catering for it, appear often in committee minutes. In 1970 it was agreed to provide saucers for smokers at monthly meetings, and in 1975 an improved plan saw one committee member responsible for bringing to the meetings a jamjar full of sand where cigarettes may be stubbed out!

Important dates in the Institute's and the nation's calendar have been marked in Buckden by the gift to the village of something to enhance the environment. Shrubs and a seat in the churchyard, roses and a seat at the Burberry Homes and a tree in the cemetery mark such occasions. A programme of daffodil planting started in 1984 continues to this day. The first bulbs were planted on the roundabout, but after police permission to cross the A1 was withdrawn, the site at the northern underpass was chosen and blooms beautifully each spring.

In 1974 the energy crisis and 'winter of discontent' saw the WI at its ingenious best. Meetings, held at that time, in a mobile classroom at the school, were warmed by two paraffin heaters brought in for the occasion and each committee member brought a flask of hot water so that tea and coffee might still be served. Its most testing time, though, came that year when, as Hostess Institute for the group of eight to which it belongs, it was required to produce refreshments in the middle of the sugar shortage! No cakes (the WI's enduring strong point) being possible, one sausage roll, one sandwich and a mince pie graced each plate that year.

The resumed minutes of 1951 reveal a keen drama group which continues to this day. For many years it had strong connections to Buckden Theatre Club, the village drama group whose own history takes it back to the Mace family: Mrs Dossie Mace who smiles out of those 1950s pictures in the WI's album, and her husband Frank.

Today, the education offered by the WI is more ambitious, supplemented as it is by Denman College in Oxfordshire which offers residential courses in exquisite needlework and embroidery, cookery and music but also, through its highly qualified teachers, a similar syllabus to Further Education Colleges throughout the country. Monthly meetings continue to instruct and entertain and offer its members friendship and support. Modern women, perhaps, do not gain the same benefits as their sisters of nearly a century ago but the value of the Women's Institute to women in rural England and Wales is reflected in the still growing membership and it is comforting to know that the WI's ideals of home and family still resonate as strongly in the on-line years of the 21stC as they did in a small community in Canada at the end of the 19thC.

Judith Armitage

Woolley, George Newnham (1815-1874), Buckden's doctor in the mid 19thC, achieved brief national fame as the debunker of the Lincolnshire New Black Death scare – see **Chapter 14**

Worley, William brought distinction to Buckden in January 1881 by being a victor in an impromptu skating championship set up in St Neots. The report of the event does not specify which William Worley it was: William junior, aged 20, a recently-married drainer living in Hardwick, or his father William senior, also a drainer and the publican of the Spread Eagle for over 30 years. A reference to experience winning out may be a clue.

Wyles, Mary and **William.** She was the daughter of Great Stukeley farm worker Arnot Pack, and came to Buckden to be a housemaid at the vicarage; he was a tailor, brought up in Hardwick by his grandmother and widowed father, a house carpenter. Perhaps their eyes first met in church: she in the vicarage pew, he in the chancel; he was a member of the choir for over seventy years. They married in 1881, and set up house in Lucks Lane. William had been apprenticed to tailor Thomas James and, after the latter's death, took over his house and business. In celebrating their diamond wedding anniversary in 1941, the *Hunts Post* said that Mr Wyles was a retiring man who enjoyed a game of bowls but did not play a large part in community affairs. This is a little unfair: as one of the Odd Fellows' representatives he helped to organise the annual Buckden Friendly Societies' Athletic Sports Day.

Mr and Mrs Wyles were both born in 1858; Mary died in 1944 and William in 1947. Their son, an apprentice tailor, had died young. Their daughter Amelia (Millie), a schoolteacher, also predeceased them; when young, she had been considered 'a very good little actress', showing 'unmistakeable dramatic ability' in entertainments put on by the National School. Her most admired performance was as Lady Fiona the Fanciful Lady in Harriet Louisa Childe-Pemberton's satirical duologue *Shattered Nerves* (1899).

Y

year of the sales: 1919. Remarkably, this year saw four of Buckden's most important properties up for auction: on 31 May, 'an old-fashioned house' with 84 acres, The Coneygarth's (sic); on 26 July, the 'unusually attractive modern freehold residence' Buckden Towers, complete with thirteen bed and dressing rooms, one bath, and 'the intensely interesting ruins of the ancient Episcopal Palace'; and on 30 August, two 'old-fashioned country residences', The Red House (two water closets and an 'ornamental garden, most prettily laid out') and The Manor House ('cowhouse and other convenient buildings').

The Towers was bought by Dr R. H. **Edleston** (q.v.), and Coneygarths was bought by Mr P. W. Priestley, who moved there from The Red House.

'Yes, We Have No Bananas' was sung at the opening of one **Women's Institute** (q.v.) meeting in the 1920s. It was the hit song from a current Broadway revue. The WI has never been as out-of-touch as its metropolitan critics like to think.

York House, High Street [MapRef 29], is a substantial town-house built in the 18thC (a chimney brick carries the date 1785). Further research is needed to establish when the name was first used and to what it relates. It seems too prosperous a residence to have been the home of the Yorke (sometimes York) family, who had a small butcher's shop nearby: see the next entry. A Charles Yorke Seawell, gentleman, lived in Buckden High Street in the mid-Victorian years, but south of the George Inn.

Among those known to have lived in York House are Sir William Power, Mayor of Hackney 1928-9, and his wife Cornelia Frances. To be more precise, the only record of their having lived there is that they both died there: she on 23 February 1944 and he on 10 June 1945. The previous occupants had been Edward and Martha Cranfield-Rose.

York Yard, High Street, once known as **Brickyard Lane** (q.v.) is, curiously, next door not to York House but to Sherwood House. A correspondent writing on the Buckden village website suggests that the yard is named after his ancestor William Yorke, a Northamptonshire-born butcher known to have been in Buckden before moving to Bedfordshire. The family business apparently continued in that county for another hundred years.

The family's progress was not quite as smooth as this description suggests. In August 1826, the creditors of 'William Yorke, late of Buckden, Huntingdonshire, butcher' were invited to a meeting in Huntingdon to sort out the distribution of his estate and effects: William was an insolvent debtor, newly discharged from confinement in the King's Bench Prison, London.

Despite this setback, a William Yorke, butcher, continues to appear in Buckden directories for both 1830 and 1839. After that there are no Yorkes or Yorks listed. However, the 1841 census places one of the village's several butchers, Robert Setchell, at or near the entrance to York Yard, and these premises remained in use as a butcher's shop into the 20thC. It seems likely, therefore, that this was indeed the site of the Yorkes' business.

Z

Zachariah was the first forename of Pc Coulson, Buckden's policeman in the years running up to the First World War. He was born in about 1876, the son of a Hilton farm bailiff, and started his working life as a farm labourer before joining the police. 'Zachariah' is a sufficiently uncommon name to confuse transcribers of the census, where he may be found under such diverse identities as 'Tachwinh Coulson' and 'Lacharial Coulson'. As his service in Buckden coincided with the St Neots magistracy's ruthless war on speeding, 'Coulson' was no doubt often preceded by even less flattering epithets in the mouths of those caught in the notorious Buckden **police trap** (q.v.).

Zombies, The This well-regarded British rock or baroque pop band was founded in 1959 and disbanded in 1968 (although some of the original members began to tour again in 2005). The band's drummer was the landlord of The Vine for a time at the end of the last century.

ΩΩΩΩΩ

An unidentified family. The photograph was with some others from Buckden.   David Thomas

PB1.1.1   The entrance to Buckden on the Great North Road. The magnificent trees on the left were in the grounds of Ivelbury House adjacent to the Vine public house. The first building on the left had been the Windmill public house. Photograph c.1935.

From the Coates Collection with permission of Wisbech & Fenland Museum

PB1.1.2 High Street 2008.   More telephones but no wires on poles with cross bars which were so prominent along main roads and railways. The magnificent trees have gone either by saw or Dutch elm disease.

PB1.2 Buckden Parish Boundary

PB1.3 A view looking northwards in 2007. One can pick out The Vine Inn, The George Hotel, The Lion Hotel, the previous vicarage, the Manor House, the present vicarage and St. Mary's church.

On the west side of the church can be seen the 1872 Towers' servants' quarters and stables and what was the kitchen garden. The knot garden, inner gatehouse and the Great Tower of the Palace are closer by. Just north of the church can be seen part of the 1959 St Hugh's church and the roofs of the Towers 1872 house. The utilitarian St Stephens Hall is on the north edge of the group of buildings. The open ground is the Little Park of the Palace.

Photograph by and courtesy of David Stephens of Old Weston

PB1.4.1 High Street c 1900. On the left note The Vine and, beyond it, the forge, the post office and The George hotel.

From the Philip Gale Collection

PB1.4.2 High Street c 1930. The Vine is more conspicuous and The George is visible after demolition of a part of the forge and the post office.

From the Coates Collection Wisbech and Fenland Museum.

PB1.5.1 The George Hotel and Lofts' antiques shop ca 1920. The George's sign is away for cleaning or restoration. Beyond the porch are the post office and the forge with The Vine public house beyond that. The AA was rating hotels from 1912 onwards. The ACU (Autocycle Union) was started in 1903.   Philip Gale Collection

PB1.5.2 2009 Due to the demolition of the post office some time after 1922 and part of the forge The Vine can be seen. The antiques shop is now part of Anne Furbank's ladies dress shop. The hotel's sign includes twelve Georges (one for each bedroom) and is hung well clear of high vehicles.

PB1.6.1 The Lion Hotel in the early 1900s. It had fewer rooms than now. The bay on the corner of Church Street was not part of it. Contrary to a onetime claim it was never a posting house. It may have accommodated the Bishop of Lincoln's staff when he was staying at the palace. Barry Jobling Collection

PB1.6.2 The Lion in 2009. In the last hundred years it has had many owners and many managers. It was owned by Trust Houses until the directors decided that they did not want hotels with less than twenty bedrooms and so sold it into private ownership.

PB1.7.1 Before 1962 the Great North Road or A1 looked like this at Hardwick Lane.

Bob Baxter

PB1.7.2 2008. The cottages occupied by members of the Gale, Clarke, Smith and Worlidge families have gone. The number of vehicles on our roads has gone up by a factor of four since the "by-pass" opened.

PB1.8.1 The school about 1920. There had been a pond on the Green but it was filled in partly to "stop children trying out their shoes" in it in 1893.   Bob Baxter.

PB1.8.2 The school in 2007 - no bell and one chimney. The Plane tree has done very well.

PB2.1.1   In the days of the Rifle Range and Hinsby's shop on the far corner of Silver Street. From the quality and style of numbering this picture is from the Wisbech and Fenland Museum's Coates Collection. The museum does not know the date but let us say the 1930s. The nearer corner shop is Peck's the butcher.

PB2.1.2   2008. Hinsby has sold his corner and the nearer was then a ladies' dress shop. The Burberry Homes and the warden's house occupy the site of the Rifle Range. There are often more parked cars in this view.

PB2.2.1 Silver Street c.1900   W.Andrews' Bakery ~ Glory. Photo supplied by David Thomas

PB2.2.2   The result of the Great Fire of 1909 ~ Misery.   From the collection of Mr. & Mrs Brian Smith

PB2.2.3   1993. The shop was last run as a bread shop and delicatessen - "Bread and Wine" by the Menchini family before it was closed and used as a family home. The building bears the redbrick string courses, a trademark of George Page the Buckden builder at the time of the fire.

PB 2.3 Doctors and General Practioners

Some of the buildings used by them in the last hundred years.

Top left:
Dr.F.E.Williams1903-1923
followed briefly by Dr. Robert
Wallace

Top right: Dr. Robert Davie
1925-1930.
Dr. Eric Jolly 1930- 1964

Centre: Dr. Michael Morris
1964-1969

Centre left: Dr. Morris and
Partners for several months
in 1993.

Centre right: Dr. Morris and
Partners in a purpose-built
surgery 1969-1993. Dr.
Morris "much appreciated the
help he received from Bill
Render in obtaining it".

Bottom: Dr. David Irwin and Partners from 1993 onwards

PB2.4.3 The late Ray Millard who chaired the committee which organised the funding and construction of the reshaping of the hall ponders the end of the years of work on opening day in1999.

PB2.4.4 John Major C.H., M.P. cuts the ribbon to mark the opening of the extended hall. Gail Robertson the Treasurer looks on.

PB2.4.1 The 1970s Village Hall just before work is started on its extension.

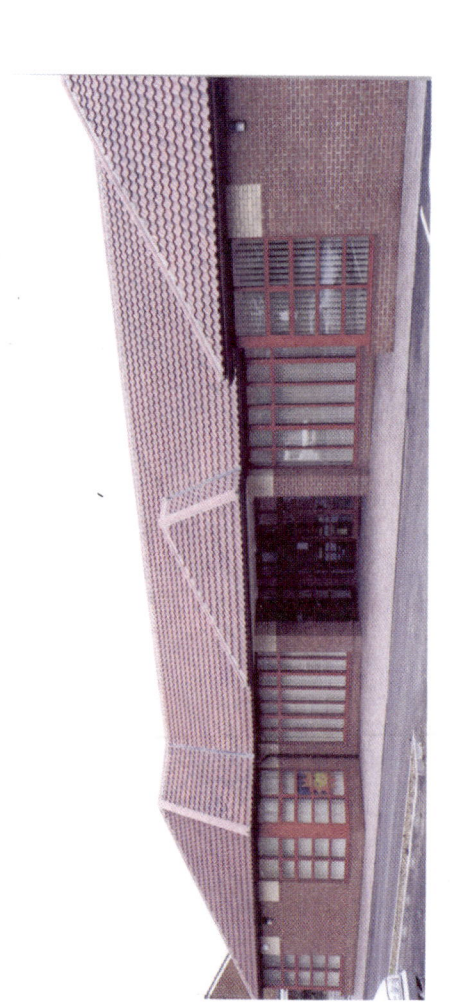

PB2.4.2 The extended village hall now to be known as the Buckden |Millennium Community Centre as the result of a substantial grant from the National Lottery. The branch of the County Library is on the left side.

PB2.4 Village Hall becomes Millennium Community Centre

PB2.5.1   1979   "The Valley" next to the playing field. The pond is believed to date back to the days when the Palace grew grapes on the adjacent vineyards and bred fish for the table.

PB2.5.2   1993 The Valley after restoration by 'Mac' and his friends known as Waders Anonymous. The painting is by Eileen O'Meara of Mollymook, New South Wales, who was sent a photograph from which she worked. The swans had mixed fortunes when nesting here due to the unwanted attention of dogs and even children.

PB2.6.1 A 1982 John Piper painting known as "Storm over Buckden". On seeing one of his earlier paintings showing similar clouds George VI is said to have remarked "You don't seem to have had much luck with the weather, Mr.Piper". Reproduced with the kind permission of Mr. Luke Piper

PB2.6.2 A 1991 lithograph by Rigby Graham . Two things to note. The man in the foreground is the poet John Clare on his walk from Epping to Helpston. It took him three days during which he had "nothing to eat except grass". While Clare has been brought in by the artist's imagination, surely the possibly female figure riding a bicycle and carrying a lawn-mower over her shoulder must have caught Graham's eye while he was here? Who was she-or he?

Reproduced with the kind permission of the artist via Goldmark Gallery

Top right: During construction of chapel by Dr Edleston 1919 onwards.
From Coates Collection Wisbech and Fenland Museum

Bottom right: Present day view with rear of St.Hugh's Church visible.

PB2.7 Buckden Palace to Buckden Towers. Views from the east

Top Left: Period before the Great Hall was demolished.
Engraving by Budge of Bedford

Bottom Left : During ownership by Sir Arthur Marshall from 1872 until 1919.
Philip Gale Collection

PB2.7 The Towers. Before 1838 to the present day.

PB2.8.1   Top left :   St Hugh of Lincoln's window in the 1956 St Hugh's Church

PB2.8.2   Top right: St Hugh from a window in the cloisters at Chester Cathedral. In the background can be seen some details of the reconstruction of Lincoln Cathedral. Hugh oversaw the start of the work which began in1192.

PB2.8.3   Centre bottom: The Katherine window in St Hugh's Church

PB3.1 Buckden's best known claims to fame can be seen in this view. St.Mary's Parish Church dates in part from the 13th century and rates one star in "England's Thousand Best Churches". The Great Tower and Inner Gatehouse are the more conspicuous parts of the palace of the Bishops of Lincoln built in the 15th century. The concrete strips adjacent to the 1956 St. Hugh's Church represent the site of the Great Hall of the palace which was demolished in 1838. The adjacent grounds are known to historians as the Little Park.

In the foreground is the 1872 house built for Sir Arthur Marshall which is now known as the Claret Centre; its owners are the Claretian Missionaries. The knot garden is a modern reconstruction supervised by William Dawson. The High Street runs across the right hand corner of the picture. The 19th century outer gatehouse and out buildings to the Towers and the Lion Hotel can be seen.

Photo: David Stephens of Old Weston

PB3.1   Historic Centre

PB3.2.1   1932 The Buckden *Pageant of the Centuries*. Miss Connie Bowtell (left) and colleague were two of a cast of about ninety! The show comprising sixteen scenes set between 1086 and 1814. It was to be held in the grounds of the Towers from July 26th to August 1st but was extended a week because of dreadful weather at the start.

Judith Addington

PB3.2.2   Not A.D. but c.400,000 B.C. A hand axe which appears to be from the early or lower Acheulian period found in Vineyard Way. The tape is graduated in inches.

Douglas & Margery Wilson via Les Button

PB3.3.1 The Towers grounds or the palace's Little Park has seen many events over the years. Dennis Burton organised several steam rallies. This one was in 1980.

PB3.3.2 The Scout Group held numerous annual donkey derbys in aid of funds, the last one being in 1990. Most of the races per meeting were between donkeys ridden bare-back by children. The leaders being heavier were only allowed to drive sulkies. Gerald Carpenter had been the leading organiser of the events and Clerk of the Course but this year Peter Mailer acted in that capacity.

PB 3.4

3rd May 1930 The Opening of the Bowling Club's Green in Silver Street

Back Row

Messrs. Butcher, Gale, Poulton, Worley,????, Spencer Hinsby, W.Milner, Johnson, E.Hinsby, J.Collyer, Turk, E.Cook, F.Rose, T.Milner

Third Row

Mesdames Butcher, Bowtell, Lofts, *Messrs.* Lofts,????, Bowtell, A. Stoneham, *Mrs.*Smith *Miss* A. Jolly, *Mesdames* Johnson, Milner, Robinson, *Miss Ivy* Dorrington, *Messrs.* Barker, W. Lovelock, ????, *Miss* Channon, *Mrs* H. Worley

Second Row – seated

Master Butcher(standing), *Mesdames* Turk, Hinsby, Collyer, G.Stoneham, Knowles, ????, Duberly, Cranfield, Bell, *Commander* Bell, *Major* Duberly, *Archdeacon* Knowles, *Mr* . W.W. Cranfield

Front Row

Messrs. F Smith, Pat Fitzgerald, *Miss* C Wayman, *Miss* J. Cowling, *Messrs.* A Robinson, J.Smith, G.Stoneham, *Sgt.* Staughton

Note: In the second row any confusion over the names of the ladies stems from the contemporary list.

PB3.4 Bowls Club 1930

PB3.5 Buckden Bowls Club 75th Anniversary Celebration on June 3rd 2004 was marked by a match against the English Bowling Association President's team.

Among the members of the Buckden Club mostly in dark jackets were:

Back Row: R. Purssord   J. Mace   A. Corn   D. West   B. Grundy   G. Robertson   R. Andrews   C. Smith.

Middle Row: P. Holmes   J. Avery   J. Price   Mark Smith   B. Crabb   M. Lee   T. Wells   G. Clark   J. Hignett   K. Spencer   Martin Smith   K. Edwards   M. Pope

Front Row: D. Francis   J. Bates   (Ian Murrell – EBA President) W. Rowlands   Brian Smith   T. Rowell

PB3.5 Bowls Club 2004

PB3.6 St. Mary's, Buckden's Parish Church, and some less common views. Whereas visitors can easily see the exterior and low level interior the angels and stained glass are much more difficult to discern.

Barry Jobling

PB 3.6 St Mary's Church Details

PB3.7 The WWII Home Guard at The Towers

Back Row: (L to R) S.Briers W.Mann J.Riseley W.Pond E.Dudley E.Simmonds G. Sabey H.Worley R.Hales W. Riseley G.Blofield P.Pepper

Middle Row: ???? E.Smith W.Throssel J.Swepstone A.Hales R.Haynes H.Pearson N.Holdsworth E.Pond T.Swepstone J.Berrill S.Mann J.Elwood

Front Row: .C.Whitmee L.Johnson L.Seaman W.Hodson W.Smith *Capt.* J.Mailer *Lt.* Cranfield-Rose J.Schnaars P.Audley S.Wayman T.Ball P.Milner?

PB3.7 The Home Guard was instituted nationally in April 1940 and was stood down in December 1944

PB3.8.1 The ancient mechanism of the church clock. The wooden frame and much of the works are original and are about 400 years old. The spindle on the right drives the hands on the two faces via five separate gear trains. The chiming mechanism works but awaits an enthusiast to connect it to one of the bells on the floor below.

PB3.8.2 This milestone survived the dualling of the Great North Road. It ought to read 61 miles but the '1' has been defaced or eroded.

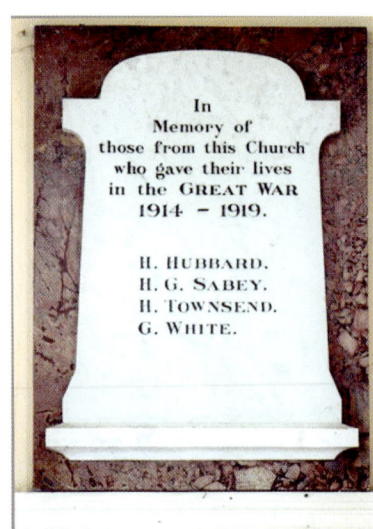

PB3.8.3 This memorial was in the Baptist Chapel in the High Street but can now be found at the Perry Baptist church.

PB3.8.4 Every self-respecting village should have its own sign. Buckden's millennium example at the start of Mill Road has its post set in a millstone.

Swans occasionally find The Valley pond a suitable place to nest but not the long pond in the Towers grounds near the church.

PB3.8.5 "The Green Memorial" in the High Street. Adjacent to the stone is a modern plaque giving details of the circumstances of the young men's deaths.

PB3.8.6 The oldest post box in the parish.

CHAPTER 1/WHY IS BUCKDEN HERE?
David Thomas

The answer, says the author, can be summed up simply enough: ice and water.

How far back into pre-history do we want to go? Would one hundred and forty million years be enough? At that time the site of Buckden was under a shallow tropical sea, in which plesiosaurs and other ancient creatures swam. The seabed was made up of clay washed down from the lands nearby and the carcasses of the sea animals. Since then it has drifted northward, until it arrived at the latitude it is in today.

Between two and a half and one million years ago, the earth became much colder with the advent of the current ice age.[1] Not all of the glacials resulted in ice covering the whole of Great Britain, but there was a time when what is now Huntingdonshire was under a thick layer of slowly moving ice. As it crawled over the underlying surface, the ice ground away the rock and transported it elsewhere, depositing the detritus when it melted in a warmer environment.

The melting proceeded fastest on the higher ground. As the ice thinned and the darker layers underneath gained more heat from the sun, so stones, sand, clay and other mineral particles were often left on the tops of hills. This is where we now find the stony clay soils known as boulder clay or glacial drift. At the same time, the valleys were carrying away the melt-water of the glaciers in huge quantities. The speed of the glacial rivers was such that the finer parts of any rocks were carried out to the ever-rising seas, leaving behind the coarser as sands and gravels. The melting of the glaciers did not take place at a steady rate. Several times the cold returned, increasing the depth of ice again. As a result, the hilltop clays and valley gravels received new deposit layers, which differed from those above and below them. These are mainly of interest to geologists, however, and do not affect the story of humans on the land.

PLESIOSAURUS ATTACKED

It was the action of ice and water, then, which left Buckden with the shape of the land as it is now: gently sloping hills to the west and the shallow valley of the river Great Ouse to the east. The boulder clay and gravel has a substratum of blue-grey Oxford clay. This clay was laid down under the sea, and is the source of the fossils that sometimes turn up in our soil, such as Gryphaea (fossil oysters informally known as the devil's toenails) and dart-shaped belemnites, the internal shells of extinct relatives of the squid and cuttlefish. Rainwater can slowly penetrate the boulder clay until it reaches the Oxford clay, but this is

---

[1] An ice age is a cyclical epoch during which a significant area of the earth's surface remains covered with a permanent ice sheet (as Antarctica still is today), while other large sheets advance and retreat, expanding during very cold periods (known as glacials), but starting to disappear during milder ones (interglacials).

impervious to water, and forces it to flow outwards and eventually form springs, which if left alone would trickle away into the gravel or down to the river.

The last glacial of the current ice age receded about twelve thousand years ago. The mineral soil was not long without any cover once the recession had started. As the temperature of the earth rose, tundra (a plain with a frozen subsoil, supporting only limited vegetation) was rapidly followed by hardy shrubs and trees; these in turn were replaced by pine forests and, eventually, deciduous forests of oak, ash, lime and other species.

Humans lived in Britain long before this exploitable landscape appeared. The early river Great Ouse flowed across what is now the North Sea to join the estuary of the present river Rhine. There was a land bridge joining Britain to the continent, and the English Channel had not yet come into existence. During the mildest interludes of the ice ages, early continental humans had therefore been able to walk to Britain, hunting and fishing for food on the way, and settle here until driven out by the return of glaciation. The discovery in Vineyard Way of a hand axe probably dating from between 400,000 and 200,000 BC suggests that some may have made it as far as Buckden: see **Acheulian hand axes** in the A to Z Section, and the opening of Chapter 2.

When Buckden was finally permanently settled, we shall never know, but it may have been by people who arrived some ten thousand years ago, following the river as the easiest way of penetrating the country. We may imagine the surprise of the first group to emerge from the forest and find fresh running water, well above the river, but with dry land above and below the springs.

Water! Water, the first essential to life, the first thing which even today space scientists look for on other planets to see if there is a possibility of life. And here, with the water, were the other necessities for a comfortable life. The forests would provide firewood, materials with which to build shelters, and a habitat for game animals. The gravels offered an easily cultivable soil to stir with a digging stick or other simple tool, to supplement the meat and fish they caught.

Water, then, the treasure in a landscape created by the ebb and flow of the great ice sheets of the glacial periods, was probably the reason for Buckden becoming, and surviving as, a permanent settlement. Over the centuries, its population rose to about 1000 and then stabilised, so we must assume that the water supply would only sustain that number. The population expanded to its present level of 3000 only after piped water reached the village in the last century. But even today, the village still has a line of springs and wells, where the underlying Oxford clay comes nearest to the surface: a vivid reminder of why Buckden is here.

CHAPTER 2/THE HISTORY OF BUCKDEN
Susan B. Edgington

The first chairman of Buckden Local History Society brings her popular *Buckden: A Short History and Plan* (1980) into the twenty-first century.

There are no written documents to give us clues as to just why the village we call Buckden is situated in this spot. We can only make guesses about when it was first settled. The oldest relic of human activity found within the parish bounds is an Acheulean axe, that is, a flint tool of the early Stone Age period. However this one survival is not very helpful: it might have been used here by Palaeolithic humans – or it might have been brought here by the movements of ice or water in the last of the ice ages.[1] Later traces of human occupation in prehistoric times are 'indistinct rectilinear enclosures' which have been distinguished in the river gravels by aerial survey and are interpreted as ancient workings: Iron Age relics have been recovered from the gravel pits.

Roman Britain

Traces of Roman settlement have been found all over Buckden: pottery has been dug up during gravel extraction, in the garden of the Red House (in 1934), and in Perry Road when the High Street bypass was built. There are rumours that during the building of houses in the area of the village called the Hoo (an Anglo-Saxon word for burial ground) cremation burials were discovered, which would argue for a substantial settlement. A formal excavation just east of Stirtloe was carried out in 1941, and finds included bones, pottery sherds, a corroded spearhead, millstone fragments, and an elephant tooth (a souvenir?). The conclusion was that there had been a settlement there, probably as early as the second century AD.

Forty years later, in the summer of 1982, a dig was carried out east of the Towers, following some surface finds, and it yielded unmistakable evidence of a Roman villa right in the middle of the (later) village: tesserae from a floor mosaic; fragments of a hypocaust tile (a hollow brick for underfloor central heating); a scatter of plaster from the walls, plus the usual pottery sherds and part of a quern for grinding corn. The site was too small to gain any impression of size, but it was certainly the property of a wealthy person, most likely a farm house managing an estate which may well have had the same boundaries as the later parish. It may have been occupied through to the end of the period of Roman settlement in 410 AD.

Anglo-Saxon Buckden

What happened in Buckden between the departure of the Romans early in the fifth century and the first written record of the village in 1086 is a mixture of deduction and speculation. The first clue to the village's pre-Conquest history is its name. The English Place-names Society lists sixteen variants or spellings: in fact the present version, Buckden, though recorded as early as 1279, only recently became the accepted one. Older people still refer to the village less elegantly as 'Bugden'. Whatever its spelling, the origin of the name is reasonably certain. 'Dene' is the Old English word for valley, and 'Bucge' the name of a person: so 'Bucge's valley'. An interesting point is that Bucge is only known as a feminine name, so we are probably looking at a settlement established by a female tribal leader.

From the place-name, and others nearby, it is probable that this area of Huntingdonshire was settled early in the post-Roman period by the Angles, a Germanic tribe who penetrated eastern England by way of the rivers: in early times it was much easier to get about by water than overland. Disembarking on the west bank of the Ouse, somewhere near the present river crossing, the invaders would see that the land nearby was low-lying and liable to flood, but there was higher ground beyond, rising to about 150 feet, which offered the two necessities for settlement: fresh water and plentiful timber. It was also good agricultural land, for both plough and pasture. It had been farmed by the Romans, but whether there were still native Britons in the area is unknown: if there were, they were either displaced or assimilated without

---

[1] For more about the axe see entry on **Acheulian hand axes** in the A to Z Section

leaving any trace. The village was established on the higher ground, away from the river, not only because of the danger of flooding, but also for reasons of security. The waterways were not only trade-routes and channels for peaceful communication, but could also carry people with less friendly intentions, and the settlement on higher ground was less vulnerable to and more defensible against such raiders. Here on the higher ground the settlers could draw water from several springs (Springfield Close is on the site of some of these); there was woodland for fuel and shelter, and there was cultivable land to grow food and graze stock.

Material confirmation that an Anglo-Saxon settlement indeed existed was found in 1961 when the by-pass was being constructed. Just north of the roundabout the site of a 'boat-shaped' building was found and investigated. Pottery sherds which included St Neots ware suggested it had been occupied during the eleventh century. Later building has undoubtedly obliterated other signs of Anglo-Saxon occupation.

Domesday Buckden

The first written reference to Buckden, as for many places, occurs in Domesday Book, the enormously detailed survey which William I ordered to be carried out following his conquest of England in 1066. People at the time felt as if they were undergoing an interrogation as thorough as on the Day of Judgment, hence the name, but the king was mainly interested in the taxable value of the lands he had conquered. From Domesday we find that in 1086 Buckden was in the Hundred of Toseland and the bishop of Lincoln was lord of the manor, holding the whole village from the king. There are problems of translation and interpretation but a modern version is: *In Buckden the bishop of Lincoln had 20 hides [a measure of land] taxable. Land for 20 ploughs. Now in lordship 5 ploughs; 37 villagers and 20 smallholders have 14 ploughs. A church and a priest. 1 mill, 30s; meadow, 84 acres; woodland pasture 1 league long and 1 league wide [a league was 1.5 miles]. Value before 1066 £20; now £16 10s.*

In some ways this is quite a typical picture. The lord of the manor farmed a quarter of the land for himself. Thirty-seven householders were 'serfs' or slaves, obliged to work for the lord; twenty others held plots of land from him and farmed on their own account. It is possible to make an approximate calculation of the village population from these figures: the 57 represent adult male householders, and experts reckon this number may be multiplied by 4.5 or 5 to estimate the total population, therefore it will have been in the region of 250 residents. The church and watermill were essential features. There was quite a large area of meadowland, managed for grazing and for hay, undoubtedly the low-lying fields near the river which were difficult to plough. The 'woodland pasture' was on the higher ground to the west, and was later developed into the bishops' deer-park.[1]

The manor was already at this time held by the bishop of Lincoln. (This disproves a persistent story, which the antiquarian Leland appears to have started in the sixteenth century – that it was transferred from the abbey of Ely.) It is thus clear that by the end of the eleventh century, some sort of episcopal residence had already been established here. This might seem odd, but the ecclesiastical map of England has altered a great deal and in those days the see of Lincoln stretched from the Humber to the Thames, so that Buckden made a good central stopping-off place for the bishops, who were expected to advise the king in London as well as carry out ecclesiastical duties in their cathedral city. A stray piece of evidence in the *Life and Miracles of St Ivo*, which was written within a few years of the Domesday survey, strongly suggests that the bishops had not only a manor house, but also a garden, for the action revolves around a 'French gardener' and his son.[2]

Medieval Buckden

During the Middle Ages a village plan must have emerged which would be recognizable today. The Great North Road formed the High Street, and in the northern part of the village it had on its east side the palace, on its west the bishops' deer-park. South of the palace was Church Street, leading east to the river Ouse. South of this junction the building now called the Lion Hotel was already in existence: a ceiling boss in the lounge is dated 1500. It shows the 'Agnus Dei' (lamb of God) and the building may have originated as a guest-house of the palace, though this is speculation. The church was close to the palace: so much so that the north aisle wall had to be buttressed to stop it subsiding into the moat. Further along on the other side of Church Street was the manor house, the frontage of which has changed little. Luck's Lane led south to Stirtloe, and Silver Street north. 'Luck' and 'Silver' were probably former landowners. Other (modern) street-names give clues to the medieval lay-out: 'Glebe Lane' where the glebe or vicarage lands once were and 'Vineyard Way' near where the bishop's vines were cultivated. Mill Lane led to the water-mills on the river. Around this residential nucleus were the village's open fields: a four-field system of rotation was

---

[1] For more on the **deer-park** see entry in the A to Z Section
[2] See **miracles** in the A to Z Section

operated, on North Field, West Field, South Field and Mill Field, with the lord of the manor and the villagers all ploughing strips of land in each field.

And what about the people who lived in Buckden during these centuries? Almost all of their names are lost, and even when known by name, their activities are forgotten (see **Chapter 20**). Famous visiting bishops included St Hugh and Bishop Grosseteste. The inhabitants of the manor house can be traced from Nicholas de Stukely who leased it in 1380 from the bishop – the Victoria County History lists his successors. But the manorial records, which could have given details of the day-to-day management of village affairs, survive only from the end of the middle ages (and are kept in Lincoln). That being so the only individuals whose deeds live after them are the outstanding miscreants who got their names into the national archives.

One such was an outstanding debtor – no less than the vicar of Buckden, Simon, who on 17 July 1337 admitted that he owed a London hosier, Robert son of Wiillam de Taverner, £24 10s. 0d. If he could not pay, the sum would be levied from his lands and chattels. How Simon incurred such an enormous debt we cannot tell but there must (surely!) have been more to it than buying hose 'on tick'. Rather later a Buckden butcher, William Mariot, was convicted of theft. In the spring of 1406 he stole a mare from its owner at Sibthorpe. To evade capture he fled to Offord church hoping to claim sanctuary, but this did not succeed and he was forced to admit his theft, worth 10 shillings, before the coroner. He was pardoned after two years, on 23 May 1408.

Alice Govy's case seems to have been more complicated. She was a Buckden housewife who appears to have fallen foul of some of her fellow villagers. In 1439 she was accused of stealing two kerchiefs and three skeins of yarn, worth two shillings, belonging to John Falconer and John Attwood, both inhabitants of Buckden. At her trial the jury found her guilty and she would probably have been put to death – had it not been discovered that she was pregnant. Alice then used her initiative to improve on the situation and petitioned Henry VI for mercy. She claimed that all her sufferings were undeserved and due solely to 'the envy and malice of enemies'. Her plea was successful and on 15 December 1439 she received a royal pardon. Whether she returned home to Buckden and outfaced her malicious neighbours we cannot tell.

Of other villagers we know even less. Robert Boteler and Geoffrey Burgeys were listed in 1372 because they were slow to pay their share towards the upkeep of the bridge at Huntingdon. An alien is listed in 1436: John Wynge of Eylan in Prussia, but how and why he landed up in this part of the country is anybody's guess.

Tudor Buckden

The sixteenth century saw one of the most dramatic episodes in Buckden's history. In July 1533, after the annulment of their marriage, Henry VIII sent Katherine of Aragon to reside in Buckden Palace, 'in a wild and sparsely populated country on the edge of the great fens', as Katherine's biographer puts it. The discarded queen was well loved by the common people of England, who thought her very ill used by Henry. She was touched when the villagers came to the gates of the palace, not asking for alms, but offering gifts of food. This local sympathy was a contributory factor to Henry's decision to move Katherine, and in December 1533 he sent the duke of Suffolk to organize this. However, the queen and her attendants resisted the attempt to force her to move, and at the same time the villagers showed their support by gathering outside the gates, not creating any disturbance, but carrying choppers and bill-hooks and looking so threatening that Suffolk did not persist for long. After a few days he returned to London and Katherine was safe for a little longer, until in May 1534 she was moved to Kimbolton. Buckden's anonymous villagers played a small part in national politics.

It is, in fact, in the sixteenth century that Buckden's inhabitants begin to emerge from anonymity. One of the wealthier was William Burberry who by his will, dated 18 March 1558, devised the rent of his lands to the poor of Buckden, to be administered 'whilst the world should endure'. This was the first of several generous charities which have made Buckden an unusually well endowed parish. From the following year (1559) we are also able to trace the lives of humbler parishioners since, in accordance with Thomas Cromwell's Act of twenty years before, the Church began to keep a systematic record of baptisms, marriages and burials. That is, the parish registers are systematic in intention, but not always in execution. In actual fact there are gaps in the first century of their keeping caused by lost pages, holes and tears in the parchment and, one suspects, clerical carelessness. Nevertheless they offer the first real opportunity of examining properly the structure of village life. By careful study we can make some realistic estimates of population figures in the days before censuses, and by painstaking work reconstruct individual families. Work that has been done along these lines suggests a population of approximately 600 at the end of the Tudor period in 1603.

Meanwhile Buckden, with its palace and its main road, could not fail to be affected by the national changes of the sixteenth century. The religious changes under Edward VI, Mary and Elizabeth Tudor brought changes of occupants to the palace, though, as is suggested above, this probably had little effect on the everyday lives of the villagers. The main difference was that after the Reformation the diocese of Lincoln was much smaller, and so Buckden became more popular and more frequently used as an episcopal residence. One result of this is that when in 1588 the country was threatened by a Spanish invasion, the bishop was very much on the spot and he seems to have enjoyed an active role in organizing the local preparations to resist the Armada. On 22 June 1588 he issued a proclamation from Buckden in his own name and that of Henry Cromwell, appointing soldiers to serve under Oliver Cromwell in case of invasion. (Both of these Cromwells were ancestors of the famous Civil War leader.) This prototype Home Guard never had to act, but the provisioning and drilling undoubtedly caused much local excitement.

Stuart Buckden

The political and religious developments of the seventeenth century were reflected in the vicissitudes of the palace. Bishop Williams (1625 - 42) undertook large-scale improvements. It is worth quoting his biographer Hackett, if only to compare his opinion of our local climate: 'He came to his seat of Bugden at disadvantage in winter; and winter cannot be more miry in any coast of England than it is round about it. He found a house... . rude, wast, untrimm'd, and in much out of the outward dress like the grange of a farmer ... This bishop did wonders in a short time . . .'

He also provided some entertainment for the villagers, though rather against his will or intention. In 1631 he allowed 'A Midsummer-Night's Dream' to be performed in the palace grounds for the local gentry. The play began at 10 o'clock on a Saturday evening but did not end until the small hours of the Sunday morning. For thus desecrating the Lord's Day the archbishop of Canterbury decreed various penalties for the participants, and a Mr. Wilson, who was blamed for instigating the project and who had played Bottom in the play, was ordered to sit in the stocks at the Porter's Lodge for the whole of the next Tuesday wearing his Ass's head and a placard round his neck:

'Good people, I have played the beast And brought ill things to pass,

I was a man but thus have made Myself a silly Asse.'

One way and another Bishop Williams certainly livened things up.

The Civil War and the period of the Protectorate was by contrast a period of destruction so far as the bishops' estate was concerned. When it was over and Bishop Sanderson was appointed his biographer Walton says he found 'a great part of it demolished, and what was left standing under a visible decay'. He initiated restoration work and his successors spent a great deal of time at the palace – Bishop Barlow, who died in 1691 and is buried in the churchyard, was known as the 'bishop of Buckden who never saw Lincoln'.

But village life in general carried on, apparently little affected by national politics. That at least is the conclusion drawn from the fact that in 1649, the year Charles I was beheaded, Buckden was busy with the restoration of the church roof, as is recorded in a carving on the rafters (see Chapter 5). This impression is confirmed by reading the Churchwardens' Account Books, where parish business was recorded through the Civil War and it hardly seems to have caused a ripple. The major loss seems to have been the ringing of the church bells: they were silent all the time Oliver Cromwell was Lord Protector. However at the Restoration in 1660 they were rung three times on the same day: for the coronation, to mark the king's birthday and in thanksgiving.

The Account Books show the everyday concerns of the seventeenth century. The Churchwardens were responsible for levying a Church rate from all but the poorest parishioners, and for a range of other activities, some of which seem a little bizarre today. They encouraged the killing of vermin, for example, by payments. A hedgehog was worth 2d., incredibly – we welcome them nowadays as eaters of smaller pests, but in those days they were believed to rob humans by sucking milk straight from the cows. By way of comparison: 18 dozen moles were only valued at 13s. 6d. in 1641, and a fox's head at 1s. in 1645. Another sign of awareness of what we now call 'ecology' was the exaction of fines for the chopping down of trees, though these were valued according to their practical uses: an ash tree felled might mean a fine of 2d., for example, while a willow (useful for basket making) was valued at 8s. The Churchwardens also had responsibility towards the poor, to wandering beggars and to any who suffered misfortune, as by fire for instance. In addition they administered the Charities which were significantly added to during the seventeenth century.

The parish registers add precious details ... or sometimes they infuriatingly fail to do so! There is a baptism entry for 2 June 1637: 'Rebecca Taylor daughter: caetera quis nescit (everyone knows the rest)' If only we did. And in 1659 when it is recorded 'William Streams and his wife were married' should we conclude that they had been living together so long that her former name had been forgotten? In 1653 the name of the 'Register' begins to be noted, the first being 'John Jakins of Bugden, barber' who was succeeded in 1655 by Henry Webb. Neither of these was responsible for the entry of 1675 which takes up a quarter of a page. Here, much ornamented with curlicues, the proud father's writing is to be seen: 'John Emerson son of Peter Emerson Vicar of Bucksden was borne on Sunday being the 23 day of January and Baptized the 29th of ffebruary being in the yeare of our Lord God 1675.' The clerk was able only to insert between the lines '& Elizabeth his wife' since this minor detail had been omitted. Sad to say the birth of a daughter the following year rated only a standard entry, as did, somewhat surprisingly, the burial of Bishop Barlow in 1691.

A name that crops up frequently in the seventeenth-century records is Rayment (a William of that name had been part of the bishop's muster in 1588 too). One of the family stands out for an act of charity. Robert Rayment, in his will dated 16 January 1661, provided for the payment of a schoolmaster who 'should yearly engage to learn the English tongue to such children of the inhabitants of Buckden, both male and female, as should be poor and unable to pay for their children's schooling, and learn such children the grounds and principles of true religion, according to the Church of England'. In 1720 it is recorded that 34 children were being taught in Buckden's charity school. This provision for the education of the poor was unusual at that time. (In 1778 Bishop Green added to it.) Another benefactor was Susannah Travill who in 1692 provided an endowment for the benefit of poor widows of the parish..

Georgian Buckden

The eighteenth century was a time of prosperity for Buckden. New methods of road building made coach travel much more comfortable and fast, and therefore more popular. The existing inn, originally the Lamb and at different times renamed the Lion and Pennant, the Lion and Lamb, and currently the Lion, was challenged by the George, built exactly facing it across the Great North Road. It was built impressively of red brick, three storeys high and fifteen windows long eventually – the brickwork shows signs of its expansion. Whatever rivalry there was between the two hostelries, the George seems to have come out on top. There is a legend that it was favoured by the notorious highwayman, Dick Turpin, who had a private emergency exit in case of trouble.

Much better authenticated is the existence of George Cartwright, who managed to combine being landlord of the George with driving the York Express daily to and from Welwyn, a seventy-mile journey. 'Peter Pry' the influential sporting writer of those days said he was an excellent driver: 'He was the idol of the road, both with old and young; while his manners on the box were respectful, communicative without impertinence, and untarnished with slang ... His excellent qualities, we are glad to notice, in conclusion, had gained their reward; he was well-to-do, lived regularly, had a happy family, and envied neither lord nor peasant.'

Some idea of just how busy Buckden High Street was in the coaching era may be gained from a schedule printed in 1839, when the age was drawing to an end. Even then there were six express coaches stopping daily at the George or the Spread Eagle on their outward and return journeys: one to Boston, two to Leeds, one to Lincoln and two to York, and 'in addition to the above, coaches from the North pass through Buckden and Eaton Socon almost hourly.' This activity naturally brought employment and prosperity to the village. There was a demand for farriers, wheelwrights, corn merchants and, of course, hostelries. All of these flourished. A most unusual establishment was one which shod geese: these were driven through warm tar and onto sand which formed a protective layer to pad their feet on the long walk to market.

A growth in its population was one consequence of the general prosperity. We can work out approximate figures from the parish registers and these suggest a population of about 700 in 1700, while the first census in 1801 recorded a population of 869, and in 1831 there were 1095 inhabitants. New houses had to be built and some of Buckden's most imposing houses belong to this period: the Red House in Church Street, a beautifully symmetrical Georgian building; the Vicarage in yellow brick with its unusual canted bay windows; Jessamine House in the High Street and Field House in Silver Street are all attractive examples.

The inhabitants of such houses, the gentry of Buckden, led a life quite separate from the ordinary villagers. They were, for example, entitled to vote in elections, and for them politics from time to time became a really lively issue. One of Buckden's vicars, the Reverend Doctor Edward Maltby (later Bishop of Durham), was at the centre of a raging controversy in 1807 when he was accused of invective in speaking against Lord Montagu's candidate in the recent election. At his own expense he published in reply 'A Letter to the Freeholders of the County of Huntingdon' in which he defended himself eloquently and set forth the electors' right ' . . . to maintain for themselves and to transmit to their children the inestimable privilege of a free and unbiased suffrage ...' These are good fighting words but we should be wary of seeing the vicar as any sort of champion of electoral reform. It seems he was as unscrupulous in his support of his own favoured candidate as were his opposition, and it has to be remembered that before 1832 the entire electoral system was very inequitable and corrupt. Moule's Huntingdonshire of 1815 gives population figures of 184 households and 973 inhabitants for Buckden, yet in the election of 1818 the Poll Book shows that only 13 freeholders voted. Politics were a pastime for the rich.

Meanwhile, how did the rest of the population live? In 1811 Parkinson's *General view of the Agriculture of the County of Huntingdonshire* appeared. It gives a great deal of information about the major landowners, of course, but also gives very interesting details about the rest of the village. The wages for an agricultural labourer were in fact below the county average: 10s. a week in winter (against 11s. 3d.) and 12s. in summer (13s. 8d.). Although prices were correspondingly low (beef at 8d. a pound for instance!) it was no easy life: 'They work from light to dark in winter, and from six to six in the spring and summer months (except harvest where they work from light till dark). The poor in general have dwellings suited to their station; and as almost every one of them grow his own potatoes and have constant employment if he pleases, they are naturally as little disposed to emigrate from Huntingdonshire, as from any other county.'

Buckdeners may in some ways have been better cared for than many others, in fact. We do not always appreciate the strength of community care in the days before the Welfare State. In the eighteenth century the gentry felt a paternalistic responsibility towards the lower orders. One intriguing example of this is the case of the Taylors. John and Mary Taylor had married in September 1717 and had four children: Mary in July 1718, but she died in infancy; Thomas in January 1720; another Mary in September 1721; and John in 1727. The three surviving children were orphaned when John and Mary died in 1729, presumably in some unusual way because they were buried on the same day, 13 April, and the parish took charge of their affairs in an extraordinary manner. The Taylors' possessions were sold and the long list of purchasers and high prices (in the Churchwarden's Account Book) suggests that most of the village turned out and bid what they could out of charity, raising between them £94 10s. 11d. The list of disbursements is equally detailed and even longer. It includes nursing, laying-out, coffins and graves for the dead, also board for the children and an apprenticeship for the girl. In all it runs to four pages. The whole record is a most unusual one, and it is intriguing to wonder what occasioned it.

More straightforward was George Swan's gift in 1766 which provided £80 to set up a workhouse. The site of this building was in Mill Road, opposite what is now Crown Cottage. It is important not to be misled, by memories of Oliver Twist for instance, into thinking Swan was anything but philanthropic. The repressive system Charles Dickens wrote about was the result of the Poor Law Amendment Act of 1834 (after which Buckden paupers were catered for by the Union Workhouse in St. Neots). In the eighteenth century individual parishes oversaw their own paupers in 'poor-houses' and judging from the records that survive Buckden was conscientious in this.

Another fascinating scrap of evidence for this care is to be found in the Parish Register: 'In April the 11th. 12th &c 1771 were inocculated for the Small Pox by Lewis Richardson of Brampton 289 Poor and 132 others of the Parish of Buckden, in all 421 of whom 5 only died 2 of them upwards of 80 years old & 3 Infants born with the Small Pox upon them. For the Poor was paid Mr. Richardson twenty one Pounds. H. Wakeman Vicar.'

That charity did not stop at home is proved by the 'Briefs' which are also noted in the Registers. These were collections taken for aid and assistance to outsiders. Several which raised particularly high sums show lists of contributors. In 1709 an eloquent appeal was made on behalf of 'the Poor Distressed Palatines (near the Rhine in Germany) more Especially the Protestants, who have sustained and layn under for several years past by the frequent Invasions of the ffrench, Whereby more than two thousand of their greatest City or Market Towns & Villages have been burnt down to the Ground so that Severall Thousands of them have been forced to leave their Native Country & seek refuge in other Nations, and of them near Eight Thousand Men Women and Children are come in and near the City of London in a poor and Miserable Condition &c.' This raised £2 10s. 8d. Like other concerns which we may have thought peculiar to the twentieth century, the refugee problem is nothing new. It seems, however, that villagers felt better able to identify with disasters nearer home, for they raised £6 18s. 8d. in September 1722 'for the Inundation in Lancashire'. The long list of names was headed by 'Edmund Lord Bishop of Lincoln £1. 1s. 0d.' and 'His Lady 10s. 6d.' and worked down to 'B. Brown £0. 0s. 2d.'

Great things were happening in the rest of England. The industrial and agricultural revolutions were changing the landscape and causing considerable distress. But here in Buckden all the evidence suggests a century of security and stability when the worst that could happen was a bad harvest. So how can we fail to quote the registrar who enjoins us in the eighteenth-century register:

'Be it Remembered ye 4th day of May
In the Year 56 was a very Snowy Day.'?

Victorian Buckden

The first decades of the nineteenth century saw the beginnings of great changes. Since medieval times methods of farming had changed little, the usual plan being open fields where landowners and leaseholders cultivated scattered strips. In Buckden the four fields were North, South, West and Mill Fields: three would usually be under cultivation while the fourth lay fallow each year. About 2500 acres (of the parish's total area of 3039) were farmed and of these the bishop of Lincoln, who was Lord of the Manor of Buckden and the Members, owned about half. The second manor, Buckden Brittains, whose lord at this time was Lawrence Reynolds, was a great deal smaller (225 acres) and there were four other people farming over 100 acres. All over England there was a move towards consolidating farming lands into fields which could be enclosed and cultivated more efficiently, and in 1813 Buckden's Enclosure Act was passed. A reading of the schedule shows that the new arrangement was by the agreement of, and largely to the advantage of, the major landowners. It is difficult to assess its effect on the ordinary villager but the parish undoubtedly began to look very different as fields were fenced and hedged.

The development which brought the greatest changes to Buckden was the coming of the railways. The opening of the Liverpool to Manchester railway in 1830 was the beginning of a transport revolution which led inevitably to a decline in the coaching trade which had underlain Buckden's Georgian prosperity.. Already in 1854 the *History, Gazetteer and Directory of the County of Huntingdon* can say Buckden is now 'a quiet insignificant place compared to what it was in coaching times, when the traffic though it was very considerable, but the many railroads which intersect the country have deprived it of this trade and support. Not one coach is now to be seen in the streets of this once bustling village. Signs of this decline in importance are visible everywhere; the most prominent is the large and mansion-like inn (the George) now divided into several tenements.'

The abrupt change in Buckden's fortunes is reflected also in the figures for its population. In 1801 (the first national census) these had reached 869. The number of inhabitants rose to 1095 by 1831 and to 1209 by 1841, but in 1851 there were only 1172 inhabitants and in the hundred years following the figure remained about a thousand. (It only increased dramatically in the 1960s.) The census returns which provide these population figures are a mine of information about the villagers of Buckden. Those of 1841 onwards list all the inhabitants by name and give details of ages, jobs and birthplaces. Using the return of 1871 and a variety of other sources (including the parish registers, post office directories, newspaper files) a local historian, Tom Lamb of Brampton, built up an amazingly detailed picture of Victorian Buckden. The two census enumerators went from house to house on foot, visiting 253 inhabited houses in all and recording a population of 1009: 474 males and 535 females. There were 260 families listed and some simple arithmetic provides the first surprise: the average family must have numbered fewer than four. This is rather different from the popular picture of the Victorian family with its tribe of children.

It is also salutary to note how many jobs you could get done without leaving Buckden. To serve 1009 villagers and travellers passing through there were: 4 butchers; 2 builders; 6 blacksmiths; 3 basketmakers; 3 bakers; 2 carriers; a coachsmith; 7 bootmakers, cordwainers and shoebinders; 6 carpenters; a coalmerchant; 2 drapers; 4 dressmakers; a dairywoman; 5 grocers; 2 general dealers; 4 gardeners; a greengrocer; a higgler; 2 lacemakers; 5 laundresses; 2 maltsters; a miller; 4 potmakers; 2 pedlars; 3 painters; a plumber and glazier; 2 seamstresses; a saddler; 2 straw bonnet makers; a thatcher; 5 tailors and a wheelwright. These were in addition to the farmers, bailiffs, shepherds, drovers and labourers on the village's eleven farms. For the scant leisure of all these people there were thirteen inns and public houses. Several still exist, but we have lost the Windmill, the Three Mill Bills, the Old Square and Compass, the Old Tap, the Black Horse, the White Horse, the Crown and the Anchor.

Another common illusion which this census shatters is the one which portrays our ancestors as people who were born, married and died in the same spot. We find that 422 out of the 1009 inhabitants were born outside Buckden: 223 in other parts of Huntingdonshire and 199 even further afield; a few came from Ireland, Scotland and France. As the population was falling, at least as many Buckden-born must have moved out of the village. The changes in transport and communications help to explain this surprising mobility. The decline may also have owed something to the great agricultural depression which was just then beginning and which tempted many British farm labourers to seek their fortunes in Canada and Australia.

The new railway system contributed to Buckden's decline, but it also, of course, served it to some extent. Two miles east of the village, in fact just outside the parish boundary, was a station on the Great Northern main line to Kings Cross called Offord and Buckden Station. A mile north of the village was Buckden Station proper on the Kettering to Cambridge branch of the Midlands Railway, which opened in 1866. This was never a busy line: for most of its existence there were three trains each weekday in each direction. Although the lack of pressure enabled the station's gardens to flourish - Buckden several times won the Best Kept Station Competition in the 1950s - the enterprise was uneconomic. Neither of Buckden's stations provided useful commuting services and both were closed down by 1962 (see **Chapter 19** for more on these two stations).

Although Buckden became a much quieter village in Victorian times, its prosperity did not decline overnight and some fine buildings were added. The almshouses in Church Street were built in a mellow version of Tudor style in 1840 with money bequeathed in 1834 by James South, who was not only a generous benefactor but a man of unusual modesty. His epitaph in the Church reads: 'Sacred to the memory of AN OFFICER, who sincerely regarded this his native village and caused an asylum to be erected, to protect Age, and to reward Industry. Reader, ask not his name. If thou approve a deed which succours the helpless, go and emulate it.'

The present Methodist chapel is also a Victorian building. The sect had come quite early to the village; its founder John Wesley actually preached here in 1781 and 1784. A small chapel was built in 1838-9 on a site next to the Lion in Church Street but a larger building was soon needed and the present site in Church Street was purchased in 1876. The foundation stone was laid in July of that year and the chapel first used for worship in November: a credit to the age of industry! The next door Sunday School room and vestries were added in 1911.

The village school – now vastly extended – was opened in 1871. The Education Act of 1870 had made provision of schooling mandatory, but in fact Buckden seems to have been well served for education even before that (see Chapter 13). That their wishes were carried out is shown by records of 1805 detailing the cost of repairs to the schoolhouse. In the 1850s Buckden boasted a school for boys, a National Society School for Girls (housed for a time in the Dining Room of the Palace), and a private 'dame school' also for girls. The 1870 Act brought its own problems. Schooling was not free to all; a payment of 4d. a week is mentioned although some free places were also available. Employers - mainly farmers - were reluctant to allow the children of their workers to receive education and parents were afraid to defy their employers and risk their jobs. Children were often marked 'absent in the fields' and, for example, on one day in April 1871 only one boy attended the first class. On another occasion thirty boys under eleven years of age were employed by the School Managers themselves at field work during school time. Not surprisingly Her Majesty's Inspector of Schools in that year was not pleased and wrote, 'The discipline of this school must be improved.'

A more humble building which provided a vital service for the village, and occasionally some incidental interest and amusement, was the new windmill built near the Great North Road in the southwest angle of Perry Road. (It was later converted into a cottage.) It was worked as a windmill until about 1888, and then an auxiliary steam engine was used for a few years. A man was killed in the 1850s when he tried to go out of a door across which the sails were working. In the 1880s a man asked the miller if he could watch Huntingdon Races (then held at Portholme) from the mill. He was strapped to a sail upside down and then raised to the top from where he declared he had an excellent view and could distinguish the jockeys' colours four miles away! The watermill on the Ouse has a much longer history, being that mentioned in the Domesday survey of 1086. Through the middle ages it was leased for a rent of ten shillings to the monks of Elstow, then after the Reformation it passed into secular ownership. In the nineteenth century it was bought by the Bowyer family who completely rebuilt it in the 1850s and converted it to steam power in the 1890s. At the beginning of the twentieth century it was modernized again and the Huntingdonshire flour it supplied to London bakers was well known for its superior quality. Today it is converted to luxury apartments.

During the nineteenth century also the Palace underwent the changes which turned it into 'The Towers'. Already in the eighteenth century Bishop Pretyman-Tomline had filled in most of the moat and provided a library. In 1837 Huntingdonshire was transferred to the diocese of Ely and in April 1838 by an Order in Council the Bishop was allowed to demolish a large part of the buildings. What remained, with the grounds, were transferred to the vicar, and it was at this time that the Palace housed a school. Finally in 1870 it passed into secular ownership. The new owner, Mr James Marshall (of Marshall and Snelgrove), found that the existing buildings were beyond repair. He filled in the remaining section of the moat and built a new house in the grounds (see Chapter 3).

And what of the people who lived in Victorian Buckden? What led the *Hunts' Post* of 1897 to make the following statement: 'The village of Buckden has enjoyed for the best part of a century the reputation of containing the most quarrelsome, cantankerous and cliquey set of people in Huntingdonshire'?

Twentieth-century Buckden

The turn of the century saw the death of Queen Victoria and the accession of Edward VII. Buckden marked the coronation by creating the green at Hunts End. This had formerly been the site of a pond and of the village stocks and pound. The trees planted at that time – lime, chestnut and plane – grew to splendid maturity, although the chestnut was replaced (by an oak) early in the present century after being damaged in a gale. In the same decade, extensive repairs to the church were carried out. The village remained a quiet place, though a certain degree of prosperity was brought back with the growing popularity of the bicycle. The first time-trial from London to York had passed along the High Street in 1872. The hardy cyclist on his solid-wheeled machine completed the journey in 42 hours and 10 minutes with an overnight stop at Stamford. Now for a brief period there were crowds of cyclists taking part in the North Road Club's road-racing events[1].

The First World War destroyed the tranquil scene. The 'lost generation' of young men who died in the conflict has become a cliché, and like every English village Buckden has its memorial. There are thirty-three names on it. It might seem invidious to single out one, but the letters V.C. after Captain John Leslie Green's name invite investigation. Green, who was born in Buckden High Street, was twenty-five when war broke out in August 1914. He had not quite finished his medical training at St. Bartholomew's Hospital, London, but he was commissioned straight away in the Royal Army Medical Corps and was soon posted as Regimental Medical Officer with the 1/5 Sherwood Foresters. He was serving with this battalion on 1st January 1916 when he married a fellow doctor, Edith Mary Nesbitt Moss. He was killed exactly six months later, one of the 19,240 young men of the British Army who lost their lives during the first day's fighting of the Battle of the Somme, 1st July 1916. For an account of his death I can do no better than to quote from the letter sent to his widow by the General Officer Commanding 139 Brigade:

I must express my intense admiration for the manner in which he met his death. He was advancing in the rear of his battalion in their assault on the German trenches. On reaching the German wire he found an officer lying seriously wounded. He moved him, under fire, into a shell hole and there dressed the wound under continuous fire and bombing from the German trenches. He then carried him back towards our lines, still under fire, though wounded himself, a matter of about 200 yards. Just before reaching our advanced trench his brother officer was hit again. Your husband started to dress his wound when he was himself shot through the head.

The General went on to express his sympathy and his opinion that the deed merited the Victoria Cross. It was awarded in October of the same year, Britain's supreme award for gallantry. Buckden therefore suffered its share of personal loss. The use of The Towers as a military hospital brought the realities of warfare close to home as well. On a lighter note: we can be sure the school children made the most of an afternoon off in 1914 to pick blackberries for jam for the soldiers.

Soon after the war, The Towers changed hands again. It was bought by Dr Robert Holmes Edleston who (again) found the old buildings ruined and neglected. He too had great plans for their restoration. In the event he carried out some excavations, renovated the gate house and rebuilt a small part of the north wing. His scheme for rebuilding the bishop's old chapel only got as far as the crypt, now the sacristy of the chapel. Edleston was devoted to the memory of Napoleon III: he wrote his biography and hoped to make a museum. This explains the mystifying inscription to the Emperor on the north wing of the Gate House; he had no other connection with the village.

Further developments in transport affected Buckden in the 1920s when motor buses began to run regular schedules. In 1921 Hinsby of St Neots was operating a service between Huntingdon and St. Neots on Thursdays and Saturdays, a year later it was four days a week, by September 1926 there was a daily service. At this time there were five buses each weekday and three on Sundays and daily commuting became a possibility. (The single fare was 6d. from Buckden to Huntingdon or St Neots.) Largely as a result of wartime demands the bus service has improved since the twenties, in contrast to many East Anglian villages' experience, though it is also vastly more expensive, of course.

There are other signs of Buckden's growing participation in the wider county scene at this time. For example, in 1927 application was made by a Miss Looker to the Huntingdon County Nursing Association for assistance in finding a suitable district nurse: 'She understood the County Association had a bicycle and

---

[1] For more on the impact of cycling on Buckden see the entries on **cycling** and **cycling clubs and cyclists** in the A to Z Section

bag they were prepared to let them have.' One fears that Buckdeners were still apt to be 'cantankerous and cliquey', though, reading in 1933 in the same minute book that Buckden and Brampton 'Definitely wished to remain as they were and would not consider amalgamating.'

Be that as it may, the 'quarrelsome' Buckdeners began the 1930s with the settlement of a very longstanding feud – and a peal of bells. The Church had, and has, five early bells, the first dating from the 16th century and inscribed 'Sca Katherina Ora Pro Nobis' (St. Katherine pray for us), and the last cast in 1627. They had been rung frequently in the seventeenth century, as the Churchwardens' Accounts show, every time the bishop arrived in the village as well as at festivals, and the ringing continued into the nineteenth century. However between 1863 and 1930 the bells were silent following a dispute between the vicar and the ringers reputed to have been about the ringers' beer allowance which it had been their custom to consume in the belfry. When the vicar banned this practice they staged a strike which lasted a very long time.

The sound of bells in 1930 was not so out-of-place as might be thought, for although the thirties were a time of world-wide depression, Buckden escaped the worst effects, which fell on industrial areas. In fact the growing popularity of the motor-car meant that Buckden benefited once again from its position on the Great North Road. Council houses were built in Silver Street and the village also spread up Perry Road. The inhabitants – still about a thousand of them – largely made their own amusements and the village boasted a rifle range, a brass band and an operatic society.

A spectacular event took place in 1932 when 'The Pageant of the Centuries' was presented at Buckden Palace in aid of the County Hospital. In sixteen scenes it showed all the royal visitors to Buckden whom we have rather neglected, from Richard the Lionheart through Edward I, James I to George III (some of their visits better authenticated than others). It also featured Cardinal Wolsey, who stayed overnight here in his period of disgrace; the two young sons of the Duke of Suffolk, Charles and Henry Brandon, who fled to Buckden to escape the sweating sickness in 1551, died of it and are buried in the churchyard; and the 'Witch of Warboys', a harmless old woman tried at Buckden in 1592 and burnt to death[1]. It was a great success. Three years later George V's Silver Jubilee was the occasion for more home-grown entertainment including a Church service, a parade of 'decorated cycles, prams etc.', sports, dancing and a bonfire as grand finale.

Once again, as a generation before, this contentment was not allowed to last: it was disrupted by the Second World War. Sixteen names were to be added to the war memorial, on supplementary blocks. Although it suffered little direct damage, the village had to cope with shortages, which it did by cultivating allotments, and play host to evacuees. Tollington School from Finsbury Park in London was evacuated to Buckden, and the Methodist Sunday School (built in 1911) became its educational centre.

The 1950s were a chance for quiet recovery between the destruction of war and the sixties' unprecedented expansion. The village was looking backwards and forwards. In 1952 Bowtells celebrated fifty years of business on the High Street site. Before 1902 there had been a shop there for at least a hundred and fifty years, but Bowtells had expanded it greatly, building the present shop with its Elizabethan-style front in 1923. Looking to the future was Mr. W. B. Carter, an ex-naval man who settled in Buckden and developed a small boat-hiring business at Buckden Mill and later bought eleven acres of land beside the river which he turned into Buckden Marina. There was a real coronation to celebrate in 1953 and in the same year and the following four Buckden crowned a May Queen in an annual Festival.

The most spectacular changes in the village's history took place in the second half of the century, during which Buckden's population has more than doubled; from 1158 in 1961 it increased to 2490 in 1975 and by 2008 to an estimated 2515. Housing the influx of people necessitated new housing estates, but these have largely been planned with care and the village centre is unspoilt. An eighteenth-century Bugdener would soon find his way about, helped by the way road-names have preserved old features of the village like the Bishop's vineyard, the glebe (vicar's land) and the manor house's gardens. The re-routing of the A1 to by-pass the village centre made the High Street less hectic. The school had to expand greatly to provide for the expanding population: in 1966 a new infant school was opened and in 1972 the junior school. The infants' section had to be extensively rebuilt after a fire in 1978. After certain vicissitudes the Palace returned to the Catholic Church and in 1956 was granted to the Claretian Order who carried out restoration work and also built a fine Roman Catholic church for the village and a parish hall. Other new facilities for the community are the recreation ground and the village hall. The *Buckden Roundabout*, a monthly newsletter produced by the joint churches, began in the 1970s and has been a great success.

In 1971 the Burberry Homes were opened to care for more of the elderly parishioners. They were built with money from Burberry's endowment and other village charities. There can surely be no more solid

---

[1] For more on this and similar events see entry on **pageants** in the A to Z Section

evidence that as the twentieth century drew to a close, Buckden, with all its changes, was still rooted very firmly in its past.

Millennial Buckden

The years either side of 2000 have seen Buckden continue to adapt to a changing world. The relentless expansion of Cambridgeshire's economy has put Buckden under pressure to provide new housing, resulting in a large development on the allotment field between the A1 and Silver Street, smaller developments within and without the built-up area of the village, and the conversion of office and other business premises (including a pub) to residential use. An increasing demand for social housing has led to two sites being developed in partnership with housing associations, one expressly intended to help Buckden people stay in their own village. Housing with support has also been provided through private investment at King George Court, built in the grounds of the George Hotel.

Road safety remains of concern as traffic continues to grow on both the east/west and the north/south axis of the village. Speed reduction and restriction measures have been introduced between the school and the green, and on Perry Road, Mill Road and the approaches to the A1 roundabout. The parish council remains deeply concerned about the consequences for Buckden's road users of such proposals as the development of Alconbury airfield and the building of a new A14 relief road between Ellington and Fen Drayton.

Buckden continues to support a remarkable range of shops for a village within easy driving distance of three major urban centres and almost on the doorstep of two market towns. Some businesses have changed hands but continue in the same trade, others have changed hands *and* the nature of their business. Only a few enterprises have ceased trading entirely. The rapidly accelerating processor speeds of personal computers gave the village a new generation of cottage industries, on which the arrival of high-sped internet access (broadband) at the Buckden exchange in June 2003 has had an impact similar to that which, in the nineteenth century, the railway had on Buckden's millers and fruit growers, enabling them to reach profitable new markets.

Buckden is lucky not only in its shops, but in its possession of a pharmacy, post office, doctors' surgery, dental surgery, school and sports facilities. The millennium brought Buckden a substantial new village hall, the envy of many a larger parish, with its meeting and recreation rooms, a fine new stage, and space for the county library branch.

At an end, finally,[1] are the long years of mineral extraction in Buckden, and also in Diddington, its neighbour to the south. They leave behind a changed landscape along the lowlands in the Great Ouse valley, with large areas of traditional farmland replaced by wetland and reedbed habitats. But on the whole, Buckden still stands in a largely unspoilt countryside, albeit an arable one with very little now to be seen in the way of livestock. Within the built-up village, too, most of its remaining green areas have escaped development in the last twenty years, and the parish council actively encourages the replacement of an ageing tree population.

Like any modern town or village, Buckden has its identity problems: older residents remember a smaller, more cohesive community where Feast Week and May Day, coronations and jubilees, weekly dances and fundraising events, were celebrations in which everyone would join: joyously, loudly and publicly. Today people are less inclined to take spontaneously to the streets[2]; through their cars, televisions and computers they have more opportunities for self-contained entertainment. Modern life tends also to discourage socializing across the age divide. To that extent, a genuine community spirit manifests itself less frequently (the last time, perhaps, being a mass meeting in the mid-1990s that saved the library from closure). But if the big events rarely stimulate a big response, the urge to be involved has certainly not disappeared: in Buckden, the community is still strengthened by the day-to-day involvement of those who care for others: voluntary car schemes for patients, the Neighbourhood Watch, the churches, those who run groups for the elderly. Unfortunately, the enthusiasm of volunteers has to battle not only against public apathy but the fear (sometimes justified) of bureaucracy, litigation and the need for costly public liability insurance.

Buckden is not unique in facing such concerns, and remains for most of its inhabitants a village well worth the living in. Or, as one resident said, looking round him in Lucks Lane cemetery, 'Not such a bad place to be dead in, either.'

---

[1] Well, for now, at least.

[2] And would probably be arrested if they did. Or run over.

Which, aptly, is a reminder that not the least pressing of the problems facing the parish in the years ahead is the need to find new burial space. Most of the people of Buckden may live longer, healthier lives than most of their forebears, but they are not immortal – yet.

CHAPTER 3/BUCKDEN'S BUILDINGS
Beth Davis

Beth Davis is an architectural historian and lecturer, and compiled the schedule of listed buildings for the Cambridgeshire resurvey in the 1980s

Introduction

Buckden has always been important as a welcome stop for travellers going to and from London. It became a pied-à-terre for the bishops of Lincoln for several hundred years: some indeed made their home here; others used it as a summer palace. Although they had several residences to choose from, Buckden was ideally situated between Lincoln and London at the 'centre' of their huge diocese. Five even chose to be buried in the parish church rather than in their cathedral.

The coaching days of the late seventeenth century brought further prosperity to Buckden with the recognisable building and rebuilding of the two great coaching inns. The railway, arriving in the mid nineteenth century, temporarily brought an end to the trade of the coaching inns but this began to recover before the end of the century with the increasing popularity of bicycling (especially long-distance road racing), a recovery consolidated in the early twentieth century by the rise of motor transportation. The Great North Road became a vital trunk road in the later twentieth century and now, as the A1 bypass, takes through traffic away from the High Street.

The buildings of Buckden reflect all these changes as well, of course, as the economic changes in the local countryside from medieval manorial control to the enclosure of the open fields in the early nineteenth century; these successive changes of land ownership have influenced new and old buildings in the town, where the fortunes of individual owners have been clearly expressed in their homes. The present day need to house an ever-growing population in the countryside is shown by the 1960s' expansion of the township on the east side with planned housing estates named with historic references to Buckden's past.

Buckden has a remarkable range of buildings; just by walking around the streets it is possible to see buildings dating from the medieval period down to our own times; it is noticeable that the materials they are built from not only vary from building to building but have varied in each century. Some buildings have been altered and extended, and others have replaced earlier buildings on ancient sites. The church and the palace, the inns and pubs, gentry houses, yeoman farmhouses, cottages and cottage rows all show this variety and are mixed together along the older village streets.

In the medieval and post medieval periods, masonry buildings of brick and stone were the most prestigious; the materials for these buildings had to be hauled from a distant source or were expensive in fuel to manufacture and were therefore not used by the common people. They found their building materials locally from the land—the woodlands and hedgerows and the farmyard. Timber-framing was the traditional form of building in Huntingdonshire up to the late seventeenth century when good building timber became scarce and brick was more easily available. Building styles changed and were clearly influenced by fashion and the technology of new materials; wealth and social needs have always played their part in the type and quality of buildings. All these variations have contributed to the characteristics that have produced such a variety in Buckden and help us to date the buildings in each century.

The survival of buildings over the centuries depended largely on their being in continuous use. It goes without saying that buildings all need to be maintained and lived in; those that were abandoned were demolished, or partly demolished and replaced. Some buildings have been recorded by deeds, maps, manorial records and surveys, and others have left their imprint in the ground to be discovered by later disturbance; but many have been forgotten. Four building surveys have been carried out in Huntingdonshire in the twentieth century. The earliest was in 1926 for the the Royal Commission's inventory of the historic monuments of Huntingdonshire, the records made at that time being kept in the National Monument Record in Swindon. The *Victoria County History for Huntingdonshire* was produced

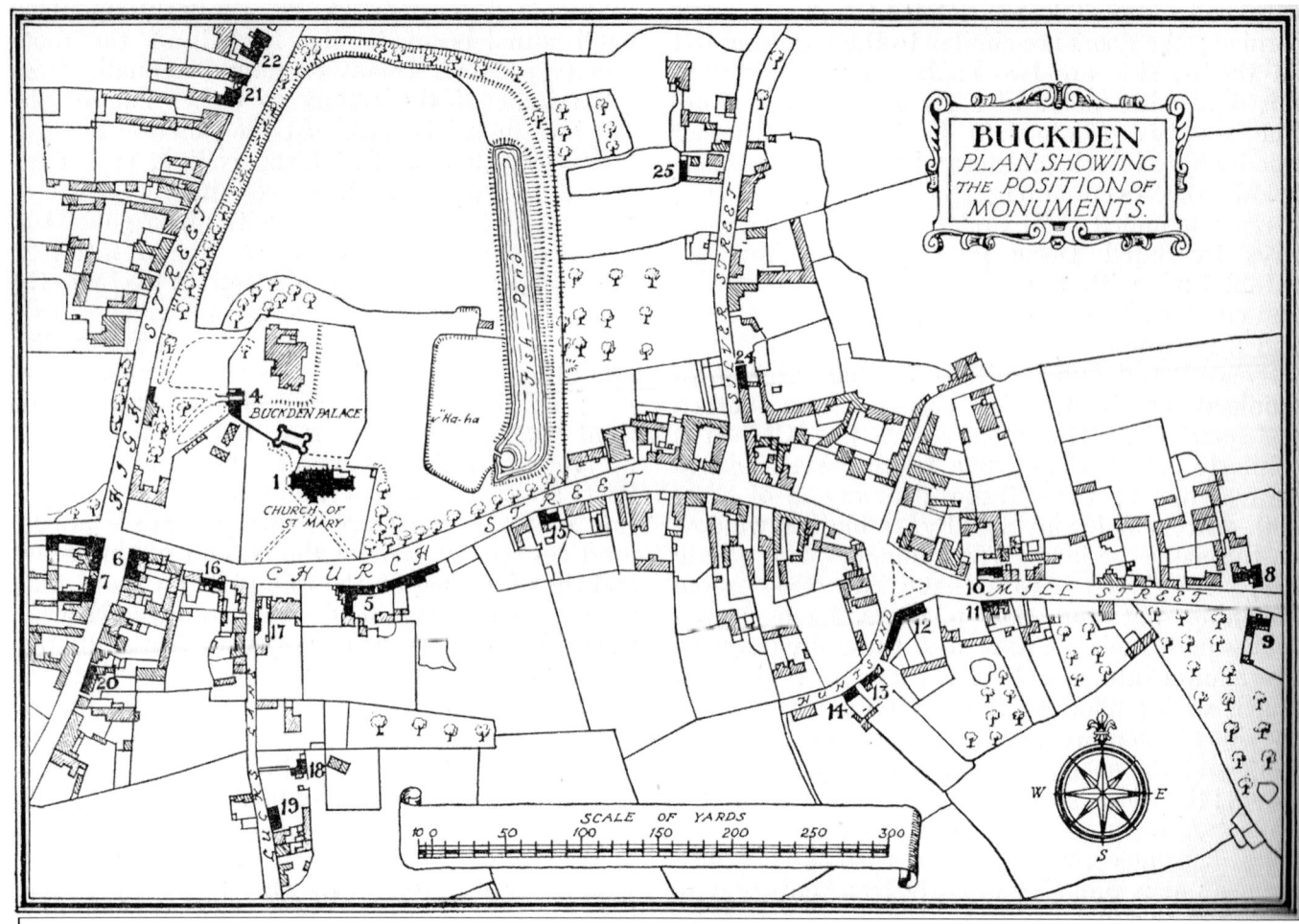

The plan of Buckden from the report from Royal Commission on Historical Monuments of 1926.
N.B. The RCH numbering is not the same as the numbering on the village plan on pages vi and vii.

in 1932, edited among others by Sidney Inskip Ladds, the Ely Diocesan architect; his records are held in the Norris Museum, St Ives. In 1968, the architectural historian Nicholas Pevsner recorded significant buildings in Buckden for *Bedfordshire and the County of Huntingdon and Peterborough* in his Buildings of England series; and the latest and most comprehensive survey was carried out for the Department of the Environment as a resurvey *List of Buildings of Special Architectural or Historic Interest* in 1983. This final survey was to produce the list of buildings (or structures) that by Act of Parliament were to be protected from inappropriate alteration or demolition. There are 63 listed buildings in Buckden, four are grade I, two are grade II* the remainder are grade II. The four grade I, nationally outstanding buildings, are the church, the Great Tower, the inner gatehouse, and the curtain wall of the former Palace of Buckden. The grade II* buildings are the Manor House in Church Street and the outer gateway of Buckden Palace and boundary wall.

This chapter is an overview of the historic buildings in their Buckden setting and is not a detailed architectural description of each building.

The Church of St Mary the Virgin

The earliest surviving building in Buckden is the church, which like the bishops' palace, has been altered and rebuilt several times from the twelfth century. The chancel was probably extended in the late thirteenth century to conform with the latest liturgical requirements, but when the whole church was largely rebuilt in the fifteenth century, the sedilia and priest's doorway in the chancel were reused and with a base to an arcade pier are reminders of that late thirteenth century date. The rebuilding of the church was carried out between 1436 and 1449 by Bishop Alnwick. The very fine Perpendicular tower appears to be independently constructed, and must be earlier than the rebuilding of the chancel and chancel arch and the aisle arcades and aisles which are contemporary with one another. As the tower does not align with the nave and aisles there is some debate as to whether there had been a change of plan after it was built for widening the church. This may be due to the proximity of the palace moat on the north side. If this was the case the south aisle was constructed before the north aisle and the adjustment to the plan was made after this. It is interesting that in the eighteenth century buttresses were needed to support the north aisle walls so there was some justification in siting the nave and aisles away from the moat. The fine fifteenth century roofs were repaired in the seventeenth century, 1649 appears on a wall plate with the initials I.I.~C.P., and 1665 is carved on one boss with the initials R.W. Other restorations were carried out in the nineteenth century and later.

The rebuilding of the nave and aisles took place possibly using much of the original building material of the earlier church, but the best quality material for the walls, that is the limestone rubble, was reserved for the chancel and the tower. The freestone for the tower and spire came from or near Barnack in Northamptonshire; some rubble stone may have come from the Lincolnshire limestone quarries. The cost of hauling the stone by bullock cart from the quarries to the river Nene, and then transporting it down the rivers Nene and Ouse must have been prodigious. The site of the hythe (riverside landing-place) for Buckden has not been established: it may have between what are now Buckden Marina and The Old Flour Mills, but the identification cannot be certain.

The local cobbles for the walls of the aisles would originally have been gleaned from the boulder clay in the open fields, they were laid in courses and like the limestone rubble walls were packed with lime mortar; you may be able to see the 'day-work' levels in the exposed walls. Most building work was seasonal and in the autumn the walls would be protected by a thatched covering. The scaffold lifts can be seen marked on the walls by the putlog holes left by the scaffold poles; the holes were usually left after the work was completed, but those on the tower and spire have been carefully filled in with matching stone. The external and internal rubble and cobble walls would originally have been plastered and limewashed: the limewash sometimes can be seen on some of the window masonry.

The master mason for the rebuilding of the church would have produced the plan and working drawings for the tower and spire, with all the architectural details. He would have had a team of layer masons constructing the walls, banker masons who cut the building stones for the walls, precisely to certain positions and marked with their individual mark, and carver masons who produced the mouldings from templates or 'moulds' which were made from his designs. It is possible that the carved window openings and tracery, and doorways and other details were produced near their quarry of origin, thus reducing the weight of the stone; this mason's yard may have been in Lincolnshire where the best limestone was still being quarried. The banker masons would work somewhere on site in a purposely built open-sided shed or lodge. The master mason would use a tracing floor to prepare his plans and designs, which may have been in the old church on a specially laid surface of lime plaster that he would use rather like a drawing board. The plans were drawn to their natural size with compasses and the set square *ad quadratum*, drawings using the square and the diagonal and *ad triangulatum* the triangle with the circle. The master mason possibly finished the finer details using chalk or lamp black.

These designs were copied onto parchment for use by the carver masons and may have been used several times by them (repeated for several windows). The scale and proportion of each element of the design for the church, tower and spire can be rediscovered today in reverse by using the same principles of geometry. The geometric patterns of the windows, arcades and doorways were then a developing tradition and details particularly of the window tracery and the proportions of the four-centred arches can be dated by comparison; the windows of St Mary the Virgin in Buckden are Perpendicular in style and beautifully proportioned. The church was meant to look like 'paradise on earth', and the crenellations of the parapets would inform passers-by that they had been granted by royal consent.

The Bishop of Lincoln's Palace

The remains of the Bishop's Palace occupy a large enclosure in Buckden on the east side of the Great North Road. This was the administrative centre of a large estate that included the manor of Spaldwick. The boundary walls survive with the gated entrance and inner gatehouse which is linked to the Great Tower by a curtain wall. The dates for these buildings are known and are recorded in the *Victoria County History*. Leyland, the Cambridge antiquarian, states that Bishop Scott, alias Rotherham (1472-80), built the new red brick tower, and Bishop Russell (1480-94) completed it and built the entrance gatehouse, enclosing all within a moat. In a survey of 1647, taken during the Commonwealth for the trustees of the sale of the bishop's lands, all the buildings are described, including the great hall and chapel with kitchen enclosure walls, the gateways, and the Great Tower referred to as the King's Lodging. Bishop Hacket, writing after the Restoration in 1660, describes the site: 'what remains of all this cost and beauty? All is dissipated, defaced, plukt to pieces to pay the army.' Many of the buildings had been pulled down during the Commonwealth

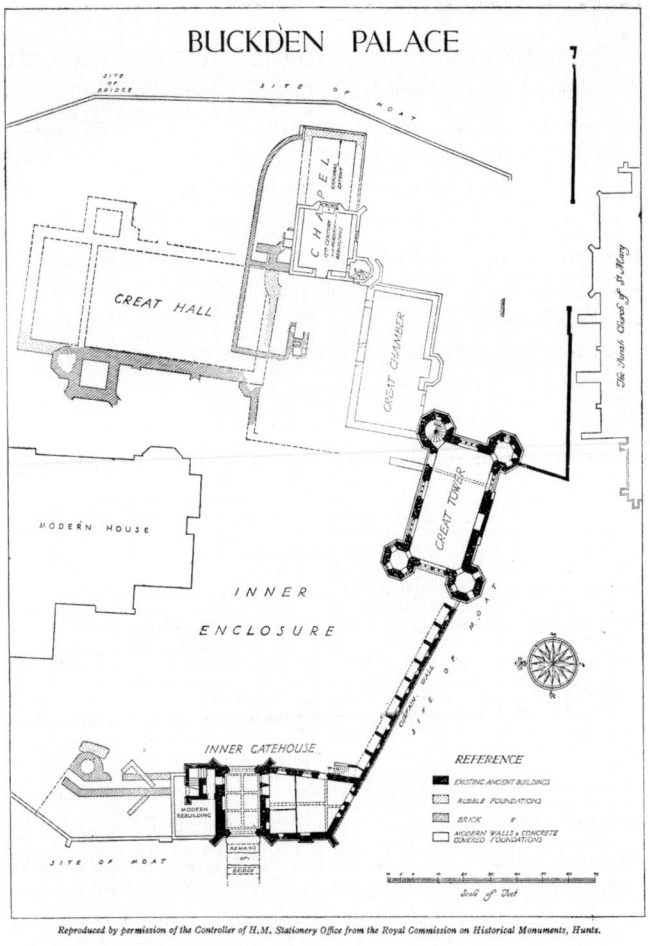

BUCKDEN PALACE

REFERENCE
EXISTING ANCIENT BUILDINGS
RUBBLE FOUNDATIONS
BRICK
MODERN WALLS & CONCRETE
COVERED FOUNDATIONS

Reproduced by permission of the Controller of H.M. Stationery Office from the Royal Commission on Historical Monuments, Hunts.

Plan from the Victoria County History

(1649-60) by Christopher Packe, a close associate of Oliver Cromwell.[1] Bishop Sanderson, who was appointed in 1660, set about repairing the buildings at his own cost, and the Palace was to remain a favourite residence of the bishops for nearly two hundred years.

Excavations have found traces of the great medieval hall and chapel which were possibly built of Barnack limestone and clunch[2], the remains of which could have been reused in the repair or remains of the inner gatehouse. Great timbers were felled from the forest of Weybridge near Huntingdon for the rebuilding of the great hall after a fire in 1291.

The surviving palace buildings are late fifteenth century in date and were constructed at the same time as other notable brick buildings in the eastern counties, particularly in Lincolnshire and locally in Cambridge. This is a time when Flemish brick makers and layers were employed by the court of Henry VII and later by Henry VIII. The Great Tower in Buckden was built as the King's Lodgings and is similar in plan though not in detail to Tattershall Castle, built for Ralf Cromwell in Lincolnshire in 1434-35. The superb quality of the bricks and the construction of the building must surely imply that a Flemish master mason was at work here in Buckden: brick building on this scale was unprecedented in Huntingdonshire at that time. The skill and intricate detail of the brickwork points to a man who was skilful in design and planning, from the manufacture of the bricks to the management of a large work force. It is possible that local people were used as labourers but Flemings were employed as the 'layers' of the bricks.

The diaper work can just be made out in the west wall of the Inner gate House. Bishop Russell's shield is clearer.

The Great Tower was built to impress visiting episcopal lords and royalty rather than for defence. The siting beside the moat may have been for reasons associated with discharge from the garderobes on the south side of the tower, which is buttressed by a great chimney stack that can be seen from the churchyard. Could this siting have been popular with the members of the parish church at that time? The bricks of the walls were laid in English bond, that is with alternating courses of headers and stretchers, while the courses laid in curved and irregular walls are in a header bond. The mortar bond is particularly thick to carry the bricks that are not perfect, but few bricks are imperfect. The openings to doorways and windows are constructed from moulded bricks reproducing the moulded details found on medieval stone masonry, but there are classical details in the clays that produced the bright red brick. The clay was

---

[1] Sir Christopher (later Lord) Packe (c. 1599–1682) was a leading City merchant, alderman, Lord Mayor and MP. In 1649 he paid some £8000 for the manor of Buckden. Despite financial scandals and the notoriety of having suggested to parliament that Cromwell should be offered the crown, he survived the return of Charles II and moved serenely into a prosperous old age.

[2] Clunch has been used for some 'stonework' details. It is a hard chalk that is easily carved and is quarried in Cambridgeshire.

98

dug before the frosts of winter and was tempered and cleaned ready for brick making in the spring. The brick makers worked in open hovels and possibly formed 1000 bricks a day using open wooden moulds. Two or more assistants prepared the clay and carried the green bricks to the hacking yard to be dried. After drying in hacks they would have been fired in clamps nearby using wood as fuel brought in from the woodland on the estate. The clamps were constructed on the ground with channels for the fuel covered by discarded bricks at the base, then the green bricks would be placed diagonally on edge about two inches apart and packed with fuel to a height of 14 feet; the firing may have taken two to three weeks as the bricks are remarkably uniform in colour showing that experienced brickmakers were involved. The moulded (shaped) bricks for the openings are a lighter red possibly because they had been made from a more refined clay. The bricks that were overburnt have a blue/black bloom and were used in the diaper work decoration.

The Four Coaching Inns

The four coaching inns, the George with its forge, the Lion, the Vine and the Spread Eagle were improved in the late seventeenth and eighteenth centuries to accommodate travellers from the Great North Road. The Lion was established by the late sixteenth century and has a great fireplace and a magnificent ceiling of oak beams with a carved boss of a Lamb inscribed with 'Agnus Dei'. It has had many alterations; the former fifteenth century jettied facade was rebuilt in both the eighteenth and nineteenth centuries. It may have been a courtyard inn similar to the George. The Vine was rebuilt in the eighteenth century and has a contemporary stable range attached to it on the west side; the outbuildings have been demolished for present day development. The George originally had a courtyard plan with galleried wings. It was re-fronted in two separate periods in the eighteenth century when the two timber-framed wings of earlier dates were retained. Alterations have been made to the brickwork of the imposing main facade of thirteen bays but the original three storeys with recessed windows and central double entrance remains. The south wing was re-fronted in about 1925, an indication, perhaps, of a flourishing trade brought about by the tourists and commercial travellers who fuelled the post-war revival in motoring.[1] The Spread Eagle further along the High Street was altered in the early eighteenth century from a seventeenth century coaching inn: its timber-framed north wing was retained (and later used as a shop) while a new main range with projecting bay windows was built. This inn closed in 2003, and both the main building and the outbuildings were converted to residential use.

Traditional Buildings

Timber framing was the preferred method of building in Buckden until the late seventeenth century when timber became scarce and often salvaged timber was used. This has given rise to a later belief that timbers with unusual features were ships timbers, which is not true. There are records of great timbers coming from the King's Forest of Weybridge, for the rebuilding of the Palace in the late thirteenth century, but generally timber for building came from the local parks, woods or hedgerows. When the Ouse was opened to navigation in the seventeenth century timber was imported from the Continent, and timber-framed buildings complete for erection may have been imported from a timber yard then. The surviving timber-framed buildings of Buckden date from the early fifteenth to the late seventeenth centuries.

The methods of timber framing had evolved over several hundreds of years and had regional characteristics. The roofs were either crown post roofs or side purlin roofs constructed without a ridge piece in Huntingdonshire and East Anglia. The wall frames were built with posts and tie beams (post and truss construction), with studs and braces forming the exposed pattern between each timber-framed bay, and these became straight braced with interrupted studs in the seventeenth century. The carpenter selected the trees from the woodland for the timber that was needed for posts and rafters etc., and prepared the timbers in the framing yard, marking the joints with Roman numerals. The types of joints used can be dated: they were all pegged with wooden pegs that were cut to shape and baked before use so that they could swell into the peg holes holding the joints tightly. The carpenter constructed the frame; the joiner constructed the windows and doors, the staircases, and panelling for the best rooms.

The farmhouse or cottage usually conformed to a traditional width of approximately 16 feet (a rod, pole or perch). The main room or the hall was usually square in plan and may have been set out first on the ground with extra bays for the parlour and service rooms (dairy or pantry) on either side; the cross passage was included in the hall on the side of the service rooms. The foundations were dug to a depth below the top soil and a plinth was built from field stones or stone rubble, above which the ground sill would be laid and the timber frame erected in sequence. The timber frame was constructed in green oak and would have

---

[1] 'After the First World War a large floating population of ex-servicemen reportedly took up travelling in preference to returning to the routines of office work.' French, M. (2005) Commercials, careers and culture: travelling salesmen in Britain 1890s-1930s. *Economic History Review* 58(2):pp. 352-377.

been allowed to season before it was completed with panels from wattles made from hedgerow material; these were daubed with a rough plaster mixed with cow dung and then coated with lime plaster. The earliest timber-framed building dating from the early fifteenth century is Bridge House[1], Church Street; it has a crown post roof and a substantial timber frame which would have been exposed; the cross wing on the west side was built later in the seventeenth century when it was fashionable to plaster over the timber-frame completely. The Manor House also has two distinct periods of timber-framing, from the late fifteenth or early sixteenth century and the early seventeenth century. The earliest part of this building may have been a court house or guildhall that later became part of a complex of buildings associated with the manor and the manor farm. It has a double jetty, one to Church Street and the other to an inner courtyard. In the early seventeenth century a large wing was added to the west gable of the jettied building reducing it in length, and later in the same century a barn was added to the east gable parallel to the road.[2] The west wing of the Manor House has some very fine examples of early seventeenth-century carved wall panels, chimney pieces and an oak staircase with turned balusters.

The Manor House.
The nearer end was added as a barn in the 17thC.

Thus both Bridge House and the Manor House demonstrate changing attitudes towards timber framing. In the fifteenth and sixteenth centuries, the timber in each building was carefully matched and meant to be seen; in the seventeenth century, however, fashion dictated that timber be hidden under plaster, not only in the exterior and interior walls of the newly-built wings, but in the existing facades as well. The plan of buildings also changed through the centuries, but in a traditional way. The cross passage between the front and rear entrance in the hall of all medieval buildings was generally chosen as the best position to build the chimneystack, which was not introduced until the late sixteenth century either in brick or timber frame, and became commonplace in the seventeenth century and later. The original front entrance, even in newly built houses and cottages, opened into a small lobby beside the chimney with a door or doors on either side leading into the main rooms. An example of this new plan can be seen in the White House, Mill Road, the doorway of which has a lobby entrance position in front of a fine seventeenth century red brick chimney stack with grouped shafts. (The shafts on the chimney stacks were called funnels in the seventeenth century.) Extensions such as a kitchen wing were often added to the rear of the main range forming a T-plan or an L-plan house, sometimes with an outshut.[3] This plan, modified, became the plan that was adopted for the early-eighteenth-century house, and for extensions to existing houses.

Eighteenth Century Rebuilding

Brick was fashionable in the eighteenth and nineteenth centuries. New houses were built on larger plots on all the main streets in Buckden, reflecting the prosperity of the township and the latest in taste. Most of these buildings, however, show individual taste in plan and detail and most are of two storeys with attics and dormer windows. Many houses retain the flush framed window rather than the recessed window frame seen in the George and the Old Vicarage, with the brick parapet dictated by statute after the Fire of London for recessed timber details in towns. Older timber-framed buildings were updated at this time with new facades and with hung sash windows and fine entrance doorways. The street side jetty to the Manor House was underbuilt in brick at this time, and a small cottage in Luck's Lane was cased in brick. The interiors of these houses may have been updated in a similar way to the newly-built houses with fine, painted joinery details, which in some cases were possibly purchased from London.

The bricks for this rebuilding may have been imported from larger brickyards beside the river Ouse or may have been made locally: there are many eighteenth-century leases in the Huntingdonshire Archives which include permissions to dig for brick and tile; there were certainly pits to the west of what is now the A1. The quality of the eighteenth-century bricks in Buckden are good; the bricks are laid in a Flemish bond, which is where the bricks alternate as headers and stretchers in each course. The openings in the walls and corners have smaller bricks set like a margin, which can be a good guide to where alterations have been

---

[1] See Chapter 6
[2] The barn was still in use (as a milking-parlour) well into the twentieth century.
[3] An outshut is an extension to a building, with a lean-to or catslide roof.

made. The bricks of the window arches, the brick band or string course of two or three courses, and the cornice details were all made from gauged bricks, specially made and rubbed to fit tightly together; they were often a brighter red colour. The mortar courses are improved with a line called a 'penny roll' or with tuck pointing using lime putty.

Most eighteenth-century houses have a symmetrical plan with a central entrance doorway, but there are a number of buildings in Buckden with side passages or archways or asymmetric facades. In the later

93, High Street

eighteenth century, yellow brick was preferred in deference to the Palladian taste; the Old Vicarage is clearly a model of this, the original vicarage, described in 1648 as being 'of timber & covered with tile', having been re-fronted in 1783 and thoroughly rebuilt in 1795; inside there is a remnant timber-framed wall. No. 93 High Street is unique in having stuccoed walls with rusticated quoins applied to the original yellow brick. The yellow brick is made from a purer clay excavated below the subsoil of the local clays, and may have come from a St Ives brickyard. The white brick of Cambridgeshire and the fens was becoming popular. In looking through the account books of Edward Gale of Buckden, we find he was supplying thousands of bricks to the Northern Railway from 1843, and to other villages for cottages. Improvement and new brick buildings within the township of Buckden continued, but the easy transportation of building materials brought to an end the use of local building materials, so that slate roofs replaced thatch. Some pantiles and plain tiles became a preferred alternative.

As a footnote it must be said that timber frame still remained the most economical building method in the eighteenth and nineteenth centuries. Timber-framed walls were sometimes built between brick gable walls or a single brick facade and as internal partition walls. The plastered timber-frame was sometimes lined out to simulate stone masonry, or limewashed a terracotta red to simulate brickwork. The timber-frame of outbuildings was usually clad in weather boards: these were elm planks in the seventeenth and eighteenth centuries, graded so that the largest were at the bottom. Later, in the nineteenth century, tarred pine boards were used. Some outbuildings such as granaries were plastered internally to seal the walls from vermin. Dairies were plastered and limewashed.

Select Bibliography
Brunskill, R.W. *Brick Building in Britain*, 1990
Brunskill, R.W. *Timber Building in Britain*, 1985
Harvey, J.   *Medieval Craftsmen*, 1975
Pacey, A.   *Medieval Architectural Drawing*, 2008
Parissien, S   *The Georgian House*, 1994
Saltzman, L.P. *Building in England Down to 1540* 1952

Surveys
Department of the Environment   *Lists of Buildings of Special Architectural or Historic Interest*, 1983
Pevsner, N. *The Buildings of England: Bedfordshire and the County of Huntingdon and Peterborough*, 1968
Royal Commission on Historical Monuments   *Huntingdonshire*, 1926
The Victoria History of the Counties of England   *A History of Huntingdonshire, Volume II*, 1932

CHAPTER 4/BUCKDEN PALACE TO BUCKDEN TOWERS
Ben Nicol And Ieuan Evans

There are many villages and small towns on the Great North Road, but few have at their centre such potent reminders of past glories as Buckden does. Two fine hotels face each other across the High Street, just as they did when the village was an important staging post in the great age of coaching. A little way up the road runs the high boundary wall of The Towers, once a palace of the bishops of Lincoln, whose presence brought fame and prosperity to Buckden.

NB The letters 'q.v.' after a name or place in the following text indicate that more information on the subject can be found in the A to Z Section.

Beginnings

Not long after the Norman Conquest in 1066, King William started to re-organise the Anglo-Saxon church. The largest diocese in the country was that of Dorchester-on-Thames in Oxfordshire, which stretched from the Midlands to the east coast and from the Thames to the Humber. One of William's first changes was to transfer the diocesan seat to Lincoln. This was over twice as far from London as Dorchester had been, promising inconvenience for the bishop, whose presence would be frequently required in Westminster: medieval bishops were an important part of government. In addition, pastoral and administrative responsibilities would require him to travel widely. Buckden, in the centre of the diocese and only sixty miles from London on the Great North Road was ripe for development as the most important of the residences that the bishop and his retinue would require during their journeys.[1]

Over the subsequent years we gather more details: there were stewponds for farming fish for the table, a warren for rabbits and a vineyard. The estate was divided in two by the Great North Road: the Little Park around the Palace and the Great Park to the west, between the road and Brampton Wood; the Great Park supported 200 head of deer at one time. It is clear Buckden had become not just a convenient stopping-off place, but a favourite residence, rivalling the Bishop's Palace in Lincoln.

For all its importance to them, some bishops failed to maintain the property, while others made singular efforts to preserve it. Three times it passed out of church hands, with mixed results. Nevertheless it has survived nine centuries of varying fortune to become a Scheduled Ancient Monument, and a busy religious training and retreat and conference centre, incorporating the local Roman Catholic parish church.

In the Middle Ages

The outstanding figure in the history of the diocese in the twelfth century is St Hugh of Lincoln, known also as Hugh of Avalon. He was born near Grenoble in about 1140. He might not have arrived in England at all, if it had not been for the murder of St Thomas of Canterbury in 1170. Full of remorse for his involvement in the crime, King Henry II founded a Carthusian priory at Witham in Somerset as a penance. When the project faltered Hugh was recommended to the king to take over as prior. Known not only for his holiness, Hugh was an able administrator, and before long the priory began to prosper and in time he was chosen to fill the vacant see of Lincoln (1186), where much work awaited his arrival, not least the rebuilding of the cathedral which had collapsed in an earthquake two years earlier. He opposed corruption and injustice and achieved much for his people. With good humour and

---

[1] Lincoln would remain the largest English diocese even after losing territory to the new sees of Ely (1109), Peterborough (1541) and Oxford (1542).

determination, he stood up to the king and afterwards to his son Richard I (the Lionheart), neither of them easy to deal with.

Although they tell us nothing about the property itself, his biographers tell us about the frequent visits he made to Buckden. It was here too that his body rested on its way to Lincoln after his death in London in 1200. The pattern was set for the residence to grow in importance.

Hugh was canonised in 1220, and there is no better saint to lend his name to today's church at The Towers. In medieval times, when few could read, it became the custom to add a symbol, or *attribute,* to the picture or statue of a saint to make recognition easier. Our reading is better nowadays, but the modern depictions of Hugh in the Inner Courtyard and the church include his swan. He came across the swan at Stow, near Lincoln, another of his residences; it is said to have been a large, fierce bird but the Bishop tamed and befriended it.

In the thirteenth century another Hugh, Hugh de Wells (1209 – 1235) replaced a largely timber building with a more permanent structure. His work was continued by the great Bishop Robert Grosseteste (1235 – 1253), who added the Great Hall. This was a sure sign that Buckden was regarded as second only to Lincoln among the numerous residences the bishops used across the centuries; estimates vary, but at least eight sites are recorded.

Grosseteste was among the leading scholars of his day; as bishop he must have been dreaded by the corrupt and incompetent, and he did not shrink from criticising Rome and the pope himself; he would also stand up for the rights of the church against Henry III. Nonetheless, the bishop was greatly respected by many in his lifetime and a petition was made for his canonisation after his death; the petition failed, perhaps because he had been too outspoken. He is still much admired and has lent his name to Grosseteste College in the city of Lincoln. He died at Buckden.

There is a report from 1291 that the work of Hugh de Wells and Robert Grosseteste had been 'lately burned by misadventure'. From then on, throughout the fourteenth and much of the fifteenth centuries, we learn little about the bishops' residence or their activities at Buckden. It was a period of important events: the Black Death, the Hundred Years War, the Wars of the Roses and the economic problems that resulted may account for this silence. Now, as the Wars of the Roses came to an end and the Tudor dynasty followed, the residence really became a palace.

Two Builder Bishops

It is appropriate to mention together here the two bishops whose achievement remains for us to admire today. In some twenty-five years they completely changed the episcopal residence into an imposing palace fit for a bishop of importance – which each of them was, both becoming Lord Chancellor (the second highest office of state, and the chief royal chaplain), a post that brought them into the king's inner circle of advisers.

Bishops Thomas Rotherham (1471-1480) and John Russell (1480-1495) held the bishopric during the reigns of Edward IV, Richard III and Henry VII. Henry was the first of the Tudor line, and we refer to the fifteenth century buildings as Tudor, even if part of the work began earlier. The Great Tower is attributed largely to Thomas Rotherham and the rest to John Russell; Russell's is the badge that decorates the south and west walls of the Inner Gatehouse.

Theirs is an early example of red and black patterned brickwork. Material for the bricks was to hand in the clay deposits of Huntingdonshire, and a kiln stood at Lymage, a site now under the western end of Grafham Water. Bricks from the kiln were also used at St Neots Priory and Diddington Church.

A third builder, Bishop William Smith (1495-1514), continued with a new chapel for the palace, but little remains for us to see today. [1]

Katherine of Aragon

Buckden's most celebrated resident to date is undoubtedly Queen Katherine of Aragon, first wife of Henry VIII. Born in 1485, she was the daughter of the dual Spanish monarchs Ferdinand of Aragon and Isabella of Castile. She was named after her great-grandmother Katherine of Lancaster (also with a K), a descendant of Edward III.

At the age of three she was betrothed to the two-year-old Arthur, son of Henry VII. They married when she was sixteen, and within months she was a widow. Two years later she was betrothed to her

---

[1] See Chapter 3 for more on the architecture of The Towers

eleven-year-old brother-in-law, Henry. They were married and crowned shortly after he ascended the throne in 1509. In twenty years of marriage she bore him six children. Only one survived, Mary.

When Henry, in the hope of fathering a male heir, made up his mind to marry Anne Boleyn, he entered into protracted legal and religious arguments to enable him to divorce Katherine. They proved more difficult than those which enabled him to marry his brother's widow in the first place. Meanwhile her presence was an embarrassment, and she was banished from court. She never ceased to declare that she was lawfully married, and refused to accept the humiliating title of Princess Dowager.

To prevent her gathering support, she was moved to six different places of confinement; Buckden was the fifth. The bishop at the time was John Longland, the king's confessor. She reached here in July 1533, and took a dislike to her latest quarters. Attempts were made to transfer her to Somersham, a place of such ill repute that the Spanish ambassador objected. Fotheringhay was equally unacceptable. It was during this time that the Duke of Suffolk was sent to remove the queen from Buckden. She locked herself inside, and the 'Men of Buckden', as they became known, armed themselves with their working tools, came to her support and sent the duke away disappointed. He was to try more successfully later, but accompanied by a band of armed men. This incident is recorded in the memorial window to Katherine in the Lady Chapel of St Hugh's Church. **See** PlatePB2.6

In May 1534 Katherine was taken to Kimbolton Castle. It was more secure than the Bishops' Palace, though somewhat more comfortable; even so, she would have found little sympathy there, for the mother of the young owner, Sir Charles Wingfield, was lady of the bedchamber to Anne Boleyn. There she lived out the rest her life, forbidden to see her daughter, or to write to the king. Write she did, an admirable and touching letter, the day before her death on 7 January 1536. People were not slow to blame Anne Boleyn for her death, but modern opinion is that she died of cancer of the heart. Her body was carried to Peterborough Abbey (now the cathedral). She was entombed under the title of Dowager Princess of Wales. Her daughter Mary was not allowed to attend, but Suffolk's daughter, the king's niece, was present. This last attempt to humiliate her was royally countered nearly four hundred years later, when Mary of Teck, Queen of George V, ordered the placing of the banners of Katherine's

---

The text of Katherine's last letter to Henry VIII

"My most dear lord, king and husband,

The hour of my death now drawing on, the tender love I owe you forceth me, my case being such, to commend myself to you, and to put you in remembrance with a few words of the health and safeguard of your soul which you ought to prefer before all worldly matters, and before the care and pampering of your body, for the which you have cast me into many calamities and yourself into many troubles.

For my part, I pardon you everything, and I wish to devoutly pray God that He will pardon you also. For the rest, I commend unto you our daughter Mary, beseeching you to be a good father unto her, as I have heretofore desired. I entreat you also, on behalf of my maids, to give them marriage portions, which is not much, they being but three. For all my other servants I solicit the wages due them, and a year more, lest they be unprovided for. Lastly, I make this vow, that mine eyes desire you above all things.

Katharine the Quene."

---

parents and husband over the tomb in Peterborough. The heraldic symbols are combined with a pomegranate, just as they are in her arms that can be seen in Buckden's memorial window. That pomegranate can also be seen on the gate of the knot garden, and miniature pomegranates grow there—in Queen Katherine's Garden, as it is now called.

From Edward VI To Queen Victoria

The mid-sixteenth century was a period of religious turmoil, and the palace came into lay hands for the first time. Under Edward VI, Bishop Henry Holbeach (1547-1552) gave up all the episcopal residences, apart from the palace of Lincoln. Buckden went to the Duke of Somerset, Edward Seymour, who as the Lord Protector of the Realm and the young king's uncle and guardian was probably the most powerful man in the kingdom. It reverted to the diocese only on his execution on 22 January 1551/2, in the reign of Mary I.[1]

John Williams, who was bishop of Lincoln from 1621 to 1641, found Buckden Palace in a dilapidated condition when he arrived in there in 1625, and began restoring buildings and making improvements to the grounds. We can still walk around the Little Park on the raised walk-way he introduced, even if it is no longer as high as the original three feet. However, in the course of a dispute with the king, Charles I, and Archbishop Laud of Canterbury, he was for three years (1637-1640) deprived of his functions and benefices and imprisoned in the Tower of London. A solicitor by the name of Richard Kilvert, who had played an underhand role in the bishop's downfall, was appointed to administer the estate at Buckden. He sold off a large amount of movable property and caused considerable damage.

Shortly after, in 1649, the estate was confiscated by the parliamentary regime and passed into private hands a second time, being sold to Alderman Sir Christopher Packe, a former lord mayor of London. He pulled down many of the buildings. He also destroyed the **deer park** (q.v.). On the restoration of the monarchy in 1660 the palace returned to the Church.

Further efforts were made to restore the property from time to time, especially by Bishop Robert Sanderson (1660-1663). Two bishops who followed him, William Fuller (1667- 1675) and Thomas Barlow (1675-1692), found the place so attractive that Fuller rarely went to Lincoln and Barlow never reached it at all. Barlow earned the title of the 'Bishop of Buckden who never saw Lincoln'. Not all their successors felt the same, however, and the palace went into a decline during the eighteenth century: Bishop Gibson (1716-1723) referred to it as merely 'a convenient old house for [the bishops'] summer residence.' A visitor reported in 1790 that 'the ancient appearance diminishes hourly, as much of the moat has lately been filled up and many walls pulled down' (John **Byng**, q.v.)

In 1836, on the recommendation of the Ecclesiastical Commissioners of England, William IV approved the reorganization of the diocese of Lincoln, and as a result Buckden, with the rest of Huntingdonshire, was transferred to the diocese of Ely. John **Kaye** (q.v.), the last bishop of Lincoln to use the Palace, left in 1837; two years later demolition began. The Palace and the north wing of the Inner Gatehouse were pulled down, the Great Tower was stripped out, and a sale of furniture took place in 1838. The remains of the property were transferred to the vicar of Buckden in 1842, and for a while an elementary school for girls and infants found a home there. At this period the Little Park was known as the 'Palace Garden and Pleasure Grounds'.

So it was that the fortunes of the Palace came to their lowest ebb in the reign of Queen Victoria. Even the books of the diocesan library, which were left behind when Kaye departed, were eventually removed to a building in Huntingdon designed to house them.

The Marshall Years

When the Ecclesiastical Commissioners sold the property to James Marshall in 1870 it passed into lay ownership for the third time. From then on it was known as Buckden Towers. The history of The Towers follows the fortunes of the Marshall family until the First World War, and a detailed account of their years at Buckden may be found in a 1999 monograph *Arthur W. Marshall, Owner of Buckden Towers* by David Thomas, past chairman of Buckden Local History Society.

Marshall had bought the estate for his son, Arthur Wellington **Marshall** (q.v.), and it was to undergo several changes during his ownership. The most important was the family home he had built in 1872. His architect, Colonel Robert Edis, proved an excellent choice; he was later called on by the Prince of Wales to make improvements to Sandringham after a fire there. Arthur Marshall's house is unexpectedly restrained for a mid-Victorian building, and shows much forethought in the architectural details which tie it in with the nearby Great Tower and Inner Gatehouse. The string-courses match those on the tower, as do the windows, with their decorative brick arches over stone lintels. The crenellation on the older buildings is picked up on the tower above the main door of the house. David Thomas's monograph describes how similar attention to detail was exercised within the house, which has good Arts and Crafts details in tiles and windows.

As a preliminary, Marshall continued the demolition of the old palace, begun some thirty years before. Now the Great Chamber and Chapel were pulled down. The remaining, western, part of the moat was filled in and the bridge demolished. The Outer Gatehouse was built at this time, and wrought-iron gates were inserted in the fifteenth-century archway. They bear the monogram AWM,

---

[1] Somerset was tried for treason. Although acquitted, he was found guilty of the lesser, but still capital, crime of bringing together men for a riot.

which also appears inside and outside the house. A curious relic can be seen here: the remains of a system of wires and rockers that connected the gateway to a bell outside the gatekeeper's bedroom in the adjoining cottage.

The north wall of what is now the Knot Garden was originally about half its present height; the brickwork and the fact that it reaches across the former moat show it to have been built in the eighteenth century. There are also initials carved in the brick with a date of 1776. The upper part of the wall, which is capped with engineering brick, is nineteenth-century work. It was probably thought necessary to support the vinehouse that rested against it until it was demolished to make room for the Knot Garden in the 1990s. By then it was in a poor condition, as were the other glasshouses there. The Marshalls used this area as a fruit and vegetable garden; old engravings show that their predecessors had done the same at the beginning of the nineteenth century.

The trees in the Little Park show us that the conifers favoured by the Victorians were no doubt planted during the Marshalls' time, especially the Wellingtonia and the other sequoia, the Californian Redwood. They were introduced from America in the 1840s and 1850s, the Wellingtonia being named in honour of Arthur, Duke of Wellington, who had died in 1852. How could Arthur Wellington Marshall resist such a tree? It has pride of place between the two gatehouses.

The Red Cross Hospital

By early 1911, Sir Arthur Marshall (as he became in 1898) and his wife had retired to Folkestone. This

Patients and nurses at The Towers hospital in WWI . The formidable matron or commandant may be Miss **Cranfield** (q.v.) of Park Farm who is known to have been prominent in the Red Cross.

Alice Whitmee

meant the house was available in 1914 for requisition as a military hospital. Another, smaller hospital was set up in the rectory of the neighbouring village of Brampton, but when the rector needed the house again at the beginning of 1917, the hospital was combined with its Buckden neighbour. Soldiers repatriated from France were placed under the care of the Red Cross. They would have been a familiar sight in the village, and they were known as the 'boys in blue' because of the bright blue jacket and trousers the convalescent soldiers wore. They enjoyed considerable support from local people, and almost every month in the *Huntingdonshire Post* the commandant would list with thanks the gifts she had received for the men. The Red Cross collecting boxes in the village hotels and public houses yielded generous offerings too.

In its years as a hospital The Towers saw nearly 2000 patients pass through the gates, and it was a proud claim that not one of them died.

The hospital closed on 23 April 1919. At a ceremony that followed, the speaker wished *au revoir* to the boys in blue: was that a slip of the tongue or a newspaper reporter's imagination? The contents of the hospital were put up for auction at the George Hotel in May. Among the many items on offer were sixteen iron bedsteads, a quantity of socks and a small lawnmower.

Sir Arthur had died in December 1918. After his will was published in April 1919, The Towers was advertised for auction at The George. It was described as 'unusually attractive and compact, in a quiet rural situation on the outskirts of an old-world village'. The features included 'the interesting ruins of the ancient episcopal palace, excellent stabling, glass houses, two cottages, ornamental water, orchard and park land'.

Robert Holmes Edleston

Dr Robert Holmes Edleston, whose home was at Gainford, County Durham, became the new owner of The Towers in 1919 and Lord of the Manor of Buckden Brittens the following year. In his time, the Manorial Court would often meet in the Inner Gatehouse of The Towers; the Court Rolls, now in the Huntingdonshire Archives, give an account of the proceedings. He would use the title 'Baron de Montalbo', awarded him by the Most Serene Republic of San Marino, for which he was consul.

Edleston was interested in archaeology and was a Fellow of the Society of Antiquaries; before long he was busy restoring parts of the old palace. His principal achievement was the rebuilding of the north wing of the Inner Gatehouse, intended to house a museum in honour of the French Emperor Napoleon III. The dedication to the Emperor above the entrance intrigues the visitor, who is surprised to learn that not only has the Emperor no connection with Buckden, but also that the building for the museum is a twentieth century construction. Edleston made a good job of blending the new with the old. He would buy material from old buildings, especially the stone door and window frames, which came from stately homes and castles being demolished in Yorkshire and County Durham. The eighteenth-century balustrade which now marks the eastern route of the old palace moat, came from a sale at Streatlam Castle, close to his Gainford home. His other major undertaking was the restoration of the crypt of the palace chapel; this work was completed by the present owners, and is the Saint Claret Chapel of Saint Hugh's Church.

Edleston did not live in The Towers, preferring to stay at the **manor house** (q.v.) when not at his home in County Durham. He maintained the Marshalls' garden, and would have fruit and vegetables sent north by rail. The Towers was requisitioned again in the Second World War. Boys from Tollington School in Muswell Hill were evacuated here to avoid the London bombing.[1] They were lodged with local families. After them it was used as a hostel for agricultural workers.

The estate passed to Alice Edleston when her brother Robert died in 1952, and the museum project was abandoned. A Roman Catholic, she presented the estate to the Catholic bishop of Northampton, in whose diocese Buckden then lay. Although no longer a bishop's palace, the property was back in religious hands. Robert Edleston may not have achieved all he hoped to do, but we should be grateful for the work he did to preserve Buckden's ancient monument.

The Claretian Missionaries

Bishop Parker of Northampton transferred the property in 1956 to the Claretian Missionaries, a Roman Catholic religious order, which takes its name from its founder, Anthony Mary Claret (1807-18 70). A Spanish missionary of extraordinary compassion and energy, he was canonised in 1950. Inspired by his example, five fellow priests became the first members of the new missionary order he created to help in his work. They were called the Congregation of the Missionary Sons of the Immaculate Heart of Mary ('the Claretians' is the name more commonly used). The letters CMF on the gates and elsewhere stand for a shorter Latin version of their name. Now the order is several thousand strong in sixty-three countries.

True to their calling, the missionaries founded a junior seminary at The Towers for the Christian education of boys soon after their arrival in 1957. The project lasted only a few years and now the work in Buckden is concentrated on running short courses for young people, often as a preparation for confirmation; offering conference facilities for adults, not necessarily Catholic; running a parish for the Bishop of East Anglia, and taking part in overseas missions.

By 1956, the fabric of the fifteenth-century buildings was in very poor condition; the Great Tower was already described as ruinous in the 1926 *Victoria County History of Huntingdonshire*, and the Inner Gatehouse needed urgent work as well. It speaks well for the efforts of the Claretians and their supporters that both tower and gatehouse are now used as working buildings, part of the complex named the Claret Centre. There is always work to do on preserving property of such age, and fundraising continues to carry conservation a stage further.

St Hugh's Church was built in 1959 as the chapel of the Claretians and became the Catholic parish church for the district in the 1960s. The choice of architect was a fortunate one. As you face the west door you are struck by the way the church harmonises with the medieval and Victorian buildings on either side. The horizontal features form a link from one building to the next; the arcaded front of the corridors picks up the same pattern along the inside of the curtain wall that joins the Great Tower to the Inner Gatehouse; the black-brick pattern on the west wall echoes those on the medieval walls: an echo repeated on the wall you see behind the altar as you go into the church.

In the north and south walls are windows by the Norfolk stained glass artist Paul Quail, showing St Hugh and St Anthony Claret. His work appears again in the Lady Chapel in two different styles. The south window is a memorial to Queen Katherine of Aragon. Beyond is the St Claret Chapel with more work by Paul Quail and a carved wooden statue of St Claret by Jane Quail. The chapel is both a haven of quiet for private meditation and a less quiet setting for the youth masses that are celebrated here. The chapel is a reminder of the days of the Bishops' Palace; it was formerly the crypt of the palace chapel, though much rebuilt.

---

[1] For more on the evacuees and their life in Buckden, see **Chapter 17.**

The western section of the moat has now been re-excavated and the bridge across it, leading to the inner gatehouse, has been restored. The Little Park with its trees, several of them subject to preservation orders, provides an open space at the heart of the village, a fit setting for an ancient monument.

The Friends of Buckden Towers

A group of local residents came together in 1975 to form a trust, named the 'Friends of Buckden Towers'. The Friends are a non-denominational registered charity dedicated to the preservation of the property for all, in fundraising and in practical ways. This includes arranging guided tours, maintaining Queen Katherine's Garden, encouraging visits by professional theatre companies, holding an annual plant sale and planning and undertaking the restoration of the park and buildings.

The following are some of the noteworthy events to have involved the Friends over the years:

[a] *Playing with Fire*, a large-cast community play commissioned jointly by the Friends and Buckden Theatre Club and performed in the courtyard of The Towers over six nights in July 1990. It was set against the background of the violent protests that affected several agricultural areas in southern England during the winter of 1830. The play was a loose interpretation of the effect of these protests on Buckden, where a group of farm labourers destroyed a threshing-machine belonging to a prominent local farmer.

[b] The Aragon Pageant, 'a feast of flowers, music and history', held in May 1995 to commemorate The Towers' most famous resident, Queen Katherine.

[c] The use of the older Towers' buildings in 1997 as a location by Ardent Productions for the filming of scenes in the second series of *Crown and Country*, in which Edward Windsor[1] traced connections between the Anglia region and his royal ancestors. Some of the Friends appeared on screen, one as an impressive Katherine of Aragon.

[d] 'Eight hundred years of music and medicine' presented in November 2000 by the Aragon Singers and friends to mark the 800th anniversary of the death of St Hugh of Lincoln.

Much has been done, but much remains to be done, which is why the Friends continue to publicise their work and future plans through regular newsletters and their website, www.fobt.org.uk.

---

[1] Edward Windsor is one of the business names used by the Queen's youngest son, HRH The Prince Edward, Earl of Wessex.

CHAPTER 5/ A HISTORY OF ST MARY'S, THE PARISH CHURCH
Barry Jobling

Why are we here?

Beautiful old church, and so alive', Ilford. 'Overwhelming', Bavaria. 'Truly, God is here', Essex. 'A lovely cup of tea', West Sussex. 'A church of outstanding beauty and with amazing angels', Cambridgeshire. These are a few of the comments from the Visitors' Book at St Mary's Church, each reflecting people's thoughts of their visit that day. As each of us enjoys different aspects and experiences when visiting old buildings - especially those of a spiritual nature - it is difficult to know how to describe St Mary's, Buckden, where God and man have been at work for around 1300 years.

While I shall focus mainly on the fabric of the church, and the events and people that have helped shape its life, it is important to remember that St Mary's is a living church serving the needs of today's community and being served by its active congregation.

The history of a village and its parish church are naturally closely entwined, please forgive any duplication with other chapters.

This church has such a cohesive feel that many have remarked that it seems to have dropped ready-made from Heaven. It is true that the building does appear to be of one character and design; this is partly due to the fact that a lot of what we see today dates from a very short period between 1432 and 1440. Credit is also due to the empathetic work of many in the intervening centuries; this work continues today with the Buckden Living Stones Project to build facilities for village use, including a kitchen and toilets. Meantime with a little diligence it is possible to find the handiwork of each of the twenty-two generations since 1437; let's have a look....

'Why are we here?' is a meaningful question to ask in a church. But long before Christianity this site was important, sitting as it does at the junction of one of the main north/south roadways in England (now the A1) and an early vital east/west crossing of the River Ouse from East Anglia and the coast (now Mill Road/Church Street). Pagan shrines or sacred sites were often located at woodland groves, springs or ponds; all three were here in antiquity, the springs and ponds remaining today. It is possible that this area was a site of worship, thanks to the combination of these physical mysteries and the roadway junction – we may never know.

Christianity came to this area during Roman times. The earliest known British Christian church plate, dating to about AD 275, was excavated twenty miles north of Buckden, at Water Newton on the Great North Road; and a coin of Emperor Tetricus of Gaul (AD 270-273) was found during excavations near the church's north wall. In nearby Godmanchester, a fourth century lead tank bearing the Chi-Rho Christian symbol has been recovered.

In AD 673, monks from Peterborough founded a monastery at Ely and began missionary work in the Ouse valley. Parishes as we know them today began to be formed around that time and there may have been sufficient population in the Buckden area to support a small wooden Christian church by about AD 700. A natural choice for its site would be in the area of a previously pagan shrine, if indeed Buckden had had one.

The Early Church

Domesday Book (1086) records that the parish and lands of Buckden belonged to the bishops of Lincoln. The early history of the diocese is complicated. In Anglo-Saxon times there was a bishop of Lindsey, whose seat was at Lincoln. In 971, the bishop of the time united this diocese with another, based on Dorchester-on-Thames in Oxfordshire. The resulting diocese of Dorchester, of which Buckden was a part, spread from the River Humber to the River Thames.

In 1066 the Saxon king, Harold, passed near Buckden heading northwards with his army to defeat the Scandinavians at Stamford Bridge. Soon after he was heading south to his death at Hastings; and the

Norman duke, William, became king. A year later, the new king rewarded one of his supporters, a Benedictine called Remigius of Fecamp, with the Dorchester bishopric. In 1072, the king ordered Dorchester to be abandoned and the seat of the diocese relocated to (and named for) Lincoln (a larger, wealthier, strategically important town). Remigius now became the first true bishop of Lincoln. The significance for Buckden was that Remigius and his successors, powerful men in the realm, now had to commute to London to attend the king, not from conveniently nearby Dorchester but all the way down the north road from Lincoln. Buckden was an ideal place to break the journey.

By this time Buckden had a prebend (a senior priest appointed by the Bishop to attend to his duties locally). In 1067, Bishop Remigius nominated Psalm 101 to be sung daily at Buckden church and by Buckden's prebend when seated in the choir of Lincoln Cathedral. Remigius allocated a different psalm to each of his prebends and canons 'to ensure that the Lincoln Psalter is said daily for the souls of the living and the dead'.

The church and its priest appear in *Domesday Book*, and Buckden manor was in the possession of the bishop of Lincoln, who had a manor house here, and it is reasonable to assume that the church and bishop's palace still occupy their original sites. The village population was then around 125.[1]

St Hugh of Lincoln (Bishop Hugh), renowned for the miracles he performed and usually portrayed with his devoted swan, often stayed at his manor house at Buckden and was popular with the villagers. He died in London in 1200 and on 12 November of that year his body lay 'with great mourning' in this church on its final journey to Lincoln.

Now we come to the earliest visible remains in the church. King John, soon after his signing of Magna Carta in 1215, permitted Hugh de Wells (Bishop of Lincoln 1209-1235) to rebuild his palace here, to build a park for hunting and to rebuild the Saxon church. King John's seemingly unusual generosity was in fact to compensate for the damages he had done both to Lincoln Cathedral and to Bishop Hugh himself. With funds from the Guild of St Mary, Hugh set to work on his new projects and by about 1230 his new church was in use. It was a large church for a small village, reflecting not only the more elaborate rituals recently introduced, but also the power and wealth of the bishop.

Certainly, the present chancel walls are those built by Hugh in c. 1230, and it is conjectured that this late Norman or Early English church was rectangular and extended to approximately where the tower is now, the previous nave walls being where the arcades rise today.

The earliest remaining feature from Hugh's church is the south doorway, still the main entrance to the church. It was not uncommon for church doorways, signifying the entry into Christ's kingdom, to be retained and reset in their rightful position when churches were remodelled. The wooden door was inserted in the 1430s, and while the bottom has rotted and been replaced, the top retains its early green paint in a stencilled pattern showing where the ornate wooden tracery once decorated this great portal. On close examination of the door face it is easy to find the carvings of initials, mainly dating to the seventeenth and eighteenth centuries. If one looks either side of the door, particularly to the left above the stone bench, more initials are visible; these are mainly the work of schoolboys from the days when school was held in the porch, and no doubt when the master was not looking.

Around 1285, in Bishop Oliver Sutton's time, further improvements were made and we can still see his vestry door arch in the chancel, retaining faint traces of medieval paintwork. The piscina, where the holy vessels were washed (note that it drains within the wall into consecrated ground), and the simple yet stylish sedilia at the east end of the chancel both date to this era. The three stone seats show a deliberate pecking order: the priest on the highest, then the deacon and the lowest being the sub-deacon's, while the bishop and prebend would have had thrones beside the altar. The priest's doorway in the south chancel wall is of the late thirteenth century also.

The lowest courses of the tower appear to be of the fourteenth century and they show the three feet (one metre) thickness of the thirteenth century south nave wall where it abutted them.

The sedilia

---

[1] Extrapolated from *Domesday*.

Buckden was not spared the Black Death in the mid-fourteenth century, its population like many in Huntingdonshire perhaps being halved. Neither was the church a safe haven, with four vicars dying during an eight-year period.

Buckden's Thomas à Becket (well....almost)

Could this church have become another Canterbury Cathedral, a place of national pilgrimage? Probably not, but on 20 June 1358 it came close.

Bishop John Gynwell of Lincoln did not approve of King Edward III's wars in France and refused to support them financially. When Edward became desperate he sent three of his knights, Thomas de Stukley, John de Tolly and Robert Bayour with a sealed letter demanding funds from Gynwell. The knights found the bishop on his knees praying before the altar of Buckden church and when he refused to accept the king's letter they threatened him 'with long knives'. Gynwell continued praying and the knights, perhaps fearing a repeat of the Becket episode 188 years earlier, left him in peace. However Edward never forgave him, and the bishop's last years were spent in obscurity.

The Great Rebuilding 1432-1440

William Gray, a wealthy and powerful man, was translated from the see of London to Lincoln in 1431. King Henry VI was ten years old, and his protectors had been fighting wars in France trying to keep hold of his possessions there; indeed Joan of Arc had been burned at the stake only the previous year. Soon Richard, Duke of York, would become Henry's protector in England, and the Wars of the Roses would start in earnest twenty years later.

But meantime Gray, nearing the end of his years, sought a lasting legacy. 'Of his many manors Buckden seems one of the most favoured' and he was a great benefactor to the church building 'as appears by his arms, which I have seen, in a great many of the windows there' (Browne Willis, 1730). Indeed, when we look around the church, a great deal of what we see today is the work or design of Bishop Gray, so much so that if he were to walk into the church today he would feel quite at home, and no doubt very pleased with his legacy.

The Nave during Feast Week 2008

Work started in 1432 and it seems that the south aisle was built first, followed soon after by the south arcade replacing the thirteenth century nave wall, then the chancel arch and the higher levels of the tower and spire. The building was constructed of limestone rubble with some cobbles and ironstone.

In places an effort has been made to lay the stone in courses but frequently it is irregular; the corner dressings, windows and the steeple are of Barnack limestone from Lincolnshire.

Finally the north arcade and aisle were completed, although it may be that this north side was not completed until perhaps thirty or forty years later.[1] We shall return to this in a little while; certainly even now among older villagers, the story is told that the son of the man who built its southern sister built the north aisle.

---

[1] There is a recent contradictory opinion concerning the date of the north aisle; an historical architect from Cambridge University believes that the north aisle windows are about 100 years older than the south aisle, dating them to c. 1330 rather than the 1480s. This does not materially affect the overall story of the church, in fact it makes it a little more exciting as we explore the building's history.

These same villagers also say that the tower, five feet thick at its base, at one time stood separately from the main building. The inside eastern wall of the tower has buttresses and an exterior drip moulding; and the north arcade meets a buttress with a straight joint showing that the arcade came later and that it joined the tower, which stood alone for a period during the rebuilding process. It is also interesting to note the outline, on the interior tower wall, of the old lower nave roof, and that the huge fifteenth century archway has been set into the earlier tower

Viewed from the chancel the tower is offset to the north, or more properly, the church is offset to the south! The lower courses of the tower date to the fourteenth century and when the south aisle and arcade were added in the 1430s they presented no problem and matched nicely to the tower. However when the north aisle and arcade came to be built it was probably realised that these would subside into the soft ground adjacent to the Palace moat (being dug around the same period in the 1480s), so they were constructed several feet south of their intended site. Likewise, it was proposed to widen the chancel to the north, but this was not done, for the same reason. We are left however, with the peculiar sights of the northeast exterior buttress supporting a non-existent wall and the east window lights squeezed together on the north side.

In co-operation with Bishop Gray, his prebend John Depyng was busy rebuilding the chancel. Depyng, a lawyer, seems to have been the constant in the church work undertaken throughout his eighteen years here. And it may have been he who encouraged the Bishop and his successors to improve St Mary's.

Around 1434, John Depyng inserted the large bright windows into the old Norman chancel walls, raised the walls to their present height and re-roofed the chancel, adding the superbly carved heavenly choir holding Psalters (possibly showing Psalm 101) and tablets. There are still traces of the original paint on these 580-year-old choristers, although their wings are 1930s replacements.

John Depyng recorded his efforts in the east window. His inscription was still visible in the eighteenth century, as parts of his stained glass inscription remained: 'Hanc cancellum fieri fecit .... Deping, hujus Ecclesiae Prebendarius AD MCC........' (which may be rendered as '[John] Depyng, Prebend of this Church AD MCC[... ...] caused this chancel to be made.'

In this same year 1434, Jan Van Eyck painted *Giovanni Arnolfini and Giovanna Cenami* (popularly known as *The Arnolfini Marriage*), a fascinating portra `Bishop Alnwick's` it of a wealthy medieval couple. If one looks closely (binoculars are useful for this) at the carved wooden figures in the corners above Buckden's chancel arch, it is plain to see that their clothing is very similar to the Arnolfini couple. Even then, Buckden's patrons were keeping up to date with the latest fashions from the Continent.

Bishop Alnwick's arms

The font with flower display during Festival or Feast Week

The carved wooden heavenly angels in the south aisle roof are rightly well known, showing musicians playing, from east to west, the lute, viol, tabor, dulcimer and hurdy-gurdy. It is believed that the carver copied these instruments from those in use in the church at the time. Beneath them, against the roof trusses, are wooden carvings of St Stephen (clutching the stones with which he was martyred) in the southeast corner and several carvings of bishops and abbots, all once richly painted and quite recognisable to the parishioners of their day. These all date to the late 1430s and are a joy to behold.

The octagonal limestone font, its blank shields once painted with benefactors' coats of arms, also dates to around this building period. Filled with holy water annually at Easter for use throughout the coming year, the font had a cover, which was locked to prevent the theft of the water for evil purposes. A modern, iron reinforced oak lid now covers the lead-lined interior.

The stone corbels supporting the south aisle roof timbers portray various grotesque faces and figures intended to illustrate sin, and its consequences, for the benefit of erring villagers! The carved faces above the north arcade, meanwhile, are quite different as they present several ladies' heads with remarkable examples of medieval hairstyles; at least one of which may be from an earlier nave as the hairstyle predates the time of this construction. Once again it is important to remember that these images would originally have been painted and have been surrounded by related frescoes depicting stories from the Bible.

Bishop Gray died in Buckden in February 1436 and, as sometimes happens with men seeking to make their mark for posterity, he left his great work unfinished.

No doubt with the ongoing encouragement of John Depyng, the bishop's successor Bishop William Alnwick completed Gray's plans. To ensure that he too was remembered, Alnwick built the clerestory; adding his 'cross moline' arms to the stone corbel angel shields. Yet he is perhaps better remembered as being the wise advisor who inspired King Henry VI to endow and build Eton School and King's College, Cambridge.

The Finishing Touches 1460-1490 and the Stained Glass

The mid-fifteenth century saw the height of worship of the Virgin Mary as the mother of God. There is evidence in the stone carving, the piscina and aumbry (a small cupboard for the Communion chalice and plate) and in the remains of stained glass, that the south aisle was a separate Lady Chapel with its own altar. There are also remains of fixings in the walls and arcade indicating where a wooden screen would have separated this chapel from the nave.

Similarly, the north aisle has its own piscina and aumbry and traces of wooden screen fittings, which again would suggest a local guild or chantry chapel there in its early history.

Around 1470 or 1480 in Bishop Rotherham's or Bishop Russell's time, a rood screen and loft were inserted into the chancel arch. The south stairway, door and upper entrance remain, as does the chiselled step cut into the chancel arch, at the top of the columns. This step or notch was inserted to accommodate the large beam necessary to bear the weight of the rood (cross) and the walkway for the choir and musicians. The screen and loft would last for only fifty or sixty years, yet the circular stairs are surprisingly well worn for such a short period of use.

As mentioned, very little remains of the original stained glass dating from this period. That which does, is intriguing, having been preserved in the upper lights of the eastern and western windows of the south aisle. They were possibly saved from destruction by being plastered over or perhaps they were too high to remove with a few swings of an iron bar, albeit the principal characters have been disfigured. Christopher Woodeforde identifies this glass as the work of the Norwich School of glassmakers, showing their trademark 'ears of barley' in rows on the ground by the angels' feet (Woodforde, 1950).

The eastern window portrays angels surrounding the Coronation of the Virgin, and the scrolls they hold contain the Latin sentences of a prose sung at Easter in the medieval church. Two of the angels stand on rings, perhaps referring to the 'living creatures' in Ezekiel 1.18.

The Annunciation of St Mary is portrayed in the west window. All the figures except one are headless, and the Archangel Gabriel is missing (Woodforde in 1972 states, knowingly, that this figure was in a private collection....). The words in the scrolls are from an anthem sung during Vespers, the evening service.

There does not appear to have been a wholesale simultaneous breaking of all the windows at Buckden, rather intermittent flurries of destruction over many years. The iconoclasms of Edward VI's reign, and later the Puritans, were responsible for the loss of some images. Indeed in the 1640s there were major expenses for window repair.

However, in a Visitation on 21 July 1684, the inspectors were still able to record 36 coats of arms in all of the main windows. And as we have already heard, in Browne Willis' publication of 1730, he states that Bishop William Gray (1431-1436) was a great benefactor of St Mary's 'as appears by his arms, which I have seen, in a great many of the windows there'. So, it would appear that persons unknown removed the remainder of the stained glass in the eighteenth or nineteenth century. Despite its loss, we are now blessed with a magnificently lit church, at its finest on a winter's day with the sun streaming almost horizontally through the south-facing windows.

The Wars of the Roses continued throughout this building period and Bishop John Russell, we must remember, in theory a neutral churchman, had been translated to Lincoln in 1480 by the Yorkist king, Edward IV; and Russell was a fervent supporter of Richard III.

The double rose boss in the porch

In Buckden, he is best known as the builder of the Tudor Buckden Palace (the Towers). In the church he was responsible for the building of the ornate south porch, c. 1485, with fine stone carvings within and without. After the battle of Bosworth Field in 1485, King Henry VII spent his first royal Christmas at Lincoln, possibly to test the loyalty of Russell. And, possibly to impress his brand new Tudor monarch, en route to Lincoln, Russell incorporated the double rose of Lancaster and York into the ceiling of Buckden church's porch: perhaps it needed some last minute colour changes! At the centre of this beautifully classic vaulting is a splendid carving of the Virgin Mary crowned and in glory, intended to represent the Assumption. The complete ceiling would have looked quite stunning to the villagers of the day in its original lavish colours, as would the interior of the church.

Around the outside of the porch is a carved string of various beasts including a monkey, a muzzled bear, a lion, a lamb, a fox stalking geese (often an uncomplimentary allegory concerning the priest and his congregation!), dogs chasing a rabbit, and a wise old owl lying on its side. Perennial favourites, however, are the little squirrels all in a row climbing each side of the entrance arch. The eroded and distorted faces on either side of the entrance were probably once of angels, although one appears to be wearing a mitre. The replacement figure of St Mary in the niche above the south entrance was commissioned in 1962 in memory of a recent vicar.

The porch has an upper room, still known as the parvis chamber, accessible by a circular stair from its interior doorway, which was used for many years as a depository for the parochial library founded in the 1690s. In the 1870s, the books were transferred to Huntingdon, together with those of the diocesan library which the vicar had inherited along with the palace in 1837. There is a somewhat puzzling reference in some hundred-year-old records that the parvis chamber also contained, at that time, the remains of an ancient font that was reputed to have been used at Queen Anne's baptism, in 1665. This association would seem most unlikely, but it possibly has a trace of truth to it; disappointingly the remains are no longer there for examination.

The Church Bells

While trying to make this history of the church a chronological one, this is probably a good time to take a break from a strict timeline and to talk about the bells.

About the same year that Leonardo da Vinci painted the *Mona Lisa*, a bell-founder called Thomas Bullisdon was casting in London Buckden's oldest bell. It must be conceded that Leonardo was probably not aware of this at the time! This, our only surviving 'Catholic' bell, was cast around 1510. It is a treble bell with the inscription around it, 'Sca Katerina ora pro nobis', 'St Katherine pray for us'. St Katherine was the patron saint of wheelwrights.

The Edwardian Inventories record church silver, vestments and bells extant in 1552. Of course, the main purpose of the Inventories was to establish the current possessions of a church and to determine 'that which is wholesome' to remain, the rest being sent to the king's London Jewel House or sold locally.

Buckden's list shows some fine vestments, two silver chalices, a large silver cross etc and six bells. The number of bells is extraordinary for a small village church.

Most Huntingdonshire churches had three or four bells; Kimbolton, Brampton and Hartford had five, but Buckden was alone with six. This can only reflect its importance, being adjacent to the bishop's palace, and the wealth of its benefactors (and not forgetting the strength of its tower). Legal permission to hang a bell was required from the diocese and the bishop would hardly have declined a licence for his own bell.

But, in the 1550s, with influential Presbyterians 'openly preaching against bells, affirming the use of them to be superstitious and abominable', it was only a matter of time before Buckden was left with one bell, the rest gone to make the king's cannon.

This is a list of the current bells with their dates, makers, tone and inscriptions:

c. 1510. Thomas Bullisdon (London). Treble. 'Sca Katherina Ora Pro Nobis' and a shield 'TB'.

1627. Wm Haulsey (St. Ives). No 5. 'John Bardar, Michel Jarmand 1627' [wardens]. Please also note the reference to this bell in the Churchwardens' Accounts appendix.

1654. Miles Graye (of Colchester. However, there are references to this bell being cast in Gamlingay). No 4. 'Miles Graye Fecit 1654'

1779. Edward Arnold. No 3. 'John Green Esq and Robt Burder Churchwardens 1779 + Edwd Arnold St Neots fecit'

c. 1790. Robert Taylor. No 2. 'John Green Esq. John Waller Churchwardens. Robt Taylor St Neots Fecit'

1997. Whitechapel Foundry (London). No 6. 'Ely Diocesan Bellringers Association – Centenary Bell - 1897-1997 – Whites of Appleton – Whitechapel Bell Founders – To the Glory of God'

In the mid-1990s it was realised that the old oak bell frame installed in the tower in 1637, while still strong, was moving in its mountings. So, it was decided as a Millennium project to raise funds for a new bell frame and for modern facilities for church and village use (i.e. a small kitchen, a meeting hall and toilets). Sufficient funds were soon generously raised and the bell frame took precedence as a tangible sign of the church's commitment. Indeed the new bell, with its five companions hanging in their new steel frame, helped ring in the third millennium after Christ's birth. The 1637 oak frame remains in situ in the tower, with its replacement two floors below. Fund-raising for the other facilities in a purpose-built extension actively continues in 2009 and the church welcomes support in any manner to assist with this venture.

The Reformation of the Church in England (and Buckden)

Many excellent and large volumes have been written about the Reformation and about what it meant to those in power, the churchmen and the common man. But for the purposes of this chapter we offer a simplified, rather informal synopsis of how this period affected Buckden church.

Henry VIII partially adopted Protestantism to suit his divorce and personal life as well as to benefit by the confiscation of the Catholic Church's wealth. When he died in 1547, his young son Edward VI carried on his work. Then on his death in 1553, Edward's half-sister, Catholic Queen Mary, tried to reverse the church-stripping process. Finally, when Mary died in 1558, her Protestant half-sister Elizabeth went back to her father's ways.

It would be tedious to read of how frequently Buckden's altar was moved and rotated, and of how the bishops fared (not well) under the differing edicts of each monarch. Bishop Longland of Lincoln (1521-47), although active in the king's divorce and happy to renounce the pope as head of the English church, had most of his land and manors seized, but was permitted to keep Buckden or what was left of it. As a wealthy church, Buckden had its silver, vestments and other valuables confiscated, and no doubt the palace was plundered too.

In 1547 Bishop Holbeche, a much-disliked man, followed Longland. He sold off major parts of the diocese, 'stripped bare' Lincoln Cathedral (and no doubt Buckden church) and, as Commissioner for Oxford, stripped the university there. He was the first Bishop of Lincoln to be married.

The 'superstitious' Lady Chapel, Guild Chapel, rood screen, loft, imagery, statues and five of the six bells had all gone. And now that the rood screen had been scrapped, rails had to be placed around the altar to protect it from the dogs in the church. Fortunately, the heavenly choir and musicians came through unscathed.

Following two Catholic bishops in Mary I's reign (1553-8), the Protestant Bishop Nicholas Bullingham in 1566 ordered the destruction of all remaining 'Popish stuff'. The following year, his wife died and was buried in Buckden church.

The 'English Sweat' and the Guinness Book of Records

Buckden used to be in the Guinness Book of Records, and the reason for this related to an obscure disease in the Middle Ages.

Sometimes incorrectly referred to today as a plague, it was a most contagious disease, which visited the English population in summer five times between 1485 and 1551, and then disappeared never to return. At the time this was called the 'English sweat' (it was almost unique to England) or sweating sickness. It started with flu-like symptoms, then profuse sweating, followed by death within 72 hours from lung congestion. The population feared it more than bubonic plague, as sweating sickness was invariably fatal.

Possibly the tomb of two Dukes of Suffolk. See the text.

In the summer of 1551, the sweat broke out near London and the widowed Duchess of Suffolk immediately took her sons Henry Brandon, Duke of Suffolk, aged 15 and his brother Charles, 14, to Cambridge where Henry had been studying at St John's College. Upon arrival they learned that the sweat had broken out there too. So they continued to flee, this time westwards and on 10 July they stopped overnight, visiting their friend Lady Margaret Neville, then resident at Buckden Palace.

But it was too late. Henry was already ill and he died on 11 July. Thus the dukedom passed immediately to his younger brother Charles, who was by now quite feverish. Poor Charles died within half-an-hour of his brother; and his peerage, according to the *Guinness Book of Records*, was the shortest-lived in English history.

Now, these were no run-of-the-mill gentry. They were half-uncles of Lady Jane Grey. And, in acknowledgement of his seniority, Henry Brandon had carried the orb at Edward VI's coronation. Hasty arrangements were made to inter them and contemporary records show that they were laid to rest in the prime nave position, just before the chancel. However, nineteenth century records, and popular history, say that these young dukes are buried beneath an old tabletop tomb in the churchyard. So which is right? Perhaps both stories are, we may never know.

There is research yet to be done, but here is one theory. The spot where the boys were originally buried is now occupied by the remains of the very influential Green family. When the family came to bury Sarah Green in October 1778, they may have found the previously unmarked remains of the dukes and, rather than lose their new prime position, the Greens arranged to re-inter the boys outside in a suitable tomb.

The tomb selected probably dates to around 1520, thirty years before the boys died, and the Greens had to 'cut & shut' it, with blank insertions in the ornate sides, to accommodate the dukes. The top is sealed with an even earlier abbot's slab, his staff still visible today. This theory would appear to fit the known facts, but any more information would be most welcome.

Whatever the truth about the boys' final resting-place, young Charles Brandon put Buckden into the record books.

Bishop Barlow and the King James Bible

James I came to the throne on Queen Elizabeth's death in 1603, and in 1608 he appointed to the see of Lincoln, William Barlow, a one-time chaplain to the late queen and one of the translators of the King James Bible (he presided over the team translating the Epistles). Barlow actively opposed the excesses of the Puritans and spoke out against them at the Hampton Court Conference in 1604; this was to bring him many enemies among the Presbyterians, and they didn't forget ...

Like many bishops, Barlow was fond of Buckden and, when he died here on 7 September 1613, he was buried beneath a fine tomb on the north side of St Mary's chancel, in accordance with his wishes. During the Civil War in 1642, however, Puritans wrecked his tomb and the effigies on it in order to settle their 38-year-old grudge. The later Bishop Thomas Barlow (no relation), when re-using some of William's tomb for his own memorial in 1691, condemned these despoilers in his epitaph as 'fanatics'.

In the late sixteenth and early seventeenth centuries, with the restoration of communion to the laity, new communion vessels were required and perhaps we should thank William Barlow for the church's earliest chalice, bearing a London silver hallmark of 1607. There is a pattern of bishops donating communion vessels to St Mary's and it would be gratifying to think of this one as his. It is a classic yet simple cup belonging to the year when Shakespeare wrote two of his best known tragedies, *King Lear* and *Macbeth*.

The Buckden Churchwardens' Accounts

We are very fortunate in Buckden that a remarkable set of books has survived and are now in the Huntingdonshire Archives; these are the Churchwardens' Accounts books for St Mary's Church and the village of Buckden. The wardens started these books in 1627 and recorded every penny collected and spent for 150 years. When coupled with the Assets and Vestry Books, they provide an excellent record of church life for over three hundred years.

The earlier records provide a view on a world quite different to our own, and the later entries give an insight into the far-sightedness and thinking of those responsible for the church and village. Another of the many benefits of these accounts, is that the clerk and wardens recorded the names of the villagers, which enables us to associate more with them and how they lived.

Naturally, when these books were started, the duties and powers of the wardens were altogether much wider than they are today. The church was the main seat of authority in the village and the wardens were responsible for raising levies or taxes, educating children, keeping law and order, caring for the poor, maintaining the church and even paying for the catching of vermin.

Please see the appendix to this chapter for more on these fascinating accounts.

The Civil War

As mentioned previously, the old bell frame containing five bells was installed in 1637, and it would see turbulent times over the next ten years.

Civil war broke out in 1642. Huntingdonshire, like much of East Anglia, was already a Puritan area with many churches following their stricter and plainer rules. It would appear that Buckden was not so severe and even leaned towards the Royalist cause, probably because of the bishop's presence here. But, by 1643 the bishop's minister, Richard Briarcliffe, had already been replaced by a Puritan one, the first of a stream of over thirty resident and itinerant ministers to preach here over the next fifteen years.

From the Accounts, we can now fill in some of the blanks in the roll of vicars: 1632-7 Jacob Brooke; 1638-9 William Lloyde; 1640 Richard Lea; 1641-2 Richard Briarcliffe; 1644-51 or 56? John Carter; 1657 Mr Sharwood; 1661-4 Giles Waring.

We cannot be certain of the damage done to the church during this period, although we do know that Bishop William Barlow's tomb was destroyed in 1642. Any remaining 'idolatrous' statues plus some of the window glass were probably removed during this time too. The walls were whitewashed as the easiest and cheapest way to cover the offending frescoes and wall paintings. It is unlikely that the perpetrators of this destruction were punished, but Buckden did have the means to correct minor offenders. The Accounts for 1646 show repairs to 'the church gate next the Stocks'. Simultaneously, repairs were also carried out to the other gate 'next Mr Powells', who was living in the Manor House; this would indicate that the stocks were by the seventeenth century west gate, a few yards to the east of the present west gate.

On the more positive side, the church got a new pulpit and box pews, more suited to the 3 or 4-hour services. Our present octagonal pulpit retains many of the geometrically patterned oak panels and the banister and newel post of that 1640s one, which stood adjacent to one of the nave columns, probably the south easternmost. The original Jacobean altar table was rediscovered in 1921 by Rev. Frederic Bodger in the old vicarage and placed in the south aisle, where in 1930 it was refurbished and re-consecrated as an altar in memory of George Page, a long-serving churchwarden.

The churchwardens, John Jackson and Cadwalader Powell, both significant landowners, levied three massive tax rates on the population in 1649 to repair the nave roof, fabric and windows. Very detailed records of the receipts and expenditure of these repairs appear in the Accounts, including payment for thirty oak trees from the former bishop's parkland. To commemorate the re-roofing, the wardens had their initials 'I.I. C.P. ANNO 1649' carved into the north roof wall plate. They replaced the former clerestory angels with plain designs on the roof panels and installed a brass candelabra suspended from a central pulley on the new roof truss. This pulley, unusually, is in the shape of a two-faced man facing east and west, both faces bearing an uncanny resemblance to King Charles!

It is important to remember that while the nave and main structure of the church were the responsibility of the wardens, the chancel's upkeep was in the care of the church's patron. This was normally, of course, the bishop of Lincoln or his prebend, but during the Commonwealth the patrons had little time for the fabric of the church.

The Restoration of the Monarchy

The monarchy was restored in 1660 and soon thereafter Charles II appointed his chaplain Robert Sanderson as Bishop of Lincoln. Sanderson, a most learned man, was the author of the Preface to the 1662 Prayer Book, and was a renowned preacher. The king commented, 'I carry my ears to hear other preachers, but I carry my conscience to hear Dr Sanderson'. This pious bishop, another Buckden admirer, stated in his will that he was to be buried beneath the altar of Buckden church 'without pomp or ceremony'. His wishes were carried out when he died in January 1663, and a fine black marble slab with his coat of arms marks his grave.

This altar table dates from the reign of Charles II

Now that the bishops were in place again, they were able to repair the chancel, which they re-roofed, retaining the fifteenth century angels, in 1665. They inserted new roof bosses, several carved with mitres, and one of which is inscribed 'R.W 1665'. The maintenance of the chancel was the responsibility of the bishops and their prebends, so it is likely that 'R.W' was on the bishop's staff, perhaps as a prebend or treasurer. A halfpenny trade token in the Norris Museum, St Ives, has a similar design of 'R.Wm'. It also bears the inscription, 'William Reeve, his halfe penny, Bugden, 1667'. This reversal of his initials and the close dates, may point to William Reeve being the renovator of the chancel roof.

Huntingdonshire was hard hit by the plague in 1665 and 1666; in July 1666 alone, fifty-two people were buried in Buckden. This was at a time when burials here averaged three or four a month. It is possible that they were buried in the churchyard, but more likely in a remote plague pit.

The Restoration also brought commercial stability and in the 1670s, the Great North Road (the High Street as it runs through Buckden) was levelled, developed and turnpiked for commercial and coaching use. This was to be the beginning of Buckden's heyday, which lasted until the coming of the railways in 1850.

St Mary's, in 1680, updated a very worthwhile facility for the entire village. They installed a new clock in the tower, and it is still keeping good time today. Thomas Powers of Wellingborough was paid £10 to build and fit the clock mechanism and its two dials facing south and west, and for an extra £14 he also supplied a set of chimes. He continued to maintain the clock until 1709. The dials have been repainted and re-gilded several times and the clock is now wound by an electric motor rather than by hand, but it happily ticks (more like, clunks) away in its large wood and iron skeleton frame.

The 'Bishop of Buckden' and the half-a-bishop

Thomas Barlow was another of those bishops who was very fond of Buckden. Shortly after his death it was recorded that from the time he was consecrated in 1675 until he died in 1692 he had rarely set foot in Lincoln but had stayed in Buckden throughout. He was, and still is, known as 'The Bishop of Buckden'.

As mentioned before, he stipulated that when the time came, parts of Bishop William Barlow's wrecked tomb were to be reused in his own monument, which can be seen on the north wall of the chancel. Although not related to William, he no doubt felt that his predecessor had been greatly maligned by the Puritans, and in his epitaph he records that William's tomb had been 'destroyed by the madness of fanatics'; a plain-speaking man, for a bishop.

Bishop Thomas Barlow's monument

The church has custody of a plain and very large chalice, hallmarked 1679, courtesy of another bishop. This prelate was at Lincoln and Buckden from 1705 until 1716 before attaining the highest position in the Church of England, when he was translated to Canterbury. Archbishop William Wake donated his own personal chalice and paten to Buckden church for the use of its congregation. The Churchwardens' Accounts in May 1717 record that they had these silver items inscribed 'for feare of being lost'. The engraving is delicate and superb and cost just 20 pence at the time.

While on the subject of church silver, we must also mention Bishop Richard Reynolds and his generosity in 1744. In his will he left 'five pounds for a silver plate or paten for the Communion Table of the Church at Bugden'. Five pounds bought a finely made paten with a pedestal having 'IHS' engraved within the sun in glory on the base, and a simple Latin inscription to the upper rim recording the donor, 'Ric: Reynolds Episc: Lincoln'.

From that same year, there remains an inscription of a very different type in the church; it reads, 'St Neots 1744, Georg Rogers' with a fleur-de-lis cipher and it can be found scratched in the easternmost window glass of the north aisle. It is the earliest of several graffiti, all in the easternmost of the north and south aisle windows, and like the others it probably represents occasions when repair work was being carried out (several also record the inscriber's trade, 'painter' et al). The effort and time taken to etch the inscriptions makes it unlikely that they were the work of a few minutes' idle time during a long sermon!

But let us return to Bishop Reynolds. When giving tours of the church, this writer likes to amuse the sightseers by saying that the church has four-and-a-half bishops interred within... Bishop Reynolds is the half-a-bishop. Not that we have his top or bottom half here, but that we cannot be certain whether he's here or not! He died on 15 January 1744 and although his previous will stated that he was to be buried in Lincoln Cathedral, where most of his predecessors lie, he made a codicil during his final illness wishing to be buried in 'Buckden Domestick Chapel'. One might take that to mean the small chapel that was within the Palace, and indeed there is no memorial to him in Buckden church. The Palace chapel was demolished in 1872, and although the present St Claret Chapel was rebuilt in 1921, in a similar manner and on the same site, there are no monuments or remains of the original building extant.

It is interesting to note however, that Reynolds' wife, who predeceased him by four years, and his daughter (died 1737), as well as his niece and nephew, are all buried beneath the chancel of St Mary's, and there are small oval brasses to commemorate them. It would be nice to think that he would want to spend eternity next to his family.

Little did the bishop know that one of his minor curates would go on to great fame in their lifetime. In March 1737, Reynolds ordained in St Mary's, a soldier's son, Laurence Sterne, and the new curate assisted at Buckden throughout the following year. Many years later, Sterne was to publish a serial novel in nine volumes entitled *The Life and Opinions of Tristram Shandy, Gentleman* which gained him instant acclaim across Europe. Unlike Reynolds, Sterne used his wife very poorly, and she probably would not have wanted to spend eternity with him!

A year after Reynolds' death, the wardens were busy having the south porch repaired, and they subsequently inserted a stone, inscribed with the date 1745 and their initials, in the porch's east wall. Perhaps the workmen stopped for a while to see George II's son, Prince William, Duke of Cumberland, heading north in Mr Gale's coach. Two hundred and sixty years later members of the Gale family are still Buckden residents. William was heading for Scotland to put down Bonnie Prince Charlie's rebellion, for which he was to be forever remembered as the 'Butcher of Culloden'.

The last bishop to be buried in the chancel was John Green in 1779 in the place he chose, the 'south east corner opposite Bishop Barlow's monument' according to his will. He has a tasteful marble monument on the south wall. Nearby is the monument of his secretary, John Hodgson (died 1822), 'who was upwards of fifty years secretary of three successive Bishops of Lincoln'.[1]

The Pews throughout the Centuries

In medieval times, most churches had no seating except for a ledge or bench running around the walls. This is where the expression 'to go to the wall' comes from, when referring to weak or ailing people, as this bench offered some comfort. There is no trace of a ledge in St Mary's, which may mean that it had a wooden bench or some other form of seating. The floor would have been of compressed earth, strewn with straw. And as the nave also doubled as the equivalent of today's village hall, it was used for all kinds of activities, meetings and even business; thus full seating was not really needed until late Elizabethan times, when benches were required to provide rest for all during the longer services.

Our closest sister church, at Diddington, still retains its Elizabethan seats, quaintly carved and with holes drilled in the seat backs to hold lighted tapers for services during the hours of darkness. The first references to Buckden's seating are in the Churchwardens' Accounts in the 1640s, when repairs were carried out to the existing benches, which were possibly similar to those at Diddington. It would also appear that new pews were installed during the Commonwealth, with higher sides to cut down on draughts during the sermons - which could last three or four hours.

In the extracts from the Churchwardens' Accounts (in this chapter's appendix), we note that in 1633 the bachelors' seat was mended. And in 1711 'A new forme for the young women to sitt on in the Church' was fabricated. Even into the Victorian era, the sexes were segregated with women on the left and men to the right of the central aisle. Single girls could not sit with married women and likewise single and married

---

[1] There is a brief biography of Hodgson in the A to Z Section.

men were sat apart also. The high-sided pews, of course, had no views to the back or sides, and thus focussed the congregation on the pulpit.

At a public Vestry meeting in the church on 12 August 1774, it was decided to re-pew the church, so as to provide more space and divide the pews more evenly, and a levy of six pence (2.5p) in the pound was accordingly collected from the villagers. But before too long these new pews were found inadequate owing to the growing population. Coupled with the desire to increase the number of pews (and thus pew rent, as pews were rented out to families), this meant that the church was re-seated again in 1838.

Fashion sometimes came to the forefront in Victorian times and as the old high and cramped box pews did not suit ladies' crinolines, it was deemed appropriate once more to replace the older pews. Consequently, while St Mary's did not suffer too much at the hands of the modernising Victorians, it again got new pews in 1886 to replace those barely fifty years old.

Our current seating dates to 1909 when the church underwent a major refit. The architect, Sidney Inskipp-Ladds, recommended new pews that would be in sympathy with the other work involved. The congregation objected to throwing away perfectly good and comfortable twenty-year-old pews, but was overruled. During the re-pewing and the plaster removal of 1909, it was discovered that the Georgians had ruthlessly mutilated the piscinae and the aisle columns, in order to get the maximum income from wall-to-wall, front-to-back pews.

Church Music

Singing and music have resounded in St Mary's from earliest times, and the tradition continues to this day. As previously noted, Bishop Remigius in 1067 required that Psalm 101 be sung in Lincoln Cathedral and Buckden church, no doubt in addition to other music. As we also saw, the carved heavenly choir above the chancel and the musicians in the south aisle probably mimicked the church choir and orchestra of the early 1400s, with their lutes, viols, dulcimers and hurdy-gurdy.

An angel playing a hurdy-gurdy

The musicians played from the rood loft, at the top of the chancel arch, from c. 1470 until its destruction c. 1530. At that time, they probably moved to the western gallery, which was constructed in the tower. This gallery remained until 1909, when it was removed to permit the west door to be opened. The parish children were also seated in the gallery, and its removal meant that they could be relocated among the congregation, where they could be better controlled!

Contemporary records during Bishop Williams' time (1621-1641) tell us that in Buckden church they had 'the Holy service of God well ordered and observed Noon and evening with music and organ and with sweetest voices'. The Churchwardens' Accounts mention selling 'the old orgyn' in the 1640s. The use of the term 'old' may indicate that a replacement had been purchased.

The present organ was installed in 1884; please see below for more detail of this instrument.

The unpopular Bishop, a selfless Officer and the Flemish Panels

Generally speaking, the nineteenth century at St Mary's seems a little flat with no great building work going on, no larger-than-life characters and little scandal, but it was a time of consolidation, caring for the church and maintaining its fabric. We shall pick up on a few items that may interest the reader.

It is ironic that the monument most visible to the seated congregation belongs to the least attractive of the bishops. A rather cold, marble figure of a grieving widow in the north aisle records the passing of the worst of the non-resident bishops, George Pelham, son of the Earl of Chichester and a social appointee. In his seven years as incumbent (1820-1827) there is no record of his visiting Buckden. Although he did visit it prior to his appointment, '[he went] sulkily down to look at Bugden...to see whether he will condescend to take it'. It was during a meeting of the nobility, at the funeral of the Duke of York in January 1827, that he caught a cold and died the following month. He was buried at the family estate near Lewes, Sussex.[1]

Overriding the strong objections of a congregation that had never seen him, his widow insisted on erecting this monument to her late husband in Buckden church. It originally stood where the organ console

---

[1] See also under **Pelham** in the A to Z Section.

is today, with the kneeling figure facing the altar. It was moved to the north aisle in 1884, when the organ was constructed, and the figure now faces south across the church.

Opposite the main entrance was a north doorway, used by the bishop's staff when he was not resident at the palace. When he was in residence, his staff worshipped with him in the Palace Chapel, except on church holy days, when all celebrated together in the church. Quite how they got across the intervening moat to the north door is open to conjecture. The door was sealed up when the intricate gothic Whitworth memorial was inserted in 1831. This memorial commemorates the life of Robert Hurst Whitworth, who took his maternal uncle's name and fortune, and died young. His sisters, who paid for the monument, are remembered to the sides of this ornate triptych. Those interested in church architecture and its various orders will be interested to note that the Whitworth memorial's designer was the architect Thomas Rickman, the man who differentiated church architectural styles and invented the terms Early English, Decorated and Perpendicular. Rickman's name appears on the left edge of the monument.

On the same wall hangs a memorial to an unnamed selfless man. It reads: -

'Sacred to the memory of an Officer who sincerely regarded this his native village and caused an asylum to be erected to protect Age and reward Industry. Reader, ask not his name, if thou approve of a deed which succours the helpless go and emulate it! Obiit 10th May 1834 aged 65 years.'

One only has to walk a few hundred yards eastwards along Church Street to find his almshouses, bearing the maxim 'Industry Rewarded, Age Protected. 1840', which are today still available to Buckden folk, aided by his legacy. Although he wished to remain anonymous, the building has been known for generations as South's Almshouses, and recently a sign was erected there to recognise his generosity and to aid visitors. Captain James South, born 1769, died 1834, soldier and philanthropist, thank you.

In keeping with the increased social conscience of the day, the Bishops' Palace was conveyed to the parish vicar in 1842. The bishop of Lincoln remained the Lord of the Manor, however, until 1862, when the Ecclesiastical Commissioners handed the manor over to the bishop of Peterborough.

It was this same vicar in 1842, Henry Sidebotham (also known as Sidebottom), who, while on a visit to the Low Countries, purchased eight sixteenth century Flemish carved oak panels of Christ's Passion and gave them to the church. The wonderfully carved panels were incorporated into modern reading desks and the minister's seat. Forgotten treasures, they are easily overlooked but they do reward close scrutiny. One can find: the Agony in the garden, the Betrayal, Pilate washing his hands, the Crowning with thorns, the Flagellation, Carrying the Cross, Ecce Homo and the Crucifixion.

The Churchyard, the loss of the Palace and a 'Misunderstanding'

The transfer of the Palace to the vicar proved to be most fortuitous within ten years. The graveyard had become very uneven, unpleasant and overfull, with no room for new interments until Rev. Daniel Haigh gave a strip of the Palace land in 1852, to extend the churchyard to the west. He had been using this land as a kitchen garden (it used to be the Bishop's Chancellor's garden) as it was conveniently placed across the road from his vicarage. This vicarage was very spacious and comfortable, being built in 1795 at a cost of £260, and very much in keeping with the position of the incumbent.

Yet the donated land could only postpone the inevitable and, after being re-levelled in 1879, the whole burial ground was closed in 1883, owing to overcrowding. It contains 388 visible memorials, a mere fraction of all the burials over seven centuries, which are estimated at around 11,000. An excellent cross-referenced list of the monumental inscriptions in the church and churchyard, detailing all the memorials at St Mary's, was compiled by the Huntingdonshire Family History Society in 1995. There are reference copies in the church and in the Huntingdonshire Archives.

In addition to the aforementioned tabletop tomb purported to contain the Dukes of Suffolk's remains, there are several notable tombs and vaults commemorating the wealthier of Buckden's population; only the well-to-do could afford stone memorials, most villagers had wooden markers that have long since decayed. Just south of the porch are several early headstones dating to the 1670s and 1680s, carved with the then fashionable skull and crossbones and hourglasses, a reminder to onlookers of the fleeting time left them. One parishioner quipped that he thought the hourglass referred to the deceased dying of boredom during an interminable sermon!

With the closing of the graveyard, the new cemetery in Lucks Lane (also known as Church Lane) was consecrated on 1 September 1883, and following two extensions is still in use today.

By 1883, the vicar had relinquished all rights to the Palace entrusted to him, having sold it in 1870 for £3500 to James Marshall, of Marshall & Snelgrove shops. Marshall, in turn, promptly pulled down the last remaining medieval buildings, including the chapel, to improve the view from his Victorian pile. Thus it was that after at least nine hundred years in the same hands, the church and Palace parted company.

To celebrate the Prince of Wales's (later King Edward VII) wedding, the church bells were rung on 10 March 1863. They would not be heard again for another sixty-seven years. 'Owing to a misunderstanding' between the Rev. Daniel Haigh and the bell-ringers, the ringers refused to ring the bells and he refused to relent. It would appear that the vicar had banned their centuries-old tradition of drinking beer in the ringing chamber. After being silent for so many years, the bells became fixed in their frame and it was necessary to re-hang them in 1928, and then have new ringers trained in how to ring them. They rang out again, for the first time in several generations, on 3 May 1930.

One wonders what the village thought of the Rev. Timothy Jones, who followed Haigh. An ambiguous entry in the Church School's Log Book for 1875 reads, 'The Vicar died on Friday night, half holiday on Tuesday afternoon'!

Church Statistics in 1885

We can get a fascinating snapshot of the village as it was 120 years ago from the Rev. Henry Roxby's statistics of June 1885: -

Total Parish population 1042, of whom 'I suppose 2/3rds labouring Class'.
Attending St. Mary's church 540. Church holds c. 400, of whom 230 pay Pew Rent
Attending Dissenting Chapels 350. (Wesleyan, Primitive Methodist and Baptist).
Neglecting worship 152.
Holy Communion first and 3rd Sundays, average 150 communicants.
41 presented at last Confirmation, 10 became communicants.
Mixed boys/girls school, 94 attend.
Infants school, 76 attend
Sunday School, 62 boys & 61 girls. 10 Sunday School teachers.
Gross income £368. Declined from £480 in 10 years due to poor seasons (harvests).

The busy 1880s

Wednesday, 28 June 1882 saw the parishioners, the wardens (Messrs Marshall and Linton) and Rev. Roxby gathered at a meeting of the Vestry (the forerunner of today's Parochial Church Council [PCC]) to consider purchasing a new organ and building a new organ chamber and vestry. The medieval vestry was too small and the contract for the rental of their current organ was about to run out, and it was thought desirable to construct a new building for the two.

With their architect they came up with an excellent plan; the westernmost chancel north window was to be retained and moved north, stone by stone, to form a transept wherein the new organ would be built. The new vestry would be entered from this transept beside the organ while retaining the thirteenth century vestry doorway in the chancel.

Much fund-raising took place for the construction; the organ alone, built by Nicholson & Lord of Walsall, costing £350 in 1884.

The impressive brass eagle lectern was donated in memory of Canon Henry Linton and used for the first time at Easter 1888. And the fifteenth century font had its corroded base replaced in 1889.

Three o'clock on the afternoon of Sunday, 24 March 1895 would not have been a good time to be sitting in church; and, fortunately, no one was. A great south-westerly gale had been blowing all day and finally, by mid afternoon the spire could take no more and its upper portions and the weathervane collapsed into the north aisle. This was not taken as any sort of omen and soon £53 5s 0d was raised to replace the spire. Tradition has it that while the steeple was being rebuilt one of the workers, named 'Long Tip' Collins, performed a headstand on the capstone! Mrs Linton kindly donated a new weathercock. Seven feet across and five feet ten inches high, it shines proudly above us still.

A combination of rusting iron inserts and sonic booms from jet aircraft in the early 1960s caused this same section of the steeple to weaken again, and the village dug deep to find £1700 to replace the top ten feet six inches in 1965. The opportunity was taken to regild the weathercock and a lightning conductor was added.

The Great Refurbishment

St Mary's did avoid the worst of Victorian meddling with its medieval fabric; still, the Edwardians really could not leave it alone. There is a letter in Cambridge University Library from the renowned local architect Sidney Inskipp-Ladds to Sir Arthur Marshall, churchwarden, dated 28 February 1908. It reads in part:

'Confirming our meeting in Buckden church yesterday. I propose to strip the plaster from the nave & aisles £100, if I strip the tower £20, and the chancel £35. I strongly recommend the same except where ancient frescoes remain & I doubt whether there are any considerable portions of frescoes in Buckden church. To reseat the nave (250 sittings) @ 35/- ea. We need to alter the floor, take it up, then concrete bed & wood block the floor all over £180; to economise we could install boards under pews for total £100-120. No monuments or memorial stones to be interfered with (per the faculty)'

The congregation at a Vestry meeting agreed to all the above except, once more, they did not want their recently furnished pews replaced. Again, they were overruled, and George Page & Sons of Buckden carried out Inskipp-Ladds' proposals in full.

Just prior to the main job going ahead, John Grundy's Warm Air Heating Apparatus Co. installed a new under-floor heating system. This involved digging a coal chute in the porch and excavating a fuel stoking space below the church floor, then fitting the furnace beneath the south part of the aisle crossing. Sufficient warm air was supplied through floor gratings that Grundy guaranteed an inside temperature of 60F degrees when it was 32F degrees outside.

Work commenced once the faculty was granted, and the old floor level was discovered three inches below the present surface but it was not possible to reuse any of the old flooring or old tiles, as only indications of them at the base of the piers, were found. Thompson & Co. of Peterborough carved the new poppy-headed seating, which is in use today.

During the stripping of the plaster from the nave walls the workers found several unexpected features. Rather surprisingly, they found the doorway to the rood loft, which had been completely plastered over.

The pulpit was moved to its present position in 1908

Also uncovered at this time were the aumbries and piscinae in the north and south aisles. The remains of some fourteenth century window tracery and a gable-cross were uncovered above the north aisle piscina. Undoubtedly, the most mysterious of the finds was that of a bearded face high up on the extreme west of the north wall of the north aisle. This early, possibly twelfth century, carved stone was reused as rubble when the wall was completed around 1480. Those who know of his presence find it comforting to have an older member of the congregation looking over their shoulder.

One has to presume that the plaster strippers did not find any medieval wall paintings, which most certainly had been there at one time; whether the frescoes had been removed during iconoclastic days or the plaster strippers were not very careful, we shall never know. Very minor traces of medieval paintwork remain in the church.

The care of the chancel now rested with the Ecclesiastical Commissioners and they were prevailed upon to take the opportunity to perform similar work at the east end of the church. Once again, Thompsons re-pewed the area, this time replacing the 1774 bishop's 'old deal pews with doors & uncomfortable straight backs'. However, when it came to stripping the chancel plaster, the original thirteenth century wall was found to be so deteriorated and unsound that parts of the south-west chancel window collapsed. The window was repaired, the wall reinforced and the plaster replaced and whitewashed.

Now that there were no high box pews remaining, the seventeenth century raised pulpit was lowered and moved to the north side of the chancel arch. The font was moved from the south aisle to the tower (it was later to be returned to its current position so that the bell ringers could ring from the ground floor of the tower). New wrought iron lamps were installed, and several small donations were made to improve the lighting, altar railings and comfort of the services.

Perhaps the most touching of these donations was the pair of brass altar candlesticks still in use, given by his sister in memory of Arthur Marshall killed in 1907 when thrown from his horse at his home in Richmond, Virginia, USA.

The Bishop of Ely presided over the reopening ceremony of the refurbished church on 29 April 1909. Even though they could not keep their well-loved pews, the parishioners had raised £1123 for the complete refitting of St Mary's.

There have been no material changes to the church in the last one hundred years. The view one gets today, on entering the church, is identical to that of 1909.

The 'Suffragist Excesses' and the First World War

Whatever might be said about the Rev. John Courtenay (vicar 1911-1921), it certainly could not be that he was boring, or politically correct by today's standards.

In November 1913, he was embroiled in local and national outrage when he locked the doors of the church both between and during services. His reasons for so doing, were 'the Suffragist excesses'. He also 'rudely treated' some female members of the congregation. He claimed that he was exercising his 'right to freehold to close the church as he thinks fit'! What exactly he thought the Suffragettes might do is unknown. He did not relent, but it seems that many of the congregation stuck by him, as will be seen later.

His character and deeds lived on after him. In the 1930s, when the church wall and bell ropes needed repair, the wardens looked for the rental income due to the parish from the church lands known as Church Wall Piece and Bell Rope Piece. Imagine their shock when they learned that this church land had been sold off during Rev. Courtenay's incumbency. The deeds of sale were never found, and the wardens were unable to recover the church properties so long after their loss.

After his death, Rev. Courtenay's widow, Bertha, petitioned the PCC to place a memorial tablet to her late husband in the chancel. She explained that, 'during his vicarage, he restored the sanctuary & chancel, removing the altar rails to their original position behind the sedilia, had reading desks moved from the nave to the chancel, and had carved beautiful oak fronts to the choir stalls in keeping with other restoration work in the nave'. But she did not have friends in high places. The Earl of Sandwich wrote from Hinchingbrooke House, objecting to the monument in the sanctuary as it was 'not a suitable place for the erection of any tablet'. He also remarked upon the proposed memorial's wording: 'there may be some local comment re the Latin inscription having a humorous significance as the incumbent had a reputation of preaching at certain members of the congregation'. The memorial's Latin translates as 'The Preacher searched to find just the right words, and what he wrote was upright and true'.

Regardless of the good earl's objections, the Parochial Church Council voted 7 to 3 in favour of the bronze plaque, which was placed in the chancel at Mrs Courtenay's expense.

A more touching memorial is that in the south aisle to Henry Usher, a private soldier in the Oxfordshire & Buckinghamshire Light Infantry Regiment. Like many of the local men, he originally enlisted in the Huntingdonshire Cyclists Battalion, a modern and popular unit, thought likely to be a favourite of the ladies! After a short while training locally, they were sent to guard the Yorkshire coast against possible invasion. Henry, along with many of his pals, found that this lacked excitement and, anxious 'not to miss the war', he transferred to the Canadian Expeditionary Force and then to the Ox & Bucks Light Infantry.

He was killed in the hell of Passchendaele in August 1917 and his body was never recovered. He was 32. It is unusual that his is the only memorial in the church to a First World War casualty, when there were thirty-three Buckden men who had paid the ultimate price for freedom. Possibly it was because his father was the church clerk or it may have been that his mother, Elizabeth, was the first to petition for a memorial. A faculty was granted and the Vestry and the vicar agreed to the marble monument that was put up in 1919.

Perhaps other petitions followed as, within a few months, the Vestry voted to have all thirty-three men commemorated on a war memorial in the churchyard; and this was unveiled in 1920. In the north aisle hangs a framed roll of honour of Buckden men who served in the Great War. Judging by the names listed and the regiments, it would seem that this list was compiled in late 1916, and parts of it updated later.

The Vestry, the body consisting of church worthies responsible for the running of the church and its related duties, was replaced on 27 December 1922 by the Parochial Church Council [PCC], which was elected by the congregation.

Within living memory

The font was removed once more in 1929, this time back to its traditional position in the south aisle by the door, in accordance with the belief that entry into Christ's church is by baptism. In the same year, electricity came to the church and electric lighting was installed.

In 1937, death-watch beetle was found to have infested the nave, south aisle and porch roofs and many boards were replaced. Fortunately, only the angels' wings were affected and they were replaced that year. The carver's daughter still recalls seeing the wings on their kitchen table, but she wasn't allowed to touch!

During the Second World War, the weekday evening services and the 8 a.m. mid-winter celebrations on Sunday morning were held on the ground floor of the church tower, which was converted into a temporary chapel by the addition of an interim ceiling and curtains. The PCC had recognised that the cost of fitting blackout curtains in the church's vast windows would be prohibitive. And to aid the war effort, the iron railings from around the tombs in the churchyard were removed in December 1941, and sent for scrapping.

The boys of Tollington School, Muswell Hill, London were evacuated to Buckden Palace on 1 September 1939 and remained until July 1942, when the worst of the Blitz was over. Some of the Old Boys still visit the church with fond memories of being marched over for Sunday service. And we have to thank their Headmaster, Dr F. W. M. Draper, for some early deciphering of the Churchwardens' Accounts and research into the lives of the bishops.

The Churchwardens' staves are particularly noteworthy, with silver heads hallmarked 1946, and donated by Major and Mrs Duberly in memory of their son. The inscription reads, 'Remember 2nd Lieut. James Duberly, Scots Guards. Killed 18.6.44'. Lieut. Duberly, with many of his comrades, was at worship in the Guards Chapel at Wellington Barracks, London when it was struck by a V1 flying bomb. The emblems to the stave tops are of a dove (a copy of the Winchester cathedral dove: this stave is for the 'Vicar's warden') and a he-goat (or buck, symbolic of Buckden, and this belongs to the 'people's warden'); nowadays, of course, both wardens are elected annually by the congregation.

Once more, Buckden men had sacrificed themselves for their fellows, and in order that they were not forgotten their sixteen names were recorded on two piers beside the First World War Memorial. In 1947, the cross was moved to align with the church tower so as to make the area more symmetrical, and a small entrance to the memorial was created in the church wall.

After the Second World War

The congregation must have got used to having services in the tower during blackout periods, as it was decided in 1948 to make a permanent room of that space; and a few of the remaining 1886 pew backs were utilised to make the screen and doors. That same year, Mrs F. C. S. Green gave two large, silver family dishes (hallmarked Edinburgh 1842) in memory of her husband, a churchwarden from 1913 to 1945. They serve a useful purpose every Sunday, as alms dishes. The Coronation chalice and its matching paten, purchased by the congregation in 1953, are also used most Sundays. In Coronation year, too, the children of the church had their own collection and they provided the silver Baptism Shell, used to this day for christenings.

Between 1955 and 1959, the roof received quite a lot of attention: the north aisle roof was replaced in its entirety and in identical form; it contained no carved work. During this time the clerestory, the upper stone level of the nave, had its windows replaced.

An anonymous church member, who had brought it home from Oberammergau, donated the well-carved wooden Crucifix above the pulpit in 1957.

Many remark on the pleasant statuette of the Virgin and Child above the porch. This is in memory of the Rev. Hugh Atkinson (1931-1950) and was sculpted by Eric Winters in 1962, to replace the statuette removed over four hundred years earlier.

Although the churchyard had been closed since 1883, there were many in the congregation who expressed a desire to have an area where they or their loved ones could be laid to rest within the consecrated grounds of St Mary's. Accordingly, a faculty was granted, in 1990, to permit the interment of ashes in a small area of the western churchyard.

The Millennium Bell

To celebrate two thousand years of Christianity the church members met in early 1995 to discuss appropriate ways of sharing their faith and reaching out to the village and others. The decision was taken to raise funds to replace the 1637 oak bell-frame, which was loose in its supports and causing the tower to move when the bells were rung, and also to provide a meeting hall, kitchen and toilet facilities for village use.

Fundraising started in earnest and by 1996 sufficient funds were in hand to commence the first part of the project, the bells. It was decided to go ahead with the bells to ensure that they would be ready in time for the year 2000. The contract was awarded to White's of Appleton to remove the current five bells and transport them to their works, where they would be retuned and rehung in a new steel frame. Additionally, to celebrate the centenary of the Ely Diocesan Bellringers' Association, they very generously offered to cast a new sixth bell for Buckden.

The bells were removed on 2 December 1996 and cleanup operations were undertaken by volunteers in the old bell chamber to remove decades of dirt and leave Thomas Parnell's oak frame of 1637 (original cost £38) in good condition and in its proper position. The Bellringers Association bell was cast at the Whitechapel Foundry on 6 February 1997 and all six bells were test assembled in their new frame at

White's soon after. In May, they were re-hung twenty feet below their original position, in order to preserve the oak frame and to reduce the risk of structural damage to the tower. The cost of the whole operation had been £30,000.

Parishioners had a wonderful day when all six bells were rung for the first time following the Service of Dedication and Celebration, which was conducted by Bishop John Dennis, on 8 June 1997.

Buckden's Living Stones

The Millennium Bell project had used up most of the funds raised; additionally the proposed meeting hall, etc. had run into problems with the planning authorities. Although the plans were finalised in 1999, a further five years were to pass before the authorities and English Heritage were able to agree on a suitable extension to the north and north-east side of the church.

The Buckden's Living Stones Appeal was formed to develop funding for the extension project and to guide the construction management, all under the authority of the PCC. The target was now £575,000 and fundraising recommenced immediately. There have been some exciting events since then including piano and organ recitals, golf days, a magnificent exhibition of quilts, open gardens at Stirtloe House, guided tours of the church, an art and sculpture exhibition, a teddy bear 'death slide', choir singing and a Sounds Spectacular.

The Appeal was launched on 9 September 2004, when for three straight days, the Bible was read non-stop by volunteers from the congregation and friends of the church. They read all 787,000 words and finished exquisitely during the Thanksgiving Service at 7:30 p.m. on Sunday, 12 September. A very generous £13,880 was raised by this event. All participants agreed that the greatest reward was the spirit of friendship and love throughout the reading.

By November 2005, £162,000 had been raised and this sum was sufficient encouragement to commence work. In October, the gravestones to the north-east of the church were moved in preparation for the below ground and foundation work. Any known descendants of those whose headstones were to be moved were contacted, and no interments were disturbed. A bonus from this preparatory work has been the discovery of four formerly buried headstones and the revelation of previously hidden details on other monuments.

All involved are hopeful that the new kitchen, toilets and meeting room will be ready for the use of village and church groups in 2010.

References & bibliography (with locations where appropriate)
NB Since mid-2009, 'Huntingdonshire Archives' has been the new title for the Huntingdon County Record Office (HCRO).

Alnwick (Bp. Wm.) Court Book & Transcript 1446-1452	Lincolnshire Archives
An Account of the Parish Church of St. Mary's Buckden 1973 & 1985	Phillip Morgan
Anglo-Saxon Chronicles. c. AD 1-1140	Public domain
British Library	London
Buckden Church Report on the Bellframe, 1994	C. Pickford
Buckden Palace	R. H. Edleston 1928
Buckden Parish Registers, 1559 - 1921 et seq.	Huntingdonshire Archives
Buckden Parish Wardens' Accounts 1627-1774, Vestry Book,	Huntingdonshire Archives
Cambs. & Hunts. Archaeological Society: Transactions & Proceedings 1890-1920	Huntingdonshire Archives & Norris Museum, St Ives

Churches and Chapels: investigating places of worship	D. Parsons 1989
Day's Solicitors Manuscripts 1750-1900	Norris Museum, St Ives
Domesday Book 1086 Huntingdonshire	J. Morris & S. Harvey 1975
Edwardian Inventories for Huntingdonshire 1552	S.C. Lomas, T. Craib 1906
Faculties & Visitations Buckden 1883-1984	Cambridge University Library
Fasti Ecclesiae Anglicanae 1066-1853	J. Le Neve 1977. Lincoln Cathedral Library
Handlist of the records of the Bishops of Lincoln 1953	K. Major
Henrician Reformation The Diocese of Lincoln under John Longland 1521-1547	M. Bowker 1981
How old is that church?	P. Cunnington 1993
Huntingdon & the Spanish Armada,	W. M. Noble
Huntingdon County Records Office (now the Huntingdonshire Archives)	Huntingdon
Huntingdon Library	Huntingdon
Hunts County News newspapers	Huntingdon Library
Hunts Post newspapers	Huntingdon Library
Inskipp-Ladds files & notes 1880-1920	Norris Museum, St Ives
Inskipp-Ladds newspaper clippings 1870-1920	Norris Museum, St Ives
Kelly's Directories	Huntingdonshire Archives
Lansdowne Manuscripts 921 (Sir Robert Cotton Collection)	British Library
Legends & Traditions of Huntingdonshire 1888	W. H. B. Saunders
Lincoln Cathedral Library and Archives	Lincoln Cathedral
Local Mediaeval Gilds (St Neots Museum)	R. Arguile
Manor & Consistory Court Books 1777-1870 et al	Northampton Archives
Norris Museum Archives	St Ives
Northants and Huntingdonshire in the twentieth century: contemporary biographies	Huntingdonshire Archives
Norwich School of Glass-painting in the Fifteenth century the	C. Woodforde 1950
Peterborough Diocesan Records 1861-1890	Northampton Archives
Pigot's Directories 1850-1870	Huntingdonshire Archives
Records of Huntingdonshire	Hunts Local History Socy.
Rolls & Register of Bp. Oliver Stone 1280-1299	Lincoln Cathedral Library (ed. 1952)
Rolls of Bp. Rich. Gravesend 1258-1279	Lincoln Cathedral Library (ed. 1925)
Royal Commission on the Historical Monuments of England 1926	National Monuments Record Centre
St Neots Advertiser newspapers	Huntingdon Library
St Mary's, Buckden Monumental Inscriptions	K. & D. Wright
Survey of Cathedrals 1730 & 1742. Annotated	Browne Willis. Lincoln Cathedral Archives
Terriers, Visitations, Surveys, Inventories etc Buckden. 16th, 17th, 18th, 19th, 20th centuries	Lincolnshire Archives, Huntingdonshire Archives, Cambridge University Library, Northants Archives, Lincoln Cathedral Library
	London
Victoria County History, Huntingdonshire 1922	
Visitation of Huntingdon 1684 (re stained glass)	Sir H. St George (ed. 1994)

APPENDIX

The Buckden Churchwardens' Accounts

When these books were started, the duties and powers of the wardens were altogether much wider than they are today. The church was the main seat of authority in the village and the wardens were responsible for raising levies or taxes, educating children, keeping law and order, caring for the poor, maintaining the church, and even paying for the catching of vermin.

Here are some extracts to give you a flavour of former days in Buckden. Some explanatory notes have been added; these are in italics ('q.v.' refers the reader to an appropriate entry in the A to Z Section). The amounts paid are shown as they were entered at the time, i.e. in pounds, shillings and pence.

1627	Mar 27	For wine bought at Huntingdon (this is the first entry in the Accounts)	£0 2s. 0d.
1627	Nov 5	Payd for ringinge ye 5th of November (celebrating the saving of Parliament from the Gunpowder Plot in 1605)	£0 4s. 0d.
1627	Mar 27	Payd ye bell founder for metal that he did put in to the mould that he had made (bell made by William Haulsey of St. Ives)	£1 2s. 4d.
1627	Mar 27	Spent at Saint Ives when we carried the bell home	£0 0s. 8d.
1627	Mar 27	Payd for washing the surplis 4 times	£0 0s. 4d.
1633		A bord for to mend the bachelers seat and the worckmanship (men and women were seated separately in church)	£0 10s. 6d.
1641		Given to a poore scoller	£0 0s. 6d.
1642		Paid for 8 dozen of moles killing	£0 6s. 0d.
1642		Laying down a grave in the church	£0 1s. 6d.
1643		Paid to the glazier for mending the windows in the year 1643	£0 10s. 0d.
1645	May	Given to a poor Irishman which was undone by the Rebels	£0 1s. 0d.
1645	Aug 24	Spent on the ringers when the King came into the County (following the Battle of Naseby. Buckden was backing both sides)	£0 4s. 8d.
1646	Mar 31	Given to a Company of Cripples upon Easter Tuesday	£0 0s. 6d.
1646	Mar 29	Paid for bread and wyne for ye Communion at Easter 1646	£1 12s. 6d
1646		Spent on the soldiers at Burr's (landlord of a Buckden inn) when they came to Henry Burder and William Luffe to help to collect a tax for (the war in) Ireland	£0 6s. 8d.
1648		Given to Tho. Shepson, John Longland's man for six hedgehogs (considered vermin)	£0 0s. 6d.
1649		Three massive tax collections to repair the church roof, fabric and windows	£169 4s.0d.
1650	May 12	For a quart of sack (sherry) sent to a stranger that had preached twice this Sunday (there were many itinerant preachers preaching in church during the Commonwealth period)	£0 1s. 6d.
1656		Paid for an owre glase (an hour glass was turned two or three times per sermon!)	£0 1s. 0d.
1663	Apr 23	Paid for a Book of Commons & a Table of Dogmas wherein what marriages are prohibited (this latter list hung in church detailing who one could not marry, it ran to some fifty exceptions)	£0 1s. 8d.
1668	July 27	Paid Mr Richard Lillingston for one year teaching at Buckden church school	£5 0s. 0d.
1690	Sep 12	Spent upon ye ringers when King William came out of Ireland (following the Battle of the Boyne)	£0 1s. 0d.
1694	Dec 4	Paid Thos Shepardson for scouring the lakes for 2 roods in Low Meadow (now Buckden Marina)	£0 2s. 4d.
1699		Paid to John Hewitt for a book against swareing	£0 1s. 0d.
1706	Jun 27	Paid to Robert Roberts for 5 days work for to help to clean and brush the church	£0 5s. 0d.
1709	Mar 9	Paid Wm Lawrence for himself and his son for sawing stone and making the door placed in the steeple	£0 2s. 6d.
1710	Mar 30	For a birch beesom (broom) had for the church	£0 0s. 2d.
1713	May 29	Spent when peace was proclaimed at Buckden (they had a street party to celebrate the end of the Wars of the Spanish Succession)	£2 18s. 9d.
1713	Nov 5	Paid for powder & shott to kill the birds in the church	£0 0s. 4d.
1717	May 17	Inscribing the chalice and paten donated by Bishop William Wake, for feare of being lost (there is a beautiful inscription on these silver vessels)	£0 4s. 0d.

1719/20		Paid William Banks for Weston paving tile for the church aisles	£10 1s. 6d.
1731	Apr 19	Paid Thomas Landell senior for cleaning the Gravell Walks in the Churchyard	£0 3s. 0d.
1732	Jan 15	Bought 2 padlocks for the church chest	£0 1s. 8d.
1764	Feb 3	Paid for a letter from Hitchin	£0 0s. 6d.
1766	Apr 28	Geo C Swan Esq paid for to build a workhouse for the poor	£80 0s. 0d.
1768	Jan 24	Paid John Plowman & John Clark for cleaning the church leads *(roof)* of snow	£0 2s. 0d.
1772	Feb 4	Paid William Stratton for a bat net	£0 2s. 0d.
1772	May 12	One year salary paid to John Plowman for cleaning the *(fire)* engine and pipes	£0 10s. 0d.
1773	Apr 29	Beer when the fire was at the Hackers *(beer was provided for those who hand-pumped the fire engine and fought the fire)*	£1 5s. 8d.
1795	July	Paid to build the new vicarage for Revd Edward Maltby *(now the Old Vicarage [q.v] opposite the church)*	£260 0s.0d.
1800	Apr 14	Dr. Mackie, Surgeon and Apothecary of Huntingdon to be paid twelve guineas per annum to attend to the Parish poor, including Midwifery. Fractures and inoculations extra. *(In 1801, the doctor's wife complained that of 22 parishes, Buckden was the only late payer. This may explain the 1802 change below)*	£12 12s. 0d.
1802	May 4	Mr. Benjamin Roberts, Surgeon and Apothecary of Buckden, to attend to the Poor, including Midwifery at £0 7s 6d each	
1803	May 9	Paid for the Huntingdon, Brampton, Offord, St. Neots and Godmanchester Fire Engines and labourers and soldiers 2 days and 2 nights *(There had been a huge fire in Buckden)*	£25 9s. 0d.
1803	June	Donations towards the loss by fire at Buckden *(received from Buckden and all surrounding towns and villages)*	£560 0s.0d.
1806	Sept	Paid John Balmer, plaisterer of Huntingdon to remove stucco from the outside of the church tower, from the parapets down to the foundation, and to re-stucco it	£130 0s.0d.
1815	July	Mary Ayers 3d, Ann Usher 3d, Mary Baker 3d, Ann Hunns 1d, Mary Middleton 3d from their Rewards at School *(subscriptions to the widows and orphans fund after the Battle of Waterloo, included these Buckden schoolgirls giving their pocket money)*	£0 1s. 1d.
1841	Apr 13	Contract for the new box pews	£230 0s.0d.
1842	Mar 5	Mr. Cartwright's *(q.v. – landlord of the George Inn)* bill for refreshments for our children confirmed at Huntingdon	£2 0s. 0d.
1842	Mar 23	New shoes for the Beadle *(forerunner of the village policeman)*	£0 6s. 0d.
1864	Apr 7	Paid Wm Gale 1 years Ringing etc *(he tolled one bell for every service and funeral)*	£1 6s. 0d.
1912	Jan 19	Printing Coronation Services *(King George V)* and National Anthem	£0 15. 4d.
1929	Nov 1	BCH Electricity Co. Installation of electric plant and light in the church	£70 15s.6d.
1930	Oct 2	Men paid to teach our men how to ring bells *(the bells had not been rung since 1863)*	£3 3s. 0d.

CHAPTER 6/BRIDGE HOUSE, CHURCH STREET: A SHORT HISTORY
Christopher Bates

Bridge House is believed to be the oldest surviving property in Buckden. The house was built in 1458 and when first completed was an open medieval hall and a building of high status. Over subsequent centuries the house has seen many changes to its structure and also to the village in which it stands. Its survival is testimony to the strength and quality of the construction. In this chapter its owner, Christopher Bates, tells the continuing story of its restoration—and in a postscript explains why in a house with a very long history you may not always be as alone as you think…

I have owned Bridge House since 2004 and have endeavoured to restore the house to its former glory, utilising wherever possible traditional materials in keeping with the original construction. These materials are able to move and breathe with the existing structure, thus ensuring its continued survival for many years to come.

During the course of this ongoing work I have made many exciting discoveries and also made many new friends in the village. I feel very fortunate to have the privilege of living in such a beautiful home in a wonderful village.

Medieval open halls

Until the middle of the sixteenth century most people of status lived in a space which was open to the roof, heated by a fire burning in a hearth built on the floor. The hall was always the largest room in the house, open from the ground to the apex of the roof, which besides being the focus of daily life for a large household was also intended as a place of assembly for the transactions of public business, such as the manorial court.

The principal features of medieval halls, despite some regional variations, were basically the same. In or near the centre of the hall was the open hearth, the smoke escaping as best it could through the small gablets at the junction of the hips and ridge of the roof. Beyond the hearth was the upper end, which was occupied by the family and contained the high table and bench. The bench was usually fixed, being no more than a long narrow plank attached to the high end wall of the hall. Most of the light in the hall came from tall unglazed mullioned windows on either side of the high table.

Halls were entered directly through a door in the front elevation (the north elevation in the case of Bridge House: the curved head of the original front entrance remains, although this is no longer the entrance to the house). A cross-passage ran between a pair of opposed doorways in the front and back walls. On one side of the passage were two doorways leading to the service accommodation at the lower end of the house, the buttery (for beer), and the pantry (for bread). The two service doorways remain in Bridge House. This is a very rare survival as so often internal alterations led to their removal. The doorways are now blocked by the insertion of a later brick chimney into the cross-passage.

On the other side of the passage there was a screen dividing it from the main hall. A visitor entering the hall through the single door from the cross-passage would first see the open fire and then, beyond, the high table.

The whole house was a hierarchical space mirroring the hierarchies of society: the servants at the lower service end, the cross-passage entrance, the screen, the lower bay of the hall with the high table beyond, and the private apartments entered from the upper end.

Bridge House, in addition to the open hall, has a cross-wing at the upper (west) end, accommodating the family on the upper floor and most probably a shop front, with workshop behind, on the ground floor. In keeping with the high-class workmanship at the upper end of the house, the front elevation of this cross-wing was jettied (upper storey projecting over the ground floor). The window at first-floor level in the front gable was of a projecting type, and the jetty was supported by a beam known as a bressummer, whose ornate carving further demonstrated the wealth and importance of the owner.

Construction of Bridge House

Oak is the predominant timber in the construction of the frame, although a fair amount of elm was also utilised, reflecting the local timber available to the original carpenters. Oak has great strength and resistance to rot, and when allowed to dry naturally is actually improved and hardened with age. Elm, when grown in woodland conditions, grows taller than oak so was employed on members where great length was required. It is somewhat inferior to oak in that it is less resistant to damp and insect attack.

Dendrochronological examination has shown that the timber was felled in 1457. It would have been worked within a year of felling, when it was still green and soft, allowing it to be cut and the joints made. As the sap dried out, the timber hardened until it was almost too hard to cut. The drying process continued after the frame had been erected, with the timber warping and twisting, causing the undulations of line found in all old timber buildings.

The trees were felled with a narrow axe. The larger trees were split into baulks and shaped with a broad axe. Timbers were usually cut from a tree just large enough to produce the section required. All the large timbers in Bridge House contain the heart of the tree, a term referred to as boxed heart, which means simply squared from a whole trunk. Smaller timbers were generally halved from the squared baulks. As the timbers were cleft, the grain of the tree ran true along the beams, giving them much greater strength than modern sawn timbers. Curved braces were cut from curved branches of larger trees. It is estimated that approximately two hundred trees would have been felled in the construction of Bridge House, varying in size from nine to eighteen inches in diameter.

With the timbers prepared, the next stage was cutting the joints. The carpenters' tools available were adzes, axes, chisels, basic planes, hammers and mallets, shell augers, scribing tools and chalk lines. Considering the basic nature of these tools, the carpenters produced work of astonishing skill and ingenuity. The joints used were mortice and tenon, half lap, or scarf, the mortice and tenon being the most important and the basis for the framework. Scarf joints were utilised to join shorter beams together to produce one continuous length. After cutting all the joints, the framework was assembled on site. Many strong arms would be needed for the rearing and building; however, the majority of members were assembled one by one. Almost all the beams could be carried by one or two men. A rope and pulley would have assisted in raising the larger beams. As the work progressed, scaffolding would have been used, consisting of poles lashed together with woven wattle panels as platforms. During erection the frame would have been supported on temporary blocks which were replaced after completion with a low stone plinth.

All the joints were held together with oak pegs driven into holes drilled through the mortice and tenons. Metal fixings were not used. The pegs were tapered so that as they were driven home the joint would be pulled tightly together.

The original roof covering would have been thatch. Reed provided the best quality thatch but wheat straw was also used. At a later date the thatch was replaced with peg tiles. These would have been produced locally from the Cambridgeshire gault clay. When fired this clay forms tiles of a distinctive yellow colour. The tiles derive their name from the small timber pegs driven through holes in the tiles and hooked over the laths. Over many years of repairing and re-roofing, a proportion of red tiles have been used producing a mixture of reds and yellows. This distinctive appearance has become known as the Huntingdonshire mix.

The panels between the timber framing were infilled with wattle and daub. This comprised a timber background fixed between the studs on to which was applied a layer of wet earth mixed with straw and cow dung. The wattle sticks were of hazel which was grown coppiced in local

A view of wattle only modernised in that plastic cable ties have been used in place of bramble bark.

woods. Growing hazel by coppicing produces many long straight sticks from each tree. Regular harvesting encourages more shoots to grow from the remaining stumps, thus increasing the yield. Brampton wood still has large areas of medieval coppice, but while it is possible that the sticks were cut from there, it is more likely they came from Buckden's deer park.[1]

Holes were drilled in the top and bottom rails of each panel and long vertical sticks were cut and sprung into these holes. V-grooves were cut into the vertical studs, then short cross-pieces were wedged into these grooves. The vertical and horizontal sticks were tied together to provide greater strength to the panel. String was not yet available to these early builders, so tough bramble strands stripped from bramble bark were used. Some of these original ties still remain, giving testament to the strength and durability of the material.

The daub was mixed on site. Usually the winter before the frame was erected on site, a large pond was dug out on site. The earth that was excavated was piled up beside the hole. Over winter the hole was allowed to fill with water. In spring time the earth was thrown back into the pond, along with chopped straw. A post was banged into the middle of the pond, to which a cow was tethered. As the cow walked round and round, the pressure from its hooves acted to mix the earth and straw adding dung as it . Once thoroughly mixed, the cow was removed and then the mixed daub dug out and applied to the wattle panels. Usually the remaining hole in the ground was left to refill with water, thus forming a permanent pond. Many ponds associated with old buildings have been formed in this way.

Once all the wattle panels were covered with daub, the exterior of the house was rendered. Most medieval timber-framed buildings were rendered to protect the framework. (It was not until Victorian times that it became fashionable to strip off the render to expose the frame.) Rough split branches were fixed to the outer faces of the frame and over this was applied a render of the same daub mixture. To provide a superior finish, a thin layer of lime plaster was utilised. Limewash was painted onto the lime plaster. The wash protects the plaster and also gives a finished colour to the exterior. During the restoration I discovered that the original limewash was an orange colour. This is a limewash containing sulphate of iron, commonly known as copperas. This was widely used in this district and gives buildings a distinctive rusty colouration.

The windows were unglazed and divided with square-section mullions set diagonally about six inches apart. It was not until the end of the sixteenth century that the manufacture of glass became widespread, and so in the place of glass, oiled cloth - preferably linen - was fixed over the openings to provide some protection from the weather. In most cases these early windows were provided with timber shutters, hinged or sliding in grooves either internally or externally.

The entrance doors were simply constructed from vertical boards of varying width, secured at the back by horizontal battens or ledges and, when the door was wide, with additional diagonal braces to prevent the door from sagging. Medieval doors had no frame and were hung directly to the opening using wrought-iron hinges.

The internal floors would have been of compacted earth, strewn with rushes and straw and perhaps treated with ox blood and ashes which produced a harder surface. The internal walls and beams would be limewashed to provide some protection and also to brighten the dark interior.

Alterations to Bridge House

When chimneys first became fashionable, they were installed in many halls, in place of the open hearth whose smoke drifted out through the roof. This led to the idea of other rooms being heated and the possibility of both an upper and lower floor having fireplaces. The roof of a hall was usually lower than any cross-wing, and most halls were altered in the sixteenth and early seventeenth centuries to raise the roof and install an upper floor. This was the beginning of a period known as the great rebuilding

Chimneys were often built in part of the cross-passage, on the back wall of the hall and on the side or back wall of a cross-wing. At the same time, glass had become cheaper, and when a hall was altered, the windows were often blocked up and new, larger frames incorporated. Halls sometimes had windows from floor to ceiling, and with the addition of a new floor, these had to be altered to accommodate two stories. The roof was often levelled up to match that on the cross-wing, and service ends were altered to provide kitchens with their own fireplaces. The rooms now started to have different uses, with more accommodation upstairs for sleeping chambers, and more private family rooms downstairs.

The main chimney in the cross-passage of Bridge House was built in 1593. At the same time an upper floor was inserted into the main hall, creating private rooms for the family upstairs. Families were no longer willing to share their daily lives with their servants and sought greater privacy, which the new first-floor rooms offered them. The chimney in the cross-wing was not constructed until 1680. This chimney

---

[1] See under **deer park** in the A to Z section.

incorporated its own bread oven to supply the needs of the family.

The mullioned windows were replaced with sash windows which slid horizontally, partly due to the low ceiling. These windows are known as Yorkshire sashes. The old window openings were usually reused for the positioning of the new glazed frames. Often these openings were enlarged.

With the blocking of the cross-passage by the new chimney, the main entrance to the house was moved and re-sited at the junction of the main wing and the cross-wing.

The earthen floors were covered with brick pamments (a type of floor tile) to provide a more serviceable flooring, and many of the internal walls and beams were limewashed with a strong Prussian blue colour, another demonstration of the owners' wealth.

In more modern times the original lime render had been replaced with a cement render and the outer walls painted with masonry paint, both unsuitable. A bathroom was installed on the first floor and also central heating in the form of electric storage heaters. Electric lighting and power sockets were installed in, I believe the 1930s. During the same period the roof timbers of the main range were unfortunately replaced with softwood rafters, probably due to failures in the original structure.

The Bridge

Bridge House takes its name from the humpback bridge that used to carry Church Street across a stream directly to the west of the main building. The stream was the overflow from large fish ponds in the grounds of Buckden Towers. There were originally three large ponds which provided a constant source of fresh fish to the residents of Buckden Palace. They were joined together to create the large lake that still remains today. It is very likely that these ponds were formed due to the digging out of the clay to be used in the manufacture of bricks on site during the construction of Buckden Palace. The stream linked the ponds with another lake which is in an area known as the Valley, which is adjacent to the modern playing fields. The stream was originally open but has since been diverted into a culvert under ground. This still runs through the garden of Bridge House and can be accessed by lifting a large stone pad. The bridge has disappeared with the piping of the stream, but the house's name serves as a reminder

Restoration

During the course of restoring the structure of Bridge House I have endeavoured to use materials and techniques sympathetic to the building. Traditional materials allow movement in the timber structure and also allow the building to breathe, which is essential to its future.

The modern cement render and the masonry paint created an impermeable layer which trapped moisture inside the building. This moisture was absorbed by the daub and also by the frame, and was unable to dry out. Modern paints used internally also exacerbated this problem. In this damp environment the timber frame suffered greatly, with the sole plate all but rotting away and the bases of all the posts decaying. The elm posts suffered much greater damage under these conditions than the oak. If left to decay in this manner, the frame would have eventually failed resulting in serious damage to the structure. Where the daub had failed, it had been replaced with a mixture of inappropriate materials: bricks, concrete blocks and plasterboard.

The kitchen extension to the rear of the cross-wing was a very poorly built single-storey structure approximately a hundred years old. As part of the listed building consent, I was granted permission to replace this with a two-storey extension consisting of a kitchen with a bedroom above. The materials used for this part were in keeping with the existing structure, handmade brick and local peg tiles. The pitch of the roof was matched to that on the cross-wing, but the roof line was set lower so that the extension is subservient to the main building. The Conservation Officer requested that the extension should be brick to be an obvious contrast to the timber frame building. Dressed splayed brick

Bridge House. Stripping of the cement mortar rendering to expose the decayed timber frame and daub has been started.

lintels were made for the window and door opening, and 'tumbling', a traditional detail, was applied to the brick courses of the gable end.

The repairs to the main building were carried out carefully by hand to avoid unnecessary disruption and loss of existing materials. The cement render was removed in sections, thus exposing the decayed framework. Where existing daub was still present, every effort was made to keep it in position. Where this was not possible, mainly due to the failure of the wattle through rotting in the damp environment, then the daub was removed and stored on site. This daub was eventually re-invigorated through the application of water and remixing with chopped straw. The daub could then be applied to the repaired wattles.

As each section of framework was exposed, the decayed timber was cleaned back. It was amazing that, though visually very poor, the timbers cores were still sound. Each piece was assessed and then new feet were spliced onto the bases of all the posts. The maximum amount of existing material was retained. The new pieces were joined with a joint called a scissor scarf which is a double sided splice joint that provides great strength. The joint tightens the more pressure is applied to it from the weight of the building.

The vertical elm posts have been restored requiring scissor scarf joints; one can be distinguished in the left hand post. The new ground beam has been inserted and awaits the replacement of the foundation brickwork!

The new posts were joined into the replacement sole plate with mortice and tenon joints. Where greater length was required the sole plate was extended by joining pieces together with half lap joints. The new sole plate was supported in place on pairs of timber wedges which were driven home to tighten the joints. Once completed, each section of frame had its brick plinth rebuilt to the underside of the sole plate. Bricks recovered from site were laid with lime mortar. When the mortar had set, the timber wedges could be removed and the building once again sat on its plinth. One section of the plinth contains square-cut stone blocks which were probably robbed from a local Norman building.

Where the wattle was missing, holes were drilled in the sole plate and new vertical hazel sticks sprung into the openings. Cross-sticks were wedged between the timber beams and the vertical and horizontal sticks tied together. The daub could then be reapplied to the wattle panels. This was carried out by two people working from either side, a messy business!

The internal floor level of the building had been raised approximately eight inches. This was probably to counteract damp problems, as over many years the outside ground level had risen considerably, by around eighteen inches. Through digging a test hole I was able to establish the original internal floor level and was granted permission to return to this level. This eased the problem of poor headroom internally.

During the course of digging out the raised floor, in which I was assisted by my dad, we uncovered many buried artefacts: coins, clay pipes, bottles, pottery and bones—mainly things that had been thrown away, but of great interest. The bones we unearthed became of much greater interest when the local police arrived, having received reports of human remains being discovered! The bones were taken away and we were most surprised when the officer returned to report that they were in fact human bones, not the animal bones that we had suspected. Luckily they were even older than the house, so the case was not pursued.

Underfloor heating was installed throughout the whole of the ground floor. This should provide a comfortable and even temperature, which will be less stressful for the house than the sudden temperature changes associated with radiators.

The roof to the rear of the main wing was failing, so the peg tiles were carefully removed and cleaned. Unfortunately the previous roofer in the 1950s had bedded them all in cement mortar where they overlapped. This created much work in cleaning off the hard cement from the old tiles. The roof was re-battened and the old tiles returned to their place. Some new handmade tiles were mixed in to account for the broken and missing tiles.

The two chimney stacks were repaired. The modern cement pointing was raked out and replaced with lime mortar. The lime mortar is softer than the bricks, so any moisture escaping from the chimney passes through the mortar and not the bricks. With cement pointing the faces of the bricks are blown off in frost. Any badly damaged brick was carefully removed and, where possible, turned around so the fresh face was showing. Where necessary the gutters and downpipes were repaired with matching cast-iron products. Most of the original gutters were cleaned up and repainted.

The front door was sympathetically repaired by splicing in replacement timber where there was a need for repairs.

The whole of the exterior walls was lathed with oak laths. These were fixed to oak counter battens fixed to the frame. Stainless steel fixings were used as the tannic acid in green oak quickly attacks plain steel. To fix the laths I used over 12,000 nails. Once they were complete, lime render was mixed on site using pre-mixed lime putty and plastering sand. These were mixed and then stored in a heap, covered with tarpaulin for at least three months. This allows the render to improve with age. After three months the render is re-mixed and at this stage goat hair is added to provide more strength.

The render was applied in three coats. The walls were protected by hessian which was hosed down daily to prevent the render from drying too quickly and to limit cracking through shrinkage. Once the render had dried, at least six coats of limewash were applied by brush, the wall first being dampened. As previously mentioned, the finish was limewash containing sulphate of iron to produce the distinctive rusty orange colour.

As the ground level outside is still higher than the internal floor level, a French drain was installed around the whole house. This consists of a perforated drainpipe buried in a trench of pea shingle. The pipe drains away from the house and I arranged it to outfall into the underground stream in the culvert. This drain carries away any water in the ground directly adjacent to the house.

I am hopeful I may be allowed to replace the missing projecting window from the front gable of the cross-wing, which is at the moment is just an opening uncovered by the removal of the modern render. Internally, there is much work left to complete, which I am now concentrating on.

A final word of thanks to all the family who have helped tremendously with their tireless support and practical help, and to my friends who have kept me cheerful throughout. A special thank you to my fantastic neighbours Richard, Melanie, Heather and Howard for their constant support and cups of tea. And finally to all the residents of Buckden, including members of the Local History Society, to whom I have so enjoyed chatting.

Ghost stories

In a house that has been occupied for five and a half centuries, there are bound to be a few residents reluctant to leave...

With a property of such age, built in 1458 during the reign of Henry VI, it is inevitable there are stories of ghosts in residence. I can only recount my personal experiences and leave it to readers to come to their own conclusions. The first night I stayed in the house, having only just moved my possessions in that day, I was sat alone in the sitting-room. The room was lit only by two small wall lights either side of the large inglenook fireplace, which at that time was bricked up to form a small grate centrally. The rest of the house was in darkness. Suddenly both lights began flashing, on off on off on off... this continued for approximately thirty seconds whereupon they returned to normal. I put this down to the old wiring but this incident was never repeated.

Peggy, a friend of the previous owner Miss Beckwith, called in to introduce herself. In the course of our chat Peggy was telling me what a lovely house Bridge House was. She recounted happy memories of her time spent here among friends. Her only reservations concerned the bedroom in the cross-wing at the front of the house. When I told Peggy that I was currently sleeping in this room she became concerned. Peggy had slept in this room when she was staying with her friend whilst she was searching for a house in Buckden.

In the morning, she was awake but lying in bed dozing with her eyes shut. The room door was closed and there was no one else in the room with her. Suddenly she became conscious of an animal having jumped up on to the bed. She could feel the weight of the animal upon her and then felt it walking up her body, turning round and round upon her chest in the manner of a dog settling down. Then the weight of the resting animal could be felt on her chest. At this point Peggy realised that she was alone in the room and opened her eyes with a start. The pressure upon her vanished and there was nothing to be seen.

One evening I invited some friends round for drinks. We had a very pleasant evening sitting in the old kitchen. One of my guests, who had an interest in the house, said that if there were ghosts I must talk to them, letting them know my plans for the restoration.

Well, after a few drinks and a long evening I bade farewell to my friends and was left alone sitting in the kitchen. Mindful of my friend's advice, and conscious that the kitchen was due to be demolished, I took this opportunity to tell anyone listening of the building work to be done. Talking out loud I discussed the alterations and re-iterated that anyone there with me was very welcome to stay once the new kitchen was completed. At this point I suggested that they could give me a sign that I wasn't alone and talking to myself. Nothing happened, so I contented myself that I had been foolish and got up to go to bed. As I left the kitchen there was a clear click noise, very noticeable as I live alone. I felt it was strange but didn't attribute it to anything. At this point I noticed another sound, it was water bubbling, beginning to boil in the electric kettle. The kettle, which stood on top of the fridge, had switched itself on and was now boiling. This was completely unexplainable. I switched it off and quickly rushed upstairs. The following morning I tried to repeat the kettle switching on, maybe it hadn't been switched off properly, but I was unable to switch it on without a definite firm click. The kettle never switched on in this manner again. I have now purchased a new kettle.

Upon returning home one afternoon I walked upstairs to the new bedroom and en suite bathroom above the kitchen. As I entered the bedroom I noticed a large puddle of water coming from under the bathroom door, which was closed. Thinking there was either a tap left on or a leak, I opened the door. The

Bridge House 2009. The exterior is almost complete. Two windows remain to be replaced.

sink was empty, but water was dripping from all around the underside of the sink. I mopped and dried up all the water expecting to discover the source of the problem. Once dry, there was no leak at all; it was only as if the sink had been allowed to overflow and then someone had switched the taps off. The house was empty and I was the only person with a key.

But this incident was due to a dodgy tap...........

All I can say is that I get a fantastic feeling that this is a very happy house and if there is anyone here with me, then I think they approve of the care and love I am investing in restoring Bridge House to its former glory.

CHAPTER 7/STIRTLOE AND THE GRANGE, CASTLE, NUNNERY OR HOUSE AND HAMLET BUILT THERE
Elspeth Thomas

In this chapter the author tells the story of Stirtloe House, which her family bought in 1970, and its surrounding area.

Stirtloe—a part of the Toseland Hundred, and at differing times paying dues to the Manor of Southoe, the Manor of Diddington, and till the early twentieth century, the Manor of Buckden

The physical features of the land suggest the origins of the house and hamlet of Stirtloe: from Steort or Sturt meaning tongue of land, and loe meaning a low hill. Old north-south droving roads hugged the edge of the flood-line of the Great Ouse, and several droving tracks can still be seen on the Parliamentary Inclosure map of 1813. These medieval roads bear little resemblance to the present day A1, whose alignment has changed periodically as improvements continue to be made to eighteenth century turnpike, twentieth century trunk road, and now dual carriageway. Morden's map of 1695 shows roads of equal size on the route of the present A1 and to the east of the present house. Until the early nineteenth century the Great Ouse would have been navigable for commercial traffic as far as Bedford but whilst Offord (confusingly called Oxford in 1780 documents) suggests a ford, the majority of road traffic between Eaton Ford and Huntingdon would have found travelling west to east difficult, and so the north-south droving routes and later the Great North Road defined the probable position of villages, farms and manor houses. One of the earliest routes joins the churches of Little Paxton, Southoe, Diddington and Buckden, dating from the eleventh century onwards: it passed along the back of Stirtloe following the line of the present public footpath bending down to join the present Lucks Lane and thence to the church, and up Silver Street towards Brampton.

The origins of a dwelling at Stirtloe are unclear. Whereas Buckden, Diddington and Southoe are recorded, there is no mention of a holding at Stirtloe in the Domesday Book.

The ownership of the land at Stirtloe, and the dwellings there, is often very confused. Stirtloe was never a separate manor, and paid feudal dues to the Manor of Southoe Winchester, then Diddington, then Buckden, and in each of these three villages there existed in medieval times two manorial holdings, with another at Broughton, still faintly visible on the modern ordnance survey map. What follows is a brief look at the major changes to the messuage at Stirtloe, which covers both land and buildings and the people who transformed the house from a grange, farm or possibly hunting lodge in the thirteenth century, to the mainly late Georgian house of the twenty-first century.

The thirteenth century

It is probable that Ralph de Quincy, Earl of Winchester, had a tenant in the grange and farm when, in 1245, he was given deer by the King and a licence to inclose land at Stert, allowed to keep the grange he had built there, and required to allow the King's deer to go in and out of the inclosure. The Earl of Winchester at this time was the owner of five manors in Southoe, Broughton and Diddington, and on his death in 1274 his estate was divided between three daughters, one third going to Margaret, Countess of Derby. Her family, de Ferrers, had an interest in the Manors of Buckden, Diddington and Southoe until the seventeenth century passing through tortuous family inheritance to the newly created Earl of Cardigan in 1661. It is likely that Margaret de Ferrers eventually owned two thirds of Ralph de Quincy's estate. The third daughter Elizabeth was married to the Earl of Buchan, a Scottish baron, who would have to have come personally to England to do homage to the King to claim seisin or possession of their inheritance.

The fifteenth century

The earliest traces of the house at Stirtloe date to between 1450 and 1500. In 1451 Elizabeth, widow of William Ferrers, was assigned South Park, Southoe, and 'Stirtgart' as dower, so one can presume that there was a dwelling included with the land separately identified. Her estate passed to her daughter, Anne, who had married William Devereux, Lord Ferrers of Chantley, in 1446. Ferrers died fighting with Richard III at Bosworth Field in 1485, one of several owners of the local manors who backed the wrong side and were killed, attainted, and even beheaded!

The wood-frame, possibly Tudor, house is now almost certainly enclosed in ancient red brick but the tie beams still exist in the indoor rooms. These beams were not used, except in roof construction, after the end of the fifteenth century, and with the wattle and daub walls still to be seen in part of the kitchen range, it is likely that a large house existed at Stirtloe around 1450 or before. This is borne out by the smoke marks on early beams in the roof where the tie beams, wall plate girth and form indicate a building constructed before bricks were readily available, and fireplaces a future import from France! There is a very large chimney built close to this part of the house which may have served both kitchen and hall, probably built after 1500 when the cost of bricks was reasonable.

The sixteenth, seventeenth and eighteenth centuries

The buildings in the hamlet of Stirtloe have been many, and recordings of them are very confused. They include Poors farm and house left by William Burberry in 1558 for the benefit of the poor in Bugden; a homestead; a brick kiln; a slaughterhouse, and a brew house—and even a Castle, mentioned in 1780, of which no convincing trace has been found. The park and gardens of the present house, created in the late eighteenth century, have a mass of foundations just beneath the surface, including a fish pond, which hearsay has as providing fish for nuns who lived at Stirtloe. The only corroboration for the dwellings at Stirtloe once being a nunnery, is the several sightings of ghosts, some of whom were said to be in nuns' habit. The most recent sightings were of Tudor ladies with lace ruffs, only the top part of whose bodies was seen. This must relate to the real problems created for ghostly figures when a 1660s house was created with two floors instead of the three floors of the early Tudor house! The feudal rights for the local manors were given to the bishops of Lincoln by Henry I after 1100, which lends the stories some credence. Except for periods of religious turbulence during the mid-sixteenth century and the seventeenth century, the bishops continued to collect rents for the land until the twentieth century.

Who lived in this large house in the sixteenth century? It is possible that members of the de Ferrers family were there after Lord Ferrers' death in 1485 until the seventeenth century: an Edward Devereux de Ferrers was taken to court in 1600-01 over the ownership of Southoe Manor by Sir Richard Dyer who had 'good and lawful' conveyance from Lady Margaret Willoughby. It is also possible that the bishops of Lincoln had use of the house: if so perhaps this was when it became the 'nunnery' of legend.

Between 1663 and 1689, and possibly earlier or later, the Dickman family lived at Stirtloe. A Jonathan Dickman inherited the house from his brother, a London lawyer. Jonathan and his wife Sarah had ten children, all christened in St Mary's Church, Buckden (one was buried in the year of his christening). The house was large enough in 1662 to be rated for tax with six hearths, later reduced to four, and in 1774 there were five hearths. Jonathan may have removed the thatch from the roof and replaced it with pantiles and wood shingles. The main roof today has a pitch of 45°, an indication of early roofing materials replaced by the present blue slates late in the eighteenth century. The seventeenth-century house was probably L-shaped, based on the original brick enclosed Tudor house and its service areas, with a new wing based on the Bath and York stone flags still to be seen in today's house: these flagstones were in fashion between 1525 and 1725. The present staircase was put in between 1760 and 1775, but the style and height of the door opening beneath it show that the Georgian stairs replaced an earlier staircase in a house built around 1640.

Soon after 1640 the fashion would have been for a house built on the 'compact plan'—that is, one in which the comfort and grandeur characteristic of a larger residence were compressed into a relatively small house. As the Dickmans had such a large family, their renovations are likely to have been intended to provide a family with rather more spacious living quarters: a 'house of substance'. Like many other people who undertake building renovation, the Dickmans seem later to be short of money and in 1684 sold 1½ acres of woodground in Stirtloe to John Rugge, gent., (son of Mrs Rugge who had eleven hearths in Buckden in 1662!). Jonathan Dickman died in 1689. In 1692, John Rugge is said to be 'of Stirtloe House', and sometime after this the house was sold to William Windress of Eaton Socon, called 'Colonel Windress' in the Buckden Manorial Roll.

Colonel Windress bought 'the capital messuage (a substantial house plus land) at Stirtloe with a close of pasture, and an orchard called the Plantation, belonging to Jonathon Dickman.' The 1750 Manorial Roll records him as still being at Stirtloe, despite his having died in 1737.[1] He left 'a capital messuage' to his relation Thomas Merriden, gentleman. In 1743 Merriden, too, died, leaving his estate to be sold and 'produce' held in trust for his sister Mary, wife of Colonel William Swan[n], but the house was still unsold at the time of her death in about 1760. Her husband had already died, in 1752: in his will he refers to himself as being 'of Sturtloe', suggesting that he and Mary were actually occupying the house. Their son, George Cornelius Swan, was admitted tenancy at the Manorial Court in 1761. He bought more land, and exchanged land in Buckden itself for Buckden Poors farm and house in Stirtloe. In July 1763 the house finally sold for £2608, having been on the market for twenty-six years, and was bought by George Alexander, Esq., the esquire suggesting he was a younger son of the nobility or in the army.

George Alexander had just inherited money from an aunt (mainly in East India Stocks). He was thus was able to buy the house and make an advantageous marriage to Mary, eldest daughter of Edward Willoughby of Aspley Hall, Nottinghamshire, in August 1763. It may be no coincidence that the Willoughby family encouraged George to buy Stirtloe House: the Ferrers family, earlier owners, were distant relatives. It may also be no coincidence that Mary's family home at Aspley had recently undergone an extensive modernisation, and that George set about the modernisation of Stirtloe and its grounds immediately, with all the enthusiasm of a young man about twenty-four years old. In 1765 and 1766 he bought eighteen elms, then sixty-one more elms plus 'a wide variety of trees' from Wood and Ingrams Nursery at Brampton—elms were 6p each!

It is likely that George Alexander built the compact plan house which still exists today, with a staircase and banister rail dated between 1760 and 1775. Existing classic windows with slender glazing bars and fine glass, a doorway with decorative capitals, pilasters and rectangular tympanum all indicate a date in the second half of the eighteenth century. It also appears to be a remodelled house rather than a new build (see 'staircase' earlier).

However, George's enthusiasm was greater than the income from his aunt's legacy (£20 per year, some East India shares, pictures and plate)! By 1770 he was running out of money and the house was mortgaged to Mary Ferrers (related to the Willoughby family) for £500. By 1774 money problems were mounting and George's father-in-law took charge of the estate on behalf of the marriage settlement trustees. Perhaps the family stayed at Stirtloe for a couple more years but then they moved to Lewisham, Kent, and the house was let, first to John Wooley and then, in 1780, to Christopher Hobson (see next paragraph). By 1788 George's wife was dead and his two daughters, Mary Martha and Helena, were probably living with their grandparents in Aspley. Helena married the nephew of the mortgagee, Mary Ferrers, while Mary Martha, a spinster at the time of her death, settled her share of the estate on Helena, reserving an income of £30 a year for her father in Lewisham. There is a wall monument in the church next to Baddesley Clinton House, just south of Birmingham, to Mrs Helena Ferrers, wife of Edward Ferrers, daughter of George Alexander of Stirtloe House, who died in 1840, aged 74 years. What a story these few bare facts suggest with the Alexanders having had advantageous marriages, elegant houses and impoverished fathers, just as in a Jane Austen novel!

The twenty-one year lease at £100 p.a. which Christopher Hobson took out in 1780 gives us the first mention of the house under its modern name. It is described as 'now' called Stirtloe House, 'lately in part rebuilt', with coach houses, stables, cowhouses, brewhouse, slaughter house, orchards, gardens, shrubberies and all other offices, outhouses and buildings. Also included were thirty acres of pasture (some already let to farmers) and, near the house itself, a messuage called 'The Castle'. This is the only mention of a castle at Stirtloe, but by 1780 it may have been a ruin with land around which gradually became a part of the gardens at Stirtloe House; this would explain the large amount of building foundations barely covered by the paths and grass of today. In view of the lack of any earlier reference to a castle, however, the name may have been fanciful, given to an earth mound, a folly or the ruin (if ruin there was) of an abandoned house or farm building—perhaps one of those destroyed in the great fire of March 1770, when a kitchen-maid burned the entire hamlet to the ground by mistake.[2]

Christopher Hobson died in 1791. There is nothing to suggest that any member (married or single) of the Alexander family returned to live in the house, and for the next twenty-four years it was occupied by tenants (or at times unoccupied). We do, however, know two of the tenants of the house during these years: Lancelot Brown[3] and Lawrence Reynolds.[1] Brown occupied it (not necessarily continuously) from the early

---

[1] His wife Eleanor had died in 1734; they are both buried in Buckden churchyard, she under the name of Ellen..
[2] Stirtloe seems to have been peculiarly susceptible to mass conflagration: it is said to have been burned down again in 1790, this time deliberately by 'malcontents', which caused fear of an uprising, this being at a time of revolutionary thinking in England, after the French Revolution.
[3] 1748-1802. Lawyer and MP (for Huntingdon 1784-7 and Huntingdonshire 1792-4); a son of 'Capability' Brown.

or mid-part of the 1790s until he died there in 1802. In his will, made shortly before his death, he instructed his executors to sell 'the lease of my house and premises at Stirtloe[...]to best advantage', together with all his books, plate, linen and furnishings (apart from two portraits of his late wife). Lawrence Reynolds leased the house for a few years, leaving when he inherited a larger estate nearby. A gazetteer of 1808 refers to Stirtloe as 'the pleasant seat of Laurence Reynolds, Esq. who was High Sheriff of Huntingdonshire in 1806'.

(It is reputed that the great landscape designer, Lancelot 'Capability' Brown, lived at Stirtloe but this is unlikely: confusion may have arisen from the fact that it was for a time the home of his son Lancelot. However, at the time the Alexander family were living at and rebuilding Stirtloe House, 'Capability' was living in Fenstanton (where he had bought the Manor in 1767), and may have been asked to advise on the small park, said in 1768 to be a small landscaped garden formed from part of Stirtloe Wood. If so, he may have suggested it to Lancelot as a convenient home.)

The house was put up for auction in 1813, when it was described as 'a substantial, spacious, well built Mansion called Stirtloe House, most delightfully situate at an agreeable distance from the great north road, near the entrance of the village of Buckden, in the County of Huntingdonshire, sixty miles from London, containing numerous chambers and sitting rooms, a spacious entrance hall, well proportioned eating room, library, and dressing room, an excellent kitchen, with all the required attached offices and good cellaring, a capital range of stabling, with coach house and outbuildings of every description, for the complete accommodation of a family of respectability, large productive walled kitchen garden, pleasure grounds, orchards, paddock and closes of rich pasture land, containing altogether about thirty acres'. This must describe the house built by the Alexander family and how wonderful it sounds, but at a very high cost to both George and Mary and their daughters. Despite the auctioneer's enticing description, the house did not sell. In May 1815, however, it was re-advertised and within two months a sale agreement had been drawn up between the owner, Helena Ferrers (nee Alexander), and John Linton, Esq., of Freiston, Lincolnshire. It was for the 'Sale of Stirtloe House, outhouses, stables, coachhouses, gardens, several closes of land. 29a adjoining. 7 cottages, gardens and land 1½a, Buckden.'. The property was 'still mainly copyhold of the Manor of Buckden , with some pieces of freehold', and the price was £5500. Stirtloe House and the Linton family were about to enter into a union that would last for over one hundred and fifty years.

The nineteenth century

The Lintons were, however, no strangers to the house. In 1789, John Linton's sister Mary had married Captain John Brown RN, brother of the Lancelot Brown who became the lessee of Stirtloe. In 1801, John Cary's map of Huntingdonshire lists the local gentry and their residences, among them John Linton Esq. at Stirtloe House. The following year, only weeks after Lancelot Brown had died, Mary's husband (now an admiral) is described as being of 'Stirtloe House, Buckden'. Since this was the time of Nelson and constant sea engagements in the Revolutionary and Napoleonic Wars with France, it is possible that with John Brown often away at sea John Linton had joined his sister at Stirtloe House. But only temporarily: during this period, other sources still describe him (in 1798, 1804 and 1815) as being 'of Freiston', where he was a considerable property owner, reputed to have been one of the first farmers to grow potatoes in the Fens.[2]

(There is a confusing document in the Cambridgeshire Archives that appears to show that in 1804, two generations of Lintons were already living in the house, including John himself, his daughter Susanne (about to be married), and his son John junior, a dragoon captain. As John junior did not achieve his captaincy until 1817 and was anyway only eight years old in 1804, this is clearly nonsense. In reality, the document (Susanne's marriage settlement) dates from 1824, the year she wed in Buckden church.)

As well as occasionally keeping his sister company, John Linton may well have been looking for a sizable house away from the damp of the Lincolnshire fens. His descendant, Robert Bruce of Low Farm, believes that John became wealthy through the draining of the fens, purchasing Freiston Priory in 1782 before his marriage in 1790 to Isabella Trollope, a relation of the literary Trollopes. Perhaps Isabella wanted to live nearer to London, to which travel from Buckden was relatively easy with five coaches a day, while for her landowner husband a coach to Boston left every morning at 4.00 a.m. from the George in Huntingdon. As well as John junior and Susanne, there were two other children, Henry and Isabella junior.

Admiral Brown died in 1808 and Mary Brown moved away (this is probably when Lawrence Reynolds took on the lease). Mary died in 1834 and is commemorated alongside her husband and his father, mother and brother Lancelot in the chancel of Fenstanton church.

By 1813, land around Stirtloe was owned or rented by John Linton, Sir James Duberly, Rev. Maltby (vicar of Buckden), A. Priestly, G. Thornhill, the Lord Bishop of Lincoln, Lawrence Reynolds Esq, and

---

[1] 1771-1839. Irritable lawyer, landed proprietor, militia captain and former student radical.
[2] Of course, the description of individuals as 'of Stirtloe House' or 'of Freiston' doesn't differentiate between their ownership or tenancy of the property, or those of the gentry with several residences.

Thomas Bowyer. Occasionally people are said to be 'of Stirtloe' as they own land not the house: this could apply to the earlier John Rugge, his son William Rugg, Thomas Williams and Israel Reynolds, all of whom are associated with the Manor in Buckden as well as Stirtloe, and may have rented or owned the messuage at Stirtloe at some time.

It is surprising with such a wealth of Linton family documents now available in the Huntingdonshire Archives, that no accounts exist of money paid for new building at Stirtloe in the nineteenth century when very considerable work was undertaken, so again only the fashion and style of the building gives an approximate date for the work.

John Linton enlarged his new 'capital mansion' considerably, adding two wings to the Georgian house, probably around 1820—the semi-circular portico entrance dates from early in the nineteenth century, as shown by the fine decoration of the pillars and the delicate curved glazing bars. The windows, some of them false, of the new north and south wings match the Georgian windows still remaining at the rear of the main block. The interior of the south wing provided a Regency-style reception room with a beautiful cornice. It was intended, no doubt, to provide a room for soirees, music and dancing, with two additional bedrooms above. To balance the front aspect of the house the north wing was built to match the south, enclosing the three storeys of the timber framed house, which was probably enclosed already in red brick. Thus John Linton created three new bedrooms for his family, the upstairs of the Tudor wing now being in use by live-in servants.

The land around the house had been scheduled for enclosure in 1813 and during the next twenty years John Linton bought land and cottages to increase his estate and park land. The house has a drive sweeping west almost into Stirtloe Park then curving east to give a dramatic approach to the front. This was probably created after the farmland around was enclosed. The drive would have been a fashionable and contemporary approach to a recently completed post-enclosure house.

John Linton died in 1834, aged eighty-three, and was succeeded by John junior. A career cavalryman, he had been with the 6th (Inniskilling) Dragoons at the battle of Waterloo in 1815, and thereafter rose through the ranks by purchase and merit to retire as a Lieutenant-Colonel. There is an impressive monument in St Mary's Church to the two John Lintons and their wives Isabella and Louisa. The funeral of the first John was obviously a grand affair since it cost £100 6s. 0d., paid to a Mrs Bryant, and changing the coat of arms on the carriage cost £2 5s. 0d., paid to a John Gilbert.

As his sister's 1824 marriage settlement indicates, John junior—henceforth referred to as Colonel Linton—may already have been living at Stirtloe well before his father died. He now inherited a very substantial house with several acres of gardens and parkland, and much agricultural land in and around Buckden. He was a bachelor at the time, and remained so until 1840, when at the age of forty-eight he married Louisa Wingfield of Rutland, who was nearly fifteen years his junior. The marriage was brief—Louisa died in 1847, aged only forty-one—and produced no children. Colonel Linton outlived her by thirty years; he did not re-marry.

Under his ownership the windows of the front of the house were altered and replaced with Victorian four-pane sashed windows of plate glass, which became fashionable following the Great Exhibition of 1851. He planted the striking Wellingtonia trees in the garden and park at the same time, probably creating a large conservatory with piped heating, and a bathroom in the house above it, and an outside toilet beside it—replacing the outdoor two-header for the gentry and single-header for the servants, still to be seen. This shows a very modern approach since interior bathrooms were only gradually introduced after 1826 and in many houses not till the twentieth century. The laundry with its chimney was also built at this time, probably on the site of the Tudor kitchens above the cellars, of which two still exist. These may have been restored in the seventeenth century or early eighteenth century. Greenhouses were built in the kitchen garden, with underground water storage fed by water from the river drawn by a windmill on the high land to the south-east of the house. So whilst the first John Linton created an imposing house, drive and garden, the second modernised, extended and improved the house and grounds. Clearly a practical man, he referred to himself after his retirement from the army as a 'farmer of 500 acres' (rather than as merely a landed proprietor).

As he entered childless into old age, the family and their advisers had begun to plan for the future of Stirtloe. The likely (and in the event, actual) heir was the colonel's brother, the Reverend Henry Linton, himself an old man, who had spent his life in the church, first as curate and vicar of Diddington and then as a canon in Oxford. He was therefore unfitted by both age and profession to take over the management of an agricultural estate. That role was allocated to his second son, another John. As early as 1861, this John had moved in with his uncle, living at Stirtloe House and working on the farm. By 1871, he had been promoted to 'farmer's assistant' and was living at Buckden Wood Farm (on what is now Perry Road). In 1877, he married Mary Louisa Gatty, whose family lived in the manor-house in Church Street.[1] In the same year, Colonel Linton died, aged eighty-five, and Stirtloe House duly passed to Henry Linton. As planned, John now took over the running of the estate, which employed twenty men and ten boys on 600 acres. He and Mary Louisa remained at Buckden Wood until at least 1881, or until Henry Linton returned to Oxford, where he died in 1886, but had moved into Stirtloe House by 1891. Mary Louisa's sister Bessie Georgiana lived there with them until 1904, when a former village doctor returned and married her in Huntingdonshire's wedding of the year.

The twentieth century

John and Mary Louisa had at least five daughters—Philippa Mary (b. 1878), Louise Linton (1879),[2] Hilda Joan (1880), Olive Horton (1881) and Irene Sherard (1892)—and two sons: Henry (1884) and Clement Arthur (1887). There is no record of the improvements John made to the house. Money may have become less plentiful: the records show parcels of land being sold from early in the twentieth century. John was succeeded by his elder son Captain Henry Linton MC MCVD DL, who inherited the house in 1911 at the age of twenty-seven, in between active service in the Boer War and the First World War. It is probable that his siblings continued to live in or visit the house over the years till his death in 1952. The garden was gradually improved with colourful flower beds and ornamental trees, but few building works were undertaken. Garages were built, bathrooms and kitchens modernised and central heating installed, but the evacuees boarded at Stirtloe House during the Second World War found it 'not the most desirable of billets'. In 1941 Captain Linton was living in the main house with his three sisters, Miss Philippa, Miss Irene and Mrs Louisa (now the widow Maude-Roxby). Below stairs there was a gamekeeper/gardener, a cook/housekeeper, a parlour maid, a gardener and handyman and a fourteen year old kitchen maid, most of whom had moved on before the end of the war. Compare these five with the seven gardeners and many other staff kept when Mr Bert Sharpe started work in the garden around 1914 at twelve years of age. The kitchen and servants' hall were below stairs, four big stone steps down to the level of the medieval house, where Captain Linton used to hang out of the window to shoot sparrows. The evacuees, three boys, hardly saw the captain, and never saw the front of the house. However Miss Philippa did lend Alec Owen some skates to use on the frozen lake in the valley, which the boys passed on their way to school, and Mrs Maude-Roxby took the boys to a concert where they sat on the front row! It must have been a very difficult time for everyone—life changing so rapidly, the disappearance of an established order for the gentry and servants, and the boys miserable away from home.[3]

When Captain Linton died in 1952, still unmarried, his brother Major [Clement] Arthur Linton continued to live in the house, but, to save death duties, the heir was to be the major's grandson, Robert Bruce, who was about six years old and living in Argentina with his mother, the daughter of Major Linton and his wife Hilda Eden. The three great-aunts spent much time at the house, but the difficulties of administering the house and estate from Argentina can be imagined. Miss Philippa suggested that the cross-wing attached to the north of the house be demolished to let more light into the kitchen, as the rooms were no longer needed for servants who now mainly came in by day from the village, and this was done in the 1950s. She and the major soldiered on, but without much help and with a leaking roof, with the spacious entrance hall of the Alexanders' house divided for warmth, and a small new kitchen created in the butler's pantry. It is easy to see why Robert Bruce decided to sell the house after his grandfather's death in 1969, keeping the parkland and estate still in the Linton family. The house was in desperate need of renovation, water running down walls when it rained, such that the local doctor didn't feel he could send in a bill, and the garden becoming more and more overgrown, with the greenhouses, walls and railings in urgent need of repair.

---

[1] In 1878 a deed was drawn up to provide Mary Louisa with an annual income of £500 for life. This may have been suggested because part of the estate was entailed.

[2] i.e., she had Linton as both her middle name and her surname.

[3] Not always miserable: see Chapter 17 in which some of the Tollington boys remember their time in Buckden.

Another enthusiastic young man, Christopher Thomas, bought the house in 1970 at a sealed bid auction, offers around £20,000 invited. (The contents of the house had been auctioned in September 1969 in a three-day sale, comprising some 1100 lots.) He and his wife, Elspeth, and their four daughters, Kathryn, Bronwen, Jo and Emma moved in. The house and gardens gradually came back to life again, this time with one gardener and one daily help. Much repair work was done to walls, conservatories, kitchen garden, and railings. Roses, shrubs and trees were planted and a modern conservatory was built, the garages improved and the interior of the house repaired and modernised. Stirtloe House is a wonderful family house and thrives with a stream of children, family and friends passing through, and each generation makes its mark and moves on.

In 2007 the house came into the ownership of the Angel family, and the Thomas grandchildren will now keep its rooms ringing with noise and laughter. The Angels will make changes to suit their lifestyle and no doubt follow the trends of current fashion as many owners have done before them.

As Mac Dowdy of the Architectural Research Group at Wolfson College writes: 'It is not surprising that Nicholas Pevsner, after a visit to the Palace, the Church, the Manor House and a good lunch at the Lion in Buckden village, looked rather quickly at the front of the house and wrote 'a semicircular stone porch of columns with fluted capitals, probably dates from late eighteenth Century.'

However like so many houses of its kind, Stirtloe House has a confusion of visual details covering many periods of history, certainly well over 500 years. From this array of architectural detail has emerged the social and economic story of a house—here is a home demonstrating the heritage of the English country house, the additive tradition.

The house as we see it today reflects the skilled workmanship of many, many craftsmen through the past 500 or more years, and the enthusiasm of those who have lived in the house to institute and carry out major improvements to the building. Everyone who has lived or will live in this lovely family home owes much to the efforts of the de Ferrers family, who probably built the Tudor house, the Dickman family, who enlarged it in Stuart times, the Alexander family whose energy created the main part of the house we see today, and the Linton family who were responsible for the modern façade and gardens. What will it look like after the next 500 years?

With very many thanks to Elizabeth Stazicker for help in tracing the residents of the house, Mac Dowdy for help in dating the building of the house, and to the local Record Office (now Huntingdonshire Archives) and many amateur historians who have helped with this account.

CHAPTER 8/CONEYGARTHS
David Thomas

Coneygarths stands out among its neighbours on the High Street by virtue of *not* being built in red brick. In telling its history, parts of this chapter draw on a paper written by the late Dr Horace Miles, with some editing to preserve continuity. His widow, Mrs Janet Miles, has kindly given her permission for it to be used.

The name

On its own, the word *coney* is a late form of *cony*, which comes via the Old French *conil* from *cuniculus*, the Latin for both a rabbit and its burrow; but in the term *coney-garth* it derives from a variant Anglo-French form, *coning*, which came into Middle English as *conyng*. It was attached to the Old English word *erthe*, meaning *earth* (i.e., the home of a burrowing animal) to describe what we now call a rabbit-warren. Over time, however, people assumed that the word (which virtually nobody would ever have seen written down) was not *conyng-erthe* but *cony-garth*. The mistake is understandable, since *garth* was a common term for a yard or enclosed place, and medieval rabbit-warrens, even when not physically enclosed, were definitely private property. Rabbits[1] were introduced into Britain in the eleventh or twelfth century to be farmed for their meat and skins. On the Buckden enclosure award map of 1813, a parcel of approximately 22 acres called 'Coneygarths' is assigned to the bishop of Lincoln, and it seems reasonable to assume that for hundreds of years the rabbits reared there had been destined for the palace kitchens just across the road.

Coneygarths (the house) has sometimes been known as Coneygarth or The Coneygarth, but the plural form is the correct one, since it stood next to two warrens, Upper Coneygarth and Lower Coneygarth (at some time before the 1850s, part of George Lane was absorbed into the lower coneygarth). How long the house has borne its present name is not known. According to a 1912 issue of the magazine *Northants and Hunts*[2], the house was once an inn called the Mitre, and was connected with the palace. Certainly, the present house, which dates from the seventeenth century, has a large cellar. If this was the site of the Mitre, the inn may well have followed the example of many other Buckden properties over the centuries, and burnt down. Given its surroundings, Coneygarths would have been a natural name to attach itself to the new house. What is certain, is that until the nineteenth century the pronunciation of the first part of the name would have followed its spelling, and rhymed with money. This would have been unacceptable to the Victorians, more alert than their predecessors to the lurking horrors of unintended obscenity; genteel lips would have framed the word to rhyme, as it still does today, with phoney.[3]

The property

An early photograph of Coneygarth [sic] in the Norris Museum collection is catalogued as showing a two-storey house with glasshouse attached, shuttered ground floor windows, and with a low wall and grass in the foreground. A fuller description of the house can be obtained from a 1983 publication in the Huntingdonshire Archives[4]. In essence it is an L-shaped seventeenth-century house, largely timber framed. It has two storeys with attics. Brick chimneys have been added, one of which has a plaque dated 1735. A fine

---

[1] Strictly speaking, they were *re*-introduced after a gap of half-a-million years, their predecessors having been wiped out by the last ice age. They may also have been temporarily present during the Roman occupation.

[2] Full title: Northants and Huntingdonshire in the 20th Century: contemporary biographies" W.T.Pike 1912.

[3] Much to the amusement, probably, of some of Buckden's less sensitive residents

[4] "List of buildings of special architectural or historic interest : District of Huntingdon, Cambridgeshire : 6 (parishes of Buckden, Diddington, Great Paxton, Hail Weston, Little Paxton, Offord Cluny, Offord D'arcy, Southoe and Midloe)" Department of the Environment, 1983.

oval window was added in the nineteenth century; it took a craftsman a week to make a new one when it had to be replaced in the 1980s. The eighteenth-century front door is six-panelled, with a bracketed triangular pediment. The doorway to the rear has a seventeenth-century studded door. Much of the interior is contemporary with the original building or from the eighteenth century. It is a large house: twelve people slept there on the night of the 1861 census, seven adults, one child and four servants.

The bishop's nephew

More than one Green family has lived in Buckden. One of them was closely associated with Coneygarths for over a hundred and fifty years. Its long connexion appears to have begun with the appointment in 1761 of Cambridge academic John Green as bishop of Lincoln. Although he preferred to live in one of his three London houses rather than Buckden (or anywhere else in his diocese), he was sufficiently attached to the village to make it known that when he died he was to be buried in St Mary's. Today some people feel that the inscription on his memorial gives an impression of one who was clever and efficient in his duties but did not inspire much affection in local people. If so, he has only himself to blame: he wrote it.

As a diocesan property, Coneygarths was at the bishop's disposal. As you do in such situations, he offered it to a member of his family: his nephew Lieutenant John Green of the 8th Dragoons. Lieutenant Green married Sarah Dixon from Ramsey in Buckden in 1766, so that could well have been the year he moved in to Coneygarths. Their marriage lasted just over nine years, during which time they had at least four children. The birth of the last in October 1778 killed Sarah at the age of thirty-eight. Just over two years later, John Green married again. In the parish register he appears as John Green Esq. This may reflect his new social status as the principal beneficiary of his uncle's will (the bishop, a bachelor, had died the previous year) rather than indicating that he had retired from the army.[1]

His second wife was Margaret Watkins, by whom he had at least two children. The first was Margaret Mary, born in 1783. She may not have been expected to live: she was baptised at home in Coneygarths and not presented in church until nearly two months later. Despite this apparently inauspicious start to life, she lived to be eighty-four.[2] The second child, born in 1789, was John George, whose life was to span most of the nineteenth century.

Major Green died in 1793, aged fifty-four, and even after death enjoyed the benefits of having a bishop in the family: he, his youngest son and both his wives (Margaret died in 1834) lie under floor slabs in the nave of St Mary's, a prominent reminder to those who survived or came after them that in their day they had been people who mattered.

The captain

John George Green followed his father into the army, joining the 21st (Royal North British Fusiliers) Regiment of Foot at the age of sixteen. Unlike his younger contemporary, John Linton of Stirtloe House, he missed the battle of Waterloo in 1815, but was with his regiment when it occupied Paris the following month. In 1816 he was commissioned into the 60th Regiment of Foot as a captain; a year or so later he married Frances Susan Urquhart of Aberdeenshire, and in 1819 transferred to the 1st Regiment of Dragoons, with whom he served in Ireland (his daughter, Margaret, was born in Dublin in 1820). He was later posted to Hampshire, where his son, Francis, was born in the summer of 1822. Soon afterwards, John George retired on half-pay and removed his family to Buckden. He had a change of career in mind. In November he was admitted to Jesus College, Cambridge, and began to study for the priesthood. This proved a mistake, and he finally settled to life at Coneygarths, putting his military experience to good use as adjutant of the Hunts Militia.[3] During the rural unrest of 1831, he was called upon to organise a corps of yeomanry to round up the rioters and bring them before the magistrates. (These events were touched on in a community play put on at The Towers in 1990; unfortunately, the demands of casting meant that Captain Green's part in quelling the uprising had to be ascribed to Colonel Linton. A quick-tempered man, the captain would not have reacted to well to this.)

His final years in the militia were not happy ones. By the 1850s he was an old man and keen to resign his post. But his financial position was such that he felt unable to do so unless he could follow the tradition

---

[1] Although he may have done and later re-enlisted. There were enough John Greens in the army at this time to make it difficult to disentangle the military career of any one of them from any other. All that is certain is that he reached the rank of major.

[2] She married Dr Maltby, vicar of Buckden and later bishop of Durham—see under **Maltby family** in the A to Z Section.

[3] The county militias, which were under civilian control, were charged with defending the homeland against invasion or internal disturbance while the professional military were overseas (this was also a way of avoiding the need for the country to maintain a large standing army, whose officers might be tempted to mount a coup d'état). By Captain Green's time they were a volunteer force, whose members continued in their civilian occupations but received regular battle training. They were paid an annual retainer and military pay while on duty.

whereby retiring adjutants nominated their own successors and in return received from them a sizeable 'consideration'. His friend and commanding officer in the militia, the Earl of Sandwich, brusquely reminded him that the practice was now banned (he also had candidates of his own to put forward for the adjutancy).

In the end, John George resigned in 1856 and lived out a presumably rather resentful retirement at Coneygarths in the company of his two unmarried daughters (his wife had died in 1845). He died in 1882, supposedly in the same bed and the same room in which he had been born ninety-four years before. During his life he had brought Buckden to the world's notice as the home of the Man with the Golden Eagle—see under **Captain Green** in the A to Z Section. Now his death, too, attracted widespread notice, for he was the last known surviving participant in Nelson's funeral, which he had attended as a boy-soldier in 1805.

The farmer

When John George died, his son Francis—who preferred to be known as Frank—was living in Field House, Silver Street. He had run the family's farming interests for nearly thirty years, taking them on while still living with his father at Coneygarths. The Greens drew most of their income from land: the government's 1873 survey of landownership showed John George had 41 acres, Frank 181 acres and his sister Margaret 52 acres. Frank's acreage was the result of his 1856 purchase of part of Hoo Farm for £9000. By 1882, however, Frank had passed the day-to-day responsibility to his eldest son, another John George, who served as a Lieutenant (later Major) in what was now called the Huntingdon Militia Rifles, as well as farming the 165 acres still in hand.[1] In 1895, John George took over the family's outstanding mortgages and with them his father's interest in Hoo Farm. Most of this land lay to the north-east of the farmhouse, where the Greenway housing estate now lies, its name being derived from the family.

After his father's death, Frank moved back to Coneygarths, where he remained until he died in 1908. The report of his funeral described him as having been a genial, well-made man, thoroughly conscientious and tenacious in his opinions. A large congregation assembled to see him off at the church, for, despite being a Commissioner of Income Tax, he was well-liked in the village, rather more widely so than his father, whose hunting down of the 1830 rioters, long service as magistrate and membership of the Huntingdonshire Association [for the suppression of poachers and other felons] would not have endeared him to some in the labouring class. Frank had a strong interest in parish affairs. He was a trustee of the Buckden Parochial Charities—indeed, *the* trustee for a time in 1885, when disputes led to all his fellows resigning—a school manager, a patron of the village cricket club, which he allowed to play in the grounds of Coneygarths, and secretary of the Buckden and Diddington Horticultural Society.

Two sons

Frank had married twice. His first wife, whom he met and married in Surrey where he was learning the art of estate management as steward to the countess de Morella, died within the year at the birth of John George. In 1864 he married Louisa La-Page Norris from Halifax, by whom he had a second son, Francis Charles Sydney (often referred to simply as 'FCS' to distinguish him from his father). FCS continued his father's interest in the welfare of the village, serving as both a county and parish councillor and as the horticultural society's secretary. He lived alone at Coneygarths, but for two servants, but until 1913 was the tenant of the Hoo Farm land his brother John George owned. John George had left Buckden in the mid-1890s for Houghton, where he lived as a man of private means and served as a JP for Huntingdon. He had two sons, both of whom were to die in the First World War—see under **Green memorial** in the A to Z Section.

The later years

The last link between the Green family and Coneygarths was broken when the house and 84 acres of land were put up for auction in May 1919. They were bought by Mr Percy Priestley, partner in the Offord and Buckden Flour Mill. He did not have to move far: he lived opposite the almshouses in Church Street. After his death in 1935, his widow stayed on, and there were several more owners over the subsequent years. Keeping an old property such as Coneygarths well maintained became increasingly difficult in the changed social and economic climate that characterised the Second World War and the decades that followed. In

---

[1] The family also had a lively interest in the 1840s railway boom. Captain Green was on the provisional committee of two small local companies, and his daughters Frances and Margaret contracted to subscribe for 250 poundsworth of shares in the London and Croydon (Orpington Branch) line, an eight-mile stretch of atmospheric railway. Unfortunately for the young ladies, the line was rejected by parliament. On the other hand the atmospheric railway system proved to be a failure so their money would have gone anyway.

the early 1960s, part of the land was sold to the Ministry of Transport for the construction of the dual carriageway that bypasses the village High Street. More of the land was sold for housing. When Dr Richard Miles, son of Horace and Janet Miles, and his wife Karen Miles took on the house in 1983, it was with a much reduced plot of ground, and they were faced with a considerable task of restoration and redecoration, inside and out, to make Coneygarths worthy of its listed building status.

The Miles family moved away in 2006.

Some trivia

The arms used by the Green family, as found in a nineteenth century bookplate, were *azure three harts trippant or*—i.e., three yellow deer walking on a blue background with their right forelegs raised. Other than the fact that yellow and blue make green, the association with the family name is not obvious.

In 1983, the district council approved a planning application for a change of use of the ground floor rooms to a private junior school.

Coneygarths 2009

CHAPTER 9/LIVING OFF THE LAND
David Thomas, Robin Gibson, W. B. Carter and others

This chapter looks at how the land in Buckden parish has been exploited over the years: not only for food production, but to provide the raw materials for local bricks and distant highways, lobster-baskets and the means of travel (horses) and, increasingly, homes and recreational space.

Land use through the ages
by David Thomas

The strongest reminder of how Buckden was farmed in the medieval period is the name Westfield. The original 'West Field' was a large parcel of land which was farmed in common but later absorbed into a single holding, Westfield Farm. This survived as a working farm into the first years of the twenty-first century. We know from the tithe map of 1799 (held at Lincoln) there were also North, Mill and South Fields. These simple names, bare of any indication of ownership (unlike, say Martins Farm), origin (as in Park Farm, once the site of the bishop's deer park) or specialised use (Little Vineyard) are characteristic of the three-field rotation that was introduced into Britain in the middle ages. Under this system, which was developed from the sixth century to the ninth century, one-third (i.e. one field) of the land under cultivation was allowed to lie fallow each year, while another third was laid down to cereals in the autumn, and the final third to oats, barley, peas and beans in the spring, for late summer harvesting. This was a marked improvement on the preceding system, under which only half the available land was under cultivation each year. Each entitled family would have had a strip in each field allocated by the landowner's bailiff. Three- or common-field farming provided basic food for the whole of each manor; it was up to each family to vary this rather restricted diet, by growing vegetables in a small garden. (As mentioned above, the tithe map shows four large fields. Four-field rotation came in the eighteenth century. But how the fourth field was brought into being and used in Buckden has not been researched.)

Oxen were used to pull the rather crude ploughs of the time: horses were then still quite small, and too many would have been needed to force the shares through the parish's notoriously heavy clays. Evidence of how these fields were ploughed can still be found in at least two fields to the west of the A1, which still have the typical ridge-and-furrow surface. Ridge-and-furrow was also visible in the river meadows until recently, but was ploughed out by using the furrows as the middle of each strip until the fields were even again. Originally, the furrows were probably drainage channels for when the river overflowed, with the ridges providing grazing animals with refuge or a means of reaching dry land.

The establishing of a Buckden residence for the bishops of Lincoln would have led to some land being taken out of food production and used for the upkeep—and probably, in the longer term, for the breeding and rearing—of horses and possibly donkeys and mules: both as pack-animals and as mounts for the bishops, their guards and those of their accompanying clerics and senior household staff whose dignity would have been impaired by having to walk with the raggle-taggle of a huge episcopal retinue. Centuries later, when Buckden became an important stage and posting stop on the Great North Road, it was from the inns that the demand came for land on which to keep and graze horses and grow their fodder (and food for the travellers). Even a small coaching-inn like the Spread Eagle had at least 30 acres of attached land, while in the 1850s the widowed landlady of the George, Mrs Elizabeth Cartwright, also had to run her inn's 104 acre farm, consisting of 11 acres of grass (the present memorial playing field) and 93 acres of 'cold, wet [and] not very productive' arable, located near the juncture of the Perry and Grafham roads.

All the George land was leased from the bishops of Lincoln until 1858, when ownership was transferred to the Ecclesiastical Commissioners. The arable acreage was then incorporated into the large neighbouring holding that later became Park Farm: the name is a reminder that the medieval bishops enclosed and coppiced much of the surrounding area to provide grazing and cover for deer—see under **deer park** in the A to Z Section. The Great Park, as it was known, was an example of sustainable multiple land use, with meat, leather and timber the by-products of a superficially unproductive recreational activity (hunting).

The bishops of Lincoln were also responsible for introducing wine-growing to the parish. This must have been some time after the late eleventh century, since the Domesday Survey of 1086 does not list Buckden among the 40 to 50 vineyard sites in southern England. Being Normans (the descendants of social-climbing Vikings who abandoned ale for wine), the early bishops would have enjoyed supplying themselves and their rich and powerful visitors with a locally-produced vintage. Today's Vineyard Way marks one of the areas where they planted their grapes; a much larger one took up the whole of what are now the memorial playing fields, then an ideal spot for growing grapes as it sloped gently and faced roughly south. At some point, production ceased in Buckden, as it did almost everywhere else in Britain. The decline of British vineyards used to be regarded as a reliable indicator of a cooling climate, but other factors are now thought to have played a part, not least easier access and distribution for superior wines from the continent (of which Buckden, on the great north-south highway and near the river, would have been well-placed to take advantage).

Hunting and wine-growing are not the only activities associated with this or earlier periods to leave their mark on village place-names: *Hardwick*, for example, would have been where a herd of either sheep or cattle was looked after in a small settlement *(wick)* dependent on a nearby town or village—in this case Buckden. The road which is now Silver Street is marked on some maps as Hoo Baulk;[1] there are still a few older inhabitants who call it the Baulk. A baulk was a green lane between two pieces of plough land, or a green strip leading to fields. In the case of the Hoo Baulk the fields would have been part of the land that became Park Farm, with the baulk probably connecting them to an estate granary on Hoo Farm. Little remains of this farmstead, except a barn and an old, substantial wall facing on to Church Street and School Lane.

We know of no determined objectors in 1330 to the continued extension of the Great Park by enclosure. But three hundred years later, the villagers were vociferous in their opposition when a bishop enclosed the Little Park—the land closest to the palace. They wanted access to the park for their cattle. For the outcome, see the A to Z entry for **riots and tumult in 1641.**

Woodland was always important to parish inhabitants both for recreation and to supply wood for various purposes. The main woods were managed on the 'coppice with standards' system: some trees (the standards) were left to grow into maturity before being felled for timber, while the rest—the coppice or underwood—was cut down on a short rotation for fencing and firewood. Often the peasants had right to collect underwood and fallen timber to meet their essential needs: as, for example, to repair fences (*hedgebote*) or for fuel (*firebote*). The latter was particularly important. An agricultural report from 1808 paints a grim picture of how the poor heated their homes:

> In the county of Huntingdon coal is principally burnt in the better kind of houses, but common faggots, black oak, turf, &c. and turf and wood, in most farmer's kitchens and offices, and in cottages among the lower classes, stubble, bean straw, reed, dried dung, &c was more common.

By about 1900, however, more of the lower classes could afford coal, and Buckden's woodland had shrunk to a small wood on the way to Perry and another on the Brampton Road. The Silver Street house called The Spinney is a reminder that there were trees there, too, until fairly recent times.

Where did the bricks come from to make the inner and outer walls and the tower of the bishops' palace? It would have cost too much to cart stone from one of the quarries near Peterborough, or to import bricks.[2] Bricks were a new and prestigious building material, and would probably been made locally. Buckden had all the necessary ingredients: clay, water, and wood for baking them. Possible worked-out clay pits are the canal in the grounds of The Towers and the lake by the playing field (The Valley). There were also pits in the fields to the west of the village but their dates are not known; some leases to dig for brick and tile clay were granted in the seventeenth century. They may have been used later for the Georgian houses that characterise Buckden's street scene.

Of the ingredients needed for mortar, sand was available from nearer the river on the flood plain, but the relatively small quantities of lime required would have had to be brought in, either by river or road (if by road, as much as possible in the summer, because there were no metalled tracks between towns and villages until the use of wheeled carriages became more common).

---

[1] Hoo itself is a variation of *hoe* or *ho*, a piece of land slightly higher than its surrounds.

[2] Although by the 1840s, the costs of manufacture and transport had fallen enough to allow the bricks for South's Almshouses to be brought in by river.

Towards the end of the eighteenth century and early in the nineteenth, the Board of Agriculture commissioned a series of local and regional reports on the agriculture of the time. The earlier ones were rather scathing about the systems of agriculture in general: essentially they were no more than a variation on the medieval three-field rotation (but reports only a few years later found that improvements had been made). At that time, Buckden's acres were broken down into arable (2060), meadow (160), pasture (200), commons (40—few parishes had any at all), and woods (40). Buckden is rarely mentioned in the reports, except in terse lists, for example:

How watered
Buckden, by good springs.
Gardens and orchards
Buckden, all gardens small, except at the Bishop's Palace.
Manures
Brampton, Brington, Broughton and Buckden. Sheep folding, and yard dung.
Roads
Buckden. Roads exceedingly good[1].
Prices of Labour &c.
Buckden, 10s. in winter, 12s. in summer.

Those Buckden wages were among the lowest in the county. Many of the labourers lived in poor cottages, often with very small gardens, and worked long hours, dawn to dark in winter and during harvest, and 6 to 6 during the rest of the year.

The grumbling opposition of much of the rural workforce to the introduction of threshing-machines and other forms of mechanization finally erupted in 1830 in the violent, widespread and apparently coordinated assault on the landed classes and their property known as the 'Captain Swing' riots. Mindful of recent and current popular uprisings on the continent, the government responded forcefully. Although the rioters were not nearly so numerous or organised as had been supposed, they inadvertently created a stereotype: the obdurate yokel who would resist any innovation. This wasn't always true. The start of the nineteenth century, for example, saw the age-old use of oxen as plough-animals[2] was coming to an end— not always through the desire of employers to adopt new methods (some strongly believed oxen still to be better suited than horses to the heavy Huntingdonshire soils), but through the 'perverseness of servants', i.e., the unwillingness of the workers to continue the old, laborious way of doing things:

'... one farmer [told me] that he had used oxen, but his men used very *unpleasant* and *refractory* expressions in his presence, and his scheme ended in the death of one ox from being overdriven, and in another being very much injured...'

As a result only one farmer in the county still used oxen.

The most significant event causing changes in Buckden farming methods was the enclosure award of the early nineteenth century, which allotted the parish's remaining unenclosed land to those who were entitled to it by long use. Only 700 of Buckden's 2500 acres had been enclosed over the preceding centuries: the enclosure movement might have been under way for many years in the rest of the country, but Buckden and some other local areas were slow to respond. Even when the Buckden award had been made (in 1813), it was not formally adopted for another seven years. We still have reminders of the award. Margetts Farm on the road to the Offords is named after the farmer to whom it was allocated. Some of the land allocated to the bishops of Lincoln is still owned by the Church Commissioners. Many smaller allocations were sold off. A small land holding cost more to enclose per acre than a large one; a smallholder without the capital to invest in fencing was likely to end up a paid labourer.

From about 1875, agriculture in general passed through a long depression, in great contrast to the previous forty years when there was much innovation, some of it by the Cranfield family, nationally-respected farmers and millers who settled in Buckden in the late 1850s. Buckden continued to have a predominantly arable economy, but there were also sheep and cattle (small dairy farms were a feature). The balance between arable and livestock was further altered by the twentieth century's two world wars. During each of these, the government set up a Wartime Agricultural Executive Committee in each county as part of its drive to grow more food. The main job of the 'War Ags', as they were known, was to assess and realise the full potential of each farm by bringing new land under the plough. It was far more productive to use the soil of old pastures - enriched by decades of manure and the rotting of grass roots - to raise crops rather than livestock. One person in Buckden spent the Second World War ploughing up fields where the farmer was unable or unwilling to respond to a compulsory ploughing order.

---

[1] Thanks to the work of the turnpike trusts. See Chapter 18.
[2] Ox shoes as well as horse-shoes have been found on land at Diddington

The second world war brought an increase in arable farming at the expense of mixed and livestock farming; its dominance remains. Another once important local farming industry, basket-making, is now remembered only in the name of The Osiers. Basket-making provided work for women in particular and jobs were much sought after. Osiers were grown in the village until the mid-twentieth century, after which the withies were sold to firms which made fish and lobster pots. Increasing mechanisation demanded bigger fields, and hedges were removed, often with a government grant. There are now rarely any cattle or sheep to be seen in the parish.

Park Farm   Peter Mailer

The horse was the main source of agricultural power until the 1930s. At Park Farm, the first Mr Cranfield had been an enthusiastic user of steam power since his arrival in 1858; yet, ironically, Park Farm was one of the last to give up its horses for tractors. (In the late twenties or early thirties, the late Bill Voss learned to plough with horses in a Park Farm field just to the west of the Great North Road. Being only about thirteen or fourteen at the time, he could drive his horses and control the plough but hadn't the strength to turn at the ends. One or other of the men who were also ploughing in the field had to come along and help him. These men earned about £2 per week.)

Today's farming is dominated by larger farms and by techniques that would have surprised our ancestors. But the acreage of cultivated land in Buckden has actually diminished. It has been eaten into by the sand and gravel industry (the worked land being more likely to be restored for wildlife habitat or leisure use than for food production). New housing has taken land both at the edges of the village and within it. Where there is still pasture, it may well be given over to horses or ponies. These are ridden for pleasure, not kept to provide power on the farm, or draw stagecoaches or carry bishops. Other recreational activities have also claimed land: for playing fields, sports areas, and a large village hall. Finally, let us remember that a substantial stretch of land (including part of what was once a large allotment field in Hardwick) now lies under the A1 dual carriageway and its verges.

Fifty years of change: a more detailed look at the last half of the twentieth century
by Robin Gibson

Until the middle of the twentieth century Buckden was a parish of farms and horticulture. Apart from the garages, the hotel trade and some gentry, most of the population were involved in these rural activities or supported them by, for example, blacksmithing. Some of these activities are described below.

Arable Farming

The London schoolboys evacuated to Buckden remember very well their work in the harvests of 1939 to 1942, but the equipment they used bore little or no resemblance to that now employed. They would also find a much narrower range of crops being grown today. Flax, for example, was once grown to provide both linseed oil and the fibres used in the manufacture of linen (which was much in demand until nylon arrived). But it is rarely seen these days, and harvested only for its oil. In wartime, when the whole plant was required, special machines were used for pulling the flax, but evacuee Ken Odell has found no example of these machines surviving anywhere in the country. The boys left graphic descriptions of harvesting peas, beans and potatoes by hand, although they seem to have escaped 'Brusselling', that most arduous of winter tasks. By the late 1930s, potatoes were being sent to Spitalfields market in London by lorry. One winter, Ken Odell hitched a lift home in one of these. He was picked up at 1.00 a.m., and endured a two-hour journey to the outskirts of London. The experience of riding in an unheated truck followed by a three mile walk in snow is not one he relished!

Park Farm—an Oliver tractor and baler   Peter Mailer

Cereal crops required a great of labour, and harvest–time photographs show gangs of a dozen or more men and boys building a stack. Now a single enormous combine and a tractor and trailer can cut a field in a few hours, eliminating or combining the separate operations of stooking, drying, carting, stack-building, and threshing. In the 1930s, the horse began to be replaced by the Fordson tractor, designed in America but built in England and Ireland. The inexorable advance of mechanisation was accelerated by the arrival of superior US-built machines such as the Oliver (the Fordson was known for its cantankerous nature).

A hundred years ago, agriculture was a major source of employment in the parish. Historian Peter Ibbett's search of the 1881 census, for example, shows that the farmers employed 69 men, 37 boys and two women (later censuses do not include such summaries, unfortunately). Now the arable farms that surround Buckden have fewer than half-a-dozen permanent employees.

Fruit

Until 1970, the growing of fruit was big business in Buckden. Frederick Brown alone had 3000 gooseberry bushes off Perry Road. The produce from these was sold to Batchelors in Manchester, sent there by rail until that service was stopped in 1959. Thereafter Paynes of Wyboston delivered the fruit to Covent Garden by road. Local domestic orders were supplied until the turn of the twenty-first century. The Browns also had 250 apple and plum trees, the fruit from which was sent to Leicester market. On a different scale, Buckden resident Eric Newman used to pick wild blackberries at a penny or a penny-halfpenny a pound as a boy to pay for new football boots at 12/6d (£0.63) a pair. The fruit was bought by Mrs Cope of Hunts End, who despatched it to James Robertson and Sons Ltd of Droylsden, for the manufacture of their famous Bramble Jelly.

Pigs and Poultry

Until the advent of intensive pig-rearing, there were numerous small holdings around the village where pigs and poultry were raised. **The Cope family** at Hunts End used to fatten pigs for market, having perhaps six dozen at a time in six successive stages of fattening. Two were kept as pets outside the pens for a time but they too had to go to market when mature enough—a sad occasion. The Copes also kept chickens and sold eggs at the rate of 120-150 dozen per week. The proceeds from these sales went towards their transport business, which was to specialise in moving cattle. As competition from factory farmers led to the pig business being phased out, the number of lorries rose from an initial two to six. This change worked well, since the drivers' return times varied so much that they could not be relied upon to be on hand to feed the pigs on time.

The Bowyer family kept about a hundred pigs, one half of them at Margetts Farm and the others at Jessamine House on the High Street. For a description of the activities of the one-time Pig-and-Poultry Club see under **Pepper, Percy. Eric Newman** farmed in Lucks Lane after returning from his service as Buckden's only Bevin Boy in the Second World War. He dismantled seven or eight redundant Nissen huts on an airfield or at the wartime Diddington hospital and re-erected them in a field bought from the Cranfield-Rose family. These were used to shelter his herd of Wessex Saddlebacks. He also kept 400 chickens, but these were in an expensive patent hen house. **Frederick Brown** kept 50-60 pigs and 500 hens to the west of the village, but this aspect of his business was ended when the land was taken by the advent of the **Buckden by-pass** (q.v.).

Osiers (Willow - *salix viminalis*) & Basket-making

Making baskets from osiers which he had grown and processed himself was turned into a highly successful enterprise by Richard Brown, Frederick Brown's great-grandfather. The son of a watchmaker, Richard was born in 1828. In due course he was apprenticed to a basket-maker. After completing his time, he worked in Cambridge (walking there and back) before buying an osier bed in Offord and starting his business in Buckden as a basket-maker. Later he added the osier beds in Lucks Lane and Mill Road.

The willows were coppiced annually to produce the wands required for basket-making. The wands were harvested in February using sickles and then retted (softened) in a water-filled pit beside Lucks Lane which was fed by the spring there. In May the wands were bundled and transported to the 'rod yard' at the

Browns' orchard west of the Great North Road. At the yard women stripped the wands and re-bundled them. In the 1930s, the price was sixpence (2.5p) a bundle. The wands were then sold, being either sent away for basket-making elsewhere or used by craftsmen in the village. Richard Furbank of Stirtloe remembers them being sent as far afield as Gloucester. By the time great-grandfather Brown died in 1912, the business had expanded to include market-gardening. His son, also Richard (1853-1915), is listed as a basket–maker and fruit grower in the parish burials register. The Browns had a shed behind Bowtells (now One-Stop) in the High Street. In this shed up to sixteen people made baskets for all manner of purposes. These were distributed locally by horse and cart. Buckden's last basket-maker, Harry Frost, had a workshop in York Yard but he worked independently of the Browns. Although blind, he continued working well into the 1940s. He died in 1948.

Dairying

Buckden has no dairy farms now, but within living memory it had four, and three purveyors of fresh milk to the village. A flavour of the dairying business including the distribution of milk may be gained from an article (reproduced later in this chapter) about Miss Gladys Mann of **Hardonian Farm**. Two of the other three farms have already been mentioned: **Park Farm** north west of the village, and **Westfield Farm** to the south. The last occupant of Westfield was Mary Mann, who succeeded her father. Their dairy cows were often pastured on the opposite side of the Great North Road. That this meant their having to cross the road twice each way each day for milking made Mr Mann rather unpopular with drivers. (It is said he did not have much time for them either.) The fourth farm was **Shooters Hollow** on Perry Road at the west boundary of the parish, now run by Mr John Mann. This branch of the Mann family also had the of use of the Little Park (The Towers field), fields north of the village and eastwards down to the river, and for a time Stirling Farm, adjacent to the clubhouse of the present Brampton Park Golf Club. Going back a generation, John Mann's father used to hand-milk in a shed near Carter's Yard in Mill Road, but later only followers grazed these fields, the milkers being kept around the farm. John's father took over the milk round of Reginald Mann of Hardonian Farm, firstly using a car and trailer, then a horse and milk-float and finally a pick-up truck. Dairying was abandoned in 1961. There were others who kept dairy cattle, some just as house cows. They included the Stockers of the Crown public house on the Great North Road and the Bowyers, who kept two cows behind Jessamine House in the High Street. Cows were also milked at the Manor House in Church Street, in a barn since converted to residential use

Other Cattle

Clearly cattle must have been regularly raised for meat in order to supply the local butchers. The transport of livestock also provided steady trade for Buckden Station and the Cope lorries. At the time of writing, cattle are still reared on Lodge Farm for the distant meat market or slaughterhouse.

Sheep

Sheep seem to have been less important to Huntingdonshire's agricultural economy than either corn or cattle: they certainly do not figure very largely in Buckden's farming, especially in recent times. An occasional shepherd is listed in nineteenth-century censuses. An early twentieth-century postcard shows sheep being driven eastwards past the almshouses in Church Street. A few sheep were occasionally agisted in the grounds of The Towers at the end of the twentieth century.

Smallholdings and Allotments

Before the arrival of incomers in the 1960s, many households grew at least some of their own vegetables and fruit. Eric Newman's uncle set up a greengrocery shop in the High Street immediately north of the Spread Eagle, but business was not good. In season Eric was sent out selling violets; his best trade was with the waitresses and maids at the Lion hotel. The present allotments behind Silver Street were preceded by those where Beaumont Drive and Wolsey Gardens are now, but they are not on new ground: the same area is marked as Allotment Gardens on the 1924 OS plan. A group of smallholdings which has entirely disappeared was in Van Diemens Lane off Mill Road; the land is now largely occupied by flooded gravel pits or the redundant routes of aggregate conveyors and site roads. No trace remains of a pair of houses about 400m from Mill Road. They, or at least their foundations, are visible in an aerial photograph of 1969. In 1871, Wood Farm on Perry Road was surveyed for the purpose of being divided into allotments—sixty-four in all, ranging between two and four acres each. It is not clear whether the proposal was ever carried out, either wholly or in part. See Chapter 10 for other areas of land under cultivation in 1924 and now.

Herbs

Mrs Elizabeth Peplow began growing herbs in 1974 at her home in Church Street, and marketed them on a small scale as 'Herbs from the Hoo'. Mrs Peplow and her husband Reginald wrote three books on herbs.

ΩΩΩΩΩ

Buckden Marina: land for leisure[1]
by W. B. Carter

(Brian Carter has written extensively on the River Great Ouse, and is the author of two well-received books on his experiences as a young naval officer during and after the D-Day landings.)

In 1949 I purchased the property known then as The Paddock, owned by Mr Robinson, which was an old granary. The old cottage had originally been a public house called The Three Mill Bills. A mill bill was a type of chisel that was used for resurfacing mill wheels. A Mrs Sabey owned the cottage before Mr Robinson. She used to hire a rowing boat from the Huntingdon boat builders Childs & Hall every summer but, due to her religious scruples, would not allow it to be hired on Sundays.

During the war, many trees had been cut down to construct airfields, and the trees were dumped on the land which later I made into a caravan site. Mr Robinson started a log business, and would go round the villages selling sacks of logs at 1/6d a time. He also was a great one for buying up old cars, giving some of them the kiss of life but the rest made the place look like a scrap yard. All the trees and the cars were removed, and I lived in a small caravan while the cottage was made habitable, the 1947 floods having come as high as its letterbox. My idea was to start a small boatyard, hiring punts, rowing boats and one motorboat. There was an old chalet and an army hut which I converted into holiday accommodation, mainly for fishermen. It was the rent from these that enabled me just to keep my head above water, for with few people owning cars and the place being somewhat out of the way, the boat hire side made little revenue.

Over the years cabin cruisers started to appear on the river, and I built the first slipway on the Ouse and those coming to use it often decided to moor with me, so gradually up to thirty cabin cruisers were moored in the basin, and the business started to get on its feet.

When Grafham Water was planned, W. & C. French, the contractors, needed a large quantity of gravel and it was decided in a combined operation they would dig the adjoining field making it a marina to my design. In 1964, in less than two years, I had the marina in good working order and all the work making landing stages, car parks, tree planting etc. was done by my own small staff, and only the large workshop was built by outside help. It was constructed purely as a boatyard with all the facilities a marina should have. My main object was to make it a quiet place where people could keep their boats and also carry out any maintenance or repair work, so an engineer joined the staff (which was only three). I was awarded the 1970 European Conservation Award by the Duke of Edinburgh and also the Sand and Gravel Award, but removed the letters from the plaque saying it had been a disused gravel pit.

In the early days the marina held just over a hundred boats, and about two-thirds of them on a fine Sunday would cruise the river system. Today the number leaving the marina is probably less than 5%, as is now found in most marinas. It is notable that the number of people cruising the river today is about the same as records show in 1970. The reason for this is probably because then boat owners generally used their craft for the holidays. Today holidays abroad have taken over and boats are somewhere to visit at a weekend—used more as a weekend retreat rather than to cruise what must be one of the prettiest rivers in the country.

The Buckden Bun

The following recipe was one of several compiled by Elizabeth Peplow of The Hoo for the fundraisers of St Mary's Church. It makes twenty-four buns

112g (4oz) self-raising flour	2 eggs
112g (4oz) margarine	2 tsps cinnamon
112g (4oz) caster sugar	50g (2oz) currants
few drops of vanilla essence	50g (2oz) sultanas
50g (2oz) ground almonds	

Put all the ingredients except the fruit and ground almonds in a large bowl and beat with an electric blender until smooth and creamy. Fold in the fruit and ground almonds. Put the mixture in greased bun trays or paper cases and bake in a hot oven (200 c/400f/Gas 6) for approximately ten minutes until they are golden brown.

---

[1]   The property referred to in this article lies between the Ouse and Mill Road, where the latter bends sharply just before the Offord and Buckden flour mills bridge.

Show Business

A passion for farming has led to decades of glory in the show ring for Gladys Mann and her host of prize-winning cattle, as James Fuller discovered in this interview, first published in *Our Time* in July 2005

Father used to go down to the river and hand-milk the cows, and then he would deliver the milk on his way home with his milk churn and measure,' says 63-year-old Gladys Mann. Gladys' father Reginald (Reggie) Mann was a familiar sight around the streets of Buckden 40 years ago, tending to his cattle herd and making sure the villagers were sufficiently supplied with milk."He took milk around Buckden for over 30 years and never had a day off," she said.

Gladys' family has lived in the Cambridgeshire village since an ancestor, Daniel Mann, a licensed victualler and groomsman, arrived there from Glemsford, in Suffolk, in the 1740s.The Manns have made the Taylors Lane area their home since purchasing 50 acres of land there in the early 1800s. Gladys was born at Hardwick House in 1942, moved to Hardonian Farm in 1964 and then to her current home, at the top of Taylors Lane, in 1983. She has two cousins who also farm in Buckden.

An only child, Gladys was schooled at Cedar House, in St Neots, and says her father wasn't convinced she would enjoy the farming life."I'd been to private school and dad didn't think I would take to it. He didn't think his daughter would do the job."He was wrong though and Gladys revelled in it, helping her father out whenever she could.

"After being to private school, the milk round was where I really learned to count," she laughs, "because if I made any mistakes with the change I would have to jump off the cart and run back."

It wasn't only farming that the young Gladys enjoyed. From the time the family bought their first cattle they began showing them."We started off with four Jerseys in 1955. when I was 13. We had Shorthorns as well, so altogether we had about 12 animals when we first started. By the time we packed up we had nearly 100. We showed first in 1955 and within a couple of years we were doing loads of shows. We did all the county shows; Cambs, Beds, Northants, Peterborough (before it became the East of England), Hunts and many others. We also did the London Dairy Show. It was absolutely fantastic.

"For six weeks in June and July we were incredibly busy. We would be in the hayfields, baling hay, carting hay; then milking the cows and going to the shows."We used to be up early when showing. I remember my first time at the Royal Norfolk Show, it was 4.45 a.m. and I was up and about and I bumped into the television presenter Gordon Moseley. He asked me if I'd help him open the programme that day. I did and I was on the TV but I never got to see it myself. I never have seen that show.

"It was a long day and by the end of it I was so exhausted I felt ill."The hard work and long days were worth it as the Manns were incredibly successful.

"We won 100 prizes every year for nearly 20 years between 1957 and 1977. We had to win because it cost so much to travel to these places. There wasn't much prize money but what there was covered our travelling."

One of the family's best animals had an unpromising start in life."We bought this bull, Horton Jolly Panther, from the Shand Kydd family in 1958. He hadn't been looked after very well at all and was in a bit of a state but my father saw something in him he liked. He was six months old and cost £15. When we got him home we took him for a long walk across the fields to pull his hocks right and began feeding him up."Within two years the animal had developed fantastically and carried off the top prize at the 1960 Royal Show at Cambridge. Five years later, he showed a handsome return on the initial investment when he was sold to the Ministry of Agriculture at Shinfield, Reading, for 600 guineas.

One of Gladys' most successful shows came just after the death of her father, in April 1977. But it was an event she nearly didn't attend."I kept saying 'I can't do the East of England' and people just kept saying 'of course you can'."I went to the show and got three firsts with three animals and a second in the Group of Three. Having won with all three animals individually I never did understand why we were second in the group, but there you go. We got champion and reserve champion of the Jersey Breed as well as champion female and reserve champion female. Then, on the Wednesday, we won supreme champion all breeds."It's little wonder that Gladys lists Peterborough's East of England Showground alongside the Royal Norfolk as her two favourite showgrounds.

But, when her mother, Joyce, suffered a heart attack in the early '80s, and following the death of her father, Gladys' cattle showing days were coming to an end. It's a hard job to keep at the top," she says. "When mother had a heart attack we decided to pack up the milking and have some beef cattle instead. We bought a Simmental and decided we would love to show her though; so we entered her for the East of England. She won first prize in the Simmental cow class. Then we went back with her - it was either the next year or the year after that - and she won again."

Around the time Gladys was attending her last cattle shows, she rekindled a love of riding and began a new business."I used to love riding ponies when I was 12 or 13; 1 used to ride the milk round pony. I did everything with that pony, carted hay, did the milk round and I rode him. We got a Shetland cross in about 1984 and someone said could they come and ride it. The business really just grew from there and I

155

had about 12 ponies at one time. I used to hire them out by the hour. It wasn't top class riding but my idea was to help everybody and in 20 years we never had any disasters."

Old habits die hard and Gladys couldn't resist showing some of her ponies."I bought a Welsh mountain Section A pony. It was a right little madam but it was OK in the right hands. I paid £200 for it and sold it in 1992 for £2,500. I haven't showed since 1992. I've got a Shetland pony now and he's quite nice, but he's just a pet."Gladys' current Noah's Ark includes the pony, a German Shepherd dog, two cats, 12 bantam hens and three cockerels.

In a lifetime of being around animals she recalls only one really nasty incident. I had the odd kick from the ponies but not long before father died we got some Ayrshires. We had them in a big yard out the back and three of them had calved."I went out there and this one cow attacked me and knocked me into the wall seven times. I crawled out of the yard black and blue."

In the last 10 years Gladys has turned her attention to organising charity pony and dog shows."I'm now doing charity stuff for the National Animal Welfare Trust. In the last 10 years I have done 30 or 40 pony shows for charity and some dog shows as well. I'm slowing down now though; I'm not going to do quite as much."

Gladys recalls her life with fondness."The main things in my life have been cows and farming. I never got married and I've always been self-employed."I like doing what I want to do and I wouldn't have been doing all this if I'd got married.

"My best and most enjoyable time was showing cattle. You are dealing with different people, friendlier. My life was Jersey cows really, the ponies was just something I kind of got into."I don't regret anything I've done, more or less. Perhaps I would have kept the Jerseys a bit longer, but that's about it." It's clear Gladys has a deep affection for Jerseys. "Some get a bit cantankerous at times but we can all do that can't we?" she laughs.

ΩΩΩΩΩ

ΩΩΩΩΩ

CHAPTER 10/GARDENING IN BUCKDEN
David Thomas, R. H. Gibson

The first part of this chapter contains a brief history of the gardening societies of Buckden, based on the booklet produced in 1993 to celebrate the Buckden Gardeners Association's first hundred years. It incorporates additional material by the booklet's author, David Thomas. In the second part, Robin Gibson deals with the village's various allotment gardens.

It is not clear exactly when Buckden's first gardening society was established. There was certainly one in existence by the late 1880s: the first annual Buckden Horticultural Society and Band of Hope Flower Show was probably held in July 1887, seeing that the second and third shows were held in July 1888 and 1889 respectively. But had the society already been active, perhaps for some years, or was it formed specifically as a show society? Whatever impulse brought it into being, its link with the local temperance movement was short-lived. In the spring of 1893, the following report appeared in the St Neots Advertiser:

'At a meeting on Thursday evening last week [20 April 1893], attended by about 80 of the inhabitants of Buckden and Diddington, Rev. H. M. Roxby in the chair, it was decided to form a horticultural society for the villages. Mr A. W. Marshall was elected President and Mr Frank J. Smith Secretary. A committee of 13 were appointed and it was resolved to hold the first Show in the grounds of Buckden Towers, on Wednesday July 12th '.

Buckden and Diddington Horticultural Society
1893

President
Mr A. W. Marshall

Vice Presidents
Rev. H. M. Roxby (Buckden)
Mr J. Linton   Mr J. C. Green   Mr A. J. Thornhill

Hon. Secretary
Mr F. J. Smith

Hon. Treasurer
Mr A. Hallett

Committee
Rev. A Hannam (Diddington)
Messrs Page Robey G. King D. Smith S. Green Looker Whitmee Copping
Hawkins Hillyer Strachan W. Stoneham F. Brightman Petfield Jnr

---

The date chosen was the Wednesday of Feast Week, a day that remained constant until 1939.

The show itself was written up in both the Hunts County News and the St Neots Advertiser. The latter reported that five hours of heavy showers had proved 'rather disastrous' to the show's finances, particularly as it kept outsiders away. Nonetheless, residents turned up in 'goodly quantities' to listen to the Buckden Brass Band as it entertained in the afternoon and then played again in the evening at a dance which was held for that year and the two subsequent years in a marquee at The Towers. In later years the show moved between The Towers, Stirtloe House, Diddington Hall and, later, Coneygarths. The venue of the show followed the presidency of the society. How many Buckden people today would walk with their exhibits in a basket or wheelbarrow in the morning, attend the show in the afternoon, and then walk back again in the evening for a dance, if it were held at Diddington?

It appears that the committee was determined to set a high standard from the beginning, as in some classes none of the entries attracted a first place and in others no award was made at all. The quantities required in some classes were very ambitious. A schedule for the show showing the first in each class reveals that the family names of some of the winners are to be found in the village today. There were no cups or trophies to be won; the only trophy I can find any record of was the rose bowl presented to Mr F. C. Sydney Green in 1906 in recognition of his services as secretary.

The way the shows were organised reflected the divisions in society, which were much deeper than today. Just as cricket then had its Gentlemen and Players, so the shows' two main sections were for Amateurs and Cottagers, a division that held until 1939. A few years after the first show, another section was added for amateurs living in the county other than at Buckden 'whether or not they employ a gardener'.

Unlike today, competitive classes for gardeners were the main rather than the sole attraction on offer. As part of feast week, the show took on something of the air of a fete. Not only was the band in attendance, but there was a baby show and sports in which the young could show off their speed and agility and their elders gamely make fools of themselves. Some of the events were positively dangerous. In 1925, the local paper reported on a 'serious accident' during the blindfolded wheelbarrow race, when Miss H. Stanyon, who was 'driving' Percy Smith, steered him into a head-on collision with another barrow, one of the Robinson family. Mr Smith's eye was badly cut and Mr Robinson was knocked unconscious. No doubt. the mortified Miss Stanyon had to run the gauntlet of some gleeful mutterings about 'lady drivers' as she sought the refuge of the tea tent.

The last show before the Second World War was an outstanding one, called by a local paper 'a red letter day in Buckden's feast week'. There were 700 entries, a record number and 150 more than the previous year. For all the forebodings of war that were already in the air during the summer of 1939, it is doubtful that anyone realised this was to be the last show of the society, and the end of the society itself. It was purely a show society, though it organised entertainment also, and except during the war years between 1915 and 1918, had put on a show every year since 1893.

Buckden Gardeners and Fertility Association

The war which killed off the Buckden and Diddington Horticultural Society, led directly to the formation of a new association. It was clear that the country was going to in desperate need of home-grown food, and a big 'DIG FOR VICTORY' campaign was started. Villages and allotment holders were encouraged to form societies to buy seeds, lime and fertilizers through one agency to save manpower at all stages. In Buckden there were also some gardens belonging to those called up which were cultivated by the older men who were still here. In 1942 the Buckden Gardeners and Fertility Association was formed. It soon became known as Buckden Gardeners Association, though this title was not formally adopted until 1958.

Commercial activities

The association made annual bulk purchases of seed potatoes, lime, soot and fertilizers, all of which it sold at little above cost price. The greatest order of seed potatoes ever submitted was for over sixteen tons. The village was also able to buy many tons of soot each year, an indication of the quantity of coal being burned in factories. Soot is, of course, a valuable source of nitrogen. Temporary storage was a recurring problem. Some of the places used were Day's the butchers, The Hoo, and Top Farm. Mr Furbank was one farmer who lent a tractor and trailer to cart the potatoes from Buckden station.

For many years after the war, members frequently raised the idea of expanding the association's commercial side, but this only became a practicable proposition in 1977, with the erection of a large shed on the parish council allotments (then sited where the houses of Wolsey Gardens and Beaufort Drive now stand). The committee rapidly realised there was a demand for many more lines than the ones traditionally traded in, and the number of items in stock grew rapidly, expanding by nearly three times in a single year. Today the association still have an annual order of seeds and seed potatoes, but about 100 other items are available during the active garden season, and others can usually be got in very quickly, making useful savings for the members.

The return of the shows

The first post-war show took place in 1947. It was divided into two sections but this was no longer a class divide: one section was for members only and the other open to all-comers. Sixty years on the whole show is open to all, but there is a section reserved for anyone who has not won a cup or other trophy.

In 1959 a Dahlia and Chrysanthemum Show was held for the first time. There were 45 entries, but in 1960 it grew to 81 entries. This show was held for the next twenty years. A Spring Show was held in 1965 and is still a main show in the programme, held at the beginning of April. The Summer Show had been failing from lack of interest. This was probably because it was a victim of the growing affluence of the 1960s and 1970s, which meant many people were out of the village during July, holidaying by the sea or abroad or simply taking the family out for the day in the car they could now afford. In 1979, therefore, it was decided to combine the Summer Show with the Dahlia and Chrysanthemum Show. The side-shows and other entertainments had already been abandoned two years before, a real break with tradition. They were replaced by the Donkey Derby held at The Towers and the Village Hall Trust's Feast Week Saturday entertainments. The Summer Show is now held on a Saturday at the beginning of September, when the main holiday is over.

Other events

The association had held discussion meetings since 1952 and probably before that, but it was only in the 1980s that it started a programme of regular monthly meetings. In the winter these usually take the form of a speaker on a topic, often illustrated with slides or video, while summer is the time for nursery or garden visits. Members have visited many of the well-known gardens in the Home Counties and the Midlands. Surprisingly, the greatest distances were travelled before the motorways were built. There is also always a seasonal social gathering at Christmas.

In 1968, after ten years on the waiting list, Buckden was the venue for the BBC's Gardeners Question Time.

And the winner is...

For many years there was only one true trophy, the Association Cup. Other section winners received a medal and a trophy donated by one or other of the gardening or homecraft magazines. Today there is a fine array of cups, shields and other trophies, some donated by members, others purchased by the committee. These are listed in the Appendix.

The future

The future of the Gardeners Association looks bright. At the time of writing, there is a waiting list for the parish allotments (allotment holders are often among the most active of the members), and current concerns about climate change and the personal and global benefits of sourcing food locally mean that parents often take up gardening at the urging of their children—who will hopefully be the association members of the future.

Allotments

During the eighteenth and early nineteenth centuries, the population of England increased rapidly in the new or expanding industrial centres. Unlike their rural forebears, these townspeople had neither the time nor the space in which to grow food, either for themselves or to sell. They were necessarily dependent on the daily import of meat, vegetables and other produce from the surrounding countryside. But their demands could not be met by the existing systems of agriculture: small holdings often made up of small parcels of land scattered throughout a parish; the strip-farming of large open fields; the grazing rights that gave people access to common land. Hence the enclosure movement, that sought to raise agricultural productivity by restricting common rights and consolidating disparate small landholdings into fewer large farms. Economies of scale now made it worthwhile for their new owners to invest in such improvements as hedging, ditching, drainage and, increasingly, mechanisation.

The Acts that implemented the enclosure changes made some provision to compensate those whom the new order had dispossessed, but it was not enough. Reformers argued that some reallocation of land was essential to save the families of labourers and small yeoman farmers from unemployment and poverty - starvation, even. But when their proposals were finally taken up, well into the nineteenth century, it was not social conscience but fear that moved the ruling class: fear induced by the intermittent revolutions shaking continental Europe and at home the increasing rural unrest epitomised by the 'Swing' riots of 1830-21 (see **machine-breaking** in the A to Z Section). By the mid-1830s, almost half of all parishes had allotment schemes; at about this time, the Buckden parish authorities invited the deserving poor to apply for allotments 'in the gravel pits' (probably off Mill Road). A succession of acts sought to ensure that no new enclosures were authorised unless land was set aside as allotments for the labouring population. In 1890 this responsibility was imposed on the county councils—which after 1894 led to disputes between them and some of the new parish councils (including Buckden's). As a result, the Small Holdings and Allotments Act 1908 shifted the responsibility down to parish, urban district and borough councils, requiring them to meet their residents' demands for allotments.

The Land Settlement Facilities Act 1919 was introduced to assist returning servicemen, and opened up allotments to all, including women, not just 'the labouring population'. It empowered parish councils to acquire land by agreement with local landowners or tenants or, with county council agreement, to buy land, or as a last resort to ask their county council to exercise its compulsory purchase powers. In Buckden the demand for allotments far exceeded the amount of suitable land available (or, rather, of land that the would-be allotment holders considered suitable). Numerous meetings were reported in the press between parish councillors and landowners, not only about the supply of land but about who was entitled to apply for an allotment or small-holding. This led to considerable ill-feeling—or as the *Hunts Post* diplomatically put it, 'Few questions have created greater interest in Buckden than the provision of allotments.' In May 1920, after a year of fruitless discussions, the Beds. and Hunts. Federation of Allotments and Smallholders called a public meeting in the Rifle Range, attended by, among many others, the local MP. The meeting was prompted by the parish council's having formally invited all who wished for an allotment to send in their names to the Clerk.[1] The chairman of the meeting, Mr F. Smith, began by saying (to general approval) that he was very pleased that the parish council had at last awakened to a sense of their responsibilities. (This was perhaps a surprising statement, given that he was himself a parish councillor!) He went on to explain that it would be better if all those who wanted allotments formed an association and submitted a single application in its name. A Federation representative supported this, pointing out that as the council's sole tenant such an association could save the parish the expense and trouble of dealing with individual allotment holders over rent collection, weed control, etc.

The immediate outcome of the meeting was the formation of a branch society for Buckden and district. The 1924 Ordnance Survey plans bear witness to the result:

Parcel No.	Area acres	Area hectares	Notes
60	5.13	2.08	Hardwick
70	1.39	0.56	Hardwick[2]
105	11.07	4.48	Now St Hugh's Road, Beaufort Drive and Wolsey Gardens
147	**2.90**	**1.17**	**Silver Street – existing**
163	1.99	0.81	Van Diemens Lane)
204	1.65	0.67	Van Diemens Lane) off Mill Road
206	5.76	2.33	Van Diemens Lane)
324	12.86	5.21	Perry Road
330	**0.78**	**0.32**	**Great North Road – existing**
	43.53	17.62	TOTAL

The demand for allotments fluctuates: it unsurprisingly increased during the Second World War (the young evacuees from London were given ground on which to produce food for their school), but as the twentieth century drew to its close, fewer people felt the need—or had the time—to grow their own food. There was little general concern when the Church Commissioners sold for housing the area of parcel 105 now under Beaufort Drive and Wolsey Gardens (there was rather more concern on the part of the existing allotment holders!). Eighty-five years on from the above table, the present area of allotments is only about 8% of the 1924 figure. Ironically, there is now a waiting-list. Concerns about food safety and food miles—and in a recession about the price of food—mean that more people see the benefit of controlling the production of what they feed to their families. It is unlikely, however, that anyone today would seek to grow a wheat crop, as some earlier allotment holders did (on their admittedly larger plots). One such enterprising 1920s grower, who raised an 'excellent piece of wheat in Taylors Lane [i.e., Hardwick] allotments ... one of the best in the district', was none other than parish councillor Mr F. Smith.

---

[1] This invitation may have been the result of an offer from the Ecclesiastical Commissioners of potential allotment land in the Big Hoo and Little Hoo, which the Parish Council had decided to accept.

[2] The Hardwick allotments often caused problems for the parish council: malodorous effluents would run off the land into Hardwick Lane, to the fury of local residents. The lane is still plagued by occasional flooding that exacerbates the damage done to its surface by heavy traffic; but at least it doesn't smell as bad.

APPENDIX
Gardeners Association Trophies
Awarded at the Spring Show

Name	Awarded for
Maurice Trophy	The best exhibit in the narcissus classes
Presidents Trophy	The best exhibit in the growing classes, other than narcissus
Association Cup	The most points in the growing classes
Bill Rowland's Shield	The winner of plate of any vegetable not listed
Hambledon Cup	The most points in the homecraft section
Stirtloe Trophy	The most points in flower arranging classes
Children's Cup	The most points in the children's classes

Awarded at the Autumn Show

Name	Awarded for
Wayman Trophy	Most points in the novice vegetable classes
Challenge Cup	Most points in the open vegetable classes
Onion Shield	Most points in the onion classes
Arthur Rivers Trophy	Best vegetable in the show
Hardonian Trophy	Best potato exhibit in the show
Peter Pullen Trophy	Heaviest yield from a single potato grown in a portable rigid container
Wally Brown Trophy	Heaviest pumpkin
Gilbank Trophy	Best display of vegetables
Peplow Cup	Most points in the fruit classes
Floral Trophy	Most points in the mixed flowers classes
Townsend Trophy	Most points in the chrysanthemums classes
Teddy Chubb Salver	Most points in the roses classes
Cannings Dahlia Trophy	Most points in the dahlia classes
George Whitlock Trophy	Most points in the pot plant classes
Maurice Trophy	Most points in the floral arrangements classes
Stanley Gale Cup	Most points in the homecraft classes
Mollicone Children's Trophy	Most points in the children's classes

CHAPTER 11/THE PARISH COUNCIL: A HISTORY OF THE GOVERNANCE OF BUCKDEN VILLAGE

Terry Hayward, OBE

The author, a past chairman and current member of Buckden Parish Council, outlines the way village affairs were managed up to the end of the nineteenth century, and looks at how far the council has fulfilled the expectations of the *Advertiser's* optimistic correspondent.

'With admirably drawn standing orders, a popular Chairman, and an able clerk, the Buckden Parish Council should get through their business very smoothly, with, let us hope credit to themselves and to the benefit of the ratepayers generally.'

St. Neots Advertiser, 9 February 1895

The parish council is a late arrival in the history of local government in England and Wales. Long before the Norman Conquest, the Saxons had a hierarchy of shire, hundred and tithing (a group of ten households) for administrative, military and judicial purposes. By 1066, local law and order was primarily maintained through the system of *frithborh* or frankpledge, under which each man in a tithing was responsible to the king for the good behaviour of every other member. The Normans adopted a modified form of frankpledge, introducing a manorial system of courts-baron (dispensing civil justice) and courts-leet (administrative bodies, which also dealt with petty offences). With the decline of feudalism, the functions of these courts gradually passed to county magistrates and parish vestries.[1]

The vestries were not established by any act of parliament, nor were their powers and composition defined by any law; but by the end of the seventeenth century they and the magistrates had come to be the rulers of rural England. Vestries were responsible for the general wellbeing of the parish; they looked after the poor, the old and the sick; they maintained the church and churchyard and managed the village pound; they waged a constant but often losing battle against sparrows, foxes and hedgehogs. For these various purposes they nominated from among themselves the appropriate officials: overseers of the poor, surveyors of highways, churchwardens, keepers of the pound, parish clerks and, in many cases, constables. Many of those chosen actually paid others to complete their tasks because very often the post could result in considerable personal cost—even physical harm—for the holder.[2]

The common, but not universal, custom was for substantial ratepayers of the village to meet once a month to deliberate on parish matters, perhaps in the church vestry but more often in an inn. Ale would be paid for out of parish rates! For the people in an eighteenth century village the real government was not parliament but the parish vestry. Perhaps it was almost inevitable that such a system sometimes led to accusations of corruption, especially where parishes were run by small executive committees known as a select vestries. These were generally self-elected and inevitably tended to grow autocratic and self-serving. In villages where the select vestry did not exist the management of village affairs was generally well-meaning but not terribly efficient.

The Local Government Act 1894 changed all of this. Thus it was that on the cold, wet evening of Tuesday, 4 December 1894, about 150 electors met in the Girls' School Room to elect Buckden's first parish council. Twenty-five residents offered themselves for election to one of the thirteen places available. Voting was done by a show of hands; it was not until 1949 that full secret ballots were held for the election of parish councillors. Meetings were held quarterly, the first in the Girls' School Room on 31 December 1894. Apart from considering the formalities of running the council, and electing a secretary, a treasurer and a

---

[1] But see the A to Z entry for Robert Holmes **Edleston**, who held manorial courts in Buckden in the 1920s.

[2] A transcript of the Buckden vestry book is held in the Huntingdonshire Archives, as is the churchwardens' accounts and memorandum book known as the Parish Book (1627-1774). For more on these accounts see the Appendix to Chapter 5 and the A to Z entry for **vermin**; for examples of the perils of being a public official see the entries for Thomas **Cope** and **pinders**.

chairman (John Linton, who was to remain in office for the next fifteen years), only one item was on the agenda: street lighting (it was later decided that none was needed). Perhaps not surprisingly the meeting was adjourned, but more surprisingly only until 1 January 1895. A special meeting was held in February, at which standing orders were agreed. These differed very little from those in place today, but included a sensible rule that no meeting would last for more than three hours.

Most activities were carried out by committees, the first being Parish Property, Footpaths and Open Spaces (including care of the cemetery and sanitary matters) and a Technical Education Committee. This last committee set up a wide ranging programme of educational courses, and to start with all the instruction was given by councillors. The initial subjects were veterinary science and farriering, bookkeeping, domestic economy, beekeeping, and poultry keeping. At later dates bread-making, cookery, ambulance, basket-making, shoemaking, carving, vocal music and sick nursing were added.[1] The early councillors obviously had a busy life and were, hopefully, multi-talented. In 1900 'military training and rifle shooting' were added to the syllabus, a response, no doubt, to the second Boer War which had begun the year before.

The number and responsibilities of these committees changed to meet circumstances over the years. In the twenty-first century they are: Planning, General Purposes, Finance, Allotments, Footpaths, and Highways and Road Safety. Councillors are, perhaps, grateful that they no longer have to run educational classes.

Meetings were short, mainly taking account of the various committee reports. Some of the agenda items would be familiar to today's councillors: footpaths, stiles, condition of road surfaces, trees, the state of the many brooks running through the village and the unsatisfactory condition of closets and vaults which ran into open sewers and ultimately into the brooks. The council had taken over from its predecessor the parish fire engine and hearse, and these responsibilities continued until the late 1930s.[2] The village also maintained a 'bathing place' and hut on the River Ouse, which was not given up until 1952. Overseers and constables were still being appointed (although both had been phased out in many parts of the country): the overseers until the 1920s and the constables until just before the Second World War. The responsibilities for the church were handed over to separately appointed churchwardens.

In 1907, in spite of the fact that there was no piped water, the council reported that 'with the exception of isolated cases of shortage there is a fair supply of water in the Parish'. Even in 1934 both Brampton and Buckden turned down a district wide water scheme. At a public meeting voting was 122 against the scheme with only 42 in support. As late as 1949 the council was urging the retention of the village pump because many villagers had no mains water and it would be a good standby for those who had. There was no sewerage system, and complaints about the dumping of 'night-soil', especially in Lucks Lane, and the pungent smell, were still being voiced in 1958 when main drainage for the village was completed. The scheme had first been agreed in 1950. The third utility was equally slow in coming to Buckden: in spite of having electric street lighting there were ongoing discussions about electricity for domestic use as recently as 1948.[3]

Neither the start nor the end of the First World War or the Second World War was recorded in the council minute books. It was not until late 1915 that any mention was made of the 'Great War', and then there were discussions about support for the Star and Garter Fund to provide accommodation for (originally) paralysed soldiers, and a fund was started for 'Christmas comforts for men of Buckden who are serving the King and Country and at present far from home'; sixty-four parcels were despatched. A War Agriculture Committee was formed, which distributed advice and seed potatoes. A notice from the Food Production Department offered rewards for killing rats, sparrows, rabbits and rooks to prevent 'deprivation committed upon crops by these pests'. In October 1917 the council was asked to nominate 'Representative Women' to assist with the setting up of a district wide nursing association to promote maternity and welfare care. Eight ladies volunteered, mainly wives of councillors or ex-councillors. The following year the council discussed the provision of cottages and smallholdings for soldiers and sailors on demobilisation at cessation of hostilities.

As early as 1936 the council discussed air-raid precautions (ARP) and first aid training and, perhaps a little macabre, purchased a new hearse. The discussion was prompted by a Home Office circular and other

---

[1] See also under **Barson** in the A-Z section.

[2] For more on the fire engine and the hearse see the A to Z entries **fires and fire-fighting equipment** and **bier** (as the hearse was more commonly known).

[3] For how Buckden's lack of utilities struck an outsider, see the appendix to this chapter,

guidance issued to local authorities the year before, instructing them to start ARP planning—but not to spend more than the bare minimum of ratepayers' money on it. One of Buckden's parish councillors, Surgeon Commander Arthur Bell, would no doubt have grumbled about such a cheeseparing attitude: he was already hard at work as the county's chief ARP officer, and in 1938 and 1939 was Hon. Sec of a national body, the Association of Air Raid Precaution Officers.

There is no mention in the council minutes of the Second World War until February 1941, when fire-watchers were appointed and a list of other civil defence duties was recorded. There were also complaints about damage caused by a 'small refugee'. In August, a Buckden and Diddington Parish Invasion Committee was formed to co-ordinate all aspects of civil defence in case of an enemy invasion. The minutes record that exercises were carried out 'to be a solemn test of the invasion arrangements'. Reserve food supplies were delivered and stored in the village, with councillors organising delivery plans. In 1943 there was a large and heated public meeting, which aired obvious disquiet about the number of people (especially male) who were not making enough effort towards the war. The minutes record a concern about 'moral laxity' especially among the young people. As at the end of the First World War, discussions started on how to provide suitable housing for returning servicemen. By 1948, thirty houses had been built in Lincoln Close.

Notwithstanding the war, the council still found time to complain about the inadequate bus service with Huntingdon and the poor mail delivery. As a footnote to war preparations, it is interesting to note that in 1951 the council was still discussing the need for civil defence and plans for the accommodation of evacuees—this time, of course, in the context of the Cold War, which was going through one of its hotting up phases, the Korean War of 1950 to 1953.

In January 1952, the council called a special public meeting to discuss 'Londoners for Huntingdonshire'. This was a London County Council suggestion that Londoners should be re-housed in Huntingdonshire over a period of twenty years. The plan was not approved. The meeting concluded that it would not be good to put city dwellers into a rural county and that 'Foreigners in London should be repatriated and emigration to the colonies should be considered.'

Throughout the 1950s there were recorded complaints about speed of traffic through the village and parking on the Great North Road (of which the village High Street was then still part). Rumours of a proposed Buckden bypass were rife. At a public meeting in 1957 the council unanimously agreed to appeal against a plan to build the bypass close to the village, its current course, because the accident black spots to the north and south of the village would still exist and it would cut the village in two. The council proposed a route from Diddington Hill to just south of Brampton Hut thus avoiding the village completely. In the event the Minister responsible decided that there was no point in holding an enquiry because seven councillors and thirty-nine villagers had written to him in favour of the route close to the village. At the next meeting of the parish council the chairman reminded councillors of their corporate responsibility and resigned!

Villagers had always been welcome to attend council meetings as observers and were on occasions allowed to speak. There had also long been the opportunity for the council chairman or a group of electors to call a parish assembly to discuss matters of concern to the community, but it was not until the early 1960s that it was decided that one should be convened annually, at which the council and village charities reported their activities and the public had the opportunity to question, complain and suggest ideas for the future of the village. There had also always been the opportunity for women to be elected on to parish councils, but again it was not until the 1960s that Buckden elected its first female councillor.

In 1956 the council initiated discussion about the War Memorial Playing Fields and the possible purchase of the Great Vineyards. In 1960 the deeds of the Memorial Playing Fields were handed over to the parish council as Custodian Trustees. In May 1967 a public meeting agreed that a new village hall should be built to replace the rifle range hall in Church Street. At the 1971 Parish Assembly, which was attended by over 200 people, the council agreed to give £10,000 towards the building of the new hall. This came into use in January 1975, under the management of the Village Hall Trust (VHT); a club was also opened to all members of the village for an annual subscription of 50p. At the preceding annual meeting of the VHT the only people present were the committee. The council and the VHT agreed to work closely together and it was decided to re-establish Feast Week. The council also instigated work on the clearance of the Valley area. During this period the council also made grants to the tennis and bowls clubs to enable them to build their own facilities.

In 1975 the council first discussed the possible provision of an office for the clerk, an ambition not realised until 2006. Throughout the 1970s there were constant fears expressed about the speed of traffic on the A1, the dangers of the crossings in the centre reservation, and the risk of accidents at the Brampton Road and Perry Road junctions on the A1. The year 1979 saw the first employment of a village handyman; up until then jobs had been completed by volunteers or contractors. The council agreed to support the newly formed drama group and the proposed new parish magazine, *The Buckden Roundabout*, whose first issue appeared in September 1979.

In 1981 the council opposed plans to move Buckden out of Huntingdonshire. As one councillor put it 'From the tenth century when King Athelstan formed the shires of Mercia, Buckden has been part of the Shire of Huntingdon ...'. In spite of the council's opposition and a petition signed by over 1000 villagers, Buckden was moved for electoral purposes into the new parliamentary constituency of South West Cambridgeshire. The constituency was abolished in 1997 and Buckden resumed its place in Huntingdonshire.

The problems of satisfying the needs of the young people of the village, especially teenagers, had often been discussed at council meetings and at the 1984 Parish Assembly the discussion topic was 'Isn't it Time that Youngsters had their Own Place?' Twelve young people attended the meeting and the names of seventy-five of the village's three hundred teenagers between eleven and eighteen had been gathered. It was agreed that money should be set aside and the VHT co-opted to work with the young people. The best intentions gae oft astray, and in spite of various abortive attempts by the council, the VHT and individuals the problem still exists.

Many councils have some form of regalia, a chairman's chain for example. This was discussed in 1985— and rejected. Also in that year the council supported the formation of a village playgroup and opposed the suggestion that there should be a dispensing chemist in the village. In 1986 the council again rejected the idea of a chemist, and started the competition for a cup for the best allotment. The following year was the last to date in which a ballot was held to elect a parish councillor. Since that date there has been no need for a ballot, because the number of candidates has never exceeded the council places available. The late 1980s also saw the council fight plans for the further extension of gravel workings in the Ouse Valley adjacent to Buckden Mill. At a Public Inquiry the council's representatives convinced the presiding Inspector that enough was enough and the diggings were restricted to their current size. The council also successfully lobbied for 'low level' reclamation for the gravel pits to the south of Mill Road. Another battle fought by the council but this time with less success was to limit the development of the Marina site. The 1980s closed with a council decision to provide the VHT with further funds to provide for repairs and refurbishment to the hall.

The final decade of the twentieth century proved a busy one for the council. Throughout the period it had the same chairman, which provided continuity and stability—although it also led to the decision in 2001 that chairmen should serve for a maximum period of three years! The first major decision was the sale of the old Mayfield/Lucks Lane rubbish tip site to the village doctors, which enabled them to build the present magnificent surgery. The money received was reserved for future village developments. In the same year the council successfully persuaded Huntingdonshire District Council to build houses and bungalows behind Smiths Drive, as low-cost and rented housing. At a stroke this emptied the Buckden waiting list for rented housing. The council successfully fought against proposals to extend the village boundaries. In 1991 the council published the first definitive booklet on the footpaths in and around Buckden, and in the same pioneering spirit followed it up in 1999 by publishing an environmental plan for the village. More renovation work was carried out in the Valley, and swans nested on the lake for the first time. After many years of argument and persuasion the council finally persuaded Cambridgeshire County Council that there should be a properly constructed slip road from the Brampton Road to Silver Street. In 1995 permission was obtained for 'Historic Buckden' signs to be erected on the A1 and in the same year an extension to the cemetery was consecrated by the Bishop of Huntingdon. The year was also marked by a public meeting to protest successfully against the potential closure of Buckden's branch of the County Library.

Perhaps one of the most far-reaching decisions made by the council was taken in 1997, when it agreed with the VHT to embark on an ambitious plan to rebuild the village hall, which was now showing its age, needed urgent repairs and was unable to meet the needs of the village. A joint committee was set up and plans were prepared. A well-attended public meeting supported the ideas and a village referendum backed both the plans and method of funding. The total cost of over £700,000 was met by a Lottery Millennium Grant, grants from the county and district councils, WREN[1], and generous donations from individuals and

---

[1] Waste Recycling Environmental Limited, a not-for-profit business that helps benefit the lives of people who live close to landfill sites by awarding grants for environmental, heritage and community projects.

village organisations. The parish council allocated the money raised from the sale of the Mayfield site, and the final £110,000 was borrowed by the council to be repaid through the village precept over a period of ten years. Not only did the new building provide much needed facilities for village clubs and societies and an extension for the Village Club, it also provided accommodation for the library and the village pre-school playgroup. At the same time as this joint venture was completed the VHT built the new sports pavilion.

Throughout the 1970s, 1980s and 1990s the council had to consider plans for the further provision of housing in the village and at each stage it was committed to trying to ensure that the houses built were not too cramped and of suitable design for a village environment. A walk around the village suggests that on the whole it succeeded in its aims. The announcement in 1997 in the new County Plan that 45,000 extra houses would be built in Cambridgeshire by 2016 sounded alarm bells. The council argued most strongly that there should be no further development in the Huntingdon and St Neots area without ensuring that there was an adequate infrastructure in place: it felt that more work was required on roads, services, police, schools, doctors' surgeries, hospital facilities etc. At the same time it again launched a defence to protect Buckden from further expansion.

When parish councils were first formed, the overseers - those hangovers from the days of the parish vestry - continued to be responsible for the collection of monies to meet the costs of the council's responsibilities. This task was later performed by the parish clerk, and later still a village precept was collected as part of the overall rates collected by the county and district councils. In 1909 the first precept was agreed at £10; it was still only £30 in 1947, in 1957 it was £140, in 1977 it was £6250 and by the late 1990s it was over £20,000. The apparently large increase is due not only to inflation and the greater demands placed on the council, but also to the fact that the village is some six to eight times larger now than it was in 1907. The precept is set by the council itself, which can set it at whatever level it wants but must observe a 'duty of responsibility'.

Throughout its history of over one hundred years the council has consisted of villagers who have tried to provide the best for their village—sometimes they have succeeded. As the chairman in the 1990s reported to an annual parish assembly, 'The council tries to act as agents for the village and sees its role as a channel through which to focus the needs of the village as a whole.'

APPENDIX

'....the loo was in a tiny shed at the end of the garden.'

The evacuation of London at the outbreak of the Second World War in September 1939 meant that a large group of schoolboys and their teachers found themselves in Buckden not as visitors entering only hotels or shops, but as long term residents intimately sharing family life in households at every level of village society. For some of the boys—from, admittedly, the comfortable suburb of Muswell Hill—there were aspects of their new life that came as a shock. The memory of them was still vivid over fifty years later for William Medhurst (Tollington School 1936-43) and Peter Allen (1936-42):

William: 'Water still came via a manual pump over the kitchen sink and whilst we did enjoy the benefit of electric lights, the loo was in a tiny shed at the end of the garden. This sanitary arrangement applied to most of the village in those days and night-soil buckets were emptied once a week by a council worker who made the rounds with a horse-drawn metal tank on wheels. Rumour had it that at the end of the week, usually every Thursday, this tank would be emptied into the river at Offord...'

Peter: 'It was a passage back in time—to long stints pumping water, doing homework by oil lamps, farms where they still used horses, and the extraordinary quiet of the countryside at night. I doubt if any of us had been aware of villages only 60 miles from London without electricity, mains water or sewers.

'But', he added, 'I am sure it was all an education in itself and an experience I should not want to have missed.'

CHAPTER 12/THE ADMINISTRATION OF THE BUCKDEN PAROCHIAL CHARITIES

Lorraine Toogood, formerly Clerk to the Trustees[1]

Buckden is fortunate in its benefactors, the men and women who in the course of the last four and a half centuries have cared enough about their fellow-residents, young and old, to help alleviate their poverty, protect their old age and provide for their education.

The first part of this chapter sets out the various benefactions that originally comprised the parochial charities, while the second briefly describes how, through consolidation and investment, they have been managed to the best effect over the years.

The original charities

The Charity of William Burberry founded by will dated 18 March 1558. The endowment of this charity consisted of land, allotments, a cottage and a garden, all in Buckden and Stirtloe, and amounting to about forty-five acres. The land was let to various tenants and the revenue distributed in doles to the poor each Good Friday. The land to the south of the roundabout on the A1, now known as the Windmill Allotments, was part of this endowment.

The Dole Charity, the origins of which are unknown. The endowment consisted of seven rent charges from various properties in the village of Buckden and the revenue was applied with the income of South's Charity.

The Charity of James South founded by will proved in the Prerogative Court of Canterbury dated 17 May 1885. The endowment consisted of the South's Almshouses and a sum of money invested in two and a half per cent Consols. The dividends, together with the income from the Dole Charity, Maltby's Charity and an annual sum received from Burberry's Charity were expended on payments of money to the almspeople, providing coal for the almshouses and keeping the building in good repair. James South was a half-pay Captain of His Majesty's 52nd Regiment of Foot, who had been born in Buckden. He left to the parish of Buckden £1500 invested in 3% Consols for the building and furnishing of 'four brick tenements to be erected in an airy situation on the said parish ground to be occupied by four of the oldest poor women and four of the oldest poor men born in the parish of Buckden. In front of the said Almshouses to be engraved on a neat octagon stone tablet 'Age protected Industry rewarded' and I give the interest ... for the purpose of keeping the said tenements in good repair and I give the further sum of £200 to be invested in the Bank of England for ever, the interest arising from which to be laid out for coals, to be equally divided between the eight inmates on every Christmas Day or the morning preceding it. I also give £40 for bibles, prayer books and other religious books to be strongly bound in calf and to remain in the said dwellings for the sole use of the occupants for ever.'

The almshouses 2009. The central plaque reads 'Age protected Industry rewarded 1840'

---

[1] Original text updated with information from the Buckden Parochial Charities' Annual Reports and Accounts 2006, 2007 and 2008.

The Charity of Susannah Travill founded by will dated 17 February 1692. The bequest was a sum of £100, the income from which was to be given to the poor widows of the parish. The money was invested in land in Ellington and Buckden. (See also the entry for **Travill, Susannah** in the A to Z Section.)

The Charity of Bishop Maltby, originally a gift of £100 to the poor of the parish. This was invested in Consols and the dividends applied with South's Charity.

In addition, there were the Allotment for Reeveman, the Allotment for Constable and the Allotment for Hayward; like the Dole Charity, they are of unknown origin.

The administration of the charities

Over the years, the land, properties and investments were sold and reinvested, and the nine charities comprising the Buckden Parochial Charities were grouped into three:

The Almshouse Charities of James South and William Burberry. These comprised two individual charities: the Charity of William Burberry for Almshouses and the Almshouse Charities of James South and William Burberry, and were funded by investments and a weekly maintenance contribution paid by the residents. The income was to be applied for the benefit of the residents of the almshouses (including the Burberry Homes), collectively or individually.

The Buckden Public Benefit Charities. These comprised three individual charities: the Allotment for Reevemen (sic), the Allotment for Hayward and the Allotment for Constable, and were funded by investments from the sale of land which formed the original endowments. The income was to be applied at the discretion of the trustees for any public purpose for the benefit of the inhabitants of the parish, for which provision could not be made from the rates.

The Buckden Relief in Need Charities. These comprised four individual charities: the Charity of William Burberry for the Poor, the Charity of Susannah Travill, the Charity of Bishop Maltby and the Dole Charity. They too were funded by investments from the sale of property and land which formed the original endowments. The income was to be applied to relieve, generally or individually, poor persons resident in the parish.

In 2006, on the advice of the Charity Commission and after due public consultation, the original nine individual charities were reduced by amalgamation to three:

The Almshouse Charities of James South and William Burberry. This was formed by merging the two individual almshouse charities named above; it took over their funding and charitable objectives.

The Allotment for Reeveman. This was formed by the incorporation of the three constituent charities of the Buckden Public Benefit Charities; it took over their funding and charitable objectives.

The Dole Charity. This was formed by the incorporation of the four constituent charities of the Buckden Relief in Need Charities; again, it took over their funding and charitable objectives.

In 2008, at the request of the trustees and after the statutory notice period, the Charity Commission agreed that the two smaller charities, the Allotment for Reeveman and the Dole Charity, could be closed and their assets transferred, in the form of grants, to the Almshouse Charities of James South and William Burberry.

The Almshouse Charities own the almshouse buildings known as South's Almshouses and the Burberry Homes, which stand to either side of the Methodist Church on Church Street. South's original four tenements have been brought up to date within their original Grade II listed building and now provide eight bedsitting-room apartments, each with its own kitchen and bathroom, for the use of single people. The Burberry Homes, more properly known as 24-38 Church Street, were built on the site of the old Rifle Range in 1969. and financed by the sale of remaining properties and land from the Burberry bequest. These homes consist of seven apartments, each comprising a sitting room, bedroom, kitchen and bathroom, and are for the use of married couples or single persons. There is also a two-storey warden's house. They are financed by remaining investments and a weekly maintenance contribution paid by the residents. Occupancy is assessed on need and residents must be able to prove a connection with Buckden and to live a fully independent life.

The Buckden Parochial Charities are administered by a committee of eight trustees, two of whom are Nominative Trustees, appointed for four-year terms by the Parish Council. They may be, but need not be, members of the Parish Council. The remainder are Co-optative Trustees who must live or carry on a business in the parish of Buckden and are appointed for a term of five years. Ordinary meetings of the trustees are held at least twice and, more usually, four times a year and it is this committee which is responsible for the policies regulating the charities, subject to the regulations of the Charities Commission and the advice of the Almshouse Association.

The committee is serviced by a Clerk who is responsible for the day to day administration of the charities. This is a voluntary position.

A part-time Warden is employed to help the residents maintain an independent lifestyle and to liaise with statutory services.

See also the A to Z Section under **parish workhouse** and **soup kitchens**.

Updated from the Buckden Parochial Charities' Annual Reports and Accounts 2006, 2007 and 2008.

2009 The Burberry Homes and warden's house on the site of the Rifle Range

CHAPTER 13/ EDUCATION IN BUCKDEN
Susan B. Edgington

Although primarily known as an academic and author specialising in medieval history, Dr Edgington also has a strong interest in local history. She was the founder Chairman of Buckden Local History Society and wrote Buckden: a short history (1980). Her other publications include Gendering the Crusades (2001) and Albert of Aachen (2007).

The Charity School

Schooling in Buckden was well established two centuries before the Elementary Education Act of 1870 made its provision statutory. In 1661, a prominent member of the community, Robert Rayment, died and in his will instructed his heirs thus:

> yearely and every yeare forever as long as the world indures pay or cause to be payd unto the Minister and Churchwardens of Buckden aforesayd for the tyme being the like summe of tenn pounds of lawfull money of England to be payd halfe yearely the first payment to be and begin six monthes after the expiracon of the first three yeare aforemenconed to be payd to such a teacher or scholemaster as shall be approved by the major part of the Jury commonly called the twenty men wch teacher or scholemaster shall yearely ingage to learne the English tongue unto such Inhabitants children both male and female as shall be poore and unable to pay for their Childrens scholeing. And that the same teachger shall learne such poore children of Bugden aforesayd in the same towne the grounds and principles of true religion according to the Church of England as the same is established by our gracious and pious prince King Charles the Second. And I desire and intreate the Minister of Buckden from tyme to tyme to see and examine such Children and to see that such teacher or scholemaster doe and performe his duty.

Robert Rayment's meticulous arrangements were not made in vain. A schoolmaster was appointed in 1665 and receipts for the money were recorded twice a year in the Churchwardens' Account Book until it ended in 1774. The list of teachers includes five members of the Burder family, in three generations. For three short periods the teacher was a woman, and for three year the vicar did the job himself, either because a suitable candidate was not available or to supplement his stipend. Most remarkably, for two years (1706-7) the post was held by a woman who was unable to sign her own name.

It is worth noting that Rayment's faith in posterity was not misplaced: his charity still exists today (albeit no longer in his name) and is used by the school to buy books and by the Church Sunday School. Following the good example of Robert Rayment there was Bishop Green, who died in 1779 and is thought to be buried in the parish church:

> John Green, Lord Bishop of Lincoln, who had in his lifetime given a house and garden in Buckden for the residence of the master of the parish school, by his will dated 17 August 1778, gave to the ministers and churchwardens of Buckden £200 in trust[...]the dividends or interests of which should be yearly paid to the schoolmaster of that parish. In teaching the poor children to read and write, such Schoolmaster[...]to be removable for any misbehaviour. *(Report of the Charity Commissioners, 1836)*

Thus at the end of the eighteenth century there was already in Buckden a parish school with a paid schoolmaster and a school-house. This was to be the nucleus for growth in the nineteenth century. The report goes on to explain that the monies:

> are paid to a schoolmaster appointed by the Minister and Churchwardens, who resides in the house given by the Bishop, which, and the parish schoolroom, are kept in repair by the Parish. The duty of the master is to instruct 30 boys, the children of settled parishioners in Buckden, gratis, and the boys are

appointed by the minister. There are usually 30 boys in attendance and they are instructed as free scholars in reading, writing and accounts and in the principles of religion, according to the doctrine of the Church of England.

Among the nineteenth century schoolmasters were the James brothers, the sons of a Fenstanton butcher (their mother). Although still listed as the master in an 1830 directory, Charles James had died the previous year, aged only 20. He was succeeded by his brother Henry (himself not yet 17), who remained in post for the next twenty-three years. There is more about them under **James** in the A to Z Section.

The National School

Girls' schooling was not mentioned by the Charity Commissioners in 1836, but it did not have to wait long for attention. In 1842, according to the Preliminary Statement submitted in 1870 concerning the existing schools, a Girls' School was founded under the aegis of the Anglican National Society.[1] The 'Endowed' school for boys and the 'National' school for girls arc listcd in (among others) Kelly's Directory for 1846 and the Post Office Directories for 1854 and 1864.

That parents accepted the idea of schooling for their children is shown by the census enumerators' returns of 1851. Under 'Occupation' the vast majority of children in the 5 to 11 age range are entered as 'scholars'. There is no doubt that this is a grossly inflated figure. Some of the children had probably never so much as stepped inside a schoolroom, and others certainly would not have attended with any regularity; but it is indicative of the expectations of the enumerators (local men), and the social pressures on the parents. It might also be inferred from the figures that boys were likely to get their schooling early, leaving at about eleven to take up employment, while girls would start later and have more chance of staying on until the age of fourteen.

It is difficult now to tell how effective the schools were, for example in teaching people to read and write. One rather rough and ready test has been devised, which is to examine the marriage registers. Here the bride and groom were required from 1754 to sign their names, or failing that, to put a mark. There are many reasons why figures derived from this source are not a reliable guide to literacy. For one thing people may be able to sign their names without being able to read or write. There have also been cases where the officiating curate obligingly signed for the parties (but not detectably in Buckden). It has been suggested too that a bride might have been reluctant to 'show up' the groom by signing when he could not—but again the evidence in Buckden does not support this. Bearing in mind all these reservations, it can be seen that in Buckden more people could sign their names than not from about 1850. Those who married in the 1850s would mostly have been at school in the 1840s (whether they grew up in Buckden or some other parish); this ties in neatly enough with the foundation of the National Schools.

The Victorian Board Schools

The 1870 Elementary Education Act, then, found Buckden already reasonably well-provided for.[2] A new school building was opened in 1871 for the National Girls' and Infants' School on land conveyed from the See of Peterborough and close to the schoolhouse that Bishop Green had given. The National School had previously been held in part of the Bishop's Palace at the other end of Church Street. From the same year, 1871, there is an excellent source for the day-to-day running of the schools: the head teachers' Log Books. The earliest and most detailed one is for the Boys' School 1871-1932, and the first part of this gives a good idea of the many problems in running a village school at the end of the nineteenth century.

For a start, numbers fluctuated a great deal: average attendance in 1871 was 45; by 1877 it had risen to 59; in 1878 it was 69; in 1884 it was 89 and there were 100 boys on the registers. The following year a reorganisation took place and the school became mixed boys and girls, with the infants and Standard I in a separate classroom. By 1889 there were 123 pupils 'on the books'. To teach them the master had the assistance of a pupil-teacher and two monitors. But the experiment of a mixed school came to an end in 1890 when the Headmaster *'reopened School as Boys Dept. Sent girls to Infants Dept.'*

For the first twenty years, until free education became a right under the 1891 Education Act, pupils were expected to pay fees. Generally these were 4d. a week, but some 'infant scholars' paid 2d. a week, and in accordance with the endowments of Rayment and Green 30 boys were taught annually absolutely free.

---

[1] Also known as SPCK, the Society was established in 1811 to promote the education of the poor. By the 1850s there were some 17,000 National Schools.

[2] The act provided for genuine mass education on a scale not seen before. The State became more interventionist and encouraged voluntary action assisted by local authorities. Elected school boards were permitted to levy money for fees and given powers to enforce attendance of most children below the age of thirteen. By 1874, over 5000 new schools had been founded.

So in 1873 an entry reads: *'The Free List revised, and vacancies filled up by boys eligible to be free.'* And in 1879: *'Admitted E.H. and C.S., gipsies, to be paid for by the parish.'* In fact income from fees ('school pence') totalled only £20 4s. 3½d. for 1879 and its collection was tedious, so that it was with relief as well as pride that the headmaster wrote *'Opened as Free School'* on 5 October 1891.

Fees or no fees, the problem of attendance cropped up regularly from 1871, when the Headmaster noted *'difficulty in working the timetable owing to irregularity; and of the bigger boys going out to field work.'*, and in August: *'Not many at School, Harvest having commenced.'* In 1873 he came closer to defining the difficulty: *'Nearly 30 boys under 11 out at field work—and the managers had promised to employ none under 10.'* When the chief farmers in the parish were also the School Managers no parent was going to risk their displeasure by refusing to allow his or her child to work in the busy season. Legislation did not help, for the same farmers were also the magistrates who in 1883 *'appear not very strict in regard to the attendance of children for they appear to stay away when they like, and Mr Worthy informed me that out of a conviction of 6 or 7 children's parents not one had paid the fine.'*[1] In June 1889, the attendance officer charged Buckden farm labourer William Carter with not sending his ten-year-old son George to school. The St Neots magistrates adjourned the case for a month; which, perhaps coincidentally, would have allowed George to continue helping with the haymaking, and then be returned to school for a few weeks' rest before the harvest began in August.

In the 1890s absences for field work became fewer and the boys' reasons, or excuses, for playing truant more diverse and ingenious. For example, in 1893: *'A very sharp frost following on floods have* [sic] *made a chance for nearly half the boys stopping away the afternoon for skating,'* and *'Many boys stopped away today there being what they consider a grand Funeral at Brampton.'* (This was the funeral of Colonel the Hon. Oliver Montagu, which was a *very* grand affair, complete with a military escort, pewfuls of dukes, earls and lesser aristocrats and gentry, and the Prince of Wales himself, mourning one of his closest companions, a gallant soldier who 'had only two misfortunes to regret during his happy, gay career': having one eye shot out by a friend, and dying in Egypt as a result of following his doctor's advice that holidaying in a warm climate would speed his recovery from flu.) In 1895 the weather was again disruptive: *'Great storm yesterday trees down in all directions and only 32 boys at school this morning all the rest out sticking.'* In 1899 the Infants' teacher recorded another diversion: *'School closed on Monday owing to the visit of Barnum and Bailey's Show to Huntingdon. Five children who came to school were dismissed.'*

There were other, rather more legitimate, amusements for which the headmaster was more or less obliged to close the school. The most contentious was the village Feast Week, the second week in July, when there were various celebrations including a Grand Flower Show. In 1871, the teacher tried to keep the school open but attendances were very low; by 1873 he gave up and granted a week's holiday. In 1885 the Headmaster tried to enforce attendance but noted: *'Teachers and attendance officers powerless.'* In 1886 he commented: *'Feast holiday very injurious to school work. Children as dense as if they had been away for 6 weeks.'* And in 1887 he complained: *'4th Standard dull at Arithmetic: this week being the Troublesome 'Feast Week' will render matters worse.'* In 1888 he finally gave in: *'The Infants Mistress has agreed in the absolute necessity of a Holiday.'*

Other annual days off were given for the Sunday School outings, both Church and Chapel, and the Club Feasts in May. Special occasions were also marked by a holiday, both national ones such as the Jubilees of 1887 and 1897 and the Queen's birthday in 1900, and local ones like the funeral of the vicar (Daniel Haigh) in 1875. A day off was also given in 1884 when the schoolmaster (George Barber) returned home to Lincolnshire to marry a fellow teacher, National Schoolmistress Rebecca Westland.

Official holiday periods amounted to only a few days at Christmas and Easter and generally five weeks in the summer. The summer holiday was not fixed in advance but was announced when the harvest was ready. If the weather was poor an extra week might be given in September to complete the field work. Here, as before, the schoolmaster was at the mercy of the school-manager farmers.

Another cause of lengthy closures was epidemic disease. There were measles (*'Arch Enemy of Elementary Schools'* the teacher calls them in 1884) in 1890 and 1897, and whooping cough in 1900. Mumps and smallpox affected attendance badly but did not necessarily lead to the school's closing altogether, as would sometimes happen in the early years of the twentieth century.

The inadequacy of the school premises must have contributed to the spread of disease. In 1871, according to the Preliminary Statement, the boys' school consisted of two rooms measuring 27' by 15' and 8'

---

[1] Alfred Worthy was a former schoolmaster, turned St Neots public official. He gave his occupations in the 1871 census as 'Relieving Officer, Registrar, Collector, Vaccination Officer &c.' The '&c.' suggests he listed them less out of pride than from weariness: they all had the potential to bring him into conflict with every section of the community.

by 20' and was 10' high at the walls, and accommodated 50+ boys. In the same year, the teacher described it as 'very close and inadequate'. It must have been a relief to write in 1880:

March 12th. Left the school on the 9th for the purpose of building being pulled down; the school is held in a large loft or granary in Mr Wm Mann's yard...

May 24th . Opened new school.

But as noted above, the number of children on the registers rose to unprecedented heights in the 1880s, and in 1889 the accommodation was again found to be inadequate:

26th July 1899 "Group II"   Brian and Verna Smith

School Room (mixed) 40' 2" by 20' 3" by 12' 2" high = at 8 ft sq per scholar, 101.6
School Room (infants) 44' 2" by 20' 4" by 13' 7" high = at 8 ft sq per scholar, 112.2.

To improve the situation a new classroom was built in 1894, 25' by 20' by 16' = (at 10 sq ft) 50 scholars. Ironically the school population began to drop not long thereafter.

Within these big rooms the children sat at long desks, up to 12' in length. In 1889 the headmaster rearranged them facing him to make instruction easier. The infants sat in a 'gallery' of seats in tiers (the little ones at the front) until it was removed in 1930.

Besides their close proximity in the classrooms, the children also faced the hazards of the 'closets' or 'offices' which were a frequent cause of complaint from the Inspectors. The boys used dry-earth type of lavatories, and the girls' drained into a cess-pit. There were many complaints about the 'flies and stench' and the probable link with diphtheria outbreaks. Many experiments with different chemicals and routines were carried out: a pupil at the school in the early 1940s remembers there being two small outbuildings, each containing two buckets, one large, one small, with wooden seats; if they were not regularly emptied, they overflowed into the playground. Hygiene was not helped by there being no water-supply to the school until 1949, and the problem was not satisfactorily solved until 1956, when 'water-borne' toilets, as the correspondence quaintly refers to them, were installed.

The premises were heated, often inadequately, by a coal-burning stove in the boys' room and by coal fires in the girls'. Later all three classrooms were heated by coke stoves, whose tops would glow red-hot in winter. To deliver the coke, the coalman simply tipped it over the wall into the playground.[1] There were lamps: a later pupil recalls two hanging from the ceiling in the boys' room but, he says, they were lit only once during his school career. Instead, the school hours were adjusted so that there was a shorter dinner hour in winter, the afternoon beginning at 1.45 p.m. and ending at 3.45 p.m.

---

[1] For most of their existence, the schools fronted Mill Road and had no rear or side entrances; what is now School Lane 'was known as Bakers Lane, a road that ran between a farm and an engineering yard and ended in open fields.

It is unfortunate that (as in this case of 'daylight-saving') the main evidence about the timetable is where alterations were made to it; nowhere is preserved a record of the teaching schedule of the school. Certainly it was operated rigidly: even such minor changes as transposing reading and writing were noted in the Log Book. Sometimes changes in the curriculum were proposed by the Inspector, as in 1874: *'The children must be taught at least twelve songs next year, none of which have a denominational character.'*

By isolating strengths and weaknesses, the inspectors' reports add further information about subjects taught: for instance geography and grammar attracted attention in 1877. There was much rote-learning and lists of poetry to be learned for the inspection appear annually in the Log Books. In 1887:

Poetry for Exam.

1st Division 'The Deserted Village'
2nd Division 'The Burial of Sir John Moore'
3rd Division 'The Inchcape Rock'
4th Division 'Good Night' and 'Good morning'[1]

Slates were used in the Infants, ruled for handwriting practice; copybooks in the Juniors. It would be possible to investigate further the sort of work done by tracing the textbooks used: Nelson's 'World' for Standard VI geography, Nelson's 'Star Reader' for Standard I and Blackie's 'Historical Reader' for Standard III are listed, for example. There are also 'National' cards for arithmetic which may have been rather demanding: *'March 26th. One child a very industrious girl has been seriously ill from anxiety (arithmetic &c): the exception not the rule.'* (1886)

'Object lessons' were also listed in the Log Books and covered such diverse topics as 'cotton', 'salt' and 'day and night'. The Girls did needlework (of course). But the teaching did not entirely lack enterprise: in 1900 the Headmaster was prepared to alter the timetable to allow the children to watch an eclipse, and there were other diversions.

The teaching staff who had to cope with all this varied almost month to month. The boys' school had a certificated master who managed with the help of monitors in 1871, but a dozen years later when it was a mixed school there were two pupil-teachers to assist him. For long periods the master had no assistance at all and it is no wonder he sometimes reached the end of his patience:

April 16th. Had to give the boy a thrashing for obstinacy.... Having the whole of the work to do myself this waste of time cannot be borne. (1895)

This same teacher survived, though his temper was notorious, to resign in 1923 after 32 years' service.

The pressure on teachers and pupils were enormous. The school managers' great influence had already been referred to. In 1889 the Headmaster wrote:

February 25th. It is the desire of Managers that the children be so efficiently instructed that they pass Standard IV (the standard for total exemption) before the age of 11. This can only be accomplished by the managers providing a <u>sufficient</u> and <u>efficient</u> teaching staff. The minimum teaching staff required by the Code will not obtain the maximum Grants, nor the above desideratum.

It is not surprising that he wrote a month later:

March 26th. Rule:- Home lessons based on the instruction at school are given daily and consist of arithmetic, grammar, spelling and memory work, and for Monday morning Scripture and Catechism.

Keeping the managers happy was a vital consideration.

The other essential was to satisfy Her Majesty's Inspector, who visited annually and examined the children On his report depended the school's grant. Curriculum was one of his concerns and in 1877 he reported that 'the Geography and Grammar were not sufficiently well known to justify a grant under Article 19(c).' And in 1886: 'The grant for Geography was barely earned; that for English was lost owing to the weakness of the fourth, fifth and sixth standards in Grammar.'

---

[1] Lord Houghton's 'Good Night and Good Morning' was a favourite for infant schools recitations. Some older readers may remember it.

It begins: and ends:

  A fair little girl sat under a tree,   And while on her pillow she softly lay,
  Sewing as long as her eyes could see;   She knew nothing more till again it was day;
  Then smoothed her work, and folded it right,   And all things said to the beautiful sun,
  And said, *Dear work, good night! good night!*   *Good morning! good morning! our work is begun!*

In other years the subject grants were awarded, but the Inspectors also criticized discipline. When the school was first inspected in 1871 the Headmaster's attention was drawn to Article 17 under which 'the grant to the whole school was endangered by an unfavourable report from H. M. Inspector' on the Infants' discipline. In spite of this threat, the pupils seem to have been controlled with only occasional resort to corporal punishment:

'Punished W. E. 3rd Standard for gross impertinence to P. T. 3 Raps on Palm of Hand with cane am glad to say such punishment is not so frequently necessary as heretofore'. (1888)

Gentler methods were also used:

'Being abusive I put her off the premises. She called me a dirty beast.

E. D. with others kept in at noon to write punishment task for disobedience. Mother came and demanded her before the work was done'. (1890)

Such entries are rare. On one occasion the Inspector complained of the boys' listlessness and the Headmaster wrote tartly: *'H.M.I. said Children appeared half asleep (not unlikely—waiting 2 hours for his appearance.'* (1881)

Besides the visits of the Government Inspectors, there were frequent checks by the vicar, who examined the registers and spoke to the children. The Diocesan Inspector visited yearly too, since the schools were Church of England, and tested the children on their catechism and knowledge of the Bible.

The Dame Schools

In addition to pleasing the various authorities, the schoolmaster had to please parents, especially when schooling was not compulsory and involved paying a fee. There were alternatives in the village. The wealthy families employed tutors or governesses, of course, and do not enter into this account.[1] There were also the 'dame schools'. Miss Frances Beaumont and her sister Laura opened a girls' seminary (boarding school) in Buckden during the 1830s, having moved to the village with their mother, Sarah, herself a schoolmistress. At some time between 1847 and 1851, the sisters moved the school to St Neots. Trade directories and censuses show that several other small private schools came and went in the nineteenth and first decade of the twentieth century, most of them for girls and very young boys. One such boy, looking back at his 1860s childhood, remembered his schoolmistress, an innkeeper's daughter, as an 'acid spinster', but he may have been prejudiced against teachers, having a surfeit of them in his own family: a sister who ran a similar school, another who taught music, a third who married a headmaster, and a brother who became a nationally-known mathematics teacher.

The schoolmasters had little good to say of these dame schools, naturally: *'Re-admitted J.W. – who has been away a year to a dame's school, and not improved.'* (1873) *'Admitted F.H. a good 7 from Mrs Bowling's Private School rather backward.'* (1878)

But on the other hand: *'A private school kept by Mrs Bowling has a good number of children. The fee is 6d a week.'* So this school definitely provided competition.[2]

The Schools in the Twentieth Century

In many respects, rather than lessening, the schools' problems increased after the turn of the century. Epidemics (of whooping cough, measles, diphtheria, mumps, influenza, jaundice) caused lengthy closures in many years. It was also much more common for children to be excluded because of scabies or 'verminous heads', though arguably higher standards of hygiene could explain this: there were inspections regularly from the School Medical Officer, the School Nurse and later (1931) the School Dentist.

Falling rolls were also a cause for concern. The downward trend of the 1890s continued and by 1907 the Boys' headmaster was worried enough to observe: *'The number of boys gets less and less. Another family left the village for London.'* There were only 40 on the books. In 1911 he reiterated: *'Number of children on books decreasing. Two families emigrated to America.'*

A different teacher in 1927 did not see the fall in numbers as part of a long-term trend; he noted: *'Sept 26th. 36 boys present out of 37. Numbers are exceptionally low owing to a very low birthrate since the war.'* A recovery in 1933 (*'70 on register—highest in 20 years'*) did not continue, and by 1943 there were only 31 boys, aged 7 to 14, being taught as one class. The step which had been fought off for so long was unavoidable: amalgamation with the Girls' and Infants Department. It was effected in 1944, anticipating the same year's Education Act by arranging for senior boys (11+) to go to Brampton and Offord schools.

---

[1] Much was expected of governesses: one who taught the Gatty sisters at the Manor House in the late 1860s had to be competent to teach 'thorough English, good French and German, music and the rudiments of Latin and Italian'.

[2] For more on the schools run by the Beaumonts and Mrs Bowling, see their respective entries in the A to Z Section.

Two world wars were bound to affect the running of the school. The first passed without comment in the Log Books until 1916 when the uncertificated teacher was called up. (After the war the managers refused to reinstate him.) Shortages began to bite soon after: *'Poetical Reader not to be supplied (War*

The Girls School c 1928   Alice Whitmee
Back Row: 1 Dorothy Waring; 2 -- Richardson; 3?; Prudence Sabey? ; 5?
Centre Row: 1 --Richardson;2 --Bull; 3 Prudence Sabey?;4 ? ;5 ? ; 6 Win Livett; 7 Doris Papworth; 8? ; 9 Vera Livett; 10 ?
Front Row: 1 Doreen Richardson; 2 – Stocker; 3 Len Bozeat; 4 Vivian Waring; 5 --Stocker; 6 Dorothy Milner; 7 --Bull?;
8 Emily Newman; 9 Jessie Haynes; 10 –Richardson?

Economy)' (1917).The shortage of coal immediately after the war was more serious because the Girls' school had to close several times when the temperature was near or below freezing point. The children probably enjoyed other aspects of wartime economy: 'Oct 12th. In accordance with a request from Government the School had a half holiday to gather blackberries. 79 lbs were gathered . . . 1253 lbs of chestnuts have also been collected.' Extra holiday was also granted for potato picking.

The day peace was announced has a dry notice in the Log Books—*'Nov 11th. Half-holiday on receiving news of the Armistice.'*—but the real story, as told by a pupil of the time, is much more lively. The children were hard at work when the windows were suddenly darkened, and when they looked up it was soldiers from the Military Hospital at the Towers, who refused to go away but like Pied Pipers led the children off to celebrate with bonfires and fun in the Palace grounds.

The Second World War was prepared for long before it arrived: plans were made in case of evacuation as early as September 1938. A year later the Headmaster recorded solemnly: *'Sept 11th. School opened today under historic conditions.'* The school did not after all have to host evacuees: *'Some 200 boys from Tollington Secondary School, Hornsey have been brought here and are now resident on the village. These will be using the Towers as a school and so our building is not required and normal hours will be worked.'*[1]

There were some private 'refugees' admitted. Helping with the potato harvest was again sanctioned, and other diversions included, intriguingly, on 30 July 1943, *'Police-Sergeant Cragill visited the school this morning and demonstrated and spoke about various bombs to the Senior and Junior Girls and Boys.'* To mark the end of the war, the local education authority gave each child one shilling to buy a celebratory ice-cream. Perhaps emboldened by this relaxation of austerity, the School Managers pressed for a school bus service for the older Buckden pupils who attended Brampton School and Huntingdon Grammar.

In spite of the setbacks of war and disease, the overall picture of the twentieth century was one of progress. Medical inspections began. From January 1935 the school participated in the 'Milk in Schools Scheme'. It cost a halfpenny for a third of a pint. A former pupil remembers that the milk did not come, as intended, in a hygienic little bottle complete with straw; the children dipped their cups into a communal

---

[1] In Chapter 17 some of the Tollington boys remember their time in Buckden.

pail.[1] School meals were served for the first time in 1949, but as early as 1929 a large table and twelve chairs had been provided for children who stayed to dinner. Electric light was installed in 1931 (at a cost of £18 6s. 1d.). The improved sanitary arrangements have been noted already.

The children's horizons were widened in many ways. From the 1910s when PT drill was strictly to keep warm and there were no organised games, it was a big step to 1930 when the boys won the County Cup Final—literally a red-letter day as far as the Head was concerned. A lively interest was taken in the activities of the Royal Family, and not only as an excuse for holidays to celebrate numerous royal weddings. In 1906: '. . . marched children to High Street to see HM the King go through to Kimbolton. Very good view motor travelling slowly past.'

In 1936: 'Jan 23rd. In order that the boys might hear the proclamation of King Edward VIII in London I fitted up my wireless in school. The broadcast came through perfectly.' (The school did not get its own wireless until 1948—over 20 years after the BBC first started schools broadcasting.)

In the last thirty years of the twentieth century, Buckden School, which is still Church of England controlled, expanded almost—but not quite—out of recognition. There was a setback in 1960 when Longsands Secondary School was opened in St Neots and only 78 pupils were left. Shortly afterwards, however, Buckden was designated a 'major expansion village' and in the 1960s the school had to enlarge to keep up with the growth in the population. A new infant school opened in 1966 and a junior school in 1972. These were both part of the existing site, but in 1968 it had looked as though the junior school would be built at the south end of the new housing development that would be Manor Gardens. Parents, teachers and school managers combined to fight the proposal, partly on the grounds of duplication of staff and facilities, and partly for reasons of safety: gravel extraction in the Ouse meadows meant there was an almost constant stream of heavy lorries along Mill Road and Church Street at that time, and families who would have a child at each site were not prepared to risk one or other of them having to go to school unaccompanied (one child had already been killed and others injured). These arguments prevailed, and through compulsory purchase enough land was made available to expand the school on the site it still occupies.

A few years later, however, the infants' section had to be extensively rebuilt after a fire, described here by Mrs June Woods, Buckden's first woman parish councillor:

In November 1978 the school suffered a disastrous fire which gutted the newly built classrooms and caused a great deal of water and smoke damage to the old buildings, although it was interesting to note that the old timbers were not affected to the same degree that the new woodwork suffered.

I saw the flames and smoke above the school roof and ran through the pathway beside KnitKnax across the green just as the glass front door blew out—I have never been so frightened in my life—and I will always remember the pathetic scraps of burnt coats and PE bags that were left hanging in the cloakroom when the emergency was over. Tribute must be paid to the outstanding way in which the entire staff including ancillary staff reacted in such a frightening emergency. Children were evacuated to various places of safety very quickly (those in the Falcon seemed to quite enjoy themselves!) and from there to their homes. Parents very kindly took in neighbours' children whose mothers were working—generally speaking there was no panic...

Due to the efforts of everyone concerned, and the many offers of books, furniture and assistance the school was back in business within seven days, and by the first anniversary of the fire in 1979 the buildings were fully restored and once more open to the public.

The children wrote some excellent accounts of these events which were displayed in Huntingdon Library, the different views expressed made very interesting reading—and the handwriting was a joy to behold.

Not everyone seems to have noticed the day's excitement, however: on her way home the exhausted headmistress dropped in to a shop not a hundred yards from the school to buy something for supper: 'I expected a stream of questions about what had happened and why and was everyone all right...instead there was not a word. It was as if all the noise, smoke, vehicles, alarms and the unusual comings and goings of children and adults had never happened!'

The twenty-first century

Well over a hundred years old and enlarged in four main phases as the village grew, Buckden school now has over three hundred children on the roll. In the main, they come from the catchment villages of Buckden, Stirtloe, Southoe and Diddington, but there is a significant number from Huntingdon and the surrounding villages. From having had only small playgrounds and no playing field at all for most of its existence, the school now has extensive grounds including a large field, three playground areas and a play fort. The field has mature trees, a football pitch, an environmental area, a wildlife area and a living willow relaxation structure. Indoors, there are ten permanent class areas—both closed-classroom and open-plan—

---

[1] The straws are confirmed by *The Times* Tuesday October 2 1934: 'one-third pint bottles of milk, with straws'; they were, however, useless when the milk froze in winter! (Editor, pers. ob.)

a well-equipped gymnasium which doubles as a dining-room, a large activity and music room and a good library. These are not all modern buildings: the 1871 National School building and the schoolmistress's house are still an integral part of the campus, a permanent reminder of the importance our nineteenth century forebears placed on universal education.

But all memories of the infants' slates and the juniors' copybooks and the headmaster's crackly valve radio have been erased by today's wi-fi computers and interactive whiteboards!

Adult and other education

Education in a community is not confined to the formal schooling of its children. Formal education for adults included the training of pupil-teachers at the school, where they received instruction from the certificated teacher outside school hours, and at classes organised by the county council. At its widest education could include library provision (in the school from 1926) or the village Reading Rooms. The latter opened in November 1891, providing somewhere members could read the more respectable newspapers, discuss the issues of the day, attend lectures, and have their cultural horizons broadened (though not, in some cases, very far: there was a hard core of members who would persist in preferring music hall songs and comic monologues to recorder duets by the Misses Linton and Gatty). In the last years of the nineteenth century, patriotic evenings devoted to the various South African Wars were hugely popular, but the educational value of 'British pluck, Boer intransigence' was perhaps limited.

The Buckden branch of the Women's Institute (WI) opened in 1919. Its committee at once set up a lending library and embarked on a programme of lectures and demonstrations designed to increase the members' self-reliance and sense of self-worth. The topics ranged from home hygiene, upholstery and poultry keeping to world geography and British history. Even more than with the Reading Rooms, there was an important social side to the WI, which let women escape the confines of home life to take part in competitions, dances and drama.

The churches (and temperance organisations) also arranged lectures or courses for adults; in addition, of course, they ran Sunday Schools, whose annual days out at the seaside were the only time some children got to see the wider world for themselves.

There were also classes organised by individuals, such as one in shorthand at the Spread Eagle which cost 1d. a time in the 1890s. Other classes were held at the school as early as 1874, when the Head noted, *'Opened Night School on 27th September.'*, but no more is known about these.

The most interesting venture on record is in the Parish Council minutes for 1896 to 1911. In this period the Technical Education Committee organised lectures in bee-keeping, farriery, poultry-keeping, shorthand, dressmaking, horticulture, ambulance (first aid), basket-making, cookery and domestic economy (where 'the audience on some occasions showed an inclination to argue the lecturer's point'). All the classes which ran were firmly practical; proposals which were not adopted included vocal music, carving and shoemaking. The income came from a grant at 4½d. per capita and the usual class size seems to have been fifteen. It would be interesting to know more about these courses which so clearly mirrored the rural preoccupations of Buckden's inhabitants. Certainly some at least of the speakers were at the top of their profession, such as James Barson, the head gardener of Hinchingbrooke House—although his series of talks did not go quite as anticipated: see his entry in the A to Z section.

The parish council runs no such courses today, but informal adult education is far from defunct. The WI still flourishes, as do groups such as the Gardening Association, the Buckden Surgery Patient's Association, the Friends of Buckden Towers, the Local History Society, and the Workers' Educational Association. With the exception of the last two, education is not their primary reason for existence, but is an important, if occasional, ancillary activity.

For the young, Buckden has a Pre-School Playgroup, a Day Nursery, and for those looking for a career in dance and drama, Stageworks, an independent performing arts college situated in the grounds of Buckden Towers.

SOURCES
Parish Registers 1559-1920
Churchwardens' Account Book 1627-1774
Rayment's Will 1661
Census Enumerators' Returns 1851
Report of the Charity Commissioners 1836
Directories:
    Pigot's 1839, Kelly's 1847, 1890, 1898, Post Office 1854, 1877
School Log Books:
    Boys 1871-1932; 1932-1944
    Infants 1896-1913
    Girls 1902-1944
School Managers, Minute Book 1903-1937 and correspondence
Admissions Register 1927-1965
Website, Buckden CE Primary School 2009
Mrs June Woods, *The Buckden Schools*, undated talk

CHAPTER 14/MEDICAL PRACTICE IN BUCKDEN: 1253 TO 1964
William Tackaberry

This chapter looks at some of the doctors (all, as it happens, male) who have looked after the wellbeing of Buckden's residents through the centuries; but it is dedicated to the women of the village. Long before organised health care became the norm, the inherited wisdom of generations of nurses, midwives and mothers was at the community's disposal. It is the fate of such women to be largely anonymous: they were not listed in trade directories (unlike the doctors, many of whom rose up the social ladder into the 'county' list); they—or more probably their husbands or fathers—rarely drew attention to their skills when completing census returns.

NB '(q.v.)' after a name or place indicates that more information may be found in the A to Z Section.

The early years

It seems unlikely now that we shall ever know who was Buckden's first resident physician. Many of the bishops of Lincoln would doubtless have had skilled healers among their entourages, whose services might have been available beyond the great man's household. But they could hardly be regarded as the village doctor. To start with, therefore, is a selection of some of the few medical men known to have been associated with Buckden, albeit briefly.

John de St Giles (*fl.* **13thC**), a Dominican friar, physician and divine, was summoned to Buckden in the late summer of 1253 to attend his friend Robert Grosseteste, bishop of Lincoln, then in his final illness. He was able to offer the dying man both physical and spiritual comfort, the latter in the form of vigorous debates about the shortcomings—as the bishop saw them—of John's order. These so engaged bishop Robert's interest that he survived until October.

Mr Richard Scrafton and **Dr Monro** were London physicians who were sent to Buckden in the week beginning 4 July 1737 to try to save the life of Thomas Jackson, Town Clerk to the City of London, who was lying at death's door at the George. A large, fat man, Jackson had been travelling up the Great North Road when he had an apoplectic fit after the weight of his body bouncing up and down in the carriage burst open a recently healed wound.[1] Neither the surgeon or the doctor could save him and he died at eleven o'clock in the evening on Wednesday, 6 July. The news reached London before nine the next morning, to the delight of the many candidates waiting to put themselves forward for his job.

Lawrence Desborough, 'late of Bugden', announced in a 1754 London newspaper advertisement that he and Edward Davis of Huntingdon had entered into practice together in the 'Several Branches of Surgery, Midwifry, and Pharmacy, [and] hope for the Continuance of all our Friends Favours'. They were setting up shop in Huntingdon, but the wording of the notice suggests that Desborough may already have been practising in Buckden. A family of that name was present in the village throughout the eighteenth century, and he may be the Lawrence Desborough who was baptised in St Mary's in October 1725.

Other doctors appear briefly in the Churchwardens' Accounts (see appendix to Chapter 5). They include Dr Mackie, Surgeon and Apothecary of Huntingdon, in 1800 and Mr Benjamin Roberts, Surgeon and Apothecary of Buckden, in 1802. From about 1820, however, rather more information becomes available about the men—and it was only men for nearly the next 150 years—who ministered to the village's medical needs.

The nineteenth century

The first of these was **Henry Waller, MRCS LSA (1787-1873)**, a rarity in that he was a Huntingdonshire man, born in Hartford. His headstone in St Mary's churchyard tells us that he was 'many

---

[1] He had been paying his compliments to some ladies in a coach when they unfortunately ran over his leg.

years surgeon of this parish', but unfortunately does not say exactly how many. He was certainly here by the time of his marriage in January 1822. He is listed in trade directories for 1830 and 1839, but does not appear in the 1841 census, although this does show his wife Jane and daughter Ellen Bennett Waller living in the High Street. Jane is said to be living on independent means—a description more usually given to an unmarried woman or a widow than to a wife, and one that suggests that Henry was on a prolonged absence from home rather than simply being missed off the census by mistake (he does not, in fact, seem to have been recorded anywhere in Britain in 1841, although Waller is so frequently mis-transcribed as Walker or Walter it is impossible to be certain). Such an absence could also explain why young Dr George Woolley, Henry's partner and successor, was not living with the family as might have been expected, but lodging further down the High Street—it would have been improper for him to remain in the Waller household in the absence of the husband and father.

However, Henry was back in Buckden to witness his daughter's marriage in 1844, and seems to have remained here until at least 1854, the year in which his wife died. By 1861 he had retired and was lodging with his unmarried sisters in Chelsea; ten years later he was living in Hemingford Grey. He died of bronchitis, at the age of 85, at Northampton's General Lunatic Asylum.

His daughter's marriage was to William Fox, a Godmanchester farmer and threshing-machine contractor 20 years her elder. Despite a spell in the Isle of Wight's Royal National Hospital for Consumption, she lived to be 79, dying in 1902.

George Newnham Woolley (1815-1874) was himself the son of a surgeon. Born in Petersfield, Hampshire, he was 15 when he was baptised, together with his two sisters and his four brothers. This crowded ceremony took place not in Hampshire but at fashionable St Luke's, Chelsea, the family having by this time moved to London. The 1841 Buckden Census finds him as a newly qualified surgeon, living in the High Street (probably in Sherwood House). However this seems to have been temporary job, possibly as a locum for the absent resident surgeon, Henry Waller. Woolley spent the next few years abroad, first in Sierra Leone and then in the West Indies, where he married the Irish-born Henrietta Charlotte Blennerhasset. Their first child was born in Kensington, in 1845 (possibly at the home of Dr Woolley, senior, who had a practice in the area). The family had settled in Buckden by 1847 when their son, George John Blennerhasset Woolley, was born. They are in the censuses for both 1851 and 1861, their home and surgery almost certainly being in one of the houses between Coneygarths and York Yard—most probably **York House** (q.v.). Dr Woolley also appears in trade directories for 1852, 1854 and 1862.

At some time during 1860s, however, the Woolleys' marriage seems to have broken up. In early 1864 George resigned from his post as the medical officer for District 6 of the St Neots Union, and was replaced by 'Dr Ballard of Buckden', which suggests that George had already given up his village practice. He then moved to the large Lincolnshire village of Bardney to become one of its GPs—but he lived in lodgings run by a sailor's wife, and his family did not join him. In December 1866, there were the beginnings of a national panic when it was rumoured that the Black Death had returned to England and was raging through Bardney. George and a colleague brought the outbreak under control and reported to the medical journal *The Lancet* that it was actually epidemic cerebro-spinal meningitis. It was deeply unpleasant, as George found out to his cost, but was not about to lay waste to the kingdom.

In his last years he suffered from heart disease. He was still in Bardney when he died in 1874, and was buried there. Mrs Woolley had moved to Hunts End and stayed on there, alone, until her death in 1883 at the age of sixty-four. She shares a grave in Buckden cemetery with her daughter Charlotte Mesmey, who appears to have married a soldier and died in Sarawak—the headstone has unfortunately sunk into the ground, obscuring this part of the inscription.

One of the Woolley children followed (almost) in his father's footsteps by becoming a dentist.

Dr Woolley's successor, **William Waddell Ballard, MD(St Andrews) MRCSEng., LSALon. (1833—1888)**, was Buckden's surgeon for nearly twenty-five years, although he lived in the village for only five of them. He was born in Folkestone, and trained and practised as an apothecary (chemist and druggist). After taking his degree he worked with Sir William Jenner, one of the leading physicians of the day. Having bought George Woolley's Buckden practice early in 1864, he got married in June of the same year. His bride was Helen Baker, the daughter of a Kentish brewer. His two eldest children were born in Buckden in 1865 and 1868. Although he is listed in an 1869 Buckden directory, he was already in the process of moving his family to Huntingdon (28 High Street, now a solicitors' office), having decided, said the *Hunts County News*, that village life could not content him for long. At some point after 1876 he shared his Buckden practice with a young Scots doctor, Donald McRitchie. But apart from a brief sojourn in Buckden, McRitchie also lived in Huntingdon, only four doors along from the Ballards. Between 1871 and 1888, therefore, Buckden appears to have had no resident doctor. The disadvantages of this were demonstrated in July 1886 when Ballard was sent for to Hardwick Lane to attend a seriously ill five year old, William Carter. By the time he got there the child had died. At the inquest held the next day at the Spread Eagle, Ballard gave it as his opinion that the boy had died of heat apoplexy from lying too long in the sun—it was an exceptionally hot month.

In Huntingdon, Ballard threw himself into public affairs, becoming an alderman in 1879 and mayor in 1886; in addition he was the President of the Literary and Scientific Institution and active in both the church and politics (as a Conservative, much to the regret of the *County News*: 'but the Doctor is—alas!—none the worse for it.'). He died at fifty-five from erysipelas. Most of Buckden's leading families were represented at his funeral in St Mary's Huntingdon: the *Hunts County Guardian* reporter assiduously noted such names as Marshall, Green, Linton, Cranfield and Roxby.

He left a widow, a daughter and two sons; his eldest son appears to have started and then abandoned medical training.

Despite being only briefly resident in Buckden. **Donald McRitchie, MB, CM (Aberdeen), LRCS & LRM (Edinburgh) (1854—1926)** may well have been the village's longest-serving doctor. He was born in Inverness, the son of a chemist and druggist. Both he and his younger brother David assisted their father in his shop before going on to medical school. Apart from a spell as an assistant physician in Aberdeen, he seems to have come straight to Huntingdonshire, primarily to work at the county hospital. He shared his house in Huntingdon with his brother (who predeceased him by many years). His reputation was that of an extraordinarily kind man, known for adjusting his fee according to his patients' circumstances (a box of matches to treat a tobacconist), and often 'forgot' to charge his poorest clients. He never married. His grave is in Huntingdon's Primrose Lane Cemetery; his last request was to be buried next to his best friend.

For six years, **Frederick Thomas Good, MD, MRCSEng, LSA (c.1855-1894)** was the senior partner in the Buckden practice of Good & Hillyer—although he never lived in the village at all. The son of a chartered accountant, he was born in Edinburgh of English parents. In 1878, he bought the practice of one of St Neots leading doctors, John Jewel Evans. He lived in Evans's house until 1883, when he moved to 20 Market Square to take over another important practice, that of the hugely popular Dr Samuel Wright, who had just died. A clearly ambitious man, he was presumably unable to resist taking on the Buckden practice when Dr Ballard died in 1888—but by then he felt the need for a partner: W. H. Hillyer, who became Buckden's first resident physician for nearly 20 years.

The two doctors shared many interests outside their work. In 1890 they were both founder members of the St Neots Golf Club, and Fred Good—such a gregarious man was surely Fred to his contemporaries—was its first secretary. The club's annual dinners were entertained with recitations by Dr Hillyer and songs from Dr Good's wife, Mary (who was also a golfer). He was also president and treasurer of the St Neots Rowing Club. There was widespread shock when he died at the age of only thirty-nine in January 1894, from complications following pneumonia. Mary and her family left the market square for Cambridge Street; she outlived her husband by over thirty years.

Now in sole practice in Buckden, **William Henry Hillyer, MD(Durham), LRCP, MRCS (1863-1945)** was a canoeist, golfer, actor, cyclist, footballer, tennis player, beekeeper, balneologist, parish councillor and Buckden's doctor through most of the 1890s. He was the son of a French-born clergyman who had trained as a missionary—although by the time William was born he was the rector of Ashby in Suffolk.[1] William had first appeared in the 1890 Buckden directory as the junior partner in Good & Hillyer, based in 'St George's Place'. This is not an address you will find on today's village street map. The 1891 census shows that it was a separate household within the building that houses the George: the 'St' presumably echoes the fact that the inn had recently been known—not for the first time—as the St George & Dragon. The occupants are twenty-seven-year-old Dr Hillyer and two elderly ladies, a housekeeper and her sister. Donald McRitchie was still appearing under the Buckden entry in trade directories, but the two doctors do not seem to have ever gone into formal partnership.

W. H. Hillyer soon moved to a large rented house on Perry Road. It had only just been erected by local builders the **Page family** (q.v.), and the doctor chose to call it 'Ellerslie' after his mother's house in Balham. From here he embarked on a life of dizzying exuberance, throwing himself into almost every social and sporting event in the village, from running the Reading Rooms, acting in plays and winning prizes in flower shows to being on the village football and cricket teams (he was a cricketing all-rounder: in a typical performance playing for the bachelors in a Single v Married match in 1897, he made the highest score (37) and had a hand in the dismissal of five husbands). It is clear he did not suffer any of the usual financial hardships facing a young doctor at the start of his career. His surgery furniture included a Chippendale

---

[1] It is not clear whether this was a change of vocation, or reflects the result of concerns about the state of the church in Suffolk.

desk; and an old resident told the late Maurice Milner that the doctor did his rounds in a pony and trap driven by a servant. Further indications of his standard of living may be found in the appendix to this chapter.

His stay in Buckden was comparatively short. He left Buckden in late 1898 (possibly finding it too dangerous: within the space of a few weeks he broke his collar-bone twice: once playing football and secondly when he was out cycling and a 'stupid pedestrian' walked into him). On 17 October 1900, he boarded the *RMS Oron*[1], bound out of Liverpool for West Africa, and exchanged the comfortable life of a rural GP for the hazards of the fever-ridden Gold Coast, where he worked as a medical officer, working for various mining companies. In a report to shareholders in 1901, the chairman of one company, Attasi Mines (Limited), praised his outstanding work. In 1904, after taking a degree at Durham University and joining a practice in East Grinstead, he returned to Buckden to claim a bride: Bessie Georgiana Gatty, a relation by marriage to the Linton family. (Love seems to have bloomed while they shared the stage in the Reading Room entertainments of the 1890s.) Theirs was the Huntingdonshire wedding of the year: the list of guests and presents stretched over a column and a half in the local papers. One of the presents was the wedding ring itself, given by a grateful Attasi Mines.

The Hillyers returned to East Grinstead but eventually settled in Hilperton, Wiltshire. Among Dr Hillyer's known publications is an article for the *British Medical Journal* on a death caused by worms (written while in Buckden); he also wrote letters to *The Times*, in one of which he blamed a resurgence of bed-bugs on the new fashion for wooden bedsteads.

The twentieth century

The Buckden practice now passed into the hands of **Frederick Edgar Williams, BA Cantab, MRCSEng, LRCPLon (1863-1923)**. He became Buckden's doctor and Medical Officer of Health for nearly twenty-five years. The son of a London architect and grandson of a physician, he was educated at Cambridge and Guy's, then worked as a house surgeon in Derbyshire and for the P. & O. line (possibly as a ship's surgeon). In 1898 he married Laura Langley and after their honeymoon brought her to their new home at **Beech Lawn** (q.v.) in Silver Street. He had the telephone number 1 Buckden, grew prize-winning roses and vegetables (or at least employed a gardener who did) and played tennis. His other relaxation was a day's shooting. An early case of his, in March 1900, took him to Offord Darcy to attend a man who had tried to kill himself. His attendance was obviously successful: a few weeks later the *St Neots Advertiser* happily reported that 'Mr E---- S----- [the paper named him in full] who attempted suicide recently, is progressing favourably'! This might be regarded as somewhat intrusive today, but Victorian newspapers simply acknowledged that death and disaster were of lasting human interest and never hesitated to report them in often grim detail: their original story on this suicide attempt had told a harrowing tale of a little girl following a trail of blood through the house until she discovered her nearly expired grandfather.

One of Dr Williams's most stressful duties during the First World War was to examine local men presenting themselves for medical assessment under Lord Derby's Group System (whereby men were encouraged to volunteer for military service before they were needed. If accepted, they returned to civilian life to await call-up. During this time they wore an armband to show that they were officially ready to 'do their bit' for King and Country.)

The Buckden practice covered a wide area, so it was not surprising to find from F. E. Williams's obituary in the *Hunts Post* that 'he was one of the first medical gentlemen to recognise the usefulness of the motor cars, and he was a familiar figure in the district driving in an enclosed car, and always accompanied by a small dog.' According to one resident, the car was a De Dion Bouton.

His death in 1923 was unexpected (except to his wife and a few close colleagues) and shocked the village. His reputation was as 'a clever, painstaking and sympathetic doctor', and he had made many friends among his patients, both in his practice and at the county hospital, where he was honorary surgeon. There was a very large attendance at his funeral

His wife remained at Beech Lawn for some years after his death. They had no children.

Dr Robert Ross Sutter of Warboys acted as locum until the arrival of **Robert Allez Rotherham Wallace, MB, ChM (Sydney), LRCP, FRCS (1888-1980)**, whose time in Buckden was to prove brief but memorable. Robert Wallace had been born in Australia, the son of an English mother and a distinguished Australian soldier of Scottish descent. He was already working at the hospital in Huntingdon

---

[1] Not a mis-print for *Orion*; it was named after a port in eastern Nigeria. Built in 1898, it continued in service until 1914, when the Germans captured it.

when Dr Williams died, and was highly regarded by his colleagues. His mother was also living in Huntingdon at the time (his father had died in Melbourne in 1915).

When he moved to Buckden, he lived, like some of his predecessors, in Sherwood House, but was allowed by Mrs Williams to take over her late husband's surgery in a cottage at Beech Lawn. A resident recalled his marked Australian accent (though wrongly ascribing it to his successor, Dr Davie, a Scot). After Dr Williams and his De Dion Bouton, his patients were surprised to find their new doctor doing his rounds on horseback, but there was nothing old-fashioned about him: his favoured off-duty transport was a motorbike, ridden in a somewhat happy-go-lucky way. He claimed to be protected from accidents by 'an automatic sense of danger'; nonetheless, the bike may have lost him his fiancée.

She was called Nancy and came from Godmanchester; *The Times* announced their engagement in May 1924. Some months later, it announced that she was now engaged to an officer of the Royal Tank Corps. It's not clear why the engagement was broken off, but perhaps an incident involving the motorbike came between them. In June 1924, Robert was brought before the Huntingdon magistrates charged with driving to the danger of the public by disobeying a traffic policeman's order to stop. He seemed a bit confused about why he had done so: he thought (he said) that the officer was waving to him, not signalling. Or was it that he had been rushing to catch a shop before it closed? Anyway, what would have been the point in stopping? If the police wanted him, they all knew where to find him. The bench was amused but unconvinced and fined him £2. Nancy's family, leading lights in the Huntingdonshire legal profession, were probably not amused; perhaps doubts began to creep in ...

By the time Nancy married her soldier in 1926, Robert had left Buckden for London. Then from 1929 until his retirement in 1969 he practised in Bishop's Stortford, where he was held in the highest regard by his patients despite his habit of keeping ferrets in his surgery. In 1966 he wrote to the *British Medical Journal* to explain how he had undertaken over 15,000 successful tonsillectomies in his career (many of them carried out on the patient's own kitchen table). He refrained from mentioning that this figure included his taking out his own tonsils with the aid of a mirror! A photograph of him in late middle age shows a robust man with a mischievous face. He had a dry wit: at an inquest on one of his Buckden patients who had died from a fall, he said that the man's symptoms were consistent with concussion. Asked to explain on what he based this opinion, he replied: 'On personal experience.'

A street called Robert Wallace Close suggests that the memory of this engaging man lives on in Bishop's Stortford.

Robert Elliott Davie, MC, MB, ChB (Glasgow) (dates unknown) succeeded Robert Wallace in 1925. He had served with the 8th Battalion Scottish Rifles during the First World War, winning his Military Cross for conspicuous gallantry and devotion to duty under heavy fire while ensuring that wounded members of his patrol were able to withdraw to safety.

He is said to have started his practice from a cottage in Church Street. Church Street is certainly his address in the 1926 telephone directory, although in 1925 he too had been living and working in Sherwood House. From 1927 until he left in 1930, he rented Oak Lawn in Mill Street as his home and surgery. The surgery was very small. The consulting room contained a desk, couch, cupboard and a bench. In the dispensary there was a pestle and mortar for the grinding of medicines. He was a much-liked doctor, known for his willingness to turn out at any time of day or night to treat rich and poor alike. When he retired in January 1930, his neighbour Archdeacon Knowles said he would miss the sound of car horn and brakes as the doctor shot out of his drive on two wheels in the early hours of the morning. The archdeacon's tribute came at the annual general meeting of the Buckden and District Branch of the British Legion; Dr Davie had been a popular and respected chairman and a grateful branch presented him with the works of Rudyard Kipling.

In 1941, Gordon Fitt of Buckden, serving with the forces 'somewhere in the east', wrote to his parents to say that he was in hospital but they were not to worry because 'to his great surprise and delight' he was in the capable hands of Dr Davie. From an entry in the British Medical Journal for 21 December 1940, it appears that the doctor himself had been wounded the previous year, having re-enlisted and been posted to the Royal Army Medical Corps

After Dr Davie came **Eric James Jolly, MB, ChB (Aberdeen) (1899-1968)**, yet another of Buckden's Scottish doctors, born in Dundee, the fifth of eight children of a Customs & Excise official. He served with the Gordon Highlanders in the First World War, reaching the rank of Second Lieutenant before being gassed and wounded in France. He qualified in 1923 and four years later joined Dr Davie's practice, buying it from him in the early 1930s and remaining Buckden's doctor until his retirement in 1964. He was fondly remembered as a 'real character', a down-to-earth man who while enjoying a pint and a game of darts at the George would offer to flatten a ganglion ('Just lay your hand on the bar') or pop round to your house later to fix that wart. His surgery at Oak Lawn was less fondly remembered: 'There was no waiting room, you sat each side of this passage, it was so narrow your knees practically touched—and it was freezing cold in winter!' 'There wasn't much privacy—you could hear him through the door shouting at patients—for their own good, mind!' But he was also a kind man – 'I'd broken my leg in a motorcycle accident and the week Dr Jolly was going to sign me off the club [ie, back to work] was the week I was going to get married. When I mentioned this, he told me I was a b-----y fool not to have told him before—and gave me another week off.'

His practice took in Brampton, and on his retirement he went there to live in the Round House on High Street, which he had previously used as a consulting room. Sadly he had only another four years left in which to enjoy the fly-fishing that was his favourite past-time.

Older residents still remember his two lively and mischievous sons.

APPENDIX: THE PROPERTY OF A GENTLEMAN BACHELOR

For most of his years in practice in Buckden, Dr William Hillyer lived and had his surgery in Ellerslie, the six-bedroomed house in Perry Road subsequently renamed Nutfield. He rented the property, but equipped and furnished it himself, and when he left Buckden to work overseas, he instructed local auctioneers, Dilley and Son, to sell the contents of the house and gardens. Their advertisement of 12 November 1898 gives a fascinating glimpse of what an unmarried, well-to-do young medical man found essential to maintain his social status and professional dignity at the turn of the century:

DILLEY AND SON have received instructions from W. H. Hillyer. Esq., who is leaving, to sell by auction on Friday, November 18th, 1898, all the Valuable Antique and Modern Household FURNITURE, including a few examples in the Chippendale, Hepplewhite, Sheraton and Queen Anne Periods, and comprising elbow and occasional chairs, card table, side table, sideboard, bedside stands, chests of drawers, and dressing glasses; excellent Walnut Frame Upright Grand Pianoforte (nearly new) [by] Monington & Weston; also excellent varnished cob size cee spring dog cart [by] Strangward, (new last year), spring cart, 2 bicycles, 2 sets harness, riding saddle and bridle, carriage and horse rugs, chaff cutter with 2 knives, root pulper, grindstone and frame, 2 sets leather pony lawn shoes, long boarded manger, 4 chicken pens, 4 heaps of carrots, 4 heaps of roots, galvanized corn bin, part stack of well-got hay, 1898 (about 7 tons); Garden Effects comprising a capital lawn mower, double gear (18in.) Green, "The Sutton" lawn mower (12in.), lawn mower, double gear, Green (22in.) edging lawn mower, 2 iron garden rolls, 8 two-light garden frames, 6 garden hand lights, quantity of iron standards, 2 wheelbarrows, 6 rolls wire netting, garden water barrow on wheels with extra tank, 6 clothes posts and 4 iron sockets; Tennis Requisites, including 3 pair 'Cavendish' poles, 8 tennis nets & tennis marker; capital Cedar Canadian Canoe, 17ft. long (maker: Burgoyne, of Kingston), with mast, sail, 4 paddles, back rests, cushions and carpets, timber and galvanized iron roof boat house, and numerous other lots; also 7 capital stocks of Bees, with 8 "Cambs," "Ivo" and other hives, and other Bee appliances.

CHAPTER 15/ THE BUCKDEN ROUNDABOUT
Brenda Steadman

The story of Buckden's community magazine is told by its founding editor, Brenda Steadman. She pays tribute to the hard work her fellow volunteers put into publishing and distributing each issue, so it is appropriate here to do the same for her: no magazine can survive for long, let alone for thirty years, without a dedicated and enthusiastic editor.

The first *Buckden Roundabout* was delivered to all 886 houses in Buckden in September 1979 and has continued to be delivered each month to every household - without missing a single issue. Over the years the village has increased in size and currently some 1300 copies are printed each month, with forty of those going to the neighbouring village of Diddington.

The
Buckden Roundabout

Volume Twenty Nine   2008

To start at the very beginning, the idea of a community magazine was raised at a meeting of the Buckden Joint Churches Committee in February 1979, chaired by the vicar of St Mary's Church, Canon Stanley Griffiths. The other three churches in the parish were represented by Father James Fischer (Catholic), the Rev. Christina Le Moignan (Methodist) and the Rev. Christopher Rule (Baptist - the High Street Baptist chapel was then still in use). But it was Canon Griffiths who was the chief instigator. He felt there was a real need for a magazine in which details of all village activities could be published, and that such a publication was within the resources of the churches, provided a keen editor and editorial committee could be obtained. The proposal was unanimously carried and the following month an inaugural meeting, to which a representative of each of the four churches was invited, was held at the temporary vicarage in Perry Road to discuss the running of such a magazine.

Things then began to happen at a rapid pace. Over the next three months the committee (Janice Church, Elizabeth Baker, Joy Mackenzie and Brenda Steadman, with Stanley in the driving seat) had not only received the backing of the Parish Council but had decided on the name: *The Buckden Roundabout*. They had negotiated with a local artist to draw up a design for the cover incorporating the Buckden roundabout junction. This effective logo included a circle of hands, depicting the 'Hands of Friendship'.

From then on it was like a rollercoaster ride, with so many aspects to be taken into consideration. It was decided that the size of the magazine should be A4 and the number of sheets for each issue should be approximately five, giving ten sides for copy. The printing problem had been solved by the generous gift of a small Roneo duplicating machine, but someone to operate it still had to be found. Prospective advertisers had also to be approached to cover the cost of the coloured covers, which were to be professionally printed each month. The number of houses in each road had to be counted, and each road would need at least one willing volunteer to distribute the magazines.

The Parish Council had provided a much appreciated donation of £100. This and an anonymous cheque for £150, along with sponsorship by the four churches, provided the magazine with the purchasing power for the paper, etc. The monthly cost of producing the magazine was estimated to be approximately £30 (this figure included the covers).

A typist was found and an editor was persuaded to take on the somewhat onerous task of putting together the contributions for the first issue. Another willing volunteer had agreed to the printing taking place in their home, and an appeal was made for anyone with a bit of time on their hands to help with the collating each month. All the village organisations and clubs were notified of the new venture and were invited to advertise events such as meetings and social events. Needless to say, everything began to fall into place at quite a rapid pace.

In the weeks leading up to the launch, Canon Griffiths wrote a short message which was delivered to all households to ensure that everyone knew that a new community magazine was to be published in the first week of September, and would be delivered free to every house in Buckden. He emphasised the way it should improve communications and encourage life together as a community, and avoid unnecessary competition and clashing of dates.

The first monthly issue – which opened with an introductory message from the late Mr Jim Davie, then Chairman of Buckden Parish Council - was collated in the kitchen at Coneygarth in the High Street and took the best part of a day to complete. After this first marathon session of collating, the production party was invited by Father Fischer to carry out future collating in the refectory at the main house of the Towers. Not only was there more space, but also a welcome cup of coffee for all who helped.

With each month things became easier, though not without the occasional setback to be overcome. The village clubs and organisations made good use of the facility, and the Parish Council was able to reach everyone in the village with the items of interest discussed at the monthly meetings. But behind the scenes there were regular hiccups with the printing, and after only a few months the duplicating machine ground to a halt with the pressure of churning out 12,000 sheets a month. At these times it was necessary to turn to the school and also the scouts for help with the use of their duplicators. Another machine had to be bought, another second-hand one, which meant having to appeal again for financial help. Thankfully, sufficient money was realised and things ran smoothly for a few more years.

The venue for the printing and the collating changed again when the printer needed to be re-housed, the new home being the Methodist Schoolroom. The work continued there for a number of years, thanks to the hospitality of the Methodist Church.

However, it was still difficulties with the unpredictable duplicators which caused the team the most concern, and eventually the Parish Council came to the rescue by taking over the financial and running costs of the magazine. It also provided a new printer (as opposed to duplicator), which is serviced on a regular basis and copes admirably with the pounding it takes each month. This was like an answer to a prayer, and since that happened, things have run like clockwork.

The *Roundabout* could not function without the dedication and professionalism of the typist who always manages to fit items into each page with such skill. As indeed, did her predecessors, all five of them, over the past thirty years. The magazine's Diary of Events provides parishioners with a record of most of the village happenings over the coming month, and is compiled very proficiently by yet another volunteer. The duplicating or printing - definitely the cause of the most frustrations over the years - has been in very capable hands at all times, with several different people taking on this onerous job since 1979.

On the last Thursday of every month a group of twelve or more volunteers gathers at the Millennium Hall to put the month's magazine together, This task now takes less than two hours - a far cry from the early days when it took at least a whole morning. The final job of the monthly production is carried out by the forty people who deliver the magazine to all the houses, again on a voluntary basis.

Thirty years is not a very long history, but thanks to the dedication of an enthusiastic team of volunteers, the people of Buckden have been made aware of most of the events in the village throughout those years and hopefully will continue to do so for many years to come.

Editor's note

In the summer of 2009, Brenda Steadman announced that the September issue of the *Roundabout* would be the last to appear under her editorship. Mrs Pamela Davenport, a former parish clerk, was named as her successor.

Brenda's long service to Buckden was recognised by an invitation to a Royal Garden Party at Buckingham Palace.

CHAPTER 16/WHERE TO GET A DRINK
David Thomas

Ale and beer have been made and drunk almost as long as barley or other cereals have been grown. Among the reasons for this are that they were often safer than water from wells or streams and had pleasant side-effects, two qualities which the early residents of Buckden would have appreciated.

NB Premises in bold type also have an entry in the A to Z Section; those followed by a map reference are marked on the street plan on page [vii].

"Beer is Best"—but good drains are better

There have been many wells and water pumps in Buckden: easy access to fresh water was the main reason for a settlement being founded here and remaining in continuous occupation for at least 2500 years. Unfortunately such settlements soon become a threat to the clean water supply that first attracted them. In the absence of planned drainage systems and sewage treatment, it is all too easy for both surface and subterranean water sources to become contaminated by human and animal waste or by the run-off from even small-scale industrial processes. Mains drainage came comparatively late to Buckden, with the first sewers being laid in 1939—not the best of timings: residents recall the work still continuing in the late 1940s and 1950s, having been suspended because of the war and the subsequent shortage of labour, construction and back-fill materials.

In the previous world of earth closets and manure heaps standing directly on the soil, the small streams marked on early OS maps as "Public Drain No.1" etc. could have offered little protection against the diseases of contaminated water. But beer could: some water-borne germs were killed when the brewing mash was boiled, others by the alcohol content of the beer. Our ancestors may not have known how beer protected them from water-borne illness, but they recognized it had a disinfectant effect not present in water. (It had other pleasant effects, too.)

Small, but plentiful, beer

Village beers were often 'small beers', that is, they had a lower alcohol content than is usual today. In the home, this made beer a suitable alternative to water for invalids, women and children;[1] but it was equally suitable for farm hands of all ages and sexes labouring in the fields, since they could drink it throughout the working day, so staving off dehydration while remaining fairly sober: William Cobbett calculated that a labouring family would need almost three times as much beer a day in the harvest months as in the winter ones.[2]

An act of 1830 (the Beer Act for short, although it also covered ale and cider) allowed any householder in England who paid rates to apply for a licence to brew beer and sell it from a public house or his own property. The government hoped that making it easier for people to buy beer than spirits (especially gin) would significantly reduce public drunkenness and riotous behaviour. The new licences were therefore made cheap to buy, incurred few running costs, and unlike those issued for existing drinking premises such as inns, alehouses and eating-houses, did not come under the jurisdiction of local magistrates. Not surprisingly, within a fortnight of the act coming into force on 10 October, several thousand licences had been applied for—and a leading clergyman who had once supported the act was grumbling that everybody was drunk, and that those who weren't singing were sprawling.

Beer and Buckden

'Beerseller' or 'beer retailer' soon became a common occupation in contemporary trade directories. Buckden was no exception: the 1854 *Post Office Directory* lists sixteen people licensed to sell alcohol, of

---

[1] But not 'little children', unless they went out to work (William Cobbett, *Cottage Economy* 1820s, more than one edition).
[2] Later in the nineteenth century, the harvesters' beer was more likely to be bought-in than home-brewed or brewed on the farm. Commercial brewers such as Paine's of St Neots would keep an eye on the weather and the progress of the crops; small advertisements would then be scattered through the local papers reminding farmers to start stocking up.

whom only six identify themselves as selling from premises we would think of as 'public houses' today. The number declined as the century went on, but over the same period beers became much more potent—which would have been something to bear in mind had you embarked on a pub crawl round all the licensed premises in late Victorian Buckden. You would have needed to make fewer stops, but the end effect would have been the same!

However much you might like to, it is no longer possible to reproduce that Victorian night out (and morning after): Buckden now has only six licensed premises: two off-licences, one pub, two hotels and the village club in the community centre. But a walk round the village can still give us an idea of just how easy it was to get a drink in, say, 1881.

A beer lover's circumambulation

Until it was demolished in January 2010 the first building on your left as you entered the village from the roundabout was a cottage that had once been a public house called the **Windmill [MapRef 20]**. Although Buckden's last working **windmill [MapRef 16]** was not far away on the other side of the Great North Road, it is thought the pub itself may have stood on the site of an earlier mill (an 1839 directory lists Richard Barton of the High Street as both a beerseller and a miller). In 1881, the Windmill's landlord was Arthur Cherry, beer seller and agricultural labourer. The Windmill was a very small house, but it was not unusual for the landlord of even a quite large pub to have two (or more) jobs, and for his wife—if he was married—to be the one who sold the beer and ejected the drunks. By 1891, Mr Cherry and his family had moved across the Great North Road to a market garden, and the pub was in the hands of William White, Jnr, publican and posting-master.[1] By the turn of the century, Mr White, too, had moved: to Church Street, to become a cab proprietor (and later a domestic coachman), and the Windmill's landlord was market gardener Edgar Cook.

As you walk on up the High Street today, the next house you pass was once the home of the village policeman: possibly a mixed blessing for the licensees of the Windmill. Barely a hundred yards further on, you find yourself at the **Vine [MapRef 21].** In 1881, it may already have announced itself by the heavy aroma of malt and hops, for this was an inn which had its own brewery, as the landlord in 1881 acknowledged, describing himself as a brewer and publican. He was Robert Crisp King, a comparatively recent arrival who would still be there in twenty years time, the last nineteenth century landlord.[2] Today there is a large blank and reinforced wall facing the road, but if you go into the car park you will see the doors and windows that may show where the brewery was.

At one time, there was apparently yet another alehouse no more than a minute's walk from the Vine, standing just beyond the forge and **goosing shed [MapRef 22]**. But by 1881, its name—if it ever had one—had disappeared and instead of a drink you would have found only Miss Sarah Mason's small school for girls and Buckden's sub-post-office. Today these, too, have gone, destroyed in the twentieth century when a new, south-facing façade was added to the next, and still thriving, licensed premises, the **George Hotel [MapRef 23]**. In 1881, you would have entered the George Inn (as it was known in 1881) by an impressively canopied door giving straight on to the pavement. At this time, it was one of the tied houses owned by Huntingdon Brewery, the profits from which helped maintain the Marshall family in the comfortable surroundings of Buckden Towers on the other side of the High Street.

It was by then no longer the mighty coaching inn it had been until the arrival of the railways thirty years before, but already the increasingly popular pastime of long-distance cycling was beginning to restore its fortunes, a process which would be completed in the early twentieth century by the advent of the motor car. (Buckden was home to an AA patrol scout by 1911). Round the corner from the George was the **Old Tap [MapRef 15]** (now part of the Anne Furbank dress shop), described in 1925 as 'the rooms used by generations of post boys, the old settles, fireplaces and adjoining stables marking the scene of former activity when the call came to ride north and south post haste.'[3] It was also said to have been frequented by the ostlers and other hotel staff in their off-duty or waiting time—and the preferred drinking place of highwaymen who could listen in to find out who was staying at the George worth holding up. There seems to be no evidence that any robbery ever took place which was initiated in the Old Tap.

The stables at the back of the George have been replaced with flats, but they once showed some very clever brickwork that would still have been visible in 1881: a rounded corner, to prevent damage to building and coaches, which gradually became square as it rose to the feed storage loft.

---

[1] A posting-master kept horses and traps or other light vehicles for hire; the hirer could return them or leave them at another inn or stable in the same 'posting line'
[2] The last landlord of the *twentieth* century was Hugh Grundy, former drummer of the sixties' rock band, The Zombies
[3] Richardson and Eberlein *The English Inn Past & Present* Batsford

Across the road from the George is the **Lion [MapRef 24]** (which like the Vine, had its own brew-room, the scene of a tragic accident in 1884—see under **Ilsley** in the A to Z Section). The oldest Buckden hostelry still in use it has been variously known as the Lion and Lamb, the White Lion, the Lion and Flag, Ye Olde Lion and the Lion Brewery. The licensee in 1881 was Henry Thomson, who described himself as a publican and engineer, the latter being a trade he shared with most of the men in his family.[1] He was the second husband of the remarkable Eliza (née Puttman), who was associated with the management of the Lion for nearly forty years. She was the wife of one licensee, Joseph Ilsley; the licensee in her own right after Joseph's early death; the wife of Henry Thomson, and the mother-in-law of Henry's successor, Augustus Shelton Thackray, brewer and 'wine & spirit & hop merchant'. When in about 1902 Thackray left the Lion to manage his brother's building company in Huntingdon, Eliza went with him and turned his family home into Ilsley House, a boarding establishment for bank clerks! Even then she retained an interest in the affairs of the Lion (but not its brewery) as it was now owned by her other son-law, Alfred H. Boutell.

Crossing carefully back to the other side of the High Street—modern traffic having replaced the 1881 hazards of runaway horses, packs of speeding penny-farthings and the dung from passing dairy cattle on their way to and from milking—your next destination is the former **Spread Eagle Inn [MapRef 33]**, a comparatively long walk. On the way you will pass **Coneygarths [MapRef 27]**, now a private house, but believed to have once—long before 1881—been called the Mitre, an appropriate name for an inn so close to the bishop's palace. The Spread was a small eighteenth-century coaching inn, with a courtyard, stabling and an older cross-wing. In the inn's heyday, this wing housed the ostlers and other staff, but in later years it was occupied by a sequence of small businesses. In 1881, the landlord was William Worley, a drainer as well as a publican, and if your visit had been in January, you might have been lucky enough to find him celebrating his victory (or possibly his son's: they had the same name) in a St Neots skating championship.

Just to the north of the Spread, the Old Falcon once stood, a humbler public house than the Spread (whose ostlers may have felt more at home drinking there). It closed in the 1840s, its buildings being used as shops and cottages until replaced by the present row of 1960s housing. In 1881, therefore, you would have had a longish walk to the **Crown [MapRef 17]**, the next public house and the last on the Great North Road before it left the village. It now stands on the other side of the A1, visible as a dark red brick building only to be reached from the High Street by a pedestrian underpass. You may wish to spare yourself the journey: it too is now a private house. The landlord in 1881, Darrington Clarke, also had a secondary business as a thatcher, employing one man, Henry Hart, who 'lived in'. (A previous landlord had been a draper and master tailor.) Its situation would at first suggest it was the local for the residents of the nearby hamlet of Hardwick, but given that it stood right beside the entrance to Park Farm, the home of the man who employed most of them, they may have preferred to retire to the Spread Eagle or the **White Horse [MapRef 46]**. This latter beer-house was much easier to reach from Hardwick in 1881 than it is today: you had only to stroll across the Great North Road and down Silver Street, originally the (Hoo) Baulk, a green lane running from Park Farm to Church Street. The junction of Silver Street and Church Street was then the focus of a number of businesses and shops: a bakery, a shoe and boot maker, a corn chandler, a slaughterhouse and a dairy to name a few. Here too was the White Horse, another house owned by the Huntingdon Brewery. Beside it was a

The White Horse
Silver Street
L R Button

forge, and most of the licensees combined the roles of landlord and smith. In 1881, it was run by John Jeakins, who had taken over both forge and pub from his father; by the time he died in 1890, the Jeakinses had been at the White Horse for forty years. Both forge and pub are now closed, but there is still the ring in the forge wall to which waiting customers tied their horses. These horses were likely to have been from local farms, rather than the coach or riding horses of the gentry. The smith probably also repaired implements.

Earlier in the nineteenth century, there had been other public houses on this stretch of Church

The Black Horse   Hunts End

Street: one, the Red Lion, was opposite the end of Silver Street. The Tiger may have been next door, whether they both sold beer at the same time I do not know.[1] The Old Square and Compass is listed in an 1847 directory against the name of Daniel Mann; Mann, a jobber and victualler, lived in Church Street, as the census four years later confirms. Turn left and then right at the green called Hunts End. To the west of the green was the **Black Horse. [MapRef 36]**. Now a private house, it has been much altered and restored. But underneath the present rendering is the timber and plaster of an old ale-house. It had closed by 1881. Nearby on Mill Road was a later Falcon. It appears in the 1881 census return, but for some reason its entry has been almost obliterated, as has the word 'publican' in its occupant's job description. Possibly it had lost its licence. If so, this was only temporary, for it finally closed in 1995. Further along still there was once an alehouse called the Quart Pot, and a short step into what is now Park Road, and probably near Swan End, was the Swan. Neither are there today.

Nor were they there in 1881, leaving Victorian pub-crawlers facing a dilemma: did they now, in the interests of completion, seek their next drink a mile down Mill Road at the (Three) Mill Bills, Buckden's furthest-flung pub (landlord: William Cornish, an employee of the nearby Bowyer and Priestley Mill)?[2] The choice is perhaps easier today: the Mill Bills is no more, nor is the Anchor, another pub known to have been somewhere on Mill Road. Better, then, to go in the other direction down Church Road and turn in to Lucks Lane, at the far end of which is a thatched cottage, that still bears the name it once had as a drinking house. It is the **Bee Hive [MapRef 38]**. Although it was once also a brewery, it had become another of Huntingdon Brewery's tied houses by 1881, and customers would have been served the company beer, not home-brew, by the occupants, agricultural labourer Frederick Lymage and his family.

The Bee Hive would have been the culmination of your Victorian forerunners' quest for the best pint in Buckden: their ninth port of call tenth if they had decided to include the Mill Bills, perhaps even eleventh if they had nipped round the back of the Falcon and wheedled a discreet half-pint out of the apparently suspended licensee. They would probably have been tempted to continue along Lucks Lane to see what Stirtloe might offer.[3] You, on the other hand, should turn right out of Lucks Lane and walk up Mayfield to the High Street. You will find yourself back where you began: opposite where the Windmill pub stood, and within sight of the Vine, the George and the Lion. It is a measure of how drinking habits have changed since 1881 that for all the ground you have covered today, your pub-crawl was effectively over in the first twenty minutes in three buildings within a few yards of each other.

What were they like?

The majority of the premises I have mentioned were not at all like our modern understanding of a public house. They were indeed private houses, where the head of household had paid £4.00 for a licence and installed a barrel in the parlour or kitchen. Their patrons would often have been friends and neighbours, sitting against the walls on rough benches round a sanded or sawdusted floor, their grumbling conversations occasionally interrupted by the arrival and departure of a small child staggering under the weight of a large jug to be filled to see Father through his evening at home. Some of the licensees would have brewed their own beer, others would have been in debt to a brewer. In addition to the Marshalls' Huntingdon Brewery, other outside brewers who have owned or leased public houses in Buckden over the years include Day & Son of St Neots, Jenkins & Jones of Huntingdon, Charles Wells of Bedford, and Greene, King & Sons of Bury St Edmunds. There were also two brewing families within the village, the Wallers and the Bowyers, the latter also millers and maltsters (i.e., they controlled the brewing process from grain to barrel).[4]

The small family beer-houses—and there are still more whose whereabouts remain a mystery: where *were* the Saracen's Head and the Hand Bells?—probably did very well when there was a public holiday, and particularly during the annual feast weeks in July. One of the Huntingdon papers near the end of the nineteenth century reported that the week at Buckden had passed off quietly, the inference being that at in some years there was a little too much liveliness—as happened in July 1900 when one well-known village character entertained a feast week crowd by taking off all his clothes 'except his shoes and stockings'!

Works consulted include

Osborne, Keith *The Brewers of Cromwell's County*, 1999

---

[1] Perhaps they were the same place, having to be re-named after an incompetent itinerant sign-painter did his worst. Such things happened.

[2] Mill bills were the tools used for dressing millstones.

[3] Nothing. The hamlet was 'dry'.

[4] Since July 2009, Buckden has, for the first time in many years, a commercial brewery within its parish boundary. The Draycott Brewery is based in Mill Road, at Low Farm **[MapRef 41]**, and produces Buckden Bronze Bitter, a CAMRA-accredited real ale in a bottle.

CHAPTER 17/FRIENDLY INVASIONS

Alan Cockburn, Robert Curtis, William Medhurst, Ken Odell, Alec Owen, Pat Paterson, Harold Randall, David Rhodes

The first invasion started even before war – the Second World War – was declared; the invaders swept in on a wave of double-decker buses. The second began three years later, its preferred transport being heavy trucks with their steering-wheels on the wrong side. This chapter describes the effect of wartime Buckden on two very different sets of newcomers: London lads and American soldiers.

Evacuation

Defence planners accepted from the early 1920s that major population centres would be bombed in any future war. At first, their overriding objective was to persuade people to behave as normally as possible, i.e. to continue living in, and going out to work from, their own homes.[1] As the 1930s progressed, however, it became clear that public morale would be better served by allowing the voluntary mass evacuation of the most vulnerable groups: children, expectant mothers and the blind. Given Huntingdonshire's good rail links to London, it is no surprise to learn that long before war was declared on 3 September 1939 discussions were underway on how the county should prepare to house, care for and, where necessary, educate evacuees.

Among those scheduled to come to the area were pupils from three schools in Tollington in North London. One of these was Tollington School, a boys' private secondary. Some of its staff and pupils were destined to spend the next two and a half years in Buckden.

'I think we'll send this lot to Buckden.'

'Destined' is perhaps not quite the right word. It suggests a rather more precise forward allocation system than was actually the case. One group of Tollington boys set out from Muswell Hill on 15 September 1939, with no idea of idea where they were going to sleep that night. For all they knew, their destination could have been the edge of London or the Scottish Highlands. One of them, David Rhodes, later wrote about why they ended up where they did:

'The train stopped at St Neots, and after being led through the latrines and given our provisions, we were packed into Eastern National buses and driven off towards the town. [...] While we were waiting on St Neots platform, I happened to hear a man—obviously one of the directors of proceedings—call out, "I think we'll send this lot to Buckden." Quite a chance remark, but what weight it carried.

'I'll have this one.'

'I remember the first impression I received of the place when, from the top of the bus, I suddenly caught sight of the church and The Towers nestling among the trees. Immediately the vision of an ancient castle floated through my mind, as I expect it did through that of many others who were not engaged at the time in playing poker. But I was given no time to dwell on this subject, for the bus drew up outside the Rifle Range and we all trooped inside. What a miserable place it was—a long, narrow room with straw piled at one end (for makeshift beds, I suppose), and smelling of nothing but dust and disuse.

'About sixteen of us lined up outside the Range, and a benevolent looking gentleman with a portly lady in attendance pointed at me and said, "I'll have this one." I realised then for the first time how cattle feel at the market, but war is war, and I was ushered away. By nightfall, we were all in different billets, scattered about the village, and were already settling down in our new homes.'

...and a large friendly dog.

The similarity to a cattle market also occurred to Alan Cockburn: 'Gently herded into the Rifle Range,

---

[1] 'Persuasion' ranged from advice on how to protect your home against bomb blast or splinters, or decontaminate your family after a gas attack, to ringing London with 100,000 troops to dissuade people from 'running away'.

really the village hall, in Church Street, we were looked over by our prospective foster-mothers, themselves supervised by efficient-looking ladies in smart WVS uniform...

'I happened to be sporting a heavy turban-like bandage covering a head-wound sustained in a playground accident the day before [...] I persuaded myself that it was the sinister-looking bandage that caused me to be the last of all to be fostered, not unreasonable considering we had arrived in a rural community, where in livestock markets damaged animals would hardly attract a buyer. An evacuee, moreover, might after all be harbouring some awful complaint like ringworm!'

He was eventually claimed by Mrs Dudley, a young mother from Monks Cottages, where he shared a room and bed with an older fellow-pupil and the rest of the small house with three adults, two infants and a large friendly dog. Although he felt perfectly at home, the billeting officers moved him on after a few days to less crowded premises.

Alec Owen remembers Buckden as a friendly place, although his first billeting got off to a bad start: 'Dick Ashby and I wound up with a family called Osborne much to Mrs O's surprise and disgust—she had expected two cute seven-year-old girls to keep her daughter company. This lady was somewhat annoyed with me because I drank the can of milk in the box of supplies which I was supposed to hand over to whomever we were to be billeted with.'[1] He, too, was soon moved on, in his case to live with the Linton family at Stirtloe House.

He had been one of the first evacuees, arriving in Buckden on Friday, 1 September. The following Sunday morning he was having an after-chapel drink from the Church Street pump when Mrs Osborne's little girl brought him the news that war had been declared.

Settling in

David Rhodes remembers that for the first few days all was confusion while the school was re-assembled. A few boys billeted at outlying farms were brought into the village, as were some of the upper school who had accidentally been sent to Abbotsley. David spent most of his time scrumping, but more formal activities were soon started up, among them compulsory walks and supervised swimming. But there were no lessons for the fortnight or so it took to complete the conversion of The Towers into suitable teaching premises.[2]

Alan Cockburn's new foster parents were John and Kate Smith of Montague House, almost opposite the village school: 'John's interests were varied; besides being a churchwarden he had a busy joinery and building business next door to Montague House, doing much work on restoration in churches. He was also undertaker, corn merchant, coal merchant and insurance agent. Jack Peacock, his clerk, kept a close eye on

"Montague House"

proceedings from the little office building near the entrance to the joinery workshop. John and Kate were a wonderfully kind and welcoming couple, tolerant and understanding of the ways of energetic boys of twelve or so, and much more like grandparents than surrogate parents.'

Alec Owen had no time to feel homesick: 'I was just too busy with my new environment.'

Then the classrooms in The Towers were ready and the long summer holiday was over.

Schooling

David Rhodes: 'I think everyone will agree that we were extremely lucky to get hold of such a suitable place for a school. When we had settled down and lessons were running smoothly, other evacuated schools were still only getting part-time education, or sitting, sixty in a class, in draughty barns. Whatever anyone may say about the disadvantages of The Towers, it would have been difficult to have found a better school under the circumstances. It was right in the centre of the village and

---

[1] According to the school's historian, Raymond Cave, the village had apparently been led to expect mothers and babies.

[2] At this time, The Towers was owned by Robert Holmes Edelston (who lived elsewhere). His solicitors complained to the County Council that 'unbeknown to our client' a school had taken up residence on his property. They received a dusty reply along the lines of ' Don't you know there's a war on?'   (Raymond Cave)

there was ample room for all the classes. The time-table was rather elastic at first, but by the end of October we were carrying on quite normally. The library and reference library were brought down and housed in specially made shelves.' He noted that despite all the upheaval and the late start, the school's exam results were, in the end, very good.

Alan Cockburn: 'The classroom that my form, IIIb, used at the start of each school day, like others was furnished with splintery benches and long deal trestle tables, their surfaces soon to be covered with inky doodles and loaded with ramparts of books which provided slight shelter from the gaze of the master in charge. In our room a defunct cooking range, a relic of the house's palmier days, occupied a recess in the wall behind Mr Huxley, biology teacher and our form master.'

Alec Owen: 'It was a squash! When the dentist came, Dr Draper was turned out of his study.'

Dr Draper

Schoolmaster's son F. W. M. Draper (1882-1968), was the headmaster of Tollington Boys School from 1922 to 1944. As a new pupil, Alec Owen had found him 'very distant. He was a scholar and had many degrees from German and French Universities as I recall. He was old-fashioned and eschewed the use of a radio, although he would listen to Winston [Churchill]'s speeches. Definitely not the hands-on kind of headmaster one is used to nowadays. He took snuff and would do so while supervising a class while some master was absent. I respected him and was a little afraid of him.'

To Alan Cockburn, too, he was 'an august, much respected figure'; but his abiding memory of his headmaster was of a robust sixty-year-old on the Diddington cricket ground, fielding at first slip in his Cambridge college cap, alert, hands at the ready for a catch, and still a good bat and off-break bowler.

Dr Draper was a Londoner through and through, born and brought up in Hackney, but he was sensitive to the hardships that could result from the sudden descent of two hundred strangers on a small rural community. In particular, he thought that the official allowance paid for an evacuee, 8s. 6d. a week, was grossly insufficient for someone having to feed and house a growing boy. He accordingly invited the boys' parents to contribute an extra five shillings a week 'to which they instantly and willingly agreed'—a reminder that the school came from the affluent suburb of Muswell Hill.[1]

Sherwood House

This large High Street house, on the corner of York Yard, had been a hotel before the war. For much of the evacuation period, it was occupied by Dr Draper, his wife Ellen Maud, a shifting population of boys and, wrote David Rhodes, 'its matron, Miss Pinkney, who rose at half past five every morning [in] summer to get breakfasts for farm workers, and it was she who had our dinners ready for us when we came home famished at night.'[2] Both he and Alan Cockburn were billeted there for a time, a mixed blessing to judge by David's ironic eulogy: 'Sherwood House! Romantic name! Enchanting mansion! When Mr Churchill has become but a memory and Hitler has been entirely forgotten, the name of Sherwood House will still remain in our minds. How could we possibly forget it? When we are middle-aged business men [...] we shall recall the big and little washes, and the squeaky pump, and the rickety billiard table, and prep, and the colony of rabbits, and the ultra-modern latrine.' It should, he proposed, be transported back to Tollington 'brick by mouldering brick' and re-erected on the school field.

Sherwood House. The white building behind was Geering's cafe in 1940.

Its inmates were fed from the school allotment, an enterprise that had amused the locals at first but in time became quite productive, not least because 'digging for victory' on the allotment replaced lines and detention as the punishment for minor breaches of school discipline.

---

[1] The Government apparently forbade the practice of supplementing the official allowance in this way, but the British don't always do what their governments tell them, even in war-time.

[2] The 'farm workers' were boys who spent their summer holidays in Buckden helping with the harvest—see below.

R and R

Alan Cockburn: 'The school was fortunate in having access to plenty of ground with short grass where we could play games. The Vineyards, a field beyond Monks Cottages, had one reasonably flat area suitable for a football pitch. Goal posts were erected, and in the lighter evenings the pitch became a favoured meeting place for anyone keen for a kickabout. Crowds of Tollington boys from the sixth form downwards, village boys and young men, numbering twenty or more on each side, would surge to and fro in friendly rivalry, owing allegiance only to the ephemeral team one happened to join for the occasion.' (Petrol shortages meant that formal matches could only rarely be played against other schools.)

'The Marathon, our rather grandly named annual cross country race, took place in the spring term over three and a bit miles down the road from Monks Cottages to Offord Mill Bridge, then south through fields to a track leading to Stirtloe and thence to the finish in the Vineyards.'

The evacuees also enjoyed winter sports, such as tobogganing, snowballing, ice-hockey (known as the 'free fight on the ice') and in 1940 a whole month of skating on the lakes in The Towers and the Valley. In the summer there was athletics, climaxing with an annual sports day held at The Towers during Feast Week, and twice a week there was cricket on the Buckden pitch in Lucks Lane ('the finest in Huntingdonshire', according to the late Maurice Milner)—until it was set aside for hay, after which matches moved to Squire Thornhill's Diddington ground. David Rhodes remembers that for practice sessions there were nets and a matting wicket at The Towers: 'the cowslip-bespangled ridges and hollows of this pitch were rather a contrast to the smooth turf of our field in London, "mais c'est la guerre".'

What with team sports, swimming in the Ouse, cycling round the countryside, a makeshift gymnasium in the Rifle Range and, for some, a weekly cup of senna tea, the boys had no excuse for not keeping fit and regular. But there was another form of exercise available, too, one which was good for them and the nation, one for which they were even paid.

To be a farmer's boy

David Rhodes realised that from the local farmers' point of view, Tollington was quite useful: 'We helped gather in the harvest. Labour was scarce, since many agricultural workers had been called up, and there was more work than ever to do. We began almost as soon as we came down here by picking beans (the money for which was rather a long time in arriving) but the real work began in the following June. Until then I believe that most of us had not realised that the peas we ate in London grew in long lines in fields, but we soon found that out. Although we picked extremely slowly at first and were amazed the speed of the local women, we soon grew more proficient in this art and by the second year most of us were old hands.

'The corn was cut in August and, although a good number of us went home for the full seven weeks, many stayed behind for at least part of the time to give the farmers a hand. If we ever became countrified, this was the time. Wielding pitchforks on the tops of swaying stacks, using the most atrocious language, wading through liquid dung, careering about the country in tractors (when they decided to start)—our own mothers wouldn't have recognised us. Ah! Those were the days, when we were able to sit in Geering's(café) with our pockets overflowing with money and lose a shilling without noticing it.[1]

'We were doing a valuable job of work, perhaps more valuable than we thought at the time. Even as it was, crops had to lie rotting in the fields because there was no one to cut them and carry them in. But not only were we serving the national interest, we were serving ourselves as well. Farm-work certainly did none of us any harm and did most of us much good. Furthermore a period of physical labour between two periods of mental labour was most refreshing.'

William Medhurst: 'A number of fifth and sixth form boys were introduced to that sturdy old machine, the Fordson tractor. We had lessons on driving and maintenance on the road side grass in Lucks Lane and when considered proficient enough were made available to local farmers for harvest work, though we were not much good at ploughing.'

Some Buckden people

One of the pleasures of the Tollington reminiscences is the numerous glimpses they give us of the people of Buckden. Alan Cockburn, in particular, has left a vivid and affectionate portrait of life with the Smith family, unfortunately too long to quote in full:

'John and Kate's cheery and energetic widowed daughter, Peggy Rogers, lived with them. She had single-handedly cultivated a half-acre of potatoes in the 1914-18 war, and now kept a poultry farm. Their eldest son, Martin, had served as an officer on the Western Front, and now farmed between Buckden and

---

[1] Poker, again? Geering's was a sweet shop and café, next door to Sherwood House.

Offord, while their second son, Ken, was in the tuberculosis hospital at Papworth Everard, where he had been for some long time.

'John picked the yellow eating apples when ripe from the tree in the back garden and stored them on racks in the cellar. Each night before bedtime he would bring a few to the table to go with a hot drink. Although the house had electricity, the supply was limited to three wall sockets, so oil lamps provided most of the illumination; and candles lit us to bed soon after the nine o'clock news on the wireless. Sometimes we tuned in to Lord Haw Haw, whose broadcasts, announced with the words "Jarmony calling, Jarmony calling!" in his unique and rather nasal tones, provoked a good deal of derision and total disbelief.

'Bath night took place at the weekend; the bath, plumbed for drainage, but without taps, stood in one corner of a big, almost empty room upstairs. A hand pump in the kitchen was the source of all our water, which we carried upstairs in buckets to the bathroom, where from a glass case in a far corner a large malevolent pike kept a baleful eye on proceedings, while from another a somewhat startled stuffed otter looked ready to plunge into the artificial waters at its feet. A gloomy oil painting of Stirtloe Park made up the rest of the furnishings.[1]

'On the night of 14 November 1940, the household, quite unusually, retired to a cupboard below the staircase. For most of the night we could hear German aircraft flying to and from some distant target. The next day we learned that Coventry had been all but destroyed.'

Making friends

In 1940, Ken Smith returned to Buckden from Papworth, still in need of nursing attention but well enough to cope with light tasks in the workshop. Two of the evacuees moved to another billet to make a bedroom available for him. Alan Cockburn, staying on, came to enjoy his company and to admire his craftsmanship. They disagreed on one thing, however: Alan, the Londoner, had come to much prefer the ways of the country; Ken, country born and bred, hankered after the city life. Sadly, his chance never came. He died in the late summer of 1943, aged 29.

Evacuee Robert Curtis also knew what it was to lose a Buckden friend. Peter Robinson was the son of the owner of Robinson's Garages and taught him to drive. Both young men held a provisional licence ('permission to go mad on the King's highways in all manner of powerful machinery'). This was a precious document because provided the war was still on, one could eventually convert it into a full licence *without having to pass the official driving test*. Robert achieved this when he was demobbed in 1947, but Peter never got the chance. He had been killed in France in 1944, a year after joining up.

Alec Owen did not make close friends with village boys of his own age: 'The Buckden kids would try to tease us. They implied that we boys thought milk came from *bottles* and not from cows. I don't think I ever rose to the bait. I never made friends with any of the local kids for some reason, probably because there were so many Tollington boys my age at school. I remember some of the Offord boys wanted to fight us (me and my little brother) but they were too big so we ran away and hurled insults at them from a safe distance.'

He did, however, have friends among the adults: 'The former village blacksmith, Mr Middleton, was a close friend of mine as was his pony Tom, who bit my behind one day as I was brushing him. Mr Middleton allowed me to help him when he took his pony and cart on the various excursions. In that way I helped an old gentleman (whose name I regretfully forget) move his apples from his orchards to various places in the village. Some of the apples never reached their destination but were gratefully received by school chums we passed on the journey. Mr Middleton's daughter Violet who lived on the High Street opposite the forge had been a nurse or nursing assistant at The Towers during the First World War when it was a convalescent home for wounded servicemen. My friendship with Mr Middleton also assisted me in getting a job as a beater when Squire Thornhill of Diddington held a pheasant shoot. I think the Squire gave me 5s. which was a princely sum for a working-class kid. I think it was the first coin I ever really earned.

'I remember Mr Frost (blind basket maker) and of course all the Stirtloe people, including the gypsies who camped down from the spinney near the house, especially the gypsy boy of my age who patiently tried to teach me to tickle trout. They roamed the country in brightly painted wagons and made clothes pegs out of hazel sticks.

'I am desperately trying to remember the name of the man who lived in the next house to the Osbornes and whose stinky pond I fell in while hunting newts in his osier bed. I wonder; do they still cut osiers?[2] Is

---

[1] Boys billeted in households without any form of bath were put on a rota for the bathroom (there was only one) at The Towers.

[2] No, sadly.

that little candy shop (Alec emigrated to Canada) still there on the south side of Church Street?[1] I was a constant customer for the little old lady who lived in the back and never seemed to have any other customers.[2]

"The little candy shop"

'Was it Miss *Cherry* in the Post Office who was Mr *Plum*'s girlfriend or was it the other way around? I remember now. Plum was the man I bought rabbits from.'[3]

Alan Cockburn: 'In the Buckden of the war years, unlike in a London suburb where one knew only a few neighbours to speak to, everyone seemed to know everyone else, so it was quite usual for Kate to stop to exchange a few words with anyone we met: Major Duberly, his wife Lady Eileen, and Mrs Duberly, his mother, who had come to stay; Mrs North, who played the church organ on Sundays and kept innumerable pets; Captain Amers, retired and always immaculately turned out, formerly a well-known leader of a north-country band, who lived in Silver Street, but soon to move to Ottery St Mary [in Devon], even further from the scene of his successes ...[4]

'Among the local shops I particularly remember Milner's grocery store in Church Street. Mr Milner and his friendly son, Walter, always courteous and helpful, even to uncouth schoolboys, were generally behind the counter. More rarely, I visited Hinsby's and the bakery on the corner of Church Street and Silver Street. Bowtell's was a much bigger grocery in the High Street, next door to the Post Office.

'A coterie of local bigwigs—Linton, Thornhill and others—used to shoot at the rooks in the grounds of the school. Despicable, I thought and hardly sporting, not much of a challenge. There was a fairly large rookery in the walnut trees adjacent to our football pitch. Can one eat rooks?'[5]

Shooting perched birds was clearly a preoccupation of the Buckden gentry. Alec Owen had been billeted in Stirtloe House, and returning there many years later, was instantly reminded of the behaviour of one of his wartime hosts: 'Captain Henry Linton used to like to hang out of the window in the servants' hall and shoot sparrows in the Wellingtonia on the lawn.' He was glad to see the great tree had survived. Captain Linton, however, had not. Alec refrained from asking if he had fallen out of the window.

'Stop that, you *horrid* little boy!'

Alan Cockburn was impressed (and amused) by the hauteur of another Linton on the end of a gun—in her case, the wrong end. Louise Linton Maude-Roxby was the Captain's sister and the widow of a distinguished First World War soldier. One day a light field gun and its crew arrived on the Hunts End green: 'They seemed to be on a goodwill mission for they positively welcomed close inspection of their equipment. Mrs Maude-Roxby, tall, well-dressed and dignified, was standing no more than a few inches from the end of the gun barrel talking quietly to the young officer in charge, when she was visibly startled by a loud hoot in her ear, issuing from the muzzle of the gun, but emanating from an urchin peering up the open breech. Her next action made the tableau complete. Laying an elegant grey-gloved hand on the muzzle, she called angrily down the barrel to the source of her fright and annoyance, "Stop that, you *horrid* little boy. You should be ashamed of yourself." It would have been so much easier to admonish him with an imperious word and glare over the gun shield. But then the delightful piquancy of the scene would have been lost ...'

---

[1] Sadly, no.

[2] Miss Florence Wallis, a wheelwright's daughter. She began her working life as a schoolteacher. Her niece Elsie married Austin Mason, one of the Tollington masters, in 1942.

[3] He raised them on the palace battlements. Alan Cockburn also kept rabbits (more conventionally housed). They were not, of course, pets. A boy has to eat.

[4] For more about Captain Amers, see his A to Z entry.

[5] Yes! Rook pie is an old English stand-by, traditionally served with gooseberry jelly and seemingly always made from six rooks. Wartime shortages rekindled interest in it, the rooks being used to eke out the occasional ration of steak. More recently, it has appeared on the menu of a fashionable London restaurant.

A saintly man

Harold Randall had particular cause to remember one Buckden resident above all the rest: John White, parish organist and choirmaster. A musical lad, Harold joined the St Mary's choir and also received Mr White's permission to try playing the church organ. His first attempt was so dire that the vicar sent post-haste to the church to find out if vandals had broken in. Despite this inauspicious start, Mr White volunteered to teach Harold, who for the rest of his time in Buckden had a lesson every Wednesday afternoon and practised every Saturday morning before a not always appreciative audience of ladies who came to dust, polish and arrange flowers. At the final evensong before the school returned to London, Harold accompanied the last hymn and played the closing voluntary. Kindly John White had seen and nurtured his potential, and enabled him to give a lifetime's service as a church organist.

'I suppose,' he wrote, 'Mr White must have died in Buckden years ago. I hope one day to find his resting place and pay my homage to a real Christian gentleman [...] He was a saintly man.'

A time of change

Ken Odell was billeted briefly with Mr and Mrs Osborne in the High Street, opposite the Vine public house: 'The house opened directly on to a narrow pavement on what was then still the Great North Road. War-time traffic thundered through the village at all hours of the day and night. I could have reached out of my bedroom window and touched those lorries as they ground their way towards London.'

For Alan Cockburn, living half-a-mile from the High Street, Buckden was a quieter place: 'The streets carried little motor traffic. John Smith's new Bedford lorry was requisitioned soon after war broke out. Jim Park, farmer, always drove his maroon Triumph saloon at a sedate five or six mph to conserve petrol. Allen Cope continued to transport livestock in his large purpose-built van.

'Horse-drawn traffic continued as usual. A sewage cart, essential as the village lacked sewers, would occasionally come by. A milk float from Mann's Farm called daily on its round. Farm carts were always moving about on some business or other. But in the autumn a long convoy, perhaps fifteen or twenty of them, each one loaded with sugar beet or some other root crop, and each accompanied by a carter, was seen passing the village school and stocking factory in the direction of Offord.[1] One of the carters was Violet Brace, our near neighbour from the row of three or four cottages called Hunts End. Violet lived there with Mrs Brace, active and sociable despite having lost the lower part of one leg, and their neighbours, Mrs Newman and her pretty blonde daughter. Violet dressed sensibly for her calling, always in a jacket, knee breeches, woollen stockings and boots, much in the style, if not the colours, of the Land Army girls—young women I did not meet until the summer of 1942, when tractor driving for the War Agricultural Committee.

'The larger farms, like Park's and Mailer's, may have had twenty or more shire horses for the various tasks on the farm, but I supposed that convoys of so many carts probably belonged to more than one farmer, and the loads were perhaps destined for onward transport from Offord Station. These carts, all of the same well-tried design, were ideally suited for the many jobs on the farm, particularly in muddy fields, where the much larger wagons would be difficult to pull. Quite unaware at the time, we were witnessing the decline of the old ways of farming, and with them the imminent disappearances of the crafts of wheelwright and blacksmith, and the last of one of the proudest sights of the year, the walking of Chivers' great dappled grey shire stallion, by its groom, round the roads, visiting the farms to serve the mares.'

Au revoir to Buckden

By 1942, school numbers had declined. The yearly exodus of fifth and sixth formers had never been matched by an intake of juniors. So, despite the war entering its darkest period, it was decided the school should return to London in the summer. Just as the original evacuation had been voluntary, so equally was repatriation. London was still being bombed, and at their parents' request forty-three of the boys stayed on in Buckden in the care of Austin and Elsie Mason.

David Rhodes, writing in the 1942 school magazine, felt that: 'With everything taken into consideration, I think we have benefited greatly by the evacuation. Country has come to understand town, and town has come to understand country. We have broadened our minds, considerably, and from a physical point of view the country has done us a tremendous amount of good.'

Alan Cockburn recalled little of the evacuation *from* Buckden, other than catching the London train at Offord and Buckden Station—a change from cycling the sixty-odd miles home, as he had sometimes done at the beginning and end of the school holidays. But he, too, was in no doubt that the boys had profited immeasurably from their experience of country life, not least because so many of Buckden's householders

---

[1] For more about the stocking factory, see its A to Z entry.

had readily and without question accepted their task of housing and caring for the crowd of young strangers who suddenly descended on them.

This did not mark the end of Tollington's association with Buckden and the Huntingdonshire countryside. Some boys returned to farm work camps in the summer holidays, one summer boarding in The Towers, and the next in a disused wooden army encampment at Brampton. In addition, many of the evacuees have visited Buckden over the last 65 years, individually or in groups. The last official reunion took place in September 2009.

Death in a wood

It would be a mistake to think that Buckden's only experience of the physical horrors of war was indirect or secondhand: news reports of the bombing of cities, the nightmares that woke a husband or son or daughter home on leave or drove a young airman to flee a dance in the Rifle Range to beat his head against a wall in rage and grief for friends lost over Germany. The reality was to hand for those who nursed or visited the wounded in evacuation hospitals, and for those who worked in the fire and rescue services.

One of the volunteers for Buckden's Auxiliary Fire Service (AFS) was sixteen-year-old Robert Curtis, a Tollington evacuee who had decided to stay on in the village. He was looking for ways to enliven his boring life as a contractor's time clerk at Graveley airfield: part of the attraction of the AFS was the chance of sharing night duty with a young female volunteer.

Many of the first incidents the AFS attended were hayrick fires, most of them out in the open countryside where no water was available, except down by the river. A fire in a farmyard might be nearer a water-supply, but was no less terrifying for that: the heat from a group of burning ricks was, in Robert's own words, 'incredible; twenty yards away it was like standing in front of your own personal crematorium— and it could easily turn into just that.'

Inevitably, however, with the USAAF as well as the RAF flying out of local airfields, the Buckden volunteers knew they would have to face a call-out to their first aircraft crash. They listened to the stories of planes returning from sorties critically short of fuel or with controls damaged and crew members wounded or dying. Some came down within sight of their home runway, unable to clear the last belt of trees; others made it back only to crash on landing.

The call came in the autumn of 1942. The reality, for Robert Curtis, was much, much worse than he could have imagined:

'Our first plane had smashed through the trees of a small wood at Diddington. We had our school cricket ground there, a very pretty rural setting. There was nothing pretty about the crash site. The plane had smashed through the trees along a hundred yard path, leaving a smoking trail of splintered branches, blackened, stunted tree trunks and bits of broken wings behind it. The tall tail told us immediately it was, had been, a Flying Fortress, and on its approach to Alconbury. Impossible to imagine this dismembered, smoking, reeking debris as one of those elegant, high-tailed birds we had so often watched above our village, taking off and climbing east to join a hundred others on another daylight mission. This returning pilot had evidently fought his plane clear of the houses, his runway in sight, but couldn't lift it past Diddington wood. Another couple of miles—another minute—and any of the ten crew still living might have been saved. But, as soon as we had the fires damped down, it was only too dreadfully clear they had all had it, and most gruesomely.

'As I saw the tattered, bloody rags through the ripped apart fuselage, I could not help dropping the fire hose from my grasp. The pilot and forward crew had not stood a chance: smouldering tree trunks were embedded in the crumpled fuselage from the cockpit to the waist gunners, their mutilated bodies all welded together with smoking wood, shattered Perspex and metal framing in a grisly embrace of death. We stood, a shocked and silent huddle, choking on the hot, smoky air, that acrid, yet sweet, smell of burnt insulation— Tufnol, it was called...

'Once the fires were out and the spilt fuel washed away, we were finished. If fire did break out again at least it would cleanse this terrible scene before the rescue crews arrived from the base. Thank god it was their job and not ours to clear away the mess.'

Buckden girls can jitterbug now...

Picture Post was a pioneering and hugely successful British weekly news magazine which ran from 1938 to 1957. It was famous for its striking use of photography and its mix of hard and soft stories. The issue of 22 September 1945 is typical. A report on a war crimes trial is accompanied by shockingly brutal illustrations of concentration camp survivors, while a few pages away is the following example of another, gentler strand, celebrating the essential decency of everyday life in town and country – in this case, Buckden.

TWO AMERICAN SOLDIERS SAY GOOD-BYE

A year and a half ago there were 2,000,000 Americans in England.
All but 150,000 have gone, and many English homes have lost a foster-son.

NEARLY two-and-a-half years ago the first American trucks, as we've learned to call them, rumbled through sleepy English village streets, hell-bent on bringing materials and men to supplement construction gangs working at top speed on airfields, army camps and Nissen hut hospitals. In the evenings, the locals began to overflow with hefty, khaki-clad fellows, whom most of us immediately mistook for officers on account of their brass buttons and "fruit salad." It took us quite a time to realise that "fruit salad" is the irreverent G.I. term for campaign ribbons and even longer to realise that "G.I." (Government Issue) covers every article, individual, routine and suggestion that emanates from the American Army. Yes, we were in for a liberal education, both of ideas and vocabulary. The Yanks were here—and when we had recovered our breath following a hearty back-slap from over-sized Texans and a "Hiya Butch" from Bronxian drugstore cowboys, we had to learn to understand and finally to enjoy this invasion by thousands of gay, brash young crusaders, bent on liberating Europe in the shortest possible time.

This is the story of two of these New World crusaders, medical corps soldiers at a military hospital in East Anglia, who have made lasting friendships with the English people in the neighbouring village of Buckden. Since they have become an integral part of the community, it is almost as if the sons and brothers of the English families were leaving, now the time has come for farewells.

T/4 (Technician 4th Grade) Norman Van Horne of Saco, Maine. and Pfc. Albert Tetrault of New Bedford, Mass, have been stationed at the hospital for two-and-a-half years now.

"This village looked pretty good to me." said Van Horne recalling his first visit. 'Al and I took off the first free evening we had and walked until we hit the nearest town. Buckden didn't look much like my idea of a town, but somehow I never got much further. I'd just come down from Iceland and when I first saw the trees in Buckden, I wanted to climb right up one of my own and stay there !"

Tetrault immediately took his new buddy in to meet Mr. and Mrs. King, the landlords of the Vine, where he had already made friends with the little daughter, "Tiger". The first thing I noticed about England was the warm beer—and I didn't like it" explained Tetrault. "I guess all the boys complain about that. But at the Vine the beer is really cold—and the welcome is warm !"

The Kings' younger daughter, Beverly, was christened after Tetrault's own baby daughter. He "sweated out" the arrival of Beverly II with the anxious father, and attended the christening ceremony. 'Van and Al both call us Mum and Pop," said Mrs. Peacock. "And do you know that on Mother's Day they brought me a beautiful flowering plant. They had to tell me what Mother's Day was—I'd never heard of it." "The look on her face just slayed me," grinned Van Horne.

You never saw a Yank who wasn't surrounded by little English kids—and in Buckden they're remembered for many more things than the traditional "gum chum." Small boys are eager to become good pitchers and a few cherish a secret ambition to get with the Brooklyn Dodgers instead of "playing for England." The G.I.s bring bats, balls and catchers' mitts from their athletic stores and take their coaching job very seriously.

Another person who will miss them is Mrs. Atkinson, the wife of the Vicar of Buckden. She is an active member of the W.V.S. and takes groups of volunteers to work up at the hospital.

"I have worked on the wards with both Van Home and Tetrault," said Mrs. Atkinson. "Nothing is too much for them to do for a patient. If we've been able to give them and their friends anything in the way of home life and family affection in our village, they've certainly given us gaiety while our own boys have been away."

There is scarcely a phase of village life in which these two and their buddies have not taken part. Every week they go to the dances in the village hall. Buckden girls can jitterbug now.

They go to the village charity fetes, and help with cocoanut shies. They have attended church services, though there is no record of their ever having taken a Sunday school class ! Van Horne even has the temerity to challenge the local darts team, and holds his own pretty well.

"I carry my own darts," he said, pulling them out of his pocket and exhibiting them with pride. "But it's real hard to beat Pop Peacock or Mr. Bull here—they're experts. Whoever loses the game buys the drinks—I've never got good enough yet to get all my beer for free in one night !"

Tetrault commented upon their early embarrassment at accepting the hospitality of the English, because of the rationing difficulties. "However, I've eaten two Christmas dinners with Mr. and Mrs. King," he told us. "They would have been really hurt if we hadn't accepted."

And now, after two-and-a-half years, this phase of life has drawn to a close for Van Horne, Tetrault and countless others. Not only in Buckden, but all over England, in a thousand English towns and villages, the Yanks are going home. And, as each American says good-bye, kissing his English "mum," and tweaking the ear as he hands out the last bit of gum to his adopted kid brother or sister, he mutters, being rather inarticulate, "Well, thanks a lot, folks." And the family replies "You're welcome !"

PAT PATERSON

The author was almost certainly Valerie 'Pat' Paterson (c. 1911-1997), an English freelance journalist, raised in Canada. After the war she moved to the USA and became a respected editor and accomplished photographer. She married Frederick G. Vosburgh, a future editor of the *National Geographic* magazine.

Seven photographs illustrated this article, taken by Francis Reiss; unfortunately he was not on the magazine's staff at the time, and they cannot be reproduced. Among them are pictures of Mr and Mrs Charles Peacock, 'Tiger' King, and the two GIs in Church Street, handing out gum to a group of boys.

This chapter has been edited, primarily by Robin Gibson, from the recollections of Alan Cockburn, Robert Curtis, William Medhurst, Ken Odell, Alec Owen, Harold Randall and David Rhodes, and from research by Raymond Cave.

Old Tollingtonians have lodged some 30,000 words of reminiscence with Buckden Local History Society, which hopes to publish them in book form; whether it does or not, it will ensure the material is placed in the Huntingdonshire Archives.

CHAPTER18/BUCKDEN IN THE TURNPIKE ERA
Peter Ibbett

The Great North Road through Buckden and the road from Buckden to Brampton and Huntingdon, are so 'ruinous and bad' that the highway authorities can no longer cope with repairs. The solution? To share costs through a private finance initiative – by setting up a turnpike trust.- well, this is 1725!

Buckden was a thriving coaching stop on a main route from London to Edinburgh during the Turnpike Era. Inns such as the George and the Spread Eagle would have been a hive of activity twenty-four hours a day as men, women, children, coachmen, guards and horses all required refreshment on their journeys north, south, east and west.

The main coaching age lasted little more than a century. A young Buckden boy in the 1720s would have seen the change from a trickle of coaches to a constant stream of humanity passing by the crumbling walls of the Towers. His son would have assumed that the hustle and bustle of the coach traffic would last for generations to come; yet his own son could have lived to hear the first steam train whistle and to witness the return of Buckden to the relative peace and quiet that his grandfather had known.

Historical Background

In 1555, the maintenance of roads in England was made the responsibility of the parishes through which they passed. Over the next hundred years, this came to be an impossible burden on parishes crossed by major highways – of which Buckden on the Great North Road was one. As wheeled traffic became increasingly frequent (and physically heavier), roads deteriorated faster than local resources could repair them. In 1663, Parliament reluctantly agreed to the temporary introduction of turnpikes or toll-gates: barriers where fees could be levied on travellers and used to supplement parish maintenance efforts. Responsibility for administering the few (six) roads turnpiked over the next forty years was given to county surveyors reporting to local justices of the peace.

In 1706, however, a new system was adopted: turnpikes controlled by trusts set up through private Acts of Parliament. A trust not only collected tolls, but could raise money via loans and private investment and could pay a good rate of interest on savings invested with them. A large number of trustees would be listed in an act, but few of them would be involved in its actual running.[1] The rest, chosen from the most trusted sections of society (such as MPs, peers and lawyers), were there to inspire investor confidence. Which they did: the number of turnpiked roads increased rapidly. One hundred and forty-one new turnpike acts were passed between 1706 and 1750, and no less than 389 between 1751 and 1772 (a period known as the Turnpike Mania, foreshadowing the similar Railway Mania of the 1840s). By 1837, there were 1116 trusts controlling around 22,000 miles of British road (18% of the estimated total) with at least 7000 gates at which tolls were taken. The Railway Era destroyed their profitability; the last trust folded in Anglesey in 1895. (Hey, 1998; Albert, 1972)

The Turnpike Road through Buckden

The road through Buckden was turnpiked in 1725 as part of the Biggleswade to Alconbury Turnpike Trust. A branch of this road ran to Huntingdon via Brampton providing a second road in the parish which was administered by the Trust.

The King's Highway on which Buckden stood was certainly in need of attention. In 1724 Daniel Defoe was moved to remark that the road between Hatfield House and Buckden was a 'most frightful way'. Along one stretch, travellers and even coaches turned off it on to private land to avoid the 'sloughs and holes, which no horse could wade through'. (Defoe, 2007)

---

[1] Extracts from the act setting up the turnpike road through Buckden are in an Appendix to this chapter. They include the names of over ninety trustees, listed in strict social order; to conduct the trust's business only seven of them needed to be present!

The Turnpike Era helped to cut the journey from London to Edinburgh from ten days in 1754 to a mere four in 1776. It also helped to stimulate business at local inns, including those at Buckden. The Turnpike Trust improved conditions for travellers, as the Hon. J. Byng noted in his Bedfordshire Tour in 1794: *'[This road] betwixt Biggleswade and Buckden [...] As a road of fine gravel it is unequalled [...] a road of unusual populousness, fertility - and pleasing views. Ten villages, or hamlets, are passed through in 16 miles!! [...] at every mile a good public house may be enter'd in case of storms, or hunger [...] The George at Buckden is also excellent.'*[1] (quoted in Houfe, 1990)

The map on the right (detail from Hinch/11/103; Huntingdonshire Archives) shows the route of the Biggleswade to Alconbury turnpike road through Buckden c. 1853. It shows the branches to Huntingdon and through the Offords, as well as the two toll-gates in the area. The main route covers 23 miles 3 furlongs 3 perches and 9 yards. The distance of the Buckden to Huntingdon branch is given as 3 miles 3 furlongs 20 perches and 0 yards.

Coaching at Buckden

The 1830 Pigot's Trade Directory states that there are 'almost hourly coaches through Buckden'. Mrs Rosa Young, (*St Neots History Society Newsletter* 69) in her research on Huntingdon Stagecoaches, uncovered information about coaches at Buckden from the Robson's Directory of 1839:

BOSTON MAIL calls at *Spread Eagle* and *George* ¼ before 12 noon, returns 2pm

LEEDS ROCKINGHAM calls at the *George* at 1 in the morning, returns 12 at night.

LEEDS UNION calls at the *Spread Eagle* at ½ past nine, returns at 1 in the morning.

LINCOLN MAIL calls at the *George* at 12 at night, returns at 2 in the morning.

YORK EXPRESS calls at the *George* at ½ past 3 am, returns at 3 in the afternoon.

YORK HIGHFLYER calls at the *Spread Eagle* at ¼ past 8, returns ¼ before 5.

'In addition coaches from the North pass through Buckden almost hourly.'

Mrs Young also notes that the London to Glasgow ROYAL MAIL; London to York ROYAL EXPRESS; London to Barton on Humber ROYAL MAIL; London to Barton on Humber 'EXPRESS'; London to Boston 'PERSEVERANCE' & 'EXPRESS'; London to Lincoln 'EXPRESS' and the London to Stamford 'REAGENT' were coaches that passed through Buckden.

The improvement of roads and trade provided work for local carriers to move goods in the area. The 1847 Kelly's Directory records local Buckden carriers as Henry Creamer (Huntingdon Wednesday/Saturday; St Neots Thursday) and John Riseley (St Ives Monday; St Neots Thursday & Huntingdon Saturday).

Toll-gates and milestones

The original edition of the OS map of the Buckden area (1834-35) shows no toll-gates in the parish of Buckden. The nearest are at Southoe, together with the 58 milestone, and at the top of Paxton Hill by the Toseland road. It would seem that going to St Neots involved paying a toll but a trip to Huntingdon did not. The 60 milestone is marked near to the Stirtloe turn and the 61 near to where Silver Street joined the A1. In the present day, there is no milestone near the Stirtloe turn, but there is one on the A1 just south of Silver Street. Its distance figure starts with a 6, but the second numeral is no longer legible. It may in fact be the

---

[1] Byng would have noted these improvements with particular satisfaction: his uncle, Pattee Byng, had been one of the founding trustees of the Biggleswade-Alconbury turnpike.

original 60 marker, given that the 62 milestone can be seen at the entrance to the waste disposal site on the Brampton road, just outside the Buckden boundary.

Records exist of the tolls paid at Southoe which give an idea of the rise and decline of the turnpike era. In 1725 the Southoe gate raised £154 15s. 7d. in tolls. By 1750 it rose to £383 15s. 7d., increasing to £517 8s. 9d. by 1769. The Hinchingbrooke map above dates from the decline of the coaching era. The Southoe tolls in 1849 were £360; in 1850 £304; in 1851 £204 and in 1852 only £180. (In contrast the Paxton gate was £170 in 1849 and £154 5s. 6d. in 1852).

The Buckden trustees

Among the ninety or so appointees to the Biggleswade to Alconbury trust are some familiar Buckden names. In some cases, this may be a coincidence, but the following inhabitants of the parish and surrounding villages may well be the persons named in the Act; if nothing else, they are from the right social background!

Robert Bell, Esq. (died and buried in Buckden, 1757)

Dr George Reynolds (lawyer-clergyman of the Stirtloe/Little Paxton Reynolds family)

George Thornhill, Esq. (of Diddington)

John Williams, Gent. (died and buried in Buckden, 1739)

William Windress, Esq. (died and buried in Buckden, 1737)

Compiled by Peter Ibbett, with grateful acknowledgements to the Huntingdon Record Office (as it was: now the Huntingdonshire Archives) and its helpful staff, and Mrs Rosa Young and the St Neots History Society and their excellent newsletter.

Sources for this chapter

Albert, William, *The Turnpike Road System in England: 1663 – 1840* (Cambridge: CUP, 1972)

Defoe, Daniel, *A Tour through the whole island of Great Britain* (London: Folio Society, 2007)

Hey, David (Editor), *The Oxford Companion to Local and Family History* (Oxford: OUP, 1998)

Houfe, Simon (Editor), *Through Visitors' Eyes: A Bedfordshire Anthology* (Dunstable: The Book Castle, 1990)

THE ACT

Anno Regni
GEORGII
REGIS

Magnæ Britanniæ, Franciæ, & Hiberniæ,
UNDECIMO.

At the Parliament Begun and Holden at *Weſtminſter*,
the Ninth Day of *October, Anno Dom.* 1722.
In the Ninth Year of the Reign of our Sovereign
Lord *GEORGE*, by the Grace of God, of
Great Britain, France, and *Ireland*, King, Defender
of the Faith, *&c.*

And from thence Continued by ſeveral Prorogations to the Twelfth
Day of *November*, 1724. Being the Third Seſſion of this preſent
Parliament.

G.   R.

DIEU ET   MONDROIT

LONDON,
Printed by *John Baſkett*, Printer to the King's moſt
Excellent Majeſty, And by the Aſſigns of *Henry
Hills*, deceas'd. 1725.

(371)

Anno Undecimo
Georgii Regis.

An Act for Repairing and Amending the Road from *Biggleswade* in the County of *Bedford*, to *Bugden*, and through *Alconberry*, to the Top of *Alconberry-Hill*, or Cross Post leading into *Sautery-Lane*, on the *York* and *Edinburgh* Road, and from the said Town of *Bugden* to the Town of *Huntingdon*, and from *Cross-Hall* in *Eaton Sokon* in the said County of *Bedford*, to *Great-Stoughton-Common* in the said County of *Huntingdon*.

Hereas the ancient Road from a *Preamble.* Town called Biggleswade in the County of Bedford, to Bugden, and by Brampton-Willows, through Alconberry, to the Top of Alconberry-Hill, or Cross Posts leading into Sautery-Lane, on the York and Edinburgh Road, and from the said Town of Bugden, to the Town of Huntingdon in the County of Huntingdon, is in many Parts thereof become so ruinous and bad, that the same cannot, by the ordinary Course appointed by the Laws and Statutes of this Realm, be sufficiently repaired and amended : Wherefore, and to the Intent the said Highway or Road may, with all convenient Speed, be effectually amended, and hereafter kept in good and sufficient Repair, so as that all Persons may travel through the same with Safety; May it please Your Majesty that it may be Enacted, and be it Enacted by the King's most Excellent Majesty, by and with the Advice and Consent of the Lords Spiritual and Temporal,

B   Aaaaa 2   and

The Act specifies a branch from 'Bugden' to Huntingdon

372   Anno Regni undecimo Georgii Regis.

and Commons, in this present Parliament assembled, and by the Authority of the same, That for the better surveying, ordering, repairing, and keeping in Repair the said Highway or Road, it shall be in the Power of William Lord Marquis of Hartington, Son and Heir Apparent of his Grace the Duke of Devonshire, John Earl Fitzwilliams in the Kingdom of Ireland, John Lord Tyrconnel in the Kingdom of Ireland, Henry Lord Morpeth, Son and Heir Apparent to the Earl of Carlisle, the Honourable Pattee Byng, the Honourable George Mordaunt, the Honourable Edward Wortley Montague, the Honourable Charles Bertie, the Honourable Charles Leigh, Esquires, Sir Rowland Alstone, Sir John Bernard, Sir Baldwyn Conyers, Sir George Downing, Sir William Dudley, Sir Gilbert Pickering, Baronets, Sir Nathaniel Gould, Sir Gilbert Heathcote, Sir Edward Lawrence, Sir Samuel Ongley, Sir William Smith, Knights, Robert Apreece, Henry Ashley, William Astell, Thomas Armstrong, William Aspinn, Nicholas Bonfoy, Thomas Bacon, John Bigg, Robert Bell, William Beecher, Thomas Brown Owin, Thomas Bromsall, George Blundall, Stephen Basely, Edward Cater, John Cater, Richard Cockaine, John Chetwood, Anthony Duncomb, John Danvers, Richard Drury, Richard Edwards of Halsy, George Edwards, John Farrer, William Fuller, William Farrer, Dennis Farrer, Humphry Fish senior, Humphry Fish junior, Charles Green, Thomas Handasyde, Roger Handasyde, George Hewitt, Richard Hillersden, George Huxley, Charnock Heron, Heylock Kingsley, Weyman Lee, Edward Leeds, Ralph Lane, Humphry Monux, James Metcalf, Francis Nalour, Colonel Francis Oldfield, Richard Orlebar, John Orlebar, Samuel Ongley, Robert Pigott, John Proby, Robert Pullegne, Joshua Palmer, Thomas Rolt, George Reynolds, Castle Sherrerd, George Thornhill, Carrier Thompson, James Torkington, William Thompson, Bromsall Throgmorton, John Whetham, John Williams, William Windress, Esquires, Clifford Handasyde, William Fullwood, Doctors of Physick, Richard Hatley, James Lovesey, and William Scarborough, Gentlemen, the Mayor and the Three senior Aldermen of Huntingdon for the time being, who are hereby nominated and appointed Trustees for putting this Act in Execution, and the Survivors of them; and that they, or any Seven or more of them, or such Person or Persons, as they, or any Seven or more of them, shall authorize and appoint, shall and may erect or cause to be erected a Gate or Gates, Turnpike or Turnpikes, in or cross any Part or Parts of the said Highway or Road, and shall receive and take the Tolls and Duties following, before any Horse, Cattle, Coach, Chariot, Chaise, or Calash, Waggon, Cart, or other Carriage whatsoever shall be permitted to pass

B   through

Trustees appointed:

They may erect Turnpikes.

The Act appoints the Trustees

206

Anno Regni undecimo Georgii Regis. 373

through the same, (videlicet) for every Coach, Chariot, *The several Tolls.*
Chaise, or Calash, drawn by Four or Six Horses, or more,
the Sum of One Shilling, and for every Coach, Chariot,
Chaise, or Calash, drawn by One, Two, or Three Horses, the
Sum of Six Pence, for every Waggon, Cart, or Carriage,
drawn by Four, Five, Six, or more Horses, the Sum of
One Shilling, and drawn by One, Two, or Three Horses
only, the Sum of Six Pence, for every Horse, Mule, or
Ass, laden or unladen (and not drawing) the Sum of One
Peny, for every Drove of Oxen or Neat Cattle, the Sum
of One Shilling and Three Pence per Score, and so in
proportion for every greater or lesser Number, for every
Drove of Calves, Hogs, Sheep, or Lambs, the Sum of
Five Pence per Score, and so in proportion for any greater
or lesser Number; which said respective Sum and Sums of
Money shall be demanded and taken in the Name of, and
as a Toll or Duty, and the Money so to be raised, as afore-
said, is and shall hereby be vested in the said Trustees, and *Toll vested in the Trustees.*
the same, and every Part thereof, shall be paid, applied,
disposed of, or assigned, to and for the several Uses, In-
tents, and Purposes, and in such Manner as is herein after mentioned and declared (the reasonable Charges expended, or to be expended, in, or about, or by reason of
passing this Act of Parliament, being first deducted;) and
they the said Trustees, or any Seven or more of them, are
hereby impowered, by themselves, or any Person or Persons by them, or any Seven or more of them, under their
Hands and Seals, thereunto authorized, to levy the Toll
or Duty hereby required to be paid, upon all and every
such Person and Persons, who shall (after Demand thereof made) neglect or refuse to pay the same, as aforesaid, by
Distress and Sale of any Horse or Horses, or other Cattle *Distress for Nonpayment.*
or Goods, upon which such Toll or Duty is by this Act im-
posed, or upon any other of the Goods and Chattels of such
Person or Persons, who ought to pay the same, and may
detain and keep the same until such Toll or Duty, with the
reasonable Charges of such Distress and Sale, shall be
paid; and it shall and may be lawful, to and for such Person or Persons so distraining, after the Space of Three
Days next after such Distress made and taken, to sell
the Goods so taken and distrained, returning the Overplus
(if any there be) upon Demand, to the Owner thereof,
after such Toll Duty, and reasonable Charges for distraining and keeping the same, shall be deducted and paid.

And be it further Enacted by the Authority aforesaid,
That if any Person or Persons whatsoever, owning, rent-
ing, or occupying any Land near unto any Turnpike to be
erected in pursuance of this Act, shall, for Gain, Reward,

Bbbb or

The Act also specifies the tolls to be charged.

CHAPTER 19/BUCKDEN AND THE RAILWAYS
Robin Gibson, with an afterword by Anne Spreckley

Livestock, fruit and vicars; a most unusual milk run, and a soldier from the wars returning: in a world now lost, the railways brought Buckden to the world and the world to Buckden.

Sad to say, but Buckden has never had its own railway station. Certainly there was one called Buckden but it was actually just in the parish of Brampton. There was also an Offord and Buckden station on the Great Northern Railway, but that was entirely in the parish of Offord. The line serving Buckden station was the Kettering, Thrapston and Huntingdon Railway, which was worked by the Midland Railway Company (latterly the London, Midland and Scottish Railway (1923-1947), and finally the Midland Region of British Railways). This did run through Buckden parish for about 1½ miles altogether, nearly all of it single track. The only other length of track in the parish - less than a hundred yards of siding - was in the yard of the Offord and Buckden Mill. This carried goods wagons drawn by horses.

Having been pedantic about the geography, it must be said that the railways were very useful to Buckden and would be yet if the stations were still open. From Buckden, the journey to Cambridge via Huntingdon, St Ives, the new town of Northstowe and the Science Park would take about 45 minutes, but that is a lost dream. If there were still a station called Offord and Buckden, the best journey time to Kings Cross would be about 50 minutes; unfortunately, it closed in 1962.[1]

Offord and Buckden Station

The station was opened in 1850, and extensively remodelled in May 1898 to accommodate an extra up-line. Making room for the new platform required the demolition of a footbridge and several buildings, including the booking office and the stationmaster's house. The residents of Buckden and The Offords petitioned the Great Northern Railway directors to take advantage of the remodelling to replace the level crossing with a traffic bridge, though they did so without much hope of success: presumably they recognised the difficulties created problems presented by the river on the west side and the houses of Station Lane on the east. According to a sarcastic aside in the *St. Neots Advertiser*, however, there was a strong possibility of a bridge being built, 'which will be good news to the inhabitants of both these important cities.'

The bridge was not built, but arguments in favour of it were revived just over a hundred years later. In 2000, a proposal for the commercial development of Alconbury Airfield aroused fears that increasingly heavy rail and road traffic would combine to cause intolerable delays at the Offord level crossing. Buckden and other parish councils argued that a traffic bridge was the only solution. Again, no bridge was built, this time because the development stalled.

Offord and Buckden was an ill-fated station for some. On the afternoon of 10 February 1853, a goods train collided head-on with a train of ballast trucks emerging from the Bowyer Brick siding south of the station. John Rigby, the goods driver, was trapped under his engine, so severely injured he was at first thought to be dead. He was dragged free by the driver and stoker of the ballast train, who had jumped clear before the crash. A pilot-engine eventually took him, not as one might expect to a hospital, but back to his home in Peterborough.

(The Offord stationmaster at the time was the newly appointed Mr Edmund Cooter, 26. In June he was moved to Hornsey station. On the 31 August, Hornsey was the scene of a not-dissimilar but far graver collision that injured many. Mr Cooter found himself accused of having caused the accident by waving a coal-train into the path of an express. He was exonerated by the subsequent inquiry: it found that Great Northern, whose safety record was poor, had failed to train him properly. His career was not harmed, and he remained with the company until he retired.)

At two a.m. on 30 September 1862, Buckden's surgeon, John Newnham Woolley, was called out to the scene of a frightful accident. The engine of a coal-train approaching the station on the up-line had been

---

[1] In the mid-1850s, the best scheduled journey time from Offord to Kings Cross was two hours thirty minutes. A non-stop special, such as the royal train, could do it in under 75 minutes.

derailed when it struck a large fly-wheel that had fallen from an earlier train carrying agricultural machinery. The engine ploughed into the wooden platform before somersaulting down an embankment. The driver and his fireman, both young men, were thrown out and crushed under the wreckage of one of the coal trucks. Both were dead by the time Dr Woolley reached them, the driver killed instantly, the less fortunate fireman lingering in agony for an hour.

Another fatality occurred on 7 September 1869, when a child of nine years, Charles Stuart Champion, was killed by a train; the details are recorded on a memorial in St Mary's church, where he is buried. In February 1930, a motorcyclist was killed on the level crossing by an express train. He was Billy Stoneham, 24, member of a well-known Buckden family.

A happier event occurred in 1902, when Private Robert Swales, a career soldier in the Bedfordshire Regiment, returned home after thirty months' service in the South African War. He was met at the station by 'a large assemblage of friends', the Buckden Brass Band, and a carriage and pair sent by Sir Arthur Marshall of Buckden Towers. His friends unharnessed the horses and accompanied by the band drew him by hand up to the Towers, where he was welcomed by Sir Arthur before being taken on to his home in Perry Road and into the expectant bosoms of his wife Mary [Wagstaff], four children and father-in-law. By this time they'd probably decided he'd missed the train.

Offord and Buckden was once widely known as the 'anglers halt', because of the many excellent fishing spots visible from the train and within walking distance of the station. It's nice to think that if Queen Victoria was looking in the right direction as the royal train bore her swiftly homewards through Offord at 4.31 p.m. on 14 October 1854, she would have glimpsed some of her subjects enjoying their own humble version of the pastime that she and dear Albert had so enjoyed during their holiday at Balmoral.[1]

Buckden Station

The Buckden station on the Brampton Road and the east-west line was opened in 1866, halfway to Brampton. It was called Brampton at the start. One suspects that if Lady Sparrow, the owner of Brampton Park, had not had her say, the line would have run further north and would have been more useful to Brampton than it was, and far less convenient to the residents of Buckden. However, Buckden it became, and it was equipped with a shunting loop, a siding, a signal-box, goods shed and cattle dock, as well as its passenger platform, the usual offices and a stationmaster's house. Thus a service for both goods and passengers could be offered down to 1959, when the line closed.

Although a passenger service was provided, it was not designed for commuters to anywhere. In 1950, the first weekday train to Cambridge left at 9.33 a.m. and arrived in that city at 10.15 a.m., early enough for a gentleman and his lady but not for the wearer of a blue or white collar. The last return trip was at 4.55 p.m. arriving in Buckden at 5.43 p.m. Such timings did suit the vicar, the Reverend Hart (1950-52), who would put his bicycle on the train and go to Cambridge to buy communion wine and bread. This gentleman was a collector of railway timetables, which were reputed to fill at least a dozen feet of shelving in the vicarage. The service of three or four passenger trains a day each way was typical during the line's life. There was an occasional seaside excursion special which called at the station, and others which passed through. Percy Pepper recalled booking trains for annual excursions by members of the Methodist chapel and their friends. (Percy knew both stations well: at Offord and Buckden he would collect the newspapers off the train from London at 7.00 a.m., and deliver them to the shop and Post Office, which at that time was adjacent to the George Hotel.)

The handling of goods was the most important part of the work of the Buckden station staff, especially when, unlike today livestock rearing was a major part of farming. Stan Smith, who took charge at Buckden in 1936 as a special-grade porter, recalled in a radio interview that eight to ten trains came daily. It is believed that half of these were pick-up goods trains, which would deliver or pick up wagons as necessary. Stan would be responsible for handling loads of hay and straw, and three or four loads a week of sheep from Scotland and cattle from, say, Leominster in Herefordshire. An informant recalls driving two bullocks to the station every Monday to catch the train for St Ives market. Another remembers consignments of hares and rabbits being despatched by train to Leicester market. Yet another has spoken of osiers and fruit being sent off.

While researching his 2001 book on the service provided at Kimbolton on the same Midland Railway line, John Slack found that a wide range of products was handled. Buckden's may have been narrower, but is likely to have included items not mentioned by Stan in his radio interview, such as guano, artificial fertilizer, cattle feeds, building materials and horse manure.[2] As regards coal, Messrs Hinsby and F. W. Smith each brought their coal supplies from the Offord station, but that is not to say that it was not also handled at Buckden. Suitable wagons can be seen in photographs in John Slack's book, and in an 1883

---

[1] Fishing, that is.
[2] Back in the nineteenth and early twentieth centuries, some horse manure had been, as it were, home-grown: the station yard was a favoured meeting place for the local hunt.

advertisement in the national press, Messrs Phillips and Lamont's Direct Supply Agency listed Buckden as one of the stations where they had arranged with 'respectable local hauliers' to deliver 'fresh wrought coals of every kind and quality' into consumers' cellars at very reasonable terms. Passing goods traffic included lengthy trains of fruit heading westwards; not all fruit in the Fens went to Chivers!

Buckden station entered the Second World War with Stan Smith now promoted to stationmaster, following the retirement of his supervisor at Grafham. He was assisted by porters Ted Lymage and Ernie Gibson. The war saw traffic through Buckden augmented by deliveries for the US Evacuation Hospital at Diddington of prefabricated hutting, with its accompanying construction personnel. Although Buckden was the nearest station, the ambulance trains delivered their casualties to Huntingdon East for unloading. Stan remembered train-loads of petrol arriving for the depot. If there were enemy aircraft about, the train drivers would stop their engines under the adjacent road bridge to hide the light from the firebox.

By 2006, the only relic of the Midland Railway remaining in the parish was the cutting that lies to the west of the A1. Although no trace of the station itself survives, the signal box - or at least its top - is now in the safe hands of the Spa Valley Railway, having been erected on a new base at their Tunbridge Wells West station (it was moved there via at least one museum). They hope one day to have it back in working order. Stan lived at the station after the line's closure and used the box as his greenhouse.

Afterword by Anne Spreckley

Mr Smith and Ted

We lived across a field from the station, and I recall that it was staffed by the stationmaster, Mr Smith, and the porter Ted (Lymage). Mr Smith epitomised all that a local stationmaster should be and I have often thought that perhaps the Reverend W. Awdry[1] had used Mr Smith as his model. He was ruddy-cheeked and had a kind twinkle in his eye for everybody, although his bearing was quite authoritative due to his portliness. Ted was the chief and only porter and the general factotum on the station, although I don't think that he was allowed to sell tickets or speak out of turn.

The station was moderately busy. At weekends in particular, many service personnel from RAF Brampton used the line, these being the days before every family and teenager had a car. During the week and depending on the season, trees, saplings and horticultural goods were loaded into the guard's van (by Teddy the porter, of course). This business came from Laxton and Bunyard, nurserymen of Brampton, the forerunners of Bickerdikes (now Frosts). The Laxton connection was to the famous nursery in Bedford, the developers of the eponymous Superb apple.

Special Delivery

One of the special services rendered by British Rail and executed by Mr Smith was the daily transportation of small quantities of mother's milk to the premature babies unit at Mill Road Maternity Hospital, Cambridge. I had left my tiny twin babies there and each day I walked across the field to the station to make sure that the precious liquid was on the 3.00 p.m. to Cambridge City Station. If I was running late Mr Smith came across the field to meet me. The bottle was given to the train guard, who had strict instructions to hand it only to a hospital porter who would be on the platform.

A very rare and unusual service given free of charge by British Railways!

Sources for this chapter

Bazley, J. H. R., *Great Northern Railway Guide to Angling Resorts* (Leeds: Chorley & Pickersgill, 1909)

Mitchell, Vic (and others), *Branch Lines around Huntingdon: Kettering to Cambridge* (Midhurst: Middleton Press, 1991) ISBN 0 9065 20 93 2

Slack, John, *The Arrival of the Midland Railway at Kimbolton, Cambridgeshire in 1866* (Ashbourne: Landmark Publishing, 2001) ISBN 1 84306 051 5

Wrottesley, John, *The Great Northern Railway* (London: Batsford, 1979) ISBN 0 7134 1592 4

Interview on BBC radio with Stan Smith, 1984

Percy Pepper's recollections, courtesy of Mr & Mrs Brian Smith

The Times August 22 1898

See also the A to Z Section under the **Great Buckden Hay Robbery**, and **railway mania**. The latter describes the consequences – good and bad – that the coming of the railways had for nineteenth-century Buckden and twenty-first century local historians.

---

[1] Creator of the *Railway Series* books about Thomas the Tank Engine and his friends.

CHAPTER 20/MEDIEVAL BUCKDEN: THREE GLIMPSES
Barry Jobling, David Thomas

Buckden is fortunate in having a set of parish registers that began four hundred and fifty years ago. There are missing and damaged pages and other omissions from the first hundred years, but the information that remains is invaluable to those researching almost any aspect of the village's history—not least in tracing the changing fortunes of individual families and in the constant movement of people in and out of the village, leaving or arriving to look for work, getting married, or taking advantage of improvements in transport.

Such research is much harder in the centuries preceding the registers, but there are some sources for the lives and occupations of earlier residents. Church historian Barry Jobling gives us a glimpse of both familiar and unfamiliar names from 1485, and David Thomas introduces us to some Buckden taxpayers from an even earlier time.

Buckden inhabitants in the fifteenth century....

From the accounts of the Parish Reeve, John Clerk, we have a list of the local men who repaired the Buckden water mill in 1485. This list of early parishioners includes a few names still present in the village today. The reeve records:

Steven Wive, Wm Brawne, John Wright, Wm Herby, Will Bacon, John Maddox, William Spalding (filling up the well), John Bylby, Bernard Here, Thomas Haynes, Edmond Blys, Wm Spanby, John Serle, Wm Fox and Thomas Parys (for making of the mill wheel, cogs and spindles).

...and in the fourteenth century

Buckden is fortunate enough to have two lists of taxpayers (technically subsidy rolls) dating from the fourteenth century. Moreover, as the two lists are five years apart, 1327 and 1332, many of the same names occur in both—or seem to occur: spelling was not standardized at the time (or for a very long time afterwards), so that what appears to be a repeated name may in fact be two different names. Conversely, what appear to be different names may in fact be the same one. In addition, clerks are human: ignorance or a wandering mind mean that mistakes have almost certainly occurred when the lists were copied.

The taxpayers were almost all male: a woman at that time could own property only as a widow, or very occasionally as a single woman who was able to make a living in her own right.

First names

The forenames on the lists are almost all in use today: the woman's name Amicia is perhaps the one that has least established itself as an indigenous choice. For men, John was by far the most popular name: there are twenty-five. Other given names represented more than once are William, Godfrey, Walter, Robert, Hugh and Nicholas. All the rest have one each.

Surnames

Because some names were so common it was necessary to distinguish between people of the same first name by some additional descriptive name; by the fourteenth century surnames were well developed. Some surnames tell us where villagers, or their ancestors, came from. The first surname on both lists is Gunild or Gyunyld, and another name on both lists is Gonild, almost certainly representing two individuals with the same surname. It comes from a female given name, the Viking Gunhildr. So for possibly three or four hundred years there had been a family with the name carried down on the female side until John or one of his male predecessors was named after his widowed mother, or single mother. It is still in use today as Gunnell, as in Sally Gunnell[1] whose family lived in St Ives. It is unlikely that she was descended from the

---

[1] Motivational speaker and former Olympic and world gold medallist (400 metres).

Buckden families, but just within the bounds of possibility. John Gynwell, bishop of Lincoln 1347–62, is mentioned elsewhere as a threatened martyr. His name possibly has the same root as the various Gunilds.

Occupational names

Other surnames derive from occupations. The first is le Hunte, pronounced Hunter in German. One of the main pastimes of the elite was hunting, and the bishops of Lincoln had a large enclosed deer park in Buckden. The hunter might make sure there were suitable deer to hunt when the bishop and other noble visitors came. He must have been good at his job to own such valuable moveable goods (maybe he was tipped well after a good day's hunting). There is also a John Perker, or Parker, in the lists: the parker was in charge of ensuring that the deer park was well stocked and maintained. Was John the parker who drove the king's deer from Weybridge and Sapley wood into the bishop's enclosure in 1354?

The second name on the lists is le Cok – the Cook, who probably managed the kitchen of the bishop's hall. This was a respected calling: the earls of Leicester, whose seat is at Holkham in Norfolk, have the surname Coke. Le Cok of Buckden had a useful taxable income.

There are two Mil(n)ewards (mill wards) in the lists. William (John) le Mileward in 1327 becomes William (John) Milneward in 1332 (Miller, Millward, Milner today). They may have been related, or perhaps one looked after the water mills and the other the windmill (if it was built by then). Both Milnewards were fairly well off, but one probably died before the second taxation day. Other occupational names are William le Colier, no doubt a charcoal burner; Henry Clerk, a lowly member of the church, perhaps a curate; another Clerk (Godfrey) paid 18 pence, showing there were opportunities to make some money even in a lowly position, or maybe he was progressing in the hierarchy and had the livings of several parishes. We cannot tell if these two were related or if perhaps one of them was employed by the bishop, as a secretary. John le Couper made barrels, probably as an independent tradesman, and since we know there was a vineyard in Buckden he may well have received at least some of his income from the bishop, though he probably also made barrels for water butts, water pails and ale casks for other villagers. John le Carter may have been a cart maker or a carter who went on a more or less regular basis to Huntingdon and St. Neots markets. Thomas le Chapman hawked his goods around from village to village. He was possibly elsewhere in 1332, since he is not in the second list. The word 'chap' in his name comes from an old English word that means to buy and sell; from it comes the 'Chipping' in place names, and Cheapside, and also 'cheap' as an adjective. William le Souter was a shoemaker. John le Shepherd probably worked for the bishop, and may have lived at Hardwick. 'Hard' denotes a herd either of sheep or cattle, and 'wick' a minor settlement of a few houses. There are Hardwicks within several Huntingdonshire parishes which were probably the sites of summer pasture for the flocks, which would spend their winters in the village proper.

John (le) Heremite is an interesting inclusion: the name means 'hermit', and it is possible he was living as an anchorite on the bishop's estate and made his wealth by alms (he was taxed at 7d and 2/-). However, some names were in the nature of nicknames, and John may just have been a recluse. One extra name appears in the second list: John le Webester, whose loom and stock of wool were his moveable goods. Usually a weaver was called Webber, as 'webster' is the female form (as 'spinster' is). It may be that John was paying tax on behalf of a woman who could not own property. John le Faukener (falconer), probably another bishop's servant, left a widow, Alice Faukener. There were many other trades in those largely self-sufficient times: the reason the trade names do not occur in the lists is probably because the tradesmen already had surnames of other sorts. The village must have had one (or more) baker, smith, butcher, and possibly a tailor, turner, thatcher and so on.

Names which indicate status

Closely allied to trade names are names which show status. John Burg, John Burges (who appears to have paid four times as much tax in 1332 as in 1327) and Hugh Freman are three. A fre(e)man was one free from service duties; a burgess was a citizen of a town, who usually paid money rents for his dwelling or business premises and who usually had civic duties to perform. William Frere was a brother: possibly a monk or friar, though neither was supposed to have (taxable) possessions. He is more likely to have been the brother of the name immediately before him.

Names from places

These—known as toponyms—fall into two categories: names from local features and names from further afield. John atte Stille, atte Welle, Attehoo, Attegrene, in the Hirne, in the Lane are six examples of people named from local landmarks. The hirne is a bend in a stream or river. The second group includes Est (east?), West, de Peterborough, Elie (Ely) and Chatteris. Robert Edeline and Robert Edyham may be the same person, and may be related to a man in the church vicar's list, Simon Ediburn. They could all be variant spellings of Edenham, a parish near Bourne in Lincolnshire. The name of Bishop Gynwell—already mentioned as possibly deriving from the Viking Gunhildr—may also be topynomal in origin: there is an area called Gynwell in Naseby, Northamptonshire.

Names from first names

Today most surnames come from given names. John and Robert Dande were not dandies, but took their name from Andrew. Dande Cosin was probably Andrew's cousin, which appears to be the only place where a relationship is fairly positive in this list. William Saunder has his name from Alexander. Aubrey and Morice are self explanatory. Catwine, as in John Catewine, is the Anglo-Norman French for Catherine. Isabella Robot did not descend from an android; almost certainly it was a misspelling of Robert. The addition of −son as in Kennison (probably son of Kenelm) is commonplace now but it seems it was just starting in the fourteenth century. Here we have only John, son of Gilbert.

Nicknames

John le Long may have been above normal height and John Grosse a big man. The Le Herls (or Erls in 1332) are most likely men who worked for an Earl, or acted in a high and mighty way, as also probably Robert Bishop. Matilda Boner appears in both lists. This could have been an occupational name, but it is more likely that it comes from the French 'bon' meaning good. It could be also from 'bon air' as in debonair. Whether the original person with the name was exceptionally affable or if the name was given in a sarcastic or facetious manner, we have to guess. If the latter perhaps her method of obtaining her income is questionable. But this is speaking ill of the dead, and perhaps maligning her unjustly.

Other names

Names for which derivations are not known are Loin'ch, Gloraunder Adaones, Morse, Hounid, and Harnchine. Canoun has a slightly different meaning from today, when it is a rank within the hierarchy of the church. Then a canon was usually a member of a religious order attached to a cathedral who undertook religious duties. If we had lists from several years later, the sons of the people on this list might have taken the fathers' name as their surname but they might have been called—for tax purposes—something different.

... and Numbers: a look at the figures

Some of our readers will remember pounds, shillings and pence. For those of you who don't: the standard coin was the penny, originally a small silver coin. Twelve pence were a shilling, and twenty shillings made up a pound. For sums up to twenty-four pence (two shillings) sums might be recorded as pence, so one shilling and sixpence would be written down as eighteen pence. Otherwise, sums would be done much as today, except you needed three columns, £ - s - d, rather than two (£ and p). As explained on page viii, the penny today bears no relationship in value to the penny of the fourteenth century.

The highest sum collected in 1327 was from John le Hunte who paid 4s. 10d.; then John Dande and Godfrey Canoun paid 3s. 6d. and 3s. 5d. respectively. John Hunte and Godfrey Canoun were almost certainly members of the retinue of the bishop who lived in Buckden, and they appear on both lists. Other high payers were probably in the same position, or were employed by the residual owner in the village who owned the Manor House. The least sum collected was from several villagers who each paid 6d. But it should be remembered that even these people had goods sufficiently valuable to make them liable to tax; there would have been others too poor ever to appear on the lists.

In 1327, when the rate was 10 per cent, the total sum collected was £3 17s 1d from sixty-five people. In 1332, however, when the subsidy was set at one fifteenth (of the value of moveable goods), the total was £5 6s 4d from fifty-five people. On average this means that each paid more than double the 1327 rate, representing an inflation rate of about 10 per cent a year. This was probably because prices had been driven up by year-on-year poor harvests (mainly the result of the weather – see below). The smaller numbers of people liable to taxation may have been caused by deaths, or by people falling below the tax threshold as a result of hardship. At least three women are on the first list—Amicia Brunis, Margaret Loin'ch, and Matilda Adaones—and not on the second, indicating they had either died or dropped below the lower limit for paying taxes.

The Weather

In 1313 the weather suddenly became colder, and there was a famine for several years. Boughton, the small village between Diddington and Little Paxton, is known to have died at this time. In 1327 there was a drought and subsequent years were also poor crop years, so some of the poorer and others died of starvation or poor health due to lack of food. The shortage of food also probably drove prices up and was the cause of the inflation, which we see in these documents.

There is one other piece of evidence which suggests that the workforce in the village was depleted at that time. The bishop of Lincoln of the time, Henry Burghersh, had the king's permission to enclose 200 acres of land to make a deer park. This was farm land, and no doubt the tenants who had not died had the spare strips in the rest of Buckden to compensate them for the loss. The land was eventually returned to agricultural use, but the time is still remembered by the name of Park Farm. For more information on the **deer park**, see entry in the A to Z Section.

Population

The difference between the figures shows that the population was probably not very stable, but when we have lists like these it is tempting to try to extrapolate population figures from them. To do this we have to assume that we can take each tax payer to be the head of a household, and multiply by a figure which represents the average household size. Historians disagree on what this variable should be, but it was probably somewhere between four and five. Taking the average of the two lists, sixty, this means a population figure of 240 to 300. However, this is probably an underestimate, and a more accurate figure cannot be found without knowing what proportion of householders were too poor to pay taxes. It was all to change anyway, after the arrival of the Black Death less than a generation later in 1348.

CHAPTER 21/BUCKDEN: A CLOSING MISCELLANY
Horace Haynes, Brian Carter, John Hebblethwaite And June Woods
Edited in part by Robin Gibson

This chapter opens with the late Horace Haynes's wonderfully vivid memories of Buckden and the ways it has changed over the last eighty years. W. B. (Brian) Carter tells the story of a vanishing fire-engine. June Woods dances to the music of Blind Ernie Bonham and remembers fundraising with the Mayoress of Buckden (her father). John Hebblethwaite, past Chairman of the Village Hall Trust, is taken to task by Horace Haynes for forgetting the true origins of the village playing-fields but redeems himself with the help of some old Buckden hands. In between, young Hales and Hardwick spin a few discs, the village plays host to a famous poet and is home to a budding songwriter, the wicked companions of a Very Bad Man are clothed in the decent obscurity of a learned language, and there are buns for tea.

Buckden as Bob Baxter and I knew it:
Horace Haynes in conversation with Bob Baxter

The last census before the Second World War showed 1087 people. There were six shops, a Post Office, two Bakers, two Butchers and two Blacksmiths as well as two butchers' vans, two fresh fish vans and two fried fish vans who visited the village on different days. Three churches: Methodist, St Mary's, and Baptist situated at the far end of the High Street. There was also a Gospel Hall, now attached to the Lion Hotel. I cannot remember this being used as a church but I do remember the Pastor, who lived at the top end of Hardwick Lane.

The School, as I remember it, had about 50 pupils, girls and boys in separate schools and an Infants School. While I was at school there was an outbreak of Yellow Jaundice and all but four or five of the pupils caught it~ and the school was closed for six weeks. I was one of the unlucky ones. You felt really ill for the first week but after that we had a jolly!

We used to play cricket on the Village Green using the trees as wickets. Cars were few and far between and we used to play Whip and Top in Church Street and the High Street. Boys rolled their marbles on the way to school.

Buckden was a friendly place and everyone knew everyone and they really helped each other. When someone died the neighbours would collect pennies for a wreath. Our older grandparents would wash and get the body ready for the undertakers on the day of the funeral. If the coffin was to pass our house the blinds would always be drawn across. We had our own undertaker in the village and the coffin was made by hand. There was no such thing as a Chapel of Rest.

We used to go to Sunday School morning and afternoon. There must have been 20 or 30 boys and girls and two or three teachers. On Sunday School Anniversary we had to take part. I remember we had to learn two new hymns. Of course our parents always attended. Our Sunday School Treat was held in the summer. We had tea on the lawn at the house just across the street and then marched to the fields where School Lane is now for sports. The men of the chapel put ropes on the trees for swings. We all left with an orange and apple each. We always had a Seaside Outing in summer and I think this was arranged with the church as well. We had three coach loads. Great Yarmouth, I remember took four hours and we had a break at Newmarket. We once went by train from Buckden station. Our mothers used to pay weekly at the chapel. I seem to remember we had our own Sunday School Hymn Books. Once hymn always sticks in my mind 'Jesus wants me for a Sunbeam'. I wonder what happened to our School Hymn Books? I went to Sunday School until I started work and then I was allowed to stay in bed, but I always had to go to evening service. This I did until I went into the RAF.

Mum always bought our clothes from a man who came for the money once a week. No different to the plastic cards of today. We always had new clothes for Easter Sunday.

There was a Buckden Brass Band who played at the Fetes and Garden Parties. The dances were held on the lawns at Stirtloe House and Beech Lawn. The Bill Heads advertising the event always added 'if wet in the Rifle Range', a saying still used today by the older villagers. Buckden Band all had uniforms and always played at the Lion Hotel on 'First Sunday', the second Sunday in July. My sister, to this day, says the only tune I played was 'Lead Kindly Light'.

Buckden was mainly agricultural and as a boy I remember there was a lot of unemployment. One other employer was the stocking factory which is now a playschool in Mill Road. It must have employed about 20 to 30 people, women and men. They came from the Offords, Southoe and Great Staughton. They made pullovers on machines they pushed by hand. At the back of the factory was a lawn and they had a good tennis club for the workforce.

Harvest time was a great time for us boys as we used to earn a few pennies driving carts bringing the corn from the field to the Stack Yard. The corn was cut by 'Binder' which tied the corn into sheaves. The Binder would be pulled by three horses. When the sheaves were dry then they would be loaded on carts and taken to the Stack Yard. The yard where I worked is now called The Barns. The yard would have about a dozen stacks by the end of the harvest. After the stack had settled down they would be thatched to keep the wet out. After about a month or so the Threshing Tackle would come and thresh the corn from the straw one stack at a time. Then the Tackle would move on to another farm. Threshing was a dirty dusty job on a par with coal mining but remember, the farm worker had no shower or bath room to get clean. I don't know how they managed it. I've said how unemployment was bad. I can remember men asking where the next threshing was so that they could get a few days work as the farmer always had to have a few extra hands at this time.

My Dad was the farm's Horse Keeper and as was expected when I left school at fourteen, I went to work there. Dad had about seven horses to look after as well as two Hunters. I left school at Easter and at the end of my first harvest I was going to plough with two horses (was it cheap labour). My Dad was in the same field with four horses and loved the work. At approximately 9.30 a.m. we would stop for half an hour for our Dockie. First we'd throw a corn sack over the horses to keep them from getting cold. We would sit on the bank of the hedgerow. Remember those Cottage loaves with a large bottom and a small top? Mum would cut the small top in half, make a hole in the top and slap a knob of butter on, and give us two thick slices of meat. This we would hold down with a piece of crust, take a knife from our pocket and eat. We would finish this with a piece of home-made cake and wash it down with cold tea—no sugar or milk. What had we used the knife for before? Did we wash our hands? (Where?). No matter what the weather was like while the ground would work we stayed out, sometimes wet through. The horses would always go home faster than they came out. In the stable Dad would mix the food up while we took the harness off and rubbed the horses down to dry them off as best we could. You always looked after the horses first. Home for dinner—my Mum's suet pudding. She would get the biggest basin she had, line it with the pudding mix, and fill it with meat and vegetables and gravy (made with Burdalls Gravy Salt I suspect). She put a top on it, covered it with muslin and cooked it in a saucepan. Another day we would perhaps have suet dumplings.

My work on the farm only lasted to my second harvest and then I was pulled off because of some medical condition. I next went to work up at the shop, Bowtells of Buckden. I must tell you a little about our shops. The tins of beans and soups weren't price marked and you didn't get a basket and help yourself. You would tell the assistant behind the counter your requirements and he would get it. Our tills didn't issue you with a ticket telling you what you had bought. Shops didn't have fridges. The cheese was kept at the back of the counter on a marble slab and covered with muslin. It was cut as you wanted it. Bacon didn't come in shrink wrap and when you fried it didn't have that horrible white stuff come out of it. It was cut on a bacon machine sliced to the thickness you wanted it with as many slices as asked for. The sides of bacon (Harris of Wiltshire English) came by rail and were hung in the bacon wire safe in the warehouse. Everything came in bulk- currants, sugar, flour, butter and lard and had to be weighed up. The goods were bought from the manufacturers direct. Then came the supermarkets and the manufacturers upped the number of items to be delivered and this stopped most of the direct deliveries. The shops then had to go to the wholesalers who, of course, upped the price and this meant the end of many small shops. Bowtells continued to thrive selling everything- groceries, ladies fashion, gents outfitting, boots and shoes and eventually furniture. The shop was eventually modernised and the size of the grocery department doubled and the rest let. The bacon still was sliced in the shop and they cooked their own ham. Now, let me tell you, when I want good bacon (no white stuff) I go to a small butchers in March. It's cut in the shop how you want and the sausages are out of this world. The A1 still came past the front door and then came the By-Pass and the new estates started. Some built on fields that were flooded half the year. The rest you know.

I didn't like these new-estates that were growing on our green fields, admittedly the extra people added a few extra pennies to my shop but as I sat in my chair after dinner with my feet up, Katie on my lap (that's my cat by the way) and reminisced about bygone days I wondered whether our chapel with its friendly congregation and new look and our own minister would be as successful as it is now if the population of the village had still been around 1250. I think not, so you see good does come out of something evil.

During the war our parents ran a dance each week to raise funds for what was called 'Forces Homecoming Fund'. They raised about £5000—a lot of money in those days. It was decided afterwards that a more permanent memorial for the boys who didn't come home would be more appropriate. After a lot of meetings and talks it was decided a Playing Field would be long lasting. The Vineyards had always been used as a sports field for the school and this was leased from the Church Commission and was eventually purchased to be called Buckden Memorial Playing Fields. A Children's Corner was fenced off and toilets built. The field sloped towards the Valley and a hard kicked ball would end up in the water. When the By-Pass was being built the foreman was approached and agreed to take the top soil to the field and level it. He was pleased to do this because of the short distance to cart the soil. My gripe: this field is now called The Millennium Playing Field and The Valley is called The Pond. This is not what our parents raised the money for but a memorial to the boys who didn't come home, and had it not been for their hard work this field would, today, be another housing estate. While a search was being made for a suitable field it was suggested that somewhere nearer the centre of the village would be better. The field where Manor Gardens is now was suggested. The help of the Cambridge Playing Fields Society was sought and they decided that the area was much too damp so the Vineyard was purchased.

Why were Bob and I asked to tell you about Buckden as it was? Well, there are not many of us left who remember Buckden as it was—peaceful and quiet. I don't need an environmental economist to tell me what is happening to rural Britain. You can see it in most villages in Huntingdonshire.

I was born in Buckden in 1923; when I don't know as I have lost my Birth Certificate. Water came from the well and was drawn up on a rope. The lavatory was twenty yards away at the bottom of the yard. There were hens at the bottom of the yard (at the time we didn't realise they were free range). There was always a Cock as it was said that if there was no cock then the eggs could have a blood spot in the yolk. I found out that was wrong when deep litter houses and hens kept in cages came about.

Milk was delivered by horse and cart from several small herds of cows. The milk was never pasteurised. The cows were milked by hand into the bucket and this was tipped into a chum and loaded on to the cart and delivered daily. The milkman brought the churn to your door and measured your requirements into your jug. Sure it went sour sometimes in the hot weather but Mum put it in a muslin bag and made cream cheese. The horse didn't need to be told to move on it just knew where to go and where to stop. We never fell ill with e-coli or other diseases. When a cow gave birth to a calf the first milk was thick and when heated in the oven with a little sugar it set like egg custard and was delicious. Now such foods are labelled unfit for human consumption.

Where the cows grazed in season the field was full of cowslips and dandelions which were picked to make wine. Have you heard the Cuckoo or the Barn Owl? I haven't. Farming and nature seemed to walk hand in hand and it's not so now. I hadn't to walk to school, it was just next door, but other boys and girls walked-across the fields from Diddington in all weathers. Did I hear you ask about a bus? The houses I passed on the way to school were all unlocked all day. Burglary was unknown in the village as we had our own Bobby who was seen biking round the village. On the way to school we passed the church and chapel. God still played an important part in the village, local farmers did not cut their corn on Sunday.

Buckden was a still sleepy village with hardly any traffic. The horses from the farm were taken to the football field in the Summer (that's the field next to Park Road). After a day's work they went on their own and would wait at the gate while the Horse Keeper caught up to let them in. In the morning, they would be waiting at the gate to be taken to the farm for their breakfast before starting day work. HH

Deejays: the early days

October 1905. It was, the members said afterwards, one of the most enjoyable evenings they had ever spent. A slap-up supper in the Lion's new club room, followed by songs, toasts, more songs, more toasts, a report from the Hon. Sec. on the most successful season in the group's history (cheers), and as the icing on the cake, the proceedings much enlivened by selections on the phonograph by young Sid Hardwick and Bob Hales, Jnr.

As the members dispersed into the autumn night, did none of them feel a slight guilt at having so much enjoyed the enthusiastic young men and their recorded tunes? A chill of foreboding that they might have been listening to the future of music: not live, but simply plucked from a pile of discs or cylinders, requiring no rehearsals, no interplay between musicians and audience, no after-the-show camaraderie over a pint?

Probably they didn't; perhaps they should have. They had, after all, been attending the annual supper of the Buckden Brass Band.

The Buckden fire engine
by Brian Carter

Some years after I established the marina, the village fire engine came up for sale. It was in a somewhat dilapidated hut which also contained a hearse which was nothing more than a trolley with four wheels, and I understood that you hired it for 3s. to wheel your loved one's coffin to the church.[1] (Offord had a magnificent hearse which had beautifully engraved glass windows.) The shed also contained the old Buckden village street lamps, two of which I purchased as well as the fire engine. This was horse-drawn with bars to the side which would be manned by eight people who raised the poles up and down to actuate the fire pump. At the back of the fire engine was a large tank which would be filled by people rushing around with buckets of water taken from the village pump or their own one if they had one. The hoses were made of leather and included leather buckets and also long rakes to pull the thatch off roofs. It gave great joy to children who would sit on the driver's seat calling it the Wells Fargo coach. I offered this to Lord Montague of Beaulieu, who declined it, but I later on sold it to a private individual. I was surprised some years later to see it featured in the national press where Lady Montague had driven it through London but had failed to empty the water out of it, making it extremely top heavy and it ended up on its side with the unfortunate pony or horse that was pulling it. Since then I have heard nothing of its whereabouts. BC

A poet in exile...

On 27 July 1909, one of the best-known poets and literary critics of the day, John William Watson, 51, met [Adeline] Maureen Pring, an 'exceedingly pretty' young Irish woman, 21, at a concert in Bath. A fortnight later he married her. A year later they came to live in Buckden.

When the Poet Laureate Alfred Tennyson died in 1892, William Watson (he rarely used his first name) had been the leading contender to succeed him. Unfortunately for Watson, Queen Victoria was in no hurry to fill the post and by the time she made up her mind in late 1895, he had fallen out of favour. His cause may not have been helped by his having once urged one of the Victoria's sons to tell his mother it was high time she abdicated. Watson's move to Buckden came at another difficult time in his life: his sudden marriage had not pleased everyone, least of all the three women with whom he was already romantically entangled, one of whom he had promised to marry; his poem savagely satirising the prime minister's wife and daughter had led to a rift between him and his friend and publisher John Lane, as well as to the cancellation of most of a lucrative American lecture tour; and worst of all, perhaps, he knew that poetic fashion was passing him by. Unsurprisingly, the title of one of the books he wrote while in Buckden was *The Muse in Exile.*

Not that it was an uncomfortable exile: the Watsons occupied a 'roomy old cottage' in Silver Street which they called Old Hollies. It had a garden big enough for William to sit and write in while Maureen played with their infant daughter, Rhona. For all William's public troubles and private fears, the Watsons' three and a half years in Buckden were as much refuge as exile. Perhaps the Parish Council should erect a plaque to the memory of this distinguished resident, if it can identify Old Hollies.[2]

...marooned on an island

There is an intriguing entry in the 1938 edition of the United States Library of Congress's Catalog of Copyright Entries, for the words and melody of an unpublished song called 'Marooned on an island'; the copyright holder is named as Louisa Gertrude Burrows, of Buckden. Did she go on to have a successful career as a songwriter? The Local History Society would be interested to learn more!

Evenings at the Rifle Range
by June Woods

It was more than an indoor rifle range. It was also a billiard hall and it had a substantial stage. It was used regularly every day and most evenings except Sundays by the various village organisations. These included the Rifle Club on Wednesdays, the Whist Club, the Youth Club (three evenings a week), the Over-Sixties, and, come the war, the Home Guard. It was also used for school meals, school medicals, and wedding receptions. Local Club Dances were held every Saturday evening and occasionally during the week. The Billiard Club was open most of the time on a casual basis—but for Men Only. Members of the opposite sex were not only banned, they were not even allowed to peek in the door!

---

[1] Look in the A to Z Section under **bier, parish** for more on the village hearse.
[2] It shouldn't be too hard. There cannot be many cottages in Silver Street with seven bedrooms and four sitting-rooms.

Although most dancing was to records (the forerunner to the disco but much more sedate), there were a number of live bands: The Squadronnaires (before they were famous), the band of the USAAF, the Fire Brigade, George Green's Blue Rhythm, Ernie Bonham (a blind pianist from St Neots) and Jack Abraham. Mrs Partington was a favourite vocalist. JW

Mr Kilvert's Buckden harem

The word *Bugden* appears only twice in the Oxford English Dictionary, each time in a quotation about the bishops' palace. The first, which mentions Katherine of Aragon, is part of an entry defining the meaning of 'life'. The second supports the definition of 'quaedam', a rare and obsolete word which describes the associates of one of Buckden's least appreciated visitors, Richard Kilvert.

The Star Chamber sent Kilvert to Buckden in 1637 to enforce payment of a fine levied by Charles I on the bishop of Lincoln, John Williams. John Hacket, the bishop's devoted memorialist, claimed that Kilvert wreaked havoc on the palace estate, selling every movable object in the place, felling timber, killing deer and drinking the palace cellars dry. According to Hacket, only £800 of the estimated £10,000 he raised was ever accounted for. The rest he squandered on the 'baggage and loose franions' who made up his *seraglia of quaedam*—the harem of wanton women which he maintained at the palace for three summers.[1]

The War Memorial Playing Fields
by John Hebblethwaite and Horace Haynes

'The Library? You want Vineyard Way, then first right into Burberry Road and you'll find the car park at the end'. Walk often along Church Street and you'll get used to acting as a human sat-nav for drivers who pull over and demand directions to the Playing Fields/ Village Club/ Millennium Centre/ Bowls Club/ Library/ Tennis Club/ Play Group... *'There should be signs,'* they grumble as they pull away. *'There are,'* you say, but to yourself so as not to aggravate, *'look: 'Village Hall.' What more do you need?')*

So having established just where the centre of village life lies, let us take a closer look at the history of those all-important playing fields, here described by John Hebblethwaite—who once made the mistake of calling them the recreation ground—and Horace Haynes, who put him right, politely but firmly:

'It's not a recreation ground; it's nothing to do with the Village Hall; and in no way at all was it paid for by the sale of the old Rifle Range! You got it wrong, John.'

I'm sorry, Horace, let's put it right then; Horace never pulls his punches!

So started the correction of matters and proper dedication of the War Memorial Playing Fields following a misleading article in the Roundabout.

A committee of interested parties was formed, including those who knew the origins, and so came together Dai Davies, Ernie Dudley, Horace Haynes, Frank Mace, Percy Pepper, Jack Riseley and myself, then chairman of the Village Hall Trust; and so started many get-togethers in Percy Pepper's bungalow on Cranfield Way. They were convivial, social evenings, when the Trust Chairman listened to many nostalgic stories and experiences of old and wartime Buckden from those who were actually there at the time.

Since the early 1920s, the old Rifle Range (now the site of the Burberry Homes) had acted as the venue for village entertainment and dances most nights of the week. Come the Second World War, such events took on even more significance as lads and lassies converged on Buckden from their various air bases in the locality—English, Irish, Scots, Welsh, Poles and Americans. Funds were gradually accumulated and various options considered, before deciding that this money should go towards establishing both a sports field and a children's play area for Buckden. We learned how some funds never arrived with the Treasurer (the committee found out that the servicemen had been paying 3d. per night for bike storage and safe keeping, but the committee was only receiving 2d) and how a post-war War Memorial Playing Fields Committee was established to invest the funds and look for suitable land.

The Towers Field was owned by the Edleston family and was eventually given to the Bishop of Northampton, who in turn gave it to the Claretian Missionary Society. It was decided that the field now under Manor Gardens was too wet, but eventually land was targeted in the old vineyard, and a small area secured for a children's play corner; this is now the car park at the front of the hall. Frank Mace was a driving force, visiting and working with the National Playing Fields Association in Cambridge, liaising with solicitors, and treading a tortuous path through the negotiations. After various open meetings, and two attempts, ten acres of land adjoining the play corner was finally purchased, and the War Memorial Playing Fields Trust was set up by the Minister of State in 1947.

---

[1] The OED also has one reference to *Buckden*, but it is the one in Yorkshire.

Horace Haynes was most anxious that it should reflect the original intentions and the land be dedicated as the War Memorial Playing Fields to indicate that it did not belong to the Parish Council, but to the people of Buckden, in memory of those war service years and of all who fought and died for their country. So it was unanimously agreed that a memorial stone would be created and dedicated.

How was this memorial stone to be obtained? Enter new residents to the village, Peter and Ann Geyelin, who were on the point of retiring from Blake and Horlock, a monumental masons' business in Enfield. With their help, Scottish granite for the stone came all the way from Galloway and was inscribed to a design by Peter. Quite a task it proved to unload and position it on the blue engineering brick plinth constructed by Ken Gale.

And so, on a rainy spring evening in 1985, the memorial was unveiled, and a hearty social in the Village Hall was enjoyed by villagers - both old and new.

So hats off to that War Memorial Playing Fields Committee of yesteryear for securing the field and valley and giving pleasure to all in perpetuity. JH   HH

The Buckden begging bowl
by June Woods

Fundraising for the playing fields took many forms. There were whist drives, socials and dances, and all the large houses took turns opening their gardens on Saturdays during the summer—a fête in the afternoon and dancing on the lawn in the evening. A set of substantial side-shows was made and became the focus of each venue, together with home-made refreshments provided by ladies of the village. Comic football and cricket matches in the Towers were very popular, with surrounding villages being encouraged to compete. All enterprising, but conventional, ways of raising money.

But then they thought up the notorious begging bowl.

This was a cup presented every Saturday evening with great ceremony and then snatched back—a grand piano leg with a large washing up bowl (metal) on one end and a baby's potty (enamel) on the other, all tastefully painted silver. The 'Mayor and Mayoress of Buckden' arrived in style in an ancient car belonging to Robinson's Garages, driven by Cliff Robinson dressed as a chauffeur. The Mayor was Mr Heffer (Gents Outfitters, now One Stop) in top hat and tails, and the Mayoress was my father, Alderman Slaughter, in the most horrendous green crinoline and ginger wig. Then began a procession round the village calling at every hostelry (there were seven) asking for donations to fill the cup (surreptitiously emptied from time to time so that it always needed topping up.) No-one was safe from this ravenous crew, which grew in numbers as the evening wore on. Unsuspecting lorry drivers who had stopped for refreshment (the village High Street was still the A1) often fell prey to these humorous highwaymen. JW

Cliff Robinson and friends on another occasion?

Alice Whitmee

Ω ΩΩΩΩ

Buckden - A Huntingdonshire Village   Appendix A

Farms -- Locations--Historic and present

All distances are to the farmstead from the High Street~Church Street Junction, "The Cross",
in a straight line unless stated otherwise.

Name	Location		Remarks
Coneygarth	High Street	100m. N	Now a private dwelling. Has also been a public house.
Coronation	South side of the Green	500m E	Also known as North's Farm. Site entirely occupied by shops or housing
Hardonian	400m off A1	600m N.W	Non-working. Previously 600m N.N.W.in Hardwick Lane
Hoo	Church Street	400m E	Now a private dwelling
Jessamine	300m off A1	600m N.W	Used to be based in High Street in house of same name.
Lodge	700m off Brampton Road	1.7km N.E	Working but affected by gravel extraction and to be severely affected further by the A14 road on its new route. Was known before 1961 as Baker's Farm
Low (2)	Stirtloe	800m S.S.E.	Working. For original farmhouse see (1)
Low(1).	Mill Road	600m E	Now private dwelling. Barns present.
Margetts	400m off Mill Road	1.6 km E	Sold to Redlands/Lafarge for gravel extraction and now sold by them to the Thornhill Estate
Martins	80m off Mill Road	1.2 km E	Private dwelling
Northfields	Not known but must have been somewhere in the North Field shown on the 1799 Tithe map. May have become Vicarage or Station Farm. This could account for the weighbridge which was in the station goods yard 300m away.		In 1901 it appears to have had a weighbridge according to the census.
Park	500m off A1	1.0km N	Working
Shooters Hill	150m(?) off Perry Road	1.2km W.S.W,	No trace of it nor access track opposite Buckden Wood turning.
Shooters Hollow	150m off Perry Road	1.5km W.S.W.	Working
Station (or Vicarage)	300m off Brampton Road	2.0km N.E.	Bought for refuse tip area. Name used by tip operators.
Stirtloe	Stirtloe	750m S	Private dwelling
Top	1.6km N.W.		Moat only remains. Combined with Park Farm
Westfield	Off A1	500m S.	Derelict. Non-working. Bought by speculator. Farmstead re-sold in 2009.
Wood	400m off Perry Road	1.1 km W	Private dwellings

This is not an exhaustive list and is mainly based on maps and censuses down to 1901.

Buckden - A Huntingdonshire Village   Appendix B

Street Names

Street	Origin or Supposed Origin of name
Aragon Close	After Katherine of **Aragon**
Bakers Lane	It was a turning off Church Street where School Lane is now. It contained workshops and some cottages and led to a field of Hoo Farm. That Lodge Farm was known as Bakers Farm before 1961 may be the origin.
Beaufort Drive	After Margaret **Beaufort** (1443-1509), mother of Henry VII and founder of Christ's and St. John's colleges, Cambridge. She visited Buckden.
Bishops Way	After the **Bishops** of Lincoln
Brampton Road	Next village of **Brampton**
Buckden Hill	The part of the Great North Road between Diddington Brook and Stirtloe Lane.
Burberry Road	Wm. **Burberry** in 1558 set up a charity for the poor of Buckden
Charles Court	Possibly after Prince **Charles**?
Church Street	St. Mary's-the Parish **Church,** and later the **Methodist Church.**
College Green	Location uncertain but is probably the present Green at Hunts End. Referred to in Kelly's Directory from 1898 onwards.
Copes Close	The **Cope** family owned the farm on which the close is built
Cranfield Way and Close	Mr. W.W.**Cranfield** and his sister gave the village the Rifle Range (q.v.) which they owned. A farmer, generous benefactor and sports enthusiast.
Falcon Way	After the **Falcon** public House in Mill Road closed in 1999 and called Crown Cottage for an unknown reason.
Field Close	After **Field** House in Silver Street
George Lane	After the **George** (and Dragon) Inn in the High Street. Once known as Pond Lane after a very large family that lived there. See Perry Road
Glebe Lane	The land was once **Glebe** land tithed to the vicar
Great North Road	It was the main road from London to "The North(East)".
Greenway	After the **Green** family (see the sons' memorial in the High Street). And Bishop **Green** of Lincoln.
Hardwick Lane	**Hardwick**- a hamlet attached to Buckden
High Street	-
Hoo Baulk	See Silver Street. (Baulk : a ridge left unploughed)
Hoo Close	After the **Hoo** in Church Street.
Hunts End and Hunts End Court	Unknown.
Ivelbury Close	After **Ivelbury** House which stood on the site
King George Court	Called **King George** Court to differentiate it from the George Hotel behind which it was built.
Lark End	Another bird between Swan and Falcon!
Leadens Lane	In 1901 Market Gardener John and wife Elizabeth **Leaden** were living here with their seven children with ages ranging from 2 months to 8 years.
Lincoln Close	After the see of **Lincoln** in which Buckden was situated until 1838
Lion Yard	After the **Lion** (and Lamb) hotel nearby
Lucks Lane	Thought to be named after a family? It was not an uncommon name in the area but it does not appear in any Buckden census.
Manor Gardens & Close	After the **Manor** House in the grounds of which part of them was built
Mayfield	A story recently circulated is that a previous lady owner with a cut-glass accent on hearing a discussion on its ownership stopped the talk by saying : 'But it's m(a)y field'. No native has ever talked of, e.g., May-pole dancing here.
Mere Lane	This was and is an unpaved track classed as a bridleway on the northern boundary of the parish. The name may be unused now. *Mereing: the definition of a boundary in relation to topographic features on the ground at the time of survey (e.g. "one metre from the road edge").*
Mill Road	The road leads to Offord and Buckden **Mill**. It was Mill Street on the 1900 OS plan. In earlier times it also led to the ford below the mill.
Monks Cottages	Possibly because someone thought that **Monks** had lived in the Bishops' Palace at one time?
Morris Close	After Dr. Michael **Morris** who was G.P. in Buckden for many years
Park Road	After the **Park** of Buckden Palace

Buckden - A Huntingdonshire Village   Appendix B (continued)

Perry Road	The road leads to the village of **Perry**. Once known as New Road. A 1695 map and Jefferys' map of 1768 shows a road heading west from the Lion corner where George Lane is now. Perhaps the Duke of Manchester decided that he needed a better connection from Kimbolton to the North Road and had a new route set out together with a good road to Grafham as now. The present very straight roads leading westwards were built before 1813 when the parish was surveyed for the Inclosure.
School Lane	Here is the modern **School**. The cul-de-sac which was here before was Baker's Lane.
Silver Street	The road from Church Street as far as Beech Lawn was Silver Street. Northwards as far as the Great North Road it used to be known as the 'Hoo Baulk'. A suggestion re the origin is that the road once led to the area of woodland reserved for coppicing and firewood since the Latin for a wood is 'silva'.
Smith Drive	Named after long-serving parish councillor Mr. Fred. **Smith** and perhaps also J.W.Smith - builder and merchant
Springfield Close	There is a **Spring** near here still. One native of the village said that the The Osiers and the Springfield Close names should be exchanged, the main spring being in The Osiers area.
St Hugh's Road	After the patron saint of the R.C. church - **St. Hugh's** at the Towers
Stirtloe	After the hamlet
Stirtloe Lane	After the hamlet
Swan End	A **Swan** was the emblem of St. Hugh (q.v.) An alehouse called the Swan is reputed to have existed at about where Vineyard Way joins Mill Road.
Taylor's Lane	Since there was no family called **Taylor** in the area at the time of the enclosure of 1813 perhaps the name is a 'modern' one. A family called Taylards once had land hereabouts but did not receive land at the Enclosure
The Barns	There were and are **Barns** ex-Low Farm adjacent. The new houses are not conversions.
The Grove	A name chosen by the builder of the houses. The ground had been called The Paddock for many decades before being sold for housing. Granted there were trees to be cut down but where are they now?
The Osiers	**Osiers** were grown here. Basket-making was a local industry but the osiers were also sent as far away as Gloucester for the same purpose.
Van Diemen's Lane	The Dutch explorer Van Diemen's name has been used in many places as well as in Buckden. For example a field in Grafham also bears his name . (The lane here is a track off Mill Road and used to serve two houses and several allotments.) Van Diemen's Land is now Tasmania. Since convicts were sometimes transported there the name may have been used to remind those of a criminal bent of what their punishment might be if apprehended.
Vineyard Way	The Bishop's Palace used to have its **Vineyards** here.
Waterworks Road	An unofficial name for the private road leading from Stirtloe Lane to the Anglian Water Pumping Station on the River Ouse which feeds Grafham Water.
Weir Close	The present opinion is that the name relates to a **weir** or weirs on the public drains nearby. The public drains are ditches which are still in use although some lengths will have been culverted or piped. From a copy of the St. Neots Local History Society magazine it appears that 'weir' there meant a pond.
Wolsey Gardens	Thomas **Wolsey** was Dean of Lincoln in1503 and Bishop in 1514 when he visited Buckden.
York Yard	After a family of butchers which lived here in the early 19th century but it moved to Bedfordshire before its name figured in directories.

Buckden - A Huntingdonshire Village   Appendix C

Telephone Users within the Parish 1937

Name	No.
Atkinson Rev. H.D, Vicarage	48
Bell Surgeon Commander , Manor ho.	45
Bowtell Bros, Grcrs , High st	8
Bowyer & Priestley Millers Offord & Buckden Mills	7
Bowyer Wm. T, Frmr, Jessamine ho	27
Brown B.A, Greenways	65
Brown E, Fmr, Buckden Wd	41
Buckden Call office	6
Buckden Farmers' Meat Co, High st	59
Buckden Hosiery Co Mfrs	20
Collyer J, Bellevue ho Church st	23
Cope A.E, Cattle Remover , Hunts End	54
Cresswell H, Gravel pits	50
Day S.C, Butcher , Church st	72
Evans Miss Gwendolen The Spinney	71
George Hotel	4
Hargreaves H, Ivelbury	60
Hildesley Rev. A.H, M.A. The Cottage Lucks lane	47
Hinsby's Coal Mchts	4
Howson Mrs. M.A, Luck *(sic)* lane	67
Jolly Eric C, Physn, Srgn, Oak Lawn	16
Knowles Archdeacon K.D, White ho	15
Linton Capt H, Stirtloe ho	24
Lion Hotel	13
L.M.S. Rly. Buckden Station Call Office	44
Looker Miss G.A, Ivelbury	60
Mailer R,	26
Park James C, Frmr	3
Police Stn	10
Priestley Mrs A.C, The Coneygarths	9
Robinson A.T, Engr, Gar	2
Robinson A.T,	22
Rose E.C, York House	52
SHELL-MEX & BP Ltd. Depot	11
Smith John W, Bldr	5
TOTALS	36

The Buckden exchange covered other villages including the Offords, the Perrys, Grafham and Ellington.

The Inclosure Map of Buckden Parish of 1813
Reproduced courtesy of Huntingdonshire Archives
The shaded areas on the original are coloured green.
By this time New Road- now Perry Road- had been built thus superseding George Lane as the route westwards from Buckden